JOURNAL FOR THE STUDY OF THE OLD TESTAMENT
SUPPLEMENT SERIES
306

Sheffield Academic Press

Israel Constructs its History

Deuteronomistic Historiography
in Recent Research

edited by
Albert de Pury, Thomas Römer
& Jean-Daniel Macchi

Journal for the Study of the Old Testament
Supplement Series 306

Original French Title—*Israël construit son histoire.*
L'historiographie deutéronomiste à la lumière
des recherches récentes
(Le Monde de la Bible, 34; Geneva: Labor et Fides, 1996)

Published by Sheffield Academic Press Ltd
Mansion House
19 Kingfield Road
Sheffield S11 9AS
England

http://www.shef-ac-press.co.uk

Typeset by Sheffield Academic Press
and
Printed on acid-free paper in Great Britain
by Bookcraft Ltd
Midsomer Norton, Bath

British Library Cataloguing in Publication Data

A catalogue record for this book is available
from the British Library

ISBN 1-84127-099-7

CONTENTS

Foreword   9
Abbreviations   15
List of Contributors   19

Part I
INTRODUCTION

THOMAS RÖMER AND ALBERT DE PURY
    Deuteronomistic Historiography (DH):
    History of Research and Debated Issues   24

Part II
ANCIENT HISTORIOGRAPHY

SARA JAPHET
    Postexilic Historiography: How and Why?   144

MARCEL DETIENNE
    A Debate on Comparative Historicities   174

JEAN-JACQUES GLASSNER
    Historical Times in Mesopotamia   189

Part III
TEXTUAL CRITICISM AND LITERARY CRITICISM

ADRIAN SCHENKER
    Jeroboam and the Division of the Kingdom in the Ancient
    Septuagint: LXX 3 Kingdoms 12.24 a-z, MT 1 Kings 11–12;
    14 and the Deuteronomistic History   214

STEPHEN PISANO
2 Samuel 5–8 and the Deuteronomist:
Textual Criticism or Literary Criticism? 258

Part IV
DIACHRONIC AND SYNCHRONIC METHODS

STEVEN L. MCKENZIE
The Trouble with Kingship 286

WALTER DIETRICH
History and Law: Deuteronomistic Historiography and
Deuteronomic Law Exemplified in the Passage from
the Period of the Judges to the Monarchical Period 315

FRANÇOISE SMYTH
When Josiah has Done his Work or the King Is Properly
Buried: A Synchronic Reading of 2 Kings 22.1–23.28 343

Part V
THE SOURCES OF DEUTERONOMISTIC HISTORIOGRAPHY

JACQUES BRIEND
The Sources of the Deuteronomic History:
Research on Joshua 1–12 360

Part VI
THE MILIEUS OF THE DEUTERONOMISTS

ERNST AXEL KNAUF
Does 'Deuteronomistic Historiography' (DH) Exist? 388

THOMAS RÖMER
Is There a Deuteronomistic Redaction in the
Book of Jeremiah? 399

Part VII
DEUTERONOMISTIC IDEOLOGY AND
THEOLOGY OF THE OLD TESTAMENT

MARTIN ROSE
Deuteronomistic Ideology and Theology
of the Old Testament 424

ANDREW D.H. MAYES
Deuteronomistic Ideology and the Theology of
the Old Testament 456

Index of References 481
Index of Authors 498

FOREWORD*

When the time came for those teaching Old Testament in the Universities of Fribourg, Neuchatel, Lausanne and Geneva to choose the theme
for the doctoral level seminar that they were in charge of setting up for
1995, the subjects that interested each of them were very diverse. After
a quick survey, without much hesitation and by common consent it was
decided to tackle a central problem in Old Testament research, 'Deuteronomistic Historiography'. Right there, it seemed to us, was situated
one of the 'frontiers' in research at the present time, and stemming from
this project we could hope for a breakthrough not only towards a new
chronology relative to the texts of the Old Testament, but also towards
a renewed understanding of Israelite religion.

What is 'Deuteronomistic Historiography' (DH)? Since the publication of Martin Noth's *Überlieferungsgeschichtliche Studien* in 1943,
this phrase has designated the lengthy literary collection that starts with
the book of Deuteronomy and extends to the Second Book of Kings, a
collection that, after Noth, has been attributed to a Judaean author of the
exilic period (sixth century BCE). And why was a new examination of
this collection so urgently required? Among the upheavals which have
affected biblical studies for a good 20 years (especially in regard to the
date of the Pentateuch and the historical evolution of Israelite religion),
the Deuteronomistic historiography thesis seemed like a fixed pole that
had escaped extensive questioning. The intent of our project therefore
was to submit the apparent scientific consensus to a new examination
by taking into account in a much more systematic way the new parameters that the discipline presents at the end of the 'agonizing revisions' of these recent years. In a certain sense, our goal was to propose
a logical follow-up to the seminar organized in 1986/87, that led to the

* Translators note: I wish to thank Dr Pamela Milne (History Department,
University of Windsor) for her technical and other help and her support in preparing
this translation. I want to thank as well Professor Walter Skakoon and Dr Moshe
Staretz (French Department, University of Windsor) for their assistance.

publication of the volume *Le Pentateuque en question* (Geneva: Labor et Fides, 1989, 2nd edn 1991).

To carry out this ambitious project, it was quite obviously necessary to make room for the greatest diversity in approaches and methods, and from this perspective we envisaged external contributions from the outset and appealed to our guests. On the one hand it was a matter of calling upon the most representative voices in each trend by encouraging them to provide us in an unedited and specific form the basic points of their present position, and on the other hand to prompt confrontations among the different protagonists, making it possible to bring to the fore the presuppositions of each position. At the same time, our constant concern was to find and make use of adequate means to ensure the best possible participation of students, both undergraduate and graduate. Accordingly, the text of each contribution was distributed in advance to a small team who were to prepare a list of questions, and even to work out replies. Overall, it could be said that this alternation of interventions by famous specialists and of reactions from a well-motivated audience largely contributed to the success of the exercise. Contrary to what we had done for the volume on the Pentateuch, we had to forego—for reasons of space—the publication of the summaries of the discussions which followed the talks.

The route followed between 13 January and 24 June 1995 is faithfully reproduced in the present volume. Only two contributions (those of J.-J. Glassner and T. Römer) could not, for various reasons, be part of the oral presentations. Nevertheless, they are an integral part of this book. As an introduction to the subject, the simplest way will be to summarize here, very succinctly, the stages of our journey.

1. On 13 January 1995, the opening session, held in Geneva, was devoted to the presentation of *the history of research* since the end of the last century. This was a presentation, worked out by the undersigned Römer and de Pury, that was supposed to be relatively detailed, insofar as there did not exist in French any complete account on the scientific debate on DH. This critical examination of a century of research will facilitate, we hope, access to the problem, as was the case for the volume on the Pentateuch. Already at this stage, we were led to call into question certain accepted ideas, both with regard to the precursors of Noth as well as with regard to the apparent solidity of the consensus since Noth.

2. At the time of our second meeting, 27–28 January 1995, which took place as did the two following at the Centre Saint Dominique (Pensier) in the Canton of Fribourg, our goal was to set about determining the situation of *ancient historiography*. Too often we begin an analysis of a biblical literary corpus without endeavouring to situate it, on the one hand, in relation to the overall sequence of biblical literature, and, on the other hand, in the context of the comparable literary production of neighbouring cultures. Sara Japhet, a specialist in Judaism of the Persian period, presented us with her view of biblical historiography beginning with the books of Chronicles and Ezra–Nehemiah. The integration of the Hellenic and Hellenistic world, often neglected in Old Testament studies, was another innovative aspect of our project. The Hellenistic scholar Marcel Detienne presented us with an unexpected journey through the different ways of understanding history in the cultures of antiquity. As for the Assyriologist, Jean-Jacques Glassner, whose contribution was only solicited after the completion of the seminar, he raises the problem of the different concepts of time that gave structure to Mesopotamian historiography and wonders about the pivotal role played in this context by the diviner. Finally, Françoise Smyth, in an address that will be published elsewhere, endeavoured to show the relationship between Semitic historiography, especially Mesopotamian, and that of Egypt. Following these presentations, a highly animated debate was set off in regard to the relevance—or non-relevance—of the term 'historiography' in designating the Deuteronomistic work.

3. Our third meeting, 24–25 February 1995, had as its theme Textual Criticism and Literary Criticism and was devoted to the problem of establishing the corpus, that is to say, to the question of textual witnesses. For this question, that just by itself would have justified the holding of a doctoral level seminar, we were able to benefit from not only the expertise but also the infrastructure of the Biblical Institute of the University of Fribourg. Using the example of the parallel history of 1 Kings 12 in the MT and the LXX, Professor Adrian Schenker gave a dazzling demonstration of the unexpected effects of textual criticism on the theories relative to the origin and cultural context of DH, with the Hebrew text often reflecting a later literary stage than the Greek version. Professor S. Pisano for his part made use of Greek and Masoretic versions of the books of Samuel, to underscore the complexity of the relationships between these two witnesses.

4. The fourth session, 28–29 April 1995, was considered by a number of the participants as one of the crucial moments of the exercise. It involved comparing the concurrent theories on *the historical origins, stages and contexts of Deuteronomistic historiography*, then evaluating the contribution of diachronic and synchronic methods to the understanding of it all. We were able to rely on the presence of two eminent representatives of the schools of Harvard and Göttingen. The first school advocates, as is known, a Josianic date for the origin of Deuteronomistic historiography, while the second has it all beginning with the Babylonian Exile. By a fortunate coincidence, the two speakers had each chosen to base their theses on the same literary corpus, the accounts on the institution of the monarchy. However, this session had a big surprise in store. Professor S.L. McKenzie, contrary to his previous publications, abandoned the Josianic dating and proposed a first edition of DH between 597 and 587 at Mizpah, therefore immediately after the first deportation. As for Walter Dietrich (Professor at the University of Berne), he remained faithful to his theses of three successive Deuteronomistic redactions, but showed himself much more optimistic than his American colleague on the possibility of reconstructing pre-Deuteronomistic documents. The contribution of Françoise Smyth on the account of the discovery of the book by Josiah (2 Kgs 22–23) was a good example of a fruitful combination of synchronic and diachronic readings.

5. 12 May 1995, at Lausanne, our session fitted in as a logical continuation of the paths opened up in our fourth session. This time our objective was to go upstream from the DH and sound ourselves out on *the sources* of the work. Professor J. Briend (Paris) chose the accounts of the conquest in the book of Joshua to support his thesis that the postexilic DH had been preceded by a Josianic collector who had gathered together some local traditions. As a pedagogic device, Professor Briend had provided the participants with pages containing his reconstruction of the oldest layer and this greatly facilitated the discussion.

6. 2 June 1995, at Neuchâtel, our meeting was devoted to the *Deuteronomistic milieus*. The interveners were Professors Rainer Albertz[1] and Ernst Axel Knauf. The first insisted on the complexity of such so-called Deuteronomistic milieus, by showing among other things that the

---

1.   Unfortunately, the contribution of R. Albertz could not appear in the present volume. The English reader may consult his article in T. Römer (ed.), *The Future of Deuteronomistic History* (BETL, 147; Leuven: Peeters, 2000), pp. 1-17.

similarity of the language could conceal profound ideological differences. He based his demonstration on a comparison between the principal theologoumenons of the DH and the Deuteronomistic editors of the book of Jeremiah. The pro-monarchic ideology continues to be dominant in the historiography, whereas hostility in regard to royalty and the Temple characterizes the Deuteronomistic Jeremiah. Knauf pointed out that he would share this opinion, but went further by questioning in a radical way the very existence of such a Deuteronomistic historiography as it had been understood by Martin Noth. For him the 'Deuteronomistic milieus' existed of course, but not a coherent literary project coming from these milieus that would cover the entirety of Deuteronomy to 2 Kings. Professor Knauf thus became the spokesperson of a line of questioning in regard to which it can be asked if it will not oblige researchers to re-examine what is understood by 'a literary work'. Finally, in order to clarify the question of the coherence or non-coherence of Deuteronomistic milieus from a still different time, we introduce here a contribution of T. Römer on the Deuteronomistic redaction of the book of Jeremiah.

7. 23–24 June 1995 was the final weekend of the doctoral level seminar and the meeting took place once again in the friendly surroundings of the Centre Saint Dominique at Pensier. It was now time to draw up the balance sheet on the exercise, and that on several levels. The chosen theme was Deuteronomistic Ideology and Theology of the Old Testament. Professors A.D.H. Mayes and M. Rose proposed, each in his own way, a well thought-out synthesis of Deuteronomic theology, with Professor Mayes putting more emphasis on the integration of this theology into a concrete sociological situation, whereas Professor Rose, in proposing a reading moving from 'the experience of failure' to a 'kerygma of redemption', placed his ideas in a more firmly theological perspective in the traditional acceptance of this term. These two presentations very well illustrate to what extent every historico-critical investigation into the texts of the Old Testament, if it is carried out without any compromise, remains in tune with the fundamental theological preoccupations of all times.

Do the origins, the nature and the historical and ideological context of Deuteronomistic historiography appear today in a clearer light? Have we reached our goal? Ultimately it will be up to the reader to decide. What we hope is that the completed journey will have given to each one, as well as to ourselves too, the desire to go back again to this historical literature of ancient Israel and to reflect on the way in which this vision of history has marked our culture and our collective unconscious.

Before concluding, we want to express our immense gratitude to all those who made possible the development and completion of this book. We thank first of all, needless to say, all the authors who gave us their assistance and whose contributions we are proud to publish today, but also all those who participated in the task of translating and revising manuscripts. Their dedication to this knew no bounds, but was shown, for weeks and months, until late into the night! Thanks are owed here especially to Mr Alain Bühlmann, Ms Florence Clerc, Mr Pietro Piffaretti and Mr Jean-Pierre Zurn, who tirelessly translated, grappled with, corrected, reread the complex texts, as well as to Ms Emmanuelle Steffek. Last but not least, our gratitude is extended to Professor Françoise Smyth: from the beginning she was our great interlocutor, then our foremost 'reader', finally, on more than one occasion our final arbiter on questions of style and choice of words. May all find here a mark of our gratitude.

ABBREVIATIONS

AAA	*Annals of Archaeology and Anthropology*
ÄAT	Ägypten und Altes Testament
AASF.B	Annales Academiae Scientiarum Fennicae, Series B
AB	Anchor Bible
ABBU	Altbabylonische Briefe in Umschrift und Übersetzung
ABD	David Noel Freedman (ed.), *The Anchor Bible Dictionary* (New York: Doubleday, 1992)
ABRL	Anchor Bible Reference Library
AfO	*Archiv für Orientforschung*
AJBI	Annual of the Japanese Biblical Association
AnBib	Analecta biblica
AOAT	Alter Orient und Altes Testament
APOT	R.H. Charles (ed.), *Apocrypha and Pseudepigrapha of the Old Testament in English* (2 vols.; Oxford: Clarendon Press, 1913)
ARM	Archives royales de Mari
ARRIM	*Annual Review of the Royal Inscriptions of Mesopotamia Project*
ATANT	Abhandlungen zur Theologie des Alten und Neuen Testaments
ATD	Das Alte Testament Deutsch
AThD	Acta Theologica Danica
ATSAT	Arbeiten zu Text und Sprache im Alten Testament
BAT	Botschaft des Alten Testaments
BDBAT	Beihefte zu den Dielheimer Blättern zum Alten Testament
BBB	Bonner biblische Beiträge
BEATAJ	Beiträge zur Erforschung des Alten Testaments und des antiken Judentums
BET	Beiträge zur biblischen Exegese und Theologie
BETL	Bibliotheca ephemeridum theologicarum lovaniensium
BEvT	Beiträge zur evangelischen Theologie
BHK	R. Kittel (ed.), *Biblia hebraica* (Stuttgart: Württembergische Bibelanstalt, 1937)
BHS	*Biblia hebraica stuttgartensia*
Bib	*Biblica*
BiOr	*Bibliotheca Orientalis*
BK	*Bibel und Kirche*

BKAT	Biblischer Kommentar: Altes Testament
BN	*Biblische Notizen*
BPO	Babylonian Planetary Omens
BTB	*Biblical Theology Bulletin*
BWANT	Beiträge zur Wissenschaft vom Alten und Neuen Testament
BZ	*Biblische Zeitschrift*
BZAW	Beihefte zur *ZAW*
BZNF	Biblische Zeitschrift. Neue Folge
CAT	Commentaire de l'Ancien Testament
CBQ	*Catholic Biblical Quarterly*
CBQMS	*Catholic Biblical Quarterly*, Monograph Series
ConBOT	Coniectanea biblica, Old Testament
CRBS	*Currents in Research: Biblical Studies*
CTh	Cahiers théologiques
DBAT	*Dielheimer Blätter zum Alten Testament*
DiTh	Dissertationen. Theologische Reihe
DLZ	*Deutsche Literaturzeitung*
EBib	Etudes bibliques
EdF	Erträge der Forschung
EHS.T	Europäische Hochschulschriften. Theologie
EstBíb	*Estudios bíblicos*
EThS	Erfurter theologische Schriften
ETL	*Ephemerides theologicae lovanienses*
ETR	*Etudes théologiques et religieuses*
FAOS	Freiburger altorientalische Studien
FAT	Forschungen zum Alten Testament
FzB	Forschung zur Bibel
FRLANT	Forschungen zur Religion und Literatur des Alten und Neuen Testaments
GThT	Gereformeerd theologisch tijdschrift
HAT	Handbuch zum Alten Testament
HSM	Harvard Semitic Monographs
HTR	*Harvard Theological Review*
IB	Interpreter's Bible
ICC	International Critical Commentary
IEJ	*Israel Exploration Journal*
Int	*Interpretation*
JA	*Journal asiatique*
JB	*Jerusalem Bible*
JBL	*Journal of Biblical Literature*
JBS	Jerusalem Bible Studies
JNES	*Journal of Near Eastern Studies*
JSOT	*Journal for the Study of the Old Testament*
JSOTSup	*Journal for the Study of the Old Testament*, Supplement Series
JTVI	*Journal of the Transactions of the Victoria Institute*

JTS	*Journal of Theological Studies*
KAT	Kurzgefaßtes exegetisches Handbuch: Altest Testament
KHAT	Kurzer Hand-Kommentar zum Alten Testament
LAPO	Littératures anciennes du Proche-Orient
LD	Lectio divina
MDP	Mémoires de la Délégation en Perse
MTA	Münsteraner theologische Abhandlungen
NCB	New Century Bible
NEB	Neue Echter Bibel
NRT	*La nouvelle revue théologique*
NSK-AT	Neuer Stuttgarter Kommentar-Altes Testament
OBO	Orbis biblicus et orientalis
OECT	Oxford Editions of Cuneiform Texts
OIP	Oriental Institute Publications
OLA	*Orientalia lovaniensia analecta*
OTG	Old Testament Guides
OTL	Old Testament Library
OTS	Oudtestamentische Studiën
PRSt	*Perspectives in Religious Studies*
PW	August Friedrich von Pauly and Georg Wissowa (eds.), *Real-Encyclopädie der classischen Altertumswissenschaft* (Stuttgart: Metzler, 1894–)
QD	Questiones Disputatae
RA	*Revue d'assyriologie et d'archéologie orientale*
RB	*Revue biblique*
RechBib	Recherches bibliques
RHPR	*Revue d'histoire et de philosophie religieuses*
RivB	*Rivista biblica*
RTP	*Revue de théologie et de philosophie*
RUB	Reclams Universität Bibliothek
SAA	State Archives of Assyria
SAAB	State Archives of Assyria. Bulletin
SB	Sources bibliques
SBAB	Stuttgarter biblische Aufsatzbände
SBB	Stuttgarter biblische Beiträge
SBLDS	SBL Dissertation Series
SBLMS	SBL Monograph Series
SBLRBS	SBL Resources for Biblical Study
SBLSCS	SBL Septuagint and Cognate Studies
SBLSP	SBL Seminar Papers
SBS	Stuttgarter Bibelstudien
SbWGF	Sitzungsberichte der wissenschaftlichen Gesellschaft an der Johann Wolfgang-Goethe Universität Frankfurt a.M.
ScrHier	*Scripta Hierosolymitana*
SCSt	Septuagint and Cognate Studies Series

SJLA	Studies in Judaism in Late Antiquity
SJOT	*Scandinavian Journal of the Old Testament*
STAT.AASF	Suomalainen Tiedeakatemian Toimituksia. Annales Academiae Scientiarum Fennicae
STDJ	Studies on the Texts of the Desert of Judah
STF	Studi e testi francescani
SThT	Studia theologica Teresianum
TBü	Theologische Bücherei
TCL	Textes cunéiformes du Louvre
ThExh	Theologische Existenz heute
ThR	*Theologische Revue*
ThSt	Theologische Studien
TLZ	*Theologische Literaturzeitung*
TRE	*Theologische Realenzyklopädie*
TZ	*Theologische Zeitschrift*
USQR	*Union Seminary Quarterly Review*
VF	*Verkündigung und Forschung*
VT	*Vetus Testamentum*
VTSup	*Vetus Testamentum*, Supplements
VVAW.L	Verhandelingen van de K. Vlaamse Academie voor Wetenschappen, Letteren en Schone Kunsten von België, Klasse der Letteren
WBC	Word Biblical Commentary
WMANT	Wissenschaftliche Monographien zum Alten und Neuen Testament
YOS	Yale Oriental Series
ZAH	*Zeitschrift für Althebraistik*
ZAW	*Zeitschrift für die alttestamentliche Wissenschaft*
ZBK.AT	Zürcher Bibel-Kommentar Altes Testament
ZTK	*Zeitschrift für Theologie und Kirche*

LIST OF CONTRIBUTORS

Jacques Briend is Professor of Old Testament at l'Institut Catholique de Paris and is the author of works on archaeology, epigraphy and the history of the ancient Near East and of Israel. His works touch as well on the most diverse aspects of biblical literature. He has particularly attracted attention because of his works on Joshua and Kings.

Marcel Detienne is Professor at Johns Hopkins University of Baltimore and Director of Research at l'École Pratique des Hautes Etudes de Paris. He is the author of numerous books on mythology, the religion and the anthropology of archaic and classical Greece.

Walter Dietrich is Professor of Old Testament at the University of Berne. He has published several works on the redaction history of the Deuteronomistic corpus, on Isaiah, on the Joseph story and, especially, on the books of Samuel.

Jean-Jacques Glassner is a researcher at CNRS and has taught Akkadian and the history of the ancient Near East in several universities. His publications deal in particular with the notion of history and destiny in the Mesopotamian world; he is the author of a French translation of the main historiographical texts of this region.

Sara Japhet is Professor of Bible at the Hebrew University in Jerusalem and has made major contributions to the study of the books of Chronicles, particularly through the publication of an important commentary on these books. She has published as well works dealing with questions of biblical historiography and of rabbinic literature.

Ernst-Axel Knauf is Professor of Hebrew and Semitic Philology at the University of Geneva and, since 1996, at the University of Berne. He is the author of books on Midian, Ishmael and the world of the Old Testament. A specialist particularly in epigraphy, in archaeology and in the history of Transjordan, he has published studies on the most diverse aspects of biblical and Near Eastern literature.

Andrew D.H. Mayes is Professor of Old Testament at Trinity College of Dublin and has contributed several works on Deuteronomistic historiography, on Deuteronomy and on the book of Judges. He is as well a leading expert on questions linked to the history of Israel.

Steven L. McKenzie is Professor of Old Testament at Rhodes College in Memphis. He has published several works on Deuteronomistic historiography, on the relation between this and the books of Chronicles and on the books of Kings. He has recently edited a collective publication devoted to the work of Martin Noth.

Stephen Pisano is Professor at the Pontifical Biblical Institute in Rome and is a specialist on the textual criticism of the Old Testament. He is a member of the committee in charge of the critical revision of the Hebrew Bible of Stuttgart and has published in particular a work on the books of Samuel.

Martin Rose is Professor of Old Testament at the University of Neuchâtel. He has published works in support of the exclusiveness of the God of Israel, on the relation between the Pentateuch and the historical books, a commentary on Deuteronomy as well as various studies on biblical hermeneutics.

Adrian Schenker is Professor of Old Testament at the University of Fribourg (Switzerland). He has published numerous works on the Hebrew text and on the Septuagint, as well as on cult, sacrifice and the central concepts of the religion of Israel. His very diverse work deals as well with exegesis and biblical theology.

Françoise Smyth is Professor of Old Testament at l'Institut Protestant de Théologie of Paris, is interested, from many angles, in the contribution of anthropology to the study of the Bible. Among her many publications, special note should be taken of an outstanding study on the promise of the land in the Old Testament and its Jewish and Christian reception.

Albert de Pury is Professor of Old Testament at the University of Geneva and editor of the present volume. He is the author of a work on the Jacob cycle and of various other studies on biblical literature, in particular on the legends about the beginnings of Israel. He edited *Le Pentateuque en question* (Geneva: Labor et Fides, 1989).

Thomas Römer is Professor of Old Testament at the University of Lausanne and editor of the present volume. He is the author of a work on the theme of the Ancestors in Deuteronomistic Historiography and of various other works, especially on the question of the redaction of biblical literature.

Part I
INTRODUCTION

DEUTERONOMISTIC HISTORIOGRAPHY (DH):
HISTORY OF RESEARCH AND DEBATED ISSUES

Thomas Römer and Albert de Pury

Anyone who is interested in the redaction of the Hebrew Bible will inevitably be confronted with the hypothesis of 'Deuteronomistic Historiography'.[1] This theory, due to Martin Noth, stipulates that the books from Deuteronomy to Kings constitute a redactional unity elaborated during the Babylonian exile. Unlike the Torah, DH therefore is not a corpus marked out by tradition but consists of an end result—nothing but an end result, though certainly a well established one—of modern exegetical research.

We might be surprised that exegetes took so long to discover the existence of such a work. However, this is easily explained. As a matter of fact, the elaboration of the theory of a DH roughly coincides with the period in which exegesis began to be interested in *Redaktions-geschichte*, that is to say in the work of redactors arranging and editing the biblical text from older material. Before the use of this method, the so-called 'historical' books were read with a certain naïvety, and it was assumed that their authors were content to describe or reproduce authentic events. It was accepted certainly that the authors in question gave a theological interpretation of the history, but hardly any interest was shown in (what could be) their literary project. This methodological shift was to a great extent brought about by Noth's research on DH. Even if Noth, as we shall see, was quite conservative in his conclusions, his initiative made it possible to understand the historical books and Deuteronomy above all as ideological constructions, and only then as sources for the history of Israel. For modern exegesis of the historical books, *Überlieferungsgeschichtliche Studien*, in which Noth elaborated in 1943 the thesis of a DH constitutes a major turning

---

1.   Abbreviated henceforth in this volume to DH.

point. That is why we will divide up the history of research into a 'before' and an 'after' Noth.

Our overview is intended to help the reader understand the present debate and to make clear what is involved. The discussion on DH and Deuteronomism in general is in no way an intellectual occupation reserved to a few experts. The various hypotheses presented imply strongly divergent views on the evolution and status of the books going from Deuteronomy to 2 Kings. To understand better how Israel constructed its history is the real intellectual challenge of this debate.

We should note too that in the upheaval of the last 20 years or so with regard to theories on the formation of the Pentateuch, we have often been tempted to present DH as *the* unshakeable pillar that still offered Old Testament studies relatively certain reference points. However, as we will see, the Noth thesis has been very quickly modified and the Deuteronomist (Dtr) of Noth is not inevitably that of his successors. Besides, today it must be noted that DH is suffering from fissures. Must these be plastered over or must the pillar be left to crumble? We will try to take a bearing and bring out the perspectives that the Deuteronomic question opens up in the current exegetical discussions.

1. *'Prehistory'*

1.1. *The Traditional View of the Books of Joshua to 2 Kings*

The books of Joshua to 2 Kings, which Jewish tradition referred to under the name of 'Former Prophets' and Christian tradition under that of 'Historical Books', did not have in traditional exegesis, it must definitely be stated, the same impact as the books of the Pentateuch, and consequently scarcely aroused the same exegetical frenzy. The reason for this relative lack of interest evidently lies in the fact that the Torah, like the Former Prophets, insists on the difference in 'canonical level' that separates these two collections of books: the entire Law is contained in the books of the Torah (Deut. 4.2; 13.1); Joshua is presented as the successor of Moses, but of inferior rank (Num. 11.28; Deut. 31.1-8, 14-23; Josh. 1.1-9), and the Pentateuch closes with a passage that declares that in any case, 'Never since has there arisen a prophet in Israel like Moses, whom Yhwh knew face to face...' (Deut. 34.10-12). For Jewish tradition at any rate, the exegetical stakes are therefore less important when beginning with the book of Joshua, and, on this point, Christian tradition—in spite of the New Testament insistence on the prophetic nature of the Scriptures—tended to follow it. We will note however that the passage from Deut. 34.10f. to Joshua 1, the opening of the collection of the *Nebiim*, clearly implies that the normative mediating authority for the transmission of the Torah as well as of the historical books is that of the prophets.

The first text to have taken up openly the question of the authority of the historical books is the famous passage of *B. Bat.* (§§14b-15a) in the Babylonian Talmud:

> Who wrote the Scriptures?—Moses wrote his own book and the section about Balaam as well as Job. Joshua wrote the book that bears his name and [the last] eight verses of the Pentateuch. Samuel wrote the book that bears his name and the book of Judges as well as Ruth... Jeremiah wrote the book that bears his name, the book of Kings and the Lamentations...

In a paragraph farther on, in the same context, the Talmud raises some possible objections:

> [You say that] Joshua wrote his book. But is it not written, *And Joshua, son of Nun, the servant of the Lord, died*? [Josh. 24.29]. [The book] was completed by Eleazar. But it is also written *And Eleazar, son of Aaron, died* [Josh. 24.33]? Phinehas completed [the book]. [You say that] Samuel wrote the book that bears his name. But is it not written *Now Samuel had died*? [1 Sam. 28.3]. The book was completed by Gad, the seer, and Nathan, the prophet.

There are several interesting points in this passage: on the one hand, each book is attributed to an author contemporaneous with the reported events—and even, as far as possible, to the principal hero in these events—but only insofar as the hero is a 'prophet'! Furthermore, we detect some beginnings of a diachronic sensibility, since the possibility is accepted that other hands might have contributed to the completion of the book. On the other hand, we perceive hardly any sensitivity in regard to thematic or stylistic characteristics: nothing is said, for example, about the specific bond that unites Deuteronomy to the historical books. At the very most we can wonder whether the attribution to Jeremiah of the book of Kings does not convey an awareness of the literary affinity between the prophetic book and the compilation of the book of Kings.

1.2. *Early Problems, First Critical Questions*

Right from the beginning of rabbinic and patristic exegesis, a certain number of questions came up in regard to the coherence and internal logic of the biblical books. In the case of the Former Prophets, these questions had to do in particular with the following problems:

- Some biblical statements are at variance with human experience. Example: the sun stopped in its course by Joshua (Josh. 10.2-14).
- Some of the behaviour of biblical heroes is contrary to Judaeo-Christian ethics. Examples: Jephthah sacrificing his daughter (Judg. 11.29-40); David bringing about the death of Uriah (2 Sam. 11-12).
- Some texts contradict others. Examples: Joshua 1–12 and Judges 1 give very different versions of the conquest of Canaan. The books of Samuel and Kings have many details that contradict the books of Chronicles.

In a context where the direct inspiration of the Scriptures is never doubted, these observations, however, did not really lead to a critical analysis, but on the contrary served to bolster and consolidate an apologetic approach.

A good example of this approach is given in the *Quaestiones* of Theodoret of Cyrene (d. 457) on the Pentateuch, Joshua, Judges, Kings, Ruth and 1 Chronicles,[2] or again in the *Thirty Questions* on the book of Kings to which Venerable Bede responded (d. 735); he is also the author of a commentary on 1 Samuel.[3] We see appearing in these writings, besides the search for a spiritual interpretation of the historical books, a pronounced interest in questions of history and geography.

This apologetic tendency will continue moreover until the Reformation and the humanistic period, and even well beyond. We can cite as an example the Lutheran Abraham Calov, a sworn enemy of Grotius,[4] who vehemently rejected the poetic interpretation (*phrasis poetica*) proposed by Grotius for Josh. 10.13 and insisted on the historical veracity of the stopping of the sun without any regard for the discoveries of

---

2. *Theodoreti Cyrensis Quaestiones in Octateuchum* (critical edition; Madrid: Seminario filológico Cardenal Cisheras, 1991). Cf. L. Diestel, *Geschichte des Alten Testamentes in der christlichen Kirche* (Jena: Mauke, 1869), pp. 133-34.

3. Beda Venerabilis, *In Regum Librum XXX Quaestiones: In Primam partem Samuelis*; cf. H. Graf Reventlow, *Epochen der Bibelauslegung. II. Von der Spätantike bis zum Ausgang des Mittelalters* (Munich: Beck, 1994), p. 122.

4. Cf. in this connection, H.-J. Kraus, *Geschichte der historisch-kritischen Erforschung des Alten Testaments* (Neukirchen–Vluyn: Neukirchener Verlag, 3rd edn, 1982), p. 53.

Copernicus.[5] Calov will have his successors throughout the history of exegesis: Hengstenberg and many others. It is understandable that this limited and essentially 'defensive' approach would have impeded in these circles any serious inquiry in regard to the stylistic and theological features of the historical books, despite the interest shown by the humanists and Reformers in the study of the Hebrew language.

1.3. *The Question of the Authors and the Formation of the Books Raised in the Period of the Reformation*

As we have seen, already in Judaism's traditional thought, it was possible to accept the intervention of a second hand after the death of the presumed author of each of the books going from Deuteronomy to Samuel. Jewish exegesis in the Middle Ages was particularly attentive to these diachronic problems. Thus, to justify his doubts regarding the provenenace of Isaiah 40–66 from the hand of the prophet Isaiah, Ibn Ezra chose the example of the book of Samuel: the death of the prophet is reported in 1 Samuel 25, which proves that all the remaining chapters have been compiled by others.[6] The Reformers who, in spite of the doctrine of divine inspiration, remained aware of the human form of Sacred Scripture, likewise raised the question of authors. In the introduction to his commentary on the book of Joshua, Calvin rejected the accepted tradition according to which Joshua himself would have been the author of his book.[7] For Calvin, that idea was not defensible, any more than the attribution of the book of Samuel to the prophet Samuel.[8] The book of Joshua could have been composed from documents compiled by the priest Eleazar.[9] Thus, even if Calvin had a contemporary of Joshua intervene, we see that the production of the book was situated for him in a later period. Still more radical theses were defended by the Catholic jurist Andreas Masius (1516–1573). In his book *Josuae imperatoris*

---

5.   Diestel, *Geschichte des Alten Testament in der christlichen Kirche*, pp. 404-405.

6.   Cf. Reventlow, *Epochen der Bibelauslegung*, II, pp. 250-51.

7.   For what follows, cf. Kraus, *Geschichte der historisch-kritischen Erforschung*, p. 17.

8.   Already in 1520, A.B. Karlstadt (1486–1541) had declared that the author of Samuel was unknown. Cf. Kraus, *Geschichte der historisch-kritischen Erforschung*, p. 30.

9.   In a certain way, Calvin takes up and radicalizes a Talmudic opinion (cf. above).

historia illustrata et explicata (1574), Masius first presents a critical edition of the *text* of Joshua, challenging the authority of the LXX. And in his commentary we find for the first time such terms as 'compilation' and 'redaction'.[10] For him, it was Ezra who, with others 'remarkable for their piety and erudition', had compiled not only the book of Joshua, but also the books of Judges and Kings. The works of Calvin and Masius indicate therefore the realization of a historical distance, and also the beginning of a sensibility about the 'priestly' character of some parts of Joshua.

1.4. *The Criticism of the Rationalists and Deists*

From the eighteenth century onward, the study of biblical texts was useful, in 'enlightened' circles, for contesting the authority of the Church. Questions of a historical and stylistic type developed. But alongside these 'classical' questions there arose a new area of inquiry, an area which would be called today ideological criticism. It became possible to take a critical stance in regard to the heroes of the historical books, even to read the accounts concerning them in a sense contrary to what was put forward by the biblical authors. Thus Thomas Morgan finds fault with the behaviour of Samuel facing Saul.[11] The prophet acted out of pique, suspecting Saul of wishing to reduce his influence over the people. As for Ahab and his wife Jezabel, Morgan considers them authentic humanists and heroes of tolerance up against the fanaticism of prophets and zealots of the Elijah type. The Babylonian Exile, finally, was nothing else but the result of a poor foreign policy.

This polemical reading of the historical books served in a way to set up the distinction between a historical event and its (often subsequent) interpretation. We become aware of the fact that the account of the institution of the monarchy in 1 Samuel 8–12, for example, is made up of different and contradictory versions of the same event and express irreconcilable opinions about it. Likewise, we find that between the books of Samuel–Kings and those of Chronicles there are differences that cannot be harmonized.[12] Thus, Spinoza, in his *Tractatus* of 1670, observes:

---

10. Such is at least the view of Kraus, *Geschichte der historisch-kritischen Erforschung*, p. 39.

11. T. Morgan, *The Moral Philosopher* (1737–40); cf. the presentation of Diestel, *Geschichte des Alten Testaments in der christlichen Kirche*, pp. 545-46.

12. Cf. the presentation of Diestel, *Geschichte des Alten Testaments in der christlichen Kirche*, pp. 520-21.

> Anyone who compares the narratives in Chronicles with the narratives in the books of Kings, will find many similar discrepancies. These there is no need for me to examine here, and still less am I called upon to treat of the Commentaries of those who endeavour to harmonize them. The Rabbis evidently let their fancy run wild.

Spinoza reached the conclusion that 'we are compelled to confess that these histories were compiled from various writers without previous arrangement and examination.'[13]

Parallel with this first historical criticism of the contents of the books, the traditional point of view about their authors was abandoned. Thomas Hobbes (1651) insists on the fact that research on the dates of the biblical books should be carried out in total independence with respect to tradition.[14] In Deuteronomy, for example, only the legislative code comes from the Mosaic period, while the discourse framework as well as the books of Joshua and Samuel must have been written much later than the period to which they refer. This is especially shown by the formula 'to this day' that recurs time and again.[15] For the books of Judges and Ruth, Hobbes seems to be the one who for the first time is thinking of a date in the exilic period. In fact, in Judg. 18.30, it is said that 'Jonathan son of Gershom, son of Moses, then his sons were priests to the tribe of the Danites until the time of the deportation from the land'. For the book of Kings, a dating in the period of the exile is, at any rate, evident.[16]

Spinoza produces roughly the same reflection—even if, for the book of Judges, he thinks rather of the monarchic period—but he goes beyond Hobbes when he raises besides the question of the coherence between the Pentateuch and the Former Prophets:

> Evidently if we consider the continuation and object of all these books, we will have no difficulty in recognizing that they are the work of a single historian, who set out to write Jewish antiquities from the most remote times up to the first destruction of Jerusalem. These books, in fact, are so closely linked that it is evident, from this point alone, that

13. Cited from B. de Spinoza, *A Theologico-Political Treatise* (trans. R.H.M. Elwes; New York: Dover Publications, Inc., 1951), pp. 138-39 (138).

14. On this point, cf. Kraus, *Geschichte der historisch-kritischen Erforschung des Alten Testaments*, pp. 57-58.

15. We already come across this same argument in Masius and in Spinoza.

16. T. Hobbes, *Leviathan*, Chapter 33. Cf. the edition of R. Tuck (Cambridge Texts in the History of Political Thought; Cambridge: Cambridge University Press, 1991), pp. 262-63.

they form one and the same account, composed by one and the same historian.[17]

Spinoza recognized too that the books from Joshua to Kings serve to confirm all the predictions of Moses in Deuteronomy: 'It is therefore evident that all these books work together for one purpose alone, which is to make known the words and commandments of Moses and to prove their excellence through an account of the events'.[18]

As far as we know, Spinoza is the first to have sensed clearly this link between Deuteronomy and the historical books, as well as the 'nomistic' character of these latter. If Deuteronomy constitutes their centre, Spinoza nevertheless supposed a great historiographical work going from Genesis to the end of 2 Kings. And this thesis, we must say, has never since lacked supporters, and this even in the most recent discussions. The idea that the author of this great historiography could be Ezra is certainly not the most original idea of the Jewish philosopher, since it probably came to him from the rabbinic tradition. It is nevertheless a fact that based on this idea, it was the postexilic period that henceforth came to mind as the most probable historical setting for the composition of the historical books, without denying, to be sure, the existence of more ancient documents.[19]

In the Catholic ecclesiastical context, it is Richard Simon who defends, in his *Histoire Critique du Vieux Testament* (1678), similar theses. Rationalist and anti-Protestant at the same time, Simon postulates the existence of a chain of traditions extending from Moses up to Ezra. In this way, he introduces as it were the idea of *Überlieferungsgeschichte*. By attributing to the 'scribes' an important part in the process of organizing and editing the historical books, Simon advances an idea that will only reappear in the debate two centuries later. It is for this reason that some like to see in Simon the founder of historico-critical exegesis.[20] We must point out, however, that his ideas on the authors of the Former Prophets were quite conservative, since he regarded Samuel as the initial author of Judges and Ruth and Jeremiah of Samuel and Kings.

17. Saisset (trans.), *Oeuvres de Spinoza*, p. 164.
18. Saisset (trans.), *Oeuvres de Spinoza*, p. 165.
19. Saisset (trans.), *Oeuvres de Spinoza*, pp. 169-70. Cf. also P. Gibert, *Petite histoire de l'exégèse biblique* (Lire la Bible, 94; Paris: Cerf, 1992), pp. 204-11.
20. Cf. Kraus, *Geschichte der Historisch-kritischen Erforschung des Alten Testaments*, pp. 65, 70; P. Gibert, *Petite histoire de l'exégèse biblique*, pp. 211-22.

1.5. Summary: The Books of Joshua–Kings on the Eve of the Birth of Historico-Critical Exegesis

Until the end of the eighteenth century, the historical books continued in their role as 'poor relatives' in respect to the great debate that was so concerned about the Mosiac authenticity of the Pentateuch. The few questions that the experts considered in regard to them focused on the following problems:

- *the author:* outside of orthodox circles, the tradition that attributed the historical books to their respective heroes or to some of their contemporaries was refuted. The chronological interval that separated the period referred to from the period of the first writing was stressed.
- *the formation of the books:* from the observation of material contradictions and stylistic differences arose the idea of the existence, in the beginning, of multiple sources or documents. The merging of these documents by compilers is the best explanation of the formation of the books.
- *the internal coherence of the books and their connection with Deuteronomy, even with the Pentateuch:* this question especially comes up in Spinoza. It is he who, even if he does not yet use the term 'Deuteronomist', discovers that the books Joshua–Kings conform to a common 'Deuteronomic' spirit.

On the eve of the birth of the historico-critical method itself, almost all the crucial points that are going to be found in research on the Prophets up to the present have thus already been turned up. But we note too the extent to which the research of that period is still prompted by intuitive judgments.

2. *The Discovery of the Deuteronomic Phenomenon*

2.1. De Wette and Vater

The work of the young Wilhelm Martin Leberecht de Wette (1780–1849) probably represents the first decisive step in the process that had to lead to the discovery of Deuteronomistic historiography, and perhaps proves Rogerson right when he sees in de Wette the 'founder of modern biblical criticism'.[21] The contribution of de Wette to research on the

---

21. On the bibliography of W.M.L. de Wette, cf. in particular R. Smend,

Pentateuch has been emphasized many times, but we are less frequently reminded that de Wette seems to have been, with Vater, the first to have used the term 'Deuteronomic' to characterize the redactional texts of the historical books.[22] Let us recall that in his 1805 thesis, de Wette—in a note at the bottom of the page!—established that the book that, according to 2 Kings 22–23, was at the origin of the reform of Josiah must correspond to the biblical book of Deuteronomy or, at least, to an earlier form of this book. Such an identification in itself was not new— the Church Fathers had already ventured assumptions going in this direction—but what was new, incontestably, was the historical con- clusion that de Wette drew from his observations: 'primitive' Deuteron- omy, he maintained, had been composed, then introduced in the Temple, as a propaganda document at the service of the Josianic reform! The book cannot therefore be dated to a period prior to the reign of Josiah (640–609). For the first time, biblical criticism had an anchorage point for the dating of the documents of the Pentateuch.[23] At the same time, de Wette divided the Pentateuch into Tetrateuch and Deuteronomy: he considered Deuteronomy, whose special character he emphasized in comparison with the other books of the Torah, as the most recent document of the Pentateuch and saw it as especially linked with the book of Joshua. He had intended to develop his ideas in the *Beiträge zur Einleitung in das Alte Testament*, but then the third volume of the commentary on the Pentateuch of Johann Severin Vater was published,[24] a commentary in which the latter insisted on the close bond

Deutsche Alttestamentler in drei Jahrhunderten (Göttingen: Vandenhoeck & Rup- recht, 1989), pp. 38-52; and J.W. Rogerson, *W.M.L. de Wette, Founder of Modern Biblical Criticism: An Intellectual Biography* (JSOTSup, 126; Sheffield: JSOT Press, 1992).

22. In most manuals, the origin of the idea of a Deuteronomistic redaction is not pinned down. O. Kaiser, for example, is content to write: 'Die Einsicht, dass...die Bücher Dtn—II Reg eine im Geist des Deuteronomiums tätige deuteronomistische (dtr) Bearbeitung erfahren haben, lässt sich bis in das 19. Jh. zurückverfolgen', (*Grundriss der Einleitung in die kanonischen und Deuterokanonischen Schriften des Alten Testaments. I. Die erzählenden Werke* [Gütersloh: Gerd Mohn, 1992], p. 86).

23. For more details, cf. S. Loersch, *Das Deuteronomium und seine Deutungen: ein forschungsgeschichtlicher Überblick* (SBS, 22; Stuttgart: Katholisches Bibel- werk, 1967), pp. 18-20; Rogerson, *W.M.L. de Wette*, pp. 39-42.

24. Cf. J. Rogerson, *Old Testament Criticism in the Nineteenth Century: England and Germany* (London: SPCK, 1984), pp. 35-36.

between Deuteronomy and the historical books and 'recognized what today are regarded as Deuteronomic glosses'.[25]

De Wette therefore rewrote his *Beiträge* in accordance with the book of Vater and published it in 1806.[26] In this work there comes to the fore—as later on in Wellhausen—a pronounced interest in the evolution of religious concepts, an interest behind which we conjecture the influence of Schelling and de Fries.[27] From then on, for de Wette, it was a question of understanding better the history of Israel, and he began his approach through a comparison between Samuel–Kings and the books of Chronicles. De Wette situated Chronicles about 330 BCE and questioned their whole historical credibility: they would have had as their only source Samuel–Kings that, for their part, must have been composed about 550 BCE. All the differences and contradictions are to be explained as ideological alterations on the part of the Chroniclers. It is interesting to note that, almost 130 years later, Noth too would follow up on his development of Deuteronomistic historiography with an analysis of the work of the Chronicler. This evaluation of the relation between Samuel–Kings and Chronicles, as Rogerson notes, was essential for modern exegesis,[28] at least up until the most recent years.[29]

It was especially in the analysis of the book of Joshua that de Wette became aware of the Deuteronomic phenomenon. Joshua is for him a late book and, as he points out in a note, permeated with the Deuteronomic style and theology.[30] It is this style that de Wette was the first to find in the other historical books as well.[31]

25. Cf. Rogerson, *Old Testament Criticism in the Nineteenth Century*, p. 35.

26. W.M.L. de Wette, *Beiträge zur Einleitung in das Alte Testament*. I. *Kritischer Versuch über die Glaubwürdigkeit der Bücher und Gesetzgebung* (Halle, 1806); II. *Kritik der israelitischen Geschichte. Erster Teil: Kritik der mosaischen Geschichte* (Halle, 1807; repr. Darmstadt: Wissenschaftliche Buchgesellschaft, 1971).

27. Cf. Rogerson, *Old Testament Criticism in the Nineteenth Century*, p. 42; Smend, *Deutsche Alttestamentler*, pp. 40, 47.

28. Rogerson, *W.M.L. de Wette*, p. 57.

29. S.L. McKenzie, *The Chronicler's Use of the Deuteronomistic History* (HSM, 33; Atlanta, GA: Scholars Press, 1985); A.G. Auld, *Kings without Privilege: David and Moses in the Story of the Bible's Kings* (Edinburgh: T. & T. Clark, 1994).

30. de Wette, *Beiträge zur Einleitung in das Alte Testament*, I, p. 137 n. 2.

31. Cf. Kraus, *Geschichte der historisch-kritischen Erforschung des Alten Testaments*, p. 176.

The work of the young de Wette makes the period of Josiah stand out as a crucial time both for the history of the religion of Israel[32] and for the formation of the historical books. By entrenching the birth of Deuteronomic ideology in the period of Josiah, de Wette has—perhaps without himself assessing the impact of his discovery—profoundly marked subsequent research.

2.2. *Towards the Idea of a Deuteronomic Composition of the Historical Books*

One of the first to take up de Wette's observations and to follow in the steps traced by him was Gramberg. In his *Histoire critique des idées religieuses de l'Ancien Testament*,[33] he presents the exilic period as fruitful for the production of Old Testament literature (Isa. 40–66; Proverbs; Job; Jonah). It is precisely in this period as well that there would have been compiled the books of Deuteronomy, Joshua and Kings, in which the whole history of the people is interpreted in light of the centralization of cult.[34]

In the same period, Karl-Heinrich Graf (1815–69) discovered the link between the books of Samuel and Kings. In a letter in 1840 to Eduard Reuss, his teacher and friend, Graf wrote: 'The books of Samuel contain a history of David in which a redactor has made additions; this redactor is at the same time the author of the books of Kings, that make up with Samuel a single work'.[35] By isolating in the books of Samuel an ancient history of David, edited in the same style found at each step in the books of Kings, Graf discovers a piece of information that will play an important role in the description of DH by Martin Noth.

Such observations were synthesized by Heinrich Ewald,[36] *enfant terrible* of German exegesis of the nineteenth century. Exactly one

---

32. The outline proposed by de Wette, absolute freedom of cult—a cult controlled by the monarchy—centralization of cult (cf. Rogerson, *W.M.L. de Wette*, pp. 59-60) is surprisingly close to that developed later by J. Wellhausen.

33. C.P.W. Gramberg, *Geschichte der Religionsideen des Alten Testaments* (2 vols.; Berlin: Duncker & Humblot, 1830), I, pp. 146-50.

34. For a presentation of the theses of C.P.W. Gramberg, cf. Rogerson, *Old Testament Criticism in the Nineteenth Century*, pp. 59-62.

35. K. Budde and H.J. Holtzmann (eds.), *Eduard Reuss' Briefwechsel mit seinem Schüler und Freunde Karl Heinrich Graf* (Giessen, 1904), p. 99.

36. Cf. J. Wellhausen, 'Heinrich Ewald', in *idem, Grundrisse zum Alten Testament* (ed. R. Smend; TBü, 8; Munich: Chr. Kaiser Verlag, 1965), pp. 120-38 (138).

hundred years before Noth, Ewald postulated a double Deuteronomic compilation of the historical books. In the first volume of his *History of Israel*, Ewald refers to the books of Genesis to Joshua as 'the great book of origins' and to those of Judges to 2 Kings (+ Ruth) as 'the great book of kings'.[37] The formation of this second 'great book' is reconstructed in the following manner: about 30 years after the separation of the two kingdoms of Israel and Judah, a Levite compiles, in a prophetic spirit, a history of the beginnings of the monarchy. This history begins with the birth of Samuel and ends perhaps in 1 Kings 12.[38] His goal would have been to describe the blessed period of the kingdom united under David.[39] The period of the Judges would have formed the subject of an initial historiographical presentation under the reign of Asa (912–871) or of Josaphat (870–846), and this would have served as a prologue to the history of the beginnings of the monarchy. Traces of this prologue would be preserved in Judges 1 and 17–21.[40] Another book referring to the period of the Judges would be hidden behind Judg. 3.7–12.15, and the Samson cycle (Judg. 13–16) would have a still different and much later origin. In the books of Kings, other documents, and especially the Elijah and Elisha cycles would have appeared between the ninth and eighth centuries.[41]

The first great compilation of the historical books combines the documents from the period of Samuel and the kings and edits them according to the 'Deuteronomic ideas' (*deuteronomische Ansichten*).[42] This

---

37. H. Ewald, *Geschichte des Volkes Israel bis Christus* (6 vols.; Göttingen: Dieterich, 1843–59). ET *History of Israel* (London, 1867–86).

38. Ewald, *Geschichte des Volkes Israel bis Christus*, I, pp. 174-90. According to Ewald, the end of this ancient history would have been suppressed at the time of the intervention of the compilers.

39. Cf. Ewald, *Geschichte des Volkes Israel bis Christus*, p. 180.

40. Ewald, *Geschichte des Volkes Israel bis Christus*, pp. 190-92.

41. Ewald, *Geschichte des Volkes Israel bis Christus*, pp. 192-95.

42. Ewald, *Geschichte des Volkes Israel bis Christus*, p. 196. We may note that Ewald accepts a Deuteronomic compilation likewise for 'the great book of origins' (Genesis–Joshua), and it is that compiler whom he refers to as the *Deuteronomiker*. This first 'Deuteronomic' compiler should not be confused however with the authors (*Schriftsteller*) influenced by Deuteronomy who are at work in 'the great book of kings' (Judges–2 Kings). The work of the first 'Deuteronomic' compiler is distinguished by the role played by the theologoumenon of 'the love of Yhwh' (up to Josh. 22.5; 23.11), whereas in the second great book, this theme is expressed by the phrase 'serve Yhwh with all your heart' (1 Sam. 7.3; 12.20, 24; 1 Kgs 2.4; 8.23,

compilation, as 1 Samuel 12 shows, must still have been produced under the monarchy, and consequently, the period of Josiah offers the most probable setting.[43] Its influence would account for the insertion especially of 1 Sam. 7.3-4; 12; 1 Kings 3; 6.11-13; 8.22-61, as well as other pieces in the same spirit.[44] In the second half of the Babylonian Exile (cf. 2 Kgs 25.27-30), a second redactor edited Judges–Kings, joining to them the book of Ruth (written by one of the exiles).[45] This exilic redactor sets out to answer 'the great and grave questions of the period: why the people found themselves subject to such great misfortunes'.[46] His hand is easily recognizable in some parenetic texts such as Judg. 2.6-23 or 2 Kgs 17.7-23.[47] It is this exilic redactor then, who prefaced the history of the monarchy with a prologue on the pre-monarchical period, the book of Judges, edited in a Deuteronomic spirit.[48] With Judg. 2.6-10 this redactor picks up the thread from the end of the book of Joshua and connects it to the final verses of the '*Deuteronomiker*' of Genesis–Joshua (Josh. 24.28-33). Despite the evidence of this explicit bond between Joshua and Judges, Ewald insists on the autonomy of his 'great book of kings' and declares in a peremptory tone: 'We would be wrong to come to the conclusion that the author would have wished to join his history book, using the book of Judges, to the book of Joshua and to the Pentateuch as a whole'.[49] The only

48; 14.8; 2 Kgs 10.31). Cf. Ewald, *Geschichte des Volkes Israel bis Christus*, p. 96 n. 1.

43. Cf. Ewald, *Geschichte des Volkes Israel bis Christus*, pp. 197-98.

44. For example 1 Sam. 2.1-10; 17; 18*; 21.11-26; 24 + 26; 28.3-5; cf. Ewald, *Geschichte des Volkes Israel bis Christus*, pp. 198-200.

45. In counting the book of Ruth among the historical books, Ewald follows, like most of his colleagues, the arrangement of the LXX (cf. *Geschichte des Volkes Israel bis Christus*, p. 203). In a general way, the LXX is often preferred to the MT. 'Die LXX welche nach dem Buch der Richter 4 Bücher der Könige zählen, zeigen wenigstens noch mehr Bewusstseyn von dem ursprünglichen Zusammenhange des grossen Werkes' (pp. 211-12).

46. Ewald, *Geschichte des Volkes Israel bis Christus*, p. 204. Noth will formulate, a hundred years later, the project of the Deuteronomist in quite comparable terms.

47. Ewald, *Geschichte des Volkes Israel bis Christus*, p. 205 n. 1.

48. Ewald, *Geschichte des Volkes Israel bis Christus*, pp. 206-207.

49. Ewald, *Geschichte des Volkes Israel bis Christus*, p. 210: 'Man würde hieraus mit Unrecht folgern, der Verfasser habe das Geschichtsbuch über die Richter mit dem B. Josua und dem Pentateuche in ein Ganzes verbinden wollen, denn er knüpft rein um eines passenden Anfanges willen an jenes Ende an, und dass jene

conclusion that Ewald draws from this assertion is that the Deuteronomic redaction of Joshua must be prior to that of Judges–Kings.

Ewald's theses received a large response in historico-critical exegesis
of the nineteenth century and were vehemently discussed. A good
example of Ewald's influence can be seen in the *Historisch-critisch
Onderzoek*[50] of Abraham Kuenen (1828–91). Kuenen begins by sub-
scribing to the observation that 'the books Judges–Kings are closely
connected together',[51] but he has no hesitation in expressing serious
reservations with regard to the conclusions of Ewald, without however
definitively rejecting them.[52] He objects, for example, that in Samuel,
the Dtr redaction is extremely restrained (limited to 1 Sam. 7; 8 and
12[53]), whereas it is present everywhere in Judges and Kings. He points
out moreover that the transition from Judges to Samuel does not take
place without a break. The fact that Judges as well as Samuel ends with
appendices is evidence instead of the autonomy of each of these
books.[54] Such objections will reappear in the stands of Fohrer, Würthwein or Westermann,[55] opposed to the unity of the DH. Kuenen is
'modern' too when he thinks of a sort of Deuteronomic 'school', and
mentions 'redactors' who 'while being different persons', would have
'worked at almost the same period and surely in the same spirit'.[56] On
reading Kuenen's work, we realize as well that the presence of the
'Deuteronomist' in the book of Joshua has become a common-place for
exegesis,[57] but the dating of this redactor still poses a problem. Refus-

---

Bücher in früheren Zeiten je zusammenhingen ist…unbeweisbar: aber gewiss folgt
daraus, dass zur Zeit des Verfassers der Deuteronomiker längst sein Werk vollendet
hatte.'

50. A. Kuenen, *Historisch-critisch onderzoek naar het ontstaan en de ver-
zameling van de boeken des Ouden Verbonds* (Leiden, 1885 [1861]). The first
volume was translated into French: *Histoire critique de l'Ancien Testament* (Paris,
1866).

51. Kuenen, *Histoire critique de l'Ancien Testament*, p. 438.

52. Kuenen concludes (*Histoire critique de l'Ancien Testament*, p. 441): 'Let us
acknowledge that we lack the facts in order to come up with a satisfactory solution'.
On several occasions, moreover, Kuenen returns to the ideas of Ewald, in particular
when he postulates a double redaction of the book of Kings (Josianic, then exilic).

53. Kuenen, *Histoire critique de l'Ancien Testament*, pp. 389-94.

54. Kuenen, *Histoire critique de l'Ancien Testament*, pp. 439-40.

55. Cf. below, §7.3.4.

56. Kuenen, *Histoire critique de l'Ancien Testament*, p. 440.

57. Kuenen, *Histoire critique de l'Ancien Testament*, pp. 333-41.

ing to locate him in the exilic period,[58] Kuenen favours a slightly pre-exilic date. But, like Ewald and most of the historico-critical exegetes, Kuenen does not manage to become aware of the 'organic' link between the Dtr redaction of Joshua and that of the following books.

How can this inability to perceive the link between Joshua and Judges be explained? The reason is probably the dominant position that the thesis of a primitive Hexateuch had acquired in exegetical circles. Inasmuch as exegetes were convinced that the 'great book of beginnings' extended from Genesis to Joshua, it was not possible to consider the Former Prophets as a unit.

2.3. *The Source 'D' and the Hexateuch*

Since de Wette[59] and Ewald,[60] the debate concerning the different explanatory models of the formation of the Pentateuch was focused, in an almost axiomatic way, on the Hexateuch and therefore had immediately incorporated the book of Joshua in its perspective. Not only did they assume that they were meeting up with the continuation of the sources of the Pentateuch in Joshua, but that they could also avail themselves of the closeness of the link between Deuteronomy and Joshua as well as of the fact that the promises of the land found their fulfillment only in the book of Joshua. There was no doubt for anyone then that Joshua should be joined to the first part of the canon and that the first great literary collection of the Bible was indeed the Hexateuch.[61]

Within this great corpus, they had set apart the source 'D', that was limited, they thought, to the 'primitive Deuteronomy' (Deut. 6.4–30.20). But what was to be done in that case with the texts that, in Genesis–Numbers, showed an undoubted affinity with 'D' (Gen. 26.5; Exod. 13; 16; 19–24; 32–34, etc.[62])? In order to reply to this question,

58. Cf. Kuenen, *Histoire critique de l'Ancien Testament*, p. 337 n. 1, where he cites Masius, Le Clerc, Herzfeld and others.

59. W.M.L. de Wette, *Lehrbuch der historisch-kritischen Einleitung in die Bibel* (Berlin, 1817).

60. H. Ewald, 'Rec. of J.J. Stähelin, "Kritische Untersuchungen über die Genesis" (1830)', in *Theologische Studien und Kritiken* 4 (1831), pp. 595-606.

61. Kraus, *Geschichte der historisch-kritischen Erforschung des Alten Testaments*, p. 178.

62. These texts are cited by J. Wellhausen, *Die Composition des Hexateuchs und der historischen Bücher des Alten Testaments* (Berlin, 3rd edn, 1899; repr. Berlin: Georg Reimer, 1963), p. 205. According to him, the Deuteronomic

they began to speak of the *Deuteronomist* (Ewald, Kuenen and others), with this Deuteronomist being understood as the author/redactor 'who fitted Deuteronomy into the narrative framework of the Hexateuch and who reworked the latter in a Deuteronomic perspective'.[63] Some wanted to identify this author/redactor with the 'Yahwist',[64] but others thought that a distinct contributor was involved, and (for Wellhausen, at any rate) one later than the 'Yahwist'. What is striking for us is the designation 'Deuteronomist' being used first in the framework of the Hexateuch, and not in regard to the historical books.[65] Furthermore, this Deuteronomist is considered to be a 'personality', since a thesis could be devoted to his concept of history.[66] While at it, they suddenly realized as well that there was a diachronic problem within Deuteronomy. Reuss's remark, for example, that Joshua 1–12; 22–24 'is later than the Deuteronomy-Code, but contemporaneous with, or rather an integral part of the Deuteronomy-Book',[67] illustrates well the necessity of defining the link between 'Deuteronomy' and the 'Deuteronomist'.[68] Thus,

redaction is most strongly represented however in Numbers and Joshua.

63. 'Der Deuteronomist, d.h. der Schriftsteller, der das Deuteronomium in das hexateuchische Geschichtsbuch eingesetzt hat, hat zugleich das letztere in deuteronomischem Sinne überarbeitet; von dieser Überarbeitung ist nun aber nicht Q [=P], sondern vielmehr JE betroffen' (Wellhausen, *Die Composition des Hexateuchs und der historischen Bücher des Alten Testaments*). Cf. before that de Wette, *Beiträge zur Einleitung in das Alte Testament*, pp. 168-70, and the authors cited by him. Cf. also J.W. Colenso, *The Pentateuch and the Book of Josua Critically Examined*, Part 5 (London, 1865), p. 53.

64. For example, J.J. Stähelin, *Kritische Untersuchungen über den Pentateuch, die Bücher Josua, Richter, Samuelis und der Könige* (Berlin, 1843).

65. As we have seen, Ewald had warned about the confusion between the 'Deuteronomist' of the Hexateuch and the Deuteronomic redaction of Judges–Kings. Cf. above, pp. 32-34.

66. H.W. Kosters, *De historie beschouwing van het Deuteronomist met den berichten in Genesis–Numeri vergleken* (Utrecht, 1868).

67. E. Reuss, *La Bible: Traduction nouvelle avec introductions et commentaires. Ancien Testament. III. L'histoire sainte et la Loi* (Paris: G. Fischbacher, 1879), p. 216.

68. We must mention too the thesis of A. Dillmann, *Die Bücher Numeri, Deuteronomium und Josua* (KAT; Leipzig: Hirzel, 2nd edn, 1886), and of C. Steuernagel, *Übersetzung und Erklärung der Bücher Deuteronomium und Josua* (HAT I/3; Göttingen: Vandenhoeck & Ruprecht, 1900), pp. 136-40, according to which the Deuteronomic texts of Joshua are not redactional elements but constitute an autonomous source.

even if all the energy put into the research concentrated on the problem of the formation of the Pentateuch, and consequently of the Hexateuch, the Deuteronomic problem could from now on no longer be ignored by researchers.

2.4. *Jeremiah and the Deuteronomists*

Soon, the 'Dtr' phenomenon was going to extend even beyond the framework of the Pentateuch and the historical books. It was in the book of Jeremiah that exegetes initially noted the presence of texts strongly resembling Deuteronomy and the other Deuteronomistic texts, as much by their style as by their themes. For Kuenen, that simply meant that the redactors of the historical books 'are individuals of the same mind as Jeremiah, acquainted with and imitating his writings'.[69] But towards the end of the 19th century, such an explanation was no longer enough to satisfy historico-critical exegesis. It was Bernhard Duhm[70] (1847–1928) who set out, in his commentary on Jeremiah,[71] the thesis of Deuteronomic redaction of this book, leaving only some 60 brief poems for the 'historical Jeremiah'. For Duhm, this Deuteronomic redaction, that gives itself away by its style, its repetitions and its theological platitudes, stretches from the exilic period down to the first century BCE. Inspired by Smend, Duhm attributed the announcement of the new covenant in Jer. 31.31-34 to this Dtr milieu and described this pericope as 'written in a style that is shoddy, clumsy, imprecise'; it appears to be the 'fantasy of a scribe for whom the highest ideal would be to have the whole Jewish people knowing the Law by heart'.[72] This quotation clearly shows the low esteem that Duhm had for the Dtr redaction. In his commentary, moreover, the redactional texts are rarely analyzed in detail. Likewise, Duhm rules out any compositional intentions on the part of the Dtr redactors: 'the book has slowly expanded,

---

69. Kuenen, *Histoire critique de l'Ancien Testament*, p. 428. Bishop Colenso goes further since he favoured the hypothesis that Deuteronomy would have been written 'as some suppose, by the hand of Jeremiah'. Cf. Colenso, *The Pentateuch and the Book of Josua Critically Examined*, Part 2, p. 359.

70. In regard to him, cf. Smend, *Deutsche Alttestamentler in drei Jahrhunderten*, pp. 114-28.

71. B. Duhm, *Das Buch Jeremia* (HAT, 11; Tübingen: J.C.B. Mohr [Paul Siebeck], 1901).

72. Duhm, *Das Buch Jeremia*, pp. 255, 258.

like a forest growing wildly... It is impossible to speak of any methodical composition'.[73]

The contempt shown by Duhm for the Dtr redactors, who were for
him 'scribes', and even 'Pharisees', is quite typical of the intellectual
and philosophical climate of his time, characterized by a mixture of
romanticism and rationalism, by a constant search for origins to escape
from 'decadence'. The achievement from this phase of the research is
that it had become commonplace to assume a Dtr redaction for some of
the prophetic books as well, even if they still did not go so far as to
raise the question of a possible redactional link between the historical
books (the Former Prophets) and the prophetic books (the Latter
Prophets).

2.5. *'Deuteronomism' in the Wake of the Triumph of the Wellhausen Paradigm*

As the theory of sources gained acceptance, thanks to Wellhausen, as
the best model to explain the Hexateuch,[74] it became common to speak
of 'D', of the Deuteronomist and of 'redactions in the spirit of Deuteronomy'. But in the case of the historical books, the dominant position
of the 'Hexateuch' concept seems to have deprived the researchers of
the leeway that would have been necessary for them to embark on an
original and thorough investigation of the redactional process responsible for the present form and arrangement of these books.

At the dawn of the twentieth century, the most common position on
the origins of the Pentateuch and the historical books is that set out in a
classical way in *Die Composition des Hexateuchs und der historischen
Bücher des Alten Testaments*, the great synthesis of Wellhausen.[75] Here
are its main tenets:

---

73. Duhm, *Das Buch Jeremia*, p. xx.

74. For more details, cf. A. de Pury and T. Römer, 'Le Pentateuque en question:
Position du problème et brève histoire de la recherche', in A. de Pury (ed.), *Le
Pentateuque en question: Les origines et la composition des cinq premiers livres de
la Bible à la lumière des recherches récentes* (Le Monde de la Bible, 19; Geneva:
Labor et Fides, 2nd edn, 1991), pp. 9-80 (22-29).

75. J. Wellhausen, *Die Composition des Hexateuchs und der historischen
Bücher des Alten Testaments* (Berlin: Georg Reimer, 1899), pp. 208-300 and the
summary pp. 300-301.

(a)   The books of Judges, Samuel and Kings[76] underwent Dtr redactions in several stages (Josianic, then exilic).

(b)   The books of Judges and Samuel were in existence before undergoing editing by the Dtr redactors;[77] this was not the case for the book of Kings.[78]

(c)   It is impossible to determine if whether, throughout the books of Judges, Samuel and Kings, we are in the presence of the same Dtr redaction or different redactions, but that question is judged unimportant.[79]

(d)   The Hexateuch underwent a Dtr redaction when the 'D' source was inserted. However, the link between this Dtr redaction of the Hexateuch and Dtr redactions of Judges–Kings did not really interest the researchers. At most, some exegetes touched on the idea of a 'great Dtr history extending from Genesis to 2 Kings'.[80]

76.   Contrary to a fairly widespread position, Wellhausen (*Die Composition des Hexateuchs*, pp. 234-35) excludes from this sequence the book of Ruth, a book that he considers late and taken into the *Ketubim* at a time when the canon of the *Nebiim* was already closed.

77.   In the case of the book of Judges, Wellhausen (*Die Composition des Hexateuchs*, p. 214) speaks of a *vordeuteronomistisches Richterbuch* that would have contained the accounts of Ehud, Deborah, Gideon, Jephthah and Samson. The typically Dtr passages are Judg. 2.6–3.6 and 10.6-16. As for Judg. 17–21, they would be post-Dtr and postexilic. Fundamental to the books of Samuel, Wellhausen (*Die Composition des Hexateuchs*, pp. 262-63) sees two stories about David, a 'Josianic' redaction in 1 Sam. 2.27-36 and, perhaps, 2 Sam. 7. The texts of 1 Sam. 7.2–8.22; 10.17-27; 11.12-14; 12.1-25, that criticize the monarchy, depend on the Dtr edition. Next come post-Dtr additions like 2 Sam. 21–24.

78.   For the book of Kings, Wellhausen is certainly willing to acknowledge sources, but he considers that the composition of the book results from the Dtr redaction. Here, Wellhausen distinguishes, following Ewald and his successors, a pre-exilic Dtr redaction and exilic and postexilic redactions. For example: 2 Kgs 17.18-21 presupposes the existence of the kingdom of Judah, whereas 17.19-20 is a Dtr insertion of the exilic period (cf. *Die Composition des Hexateuchs*, p. 298). The difference between the two Dtr redactions is perceptible not only from their divergent historical contexts, but also in their different concepts of the Torah. For example: in 2 Kgs 17.13, the Torah is sent by the prophets, whereas in 17.37, there is question of a written Torah.

79.   'Ob sie überall von der selben Hand oder von den selben Händen herrührt, ist gleichgiltig' (Wellhausen, *Die Composition des Hexateuchs*, p. 301).

80.   Along this line, cf. already Ernst Bertheau, *Die Bücher Richter und Ruth* (Leipzig, 1845), pp. xxiii-xxxii; E. Sellin, *Einleitung in das Alte Testament*

In conclusion, we notice that already in the time of Wellhausen almost all the observations had already been formulated on which Noth and his successors were going to build their hypothesis.[81] The fact that it was necessary to wait almost half a century for this is explained, not only by the a priori assumption that the 'Hexateuch' inevitably represented a basic unit, but also by the methodological predominance of literary criticism (source criticism), a method for which *Formgeschichte* and *Redaktionsgeschichte* were soon going to provide the necessary corrective.

3. The Thesis of a Deuteronomistic Historiography

When Noth published his *Überlieferungsgeschichtliche Studien (ÜSt)* in 1943, he could therefore take advantage of a good number of observations made from the time of de Wette up to that of Wellhausen. The utilization of these observations in the service of an original concept and their integration in a system of new coordinates were made possible by the following phenomena.

3.1. *The Antecedent Conditions for Überlieferungsgeschichtliche Studien*

3.1.1. *The Overtaking of Literarkritik by Formgeschichte*
In the Wellhausenian system, the approach to the books of the Old Testament took place exclusively from the perspective of literary criticism.[82] Of course, the proposed solutions too remained within the

(Leipzig, 1910), pp. 67-68; A. Meinhold, *Einführung in das Alte Testament* (Giessen, 3rd edn, 1932 [1919]), p. 219 (where he notes that the Dtr redaction is very limited in the history of the patriarchs).

   81. In French-speaking countries, Wellhausen's theses on the Dtr question had been disseminated as early as 1905 by Lucien Gautier, who, in his *Introduction à l'AT*, summarized its position as follows: 'The Deuteronomistic school has strongly made its imprint on the narratives in the book of Joshua; it has drawn up the plan of the book of Judges...it has not remained peripheral to the redaction of the book of Samuel, where, it is true, its intervention is felt to a lesser degree; finally, it was given a free hand in the composition of the book of Kings... Fortunately the work of the Deuteronomistic school has remained at a more superficial level. It has not transformed the traditional narratives and has not even made them undergo important modifications.' Cf. L. Gautier, *Introduction à l'Ancien Testament*, I (2 vols.; Lausanne: Payot, 3rd edn, 1939 [1905]), pp. 309-10.

   82. In the sense of German 'Literarkritik.'

confines of this method. Scholars thought they could explain tensions, contradictions and inconsistencies by regarding them as resulting from the combination of parallel documents and by attributing them to redactors who were not very talented. This model was applied as well to the historical books. It mattered little whether the same documents were found there as in the Hexateuch[83] or if other documents were found to be present there;[84] in any case, the explanatory model remained the same. This model, based on methodological dogmatism,[85] suffers in particular from the lack of any sociological reflection on the circumstances of the production and formation of the biblical books.

The criticism of literary genres or form criticism (*Formgeschichte*) endeavours to provide a remedy for this shortcoming. Thanks to this method, it became possible to appreciate better the stylistic and ideological features of different literary collections. Thus Hugo Gressman, who like his teacher Hermann Gunkel, continued to support the Wellhausenian paradigm in addition to (or in spite of) his interest in forms, published a commentary on Joshua in which he insisted on the etiological nature of the conquest legends and postulated a preliterary origin for these legends.[86]

For the books of Samuel, the new orientation in exegesis appears in an exemplary way in the study of Leonhard Rost on the literary work devoted to the Davidic succession.[87] Rost presents 2 Samuel 6–2 Kings

83. In this case they spoke of an Octateuch or of an Enneateuch. Cf. K. Budde, *Das Buch der Richter* (KHCAT, 7; Freiburg, 1897), pp. xii-xv; G. Hölscher, 'Das Buch der Könige, seine Quellen und seine Redaktion', in H. Schmidt (ed.), *Eycharisterion: Studien zur Literatur des Alten und des Neuen Testaments* (Festschrift H. Gunkel; FRLANT, 36; Göttingen: Vandehoeck & Ruprecht, 1923), pp. 158-213. For other supporters of this theory, cf. G. Hölscher, *Geschichtsschreibung in Israel: Untersuchungen zum Jahwisten und Elohisten* (Lund: C.W.K. Gleerup, 1952), pp. 7-17.

84. R. Pfeiffer, *Introduction to the Old Testament* (New York: Harpers, 3rd edn, 1950 [1941]), pp. 314-412; H.H. Rowley, *The Growth of the Old Testament* (London: Hutchinson's University Library, 1950). These two authors used the sigla 'J' and 'E' for Judges and Samuel without claiming the identity of these sources with those of the Hexateuch.

85. Each problem of internal logic presented by a text was resolved immediately by the distribution of 'contradictory' elements over several documents.

86. H. Gressmann, *Die Anfänge Israels* (SAT I/2; Göttingen: Vandenhoeck & Ruprecht, 2nd edn, 1922).

87. L. Rost, *Die Überlieferung von der Thronnachfolge Davids* (BWANT, 3.6; Stuttgart: Kohlhammer, 1926), reprinted in L. Rost, *Das Kleine Credo und andere*

2 as an independent literary unit with its own prehistory. The author of this history, whom Rost sometimes compares with Herodotus,[88] would have had available the following documents (*Unterquellen*): the history of the ark, the oracle of Nathan, the account of the war against the Ammonites and the history of the succession. Rost's conclusions happen to be in sharp contradiction to those that come from the application of the theory of sources to Samuel–Kings,[89] but in particular they reveal a new sensitivity to the stylistic and theological characteristics of the historical books. It is certainly not an accident that Noth, in his analysis of the books of Samuel, frequently cites Rost's work.

3.1.2. *Albrecht Alt and the Work on Joshua*

For the Dtr question, the book of Joshua has for a long time had a decisive role. It was in Joshua that the presence of texts of a 'Deuteronomic' type was first detected. Next, the joining of Joshua to the Pentateuch blocked research on the historical books for a long time, as we have seen. It is due to the research of Gressmann, Alt and Noth[90] on Joshua that freedom from the Hexateuch straitjacket was finally possible.

In 1936, Albrecht Alt, Noth's teacher, published an article on Joshua in which he emphasized the independence of the Benjaminite collection that he detected behind the narratives of Joshua 2–9 and that he surmised to have been handed down at the sanctuary of Gilgal.[91] Ten years earlier, in the second part of the book of Joshua, Alt had detected the presence of a list of tribal boundaries going back to the premonarchical period, as well as a survey document from the period of Joshua.[92]

In his commentary on Joshua that appeared in 1938 and had been prepared for in the edition of the fascicle of Joshua for the BHK in 1936,

---

Studien zum Alten Testament (Heidelberg: Quelle & Meyer, 1965), pp. 119-253.

88. Rost, *Das Kleine Credo*, p. 213.

89. Rost takes note of this himself: *Das Kleine Credo*, p. 243.

90. Cf. E. Jenni, 'Zwei Jahrzehnte Forschung an den Büchern Josua bis Könige', *ThR* 27 (1961), pp. 1-32, 97-146 (120-22).

91. A. Alt, 'Josua', in P. Volz *et al.* (eds.), *Wesen und Werden des Alten Testaments* (BZAW, 66; Berlin, 1936), pp. 13-29 = A. Alt, *Kleine Schriften zur Geschichte des Volkes Israel*, I (3 vols.; Munich: Beck, 1953), pp. 176-92.

92. A. Alt, 'Das System der Stammesgrenzen im Buche Josua', in A. Jirku (ed.), *Beiträge zur Religionsgeschichte und Archäologie Palästinas* (Festschrift E. Sellin; Leipzig: 1927), pp. 13-24, = A. Alt, *Kleine Schriften*, I (Munich: Beck, 1953), pp. 193-202; *idem*, 'Judas Gaue unter Josia', *PJ* 21 (1925), pp. 100-16.

Noth took up again all the theses of his teacher. But unlike Alt, he was also interested in redactional and compositional questions, and he reached the conclusion that the thesis of the presence of sources of the Pentateuch in the book of Joshua is untenable.[93] Noth thus dealt a 'fatal blow'[94] to the theory of the Hexateuch. But what should be put in place of the late Hexateuch? Five years later, it is Noth himself who will give the answer.

3.2. *Deuteronomistic Historiography according to Martin Noth*

In the midst of the Second World War, cut off at Königsberg, far from the great university libraries, Martin Noth conceived of, composed and published, under a delightfully unimaginative title, a brilliant little work: *Studies on the History of Traditions: First Part.*[95] In retrospect, we can say that it is probably the book that, in the course of this century, will have influenced most profoundly and most enduringly Old Testament studies. The novelty of this work resides in the fact that for the first time, it was a matter not so much of identifying or of distinguishing the redactional layers but of raising a question about the *literary plan* that had controlled that redaction.

Noth's fundamental thesis is set out in the first 12 pages of the book. The historical tradition of the Old Testament, Noth points out, has come down to us in great works of 'compilation' (*Sammelwerke*): on each occasion, older literary materials have been collected and placed in a redactional setting that determined their arrangement, presentation and interpretation. Three great *Sammelwerke* have come down to us: the Pentateuch, the Deuteronomistic historiography and the Chronicles historiography. But unlike the Pentateuch and the Chronicles historiography, whose outlines are obvious at a first glance, the Deuteronomistic historiography needs first of all to be 'discovered', before being

---

93. M. Noth, *Das Buch Josua* (HAT, I.7; Tübingen: J.C.B. Mohr, 2nd edn, 1953 [1938]), p. 16.

94. This expression comes from A. Gelin, *Josué traduit et commenté* (LSTB, III; Paris, 2nd edn, 1955 [1949]), p. 12.

95. M. Noth *Überlieferungsgeschichtliche Studien. I. Die sammelnden und bearbeitenden Geschichtswerke im Alten Testament* (Schriften der Königsberger Gelehrten Gesellschaft. Geisteswissenschaftliche Klasse, 18; Halle, Germany: Max Niemeyer Verlag, 1943; repr. Tübingen, 1957; Darmstadt, 1963) (cited as *ÜSt*). ET *The Deuteronomistic History* (JSOTSup, 15; Sheffield: JSOT Press, 2nd edn, 1991 [1981]).

able to be grasped in its unity and coherence.[96] And it is precisely to this discovery that Noth invites his reader in the first part of his *Studies*.[97]

It has been a very long time since anyone continued to question, Noth points out, the presence in the books of Joshua, Judges, Samuel and Ruth of a certain number of passages, long or short, that indicate a close relationship with the law of Deuteronomy and with the parenetic discourses that surround that law. Moreover, it is because of that 'filiation' that these passages have been called 'Deuteronomistic'. Noth accepted this usage, but established—in a note at the bottom of the page[98]—the system of sigla that was going to establish itself, at least in German exegesis, until the present day. The siglum 'Dtr' designates not only the collector/author responsible for having conceived and constructed the great historiographical work, but also the passages within that work that must be attributed to him in particular. This siglum 'Dtr'—for Deuteronom*ist*—takes over from the more vague siglum 'D' generally used by Noth's predecessors to refer to the strata similar to Deuteronomy. After Noth, when exegetes began to try to distinguish within the Dtr redaction the successive literary strata, the Dtr of Noth will become 'DtrG' (*die deuteronomistische Grundschrift*, the Basic Deuteronomistic Text) or 'DtrH' (*der deuteronomistische Historiker*, the Deuteronomistic Historian), in order to distinguish the originator of the work from the later revisers, who will find themselves attributed sigla such as DtrP, DtrN, DtrL, and so on (cf. below). For Noth, the siglum 'Dt' refers to the Law of Deuteronomy with its parenetic framing passages, and the siglum 'Dtn' refers to the canonical book of Deuteronomy. In these last two cases, the adjective (Dt) is Deuteronom*ic*!

The Dtr passages detected long ago in the historical books are recognizable by linguistic and thematic criteria. The style of these passages is very simple, repetitive, full of stereotyped expressions, and Noth gives up on making anew an inventory of them. What holds his attention on

96. Noth, *ÜSt*, p. 2.

97. Noth, *ÜSt*, pp. 3-110. The second part of the book (pp. 110-80) is given over to the Chronicler. The inquiry into the history of the traditions of the Pentateuch is taken up, in a proleptic way, in an appendix entitled 'Die "Priesterschrift" und die Redaktion des Pentateuch' (pp. 180-217), but it was to be the subject, principally, of a new book that appeared five years later, and that, rather than being entitled *ÜSt Zweiter Teil*, as would be expected, had as its title *Überlieferungsgeschichte des Pentateuch* (Stuttgart: Kohlhammer, 1948; Darmstadt, 1960).

98. Noth, *ÜSt*, p. 4 n. 1.

the other hand, and in this his approach is original, is the *function* of
these passages in their broad context. Noth observes, in fact, that the
most representative of these passages takes the form of a *discourse* put
in the mouth of the principal heroes of the narrative, and that these
discourses, interspersed throughout the history from the entrance of the
Israelites into the land under the leadership of Joshua up to the dedication of the Temple of Solomon, make it possible to structure and interpret the succession of historical periods, and that in a form that looks to
the past as well as to the future. Thus, the entry of the Israelites is
introduced, in Joshua 1, by a discourse of God, then of Joshua, setting
the goal of conquest of the land; and this conquest finds its outcome in
the farewell discourse of Joshua in Joshua 23. In this discourse of
Joshua are formulated Yhwh's requirements so that Israel can live in
the land in peace. The period of the Judges itself will be marked again
by a discourse. In 1 Samuel 12, Samuel draws up an outline of the history since the coming out of Egypt and addresses a serious warning to
the people and to ('their') king. Finally, after the construction of the
Temple, king Solomon gives a discourse in the form of a prayer (1 Kgs
8.14-53), while insisting on the meaning of the Temple for the present
and for the future.

Alongside these discourses, Noth finds some personal historical
reflections formulated by the narrator. In Joshua 12, there is a recapitu-
lation of the conquest of Canaan; in Judg. 2.11-23, a foreshadowing of
the period of the Judges, characterized by the recurrent failings of Israel
and the salvific interventions of Yhwh raising up the Judges. In 2 Kgs
17.7-23, we have a retrospective reflection on the ruin of the Northern
Kingdom. Perhaps Dtr has recourse to these 'considerations' when there
was no hero sufficiently important available to shoulder responsibility
for the discourse.

Noth thinks that there emerge, as much from the discourses as from
the reflections, such a unity of perspective and such a linguistic homogeneity that we must be in the presence of a real *author*. More
precisely, the one who presents these discourses is an artisan of a presentation of Israel's past that conforms to a perfectly coherent theology
of history. The principal *leitmotiv* of this history is the obedience or disobedience of Israel. Each time the stake is to know if Israel has
'listened' to the voice of God.

The Dtr is an author too in the sense that he does not work, like the
redactors who will succeed him, with a pre-existing narrative frame-

work, but that he himself arranges among themselves the blocks of previously autonomous narratives and *constructs* the presentation of the
history and prescribes the limits of its periods. That delimitation still
does not coincide with that of the future biblical books, since the period
of the 'conquest' comes to an end in Joshua 23, the period of the Judges
in 1 Samuel 12, and that of the first kings in 1 Kgs 8.14-53.

The ancient materials used by the Dtr to construct his history, are of a
very diverse nature. We find there among other things etiological narratives of conquest in Joshua 2–9, the heroic deeds of the book of
Judges, the monarchical narratives of 1 and 2 Samuel, prophetic legends
as well as royal annals in 1 and 2 Kings. These traditional materials
reveal points of view totally different from those of the redaction and
seem to have scarcely ever been connected among themselves before
the work of the Dtr. Conseqently, the assembling and the structuring of
the collection should be exclusively attributed to the Dtr. The Dtr is at
the same time a redactor and an author completely on his own, who
makes use, with great sense of respect,[99] of numerous pre-existing
pieces but links them together and gives them a coherence thanks to
textual links of his own. He thus creates a truly original historiographical work. By the way, Noth elsewhere compares the Dtr to Greek
historians of the fifth/fourth centuries BCE whom he considers his
closest colleagues.[100]

3.2.1. *End, Beginning and Coherence of DH*
For Noth, the ending of the DH corresponds to that of the Second Book
of Kings. In fact, 2 Kgs 25.26 appears to him to be its 'natural' ending,
since all the events driving Israel into exile have then been recounted.
The final note about the rehabilitation of Jehoiachin (2 Kgs 25.27-30),
although it could be considered mitigating, in no way represents a
fundamental change in destiny for Israel. It too, therefore, can be attributed to the Dtr. It is on this basis that Noth can determine its terminus
a quo, namely 562, after the rehabilitation of Jehoiachin.[101]

The beginning of the DH is, for its part, more difficult to establish,
and we can consider that Noth situates it in Deuteronomy 1 because he
could imagine it nowhere else. In his investigation of the incipit of the

99. Noth compares his Dtr to an 'honest broker'.
100. Noth, *ÜSt*, p. 12.
101. Noth, *ÜSt*, p. 12.

DH, he essentially proceeds by *via negationis*. On the one hand, the beginning cannot be between Genesis and Numbers, since, in spite of some secondary Dtr alterations, he detects no trace of a coherent Dtr redaction comparable to that found between Deuteronomy and 2 Kings. On the other hand, the DH cannot really open with the first chapter of Joshua, since this book presupposes at the same time the Mosaic history and the conquests by the Transjordanian tribes related in Deuteronomy. Furthermore, Joshua contains a certain number of explicit cross-references to Deuteronomy.[102]

Deuteronomy, presented as a long discourse of Moses culminating in the proclamation of the Law, provides an altogether logical pro-grammatic introduction to Joshua–2 Kings. Therefore it is the historical summary of Deuteronomy 1–3 that constitutes the real introduction to the DH. That introduction was placed by the Dtr before the procla-mation of the Deuteronomic law (Deut. 4–30) that, according to him, is made up in large part of Deuteronomic material going back to the eighth or seventh century. The farewells and the account of the death of Moses in Deuteronomy 31 and 34, composed by the Dtr, introduce the conquest by Joshua, while insisting repeatedly on the importance of fidelity to 'this law' (Deut. 12–26). Moreover, it is this fidelity that will constitute the decisive criterion according to which the conduct of Israel will be judged throughout the entire DH.

3.2.2. *The Governing Ideas of the Dtr Concept of History*
For Noth, the DH is essentially aimed at understanding and explaining the end of the kingdom of Judah as well as the exile in Babylon. Faced with these dramatic events of which he had been a witness and that seemed to bring an end to the existence of the people of Yhwh, the Dtr tries to interpret the catastrophe: he sees in it the fruit of the apostasy of the people. Neither the warnings nor the repeated chastisements of God had led the people to a lasting change in conduct. One could say that the lessons of history had turned out to be useless for Israel. The end of Judah is seen by the Dtr as the ultimate chastisement of God, the final expression of divine justice.

The great theological themes of the proposal of a covenant between God and the people or the promise of a land flowing with milk and honey are subject according to the Dtr to one condition: the people must

---

102. For example, Josh. 8.30-35 refers to Deut. 11.29-30.

in return be faithful to the Law. Now, it is the infidelity of the people that is going to permit the Dtr to justify the divine sanction of the exile. In this sense, the DH can be considered a *theodicy*.

While the Dtr insists frequently, as we have seen, on the importance of the Law, he shows on the contrary a very restrained interest in the cult. Thus, the ark is just a receptacle for the tablets of the Law, and the temple is the place where God makes his name reside, the place of prayer rather than the place of sacrifices (cf. 1 Kgs 8).

In Noth's eyes, the Dtr pronounces such a sombre judgment on the history of Israel that he seems to preserve no perspective on the future, and, especially, to be sustained by no hope about the future restoration of Israel. On this point, Noth's Dtr is sharply distinguished from his contemporaries, Second Isaiah or the prophet Ezekiel. Like them, he tries to make sense of the catastrophe, but unlike them, he does not allow himself to go beyond the spirit of the great pre-exilic prophets: the end is the expression of divine chastisement.

Noth also ponders over the identity of this Dtr. Now, contrary to the conclusions of many later works, he does not think that he should distinguish several Dtr layers nor even envisage the existence of a Dtr milieu. For him, the author of DH is just one person, who is neither a member of the clergy nor of the official intelligentsia. He depends on no institution and has to render an account to no one. The reasons impelling the Dtr to compose his work remain therefore personal and unknown. Noth apparently thought of Dtr as a solitary intellectual who, on the day following the catastrophe, cut off in his study,[103] set to work to draw up an assessment of the situation. We cannot refrain from thinking that Dtr's vision of the situation reflects a little the very situation of Noth himself. In fact, Noth composed his *ÜSt* just as the war of extermination instigated by his own people was ravaging Europe and Germany. Just like his Dtr, Noth felt himself indebted to no institution, and it is tempting to think that the pessimism facing the future that he attributes to Dtr corresponded to his analysis of the contemporary situation.

The historical and sociological situation of the author of the *ÜSt* therefore makes it possible, perhaps, to understand better some of his statements on Dtr that are challenged today. However, as the history of

---

103. Noth locates his author rather in Palestine than in the Babylonian exile where access to the sources would have been less easy; cf. *ÜSt*, p. 110 n. 1.

the reception of Noth's thesis will show, this putting of its author in context does not permit on any account discrediting it globally (cf. below). What is more, Noth's redactional approach was to find itself supported, in an independent way, by the publication of A. Jepsen's book on the history of the redaction of the books of Kings.

3.3. *Confirmation of Noth's Thesis by A. Jepsen and I. Engnell*

In 1939, Alfred Jepsen completed his work on the sources and formation of the book of Kings. Because of the war and then the economic situation of East Germany, this book did not appear until 1953.[104] Meanwhile, Noth's studies had been published, and Jepsen could make himself acquainted with them. As Jepsen notes in the postscript to his book and in some additional notes composed in 1953,[105] his view of the redactional history of the book of Kings entirely confirms the existence of the DH as Noth imagined it.

At the origin of the book of Kings there were, according to Jepsen, two documents: a royal chronicle and some annals of the kings of Israel and of Judah. The royal chronicle, containing a synchronic enumeration of the different reigns, of which Jepsen proposes a reconstruction,[106] would have been written between 705 and 701, after the fall of the Northern Kingdom.[107] As for the royal annals, they would relate in more of a narrative form the history of the kings and, especially, that of the Temple beginning with the reign of Solomon. Jepsen thinks that that work came out during the reign of Manasseh, at a time when Assyrian domination loomed as a grave threat to the survival of the kingdom of Judah and the cult of Yhwh.

In terms of the analysis of Jepsen, these two sources had been combined and reworked by two successive redactors. After the catastrophe of 587 (towards 580), a redactor from priestly circles (R^I) wrote a history of the kingdom: he took as a base the royal chronicle,[108] that he

---

104. A. Jepsen, *Die Quellen des Königsbuches* (Halle: Niemeyer, 2nd edn, 1956 [1953]).

105. For example, pp. 105 and 116.

106. Jepsen, *Die Quellen*, pp. 30-36.

107. Jepsen, *Die Quellen*, p. 38.

108. Jepsen envisages the possibility that that history of the monarchy already includes a part of the Davidic traditions as well as Judg. 1 and 17–21; cf. *Die Quellen*, p. 68.

enriched with excerpts from the book of annals, by imprinting on the whole his own pessimistic vision of the history of the worship of Yhwh during the reign of the kings. The ending of that edition is found in 2 Kgs 25.21.[109] This royal history is reworked about 550[110] by a redactor of prophetic inspiration (R[II]), influenced especially by Hosea and Jeremiah. R[II] was not content with a new edition of the book of Kings but, by taking the Deuteronomy revised by his hands as a foundation, he constructed a presentation of the history of Israel going from the Mosaic period up to the end of the kingdom of Judah. Thus, R[II] had augmented the history of the kings with an immense prologue containing Deuteronomy, the accounts of the conquest in Joshua, the traditions on Samuel, the history of David and especially the history of the succession, as well as the prophetic accounts of Northern origin.[111] R[II] therefore closely resembles Noth's Dtr, and Jepsen expressly proposes to see there the same author.[112] Like Noth, Jepsen considers R[II] = Dtr as an individual and places his activity in Palestine, more precisely at Mizpah.[113] The two researchers are also in agreement in considering the post-Dtr redactional interventions rather minimal.[114]

In a very laudatory review that Jepsen devotes to *Überlieferungsgeschichtliche Studien*,[115] he furthermore affirms even more strongly than Noth the literary consistency of the DH. We can actually only find great convergence between the results of Jepsen's research and that of Noth. However, Jepsen goes much further than Noth in the preciseness with which he thinks he can identify, in the book of Kings, the sources and a pre-Dtr redaction. Furthermore, he postulates two exilic redactors for 1 and 2 Kings. It was in this way that, without wanting to, he prepared the way not only for those who postulate two or several Dtr

109. Jepsen, *Die Quellen*, pp. 60-77.

110. Like Noth, Jepsen considers that the account of the rehabilitation of Jehoiachin (561) provides the terminus *a quo*, and the end of the Babylonian Empire in 539 the terminus *ante quem*; cf. *Die Quellen*, p. 94.

111. Jepsen, *Die Quellen*, pp. 76-101.

112. Jepsen, *Die Quellen*, p. 105.

113. Jepsen, *Die Quellen*, pp. 94-95.

114. Jepsen especially envisages a Levitical redaction toward the end of the sixth century. He attributes to this redaction texts such as 1 Kgs 12.21-24, 31–13.34; 2 Kgs 17.24-33, 41; cf. *Die Quellen*, pp. 102-104.

115. Published in *DLZ* 71 (1950), cols. 481-85.

layers,[116] but also for those who distinguish pre-Dtr redactions within the historical books (cf. below).

The great Scandinavian exegete Ivan Engnell provides an indirect confirmation of the Nothian concept.[117] While rejecting literary criticism and considering Old Testament literature to be thoroughly 'oral', Engnell makes, like Noth, a very clear distinction between the Tetrateuch on the one hand, (called the 'P-work'), and on the other the books of Deuteronomy to 2 Kings (called the 'D-work'). In his work which appeared two years after that of Noth,[118] Engnell insists as well on the fact that D = Dtr went back to many older traditions while managing to maintain a great consistency in style and thought.

The fact that three researchers, working with very different exegetical methods and presuppositions, would have ended up with the discovery of a Dtr redaction affecting the whole complex of Deuteronomy–2 Kings could only confirm the birth of a new explanatory model for the historical books of the Old Testament.

4. *The First Reactions to Martin Noth's Thesis*

Since the *Überlieferungsgeschichtliche Studien* appeared during the war and in a very limited printing, we find practically no reaction to the initial publication of this work. It was only after the appearance of a reprint in 1957 that the book really started its 'career'. And Ernst Jenni[119] is right in emphasizing that it was only at the beginning of the 1960s that the DH thesis became largely dominant, at least in exegesis in the German-speaking world. In this context, therefore, almost 20 years after the appearance of the book, the first reactions can be classified in three categories: (1) acceptance of the thesis with minor

116. The priestly redactor from the beginning of the exile, according to Jepsen, would be responsible for a certain number of texts that Noth had attributed to the Dtr (for example, 1 Kgs 8.31-61*; 12.28; the assessment of kings in comparison to David).

117. Unfortunately Engnell's publications are not easily accessible. We may mention the English translation of some of his major articles: *A Rigid Scrutiny: Critical Essays on the Old Testament* (trans. and ed. J.T. Willis; Nashville: Vanderbilt University Press, 1969).

118. I. Engnell, *Gamla testamentet, en traditionshistorik inledning*, I (Stockholm: Svensk Krykans Diakonistyrelses, 1945); cf. especially, pp. 168-259.

119. Jenni, 'Zwei Jahrzehnte Forschung an den Büchern Josua bis Könige', pp. 116-17.

modifications; (2) positive reaction to the thesis but at the price of modifications on basic questions; and (3) total rejection.

4.1. *Acceptance of the Thesis with Minor Modifications*

Noth's thesis was taken up without alteration in a majority of the commentaries on the historical books as well as in numerous articles in theological dictionaries.[120] Among the most loyal Nothians, we may mention Fichtner, Macholz and Boecker.[121] Boecker, in particular, endeavours to confirm Noth's thesis according to which the variations in perspective on the origins of the monarchy in 1 Samuel 8–12 are explained by a dialectical, if not ambivalent, attitude of the Dtr to the subject of the monarchy. Some Dtr texts (1 Sam. 8; 10.17-19; 12) alternated with older narratives taken up by the Dtr to underscore the ambiguity of this institution.[122] Curiously, these are precisely the texts that will prove to be one of the 'Achilles heels'[123] of Noth's thesis.

Most of the researchers who sided with Noth's thesis did not do it, however, without proposing some modifications in perspective, and that especially on three points: the question of the author, the localization of the undertaking and the aim of the work.

4.1.1. *The Question of Author*

In his commentaries on Joshua, Judges and Samuel,[124] Hertzberg expresses doubts on the possibility of considering the Dtr to be a unique individual. Rather than postulate an individual author, Hertzberg thinks

---

120. For more details, cf. Jenni, 'Zwei Jahrzehnte Forschung an den Büchern Josua bis Könige', p. 117.

121. J. Fichtner, *Das erste Buch der Könige* (BAT, 12.1; Stuttgart: Calwer Verlag, 1964), pp. 15-31. This work was edited posthumously by K.D. Fricke. Fichtner actually combines the conclusions of Jepsen and of Noth; G. Chr. Macholz, 'Israel und das Land' (unpublished habilitation thesis) (Heidelberg, 1969); H.J. Boecker, *Die Beurteilung der Anfänge des Königtums in den deuteronomistischen Abschnitten des 1. Samuelbuches: Ein Beitrag zum Problem der 'deuteronomistischen Geschichtswerks'* (WMANT, 31; Neukirchen–Vluyn: Neukirchener Verlag, 1969).

122. On this subject, cf. T. Römer, 'Le mouvement deutéronomiste face à la royauté: monarchistes ou anarchistes?', *Lumière et Vie* 178 (1986), pp. 13-27.

123. The expression comes from A.N. Radjawane, 'Das deuteronomistische Geschichtswerk: Ein Forschungsbericht', *ThR* 38 (1974), pp. 177-216 (191).

124. H.W. Hertzberg, *Die Bücher Josua, Richter, Ruth* (ATD, 9; Göttingen: Vandenhoeck & Ruprecht, 1956), p. 9.

of Dtr 'circles',[125] people recruited from among Judaeans who had not been exiled.

4.1.2. *The Problem of Localization*
The majority of authors in the 1960s supported Noth's idea (contained in a footnote!) that the Dtr did not belong to the exiles and composed his work in Palestine, the reason given being the documents to which they supposed he must have had access. In his thesis of 1957,[126] Hermann was one of the first to situate the Dtr in the Babylonian *Golah*. He was followed on this point by Soggin,[127] Ackroyd[128] (with some hesitations) and others.[129]

4.1.3. *The Perception of the Intention of the Work*
Noth, as we have seen, considered that the Dtr was motivated above all by the need to explain the national catastrophe, and that there was no indication in his work enabling us to presuppose that he had any hope about the re-establishment of the people.[130] But earlier Enno Janssen, who nevertheless worked hard to establish Noth's thesis definitively, had some hesitations on this subject. As he saw it, the Dtr went back to the parenetic style of the Deuteronomic preaching, and this style in itself was not compatible with an exclusively negative objective.[131] Hans-Walter Wolff[132] and Walter Brueggemann[133] took a still further

125. Several other authors move in the same direction; cf. Radjawane, 'Das deuteronomistische Geschichtswerk', p. 212.

126. W. Hermann, 'Die Bedeutung der Propheten im Geschichtsaufriss des Deuteronomisten' (Dissertation, Berlin, 1957), pp. 7-8.

127. J.A. Soggin, 'Deuteronomistische Geschichtsauslegung während des babylonischen Exils', in F. Christ (ed.), *Oikonomia: Heilsgeschichte als Thema der Theologie* (Festschrift O. Cullmann; Hamburg: Bergstedt, 1967), pp. 11-17.

128. P.R. Ackroyd, *Exile and Restoration: A Study of Hebrew Thought of the Sixth Century B.C.* (OTL; London: SCM Press, 1968).

129. Cf. for example, E.W. Nicholson, *Preaching to the Exiles: A Study of the Prose Tradition in the Book of Jeremiah* (Oxford: Clarendon Press, 1970), pp. 118-23.

130. Noth developed this perspective in his article 'Zur Geschichtsauffassung der Deuteronomisten', in A.Z.V. Togan (ed.), *Proceedings of the 22th Congress of Orientalists* (Istanbul: Yalçin Matbaasi, 1951), pp. 558-66.

131. E. Janssen, *Juda in der Exilszeit: Ein Beitrag zur Frage nach der Entstehung des Judentums* (FRLANT, 51; Göttingen: Vandenhoeck & Ruprecht, 1956), pp. 73-76, 107-109.

132. H.W. Wolff, 'Das Kerygma des deuteronomistischen Geschichtswerks',

step: embarking on research into the 'kerygma' of Dtr, Wolff found it in the theme of the invitation to return (שוב), that is to say in the call to conversion of the persons addressed in the work (cf. for example Deut. 4.25-31; 30.10; 1 Kgs 8.51). It must be noted, however, that most of the passages referred to by Wolff had been considered by Noth as 'secondary', which Wolff, moreover, did not question. But on the question of the intention of the Dtr, it is von Rad who took a position most distant from that of Noth. For the Lutheran theologian, the DH quite naturally integrated the Law *and* the Gospel, with this being expressed particularly in 2 Samuel 7. Did not Nathan's oracle indeed confer—after the catastrophe—on the Dtr enterprise a messianic and eschatological meaning? These messianic tones are perceived by von Rad at the end of the work as well,[134] in 2 Kgs 25.27-30. In fact, the position of von Rad in regard to Noth's thesis in general could have led us to situate him instead under the following heading.

4.2. *Positive Reaction to the Noth Thesis, but at the Cost of Fundamental Modifications*

For von Rad, we may suspect, the thesis of a Dtr historiographical work could only run counter to the idea that he himself had developed on the primitive form of the Hexateuch.[135] Even if Noth continued to hold as probable that the ancient sources of the Pentateuch would have ended with an account of the conquest of the land,[136] he no longer thought that these accounts would have been present in the book of Joshua, and especially he insisted on the fact that P, itself, had related events only up to the death of Moses.[137] In spite of this difference, von Rad greeted

---

ZAW 73 (1961), pp. 171-86 = *Gesammelte Studien zum Alten Testament* (TBü, 22; Munich: Chr. Kaiser Verlag, 1964), pp. 308-24.

133. W. Brueggemann, 'The Kerygma of the Deuteronomic Historian', *Int* 22 (1968), pp. 387-402.

134. G. von Rad, *Theologie des Alten Testaments*, I (2 vols.; Munich: Chr. Kaiser Verlag, 1957), pp. 355-56; French translation: *Théologie de l'Ancien Testament*, I (Geneva: Labor et Fides, 1957); English translation: *Old Testament Theology* (2 vols.; trans. D.M.G. Stalker; New York: Harper & Row, 1962).

135. G. von Rad, *Das formgeschichtliche Problem des Hexateuch* (BWANT, 78; Stuttgart: Kohlhammer, 1938) = *Gesammelte Studien zum Alten Testament* (TBü, 8; Munich: Chr. Kaiser Verlag, 4th edn, 1971), pp. 9-86.

136. Noth, *ÜSt*, pp. 211-17.

137. Noth, *ÜSt*, p. 205.

the publication of Noth's work as 'closing a shameful gap' in Old Testament studies.[138] This did not prevent him from remaining very critical with regard to the view of sources following from Noth's theory.[139] For von Rad, the book of Joshua remained the natural outcome of the Pentateuch, and in his opinion, the existence of the Hexateuch had to be reaffirmed for reasons provided by literary criticism as well as by the history of forms. Perhaps too Noth's thesis fitted in poorly with the (Barthian) history of salvation theology,[140] as von Rad continued, certainly in modified forms, to retain it in his thinking.[141]

Aage Bentzen too will consider that the weak point in Noth's theory lies in the idea of a Tetrateuch: this would remain 'a torso without the scopus (*sic*) so clearly indicated in the Patriarchal and Mosaic Story'.[142] Bentzen consequently became the advocate of a compromise: the Dtr would have integrated into his work the end of the Hexateuch (Joshua). It is this ending (Joshua and Judges 1) as well that would represent the nucleus from which J and E would have constructed their narrative.[143] This proposal, probably premature,[144] achieved no success at the time.

Otto Kaiser, in the first edition of his introduction to the Old Testament,[145] affirmed his agreement with the theory of the DH, but hastened to specify everything in this theory that presented problems for him. Three objections especially were made to Noth's hypothesis: (1) If, as Noth claims, the DH takes its inspiration from Dt, it cannot be dated to the exilic period, since Kaiser, following Hölscher and others, places

---

138. G. von Rad, *Deuteronomium-Studien* (FRLANT, 58; Göttingen: Vandenhoeck & Ruprecht, 1947), p. 52; ET *Studies in Deuteronomy* (London: SCM Press, 1953); cf. as well *idem*, 'Hexateuch oder Pentateuch', *VF* 1 (1947–48), pp. 52-56.

139. Von Rad blames Noth, among others, for an arbitrary attribution of many texts to 'P^s', namely, to layers not belonging to the original priestly document. Cf. von Rad, 'Hexateuch oder Pentateuch', p. 54.

140. Smend, *Deutsche Alttestamentler in drei Jahrhunderten*, p. 259, notes also Noth's reservations in regard to Barth's theology.

141. Cf. A. de Pury and E.A. Knauf, 'La théologie de l'Ancien Testament: kérygmatique ou descriptive?', *ETR* 70 (1995), pp. 323-34.

142. A. Bentzen, *Introduction to the Old Testament*, II (2 vols.; Copenhagen: G.E.C. Gad, 1948), p. 75.

143. Bentzen, *Introduction to the Old Testament*, pp. 76, 85.

144. As we will see, the idea that J and E developed from Joshua, namely, from the Dtr construction, is today one of the great theses at the centre of the debate.

145. O. Kaiser, *Einleitung in das Alte Testament* (Gütersloh: Gerd Mohn, 1969), pp. 100-40.

the origin of Dt itself in the exilic period.[146] (2) In many texts the problems of literary criticism are so complex that they cannot be resolved merely by a distinction between a 'source' and a 'Dtr redaction'. (3) The Dtr redaction proves to be of a completely different nature according to the books where an attempt to pick it out is made: present everywhere in Kings, it is practically nonexistent in the books of Samuel. These two latter observations are frequently found in authors who reject Noth's theory.

4.3. *Total Rejection of Noth's Thesis*

The critical voices raised most strongly against Noth's thesis were those of Eissfeldt, Weiser and Fohrer.

4.3.1. *Eissfeldt and the Priority of Literarkritik*

In the criticisms of Eissfeldt[147] and Fohrer,[148] we meet right away the problem of the Hexateuch-Tetrateuch alternative already mentioned by von Rad, but this is no longer perceived as being surmountable by compromise measures. In a more global way, it is the hierarchy of exegetical methods in Noth's work that is contested: he is criticized for putting *Redaktionsgeschichte* before *Literarkritik*. Eissfeldt who, in every aspect of exegesis, found himself at opposite poles from Noth,[149] criticizes him for his neglect of diachronic problems. Thus, for example, in Joshua 1–3: if Joshua 1 and 3.2-4b are derived from the Dtr, how in that case can the tension between 1.11 (announcement of the crossing of the Jordan the third day) and 3.2 (after three days the scribes announce the future crossing) be explained, and that without even taking into account the story of the spies in Joshua 2 (that

146. Kaiser, *Einleitung in das Alte Testament*, pp. 108-109. Today he seems to have changed his opinion; cf. O. Kaiser, *Grundriss der Einleitung in die kanonischen und deuterokanonischen Schriften des Alten Testaments. I. Die erzählenden Werke* (Gütersloh: Gerd Mohn, 1992), pp. 96-97.

147. O. Eissfeldt, *Geschichtschreibung im Alten Testament: Ein kritischer Bericht* (Berlin: Evangelische Verlagsanstalt, 1948); *idem*, *Einleitung in das Alte Testament* (Tübingen: J.C.B. Mohr, 3rd edn, 1964), pp. 321-30.

148. G. Fohrer, *Einleitung in das Alte Testament* (Heidelberg: Quelle & Meyer, 1969), pp. 209-11.

149. According to the formulation of Smend, *Deutsche Alttestamentler in drei Jahrhunderten*, p. 268.

presupposes an even longer lapse of time)?[150] In a general way Eissfeldt cannot see how a historiographical work could have come into existence in the period of the exile, a period when literary activities, according to him, were exclusively of a cultic and ritual order.[151] As we see, the theory of the decadence of Judaism still had a bright future before it, even after the Second World War.

4.3.2. *Weiser and the Independence of the Dtr Redactors*

Artur Weiser for his part stressed the different character of the Dtr redaction in each of the historical books.[152] In his opinion, the following observations were essential: the book of Joshua is linked to the Pentateuch, with the Dtr redaction being limited and secondary. The book of Judges, in 2.6–16.31, shows clearly the signs of a Dtr redaction; this one took place during the exile, using a pre-Dtr source. As for the books of Samuel, they display a complex redactional history in the midst of which the Dtr redaction scarcely appears at all. On the other hand, the Dtr imprint is most clearly perceptible in the books of Kings. In Kings, two Dtr redactions are distinguishable, one Josianic, the other exilic. For Weiser (as for Fohrer), a Dtr milieu indeed existed therefore, but a DH did not exist: each book has its own history, and the books extending from Deuteronomy to 2 Kings cannot in any case be considered a historiographical work as Noth had imagined it.[153]

As such, these attempts to question the very existence of a DH remain upon the whole quite marginal. Most of the observations made by the adversaries of Noth on the diachronic level or on that of the history of redaction are, however, going to resurface in the proposals

---

150. Eissfeldt, *Geschichtschreibung im Alten Testament*, pp. 27-29. The other example chosen by Eissfeldt is that of the pro- and antimonarchical texts in 1 Sam. 7–12.

151. Eissfeldt, *Geschichtschreibung im Alten Testament*, p. 44.

152. A. Weiser, *Einleitung in das Alte Testament* (Göttingen:Vandenhoeck & Ruprecht, 1963), pp. 117-66; cf. as well von Rad, *Theologie*, I, pp. 340-59; Fohrer, *Einleitung in das Alte Testament*, p. 211.

153. We may note that this argumentation has recently been updated by Ernst Würthwein and Claus Westermann with the intention of contesting the existence of DH. Cf. C. Westermann, *Die Geschichtsbücher des Alten Testaments: Gab es ein deuteronomistisches Geschichtswerk?* (TBü, 87; Gütersloh: Chr. Kaiser Verlag-Gütersloher Verlagshaus, 1994).

for modification that will mark the next phase of the history of research in the 1970s and 1980s.[154]

5. *Proposals for a Diachronic Differentiation in the DH Edifice*

Noth himself had already made the observation—without stopping to go into details—that many Dtr texts reveal the intervention of two, even of many hands in the redactional process. Thus, in Joshua 1,[155] Yhwh's address to Joshua ends, in its first phase, with the exhortation of v. 6: 'Be strong and courageous; for you shall give the people possession of the land that I swore to their ancestors that I should give to them.' In Josh. 1.1-6, Joshua is installed as military leader in a spirit entirely in conformity with the account of the conquest that is going to follow. Now, v. 7 continues in these terms: 'Be strong and courageous, being careful to act according to all[156] that Moses my servant laid down for you... This book of the Torah shall not be far from your mouth; you shall murmur it day and night...' In this second passage, Joshua, from a charismatic leader, has become an examplary follower of the Torah, and the warlike context has almost entirely disappeared.

Let us take another example: Judges 3,[157] a key text for DH, contains a reflection on the fact that all the enemies of Israel have not been wiped out or expelled from Canaan. This text (which moreover contradicts Josh. 21.43-45, a passage, likewise Dtr, that asserts that all the land is handed over by Yhwh to Israel) gives two different explanations of this established fact. According to v. 2, this was only to teach the art of war to the generations of Israelites who had not had the occasion of being initiated into it, whereas according to v. 4, it was a matter of a

---

154. For this period, cf. as well the following histories of research: L.V. Alexander, *The Origin and Development of the Deuteronomistic History Theory and its Significance for Biblical Interpretation* (Ann Arbor: University of Michigan, 1993); H.D. Preuss, 'Zum deuteronomistischen Geschichtswerk', *ThR* 58 (1993), pp. 229-64; 341-95; L. Laberge, 'Le Deutéronomiste', in L. Laberge and M. Gourgues (eds.), *'De bien des manières'. La recherche biblique aux abords du XXIe siècle. Actes du Cinquantenaire de l'ACEBAC* (LD, 163; Paris: Cerf, 1995), pp. 47-77; D.A. Knight, 'Deuteronomy and the Deuteronomists', in J.L. Mays *et al.* (eds.), *Old Testament Interpretation: Past, Present, Future. Essays in Honor of Gene M. Tucker* (Edinburgh: T. & T. Clark, 1995), pp. 61-79.

155. Noth, *ÜSt*, p. 41 and n. 4.

156. MT specifies: 'according to all the Law'.

157. Noth, *ÜSt*, pp. 7-8.

proof 'to know whether the Israelites would obey the commandments that Yhwh had laid down to their ancestors'.

To the observation of these internal inconsistencies in the 'Dtr' texts are added the findings, already mentioned, of differences in the Dtr attitude in regard to the monarchy and, more particularly, in regard to personages like David or Solomon, or again the absence of clear indications on the possibility of a future after the catastrophe. We notice in addition a certain alternation between optimistic, even triumphalistic texts, and texts that are irremediably pessimistic.

There comes up too the problem of where the work ends. Would the Dtr historian, who is usually quite long winded and comments on each period with a detailed 'meditative discourse', really be satisfied with an episode as marginal and an ending as abrupt as that offered us in 2 Kgs 25.27-30 for the closing of his work? Or must we seek the 'real end' elsewhere?

The systematization of all these questions and of the observations that are connected to them has led, starting from the end of the 1960s, to two explanatory models that, while being presented as prolongations of Noth's thesis, nonetheless modify its parameters, each in its own way.

5.1. *The School of F.M. Cross and the Thesis of a Double Dtr Redaction*

In a 1968 article, republished in 1973, Frank M. Cross[158] returned to the old idea[159] of a double redaction of the Dtr historiography, the first Josianic, the second Exilic. His arguments were the following:

The books of Kings and Samuel are marked by two major themes: the sin of Jeroboam, which culminates in the fall of Samaria (2 Kgs 17.1, 23) and the promise of an eternal Davidic dynasty (2 Sam. 7). These two thematic lines converge in the reign of Josiah,[160] because Josiah is the one who definitively demolished the altar at Bethel, and thus abolished the sin of Jeroboam (2 Kgs 23.15). He is also the exemplary Davidic offspring (2 Kgs 22.2; 23.25). The reign of Josiah

158. F.M. Cross, 'The Themes of the Book of Kings and the Structure of the Deuteronomistic History', in *idem, Canaanite Myth and Hebrew Epic* (Cambridge, MA: Harvard University Press, 1973), pp. 274-89.

159. Cf. above, §2.2. The same approach is found for example in the commentaries of John Gray: J. Gray, *I & II Kings* (OTL; London: Oliphants, 1970); *Joshua, Judges, Ruth* (NCB; London: Oliphants, 1967; rev. edn, 1986).

160. Cross, 'The Themes of the Book of Kings', pp. 283-84.

corresponds therefore with the logical finale of the first edition of the DH, whose conclusion is found in 2 Kgs 23.25 (this verse forms besides an *inclusio* with Deut. 6.4-5). From this perspective, DH seems to be originally a piece of propaganda in favour of Josiah, a work meant to celebrate his political and religious innovations. Consequently, 2 Kgs 23.26–25.30 comes from a different hand: these two chapters belong to a second edition of DH, an edition in the exilic period from the hand of a redactor (Dtr^2) who, because of the shock of the disaster, would have provided the work with a laconic ending and thus transformed the propaganda document into an announcement of mourning.

If Cross can develop such a thesis, it is because he attributes in the setting of the DH, unlike Noth (but in secret agreement with von Rad?), a decisive role to Nathan's oracle (2 Sam. 7).[161] We will take note too that the thesis is almost exclusively constructed from the book of Kings. This book will play from now on a more and more central role in the debate on the profile of the DH. The thesis of Cross—and in particular the idea of a first Josianic redaction—will be confirmed and refined by the works of many researchers. Thus Nelson, who will try to support the thematic arguments of Cross through detailed literary analyses, carries out at the beginning of his 1973 work[162] an investigation of the formulas of appreciation of the monarchy in 1 and 2 Kings, an investigation that will lead him to take note of an obvious break in style for the reigns that follow that of Josiah: the formulas, after that point become more rigid, less 'Deuteronomistic', and their rubber-stamp character gives away their provenance from an 'Exilic editor'. Nelson attributes to this layer among others the following texts: Deut. 4.19-20; Josh. 24.1-28; Judg. 2.1-5; 6.7-10; 1 Kgs 8.44-51; 9.6-9; 2 Kgs 17.7-20, [24-34a], 34b-40; 22.16-17, 20b; 23.4b-5, 19-20, 24[?], 26-30; 23.21–25.30. In the description of the two editions, Nelson is in total agreement with Cross: the Exilic editor would have transformed a triumphalist writing[163] into a doxology of judgment.[164] Friedman, for his part,

---

161. Contrary to the older criticism (Kuenen, Nowack), Noth had decreed that it was impossible to attribute 2 Sam. 7 to the Dtr. Only vv. 13a and 22-24 were, for him, of Dtr origin. Later, Noth also added vv. 8-10. Cf. M. Noth, 'David und Israel in 2 Sam 7', in *idem, Gesammelte Studien zum A.T.* (TBü, 6; Munich: Chr. Kaiser Verlag, 1960), pp. 334-45.

162. This work was only published in 1981: R.D. Nelson, *The Double Redaction of the Deuteronomistic History* (JSOTSup, 18; Sheffield: JSOT Press), 1981.

163. Nelson points out that the Josianic editor sets up numerous parallels among

makes the same observations as Nelson, without apparently knowing the work of the latter.[165] For him too, the ending of the Josianic edition (Dtr[1]) is found in 2 Kgs 23.25, since we no longer encounter the theme of the high places (*bamôt*) nor the reference to David as an ideal king. In regard to the Exilic tradition (Dtr[2]), Friedman considers that it ends in 2 Kgs 25.26 with the mention of the descent of the people to Egypt.[166] It is actually with the return to Egypt that the curses of Deuteronomy 28 are realized: 'Dtr[2] tells the story from Egypt to Egypt'.[167] The appendix of 2 Kgs 25.27-30 would consequently be considered an addition due to a member of the Babylonian *golah*. Nelson and Friedman have a tendency besides to reduce somewhat the number of texts attributed by Cross to Dtr[2].[168] For them, the fact that the Davidic promise would be conditional does not necessarily presuppose the exile, since that conditionality can be explained in the Josianic period by taking into account the events of 722. Besides, the threat of exile does not necessarily presuppose the reality of the latter, since the announcement of such a calamity is not only a standard element but practically an obligatory one in vassal treaties.[169]

That being said, there are, among the disciples of Cross, those too who take the opposite position and very massively increase the portion attributed to the Exilic redaction. In this direction, we will mention among others the works of Levenson,[170] Boling,[171] Peckham[172] and Mayes.[173]

Moses, Joshua and Josiah; cf. Nelson, *The Double Redaction*, p. 125.

164. Nelson, *The Double Redaction*, pp. 121-23.

165. R.E. Friedman, *The Exile and Biblical Narrative: The Formation of the Deuteronomistic and Priestly Codes* (HSM, 22; Atlanta: Scholars Press, 1981).

166. Friedman, *The Exile and Biblical Narrative*, p. 35.

167. Friedman, *The Exile and Biblical Narrative*, p. 36.

168. Cf. the list of Dtr[2] texts in Friedman, *The Exile and Biblical Narrative*, pp. 25-26.

169. For a more detailed presentation of these arguments, cf. S.L. McKenzie, 'Deuteronomistic History', *ABD*, II, pp. 160-68 (164).

170. J.D. Levenson, 'Who inserted the Book of the Torah?', *HTR* 68 (1975), pp. 203-33; *idem*, 'From Temple to Synagogue: 1 Kings 8', in B. Halpern and J. Levenson (eds.), *Traditions in Transformation: Turning Points in Biblical Faith* (Festschrift F.M. Cross; Winona Lake, IN: Eisenbrauns, 1981), pp. 143-66.

171. R.G. Boling, *Judges* (AB, 6A; Garden City, NY: Doubleday, 1975); *idem*, *Joshua* (AB, 6; Garden City, NY: Doubleday, 1982).

What is appealing in the hypothesis of Cross and his students, all lumped together, is that it works from a simple model: a Josianic historiography taken up again by an Exilic editor! It is a thesis that puts us in the presence of two Dtr editions, each having its own outlook and belonging to two clearly distinct phases of the history of Israel. However, we cannot help noticing a certain cleavage between Anglo-Saxon and German exegetes. Whereas the thesis of Cross has largely become established in the United States and in the English-speaking world, it has few supporters among German specialists, almost all of whom have remained sceptical in regard to a Josianic DH. Among those who have openly gone over to it are Helga Weippert[174] and Rendtorff.[175]

We will go back over the evaluation of Cross's model, but we can already point out the main questions that have been raised by critics of this model: is an end of the work in 2 Kgs 23.25 conceivable? How do

172. B. Peckham, *The Composition of the Deuteronomistic History* (HSM, 35; Atlanta: Scholars Press, 1985). Peckham is difficult to 'classify', since he has a quite eccentric view of things. For him, Dtr[1] was composed in the period of Ezekiah with the goal of providing a continuation of the Yahwist. P would have been composed following this, in order to offer an alternative to J. As for E, it would be a work intended to compete with Dtr[1]. In the exilic period, it was Dtr[2] that would have gathered together all these sources so as to form the great work that extends from Genesis to 2 Kings. For a critique of this theory ('creative but highly idiosyncratic'), cf. McKenzie, 'Deuteronomistic History', p. 164. In his later book, *History and Prophecy: The Development of Late Judean Literary Traditions* (ABRL; New York: Doubleday, 1993), Peckham has become more prudent in regard to sources and insists instead on Dtr[2] as an 'author'.

173. A.D.H. Mayes, *The Story of Israel between Settlement and Exile: A Redactional Study of the Deuteronomistic History* (London: SCM Press, 1983). Mayes has provided a detailed reconstruction of the redactional history of DH. His approach can be considered a 'model' of compromise and will be presented later.

174. H. Weippert, 'Das deuteronomistische Geschichtswerk: Sein Ziel und Ende in der neuren Forschung', *ThR* 50 (1985), pp. 213-49.

175. R. Rendtorff, *Das Alte Testament: eine Einführung* (Neukirchen–Vluyn: Neukirchener Verlag, 1983); ET *The Old Testament: An Introduction* (London: SCM Press, 1985); French translation by F. Smyth and H. Winkler, *Introduction à l'Ancien Testament* (Paris: Cerf, 1989), pp. 313-15. Rendtorff remains prudent and describes Cross's thesis as 'attractive'. Recently, several German works seem to have been won over to Cross's model. Cf. A. Moenikes, 'Zur Redaktionsgeschichte des sogenannten deuteronomistischen Geschichtswerks', *ZAW* 104 (1992), pp. 333-48; H.-J. Stipp, *Jeremia im Parteienstreit: Studien zur Textentwicklung von Jer 26, 36-43 und 45 als Beitrag zur Geschichte Jeremias, seines Buches und judäischer Parteien im 6. Jahrhundert* (BBB, 82; Frankfurt a.M.: Hain, 1992).

we explain the omnipresence of allusions to the exile in the DH? Is not the effect of the attempt to reduce the genesis of DH to two main steps an improper simplification of the diachronic and thematic complexity still perceptible within this great historiographical corpus? Questions of this sort have led to a model of what is currently called 'the Göttingen School', of which we must now speak.

5.2. *The Göttingen School and the Theory of Successive Layers*

The second diachronic model proposing a modification of Martin Noth's thesis comes from Göttingen, insofar as it was elaborated by Rudolf Smend, Jr and his students Walter Dietrich and Timo Veijola. The starting point for this model can be located in a 1971 article, in which Smend presented an analysis of Joshua 1; 13; 23–24, as well as of Judg. 1-2.5.[176] In those texts recognized by Noth as Dtr, Smend discovered additions in Josh. 1.7-9; 13.1bβ-6; 23; Judg. 1.1–2.9, 17, 20-21, 23. In these passages, a conception of the conquest actually different from that which characterized the surrounding verses was expressed. According to the first edition of the DH, Joshua had conquered the entire country and had completely exterminated the ancient inhabitants. In the secondary passages detected by Smend, on the contrary, the conquest was not considered complete, and a great number of the former inhabitants were living in the land. Furthermore, these additions were seen to be preoccupied with the obedience of the Israelites with regard to the Law. Smend proposed therefore to subdivide the Dtr redaction into two successive layers, for which he assigned the following sigla: DtrH[177] (Deuteronomistic historian, the creator of the work in its first edition) and DtrN (the Nomistic redactor insisting on the role of the Law, who re-edited DtrH, correcting it and adding other material). For Smend, there was no doubt that DtrH should be situated in the exilic

176. R. Smend, 'Das Gesetz und die Völker: Ein Beitrag zur deuteronomistischen Redaktionsgeschichte', in H.W. Wolff (ed.), *Probleme biblischer Theologie: G. von Rad zum 70. Geburtstag* (Munich: Chr. Kaiser Verlag, 1971), pp. 494-509.

177. Following Noth, Smend had at first, in his 1971 article, called the first redactor 'DtrG', but subsequently and to avoid confusion between *Geschichtsschreiber* (the historiographer) and *Geschichtswerk* (the historiographical work), Smend adopted Dietrich's suggestion: 'DH' (*der deuteronomistische Historiker*, therefore the historiographer). Cf. W. Dietrich, 'David in Überlieferung und Geschichte', *VF* 22 (1977), pp. 44-48 (48 n. 11).

period, and more precisely around 560.[178] In spite of his insistence on
two redactional levels, it was well and truly a different model to that of
Cross—and basically closer to Noth's—that made its appearance in the
exegetical debate. DtrH as a matter of fact took over from the Dtr of
Noth, not only with regard to the initial literary project, but also with
regard to its theological intention. For Smend as for Noth, the goal of
DrtrH was to explain to the people the catastrophe of the exile, even if
Smend relativized somewhat the darkness of the picture painted by
Noth.[179]

Smend had elaborated his thesis from a very small number of texts,
and these texts, moreover, had always been the subject of divergent
diachronic explanations.[180] It remains no less true that with this brief
article, Smend provided a base for the construction of a new diachronic
hypothesis that made it possible to integrate better the texts that Noth
had often described as 'secondary additions'.

The way opened by Smend has been followed by his students
Dietrich and Veijola. It really seems that the book of Kings must contain the solution to the problem of the dating of the first Dtr. Consequently, it is that book which Dietrich chooses as his starting point.[181]
Throughout 1–2 Kings, Dietrich discovers—making use of literary-
critical techniques—a series of discourses containing prophetic judgments structured according to a recurrent outline and followed,
generally some chapters later, by a notice reporting the fulfilment of the
predicted judgment (*Erfüllungsvermerke*).[182] These texts, which are distinguished by a Dtr style and an intense interest in the role of the
prophets and in the prophetic word, constitute, according to him, a
specific Dtr redactional layer that he designated by the siglum 'DtrP'
(the prophetic Deuteronomist). The texts that Dietrich attributed to DtrP
are the following:[183]

178. Cf. R. Smend, *Die Entstehung des Alten Testaments* (Stuttgart: Kohlhammer, 1978), p. 124.
179. Cf. Smend, *Die Entstehung des Alten Testaments*, p. 124.
180. Cf. the remark of McKenzie, 'Deuteronomistic History', p. 163.
181. W. Dietrich, *Prophetie und Geschichte: Eine redaktionsgeschichtliche
Untersuchung zum deuteronomistischen Geschichtswerk* (FRLANT, 108; Göttingen: Vandenhoeck & Ruprecht, 1972).
182. In this connection, cf. already G. von Rad, 'Die deuteronomistische
Geschichtstheologie in den Königsbüchern', in *idem*, *Deuteronomium-Studien*, Teil
B; also in *Gesammelte Studien zum A.T.*, pp. 189-204.
183. For a detailed summary of the diachronic operations of Dietrich, cf.

Judgment Discourse:	Notice of Fulfilment
1 Kgs 14.7, 8a, 9b-11, 13b	1 Kgs 15.29
1 Kgs 16.1-4	1 Kgs 16.11-12
1 Kgs 21.19b, 20bβ-24; 22.38	2 Kgs 10.17a
2 Kgs 9.7-10a	2 Kgs 9.36
2 Kgs 21.10-14	2 Kgs 24.2
2 Kgs 22.15-18	

For Dietrich, DtrP is at the same time author and redactor, since he has integrated into DH pre-Dtr material (for example, the Elijah and Elisha cycles) but also, in 1–2 Samuel, accounts of his own choice, among others the nucleus of 2 Samuel 12. DtrP would be prompted by the need to instil in the reader the conviction that the word of Yhwh's prophet was accomplished without any exception.[184] According to DtrP, history would be nothing else but the fulfilment of predictions (*Weissagungen*). Because of his tendency to systematize the prophetic word, he would have confined it within a 'rigid corset'.[185] As Dietrich saw it, DtrP is situated between DtrH and DtrN and would hardly have come up before the book of Samuel. For the three layers of DH, Dietrich proposes a quite tight dating:[186] DtrH, that (contrary to Smend's opinion) would have its ending in 2 Kgs 25.21, would have been composed about 580, while the epilogue concerning the rehabilitation of Jehoiachin would be the work of DtrN, itself dated about 560, which leaves space for DtrP between these two dates. Dietrich localizes his DtrP in Palestine, probably at Jerusalem, but on this point he seems to remain under the influence of Noth, since he does not present any new arguments in favour of this assertion.

Veijola, for his part, devotes himself more particularly to DtrN, especially in the books of Samuel and Kings.[187] While practising *Literarkritik* as well, Veijola gives an important place to *Ideologiekritik*, to underscore the differences in ideological sensitivity among the

F. Langlamet's review, *RB* 81 (1974), pp. 601-604.

184. Dietrich, *Prophetie und Geschichte*, p. 107.

185. Dietrich, *Prophetie und Geschichte*, p. 109.

186. Dietrich, *Prophetie und Geschichte*, pp. 143-44.

187. T. Veijola, *Die ewige Dynastie: David und die Entstehung seiner Dynastie nach der deuteronomistischen Darstellung* (STAT.AASF, 193; Helsinki: Suomaleinen Tiedeakatemia, 1975); *idem, Das Königtum in der Beurteilung der deuteronomistischen Historiographie. Eine redaktionsgeschichtliche Untersuchung* (STAT.AASF, 198; Helsinki: Suomaleinen Tiedeakatemia, 1977).

redactors of the DH. It is therefore in relation to their view of the monarchy that the 'voices' perceptible in the Dtr redaction will be appraised.[188] The texts favourable to the establishment of the monarchy in 1 Samuel 8–12—and therefore favourable to the Davidic dynasty— are due to DtrH. He would make an effort to legitimate the Davidic dynasty by repeated referrals to a divine promise made to David (1 Sam. 25.28, 30; 2 Sam. 3.9-10, 18; 5.2; 7.11b, 13, 16), without how- ever thinking it necessary to provide the readers with the *foundation* of these 'reminders' (*Textgrundlage*).[189] DtrP, on the other hand, would have a negative vision of the monarchy and it is he who would have painted the portrait of David in the grip of sin. As for DtrN, he too would judge the monarchy in a very critical manner (1 Sam. 8.6-22; 1 Sam. 12). But, unlike DtrP, he would attempt to 'whitewash' the royal founders of the dynasty, David and Solomon, as can be seen in 1 Kgs 1.35-37, 46-48; 2.3, 4aβ. DtrN would therefore not exclude future pros- pects for the Davidic dynasty, on condition that the descendants of the Davidic line obeyed the Mosaic law.

In a general way, we see that Veijola considerably increases the proportion of texts attributed to different phases of the Dtr redaction, especially in Samuel.[190] The pronounced presence of Dtr redactional interventions in 2 Samuel 5–8 would tend to prove, according to him, that the great pre-Dtr collections, the history of the rise and the history of the succession of David, would only have been joined one to the other at the time of the Dtr redaction. Following the example of Noth and Smend, Veijola thinks he can localize the literary activity of the Dtr redactors in Palestine, probably at Mizpah.[191]

---

188. For a summary of the distribution of Dtr layers according to Veijola, cf. Dietrich, 'David in Überlieferung und Geschichte', p. 49.

189. Veijola, *Die ewige Dynastie*, pp. 79, 133.

190. As a 'precursor' in this attempt, we could cite R.A. Carlson, *David, the Chosen King: A Traditio-Historical Approach to the Second Book of Samuel* (Stockholm: Almqvist & Wiksell, 1964). Influenced by the Scandinavian school, Carlson all the same renounces processes of the 'literary critical' type. Cf. in regard to this, T. Veijola, 'Remarks of an Outsider Concerning Scandinavian Tradition History with Emphasis on the Davidic Tradition', in K. Jeppesen and B. Otzen (eds.), *The Productions of Time: Tradition History in Old Testament Scholarship* (Sheffield: Almond Press, 1984), pp. 29-51.

191. Thus, what Noth had indicated as a possibility in the last footnote of his foundational book was transformed little by little into certitude for a good number of his 'faithful'. 'The fact that the Dtr had access to such a variety of literary

Many researchers were won over to this thesis of a triple edition of the DH. We may mention, among others, Hermann Spieckermann,[192] Christoph Levin,[193] Fabrizio Foresti,[194] Ernst Würthwein,[195] J. Alberto Soggin,[196] Rainer Bickert,[197] Otto Kaiser,[198] Uwe Becker,[199] and in the English-speaking world, Ralph Klein,[200] Wolfgang Roth,[201] Ehud Ben-Zvi.[202] Of course, all these exegetes do not understand Smend's model in an exactly identical way: differences come up particularly over the question of localizing the redactions (Palestine or Babylon?) and even more, with regard to the notion of DtrN. Whereas Dietrich and others date DtrN to the exilic period, Smend, Würthwein, Kaiser and Levin understand DtrN rather as a siglum covering redactional interventions

sources might suggest that he had stayed behind in the homeland rather than being deported'. Noth, *The Deuteronomistic History*, p. 142 n. 9.

192. H. Spieckermann, *Juda unter Assur in der Sargonidenzeit* (FRLANT, 129; Göttingen: Vandenhoeck & Rupecht, 1982).

193. C. Levin, *Der Sturz der Königin Atalja: Ein Kapitel zur Geschichte Judas im 9. Jahrhundert v. Chr.* (SBS, 105; Stuttgart: Katholisches Bibelwerk, 1982).

194. F. Foresti, *The Rejection of Saul in the Perspective of the Deuteronomistic School: A Study of 1 Sam. 15 and Related Texts* (SThT, 5; Rome: Ed. del Teresianum, 1984).

195. E. Würthwein, *Die Bücher der Könige. 1 Kön 1–16* (ATD, 11.1; Göttingen: Vandenhoeck & Ruprecht, 1977); *1 Kön 17–2 Kön 25* (ATD, 11.2; Göttingen: Vandenhoeck & Ruprecht, 1984).

196. J.A. Soggin, *Joshua: A Commentary* (OTL; Philadelphia: Westminster, 1972). In his *Introduction to the Old Testament* (Louisville, KY: Westminster / John Knox Press, 1989), pp. 178-84, he seems much more reserved.

197. R. Bickert, 'Die Geschichte und das Handeln Jahwes: Zur Eigenart einer deuteronomistischen Offenbarungsauffassung in den Samuelbüchern', in A.H.J. Gunneweg and O. Kaiser (eds.), *Textgemäss, Aufsätze und Beiträge zur Hermeneutik des Alten Testaments* (Festschrift E. Würthwein; Göttingen: Vandenhoeck & Ruprecht, 1979), pp. 2-27.

198. O. Kaiser, *Grundriss der Einleitung in die kanonischen und deuterokanonischen Schriften des Alten Testaments*, I (3 vols.; Gütersloh: Gerd Mohn, 1992), pp. 85-139.

199. U. Becker, *Richterzeit und Königtum: Redaktionsgeschichtliche Studien zum Richterbuch* (BZAW, 192; Berlin: W. de Gruyter, 1990).

200. R.W. Klein, *1 Samuel* (WBC, 10; Waco, TX: Word Books, 1983).

201. W. Roth, 'Deuteronomistisches Geschichtswerk/Deuteronomistische Schule', *TRE* 8 (1981), pp. 543-52.

202. E. Ben-Zvi, 'The Account of the Reign of Manasseh in II Reg 21, 1-18 and the Redactional Unity of the Book of Kings', *ZAW* 102 (1991), pp. 335-74.

that could have taken place all through the Persian period.[203] According to Smend, DtrN should perhaps be identified with the Dtr redaction of the Pentateuch and would have therefore attempted to edit the great history extending from Genesis to 2 Kings.[204] The most extreme dates are those that have been proposed by Levin, who situates the final interventions of DtrN in the second half of the fourth century.

The risk in this new tendency is that the Dtr layers begin to multiply. We notice too some inflation of new sigla to catalogue all the levels and sublevels that need to be recognized: to refer, for example, to the final Dtr interventions in Deuteronomy–2 Kings, Lohfink[205] speaks of 'DtrÜ' (*deuteronomistischer Überarbeiter*) and Kaiser[206] of 'DtrS' (*Spätdeuteronomistische Redaktion*). This tendency cannot help but recall the exacerbation with the literary criticism that was produced in Pentateuchal studies three-quarters of a century earlier and that likewise had as a consequence a multiplication of sources and sigla.[207] The attribution of texts to one of these multiple levels risks therefore being done according to more and more arbitrary criteria and leads to allocations that are less and less verifiable. Besides, we note that the terminus *a quo* for the starting up of the DH invariably remains, for the Göttingen school, the first deportation of 597. The possibility of a pre-exilic date for certain texts with a Dtr appearance is not even considered. All this indicates that his theory—just like that of Cross—could have ideological presuppositions, but these have rarely been explained or discussed.

5.3. *The Exegetical and Ideological Presuppositions of the Models of Cross and Smend*

The supporters of a first edition of the DH under Josiah often emphasize the fact that their model remains close to that of Noth since they simply

203. Smend ('Das Gesetz und die Völker') had already proposed subdividing DtrN into $DtrN_1$, $DtrN_2$, ...etc.

204. We will go back over the problem of a Dtr redaction (or redactions) of the Pentateuch; cf. below, §6.2.

205. N. Lohfink, 'Kerygmata des deuteronomistischen Geschichtswerks', in J. Jeremias and L. Perlitt, *Die Botschaft und die Boten* (Festschrift H.W. Wolff; Neukirchen–Vluyn: Neukirchener Verlag, 1981), pp. 87-100.

206. Kaiser, *Grundriss der Einleitung*, I, p. 85.

207. On this subject, cf. de Pury and Römer, 'Le Pentateuque en question', pp. 29-31.

distinguish between the main edition (Dtr[1]) and secondary additions.[208] The fact nonetheless remains that moving the origin of the DH to the reign of Josiah entirely changes the vision that Noth had of the Dtr undertaking. The DH that, according to Noth, had as its goal—and its entire reason for existing!—the offering of an explanation for the catastrophe of the exile, indeed a theodicy facing the disaster that had struck Israel, is transformed by Cross into a triumphal historiography, indeed into a document of royal propaganda! Cross develops his whole argument from texts that highlight the Davidic monarchy, whereas Noth was not excessively preoccupied with the role of the monarchy in the DH. Whereas for Noth's DH the exile was the central event, from which the very Dtr enterprise was set in motion, for Cross and his students, the texts that bring up the exile are to be understood as theological additions of little significance.

We cannot refrain from questioning the role played in the genesis of the Anglo-Saxon model by the great admiration that Cross clearly has for king Josiah and his reform projects. It is almost a fascination, and we perceive in his work an optimistic theology, not so distant, after all, from the spirit of American Puritanism. The approach to the texts is positivist: Cross and his students consider that, with only some exceptions, the book of Kings relates events that are really historical. On the methodological level, literary criticism does not play an important role, and the arguments from which the theory is constructed are most often of a thematic order.

The Smend school, on the other hand, bases all its efforts on dividing up the text into layers, whereas the description and evaluation of the overall *project* as well as its geographical and socio-historical circumstances instead remain on the fringe. Under some of its aspects, the triple redaction of the DH common to this school can be put in relation with the analysis of the book of Kings as it has been elaborated by Jepsen, who too had ended up distinguishing three main editions.[209] What is particularly interesting is—as Smend himself had observed[210]—that

208. In reality, Cross is closer to Kuenen, Wellhausen and some of their contemporaries who had postulated a first pre-exilic redaction of Kings, followed by a second exilic redaction.

209. For Jepsen (*Die Quellen des Königsbuches*), it is true, the first of these three editions was still pre-exilic.

210. R. Smend, *Die Entstehung des Alten Testaments* (Stuttgart: W. Kohlhammer, 1978), p. 124.

the description of DH according to the stages DtrH—DtrP—DtrN implies the chronological sequence 'History—Prophecy—Law', a sequence that surprisingly resembles the Wellhausenian idea on the religious evolution of Israel through its Old Testament history, and we can even ask whether Smend's model does not attempt, without realizing it, to apply the Pentateuchal documentary theory to the historical books.[211] At least we see that a clear choice has been made in favour of the priority of *history* in relation to the *Law*, and that option goes so far as to persuade some exegetes to question the presence of the Deuteronomistic code within the first edition of the DH—thus Preuss[212] among others—a position that is quite difficult to defend.[213]

The two principal modifications of the Noth thesis, as we see it, are not free from theological and exegetical presuppositions, presuppositions that the protagonists of modifications have not really explained.

6. *The Broadening of Deuteronomistic Redactions to Other Literary Corpora*

For Noth, the work of the Dtr was clearly limited to the edition of the books Deuteronomy–2 Kings. Of course, in his commentaries on Exodus and Numbers, he noted for certain texts some 'additions in the Dtr style', without however bringing these texts together with the Dtr edition of the historical books.

For certain books, in particular Jeremiah, the redaction of a very large number of texts has long been attributed to Dtr hands.[214] But it is only when *Redaktionsgeschichte* gains the entire attention of Old Testament

211. The 'J' historian of the classical documentary theory would correspond quite well to the DtrH of Smend. 'E', whose relationship with the prophetic movement has often been emphasized, would have its counterpart in DtrP, and 'D' and 'P', whose legalism Protestant exegesis always liked to stress, would find their parallel in the legalism of DtrN.

212. H.D. Preuss, *Deuteronomium* (EdF, 164; Darmstadt: Wissenschaftliche Buchgesellschaft, 1982), pp. 22, 84. This idea is met as well among some representatives of the Cross school; cf. J. Levenson, 'Who Inserted the Book of the Torah?', *HTR* 68 (1975), pp. 203-33.

213. Cf., for example, the critical remarks of M. O'Brien, *The Deuteronomistic History Hypothesis: A Reassessment* (OBO, 92; Freiburg: Universitätsverlag; Göttingen: Vandenhoeck & Ruprecht, 1989), pp. 56-66.

214. Especially since Duhm's commentary on Jeremiah (*Das Buch Jeremia*, 1901); cf. above, n. 71.

exegesis that the question of such Dtr redactions (and their links with DH) comes up with some vehemence.

6.1. *Deuteronomistic Redactions in the Prophetic Corpus*

6.1.1. *Amos*

It was probably an article of W.H. Schmidt[215] that attracted the attention of researchers on the Dtr phenomenon in the prophetic books. In this study, Schmidt detected in verses 1.1*, 2, 9-13; 2.4-5, 10-12; 3.1*, 3, 7; 5.25-26 ideological and stylistic parallels with DH and attributed them to a Dtr redaction. Gese added to these 9.7-8 as well.[216] Thus, the rare evocations of history (such as the coming out of Egypt and the sojourn in the desert) in Amos would be due to a Dtr revision. The idea of a Dtr redaction in the book of Amos was taken up again by a majority of exegetes thanks to the commentary of Wolff.[217] As for Vermeylen, he detects in Amos a Dtr redaction from the period of Josiah and another from the exilic period.[218] The debate on the book of Amos at present has not really reached a consensus about the formation of the book, but the presence of Dtr elements is no longer really questioned.[219] What the relation is between these texts and the DH still has to be made clear.

6.1.2. *Hosea*

Traditionally, the similarities existing between the book of Hosea and that of Deuteronomy (for example, covenant theology, the importance of the Exodus, the polemic against the high places...[220]), even the books

215. W.H. Schmidt, 'Die deuteronomistische Redaktion des Amosbuches: Zu den theologischen Unterschieden zwischen dem Prophetenwort und dem Sammler', *ZAW* 77 (1965), pp. 168-93.

216. H. Gese, 'Das Problem von Amos 9, 7', in A.H.J. Gunneweg and O. Kaiser (eds.), *Textgemäss: Aufsätze und Beiträge zur Hermeneutik des Alten Testaments* (Festschrift E. Würthwein; Göttingen: Vandenhoeck & Ruprecht, 1979), pp. 33-38 = H. Gese, *Alttestamentliche Studien* (Tübingen: J.C.B. Mohr, 1981), pp. 116-21.

217. H.W. Wolff, *Joel und Amos* (BKAT, 14.2; Neukirchen–Vluyn: Neukirchener Verlag, 1985). ET *Joel and Amos: A Commentary on the Books of the Prophets Joel and Amos* (Hermeneia; Philadelphia: Fortress Press, 1984).

218. J. Vermeylen, *Du prophète Isaïe à l'apocalyptique*, II (2 vols.; EBib, 1; Paris: J. Gabalda, 1978).

219. For a general survey of the present discussion, cf. O. Kaiser, *Grundriss der Einleitung in die kanonischen und deuterokanonischen Schriften des Alten Testaments*, II (3 vols.; Gütersloh: Gerd Mohn, 1992), pp. 118-26.

220. Cf. the synopsis in M. Weinfeld, *Deuteronomy and the Deuteronomic*

of DH, were accounted for by imputing to Hosea the spiritual paternity of the Deuteronomistic movement.[221] The texts to be assigned to later (Dtr) redactions were therefore not very numerous.

But as the thesis of a Deuteronomy originating from Northern levitical-prophetic circles was no longer self-evident, it became possible to return to the problem of the Dt or Dtr construction of the book of Hosea. As a result, Gale A. Yee in 1978 reached a conclusion diametrically opposed to the classical consensus.[222] The book of Hosea would first and foremost be the result of two important Dtr redactions: R_1 (in the time of Josiah) and R_2 (in the period of the exile); R_2, whom Yee considers to be the final redactor of Hosea, would in particular have especially framed the book with 1.1 and 14.10, and would have inserted the salvation oracles as well. In Hosea 12, Jacob becomes the symbol of a necessary repentance and the Exodus appears as the image of the liberation from exile.[223] The importance of the Dtr texts is underscored too in the analysis of chs. 4 and 11 by Nissinen,[224] to such an extent that it becomes almost impossible to detect the specifically Hosean texts. Unlike Yee, he opts for late Dtr redactions, from the end of the exile, even from the beginning of the postexilic period.

At present, most exegetes remain sceptical when faced with such a reversal of values.[225] We find a diametrically opposite position to Yee or Nissinen in Naumann,[226] who attributes only a half-verse (8.1b) of

School (Oxford: Clarendon Press, 1972), pp. 320-64 (364).

221. This was the classical thesis defended especially by A. Alt, 'Die Heimat des Deuteronomiums', *Kleine Schriften zur Geschichte des Volkes Israel*, II (Munich: Beck, 1954), pp. 250-75.

222. G. Yee, *Composition and Tradition in the Book of Hosea: A Redaction Critical Investigation* (SBLDS, 102; Atlanta: Scholars Press, 1987).

223. Yee attributes the following texts to R_2: 1.1, 5, 6bβ-7; 2.1-3, 8-9, 10b, 15b-18aα, 19-20, 22b-25; 3.1-5; 4.3, 6a, 7-12a.bβ-13a, 14, 16b, 17b; 5.2b, 4, 13b, 15–6.3; 6.5, 11b–7.1*; 7.4, 10b, 12a*.b, 15*, 16; 8.4b–5aα, 6*-7, 13-14; 9.2-4, 6, 8-9, 14, 17; 10.9-10, 12, 13b-14; 11.1-11; 12.1b, 5-7, 10-12, 14; 13.14; 14.2-10; cf. the summary table, pp. 315-17.

224. M. Nissinen, *Prophetie, Redaktion und Fortschreibung im Hoseabuch: Studien zum Werdegang eines Prophetenbuches im Lichte von Hos 4 und 11* (AOAT, 231; Kevelaer: Buxton & B.; Neukirchen–Vluyn: Neukirchener Verlag, 1991).

225. Cf. A. de Pury, 'Osée 12 et ses implications pour le débat actuel sur le Pentateuque', in P. Haudebert (ed.), *Le Pentateuque: Débats et recherches* (LD, 151; Paris: Cerf, 1992), pp. 175-207 (181-82).

226. Cf. T. Naumann, *Hoseas Erben: Strukturen der Nachinterpretation im Buch*

the book of Hosea to the Dtr! Hosea is thus a typical example of the difficulty we encounter in finding criteria for differenciating the pre-Dtr, Dtr, even late Dtr texts within the prophetic corpus.

6.1.3. *Jeremiah*

There is no doubt about the presence of Deuteronomistic texts in Jeremiah and many works have been devoted to this subject.[227] It suffices to compare, for example, the discourse on the Temple in Jeremiah 7 with the Dtr discourse on the Temple put in the mouth of Solomon in 1 Kings 8. The similarities between the prose discourses (source 'C' of Mowinckel and of Rudolph) have sometimes been explained as the use of a 'theological language' fashionable in the seventh / sixth centuries (H. Weippert and others[228]). However, this thesis, aimed perhaps at saving the prose texts for the 'historical Jeremiah', does not sufficiently take into account the differences between the oracles in verse and the sermons in prose, nor the close parallels that we can observe between these latter and the style and phraseology of DH. It seems consequently wiser to postulate, with Nicholson, Thiel and others,[229] one, even two important Dtr redactions. There too the following question comes up: can we put these redactions into contact with the circles producing

Hosea (BWANT, 131; Stuttgart: W. Kohlhammer, 1991). For a rather conservative view, cf. as well D.R. Daniels, *Hosea and Salvation History: The Early Traditions of Israel in the Prophecy of Hosea* (BZAW, 191; Berlin: W. de Gruyter, 1990).

227. For the history of research, cf. S. Herrmann, *Der Prophet Jeremia und das Buch* (EdF, 271: Darmstadt: Wissenschaftliche Buchgesellschaft, 1990).

228. H. Weippert, *Die Prosareden des Jeremiabuches* (BZAW, 132; Berlin: W. de Gruyter, 1973); W.L. Holladay, *Jeremiah 1: A Commentary on the Book of the Prophet Jeremiah 1–25* (Hermeneia; Philadelphia: Fortress Press, 1986); *idem, Jeremiah 2: A Commentary on the Book of the Prophet Jeremiah Chapters 26–52* (Hermeneia; Minneapolis: Fortress Press, 1989); A. Weiser, *Das Buch des Propheten Jeremia: Kapitel 1–25.13* (ATD, 20; Göttingen: Vandenhoeck & Ruprecht, 1952); *idem, Das Buch des Propheten Jeremia: Jeremia 25.15–52.34* (ATD, 21; Göttingen: Vandenhoeck & Ruprecht, 1955).

229. E.W. Nicholson, *Preaching to the Exiles: A Study of the Prose Tradition in the Book of Jeremiah* (Oxford: Basil Blackwell, 1970); W. Thiel, *Die deuteronomistische Redaktion von Jeremia 1–25* (WMANT, 41; Neukirchen–Vluyn: Neukirchener Verlag, 1973); *idem, Die deuteronomistische Redaktion von Jeremia 26–45* (WMANT, 52; Neukirchen–Vluyn: Neukirchener Verlag, 1981). Cf. as well the commentaries of J.P. Hyatt, *The Book of Jeremiah* (IB; New York: Doubleday, 1956), and S. Herrmann, *Jeremia* (BKAT, 12.1; Neukirchen–Vluyn: Neukirchener Verlag, 1986).

DH[230] or must we instead, with McKane or Carroll, adopt the 'snow-ball' hypothesis (*rolling-corpus-hypothesis*) and postulate additions and successive updatings—that we really cannot precisely localize?[231]

Textual criticism of the book of Jeremiah[232] could confirm this theory. The text of Jeremiah represented by the Greek versions (20 per cent briefer than the MT) seems to be based on a Hebrew *Vorlage* different from the MT. The 'pluses' of the MT are often composed in a Dtr style (but differing from the DH),[233] which indicates that there was use of Dtr phraseology during the Persian and even the Hellenistic periods. On the other hand, there exist intentional cross-references between certain Dtr texts (for example, between the breaking of the covenant in Jeremiah 11 and the announcement of the new covenant in 31.31-34,[234] or between chs. 7; 25 and 35)—which would be a point in favour of a redactional activity with a global intention. Kaiser is probably right in observing that the Dtr redactions of Jeremiah share with the DH the concern to provide a theological explanation of the catastrophe of the

230. According to Thiel, the Dtr redaction of Jeremiah presupposes DH in its exilic form. Römer had put forward the hypothesis that the first Dtr redaction of Jeremiah could have come from the same hands as the exilic edition of DH, while JerD[2] would be later than Dtr[2] (cf. *Israels Väter: Untersuchungen zur Väter-thematik im Deuteronomium und in der deuteronomistischen Tradition* [OBO, 99; Göttingen: Vandenhoeck & Ruprecht, 1990], pp. 485-91).

231. W. McKane, *Jeremiah*, I (ICC; Edinburgh: T. & T. Clark, 1986). R.P. Carroll, *From Chaos to Covenant: Uses of Prophecy in the Book of Jeremiah* (London: SCM Press, 1981); *idem*, *Jeremiah* (OTL; London: SCM Press, 1986); *idem*, *Jeremiah* (OTG, Sheffield: JSOT Press, 1989). Cf. as well C. Levin, *Die Verheissung des neuen Bundes in ihrem theologiegeschichtlichen Zusammenhang ausgelegt* (FRLANT, 137; Göttingen: Vandenhoeck & Ruprecht, 1985).

232. On this subject, cf. among others Y. Goldman, *Prophétie et royauté au retour de l'exil: les origines littéraires de la forme massorétique du livre de Jérémie* (OBO, 118; Freiburg: Universitätsverlag; Göttingen: Vandenhoeck & Ruprecht, 1992); E. Tov, 'L'incidence de la critique textuelle sur la critique littéraire dans le livre de Jérémie', *RB* 79 (1972), pp. 189-99; P.-M. Bogaert, 'Le livre de Jérémie en perspective: Les deux rédactions antiques selon les travaux en cours', *RB* 101 (1994), pp. 363-406; S. Sonderlund, *The Greek Text of Jeremiah: A Revised Hypothesis* (JSOTSup, 47; Sheffield: JSOT Press, 1985).

233. Cf. the work of L. Stulman, *The Prose Sermons of Jeremiah: A Redescription of the Correspondences with Deuteronomistic Literature in the Light of Recent Textcritical Research* (SBLDS, 83; Atlanta: Scholars Press, 1986).

234. Cf. T. Römer, 'Les "anciens" pères (Jér 11, 10) et la "nouvelle" alliance (Jér 31, 31)', *BN* 59 (1991), pp. 23-27.

exile.[235] There are, however, differences between the DH and some Dtr texts of Jeremiah (which insist a great deal, for example, on the 'sin of the ancestors'—see among others 7.25-26; 44.9-10—while being much more optimistic than the DH in regard to the future—see, for example, 16.14-15; 31.31-34). We must point out as well the problem of the absence of the prophet Jeremiah from the DH (see on the other hand 2 Chron. 36!). That perhaps indicates that the message of the 'historical Jeremiah' was not entirely in conformity with Deuteronomistic ideas. How must we in that case interpret the redaction of certain parts of the book 'in the spirit of the *golah*', as it has been interpeted by Pohlmann and Seitz?[236] Must it be classified as a Dtr redaction or not? Or again, must we imagine that within the 'Dtr party', there would have been a number of different tendencies?

6.1.4. *Other Prophetic Books*
Among the pre-exilic prophets, it is especially for Micah that some exegetes have postulated a Dtr redaction.[237] Otto considers that the collection Micah 1–3 comes from an exilic redactor who would have had at his disposal a few prophetic oracles.[238] Likewise, the collection Micah 6–7 is constructed round the Dtr indictment of 6.9-16*, introduced in 6.2-8 by a sermon containing a typically Dtr vision of history. We find a similar opinion in Vermeylen, who thinks there were two Dtr redactions and attributes 6.2-8 to 'Dtr 575'.[239] The hypothesis that the present book of Micah would have stemmed from one or several Dtr

235. Kaiser, *Grundriss der Einleitung*, II, p. 72.

236. K.F. Pohlmann, *Studien zum Jeremiabuch* (FRLANT, 118; Göttingen: Vandenhoeck & Ruprecht, 1978). C.R. Seitz, *Theology in Conflict: Reactions to the Exile in the Book of Jeremiah* (BZAW, 176; Berlin: W. de Gruyter, 1989). Pohlmann situates his redaction centred on the *golah* in Jer. 24 and 37–44 in the period of Ezra–Nehemiah, while Seitz thinks that the Jeremian tradition favourable to the non-exiles would have been reinterpeted in circles of the Babylonian *golah* during the exile.

237. For example, J. Jeremias, 'Die Deutung der Gerichtsworte Michas in der Exilszeit', *ZAW* 83 (1971), pp. 330-54; B. Renaud, *La formation du livre de Michée: tradition et actualisation* (EBib; Paris: J. Gabalda, 1977), pp. 387-99; Vermeylen, *Du prophète Isaïe à l'apocalyptique*, II, pp. 570-600.

238. E. Otto, 'Techniken der Rechtssatzredaktion israelitischer Rechtsbücher in der Redaktion des Prophetenbuches Micha', *SJOT* 2 (1991), pp. 119-50.

239. J. Vermeylen, *Le Dieu de la promesse et le Dieu de l'alliance* (LD, 126; Paris: Cerf, 1986), p. 130.

redactions seems to be to some extent the general opinion.[240] Such is not the case for the book of Zephaniah. Seybold[241] thought he could identify a Dtr redaction in this book, unlike E. Ben-Zvi[242] who, for his part, considered Zephaniah an apocryphal book from the exilic to post-exilic period without managing however to identify in it a typically Dtr style or ideology.

The question of a Dtr redaction of the book of Isaiah, and particularly of Isaiah 1–39, is the subject of intense debate. Barth had situated the unconditional oracles of salvation in Isaiah 1–39 in the period of Josiah and had thus made conceivable the existence of a connection with the Dtr milieu.[243] In the same period, the thesis of Vermeylen[244] came out in which he identified several Dtr redactions in Isaiah, for example 'Dtr 575': 1.2-7 (lawsuit against the people after the catastrophe); 1.18-20 (Yhwh had offered one last chance of salvation that the people did not grasp). 'Dtr 525': 1.21-26 (+ 1.10-17?) (the misfortune is no longer caused through the fault of all the people but by the corrupt leaders). Kaiser, Sweeney and others[245] have considerably increased the number of (post)exilic texts in Isaiah 1–39, while remaining quite vague regarding the connections of these redactions with the Dtr milieu. But the tendency to postulate Dtr redactions in a more or less abstract way in

240. Cf. again recently M. Alvarez Barredo, *Relecturas deuteronomisticas de Amos, Miqueas y Jeremias* (Serie Mayor, 10; Murcia: Publicaciones del Instituto Theologico Franciscano, 1993), pp. 83-122.

241. K. Seybold, *Satirische Prophetie: Studien zum Buch Zefanja* (SBS, 120; Stuttgart: Katholisches Bibelwerk, 1985).

242. E. Ben-Zvi, *A Historical-Critical Study of the Book of Zephaniah* (BZAW, 198; Berlin: W. de Gruyter, 1991).

243. H. Barth, *Die Jesaja-Worte in der Josia-Zeit: Israel und Assur als Thema einer produktiven Neuinterpretation der Jesajaüberlieferung* (WMANT, 48; Neu-kirchen–Vluyn: Neukirchener Verlag, 1977). See as well R.E. Clements, *Isaiah and the Deliverance of Jerusalem: A Study in the Interpretation of Prophecy in the Old Testament* (JSOTSup, 13; Sheffield: JSOT Press, 1984).

244. Vermeylen, *Du prophète Isaïe à l'apocalyptique*. Cf. especially vol. II, pp. 693-709 and likewise *Le Dieu de la promesse*, pp. 128-31.

245. O. Kaiser, *Das Buch des Propheten Jesaja: Kapitel 1–12* (ATD, 17; Göt-tingen: Vandenhoeck & Ruprecht, 1981); *Der Prophet Jesaja: Kapitel 13–39* (ATD, 18; Göttingen: Vandenhoeck & Ruprecht, 1983); M.A. Sweeney, *Isaiah 1–4 and the Postexilic Understanding of the Isaianic Tradition* (BZAW, 171; Berlin: W. de Gruyter, 1988). Cf. as well W. Werner, *Eschatologische Texte in Jesaja 1–39* (FzB, 46; Würzburg: Echter Verlag, 1986): and R. Kilian, *Jesaja 1–12* (NEB, 17; Würzburg: Echter Verlag, 1986), pp. 14-17.

the book of Isaiah (1–39) has been sharply criticized by Perlitt and Brekelmans.[246] The arguments put forward by these researchers do not lack weight: can we be satisfied with interpreting every report of infidelity to Yhwh or every exhortation to take stock of themselves as the infallible sign of a Dtr hand, and that, even in the absence of any phraseology, any style or any other link making it possible to establish a connection with the Dtr?[247] Do we not run the risk of falling into a sort of pan-Deuteronomism or of a 'Deuterono-mystique', a danger that some have already perceived in the debate on the Pentateuch? That discussion at any rate underscores the need to define clearly the criteria making it possible to identify a redaction as Deuteronomistic.

The book of Ezekiel presents a similar problem. Despite the absence of a consensus in regard to the formation of the book,[248] many researchers agree on the existence of one or more redactions defending the interests of the *golah*.[249] Is there a link with Deuteronomistic milieus? Some texts, as for example Ezek. 2.3-7 or Ezekiel 20 reflect the Dtr style and ideology. Must they for all that be qualified as Dtr (thus Liwak[250]), or should we see in Ezekiel 20[251] a polemic against the Dtr

246. L. Perlitt, 'Jesaja und die Deuteronomisten', in V. Fritz *et al.* (eds.), *Prophet und Prophetenbuch: Festschrift für O. Kaiser zum 65. Geburtstag* (BZAW, 185; Berlin: W. de Gruyter, 1989), pp. 133-49 = *Deuteronomium-Studien* (FAT, 8; Tübingen: J.C.B. Mohr, 1994), pp. 157-71; C. Brekelmans, 'Deuteronomistic Influence in Isaiah 1–12', in J. Vermeylen (ed.), *The Book of Isaiah: Le livre d'Isaïe. Les oracles et leurs relectures. Unité et complexité de l'ouvrage* (BETL, 81; Leuven: Leuven University Press, 1989), pp. 167-76.

247. Can we really declare, as Vermeylen does, that the 'Song of the Vineyard' in Isa. 5 is a Dtr text?

248. Cf. for example the state of the question by K.F. Pohlmann in Kaiser, *Grundriss der Einleitung*, II, pp. 82-102.

249. See in particular J. Garscha, *Studien zum Ezechielbuch: Eine redaktionskritische Untersuchung von Ez 1–39* (EHS.T, 23; Bern: Peter Lang, 1974); T. Krüger, *Geschichtskonzepte im Ezechielbuch* (BZAW, 180; Berlin: W. de Gruyter, 1989); K.F. Pohlmann, *Ezechielstudien* (BZAW, 202; Berlin: W. de Gruyter, 1992).

250. R. Liwak, 'Überlieferungsgeschichtliche Probleme des Ezechielbuches: Eine Studie zu postezechielischen Interpretationem und Komposition' (Dissertation; Bochum, 1976).

251. Entire mongraphs have been devoted to this chapter. Cf. J. Lust, *Traditie, redactie en kerygma bij Ezechiel: Een analyse van Ez., XX, 1–26* (VVAW. L 31.65; Brussel: Paleis der Academiën, 1969); F. Sedlmaier, *Studien zur Komposition und Theologie von Ezechiel 20* (SBB, 21; Stuttgart: Katholisches Bibelwerk, 1990).

school (thus Pons[252])? This last text is especially interesting, since it seems to combine Dtr and priestly preoccupations: this would be an indication of a possible revival or imitation of the Dtr style and ideology other than in the Dtr milieu *stricto sensu*.

The 'survival' of Dtr themes toward the end of the Persian period, even in the Hellenistic period, is clearly attested moreover in the last books of the Twelve Prophets, particularly Zechariah and Malachi.[253]

6.1.5. *Brief Summary*

The fact that some prophetic books (Jeremiah, Amos, Micah, Hosea) would have undergone one or several Dtr redactions seems to be accepted by a large number of exegetes. Consequently, we can ask whether the circle that edited the DH did not likewise produce a first 'canon' of prophetic books, with the objective of supporting its theological program not only on the presentation of the history of Israel but also in the publication of the preaching of the great prophets. The determination of the nature and of the bonds uniting the Dtr redactions of the prophets and those of DH remains a *desideratum* of current research.

6.2. *Deuteronomistic Redactions in the Tetrateuch*

Noth had situated the beginning of DH in the book of Deuteronomy, and this by *via negationis*. According to him, there were no important traces of Dtr style in Genesis–Numbers, which would rule out these books belonging to DH. Of course, since Wellhausen, and even before him, it had been pointed out that certain texts, particularly in Exodus and Numbers, had a Dt or Dtr construction; the Yahwist had often been compared to the Deuteronomist, but it is only since the 1970s that exegetes began to focus their attention on the phenomenon of Dtr texts in the Tetrateuch.[254]

252. 'Le vocabulaire d'Ez 20: Le prophète s'oppose à la vision deutéronomiste de l'histoire', in J. Lust (ed.), *Ezekiel and his Book: Textual and Literary Criticism and their Interrelation* (BETL, 74; Leuven: Leuven University Press / Peeters, 1986), pp. 214-33.

253. For Zechariah, cf. R.F. Person, *Second Zechariah and the Deuteronomic School* (JSOTSup, 167; Sheffield: JSOT Press, 1993); for Malachi, cf. A.S. van der Woude, 'Seid nicht wie eure Väter! Bemerkungen zu Sacharja 1,5 und seinem Kontext', in J.A. Emerton (ed.), *Prophecy* (Festschrift G. Fohrer; BZAW, 150; Berlin: W. de Gruyter, 1980), pp. 163-73.

254. For the review that follows, we will make do with a brief survey since we

6.2.1. *The Classical Solution: 'Proto-Deuteronomic' Texts*

The existence of 'proto-Deuteronomic' texts was and still is defended by some researchers who hold the traditional documentary hypothesis (J—E—D—P) to explain the formation of the Pentateuch (Brekelmans, Loza, Skweres and, very recently, Chan[255]). The 'Dt' texts of the Tetrateuch are then considered the 'missing link' between JE and D and as the precursors of the Dt movement. In the framework of the theory of documents, this way of thinking had a certain logic, but with a closer examination of the supposed proto-Dt texts, numerous problems become apparent.[256] Thus the so-called proto-Dt verses of the spy episode in Numbers 13–14 are doubtless later than the Dtr version of Deuteronomy 1. But Deut. 1.19-33 actually makes no allusion to the great intercessory prayer of Num. 14.13-19 and the remark about Yhwh being angry with Moses (Deut. 1.37) would be hard to understand if the version of Numbers 13–14 was already known to the author of Deuteronomy 1.[257] Or, to take another example, when a text such as Exod. 13.3-16 includes at the same time Dtr turns of phrase and phrases dear to P, frequent in postexilic literature,[258] can we still consider this pericope as proto-Dt? Because of problems of this kind it has become necessary to propose other solutions to the question of the presence of

---

have dealt with this point in detail in *Le Pentateuque en question*, pp. 58-67.

255. C. Brekelmans, 'Eléments deutéronomiques dans le Pentateuque', in C. Hauret (ed.), *Aux grands carrefours de la révélation et de l'exégèse de l'Ancien Testament* (RechBib, 8; Bruges: Desclée de Brouwer, 1967), pp. 77-91; J. Loza, 'Exode XXXII et la rédaction JE', *VT* 23 (1973), pp. 31-55; A. Reichert, 'Der Jehowist im Buch Exodus' (Doctoral Thesis; Tübingen, 1972); D.E. Skweres, *Die Rückverweise im Buch Deuteronomium* (AnBib, 79; Rome: Pontifical Biblical Institute Press, 1979); M.Z. Brettler, 'The Promise of the Land of Israel to the Patriarchs in the Pentateuch', *Shnaton* 5-6 (1978–79), pp. vii-xxiv; T.-K. Chan, *La vocation de Moïse (Ex 3 & 4). Recherche sur la rédaction dite deutéronomique du Tétrateuque* (Brussels: Thanh-Long, 1993).

256. Cf. for example the remarks of E. Blum, *Studien zur Komposition des Pentateuch* (BZAW, 189; Berlin: W. de Gruyter, 1990), pp. 166-76.

257. Cf. in particular M. Rose, *Deuteronomist und Jahwist: Untersuchungen zu den Berührungspunkten beider Literaturwerke* (ATANT, 67; Zürich: Theologischer Verlag, 1981), and *idem*, 'La croissance du corpus historiographique de la Bible— une proposition', *RTP* 118 (1986), pp. 217-36.

258. Cf. M. Caloz, 'Exode XIII, 3-16 et son rapport au Deutéronome', *RB* 75 (1968), pp. 5-62; Caloz defends the idea of a 'proto-Dt' redaction while taking note of the connections of this text with postexilic literature.

Dtr elements in the Tetrateuch. Thus in 1962, Fuss[259] already spoke, in a general way, of a 'Dtr redaction of the Pentateuch', leaving open the question of the connection of this redaction with DH. Others attempted to clarify the nature of this connection.

6.2.2. *The Yahwist as Deuteronomist*
It was through the influence of his teacher Schmid,[260] who had insisted on the stylistic and theological closeness of 'J' and DH, that Rose[261] made a revolutionary proposal for that time: should not the Yahwist be later than DH? Should not the Yahwist be considered a Dtr of the second or third generation? By insisting on the fact that the 'J' texts that have parallels in Deuteronomy or in Joshua presuppose the latter, Rose tries to establish that 'J' was from the beginning a prologue for DH and its principal goal was to correct or tone down the Dtr insistence on the law. Thus, if 'J' adds the patriarchal narratives and the epic of the Exodus, it was to bring to the fore the primacy of divine grace. And if he places the history of beginnings as the opening of his work, it was to show that humans are incapable of fulfilling the law. A similar hypothesis had already been envisaged by Bentzen, who thought that the accounts of the Patriarchs and of the Exodus had been placed ahead of the accounts of the conquest as a sort of prologue.[262]

Van Seters reaches a similar conclusion,[263] but, unlike Rose, he insists on the parallels that exist between 'J' and the Greek historians. While maintaining that 'J' is later than DH, Van Seters points out that important differences exist between 'J' and DH, so much so that it

259. W. Fuss, *Die deuteronomistische Pentateuchredaktion in Exodus 3–17* (BZAW, 126; Berlin: W. de Gruyter, 1962).
260. H.H. Schmid, *Der sogennante Jahwist: Beobachtungen und Fragen zur Pentateuchforschung* (Zürich: Theologischer Verlag, 1976).
261. Rose, *Deuteronomist und Jahwist.*
262. Bentzen, *Introduction to the Old Testament*, II, p. 85: 'They both (= J/E) wrote their "History of Salvation" as "pre-history" to the story of the fulfilment of the promises'.
263. Among Van Seters's numerous publications, see especially: *Der Yahwist als Historiker* (ThSt, 134, Zürich: Theologischer Verlag, 1987); *Prologue to History: The Yahwist as Historian in Genesis* (Louisville, KY: Westminster/John Knox Press; Zurich: Theologischer Verlag, 1992); *The Life of Moses: The Yahwist as Historian in Exodus–Numbers* (Louisville, KY: Westminster/John Knox Press; Kampen: Kok, 1994).

should not be too necessary to compare one with the other.[264]

The positions of Rose and Van Seters have been adopted by some exegetes,[265] but they are far from being unanimous. Can we actually say that all the texts formerly called J/E are Dtr or (post)exilic? Is there still need to subject the non-priestly material of the Tetrateuch to a more differentiated analysis?

6.2.3. *The 'D' Composition*

The term 'D composition' was coined by Blum. In two voluminous works,[266] this author attempted to explain the formation of the Pentateuch starting from a blending process. The Pentateuch would be the result of the fusion between two *Kompositionsschichten*: D and P. Blum is here taking up again an idea of his teacher Rendtorff,[267] for whom the 'major units' of the Pentateuch, independent from one another, would have been linked up thanks to two redactions: 'Deutero-nomic' (with the exception of the cycle on origins) and 'Priestly'. For Blum, there was no doubt that the *D composition* is later than DH. He admits of course that the authors of this composition (on whose identi-ties he remains quite vague) had integrated older texts (for instance, a *Vita Mosis*, or an exploit of Jacob), but he foregoes delimiting these

---

264. Cf. J. Van Seters, 'The So-Called Deuteronomistic Redaction of the Penta-teuch', in J.A. Emerton (ed.), *Congress Volume Leuven 1989* (VTSup, 43; Leiden: E.J. Brill, 1991), pp. 58-77; *idem*, 'The Theology of the Yahwist: A Preliminary Sketch', in I. Kottsieper *et al.* (eds.), *'Wer ist wie du, HERR, unter den Göttern?' Studien zur Theologie und Religionsgeschichte Israels* (Festschrift O. Kaiser; Göt-tingen: Vandenhoeck & Ruprecht, 1994), pp. 219-28. Recently, C. Levin (*Der Jah-wist* [FRLANT, 157; Göttingen: Vandenhoeck & Ruprecht, 1993]) has gone even further, since he considers his Yahwist as a 'liberal' theologian—as Van Seters had already done to some extent—defending popular religion against the Dtr orthodox.

265. Cf. F.H. Cryer, 'On the Relationship between the Yahwistic and the Deuter-onomistic Histories', *BN* 29 (1985), pp. 58-74; R. Kilian, 'Nachtrag und Neuorient-ierung: Anmerkungen zum Jahwisten in den Abrahamzählungen', in M. Görg (ed.), *Die Väter Israels: Beiträge zur Theologie Patriarchenüberlieferungen im Alten Testament* (Festschrift J. Scharbert; Stuttgart: Katholisches Bibelwerk, 1989), pp. 155-67.

266. E. Blum, *Die Composition der Vätergeschichte* (WMANT, 57; Neukirchen–Vluyn: Neukirchener Verlag, 1984) and *idem*, *Studien zur Komposition des Penta-teuch* (BZAW, 189; Berlin: W. de Gruyter, 1990).

267. R. Rendtorff, *Das überlieferungsgeschichtliche Problem des Pentateuch* (BZAW, 147; Berlin: W. de Gruyter, 1976); ET *The Problem of the Process of Transmission in the Pentateuch* (JSOTSup, 89; Sheffield: JSOTPress, 1990).

sources in detail and is content to describe their 'diachronic reliefs'. This model, that has been adopted by Johnstone, Albertz, Crüsemann and others,[268] makes it possible to situate in a coherent way the Dtr texts of the Tetrateuch while avoiding the danger of 'pan-Deuteronomism'. But can we consider that the texts attributed to the D 'composers' all belong to the same literary level? Lohfink, for example, has criticized Blum for examining the relation between the D composition and DH without taking into consideration the diachrony within Deuteronomy itself.[269]

Blum considers that his D composition is actually later than DH, but he admits also that *subsequent* to that there had been redactional interventions, at the same time in the collection that goes from Deuteronomy to 2 Kings (for example, Joshua 24 that, according to Blum, would be a post-Dtr attempt to create a sort of Hexateuch) and in the D composition itself (for example, Exod. 18).[270] He speaks several times of redactional intrusions between the D composition and DH. The debate focusing on the existence of a 'great Dtr historiography'[271] going from Genesis to 2 Kings is thus revived.

6.2.4. *The Connection between DH and the 'Deuteronomic Tetrateuch'*
R. Smend had foreseen the possibility that DtrN had intervened as well in Genesis–Numbers, editing in this way the collection of Genesis to 2 Kings.[272]

A comparable position was adopted by Vermeylen[273] who distinguished four Dtrs that he thinks he can date quite precisely: Dtr 585;

268. W. Johnstone, *Exodus* (OTG; Sheffield: JSOT Press, 1990); R. Albertz, *Religionsgeschichte Israels in alttestamentlicher Zeit* (ATD Ergänzungsreihe 8.1-2; Göttingen: Vandenhoeck & Ruprecht, 1992), pp. 504-35; F. Crüsemann, *Die Tora: Theologie und Sozialgeschichte des alttestamentlichen Gesetzes* (Munich: Chr. Kaiser Verlag, 1992), pp. 381-425.
269. N. Lohfink, 'Deutéronome et Pentateuque', in P. Haudebert (ed.), *Le Pentateuque: Débats et recherches* (LD, 151; Paris: Cerf, 1992), pp. 35-64 (37).
270. Blum, *Studien zur Komposition des Pentateuch*, pp. 363-65.
271. Cf. as well Rendtorff, *Introduction à l'Ancien Testament*, pp. 313-14.
272. Smend, *Die Enstehung des Alten Testaments*, p. 125.
273. Vermeylen, *Le Dieu de la promesse*; cf. as well *idem*, 'L'affaire du veau d'or (Ex 32-34): Une clé pour la "question deutéronomiste"?', *ZAW* 97 (1985), pp. 1-23 and 'Les sections narratives de Deut. 5–11 et leur relation à Ex 19–34', in N. Lohfink (ed.), *Das Deuteronomium: Entstehung, Gestalt und Botschaft* (BETL, 68; Leuven: Leuven University Press, 1985), pp. 147-207.

Dtr 575; Dtr 560; Dtr 525. His proposal, 'as a hypothesis', is 'to attribute the formation of the "Deuteronomistic history" to the same redactors'[274] as for the Dtr texts of the Tetrateuch. Furthermore, he finds these redactors in some prophetic books as well (cf. above). With regard to the Pentateuch, only Dtr 585 is clearly identifiable, according to Vermeylen, in the rereading of the Decalogue (Exod. 20.2-6) and in the episode of the golden calf.[275] For Dtr 585 and for 575 too, it was a matter of responding to the questioning of Yahweh following the disaster. Dtr 575 began his work in Genesis 3. He insists on the fact that the divine sanction is not arbitrary, but fits in with human responsibility. The end of Dtr 575 is found in 2 Kgs 25.21. Among the many texts that must be attributed to this great author would be: Gen. 18.16-33, the episode of the confrontation between Pharoah and Moses and the plagues in Egypt, the first framing of the Deuteronomic Code (Deut. 4.44–5.27*; 9.9-29*; 10.1-15; 31.9-12*), the presentation of the period of the Judges (Judg. 2.11-19), the notices evaluating the kings of Israel and Judah, and the commentary on the fall of Samaria (2 Kgs 17.7-23) that 'justifies at the same time the fall of Judah, that takes no notice of this terrible warning'.[276]

Dtr 560 expresses the perspective of the second generation of the exilic period. It comes up first of all in the account of the call of Moses (Exod. 3.7-8*; 4.1*, 5, 8-9) and in the Pentateuchal texts addressed to the generation that has the possibility of entering the land (for example, Exod 13.3-16; 34.8-10a, 11-12, 14-28a). It was Dtr 560 as well elaborated the most important part of Deut. 1–4; 6.2–9.6* as well as the 'we' texts, in which the redactor insists on the distinction of generations (5.2-3; 29.13-14, 28). In Joshua to 2 Kings, the following texts, among others, come from Dtr 560: Joshua 23; Judg. 2.6-10 (arrival of a new generation); 1 Kgs 8.22-61. Finally, it is most certainly Dtr 560 who composed the conclusion in 2 Kgs 25.22-30. According to Vermeylen, the rehabilitation of Jehoiachin 'appears as a sort of presage of the imminent end of the nation's misfortune'.[277]

As for Dtr 525, it is to be situated at the time of the return of the deportees and serves as a vehicle for an 'anti-*golah*' (!) ideology aimed

274. Vermeylen, *Le Dieu de la promesse*, p. 123.
275. Vermeylen attributes to it: 32.7-8a, 9-15*, 19-20bα, 20-32a, 34*; 34.1, 4*, 28b-29a*.
276. Vermeylen, *Le Dieu de la promesse*, p. 125.
277. Vermeylen, *Le Dieu de la promesse*, p. 126.

at establishing 'that the deportees form...the wicked group responsible for the misfortunes of Israel'.[278] Thus, Dtr 525 contrasts in Gen. 4.17-24 the group of the wicked, who must disappear, with Enosh invoking the name of Yahweh (4.25-26) and with Noah the Just (5.28b-29, since these verses constitute, in the Dtr work, the immediate continuation of 4.26). In the cycle of Patriarchs, Dtr 525 develops the motif of the promise, and it is probably he who gave to Deuteronomy its definitive look and made it the conclusion of the Pentateuch in its present form (Vermeylen unfortunately does not specify the reasons for this). In Joshua–2 Kings, Dtr 525 elaborated the anti-monarchical texts (1 Sam. 8 + 12). He tends also to be critical of the cult and the Temple.

The approach of Vermeylen is, as far as we know, one of those that examines in the most precise and comprehensive way the bond uniting the Dtr texts of Genesis–Numbers and those of the Deuteronomy–2 Kings corpus. The very ambition of his project perhaps explains the fact that his thesis does not give the impression of being very complete as yet, with assertions often taking precedence over argumentation. Several questions would call for further study: the criterion for attributing a text to such or such a Dtr, if not to the Dtr redaction in general. Can we really distinguish so clearly four Dtr redactions? And what is it that makes possible the affirmation that the (final) Dtr redaction was hostile to the Babylonian *golah*? Let us simply recall that for many exegetes, it is precisely the *golah* that has a better chance of corresponding to the milieu in which the Dtr redactions originated. This leads us directly to the present debate on DH.

7. Deuteronomistic Historiography in the Current Debate

7.1. The Problem of the Transmission of the Text of DH

Textual criticism is a discipline as old as the Masoretes, who were fully aware of the problems that the transmission of the text could pose.

During the period of the Reformation and of Humanism there was a strong awareness of the diversity of manuscripts as well as of the disparity that could exist, especially between the Greek translations (LXX) and the MT. But these observations were especially made by those who challenged the doctrine of inspiration. On the other hand, the Reformers for their part favoured the *Veritas hebraica* (under the form

---

278. Vermeylen, *Le Dieu de la promesse*, p. 117.

of the *textus receptus*), and that hardly contributed to the creation of a favourable climate for research on the other witnesses to the biblical text.

For the books of Joshua–2 Kings, modern textual criticism began in the nineteenth century. Mention must especially be made of the commentary of Thenius on the books of Samuel[279] and the investigation by J. Hollenberg on the Alexandrian translation of Joshua.[280] The books of Deuteronomy and Judges (and in a certain way those of Kings) presented fewer problems for the exegetes and philologists: the MT is quite well preserved in their case and the disparities between the diffferent textual witnesses did not immediately attract attention.

According to Pisano,[281] it is Thenius who is behind the high evaluation of the text of the LXX. For Joshua, it is Holmes, followed by Cooke, who advocates the superiority of the Greek text.[282] We notice subsequently some enthusiasm for the attempts to reconstruct the 'original' text, even correcting the MT according to the LXX. However, already in 1863, de Lagarde remarks that the supposed LXX is the result of many recensions, and therefore it is necessary to elucidate the history of these recensions before being able to utilize the Greek versions for the reconstruction of a 'better' text.[283] Thus begins a long and exacting study of the internal history of the LXX. But that research hardly affects the exegetical work dealing with the books of DH, for which, as Auld

---

279. O. Thenius, *Die Bücher Samuels* (KAT, 4; Leipzig: S. Hirzel, 1864).

280. J. Hollenberg, *Der Charakter der alexandrinischen Übersetzung des Buches Josua und ihr textkritischer Wert* (Moers, 1876). For Jeremiah, it was F.C. Movers who, from 1837, had postulated that the 'minuses' of the LXX in the book of Jeremiah were to be explained by a *Vorlage* earlier than that of the MT (see *De utriusque recensionis vaticiniorum Ieremiae* [Hamburg, 1837]).

281. S. Pisano, *Additions or Omissions in the Book of Samuel: The Significant Pluses and Minuses in the Massoretic, LXX and Qumran Texts* (OBO, 57; Göttingen: Vandenhoeck & Ruprecht, 1984), p. 3. Cf. pp. 2-10, for a history of the research on the textual criticism of the books of Samuel.

282. S. Holmes, *Joshua, the Hebrew and the Greek Texts* (Cambridge: Cambridge University Press, 1914); G.A. Cooke, *The Book of Joshua* (Cambridge: Cambridge University Press, 1917). Cf. as well, on this subject, A.G. Auld, 'Joshua: The Hebrew and Greek Texts', in J.A. Emerton (ed.), *Studies in the Historical Books of the Old Testament* (VTSup, 30; Leiden: E.J. Brill, 1979), pp. 1-14.

283. Cf. Paul de Lagarde, *Anmerkungen zur griechischen Übersetzung der Proverbien* (Leipzig, 1863), p. 2. Cf. as well J. Wellhausen, *Der Text der Bücher Samuelis* (Göttingen: Vandenhoeck & Ruprecht, 1871).

points out, researchers go back to take the *Veritas hebraica* for a starting point.[284]

It is the discovery of the Dead Sea Hebrew manuscripts that causes interest to be revived in the Greek witnesses of the biblical text. Some Qumran biblical manuscripts have more affinities with the Greek text than with the Masoretic text. For fifteen years or so, specialists in textual criticism have pointed out that for some of the books compiled by the Dtr, the differences between the LXX* (*prima manus*) and the MT could have effects on the question of the internal diachrony of the Dtr redactional work. But, strangely, exegetes who are non-specialists in the LXX have scarcely taken advantage of these observations. We cannot present this volume of work in detail here;[285] so we will make do with some general remarks.

The clearest case is doubtless that of Jeremiah.[286] It seems to be accepted today that the Greek text (A version) of Jeremiah reflects a different Hebrew text (B version) to that of the MT (C version). According to Stulman,[287] the texts of Jeremiah belonging to Mowinckel's source 'C' would have a more pronounced Dtr character than version A (short text). The MT would have a tendency to 'dilute' the Dtr style by using a more stereotyped language, a language that would indicate a later stage in the redaction and would point to late redactors that we should for that reason no longer call Dtr. According to Stulman, the LXX would reflect the text of the Dtr redaction in the period of the exile, while the Hebrew text (B version) would express the preoccupations of the descendants of the *golah* returned to the land. Goldman has confirmed the thesis of two successive redactions of the book of Jeremiah (cf. Bogaert and Schenker as well[288]): the *Vorlage* of the LXX would have undergone a Dtr redaction during the exile, while the Hebrew text would present a 'restoration redaction' that should be situated between 515 and 445.

---

284. Cf. Auld, 'Joshua', p. 2.

285. Cf. on this subject too the contributions of Pisano and Schenker in this volume.

286. For a brief presentation, cf. Goldman, *Prophetie et royauté*, pp. 1-3.

287. Stulman, *The Prose Sermons of Jeremiah*.

288. P.M. Bogaert, 'Les mécanismes rédactionnels en Jér 10, 1-16 (LXX and MT) et la signification des suppléments', in P.M. Bogaert (ed.), *Le livre de Jérémie: Le prophète et son milieu. Les oracles et leur transmission* (BETL, 54; Leuven: Leuven University Press; Peeters, 1981), pp. 222-38; A. Schenker, 'Nebukadnezzars Metamorphose vom Unterjocher zum Gottesknecht', *RB* 89 (1982), pp. 498-527.

Even if the dating of the final form of the MT to the Persian period remains debatable,[289] such studies doubtless make it possible to work out better the redactional stages of the book. Unfortunately, Thiel who personally postulates two redactions of the Dtr type in the book of Jeremiah, has not tried to confront that idea with the works on the LXX; quite the contrary, he regards, almost systematically, the LXX as secondary compared to the MT, and he is not alone to do so.

Let us turn to the books of the DH: the LXX* of the book of Joshua (whose text is shorter than the MT by 5 per cent) could have been based on a Hebrew text earlier than the MT, but it is just as possible that the relationship between the LXX and the MT would be more complex.[290] We note in the 'pluses' of the MT some elements of stereotyped Dtr vocabulary; thus, these passages strengthen the designation of Yhwh as אלהיכם (five times).[291] Likewise, Moses is called 'servant of Yhwh' more often in the MT than in the LXX,[292] as is shown, for example, in the case of Josh. 1.15:

LXX*: 'You shall return to the land that is yours to possess that Moses gave you'.

MT: 'You shall return to the land that is yours to possess that Moses, the servant of Yhwh, gave you, and you will take possession of it'.

---

289. A. Schenker, 'La rédaction longue du livre de Jérémie doit-elle être datée du temps des premiers Hasmonéens?', *ETL* 70 (1994), pp. 281-93, now looks to the Hasmonaean period for the MT.

290. See among others: Auld, 'Joshua'; E. Tov, 'The Growth of the Book of Joshua in the Light of the Evidence of the LXX Translation', *ScrHier* 31 (1986), pp. 321-39; A. Rofé, 'The Editing of the Book of Joshua in the Light of 4Q Josh.ᵃ', in G.J. Brooke and F. Garcia Martínez (eds.), *New Qumran Texts and Studies: Proceedings of the First Meeting of the International Organization for Qumran Studies, Paris, 1992* (STDJ, 15; Leiden: E.J. Brill, 1994), pp. 73-80. For a more balanced view, cf. S. Sipilä, 'The Septuagint Version of Joshua 3–4', in C.E. Cox (ed.), *VII Congress of the International Organization for Septuagint and Cognate Studies Leuven 1989* (SBLSCS, 317; Atlanta: Scholars Press, 1991), pp. 63-74; K. Bieberstein, *Josua—Jordan—Jericho: Archäologie, Geschichte und Theologie der Landnahmeerzählungen. Josua 1–6* (OBO, 143; Göttingen: Vandenhoeck & Ruprecht, 1995). V. Fritz, *Das Buch Josua* (HAT, I.7; Tübingen: J.C.B. Mohr, 1994), pp. 1-2 wishes, in the present state of research, to give the priority to the MT.

291. Cf. the chart of Auld, 'Joshua', p. 11; however, in Josh. 1.11, the phrase 'the God of your ancestors' (LXX) has become 'your God' in the MT.

292. Cf. the list in E. Tov, *Textual Criticism of the Hebrew Bible* (Minneapolis: Fortress Press; Assen: Van Gorcum, 1992), p. 328.

Let us mention Joshua 20 as well, much briefer in the text of the LXX. According to Tov, the expansions in the MT would be very close to Deuteronomy (especially Deuteronomy 19), while the rest of the chapter reflects priestly style (see the parallels in Numbers 35). We would have then the trace of a post-priestly redaction, taking up again the Dtr style. According to Tov, the variations between the LXX and the MT would indicate two different stages of the Dtr edition of the book.[293]

The history of the LXX text of the books of Samuel is very complex,[294] and its status compared to the MT is vigorously discussed by the specialists.[295] The most striking case is the story of David and Goliath (1 Samuel 16–18[296]), where the text of the LXX is 40 per cent shorter than the MT. According to Barthélemy, Pisano and others, the LXX here would have shortened a longer text corresponding *grosso modo* to the MT; on the other hand, Tov, Lust and others think that there is little probability that a translator would have taken such an initiative.[297]

293. Cf. Tov, *Textual Criticism of the Hebrew Bible*, p. 332. For Joshua 20, cf. also A. Rofé, 'Joshua 20 Historico-Literary Criticism Illustrated', in J.H. Tigay (ed.), *Empirical Models for Biblical Criticism* (Philadelphia: University of Pennsylvania Press, 1985), pp. 131-47.

294. Cf. in particular, A. Aejmelaeus, 'The Septuagint of I Samuel', in *idem*, *On the Trail of the Septuagint Translators: Collected Essays* (Kampen: Kok, 1993). In French, see A. Caquot and P. de Robert, *Les livres de Samuel* (CAT, 6; Geneva: Labor et Fides, 1994), pp. 9-12.

295. For the problems of the so-called 'Proto-Lucian' recension, cf. D. Barthelemy, *Les devanciers d'Aquila* (VTSup, 10; Leiden: E.J. Brill, 1963), pp. 92-109; *idem*, 'A Reexamination of the Textual Problems in 2 Sam. 11, 2–1 Kgs 2, 11 in the Light of Certain Criticism of *Les devanciers d'Aquila*', in R.A. Kraft (ed.), *Proceedings Nineteen Hundred and Seventy-Two* (SCSt, 2; Missoula, MT: University of Montana), pp. 16-89.

296. We could of course mention as well 1 Sam. 11, where 4Q Sam.—close to the 'Proto-Lucian version'—presents a long and coherent text, that would have been lost in the MT through corruption. Cf. F.M. Cross, 'The Ammonite Oppression of the Tribes of Gad and Reuben: Missing Verses from 1 Samuel 11 Found in 4Q Samuel[a]', in E. Tov (ed.), *The Hebrew and Greek Texts of Samuel: 1980 Proceedings IOCS* (Jerusalem: Academon, 1980), pp. 105-19; A. Rofé, 'The Acts of Nahash According to 4Q Sam.[a]', *IEJ* 32 (1982), pp. 129-33; Tov, *Textual Criticism of the Hebrew Bible*, pp. 342-44. But this problem does not have direct relevance for the question of Dtr redactions.

297. Cf. in particular the discussion in the collective work: D. Barthelemy *et al.*, *The Story of David and Goliath, Textual and Literary Criticism* (OBO, 1973; Göttingen: Vandenhoeck & Ruprecht, 1986).

As for the books of Kings, we will merely mention the most remarkable example: that of the LXX supplement in 3 Kgs 12.24 a-z, dealing with details of the reign of Jeroboam (we find some parallels to this text in 1 Kgs 11; 12 and 14 MT).[298] Contrary to the classical vision which maintains that we would be dealing with a sort of late midrash, Debus[299] and Trebolle[300] have shown that the 'plus' of the LXX stands out because of the absence of all Dtr language and thus would indicate a pre-Dtr stage (according to Trebolle, a prophetic redaction) in the composition of the book of Kings. Now, McKenzie has re-examined this text which, according to him, is based on a Hebrew *Vorlage*. For him, it leaves no doubt that the expansion of the LXX already pre-supposed a Dtr redaction.[301] For Talshir, 3 Kings 12 LXX definitely had at his disposal a Dtr type Hebrew *Vorlage*, somewhat different from the Dtr redaction of the MT.[302]

These few examples show to what extent the domains of the history of the text and of the history of redactions can end up interpenetrated.[303] If it should come about that, with the help of comparisons among different textual witnesses, to ascertain the existence of several stages of Dtr (or post-Dtr) redaction could be ascertained, the historico-critical study of DH could free itself a little more from part of the subjectivity inevitably inherent in all stylistic analysis and would have surely acquired a tool for renewed work.

298. This text is presented and discussed in detail in the contribution of Schenker in this volume.

299. J. Debus, *Die Sünde Jeroboams* (FRLANT, 93; Göttingen: Vandenhoeck & Ruprecht, 1967), p. 90.

300. J.C. Trebolle Barrera, *Salomón y Jeroboán. Historia de la rencensión y redacción de 1 Reges 2-12, 14* (Bibliotheca Salmanticensis, Dissertationes 3; Salamanca, 1980).

301. S.L. McKenzie, *The Trouble with Kings: The Composition of the Book of Kings in the Deuteronomistic History* (VTSup, 42; Leiden: E.J. Brill, 1991), pp. 21-40.

302. Zipora Talshir, 'Is the Alternate Tradition of the Division of the Kingdom (3 Kgds 12:24a-z) non-Deuteronomistic?', in G.J. Brooke and B. Lindars (eds.), *Septuagint, Scrolls and Cognate Writings: Papers Presented to the International Symposium on the Septuagint and its Relations to the Dead Sea Scrolls and Other Writings* (Atlanta: Scholars Press, 1992), pp. 599-621.

303. Cf. on this subject Tov, *Criticism of the Hebrew Bible*, p. 169.

7.2. The Problem of the Dating of DH and of its Original End

The question of the dating of DH continues to divide the schools of Cross and Smend. To defend their respective dating, the supporters of a Josianic DH are obliged to put the original end at the latest in 2 Kgs 23.25, and the defenders of a first exilic edition somewhere in 2 Kings 24 or 25. However, even within the two schools, the opinions remain divided on the subject of the *precise* end of the first edition of the DH.

Thus, among recent authors of the Cross school, Provan[304] places the end of the Josianic DH in 2 Kgs 19.37 (reign of Hezekiah), while McKenzie and O'Brien have in mind 2 Kgs 23.23 (celebration of the Passover).[305] As for Vanoni, he returns to the classical thesis of an end in 2 Kgs 23.25.[306]

Among those who favour the hypothesis of a first exilic edition, we find too a multitude of proposals:

According to Seitz, the first Dtr edition of the book of Kings would have ended in 2 Kings 24,[307] immediately after the first deportation of 597. For Würthwein, the first Dtr layer in Kings ended in 2 Kgs 25.7* (exile of Zedekiah).[308] Dietrich, Spronk and others set the original end of DH in 2 Kgs 25.21 ('Thus Judah was deported far from its land'),[309]

---

304. I.W. Provan, *Hezekiah and the Book of Kings: A Contribution to the Debate about the Composition of the Deuteronomistic History* (BZAW, 172; Berlin: W. de Gruyter, 1988). Cf. too B. Peckham, *History and Prophecy: The Development of Late Judean Literary Traditions* (ABRL; New York: Doubleday, 1993), pp. 49-51.

305. S.L. McKenzie, *The Chronicler's Use of the Deuteronomistic History* (HSM, 33; 2 vols.; Atlanta: Scholars Press, 1985), p. 191. See on the other hand McKenzie, *The Trouble with Kings*, p. 115. O'Brien, *The Deuteronomistic History Hypothesis*, p. 267. See now too G.N. Knoppers, *Two Nations Under God: The Deuteronomistic History of Solomon and the Dual Monarchies* (HSM, 52; 2 vols.; Atlanta: Scholars Press, 1993–1994), II, p. 215.

306. G. Vanoni, 'Beobachtungen zur deuteronomistischen Terminologie in 2Kön 23,25–25,30', in N. Lohfink (ed.), *Das Deuteronomium: Entstehung, Gestalt und Botschaft* (BETL, 68; Leuven: Leuven University Press, 1985), pp. 357-62. Cf. as well Preuss, 'DtrG', p. 387.

307. Seitz, *Theology in Conflict*, pp. 167-69.

308. Würthwein, *Die Bücher der Könige*. Cf. the reconstruction of this layer, pp. 505-15.

309. Dietrich, *Prophetie und Geschichte*, pp. 140-41; K. Spronk, 'Aanhangsel of uitvloeisel', *GThT* 88 (1988), pp. 162-70; K.F. Pohlmann, 'Erwägungen zum Schlusskapitel des deuteronomistischen Geschichtswerk. Oder: Warum wird der Prophet Jeremia in 2 Kön 22–25 nicht erwähnt?', in Gunneweg and Kaiser (eds.),

unlike the Nothian vision for which, as we have seen, the present end of the book of Kings (rehabilitation of Jehoiachin) coincides with the end of the DH.

These various options have, of course, consequences for the way in which the authors conceive the intention and the ideology of the DH.

For a very long time, the confrontation between the supporters of a Josianic dating and those of an exilic dating took on the appearances of a holy war. But recently some works have been published that could open the door to a compromise between the Harvard and Göttingen schools.

We thus take note that some exegetes influenced by the Cross approach acknowledge increasingly a number of Dtr texts as *exilic*. Mayes certainly postulates a Josianic historian, but he attributes more texts to a 'Deuteronomistic editor' close to Second Isaiah.[310] The insistence on the Law in this editor brings him remarkably close to the DtrN of Göttingen. O'Brien too finds—after a Josianic edition—three important exilic redactions of the DH.[311] The work of McKenzie on the books of Kings likewise effects a modification of Cross's model,[312] insofar as the Josianic version of DH is extremely reduced. McKenzie actually attributes to the post-Dtr redactors numerous texts that were formerly considered ancient texts integrated by the first Dtr into his narrative framework. Incidentally, he continues to advance (or recall) solid arguments that argue in favour of a *Josianic* edition of the books of Kings. Whence the question: does this still necessarily imply a Josianic DH (Deuteronomy–2 Kings)?

For this problem, the work of Provan is especially worthy of our attention. Provan too starts from a study of the book of Kings. His analysis of the mentions of the במות, the 'high places', leads him to situate the end of the Josianic edition in 2 Kings 18–19 (see above). But what was the extent of this first pro-monarchic edition of DH? For Provan, it only included, besides the books of Kings, the stories of the rise to power and the succession of David, themselves introduced by the story of Samuel (without the anti-monarchic texts in 1 Sam. 7–12). So,

---

Textgemäss. Aufsätze und Beiträge zur Hermeneutik des Alten Testaments, pp. 94-109.

310. Mayes, *The Story of Israel between Settlement and Exile*.

311. O'Brien, *The Deuteronomistic History Hypothesis*.

312. See the remarks on this subject of Preuss, 'DtrG', pp. 376-77.

in the time of Josiah, DH consisted of just Samuel and Kings![313] Deuteronomy, Joshua and Judges were only added to it by exilic editors! So can we still speak, for the period of Josiah, of a DH in the sense intended by Noth, when, if we follow Provan, more than half of this historiography still does not appear in it?

Provan's results moreover come close in an interesting way to the point of view of Lohfink on DH: in an article in 1981, Lohfink had introduced the new siglum 'DtrL' (*Landeroberungserzählung*, 'narrative of the conquest'),[314] by which he intends to designate the edition of Deuteronomy 1–Joshua 22*, an edition that he proposes to situate in the time of Josiah. In Lohfink's view, this collection would be a propaganda document in favour of the expansionist policy of Josiah. Lohfink accepts as well the idea of a Josianic edition of the book of Kings, without the latter already making up a unit with 'DtrL'.

We could eventually therefore come to a sort of compromise[315]: by situating the beginnings of the literary activity of the Dtr milieu in the time of Josiah (perhaps even before, as far as the primitive Deut. is concerned?), it is possible to imagine the establishment of a small library of texts containing propaganda in favour of the ('Dtr') policy of Josiah. That library would comprise Deuteronomy, perhaps a version of the conquest account exactly copying the Assyrian model (Joshua), and an edition of Kings (+ Samuel*?) showing that Josiah is a worthy successor of David. To this even some texts of the Tetrateuch could have been added, for example, a *Vita Mosis* (such as that made plausible by Blum[316]). The organization of some of these collections into a great history (DH) would only have taken place in the period of the exile, and it is after the catastrophe that a literature, conceived originally as propa-

313. Provan, *Hezekiah and the Book of Kings*, p. 168 n. 30, envisages the possibility that Judg. 17–21 would have formed part of it.
314. Lohfink, 'Kerygmata des deuteronomistischen Geschichtswerkes', pp. 87-100 = *Studien zum Deuteronomium und zur deuteronomistischen Literatur*, II (SBAB, 12; Stuttgart: Katholisches Bibelwerk, 1991), pp. 125-41; cf. as well his 'Deutéronome et Pentateuque', in Haudebert (ed.), *Le Pentateuque*, pp. 38-42, where he appears however more critical with regard to the Göttingen model.
315. For an appeal for compromise, cf. too E. Cortese, 'Theories Concerning Dtr: A Possible Rapprochement', in C. Brekelmans and J. Lust (eds.), *Pentateuchal and Deuteronomistic Studies: Papers Read at the XIIth IOSOT Congress Leuven 1989* (BETL, 94; Leuven: Leuven University Press & Peeters, 1990), pp. 179-90.
316. Blum, *Studien zur Komposition des Pentateuch*, pp. 208-18.

ganda, would have been put at the service of an attempt at a theodicy.[317]

Could such a consensus come to pass? It is doubtless too early to say. We notice at present among the supporters of the Smendian model as well as among the 'neo-Nothians' (Hoffmann, Van Seters; see below) some reluctance about considering (save for Deuteronomy) the possibility of an important literary activity at the time of Josiah.

The discussion of the dating of DH especially revolves around the pre-exilic / exilic alternative. Noth had decided that the end of 2 Kings 25 (the release of Jehoiachin) definitely attested to an exilic redaction of DH, all the more so since there is no indication in it about the arrival of the Persians or the possibility of a return from exile. That *interpretatio exilica* of 2 Kgs 25.27-30 has been taken up by the majority of exegetes.[318] Now however, Würthwein has drawn attention to the fact that this passage contains neither typically Dtr style nor its preoccupations.[319] But why then would it have been added to DH? We can compare the fate of Jehoiachin in these verses to that of a Mordecai, or of a Daniel or of a Joseph having a career in foreign courts.[320] It could have been a justification of the diaspora, that would bring us round to the thesis of a (Dtr or post-Dtr) revision of DH in the Persian period. However, it must be clearly acknowledged that we find scarcely any allusions to the Achaemenid period in Deuteronomy to 2 Kings.

7.3. *The Problem of the Unity and Coherence of the Work*

7.3.1. *The Proliferation of Dtr Layers*
As we have already remarked, some scholars at present are fond of multiplying Dtr layers. New sigla are created (DtrÜ, DtrS and so on), when DtrN is not being divided into DtrN^1, DtrN^2 and so forth. Thus, Stahl ended up distinguishing ten Dtr layers,[321] while Perlitt's students,

317. On this subject see T. Römer, 'Historiographies et mythes d'origines dans l'Ancien Testament', in M. Detienne (ed.), *Transcrire les mythologies* (Paris: Albin Michel, 1994), pp. 142-48 and 236-37.

318. Cf. recently for example B. Becking, 'Jehojachin's Amnesty, Salvation for Israel: Notes on 2 Kings 25, 27-30', in Brekelmans and Lust (eds.), *Pentateuchal and Deuteronomistic Studies*, pp. 283-93.

319. Würthwein, *Die Bücher der Könige*, p. 484.

320. Cf. T. Römer, 'Transformations in Deuteronomistic and Biblical Historiography: On "Book-Finding" and other Literary Strategies', *ZAW* 109 (1997), pp. 1-11.

321. In an unpublished dissertation: 'Aspekte der Geschichte dtr Theologie. Zur

in helping their teacher prepare his commentary on Deuteronomy, identified so many layers in it that it became impossible to count them or
attribute sigla to them.[322]

Faced with this situation where the results of criticism risk getting
beyond any control, it is very easy to understand the scepticism of
Albertz[323] who proposes making do with the idea of a Dtr group. The
'tensions' that can be discerned within some Dtr texts would simply be
the echo of internal debates in Dtr circles, without it being possible to
identify the spokespersons for such or such an opinion. For Rofé, the
ideological contradictions within the historical books bear witness to
the reunion of two historiographical works: an Ephraimite history originating in the North and a Josianic DH.[324]

These last few years, we notice besides an increasing number of publications favouring the 'final' form of such or such a part of the DH (for
example, Eslinger on Joshua–2 Kings,[325] or Berges and Diana Edelman
on the story of Saul[326]). What we have here—at least partially—is a
reaction to a diachronic criticism that runs the risk of losing sight of the
biblical text in its completed form.

7.3.2. *Priority Given to Synchronic Methods*

Under the impact of structuralism in the French and English-speaking
worlds or in rallying, more simply, to the concept of 'close reading' or

---

Traditionsgeschichte der Terminologie und zur Redaktionsgeschichte der Re-
dekomposition' (Jena, 1982). Cf. the review in *TLZ* 108 (1983), cols. 74-76.

322. Cf. in particular R. Achenbach, *Israel zwischen Verheissung und Gebot:
Literarkritische Untersuchungen zu Deuteronomium 5–11* (EHS.T, 422; Frankfurt:
Peter Lang, 1991).

323. R. Albertz, 'Die Intentionen und Träger des deuteronomistischen Geschichtswerks', in R. Albertz, F.W. Golka and J. Kegler (eds.), *Schöpfung und Befreiung*:
Für Claus Westermann zum 80. Geburtstag (Stuttgart: Calwer Verlag, 1989),
pp. 37-53.

324. A. Rofé, 'Ephraimite Versus Deuteronomistic History', in D. Garrone and
F. Israel (eds.), *Storia e tradizioni di Israele: Scritti in onore di J. Alberto Soggin*
(Brescia: Paideia, 1991), pp. 221-35.

325. L. Eslinger, *Into the Hands of the Living God* (JSOTSup, 84; Bible and
Literature Series, 24; Sheffield: Almond Press, 1989).

326. U. Berges, *Die Verwerfung Sauls: Eine thematische Untersuchung* (Fzb, 61;
Würzburg: Echter, 1989); D. Edelman, *King Saul in the Historiography of Judah*
(JSOTSup, 121; Sheffield: JSOT Press, 1991).

'narratology',[327] some authors have begun to reject, in a more or less categorical manner, the differenciation of literary levels within DH. Thus, Polzin, in elaborating a trilogy on DH,[328] strongly criticizes historico-critical exegesis for being an obstacle to an appropriate perception of the structure of DH and of the message of the Dtr—through its shallow and useless pursuit of redactional layers, that are themselves illusory. It is this message that he proposes to bring out by means of a 'holistic' analysis. The efficacy of his method, however, is not clearly evident. When Polzin observes, for example, that the author of Deut. intends, by means of the Mosaic fiction, to present himself as the true mediator of the divine word, what else is he doing but repeating evidence recognized by everybody (and brought to light in the first place by historico-critical exegesis)? And when, while describing diachronic exegesis, he can write: 'That corpus of the Hebrew Bible that stretches from the Book of Deuteronomy through 2 Kings is called the Deuteronomistic History',[329] he is depending on a result from historico-critical exegesis and not on the traditional tripartition of the Hebrew Bible.

Hoffman too favours a synchronic reading of DH, while at the same time recognizing the possibility of later redactional interventions in the first edition of the DH.[330] He wonders about its structure and reaches the conclusion that this great literary work ensures its consistency through the theme of cultic 'reforms and counter-reforms', with DH being framed by two exemplary reformers, Moses and Josiah. For Hoffmann, the reform of Josiah constitutes the apotheosis of the entire work. That does not imply in any way, however, the pre-exilic origin of DH, since the idealized presentation of the reign of Josiah has the precise goal of proposing a model for a new start after the exile. Hoffmann criticizes Noth for some ambiguity in his description of the Dtr—does

327. Cf., for example, D.N. Fewell and D.M. Gunn, *Gender, Power and Promise: The Subject of the Bible's First Story* (Nashville: Abingdon Press, 1993).

328. R. Polzin, *Moses and the Deuteronomist: A Literary Study of the Deuteronomic History*. I. *Deuteronomy, Joshua, Judges* (New York: Seabury, 1980); *idem, Samuel and the Deuteronomist: A Literary Study of the Deuteronomic History*. II. *1 Samuel* (San Francisco: Harper & Row, 1989); *idem, David and the Deuteronomist: A Literary Study of the Deuteronomic History: 2 Samuel* (Indiana Studies in Biblical Literature; Bloomington: Indiana University Press, 1993).

329. Polzin, *Moses and the Deuteronomist,*. I, p. 18.

330. H.-D. Hoffmann, *Reform und Reformen: Untersuchungen zu einem Grundthema der deuteronomistischen Geschichtsschreibung* (ATANT, 66; Zürich: Theologischer Verlag, 1980).

he see in him an author or a redactor?—and he himself very clearly opts
in favour of a Dtr-author, who conceives and realizes a historiographic
project in the service of a well-defined cause. In this, Hoffmann comes
very close to Van Seters.[331]

7.3.3. *The Deuteronomist as a Historian*

In his 1983 work, *In Search of History*, John Van Seters stands firmly
by the idea of one Dtr 'historiographer' only, thus showing himself
faithful to Noth. Nevertheless, his position differs from Noth's on two
important points:

1. Van Seters is much more sceptical than Noth as regards the
existence of ancient written sources that the Dtr would have taken up
and retouched slightly; he is thinking rather of traditions whose outlines
remain quite blurred. In this context, Van Seters considers that the so
called 'history of the succession of David' does not represent in any
case, as the common opinion would have it, the beginnings of historiography in Israel, but is on the contrary a postexilic addition to DH in
order to underline the negative aspects of the figure of David and
counter the Davidic messianism of the Persian period.[332] In a general
way, Van Seters sees in DH more of an ideological construction than a
source that makes it possible to reconstruct the 'true' history of Judah.

2. According to Van Seters, it is by turning our eyes toward Greece
that we discover the most revealing parallels to DH. Like Herodotus, of
whom he was perhaps even the precursor, the Dtr was both an author
and an editor, collecting and organizing different traditions in order to
make the first historiographical work of the ancient Near East. But,
unlike Noth's Dtr, that of Van Seters does not simply play the role of an
'honest broker' in relation to the sources; he is rather a creative writer
who does not hesitate to fill in the gaps in tradition with his own ideas.

Since he understands Dtr as an individual historian, Van Seters does
not attach too much importance to the eventual additions that would

331. An approach comparable to Hoffmann's has just been proposed by E.T.
Mullen, *Narrative History and Ethnic Boundaries: The Deuteronomistic Historian
and the Creation of Israelite National Identity* (Semeia Studies; Atlanta: Scholars
Press, 1993). He considers the DH under its final form as an exilic work that constitutes a 'two-way vision: it looks to the past to understand the present and to the
future to restore the ideals that have been described as part of that past' (p. 228).

332. Cf. J. Van Seters, *In Search of History* (New Haven: Yale University Press,
1983), pp. 317-21, for more details; cf. below §7.5.4.4.

have been made to the *editio princeps* of DH. A similar position is adopted by McKenzie (with the difference that for him—at least in his publications prior to his contribution to the present volume[333]—the Dtr is Josianic). According to his analysis, the 'Dtr[2]' texts in Kings are not an indication of a second redaction elaborated in a systematic way: they are instead isolated additions.[334] Being content with a distinction of a general nature between 'Dtr[1]' and 'Dtr[2]' can actually seem profitable. This is also the position of Rose, who advocates a distinction between an 'ancient Deuteronomistic level' and a 'recent Deuteronomistic level'.[335] 'Dtr[2]' would therefore group together all the additions to the first edition of the DH. There would remain in suspense the question, a perfectly legitimate one, of knowing whether behind the siglum 'Dtr[2]' there was not hidden a second great historiographical project, a second redaction that too would have had as its goal a coherent presentation of Israel's history. It would in that case be conceivable that the edition of the 'great Dtr history', namely Genesis–2 Kings, should be attributed to 'Dtr[2]'.

That brings up again the question of the coherence, if not the existence, of the Dtr redaction(s). Now, it is precisely this coherence that has recently found itself under critical fire, even total contestation.

7.3.4. *The Questioning of the Cohesion, even the Existence of DH*

Recently, Würthwein[336] has challenged the coherence of DH. In his opinion, we would not be dealing with a unified work, but with a blend of successive Dtr redactions.[337] This literary activity would have begun with an exilic edition of the history of the monarchy (from Solomon to Zedekiah). Other Dtr redactors would then have preceded this history of

---

333. Cf. however his contribution to this volume.

334. Cf. McKenzie, *The Trouble with Kings*, pp. 135-45.

335. Cf. Rose, 'La croissance du corpus historiographique de la Bible', pp. 224-25. Cf. as well T. Römer, 'Le Deutéronome à la quête des origines', in Haudebert (ed.), *Le Pentateuque*, pp. 65-98 (71).

336. E. Würthwein, 'Erwägungen zum sog. Deuteronomistischen Geschichtswerk. Eine Skizze', in E. Würthwein, *Studien zum deuteronomistischen Geschichtswerk* (BZAW, 227; Berlin: W. de Gruyter, 1994), pp. 1-11.

337. Cf. now as well E. Eynikel, *The Reform of King Josiah and the Composition of the Deuteronomistic History* (OTS, 33; Leiden: E.J. Brill, 1996). According to him: 'At best we can speak of a dtr redaction in which the historical books are parenetically interpreted' (p. 361). But in what way is that parenetic interpretation opposed to the idea of a DH?

the monarchy with some traditions on the rise to power and the succession of David (Würthwein speaks of a 'second block'). Later, other postexilic Dtr redactors would have created the history of the Judges by way of a new prologue (Judg. 2.11–12.6*, a 'third block'). Each time the theological idea was changed. In the book of Judges, for example, the concept of history is cyclic, unlike that of the book(s) of Kings; furthermore, it is the entire people who do evil in the eyes of Yhwh and not only their kings. Finally, well after the end of the exile, the hope of being free again in the homeland would have given rise to the Dtr composition of Joshua 1–11 ('fourth block'). In this fresco painted by Würthwein, we indeed witness the growth, with the passing epochs, of a literary corpus, but it is no longer a question of the birth of a coherent historiographic project. The whole thing becomes more complicated when Würthwein distinguishes within these blocks several Dtr redactors, whom he designates with the sigla DtrP and DtrN. The big absentee from the debate is the book of Deuteronomy itself. In elaborating his theory, Würthwein does not express an opinion on the status of this book.

We will notice that Würthwein takes up again the first objections that had been raised against Noth's thesis by authors such as Fohrer, Weiser or von Rad. This is likewise the situation with Westermann,[338] whose challenging of DH appeared at almost the same time as the article of Würthwein. Westermann too insists on the differences in character and ideology that separate the Dtr texts in Judges, Samuel and Kings. His perspective is, on the other hand, more 'conservative' in as much as he thinks that he can, by insisting on the role of oral tradition, remain in contact with the 'events related'.

The questioning of the existence of DH is becoming more extensive.[339] Is it a brief burst of 'deconstructionism', or must the idea of a coherent literary collection going from Deuteronomy to the historical books be finally abandoned? In any case, it will always be necessary to explain the many internal cross-references to Deuteronomy–2 Kings, references that would make no sense, it seems to us, if they did not fit into a comprehensive redactional project covering the whole Dtr complex.

338. C. Westermann, *Die Geschichtsbücher des Alten Testaments*.

339. Cf. A.G. Auld, 'What Makes Judges Deuteronomistic?', in *idem, Joshua Retold: Synoptic Perspectives* (Edinburgh: T. & T. Clark, 1998), pp. 120-26; cf. as well the contribution of E.A. Knauf in the present volume.

The problem of the introduction to DH must be taken up again as well. Let us recall, once again, that Noth had proposed Deuteronomy as an opening, by *via negationis*. Würthwein himself speaks of the collection Joshua–2 Kings as if Deuteronomy did not exist.

Already in 1975, Mittmann had challenged the thesis of Noth, who saw in Deuteronomy 1–3(4) the introduction to DH.[340] For Mittmann, these chapters introduced the Deuteronomic Code alone. In fact, one could ask whether Deut. 1.5-18 (reminder of Horeb) provides an adequate introduction to a historiographical work that continues to the end of 2 Kings. Would it not be more judicious, Mittmann asks, to begin this great history with the events related in the book of Exodus?[341] From this perspective, would the solution not be to consider Deuteronomy 1–3 as an addition that had been made at the time of the insertion of Deuteronomy into the Torah?[342] DH would thus be deprived of its classical introduction. But that would practically lead us back to the start. One should not forget that there actually exist many links between the basic Dtr layer in Deuteronomy 1–3; 31 and Joshua 1.[343] Joshua 1.6 actually repeats almost word for word Deut. 31.7. The order that Joshua gives to the Transjordanian tribes in Josh. 1.12 corresponds to Deut. 3.18-20 (cf. the reference in Josh. 1.13). And Deut. 3.12-22, which reports the conquest of Transjordan, gives orders for the future conquest and relates the investiture of Joshua, makes sense only if this discourse leads on to a sequel such as we find developed in the book of Joshua. Thus, Deuteronomy serves as an introduction, at least partially, to a literary collection that immediately surpasses the limits of the book of Deuteronomy alone.[344] The existence of a link—of whatever sort it

---

340. S. Mittmann, *Deuteronomium 1,1–6,3: Literarkritisch und traditions-geschichtlich untersucht* (BZAW, 139; Berlin: W. de Gruyter, 1975), especially pp. 177-78.

341. Mittmann, *Deuteronomium, 1,1–6,3*, p. 178.

342. As Fohrer had envisaged in his *Einleitung in das Alte Testament*.

343. Cf. the arguments of L. Schmidt, 'Deuteronomistisches Geschichtswerk', in H.J. Boecker *et al.*, *Altes Testament* (Neukirchener Arbeitsbücher; Neukirchen–Vluyn: Neukirchener Verlag, 1983), pp. 101-14 (104). Cf. as well his explanations of the different 'conceptions' of history in DH.

344. We could cite still other cross-references within Deuteronomy that prepare for and presuppose the subsequent books: the construction of a sanctuary on Mt Ebal at the time of the entry into the land (Deut. 11.29) is carried out in Josh. 8.30; the warnings of Deut. 6.12-19 very clearly prepare for the remarks on the subject of the disobedience of the people in Judg. 2.12-23 (cf. Römer, *Israels Väter*, p. 301).

might be—between Deuteronomy and the books that follow it seems to us therefore difficult to question.

7.4. *The Problem of the Localization and Identity of the Deuteronomists*

In the recent publications, the question of the location and identity of the Deuteronomists has often been relegated to footnotes. The response to this question, however, has considerable significance for our way of understanding DH and of visualizing an eventual succession of Dtr redactions. After the publication of Weinfeld's book in 1972, a number of scholars were won over to the hypothesis according to which the first Deuteronomists were courtiers in Jerusalem who had begun their activities in the reign of Ezekiah.[345] The idea of a Northern origin of the Deuteronomists, seen as refugees stemming from a prophetical-Levitical milieu,[346] lost its attraction. This idea is still defended, however, by Roth, who thinks of Levites located just about everywhere in the country and oriented towards the Jerusalem temple.[347]

The insistence of Weinfeld and his supporters on the activity of 'scribal circles' has been considered somewhat excessive. If the analogies between Deuteronomy and the Wisdom literature, presented by Weinfeld, are actually indisputable, the fact remains that the Wisdom literature, unlike the books of the DH, is in no way interested in the historical traditions. Albertz and others have therefore proposed thinking instead of a sort of Dtr 'coalition'[348] that would have grouped together Jerusalemite priests, prophets and 'laity' (generally high-ranking officials). By using 2 Kings 22–23 and some texts in Jeremiah (especially chs. 28 and 36) as historical documents, Albertz can even

The curses of Deut. 28 prepare for the exile of the people related in 2 Kgs 17 and 25. See besides the many allusions to the crossing of the Jordan in Deuteronomy.

345. Weinfeld, *Deuteronomy and the Deuteronomic School*, pp. 148-71; Weinfeld especially bases his argument on the strong influence and assimilation of Assyrian culture in Deuteronomy. See too N. Lohfink, 'Culture Shock and Theology: A Discussion of Theology as a Cultural and Sociological Phenomenon Based on the Example of Deuteronomic Law', *BTB* 7 (1977), pp. 12-22.

346. Cf. as well E.W. Nicholson, *Deuteronomy and Tradition* (Oxford: Basil Blackwell, 1967).

347. Roth, 'Deuteronomistisches Geschichtswerk/Deuteronomistische Schule', p. 547.

348. Albertz, 'Die Intentionen und Träger des deuteronomistischen Geschichtswerks', pp. 48-49; R.E. Clements, *Deuteronomy* (OTG; Sheffield: JSOT Press, 1989); Blum, *Studien zur Komposition des Pentateuch*, pp. 341-42.

name these Deuteronomists: after the failure of the Josianic reform, we find among them the descendants of the priest Hilkiah, prophets like Hananiah (who announces the imminent return of Jeconiah, Jer. 28.1-4), families of royal officials like that of Malchiah and Shemaiah, who are hostile to Jeremiah, as well as that part of the Jewish aristocracy (עם־הארץ) who supported, before 587, a nationalist and anti-Babylonian policy. After the catastrophe of the exile, this group edits the DH while trying to assume responsibility for the failure of its nationalist policy: they accepted the judgment while maintaining a certain 'nationalist' ideology. The thesis of Albertz is appealing, since it manages to give some depth to the Deuteronomists. However, it raises some questions: if the Deuteronomists were at this time royalists, why does the only text mentioning the king in Deuteronomy (Deut. 17) transform him into a reader of the Torah? If the Deuteronomists taken as a whole were hostile to Jeremiah, why does the book of Jermiah show traces of a Dtr redaction? Albertz,[349] Stipp[350] and others speak of a conflict within the Dtr movement. Another question: can we really describe the editors of DH as 'thoroughgoing oppressors' if we take into account the interest that some Dt/Dtr texts show in peasant debtors and in the disadvantaged of society (Deut. 15)?[351] We must think too about an adequate sociological definition of these Deuteronomists. We note a great lack of clarity on this subject in the present discussion. Is it a matter of a 'school', of a 'group', of a 'party', of a 'movement'?[352] Perhaps the exegetes should work in a more interdisciplinary way on this point.

If we accept the hypothesis of activity by the Deuteronomists before the exile, there is (almost) no doubt about their localization in Jerusalem. As for the question of the location of the *exilic* Deuteronomists, that is still the object of great debate. Noth and a good number of his students postulated a localization of the Deuteronomists in Palestine,

---

349. Cf. 'Die Intentionen und Träger des deuteronomistischen Geschichtswerks'.

350. Stipp, *Jeremia im Parteienstreit*.

351. Cf. in particular Crüsemann, *Die Tora*, pp. 311-14, as well as the remarks of Blum (*Studien zur Komposition des Pentateuch*, pp. 342-43) with regard to Albertz.

352. Cf. on this subject N. Lohfink, 'Gab es eine deuteronomistische Bewegung?', in W. Gross (ed.), *Jeremia und die 'Deuteronomistische Bewegung'* (BBB, 98; Weinheim: Beltz Athenäum, 1995), pp. 313-82, ET: 'Was There a Deuteronomistic Movement?', in L.S. Schearing and S.L. McKenzie (eds.), *Those Elusive Deuteronomists: The Phenomenon of Pan-Deuteronium* (JSOTSup, 268; Sheffield: Sheffield Academic Press, 1999), pp. 36-66.

more precisely at Mizpah (residence of Gedaliah). Their principal argument was that the redaction of a historiography like the DH would presuppose recourse to a great number of documents. Now, access to the documents was easier to imagine in the homeland than in distant Babylon. But this idea, while it still appears in recent authors (for example, in Albertz, Veijola[353]), is nevertheless contested more and more (Pohlmann, Blum and others).[354] Many texts of DH actually reveal a viewpoint of exiles (for example, the temple as the place in which direction they pray, 1 Kgs 8.33-53; or, in the same text, as already in Deut. 28, the curses announcing the expulsion outside the country). If 2 Kgs 25.21-26 is part of the exilic edition of DH, we do not see how that vision of a total depopulation of the country could have been that of non-exiled Judaeans. We definitely have here the trace of a pro-*golah* ideology, of an attitude that appears too in some Dtr texts of Jeremiah. Consequently there are strong presumptions for situating the Deuteronomists among the exiles in Babylon; however, the discussion is not closed.

7.5. *The Problem of Sources*

The question of sources available to the Dtr redactor(s) is likewise the subject of various hypotheses with regard to the function and genius of the Deuteronomists. Furthermore, the questions of pre-Deuteronomistic sources or documents comes up in a different way for each book. In the limits of this article, we must be content with a brief survey.

7.5.1. *Deuteronomy*[355]
7.5.1.1. Numeruswechsel *and Primitive Deuteronomy*. For a long time, Old Testament criticism has considered that the alternation of the

---

353. Albertz, 'Die Intentionen und Träger des deuteronomistischen Geschichtswerks', p. 49; T. Veijola, *Verheissung in der Krise: Studien zur Literatur und Theologie der Exilszeit anhand des 89. Psalms* (STAT.AASF, 220; Helsinki: Suomaleinen Tiedeakatemia, 1982), pp. 177-90.

354. Pohlmann, 'Erwägungen zum Schlusskapitel des deuteronomistischen Geschichtswerks'; Blum, *Studien zur Komposition des Pentateuch*, pp. 339-40; J.A. Soggin, *Introduzione all'Antico Testamento* (Brescia: Paideia, 1987), p. 215; Friedman, *The Exile and Biblical Narrative*, p. 34.

355. For more details, cf. T. Römer, 'The Book of Deuteronomy', in S.L. McKenzie and M.P. Graham (eds.), *The History of Israel's Traditions: The Heritage of Martin Noth* (JSOTSup, 182; Sheffield: Sheffield Academic Press, 1994), pp. 178-212, and *idem*, 'Approches exégétiques du Deutéronome: Brève histoire de

address formulas of Deuteronomy, sometimes in the second person singular, sometimes in the second person plural, constitutes a criterion that makes it possible to determine the stages in the formation of the book.[356] In 1962, Minette de Tillesse, who considers himself one of the most faithful continuators of Noth,[357] systematically applied this principle to Deuteronomy, maintaining that all the sections of Deuteronomy 5–30 containing plural addresses were due to the Deuteronomist, and that the passages written in the singular went back to the original Deuteronomy that the Dtr would have had at his disposition.[358] But quite rapidly, the work of Minette de Tillesse has proved too schematic, and literary criticism, making use of the criterion of the *Numeruswechsel*, produces a multiplicity of Deuteronomic and Deuteronomistic layers[359] escaping all control. What is more, there have been several voices maintaining that this alternation should be explained differently. For Buis and Leclerq, this phenomenon reflects a strategy of oral discourse and is found in other cultures.[360] Lohfink interpreted the *Numeruswechsel* as a result of the style of the authors of Deuteronomy.[361] It actually seems risky to make use of the *Numeruswechsel* as an automatic criterion to reconstruct the pre-Deuteronomistic

la recherche sur le Deutéronome depuis Martin Noth', *RHPR* 75 (1995), pp. 153-75; M.A. O'Brien, 'The Book of Deuteronomy', *CRBS* 3 (1995), pp. 95-128.

356. For the history of the research on the *Numeruswechsel* before Noth, cf. C. Begg, 'The Significance of the Numeruswechsel in Deuteronomy: The "Pre-History" of the Question', *ETL* 55 (1979), pp. 116-24.

357. Cf. what he writes in the 'supplements' to the Portuguese translation of the *Studien* in the *Revista Biblica Brasileira* 10 (1993), pp. 229-67.

358. G. Minette de Tillesse, 'Sections "Tu" et Sections "Vous" dans le Deutéronome', *VT* 12 (1962), pp. 29-87; *idem*, 'Martin Noth et la "Redaktionsgeschichte" des livres historiques', in C. Hauret (ed.), *Aux grands carrefours de la révélation et de l'exégèse de l'Ancien Testament* (RechBib, 8; Paris: Desclée de Brouwer, 1967), pp. 51-75.

359. Cf. in particular F. García López, 'Analyse littéraire de Deutéronome V–XI', *RB* 84 (1977), pp. 481-522; 85 (1978) pp. 5-49, and Y. Suzuki, *The 'Numeruswechsel' Sections in Deuteronomy* (Ann Arbor, MI; London, 1982); *Linguistic Studies in Deuteronomy* (in Japanese) (Tokyo, 1987); he finds ten different layers in Deuteronomy; cf. the presentation of K.-H. Walkenhorst, 'Neueste Deuteronomiumforschung in Japan', *BZ* 33 (1989), pp. 81-92.

360. P. Buis and J. Leclerq, *Le Deutéronome* (SB; Paris: J. Gabalda, 1963), p. 9.

361. N. Lohfink, *Das Hauptgebot: Eine Untersuchung literarischer Einleitungsfragen zu Dtn 5–11* (AnBib, 20; Rome: Pontifical Biblical Institute Press, 1963), pp. 239-58.

Deuteronomy. That however does not mean that *all* the occurrences of the *Numeruswechsel* are to be explained on the basis of stylistic arguments, as Lohfink, Braulik and others maintain.

But let us return to the problem of the primitive Deuteronomy. For many researchers the first edition was written in the time of Ezekiah.[362] Others consider as more probable the idea that the original had been produced by supporters of Josiah as a propaganda document for his reform.[363] Even if the link between the book mentioned in 2 Kings 22 and the book of Deuteronomy has remained a near certainty in critical exegesis, the research on this subject since Noth has prompted some doubts. Recently, Eleanore Reuter has questioned this link, arguing that the book of the Josianic reform must be the Book of the Covenant (Exod. 20.22–23.33).[364] According to her, the original Deuteronomy was written just at the time of the Josianic reform or a little later. But it is difficult to support this thesis owing to the fact that there is no precise relationship connecting Exod. 20.22–23.33 to the account in 2 Kings 22–23,[365] a text which, for its part, would clearly make an allusion to Deuteronomy. The real problem is that of the historicity, even the function of 2 Kings 22–23. It has been realized for a long time that the account, in its present form, is due to a Dtr redactor who attempted to endow the Deuteronomic movement with an origin myth.[366] Now, as Diebner and Nauerth have shown, the motif of the discovery of a 'divine' book actually corresponds, in antiquity, to a classical literary strategy whose goal is in general to legitimate changes in the social and religious order.[367] Even if a 'reform' was carried out in Josiah's reign

362. For example N. Lohfink, 'Culture Shock and Theology'; M. Weinfeld, *Deuteronomy* (AB, 5A; Garden City, NY: Doubleday, 1991), pp. 44-54; F. García López, *Le Deutéronome: Une loi prêchée* (Cahiers Evangile, 63; Paris: Cerf, 1988), p. 10.

363. Clements, *Deuteronomy*, p. 71; Y. Suzuki, 'A New Aspect of the Occupation Policy by King Josiah', *AJBI* 18 (1992), pp. 31-61.

364. E. Reuter, *Kultzentralisation: Entstehung und Theologie von Dtn 12* (Athenäums Monographien, Theologie, BBB, 87; Frankfurt: A. Hain, 1993), pp. 243-58.

365. Cf. N. Lohfink, 'Gibt es eine deuteronomistische Bearbeitung im Bundesbuch?', in Brekelmans and Lust (eds.), *Pentateuchal and Deuteronomistic Studies*, pp. 91-113.

366. We cannot enter here into the debate on the redactional history of this text; cf. K. Visaticki, *Die Reform des Josija und die religiöse Heterodoxie in Israel* (Dissertationen, Theologische Reihe, 21; St. Ottilien: EOS Verlag, 1987).

367. B.J. Diebner and C. Nauerth, 'Die Inventio des התורה ספר in 2Kön 22.

(and there is no need to doubt it), it is not certain that such a reform had been activated by the discovery of a book. It is more likely that the original Deuteronomy would have been written with the intention of accompanying and legitimating the policy of Josiah.[368] However that may be, the reconstruction of an *Ur-Deuteronomium* remains an open question. Recently, Achenbach has analysed Deuteronomy 5–11. He has detected there an impressive number of Deuteronomistic, late Deuteronomistic and post-Deuteronomistic layers,[369] which he gives up even counting. In one sense, Achenbach confirms the quite common idea that the original introduction to the Deuteronomic law begins in Deut. 6.4-5, 10-13. But this text already belongs to the exilic period.[370] Finally, there is not, according to him, a pre-exilic introduction to the Deuteronomic Code in Deut. 12.2–26.15, the code that forms the essential nucleus of the primitive Deuteronomy.[371] Now, even within this Code, the exegetes discover more and more exilic texts.

7.5.1.2. *The Diachronic Works on the Law Code.* Numerous works have been devoted to the legislative collections from which the Deuteronomic code was born. Merendino, Seitz, L'Hour and others,[372]

Struktur, Intention und Funktion von Auffindungslegenden', *DBAT* 18 (1984), pp. 95-118.

368. Cf. for this opinion A.D.H. Mayes, *Deuteronomy* (NCB; Grand Rapids: Eerdmans; London: Morgan & Scott, 1981) pp. 102-103, and Reuter, *Kultzentralisation*, p. 258.

369. Achenbach, *Israel zwischen Verheissung und Gebot*. This author has recourse quite often to the *Numeruswechsel* criterion. According to him, the basic text, written in the singular, was reworked with a redaction in the plural before several new redactions in the singular would have taken place.

370. Achenbach thinks that Deut. 6.4-5, 10-13 is more recent than Josh. 24 and older than Josh. 23. See *Israel zwischen Verheissung und Gebot*, pp. 180-82.

371. A consensus in regard to the original Deuteronomy can only be hoped for in an eschatological perspective. Cf. the different reconstructions of Mayes, *Deuteronomy*, p. 48; Preuss, *Deuteronomium*, pp. 49-61; O. Kaiser, *Einleitung in das Alte Testament* (Gütersloh: Gerd Mohn, 1984), pp. 134-35.

372. R.P. Merendino, *Das deuteronomische Gesetz: Eine literarkritische, gattungs- und überlieferungsgeschichtliche Untersuchung zu Dtn 12–26* (BBB, 31; Bonn: P. Hansen, 1969); G. Seitz, *Redaktionsgeschichtliche Studien zum Deuteronomium* (BWANT, 93, Stuttgart: Kohlhammer, 1971); J. L'Hour, 'Une législation criminelle dans le Deutéronome', *Bib* 44 (1963), pp. 1-28; cf. as well G. Nebeling, 'Die Schichten des deuteronomischen Gesetzeskorpus: Eine traditions- und redaktionsgeschichtliche Analyse von Dtn 12–26' (Dissertation, Münster, 1970). The

postulated the existence of the following collections: the *tô'ebâ* ('ab-
horrent') laws (Deut. 16.21–17.1; 18.10-12a; 22.5; 23.18-19b; 25.13-
16); the *bi'artâ* ('purging') laws (13.2-6; 17.2-7; 19.16-19; 21.8-21;
22.13-21, 23-27; 24.7), the warfare laws (20; 21.10-14; 23.10-15;
25.17-19), the 'social laws' (15.22-24) and the laws on centralization
(12; 14.22-27; 15.19-23; 16.1-15; 17.8-13; 18.1-8; 26.1-11). Very
quickly, it becomes clear that some 'collections' (on centralization, war,
social issues) were closely connected to Deuteronomistic ideology,
which presents difficulties for the idea of a possible pre-Deuteronomic
origin. Even if the possibility of pre-Deuteronomic laws in Deut. 12.2–
26.15 cannot be excluded and remains fairly probable, today's research
is clearly more cautious with regard to the existence of ancient collections. We notice therefore a marked tendency to date certain parts of
the legislative material in the exilic period. Lohfink, Braulik and others
consider that the laws about those in authority (16.18–18.22) as well as
the collection in chs. 19–25 come from exilic and postexilic redactions,[373] which considerably reduces the dimensions of the book of
Josianic or pre-Josianic law. Most of the prescriptions contained in the
Deuteronomic code can therefore no longer be interpreted as concrete
legal measures—that would have had, at a certain point, 'force of
law'—but they are understood rather as theoretical and theological
postulates, describing the ideal Deuteronomistic society.[374] McBride
and Crüsemann[375] vigorously take issue with this view. For these
authors, the law of Deuteronomy is not utopian but reflects the political

existence of independent pre-Dtr collections has already been postulated by Steuernagel. For a history of the research cf. Preuss, *Deuteronomium*, pp. 103-48.

373. N. Lohfink, 'Die Sicherung der Wirksamkeit des Gotteswortes durch das
Prinzip der Schriftlichkeit der Tora und durch das Prinzip der Gewaltenteilung nach
den Ämtergesetzen des Buches Deuteronomium (Dt 16, 18–18, 22)', in H. Wolter
(ed.), *Testimonium Veritati* (Festschrift W. Kempf; Frankfurt: Knecht, 1971),
pp. 143-55 = *Studien zum Deuteronomium und zur deuteronomistischen Literatur*, I
(SBAB, 8; Stuttgart: Katholisches Bibelwerk, 1990), pp. 305-23; G. Braulik, *Die
deuteronomischen Gesetze und der Dekalog: Studien zum Aufbau von Deuteronomium 12–26* (SBS, 145; Stuttgart: Katholisches Bibelwerk, 1991). U. Rüterswörden
has a more qualified approach, *Von der politischen Gemeinschaft zur Gemeinde:
Studien zu Dt 16, 1–18, 22* (BBB, 65; Frankfurt: Athenäum, 1987).

374. This was a common interpretation of Deut. 12.2–26.15 at the beginning of
the twentieth century.

375. S. McBride, 'Polity of the Covenant People: The Book of Deuteronomy',
Int 41 (1987), pp. 229-44; Crüsemann, *Die Tora*.

constitution of the landowners who backed the Josianic reform. This debate brings to light a methodological problem affecting the interpretation of the legal texts of the Old Testament. Were they written to serve as a constitution or with a homiletical view? What are the criteria that make it possible to situate them in history?

7.5.1.3. *The Assyrian Influences.* It is Weinfeld[376] who, followed by many others, has brought out the influence of Assyrian treaties on the composition of Deuteronomy. Since then, the structure of Deuteronomy has often been described as being a copy of an Assyrian treaty, but that approach as well runs into serious objections and has given rise to criticisms.[377] On the one hand, almost all the known Assyrian treaties[378] have come down to us in fragmentary conditions, so that it is difficult to draw up a standard model for these texts. On the other hand, the structure proposed for Deuteronomy on the basis of this supposed model is quite superficial and presupposes the book in its Deuteronomistic and exilic form. The original Deuteronomy (6.4-9; 12-26*; 28-30* [?]) does not really display all the elements that we find in the Assyrian (or other) vassal treaties. But it is clear as well that significant convergences exist between Deuteronomy and the tradition of Near Eastern treaties; we easily recognize there some elements of the terminology proper to vassal treaties. The cursing formulas in Deut. 28.20-57, for example, have such pronounced affinities with the treaties of Esarhaddon[379] that there is necessarily a literary influence. We must therefore admit 'that treaty forms and vocabulary have influenced the form, vocabulary and the ideas of the book';[380] there is therefore an affinity about which it is

376. Weinfeld, *Deuteronomy and the Deuteronomic School*, pp. 59-157.

377. Cf. L. Perlitt, *Bundestheologie im Alten Testament* (WMANT, 36; Neukirchen–Vluyn: Neukirchener Verlag, 1969), in particular pp. 93-101.

378. We have at our disposal recent French and English translation of these treaties: S. Parpola and K. Watanabe, *Neo-Assyrian Treaties and Loyalty Oaths* (State Archives of Assyria, II; Helsinki: Helsinki University Press, 1988); J. Briend *et al.*, *Traités et serments dans le Proche-Orient Ancien* (Supplement au Cahier Evangile, 81; Paris: Cerf, 1992).

379. Cf. the synopsis of Preuss, *Deuteronomium*, pp. 72-73 and, in a detailed way, H.U. Steymans, *Deuteronomium 28 und die adê zur Thronfolgeregelung Asarhaddons: Segen und Fluch im Alten Orient und in Israel* (OBO, 145; Göttingen: Vandenhoeck & Ruprecht, 1995).

380. Mayes, *Deuteronomy*, p. 34.

consequently legitimate to analyse the ideological implications. If the Josianic or even exilic authors of Deuteronomy borrow their rhetoric and their ideology from Assyrian treaties and rethink the Yahwistic religion according to the model of a vassal treaty, they can only do it, as Lohfink has suggested, with a subversive intention:[381] the suzerain of Israel is not the king of Assyria or of Babylon, but Yhwh, the unique Lord of his people!

7.5.2. *The Book of Joshua*[382]

As we have recalled, it was in working on Joshua that Noth came to postulate the existence of DH, particularly after having taken note of the absence of the Pentateuchal sources in this book. The genesis of the book presented itself to him in a quite simple manner. Noth distinguished two parts (chs. 2–12 and 13–22), as well as a Deuteronomistic introduction and conclusion (1; 23[24]). The narrative part in chs. 2–12 was originally for him a Benjaminite collection of conquest accounts, etiological in nature, going back to the premonarchic period. These accounts were edited and adapted for a pan-Israelite perspective by a ninth-century *Sammler* (collector) who introduced Joshua as the principal hero. Four centuries later, the Deuteronomist went back to this collection and reworked it (for example, 8.30-35). Chapters 13–22, which contained documents of the premonarchic and Josianic periods, did not yet form part of the book but were introduced afterwards by an *Ergänzer* (supplementer), just like Joshua 24. The end of the Deuteronomistic edition of the book is found in 21.43-45; 22.1-6 and 23.

7.5.2.1. *The Accounts of the Conquest.*

Noth's theory on the formation of Joshua 2–12, still repeated in a good number of commentaries, is no longer the unanimous opinion. It is particularly the idea of a ninth-century collection (Josh. 2–8) that seems suspect. For Rose,[383] these

---

381. Cf. the stimulating article of Lohfink, 'Culture Shock and Theology'.
382. For more details, cf. B. Peckham, 'The Significance of the Book of Joshua in Noth's Theory of the Deuteronomistic History', in McKenzie and Graham (eds.), *The History of Israel's Traditions*, pp. 213-34; A.G. Auld, 'Reading Joshua After Kings', in J. Davies *et al.*, *Words Remembered, Texts Renewed: Essays in Honour of J.F.A. Sawyer* (JSOTSup, 195; Sheffield: Sheffield Academic Press, 1995), pp. 167-81; A.W.H. Curtis, *Joshua* (OTG; Sheffield: JSOT Press, 1994).
383. Rose, *Deuteronomist und Jahwist*.

accounts are explained much better in a context where the territory of Benjamin and of the North is threatened, which is the case after the fall of Samaria in 722. Ottoson, while admitting the utilization of ancient material, attributes the edition of these accounts to a Deuteronomist whom he situates in the Josianic period; the book of Joshua would be a programmatic writing in favour of the restoration of the Davidic dynasty under Josiah.[384] The Josianic dating of Joshua 2–12, that Lohfink and Knauf[385] defend as well, could be corroborated by its numerous parallels with the Assyrian conquest accounts, as has been brought to light by Younger.[386] In this context, we may cite too the commentary of Fritz replacing that of Noth in the HAT series.[387] Unlike Noth, Fritz considers the whole basic account of Joshua 1–12 as the work of the Deuteronomistic historian. DtrH would have had at his disposal some oral traditions, but only for the story of the spies (Josh. 2), the conquest of Ai (Josh. 8) and the end of the enemy kings at Makedah (Josh. 10). Fritz, however, leaves the question of the dating (Josianic or exilic) open. Van Seters,[388] for his part, comes out in favour of an exilic dating not only for the redaction but also for the nucleus of chs. 1–12: he actually regards these conquest accounts as an invention of an exilic Deuteronomist who would have been inspired by Assyrian and Babylonian accounts of conquest. As for Briend,[389] he goes back to Noth's tripartite model by carrying out a chronological displacement: the compiler is situated towards the end of the monarchy, while the Deuteronomistic redaction, characterized by 'a rhetoric of conquest', dates from the beginning of the postexilic period. The debate on the dating of these texts reveals some hesitation in regard to their primary purpose: is it a question of propaganda for Josianic expansionism or are we rather in

---

384. M. Ottoson, *Josuaboken: en programskrift för davidisk restauration* (Acta Universitatis Upsaliensis, I; Uppsala: Almqvist & Wiksell, 1991).

385. Lohfink, 'Kerygmata des deuteronomistischen Geschichtswerkes'; E.A. Knauf, *Die Umwelt des Alten Testaments* (NSK-AT, 29; Stuttgart: Katholisches Bibelwerk, 1994), p. 134.

386. K.L. Younger, *Ancient Conquest Accounts: A Study in Ancient Near Eastern and Biblical History Writing* (JSOTSup, 98; Sheffield: JSOT Press, 1990).

387. Fritz, *Das Buch Josua*.

388. Van Seters, *In Search of History*, pp. 324-31.

389. Cf. his contribution in this volume.

the presence of a parenesis destined for an audience demoralized and deprived of its country?

What is more, many authors insist on the literary complexity of these accounts. Floss finds in Joshua 2 a pre-Deuteronomistic layer, two Deuteronomistic layers and the interventions of a final redactor.[390] As for Joshua 6, we may discern there, according to Schwienhorst, an ancient account, a Jahwist redaction, then DtrH, DtrP, DtrN as well as various post-Deuteronomistic additions.[391] There doubtless too would have been numerous post-Deuteronomistic interventions in the rest of the book, particularly in the texts on the crossing of the Jordan (3–4) or in the account of the circumcision. According to Van Seters, in these latter texts, we would have a 'P',[392] which could signify in some way a return to the idea of a Hexateuch including the book of Joshua, the very idea that Noth had so vigorously contested! Fritz, on the other hand, describes the post-Deuteronomistic elements in these texts as 'various additions' and thus chooses to put up with a certain vagueness.

7.5.2.2. *The Lists.* The position of Noth, for whom the unit Joshua 13–22 did not form part of DH, raises a difficulty. The programmatic text of Joshua 1 (Deuteronomistic) actually sets forth a double programme for Joshua: conquest and distribution of the land. It seems logical therefore that DH would have included texts relating to the dividing up of the country, as Smend and Auld have emphasized.[393] It remains to be seen whether the Deuteronomist was content with 13.1-7 or integrated other material whose origin still has to be made clear.[394] A number of

390. J.P. Floss, *Kunden oder Kundschafter? Literaturwissenschaftliche Untersuchung zu Jos 2* (2 vols.; ATSAT 16 and 26; St. Ottilien: EOS, 1982 and 1986).

391. L. Schwienhorst, *Die Eroberung Jerichos: Exegetische Untersuchung zu Josua 6* (SBS, 122; Stuttgart: Katholisches Bibelwerk, 1986).

392. Van Seters, *In Search of History*, pp. 325-26.

393. Smend, 'Das Gesetz und die Völker', p. 97; A.G. Auld, *Joshua, Moses and the Land. Tetrateuch—Pentateuch—Hexateuch in a Generation since 1938* (Edinburgh: T. & T. Clark, 1980), pp. 52-71; cf. on the other hand M. Wust, *Untersuchungen zu den siedlungsgeographischen Texten des Alten Testaments. I. Ostjordanland* (Tübinger Atlas des Vorderen Orients, B, 9; Wiesbaden: Dr. Ludwig Reichert, 1975), pp. 213-15.

394. It is often said that lists like those of Josh. 14–22 do not invent themselves. This is possibly true, but that does not solve in any way the problem of their origin. Some authors think, following Noth, of documents going back to the pre-monarchic period, while others would see here various documents covering the period from

commentators, having observed that these documents appear in priestly garb (for example 14.1-5; 19.49-51), have gone back to attributing these texts to P (cf. among others, Mowinckel and recently Van Seters), a current option before Noth. Cortese has re-examined the question.[395] According to him, the Priestly redaction in Joshua 13–21 is later than P (P^S), but would have integrated older documents, among others an *Urdokument* of the Salomonic period that he even attributes to the 'J' source. Cortese actually tries to reactivate the idea of a Hexateuch, without wishing to question the thesis of a DH. But the question can be asked differently as well: if there really had been a Priestly intervention in Joshua—but not in the subsequent books of the DH—would that indicate that the Priestly school had wanted to separate Joshua from what followed? Or rather that Joshua was conceived first and that it had—in some circles at least, or in some periods—a circulation independent from that of the following books?

7.5.2.3. *The Problem of the Ending of the Book.* The book of Joshua comes to an end with two farewell discourses. For Noth, Joshua 23 belongs to the Deuteronomistic discourse, while Joshua 24, although pre-Deuteronomistic in origin, was added afterwards.[396] Joshua 24 was later considered an ancient text that would have preserved the memory of a pre-monarchic assembly at Shechem,[397] an opinion still recently defended by Koopmans.[398] However Joshua 24, in its present form,

David to Ezekiah. This is the opinion of Z. Kallai (Kleinmann), *Historical Geography of the Bible: The Tribal Territories of Israel* (Jerusalem: Magnes Press, 1986) (cf. as well the presentation of the different options in T. Butler, *Joshua* [WBC, 7; Waco, TX: Word Books, 1983], pp. 143-44). As for Fritz, he sees in these lists the reflection of 'administrative measures of the royal period, without it being possible to discern yet their causes and effects' (*Das Buch Josua*, p. 8).

395. E. Cortese, *Josua 13–21. Ein priesterschriftlicher Abschnitt im deuteronomistischen Geschichtswerk* (OBO, 94; Göttingen: Vandenhoeck & Ruprecht, 1990).

396. Cf. Noth, *Das Buch Josua*, p. 139; *ÜSt*, p. 9.

397. Cf. for example, G. Schmitt, *Der Landtag von Sichem* (Arbeiten zur Theologie I.15; Stuttgart: Calwer Verlag, 1964).

398. W.T. Koopmans, *Joshua 24 as Poetic Narrative* (JSOTSup, 93; Sheffield: JSOT Press, 1990). Koopmans offers a very complete history of the research on this chapter. He affirms that Josh. 24 'supports...the historical likelihood of the contention that Joshua held an assembly at Shechem to impress upon the Israelites the need to affirm exclusive allegiance to Yahweh' (p. 419).

contains numerous Deuteronomistic themes and terms, which has led
the school of Göttingen to attribute Joshua 24 to DtrH and ch. 23 to
DtrN.[399] But that solution comes up against the fact that Joshua 24
contains as well some non-Deuteronomistic elements (for example the
motif of the ancestors beyond the Euphrates and the priestly vocabulary, in vv. 3 and 4 among others).[400] Furthermore, a close parallel to
Joshua 24 is found in Nehemiah 9. It seems quite logical therefore to
attribute Joshua 24 to a post-Deuteronomistic author-redactor, as many
exegetes at present do.[401] The Deuteronomistic end of Joshua would be
found therefore in 23, while 24 (with Judg. 1.1–2.5) would be an
attempt to interrupt the Deuteronomistic thread (and, who knows, to
make Joshua 1–24 a separate book?).

7.5.3. *The Book of Judges*[402]

According to Noth, the Deuteronomist had two sources available to
construct an age of the Judges: a list of 'Minor Judges', and a collection
of heroic legends. Since Jephthah is the only individual to appear in
both documents, we understand that the Deuteronomist would have
taken the initiative to combine the two sources. It is he, therefore, who
in this way transformed into (judges) the charismatic heroes of the
heroic legends. The Deuteronomist introduced the period of the Judges
with the programmatic considerations of Judg. 2.6-23 and had the
ancient cycle preceded by the story of Othniel, a narrative created *ad
hoc*. For Noth, the Dtr edition of Judges only consisted of the corpus

399. Cf. Smend, 'Das Gesetz und die Völker', pp. 501-504.

400. Cf. too J. L'Hour, 'L'alliance de Sichem', *RB* 69 (1962), pp. 5-36.

401. J. Van Seters, 'Joshua 24 and the Problem of Tradition in the Old Testa-
ment', in W.B. Barrick and J.R. Spencer (eds.), *In the Shelter of Elyon: Essays on
Ancient Palestinian Life and Literature in Honor of G.W. Ahlström* (JSOTSup, 31;
Sheffield: JSOT Press, 1984), pp. 139-58; Blum, *Die Komposition der Väter-
geschichte*, p. 59; C. Levin, *Die Verheissung des neuen Bundes in ihrem theologie-
geschichtlichen Zusammenhang ausgelegt* (FRLANT, 137; Göttingen: Vandenhoeck
& Ruprecht, 1985), pp. 114-15; Römer, *Israels Väter*, pp. 320-30; U. Becker,
Richterzeit und Königtum: Redaktionsgeschichtliche Studien zum Richterbuch
(BZAW, 192; Berlin/New York: W. de Gruyter, 1990), pp. 69-70; M. Anbar, *Josué
et l'alliance de Sichem (Josué 24:1-28)* (BET, 25; Frankfurt: Peter Lang, 1992).

402. For more details, cf. R. Bartelmus, 'Forschung am Richterbuch seit Martin
Noth', *ThR* 56 (1991), pp. 221-59; M. O'Brien, 'Judges and the Deuteronomistic
History', in McKenzie and Graham (eds.), *The History of Israel's Traditions*,
pp. 235-59.

Judg. 2.6–13.1. Neither the Samson cycle nor the 'shocking chronicle' of chs. 17–21 formed part of it. This material, although ancient, was added later. Here once again, Noth continues to be extremely evasive about the circumstances that could have brought about these additions.

7.5.3.1. *W. Richter and the 'Book of Saviours'*. If we accept Noth's thesis on the formation of the book, it brings up the question of the Deuteronomist's access to the ancient and scattered material just mentioned. Is it not more logical to suppose an intermediate stage? That stage presents itself, according to Richter,[403] in the form of an Israelite 'Book of Saviours' (*Retterbuch*), a narrative cycle that dates from the period of Jehu (ninth century) and arises from a strongly anti-monarchical ideology. This book would have included the story of Ehud (3.15-26) the episode of Jael (4.17-22*), the accounts about Gideon (7.11b, 13-21; 8.5-9, 14-21a) and a conclusion in 9.56. It would have been filled out later by a first redactor especially interested in the theme of the 'war of Yhwh' (3.13, 27-29; 4.4a, 6-9, 11, 17b; 6.2b-5, 11b-17, 25-27a, 31b, 32-34; 7.1, 3-11a, 22-25; 8.3-4, 10-14, 22-23, 29, 31; 9.1-7, 16a, 19b-21, 23-24, 41-45, 56-57). Again, before its insertion into the DH, the Book of Saviours would have gone through two Deuteronomistic editions: RDt₁, responsible for the narrative outline (in 3.12, 14, 15a, 30; 4.1a, 2-3, 23-24; 5.31; 6.1-2a; 8.28), and RDt₂, author of the exemplary narrative of 3.7-11* placed as an opening to the book. It is all finally taken up again in the DH and completed, subsequently, by the post-Deuteronomistic additions. Unlike Noth, Richter thinks that Judges 13–16 formed part of DH. The Deuteronomist would have integrated the story of Samson in order to demonstrate, as he does too at the beginning of Samuel, that the institution of the Judges had to disappear because of the decadence into which it had eventually sunk.

Richter's thesis had enormous success and marginalized other attempts to retrace the pre-Deuteronomistic formation of Judges.[404] It is

403. W. Richter, *Traditionsgeschichtliche Untersuchungen zum Richterbuch* (BBB, 18; Bonn: Peter Hanstein, 1963); *idem, Die Bearbeitungen des 'Retterbuches' in der deuteronomischen Epoche* (BBB, 21; Bonn: Peter Hanstein, 1964).

404. For example, W. Beyerlin, 'Gattung und Herkunft des Rahmens im Richterbuch', in E. Würthwein and O. Kaiser (eds.), *Tradition und Situation: Studien zur alttestamentlichen Prophetie, A. Weiser zum 70. Geburtstag* (Göttingen: Vandenhoeck & Ruprecht, 1963), pp. 1-29; M. Weinfeld, 'The Period of the Conquest and of the Judges as Seen by the Earlier and Later Sources', *VT* 17 (1967), pp. 93-113.

adopted in many commentaries, monographs and introductions.[405] Nevertheless, for some time now, there has no longer been agreement about the idea of a Saviour Collection (*Retterbuch*). Thus, Van Seters rejects any possibility of reconstructing a pre-Deuteronomistic book of Judges.[406] The most extensive—and the most detailed—attack against the *Retterbuch* has been led by Becker[407] who finds no evidence in Judges of a pre-Deuteronomistic collection. According to him, the Deuteronomist would only have had at his disposal some scattered material: Ehud (3.16-26*), the Canticle of Deborah (5*), Gideon (6.11a*, 18-24a*; 7.11-16*, 16-22*; 8.5-21*), Abimelech (9.25-41, 50-54; 9.8-15a), a list of five judges (10.1-5; 12.8-15), Jephthah (11.1-11a), as well as a large part of the Samson cycle. This material would have been gathered together by the author of DH, to be completed by the post-Deuteronomistic redactors and by a redactor close to the milieu of the final redaction of the Pentateuch. Becker's position, also adopted by Lindars,[408] indicates a return to Noth, even a radicalization of the Nothian position. We seem to have come full circle, but the questions raised by Richter and others remain. In our opinion, the best argument for the existence, in one form or another, of a book or a *cycle* of pre-Deuteronomistic accounts remains the fact that all the episodes of Judges 3–12 are situated in the geographic horizon of the Northern Kingdom. What Judaean Deuteronomist, whether Josianic or exilic, would have accomplished the amazing feat of ignoring so completely

---

Weinfeld defends the old idea that J and E are found in Judges. R.G. Boling, *Judges* (AB, 6A; New York: Doubleday, 1975), postulated four stages: (1) composition of independent narrative units that are gathered together in an epic (when?); (2) an edition of a didactic collection of the eighth century; (3) incorporation in the DH in the Josianic period; (4) revision at the time of the exilic edition of DH.

405. For example, J.A. Soggin, *Le livre des Juges* (CAT, 5b; Geneva: Labor et Fides, 1987); J. Gray, *Joshua, Judges, Ruth* (NCBC; Grand Rapids: Eerdmans; Basingstoke: Marshall Morgan & Scott, 1986); Mayes, *The Story of Israel between Settlement and Exile*, pp. 58-80; *Judges*, pp. 20-27; O'Brien, *The Deuteronomistic History Hypothesis*, pp. 82-98; Smend, *Die Entstehung des Alten Testaments*, pp. 126-27; G. Fohrer, *Das Alte Testament*, I (3 vols.; Gütersloh: Gerd Mohn, 1980), pp. 94-95.

406. Van Seters, *In Search of History*, pp. 343-44.

407. Becker, *Richterzeit und Königtum*.

408. B. Lindars, *Judges 1–5. A New Translation and Commentary* (Edinburgh: T. & T. Clark, 1995), p. 174.

the familiar setting of the kingdom of Judah, if he was really the author of these accounts?

7.5.3.2. The Introduction in 1.1–2.5. There is quite a consensus on the fact that the Deuteronomistic edition of Judges begins with 2.6-10. The sequence of 1.1–2.5 would not have formed part of DH. Does this text contain ancient material preserving the historical memory of an aborted conquest, as has often been thought, following Noth (for example Cortese[409])? Van Seters attributes this section to 'P',[410] an opinion that goes against the research current in recent years. Younger compared Judges 1 with Assyrian inscriptions and found there the same formal structure and the same aesthetic criteria.[411] According to Auld, we have in this section a post-Deuteronomistic construction that would have attempted to correct the Deuteronomistic conquest-ideology and would perhaps be 'contemporaneous with the division of the long Deuteronomistic History into the now familiar separate book'.[412] Judges 1 remains one of those examples whose probably late literary form does not rule out a certain historical relevance (at least in regard to the late entry of cities into the Israelite orbit).

7.5.3.3. The Heroic Accounts. We cannot give a detailed account of the discussion concerning the different heroes of Judges 3–16. We will simply recall the most important points. The Canticle of *Deborah* has certainly caused the most ink to flow. Traditionally considered one of the oldest texts of the Old Testament, we meet today all sorts of dating, going from the twelfth century down to the fourth century BCE. Among the most recent authors, Bechmann has proposed dating it toward the end of the monarchy,[413] but Knauf has advanced an impressive series of arguments for maintaining a relatively ancient date for this poem: he

---

409. E. Cortese, 'Gios. 21 e Guid. 1 (TM o LXX?) e l' "abottonatura" del 'Tetrateuco" con l' "Opera Deuteronomistica" ', *RivB* 33 (1985), pp. 375-94.

410. Van Seters, *In Search of History*, pp. 337-40.

411. K.L. Younger, Jr, 'Judges 1 in its Near Eastern Literary Context', in A.R. Millard (ed.), *Faith, Tradition and History: Old Testament Historiography in its Near Eastern Context* (Winona Lake, IN: Eisenbrauns, 1994), pp. 207-27.

412. A.G. Auld, 'Judges 1 and History: A Reconsideration', *VT* 25 (1975), pp. 261-85 (285).

413. U. Bechmann, *Das Deboralied zwischen Geschichte und Fiktion: Eine exegetische Untersuchung zu Richter 5* (DiTh, 33; St. Ottilien: EOS, 1989), p. 212: '…perhaps under Josiah'.

puts the origin of Judges 5 in the tenth century, in the sphere of influence of Ishbaal.[414] It is therefore very probable that the Deuteronomist had access to this poem. It remains to be determined whether the account in prose was already attached to it. According to de Pury,[415] Judges 3; 4.17-22; 5.24-27 and 6.25-32 have in common the theme of the breaking of social taboos in the name of Yhwh. We would therefore have there a short collection stemming from anti-clan circles and bearers of an exclusivist Yahwism in the Northern kingdom.

The nucleus of the *Gideon* cycle is also considered to be pre-Deuteronomistic, and Auld's thesis for whom the whole of Judges 6–8 is a post-Deuteronomistic composition from the Persian period[416] is not likely to be followed very much.[417] Nevertheless, there is no consensus on the extent of the pre-Deuteronomistic version;[418] did this come from circles hostile to the monarchy as has often been maintained?

Jephthah was the key personage for Noth in the formation of the book. According to Richter,[419] the story of Jephthah did not form part of the initial 'Book of Saviours' (*Retterbuch*), and the different traditions on this ambiguous personage were gathered together by a redactor (*Bearbeiter*) who was a contemporary of the 'Elohist' (eighth–seventh centuries) and were added to the 'Book of Saviours'. The Deuteronomist would have integrated 10.17–12.6 into his work while providing 10.1-16 and 12.7-15 as a framework. Becker on the other hand considers the story of the sacrifice in 11.30-31, 34-40 as post-Deuteronomistic.[420]

414. E.A. Knauf, in a study to appear; cf. meanwhile *idem, Die Umwelt des Alten Testaments*, pp. 229-30. Cf. as well H.-D. Neef, 'Der Stil des Deboraliedes (Ri 5)', *ZAH* 8 (1995), pp. 275-93, who proposes a date about 1025 BCE.

415. A. de Pury, 'Le raid de Gédéon (Juges 6, 25-32) et l'histoire de l'exclusivisme yahwiste', in T. Römer (éd.), *Lectio difficilior probabilior? Mélanges offerts à Françoise Smyth-Florentin* (BDBAT, 12, Heidelberg: Wiss.-theol. Seminar, 1991), pp. 173-205.

416. A.G. Auld, 'Gideon: Hacking at the Heart of the Old Testament', *VT* 39 (1989), pp. 257-67.

417. Cf. for example the critical comments of de Pury, 'Le raid de Gédéon', p. 182-83 n. 27.

418. The accounts of Gideon's vocation and the destruction of the altar of Baal are especially discussed.

419. W. Richter, 'Die Überlieferungen um Jephtha. Ri 10, 17–12, 6', *Bib* 47 (1966), pp. 485-556.

420. Becker, *Richterzeit und Königtum*, p. 221.

The *Samson* cycle certainly underwent an independent transmission before being inserted—by a Deuteronomist or a later editor—into the book of Judges. What explanation can be given for the parallels with the Hercules traditions as pointed out by Bartelmus and others?[421] Must it be concluded that Judges 13–16 would be a Hellenistic composition? It is conceivable too that Hercules and Samson both go back to a common mythical background from the end of the second millennium.

7.5.3.4. The List of 10.1-5 and 12.7-15. There is no doubt that the names of the 'Minor Judges' in Judg. 10.1-5 and 12.7-15 go back originally to a single list. But where does it come from? Is it really a vestige of the pre-monarchic period and what was its function?[422] Noth[423] saw in the 'Minor Judges' magistrates or government officials of the Israelite tribal league, but this interpretation is linked up with another hypothesis of Noth, today abandoned, that of the amphictyony. Today, it is not clear what to do with these individuals. Lemche thinks that 'the names appearing in these lists do not belong to historical personalities but refer to some unknown (to us) ancestors' who were probably venerated round their tombs.[424] Görg even speaks of a 'fictitious and post-Deuteronomistic tendency' and he considers that we are in the presence of names invented by an author who wanted to stress the duration of the institution.[425]

7.5.3.5. The Appendix in 17–21. These chapters seem to legitimize the monarchy by presenting the period of the Judges as totally abominable. Notwithstanding Noth, Smend's disciples attributed these texts to DtrH

421. R. Bartelmus, *Heroentum in Israel und seiner Umwelt: Eine traditionsgeschichtliche Untersuchung zu Gen. 6, 1-4 und verwandten Texten im Alten Testament und in der altorientalischen Literatur* (ATANT, 65; Zürich: Theologischer Verlag, 1979); O. Margalith, 'The Legends of Samson/Heracles', *VT* 37 (1987), pp. 63-70; C. Nauerth, 'Samsons Taten—motivgeschichtlich untersucht', *DBAT* 21 (1985), pp. 94-120.

422. For the various opinions, cf. H.N. Rösel, 'Die "Richter Israels": Rückblick und neuer Ansatz', *BZNF* 25 (1981), pp. 180-203.

423. M. Noth, 'Das Amt des "Richters Israels" ', in W. Baumgartner *et al.* (eds.), *Festschrift Alfred Bertholet* (Tübingen: J.C.B. Mohr, 1950), pp. 404-17 = *Ges. Studien zum A.T. I* (TB, 39; Munich: Kaiser, 1969), pp. 71-85.

424. N.P. Lemche, 'The Judges—Once More', *BN* 20 (1983), pp. 47-55 (54).

425. M. Görg, *Richter* (NEB, 31; Würzburg: Echter Verlag, 1993), p. 6; cf. as well pp. 59 and 70-71.

(which they consider pro-monarchic since they attribute the anti-monarchic passages to DtrN).[426] There is actually little Dtr terminology in these chapters; and their 'archaic' character has often been referred to by those who see in them ancient traditions. Their historical content is discussed as well. Niemann,[427] for example, thinks that it is possible, on the basis of Judges 17–18, to reconstruct the history of the migration of the Danites in the twelfth century. Dohmen and Amit[428] see in these chapters instead a polemic against the sanctuaries of Bethel and Dan: this polemic could date from the seventh century (Amit), but it is also in conformity with the spirit of the Deuteronomists (Dohmen). This account, which makes Dan an anti-sanctuary, actually presupposes the Dtr ideology of the cult centralization, for which reason Görg considers Judges 17–18 a late Dtr work.[429]

Judges 19 is a defence of the monarchy, as is shown by Jüngling[430] who proposes at the same time, but perhaps less convincingly, to date it to the period of David. He thus separates Judges 19 from chs. 20–21 that would themselves be Deuteronomistic.[431] Judges 19–21 can be read as a caricature of the prehistory of Israel,[432] but is this caricature directed at the anarchy that preceded the monarchy—in the sense of 19.1; 21.25—or is it being ironical about what happens when a central power tries to impose its law in the villages?

Judges 17–21 interrupts the continuity of DH and in this way occupies a position analogous to that of the appendix of 2 Samuel 21–24 at the end of the books of Samuel. So Noth was probably right to exclude

426. Cf. among others Veijola, *Das Königtum in der Beurteilung der deuteronomistischen Historiographie*, passim.

427. H.M. Niemann, *Die Daniten: Studien zur Geschichte eines altisraelitischen Stammes* (FRLANT, 135; Göttingen: Vandenhoeck & Ruprecht, 1985).

428. C. Dohmen, 'Das Heiligtum von Dan: Aspekte religionsgeschichtlicher Darstellung im deuteronomistischen Geschichtswerk', *BN* 17 (1982), pp. 17-22; Y. Amit, 'Hidden Polemic in the Conquest of Dan: Judges xvii-xviii', *VT* 40 (1990), pp. 4-20.

429. Görg, *Richter*, p. 90.

430. H.W. Jüngling, *Richter 19—ein Plädoyer für das Königtum: Stilkritische Analyse der Tendenzerzählung Ri 19,1-30a; 21,25* (AnBib, 84; Rome: Pontifical Biblical Institute Press, 1981).

431. Cf. the critical remarks of Bartelmus, 'Forschung am Richterbuch seit Martin Noth', p. 252 and Preuss, 'DtrG', p. 261.

432. Cf. H. Specht, 'Die Abraham-Lot-Erzählung' (Dissertation; Munich, 1983), p. 152.

Judges 17–21 from the first edition of DH, but that does not prejudge in any way the origin of these accounts.

7.5.4. *The Books of Samuel.*[433]

1–2 Samuel are the books in DH in which the Dtr redaction is least perceptible. For Noth and the majority of exegetes, this indicates that the Deuteronomist had available already written documents that were taken over in his work just as they were.

7.5.4.1. *The Traditions about Samuel and the History of the Ark.* The history of the traditions about Samuel arose according to Mommer[434] in the following way: We can first of all isolate a brief cycle: chs. 1–4* and 7* recounting the youth and the career of Samuel;[435] this account was produced in the ninth/eighth centuries in prophetic circles. Briend is sceptical of such an early date: according to him the primitive account of chs. 1–3 is 'relatively late' and 'presupposes the prophetic experience of the prophets of the 8th century... We can at best date the text to the end of the 8th century'.[436] On the other hand there is a certain unanimity in regard to the unobtrusiveness of the Deuteronomistic

433. For more details, cf. P.K. McCarter, Jr, 'The Books of Samuel', in McKenzie and Graham, *The History of Israel's Traditions*, pp. 260-80; W. Dietrich and T. Naumann, *Die Samuelbücher* (EdF, 287; Darmstadt: Wissenschaftliche Buchgesellschaft, 1995).

434. P. Mommer, *Samuel: Geschichte und Überlieferung* (WMANT, 63; Neukirchen–Vluyn: Neukirchener Verlag, 1991).

435. This cycle would have had a prehistory too (cf. Mommer, *Samuel*, pp. 13-15). Mommer sets apart the accounts on the youth of Samuel, 1.1-3a, 4-28; 2.19-21a; 3, from an anti-Shiloh account, 1.3b; 2.12-17, 22-25; cf. in the same sense W. Dietrich, *David, Saul und die Propheten: Das Verhältnis von Religion und Politik nach den prophetischen Überlieferungen vom frühesten Königtum in Israel* (BWANT, 122; Stuttgart: Kohlhammer, 1987), pp. 11-13. We cannot summarize the discussion on the Canticle of Anna. P. Mathys considers this text as a post-Deuteronomistic insertion composed *ad hoc* for its present context (*Dichter und Beter: Theologen aus spätalttestamentlicher Zeit* [OBO, 132; Göttingen: Vandenhoeck & Ruprecht, 1994], pp. 126-28); cf. also R.J. Tournay, 'Le cantique d'Anne: I Samuel II. 1-10', in P. Cassetti *et al.*, *Mélanges Dominique Barthélemy: Etudes bibliques offertes à l'occasion de son 60e anniversaire* (OBO, 38; Göttingen: Vandenhoeck & Ruprecht, 1981), pp. 554-76.

436. J. Briend, *Dieu dans l'Ecriture* (LD, 150; Paris: Cerf, 1992), pp. 51-68 (66). This important study is overlooked in the *Erträge der Forschung* of Dietrich and Naumann (*Die Samuelbücher*).

redaction of this collection, a presence perceptible nevertheless in 2.27-36.[437]

The story of the Ark in 1 Samuel 4–6 and 2 Samuel 6 is traditionally considered an independent document since Samuel's name does not appear. But to the extent that 1 Samuel 4 presupposes the preceding episodes, it is definitely necessary to raise the problem of the beginning of that story. So Miller and Roberts as well as Dietrich imagine the beginning of the story of the Ark in 1 Sam. 1.3b; 2.12-16. 22-25.[438] The dating is a subject of discussion too. According to Schicklberger, it is necessary to think of the end of the eighth century,[439] the story of the ark presupposing at the same time classical prophecy and the Exodus epic. Smelik places the account in the sixth century and sees in it a parable of the Babylonian exile.[440] This might have been the function of the Ark story within DH, but was that its first function?[441] We may note too that Gordon expresses doubts about the original independence of this theme.[442]

7.5.4.2. *Saul and the Birth of the Monarchy.* Due to the influence of Wellhausen and Noth, the pro-monarchic texts in 1 Samuel 8–12 were generally held to be 'ancient', while the critical texts were attributed to the Deuteronomist. Veijola has transferred the tension between the partisans and opponents of the monarchy in 1 Samuel 8–12 to the very interior of the Deuteronomistic school: the texts favourable to the monarchy he attributes to DtrG, and the critical passages, to DtrN![443] This solution to the problem is not unanimously accepted, even by members

437. Cf. Veijola, *Die ewige Dynastie*, pp. 35-36; Römer, *Israels Väter*, pp. 277-79.

438. P.D. Miller and J.J.M. Roberts, *The Hand of the Lord: A Reassessment of the 'Ark Narrative' of I Samuel* (Baltimore: The Johns Hopkins University Press, 1977); Dietrich, *David, Saul und die Propheten*, pp. 78-80.

439. F. Schicklberger, *Die Ladeerzählungen des ersten Samuelbuches: Eine literaturwissenschaftliche und theologiegeschichtliche Untersuchung* (FzB, 7; Würzburg: Echter Verlag, 1973).

440. K.A.D. Smelik, 'The Ark Narrative Reconsidered', in A.S. van der Woude (ed.), *New Avenues in the Study of the Old Testament* (OTS, 25; Leiden: E.J. Brill, 1989), pp. 128-44. Cf. before that G.W. Ahlström, 'The Travels of the Ark: A Religio-Political Composition', *JNES* 43 (1984), pp. 141-49.

441. Cf. the remarks of Dietrich and Naumann, *Die Samuelbücher*, p. 138.

442. Gordon, *Samuel*, p. 33.

443. Cf. §5.2, esp. p. 66.

of the Göttingen school. Thus Dietrich and Mommer think that they can find in 1 Samuel 7–8; 10.17-27, even in 12, some pre-Deuteronomistic texts that would have formed part of the story of Samuel and of Saul, originating in the Northern Kingdom.[444] However, authors such as McCarter or Campbell,[445] who find in 1 Samuel 'prophetic records' dating from the ninth century, are of the opinion that the anti-monarchic material is better explained in an exilic context. That opinion is shared by McKenzie.[446]

The accounts of the tragic reign of Saul produce the same variety in the assessments. There are those who remain fairly optimistic about the possibility of recognizing, behind the present text, an ancient framework favourable to Saul, an account that was later revised by the supporters of David.[447] And there are those who would only see, behind the memories of the tragic figure of the first king of Israel, a late composition.[448]

7.5.4.3. *The Rise of David.* As we have seen, Rost considered the whole of 1 Samuel 16–2 Samuel 5 as an independent and very ancient historiographical work. Noth sided with this thesis: for him the Deuteronomist had reproduced this ancient story practically just as it is. The difficulty is that the beginning and end of this narrative are not clearly indicated; in addition, the literary unity of the story is perhaps not as incontestable as Rost thought.[449] Van der Lingen,[450] for example, recognized two distinct documents within this collection: a document A that he considered a piece of Davidic propaganda (1 Sam. 17–19*; 23–25; 27; 29–30; 2 Sam. 1–5*) and a document B from the North aimed at explaining the inexplicable destiny of Saul (1 Sam. 11–14*; 16–22*; 26; 28; 31). These two documents would have been combined by a Judaean redactor (R[II]) who, at the same time, made of Saul an

444. Dietrich, *David, Saul und die Propheten*; P. Mommer, *Samuel*.

445. P.K. McCarter, Jr, *1 Samuel* (AB, 8; Garden City, NY: Doubleday, 1980); A.F. Campbell, *Of Prophets and Kings: A Ninth-Century Document (1 Samuel 1–2 Kings 10)* (CBQMS, 17; Washington: Catholic Biblical Association, 1986).

446. Cf. his contribution to this volume.

447. Cf. Dietrich, *David, Saul und die Propheten*; Mommer, *Samuel*.

448. Foresti, *The Rejection of Saul*; F. Stolz, *Das erste und zweite Buch Samuel* (ZBK.AT, 9; Zürich: Theologischer Verlag, 1981), pp. 99-100.

449. For more details, cf. Dietrich and Naumann, *Die Samuelbücher*, pp. 66-70.

450. A. Van der Lingen, *David en Saul in I Samuel 16–II Samuel 5: Verhalen in politik en religie* (Haag: Boekencentrum, 1983).

incompetent and wicked king. A post-Deuteronomistic redactor (R[III])
would have accentuated the theological interpretations. For Kaiser, who
revives an idea of Wellhausen, there is at the root of 1 Samuel 16–
2 Samuel 5 a primitive account that dates from the end of the tenth or
from the ninth century.[451] There follows a first redaction, still pre-
Deuteronomistic, after the fall of Samaria, then the integration of the
whole into DH. We note therefore a certain unanimity regarding the
relatively early age of the first setting of this story. There are still two
questions remaining: is it simply a matter of a piece of pro-Davidic
propaganda, and what part of the present form of this text comes from
the Deuteronomists?

7.5.4.4. *The Succession of David.*[452] The relative unanimity concerning
the story of the rise of David disappears when we turn our attention to
the so-called history of the succession of David. According to Rost, this
collection is made up of 2 Sam. 6.16, 20-23; 7.11b, 16; 9–20 and
1 Kings 1–2. Here again, the first question concerns the beginning and
end of the work, especially the beginning. No chapter gives a satisfactory introduction to this collection that could be presumed to be independent of its present context. In that case, must we conclude that the
original incipit has been lost[453] or altered at the time of the insertion of
the collection into DH? Another problem is that of the ideology of the
story of the succession: for or against David? For or against Solomon?
Or then: for David and against Solomon? Or against the monarchy as an
institution? Is it a matter of a 'historiography' or of a novelistic epic?
Some resort to a diachronic model to account for the multiplicity of
aspects. Thus McCarter[454] supposes a conglomerate of several documents (revolt of Absolom, the story of the Gabaonites, etc.) that would
have been gathered together in the Salomonic period, then revised on
three occasions (prophetic redaction, Dtr[1], Dtr[2]). For Langlamet,[455] the

---

451. O. Kaiser, 'David und Jonathan: Tradition, Redaktion und Geschichte in
I Sam. 16–20. Ein Versuch', *ETL* 66 (1990), pp. 281-96.

452. See now: A. de Pury and T. Römer, *Die sogenannte Thronfolgegeschichte
Davids: Neue Einsichten und Anfragen* (OBO, 176; Freiburg: Universitätsverlag;
Göttingen: Vandenhoeck & Ruprecht, 2000).

453. Already J. Wellhausen, 'Der Anfang ist nicht erhalten', *Die Composition
des Hexateuchs und der historischen Bücher des Alten Testaments*, p. 256.

454. McCarter, Jr, *I Samuel*.

455. Langlamet has developed his hypothesis in numerous articles that appeared
between 1976 and 1984 in *RB*. Cf. among others 'Pour ou contre Salomon? La

kernel of the collection is found in a story of Absalom. That story was integrated in the first history of the succession ('S1': 2 Sam. 10–12*; 13–14* (?); 15–20*; 1 Kgs 1–2.35). It is hostile to the usurpation of the throne by Solomon and was edited even during the latter's reign. The same author composed, some years later, a second history of the succession ('S2'), to reinforce the negative image of Solomon. Next comes 'S3', from the hand of a Jerusalem priest, who, for his part, attempts in the seventh century a theological legitimation of Solomon, builder of the Temple. The opposition manifesto becomes a piece of royal propaganda! The collection is later lightly retouched by Dtr redactors. The works of Würthwein and Veijola seem to confirm that the first version of the history of the succession gives a very negative image of David and Solomon. All the texts legitimating the Davidic dynasty would have to be considered Dtr creations. But when must this first version be dated? In the same period as the supposed events? This thesis is being contested more and more. Thus Gunn, following Whybray, Ackroyd and others,[456] considers 2 Samuel 7–21 not as historiography but as a romance, 'a story told for the purpose of serious entertainment',[457] written centuries after the birth of the Israelite monarchy, and resembling in some way the royal histories of Shakespeare. Kaiser thinks of a redaction between the end of the eighth and the sixth century.[458]

It is most probably Van Seters who has attempted to shake up most radically the traditional view of things. For him, it is simply impossible that the Deuteronomist, who made use of David, in Kings, as the model for the evaluation of all his successors, could report stories so little flattering of David as that, for example, of the murder of Uriah. He deduces from this that the Court History of David (2 Samuel 2–4; 9–20; 1 Kings 1–2) must be a post-Deuteronomistic insertion that never had an independent existence, and he estimates that this history could not

rédaction prosalomonienne de IRois I–II', *RB* 83 (1976), pp. 321-79, 481-528; 'David, fils de Jessé: Une édition prédeutéronomiste de l'Histoire de la succession', *RB* 89 (1982), pp. 5-47.

456. R.N. Whybray, *The Succession Narrative: A Study of II Samuel 9–20; I Kings 1 and 2* (SBT, 2.9; London: SCM Press, 1968); P.R. Ackroyd, 'The Succession Narrative (so-called)', *Int* 35 (1981), pp. 383-96; O. Eissfeldt, *Einleitung in das Alte Testament*, p. 187.

457. D.M. Gunn, *The Story of King David: Genre and Interpretation* (JSOTSup, 6; Sheffield: JSOT Press, 1978), p. 62.

458. O. Kaiser, 'Beobachtungen zur sogenannten Thronnachfolgeerzählung', *ETL* 64 (1988), pp. 5-20.

have been written before 550, all the more so since 'the events may all be imaginary'.[459] This 'court history' would have been inserted into DH in order to counter any royal ideology and, at the end of the exile, the first messianic tendencies that might crystallize round the figure of David. For Van Seters, DH went directly from 2 Samuel 8 (with a note about the birth of Solomon?) to 1 Kgs 2.1-4, 10-12, 46b. This hypothesis of Van Seters, appealing because of its radicality and efficacy—it resolves the problem of coherence by doing away with the contentious texts!—raises just as many grave difficulties, and has been met with much scepticism.

7.5.5. *The Books of Kings*[460]

According to Noth, the Deuteronomist had available several sources for recording the history of Solomon[461] and that of the two kingdoms: particularly royal annals, various lists, as well as traditional accounts, such as those of Elijah and Elisha, and so on. In his commentary on 1 Kings 1–16, which appeared in 1968,[462] Noth makes clear that the link between the history of the succession and the history of Solomon already existed before the intervention of the Deuteronomist. The latter nevertheless remains for him the real creator of the book(s) of Kings, using his sources selectively and with great freedom. It is the Deuteronomist who, according to Noth, created the framework that introduces and concludes each reign and as a result gives its structure to the book. Many exegetes have attempted, however, to give more weight to the sources.

7.5.5.1. *The Reign of Solomon.* Görg has interpreted the history of Solomon according to the Egyptian model of 'royal short stories' (*Königsnovelle*).[463] The primitive account in 1 Kings 3–11 could be quite old,

459. Van Seters, *In Search of History*, p. 287.
460. Cf. too S.L. McKenzie, 'The Books of Kings in the Deuteronomistic History', in McKenzie and Graham (eds.), *The History of Israel's Traditions*, pp. 281-307 and E. Noort, 'Omgaan met Koningen: Tendenzen in de Exegetische Literatur', *GThT* 88 (1988), pp. 66-81.
461. We may recall that Noth, following Rost, considers 1 Kgs 1–2 as the conclusion of the history of the Davidic succession.
462. M. Noth, *I Könige 1–16* (BK, 9.1; Neukirchen–Vluyn: Neukirchener Verlag, 1968).
463. M. Görg, *Gott-König-Reden in Israel und Ägypten* (BWANT, 105; Stuttgart: Kohlhammer, 1975).

written to glorify the reign of Solomon. Helen Kenik supports the idea of a pre-Deuteronomistic *Königsnovelle*; she envisages as well oral traditions that would have been available to the Deuteronomist, but insists, however, on the importance of the Dtr redaction. For her, 1 Kgs 3.4-15, an account in which many researchers find a pre-Dtr kernel, was entirely composed by the Deuteronomist to prepare for the accounts of the two exemplary kings, Hezekiah and Josiah.[464] Wälchli as well thinks of the possibility to reconstruct a pre-Deuteronomistic history of Solomon, put into writing in the period of Hezekiah.[465] It is difficult therefore to use 1 Kings 3–11 for the historical reconstruction of the reign of Solomon. Likewise, Knauf insists on the fact that the description of the Solomonic empire is modeled on that of Assyria.[466] The precise reconstruction of an eventual pre-Deuteronomistic Solomonian history turns out to be a difficult undertaking.

7.5.5.2. *The Accounts of the Reigns from Solomon to Josiah.* In the context of this study, it is impossible to discuss the sources for each reign. It is commonly admitted that the Deuteronomist would have made use of annals about these reigns, but there is debate over his fidelity to his sources. We will make do here with the mention of a few accounts of exemplary reigns.

Great confidence in literary criticism enables Minokami[467] to reconstruct almost to the half-verse, the primitive version on Jehu's reign: 2 Kgs 9.1-6*, 10b-12bα, 13, 16aα, 17-21bα*, 22abα, 23a, 24, 30, 35; 10.1bαβ*, 2-3, 7-9, 12a*. This account, contemporaneous with the events, would have been written to justify Jehu's coup. But this coup

464. H.A. Kenik, *Design for Kingship: The Deuteronomistic Narrative Technique in 1 Kings 3:4-15* (SBLDS, 69; Chico, CA: Scholars Press, 1983); cf. as well D.M. Carr, *From D to Q: A Study of Early Jewish Interpretations of Solomon's Dream at Gibeon* (SBLMS, 44; Atlanta: Scholars Press, 1991); R.E. Clements, 'Solomon and the Origins of Wisdom in Israel', *PRSt* 15 (1988), pp. 23-35.

465. S.H. Wälchli, *Der weise König Salomo: Eine Studie zu den Erzählungen von der Weisheit Salomos in ihrem alttestamentlichen und altorientalischen Kontext* (BWANT, 141; Stuttgart: Kohlhammer, 1999).

466. E.A. Knauf, 'Das zehnte Jahrhundert: Ein Kapitel Vorgeschichte Israels', in *Heidel-Berger-Apokryphen* (Festschrift K. Berger; Heidelberg: Carl Winter, 1990), pp. 156-61.

467. Y. Minokami, *Die Revolution des Jehu* (GTA, 38; Göttingen: Vandenhoeck & Ruprecht, 1989); for a summary in French, cf. the review of T. Römer in *ETR* 65 (1990), pp. 435-36.

did not have religious, anti-Baal motivations: this vision of events is the work of many Dtr and post-Dtr redactions that Minokami tries hard to delimit. His reconstruction seems to be somewhat arbitrary, as is shown in the analysis of Barré, for whom the basic account already demanded the exclusive veneration of Yhwh.[468]

We see similar hesitation about the reign and fall of Athaliah, 2 Kings 11–12.[469] While authors such as Timm have some confidence in the historicity of the the sources used by the Deuteronomist, Levin sees in 2 Kings 11–12 a radical reinterpretation of the facts due to Dtr and post-Dtr redactors.[470]

2 Kings 18–20, the account of the reign of Hezekiah, has been extensively analyzed and commented on.[471] Following Stade,[472] three pre-Dtr sources are distinguished: some annals and two accounts of the liberation of Jerusalem: B_1 (18.17-19, 9a, 36-37*) and B_2 (19.9b-36*). This distribution is met in Gonçalves, Spieckermann and Camp.[473] For these authors, 18.13b-16 contains a reliable account of Sennacherib's expedition. As for the reference to Hezekiah's reform, Camp considers it first of all a construction of various Dtr redactors. The ancient sources (18.4, 7-8*; 20.12a, 13) show that it would amount to some symbolic actions of an anti-Assyrian character. The classical dating of the three sources of 2 Kings 18–20 has been abandoned by Hardmeier and Ruprecht. For them, the first version would have been written in 588, on the

468. L.M. Barré, *The Rhetoric of Political Persuasion: The Narrative Artistry and Political Intentions of 2 Kings 9–11* (CBQMS, 20; Washington: Catholic Biblical Association, 1988).

469. Cf. L.S. Schearing, 'Models, Monarchs and Misconceptions: Athalia and Joash of Judah' (PhD dissertation, Emory University, 1992).

470. S. Timm, *Die Dynastie Omri: Quellen und Untersuchungen zur Geschichte Israels im 9. Jahrhundert vor Christus* (FRLANT, 124; Göttingen: Vandenhoeck & Ruprecht, 1982); C. Levin, *Der Sturz der Königin Atalja: Ein Kapitel zur Geschichte Judas im 9. Jahrundert v. Chr.* (SBS, 105; Stuttgart: Katholisches Bibelwerk, 1982).

471. Preuss, 'DtrG', p. 380, thinks that these chapters occupy a key position in the present debate on DH.

472. B. Stade, 'Anmerkungen zu 2 Kö. 15–21', *ZAW* 6 (1886), pp. 156-89.

473. F.C. Gonçalves, *L'expédition de Sennachérib en Palestine dans la littérature hébraïque ancienne* (EBib NS, 7; Louvain-la-Neuve: Institut orientaliste de l'Université catholique de Louvain, 1986); Spieckermann, *Juda unter Assur in der Sargonidenzeit*; L. Camp, *Hiskija und Hiskijabild: Analyse und Interpretation von 2 Kön 18–20* (MTA, 9: Altenberge: Telos, 1990).

eve of the fall of Jerusalem. The author would have recounted the events of 701 in order to encourage its addressees, in despair because of the Babylonian threat.[474] This account (according to Ruprecht: 2 Kgs 18.13, 17-19.9a, 36-37 + 20.1-18) would have circulated independently at first before being integrated into DH. Ruprecht envisages as well some additions in the postexilic period. If this new approach were to prevail, it would mean that the first account on Hezekiah would be more or less contemporaneous with the beginning of the Dtr school.

The interpretation of the account of the reign of Josiah varies according to the dating of the first edition of DH.[475] If the latter is situated in the Josianic period, 2 Kings 22–23 is due to the Deuteronomists and constitutes the conclusion of their work; if an exilic date for DH is maintained, the question of a pre-Dtr source for 2 Kings 22–23 must be considered. It is impossible to summarize the countless studies devoted to this subject.[476] Numerous authors find written sources in 2 Kings 22–23 from the time of Josiah.[477] Thus, Lohfink finds at the base of this text a 'short historical account' (*historische Kurzgeschichte*), comparable to Jeremiah 26 and 36, that preserved reliable historical information.[478]

---

474. C. Hardmeier, *Prophetie im Streit vor dem Untergang Judas. Erzählkommunikative Studien zur Entstehungssituation der Jesaja- und Jeremiaerzählungen in II Reg 18–20 und Jer 37–40* (BZAW, 187; Berlin: W. de Gruyter, 1990); E. Ruprecht, 'Die ursprüngliche Komposition der Hiskia-Jesaja-Erzählungen und ihre Umstrukturierung durch den Verfasser des deuteronomistischen Geschichtswerkes', *ZTK* 87 (1990), pp. 33-66.

475. For further details, cf. above §5.

476. For a recent bibliography, cf. Preuss, 'DtrG', p. 246-50 and McKenzie, 'The Book of Kings in the Deuteronomistic History', pp. 294-95 nn. 2 and 3. We can add to this: H. Niehr, 'Die Reform des Joschija: Methodische, historische und religionsgeschichtliche Aspekte', in Gross (ed.), *Jeremia und die 'deuteronomistische Bewegung'*, pp. 33-54; C. Uehlinger, 'Gab es eine joschijanische Kultreform? Plädoyer für ein begründetes Minimum', in W. Gross (ed.), *Jeremia und die 'deuteronomistische Bewegung'*, pp. 57-89; G.G. Dever, 'The Silence of the Text: An Archaeological Commentary on 2 Kings 23', in M.D. Coogan *et al.* (eds.), *Scripture and Other Artifacts: Essays in Honor of Philip J. King* (Louisville, KY: Westminster / John Knox Press, 1994), pp. 143-68; Eynikel, *The Reform of King Josiah and the Composition of the Deuteronomistic History*.

477. For example, W. Dietrich, 'Josia und das Gesetzbuch (2 Reg. xxxii)', *VT* 27 (1977), pp. 13-35; M. Rose, 'Bemerkungen zum historischen Fundament des Josia-Bildes in II Reg', *ZAW* 89 (1977), pp. 50-63.

478. N. Lohfink, 'The Cult Reform of Josiah of Judah: 2 Kings 22–23 as a Source for the History of Israelite Religion', in P.D. Miller *et al.* (eds.), *Ancient*

However, many exegetes have emphasized the 'ideal' and constructed character of the account of the Josianic reform.[479] Thus, the motif of the discovered book is a widespread literary motif in the ancient Near East.[480] We have first of all then in 2 Kings 22–23 the 'origin story' of the Deuteronomistic movement,[481] which necessitates great prudence in utilizing this text for a reconstruction of the historical reign of Josiah.

7.5.5.3. *The Prophetic Accounts.* Following Noth, the accounts about Elijah and Elisha in particular were considered to be traditional material integrated by the Deuteronomist into his work. Thus, A. Campbell proposes the reconstruction of a *prophetic record*, that would contain the story of Samuel, the narratives about Elijah and Elisha and would conclude with the revolt of Jehu. This event provides him with an argument on dating.[482] The reconstruction of such a document going back to the ninth century BCE does not, however, lead to general agreement. Many works have emphasized the late character of some of the prophetic accounts in Kings. Schmitt sees a very complicated redactional history for the Elisha cycle. According to him, the greatest part of the tradition on Elisha was only inserted into Kings after the Dtr edition. In DH, only the account of Jehu's revolt (2 Kings 9–10) alludes to Elisha.[483] This thesis was confirmed, despite some differences in detail, by the analysis of Stipp.[484] Rofé insists on the legendary character of the

Israelite Religion: Essays in Honor of F.M. Cross (Philadelphia: Fortress Press, 1987), pp. 459-75.

479. For example, Hoffmann, *Reform und Reformen*, pp. 169-203; C. Levin, 'Joschija im deuteronomistischen Geschichtswerk', *ZAW* 96 (1984), pp. 351-71. C. Minette de Tillesse, 'Joiaqim, repoussoir du "Pieux" Josiah: Parallélismes entre II Reg 22 et Jer 36', *ZAW* 105 (1993), pp. 352-76.

480. Diebner and Nauerth, 'Die Inventio des הַתּוֹרָה סֵפֶר in 2Kön 22'; Römer, 'Transformations in Deuteronomistic and Biblical Historiography'.

481. Cf. J.P. Sonnet, 'Le livre "trouvé", 2 Rois 22 dans sa finalité narrative', *NRT* 116 (1994), pp. 836-61; cf. too the contribution of F. Smyth in the present volume.

482. Campbell, *Of Prophets and Kings*. He is followed by O'Brien, *The Deuteronomistic Hypothesis*. For a mostly historical reading of the texts on Elisha, cf. R.D. Moore, *God Saves: Lessons from the Elisha Stories* (JSOTSup, 95; Sheffield: JSOT Press, 1990), and A. Lemaire, 'Joas, roi d'Israël et la première rédaction du cycle d'Elisée', in Brekelmans and Lust (eds.), *Pentateuchal and Deuteronomistic Studies*, pp. 245-54.

483. H.C. Schmitt, *Elisa: Traditionsgeschichtliche Untersuchungen zur vorklass-ischen nordisraelitischen Prophetie* (Gütersloh: Gerd Mohn, 1972).

484. Stipp, *Elischa—Propheten—Gottesmänner: Die Kompositionsgeschichte*

accounts on Elijah and Elisha and the anonymous prophet in 1 Kings 13. These accounts, which he considers late, are comparable to the legends of the saints in Christianity.[485] McKenzie, in his work on the book of Kings, reaches the conclusion that almost all the prophetic accounts contained in 1 Kings 13 and 2 Kings 13 are post-Deuteronomistic insertions.[486] That means that the Deuteronomistic history of the monarchy was shorter than commonly supposed and that the first Deuteronomist was interested in the prophets only insofar as they transmitted the divine word. If the prophetic cycles were only added afterwards, we should reconsider the link between prophecy and Deuteronomism.[487]

7.5.5.4. The Problem of a Pre-Deuteronomistic Edition of Kings. In analyzing the stereotypical appraisals of the different kings, H. Weippert reached the conclusion that these formulas indicate that three redactors were involved, the oldest of whom would be from the period of Hezekiah.[488] Other exegetes have tried to go back even earlier in the reconstruction of a pre-Deuteronomistic book of Kings. Lemaire proposes a first composition in the period of Jehoshaphat about 850. This book would have been made up of the history of David and Solomon, then the history of the two kingdoms of Judah and Israel up to their reconciliation (cf. 1 Kgs 22.45).[489] The analyses of Weippert and of

des Elischazyklus und verwandter Texte, rekonstruiert auf der Basis von Text- und Literarkritik zu 1 Kön 20. 22 und 2 Kön 2–7 (ATSAT, 24; St. Ottilien: EOS, 1987).

485. A. Rofé, *The Prophetical Stories: The Narratives about the Prophets in the Hebrew Bible. Their Literary Types and History* (Jerusalem: Magnes Press, 1988); *idem*, 'The Vineyard of Naboth: The Origin and the Message of the Story', *VT* 28 (1988), pp. 89-104.

486. McKenzie, *The Trouble with Kings*; cf. particularly pp. 80-100.

487. According to McKenzie, these accounts were inserted 'essentially as a group' (*The Trouble with Kings*, p. 99 n. 24). He does not specify, however, whether that insertion was made in the setting of a redaction in a Deuteronomistic style (for example, 'DtrP') or if it was a matter of a redaction that can no longer be characterized as Deuteronomistic.

488. H. Weippert, 'Die "deuteronomistischen" Beurteilungen der Könige von Israel und Juda und das Problem der Redaktion der Königbücher', *Bib* 53 (1972), pp. 301-39; cf. as well W.B. Barrick, 'On the 'Removal of the "High" Places' in 1–2 Kings', *Bib* 55 (1974), pp. 257-59.

489. A. Lemaire, 'Vers l'histoire de la redaction des livres des Rois', *ZAW* 98 (1986), pp. 221-36; cf. as well *idem*, 'Joas, roi d'Israël et la première rédaction du cycle d'Elisée'. We should note in passing that the reference to Provan in this last

Lemaire depend on many exegetical and historical presuppositions.[490] Most exegetes do not actually venture into the reconstruction of a pre-Deuteronomistic edition of the book of Kings, even if such a possibility is not definitely excluded.

8. *Summary and Perspectives*

Research on DH, even on Deuteronomism in general, finds itself today in a paradoxical situation. At first sight, we get the impression that the 'Deuteronomistic fact' is well established. But after a closer look, it turns out that the definitions of DH are legion and not always compatible with one another. How can we define what is Deuteronomic, Deuteronomistic and what is not?[491] We must doubtless combine diachronic, stylistic and ideological criteria.[492] But defining the ideology of a work is a perhaps rash undertaking. Let us then begin our summary with this question.

8.1. *Ideology and Theology*

To characterize the theology or ideology of the Deuteronomistic work[493] depends at least partially on diachronic options. If we accept the existence of a first edition of DH in the period of Josiah, that work very likely displays a 'triumphalist' vision prompted by a promising international situation and the political energy of this monarch. If we consider on the contrary that the first editon of DH dates from the exilic period, the work should then be considered a theodicy.

What is surprising in the whole debate is that the same work could be

article is wrong, since the latter is in no way defending an edition of the book of Kings in the time of Hezekiah.

490. Lemaire's argumentation is circular. He reconstructs the history of Israel and Judah from the book of Kings and then uses this reconstruction to situate in it the different stages of the pre-Deuteronomistic edition of Kings. For a critique of the theses of H. Weippert, cf. E. Cortese, 'Lo schema deuteronomistico per i re di Giuda e d'Israele', *Bib* 56 (1975), pp. 37-52 and Römer, *Israels Väter*, pp. 282-85.

491. Cf. R. Coggins, 'What does "Deuteronomistic" Mean?', in Davies (ed.), *Words Remembered*, pp. 135-48.

492. Cf. A.F. Campbell, 'Martin Noth and the Deuteronomistic History', in McKenzie and Graham (eds.), *The History of Israel's Traditions*, pp. 31-62 (55).

493. Cf. as well the articles of A.D.H. Mayes and of M. Rose in the present volume.

perceived in two such opposite ways. There is no doubt that the two readings find some points for support in the text itself. The whole question, consequently, is to know how to explain the juxtaposition of these two aspects. Would there have been a transformation of a piece of propaganda into an act of repentance and a theodicy?

The question of future prospects presented in an exilic edition of DH remains very much under discussion. Can we really actually imagine that such a historiography would have been composed in order to explain Judah's national catastrophe? Many authors consider this Nothian hypothesis improbable.

On the basis of texts like Deut. 4.30 or 1 Kgs 8.46-50, it has often been claimed that the hope of a restoration was not foreign to the Dtr programme. Nevertheless, as these texts seem to belong to a late phase of the redaction (Dtr$_2$ or DtrN), the question remains open for the first exilic edition. The conclusion of DH in 2 Kings 25 recounting the restoration of Jehoiachin to favour at the Babylonian court plays a preponderant role in the discussion of the intention of the work. Many exegetes see in it the more or less discreet hope of an imminent restoration of Israel.[494] Nevertheless, it seems difficult to define the intention of a work only on the basis of its conclusion, all the more so since 2 Kgs 25.27-30 probably does not constitute the original conclusion of the exilic edition of DH. We must wonder too about the important role played by the references to the exodus within DH. Do these references to the tradition of the people liberated by Yhwh imply the hope of a new exodus, or is it a matter of merely showing that the people and its heads were incapable of responding to this original salvific act to which Israel owes its birth?

In our opinion, the question is not so much of knowing whether it is hope or rather despair that determines the future prospects of DH. What seems to us more important is to take the measure of the *kairos* (providential moment) of DH—or of the *kairoi*, since there were doubtless several of them. Whether the beginning of the work is situated in the Josianic period or not, quite obviously the fateful hour (*Sternstunde*) of the DH is found in the span of time covering the collapse of the kingdom of Judah, the destruction of the Temple and the exile of the Judaeans. These are the events from which the history must be con-

---

494. Dietrich, *Prophetie und Geschichte*, p. 142; C. Begg, 'The Significance of Jehoiakim's Release: A New Proposal', *JSOT* 36 (1986), pp. 52-53; Nelson, *The Double Redaction of the Deuteronomistic History*, p. 123.

templated, interpreted, 'constructed'! It is curious that these key events occupy only a marginal and almost negligible place in the work: in the great DH, the account of the fall of Jerusalem does not even fill a chapter. (Imagine how much different things would have been, if it were Flavius Josephus who had been the chronicler!) From this pivotal event onwards, it is therefore no longer the isolated event or the episode, that interests those in charge of DH. They are well aware that it is not a particular strategic decision, a specific act of bravery, or some chance in circumstance that could change the course of events, and it is therefore unnecessary to linger over details. What is of interest to them is that which, in our century, Fernand Braudel has called the 'long duration', the slow, long-lasting, seemingly at times inexorable evolutions: for Braudel, the history of spaces, of commercial routes, of mentalities; for DH, the history of Yhwh and of Israel. What happened in 587—what for the Deuteronomist or the Deuteronomists had just happened—that has been brewing for centuries, and almost since the very beginnings. Such, in spite of their varying positions, is their common conviction.

It is well known, and has often been said, that catastrophe—or the threat of catastrophe—sharpens the perception and provides a stimulus: it is necessary to preserve what has taken place, to recall what is in danger of being forgotten, to preserve what is on the way to foundering. It is at the moment when a dialect is dying that they compose its dictionary, it is once a community disappears that they set out to write its history.[495] The biblical historiography, as it has come down to us, is born of this catastrophe and lives from the crisis that follows.[496] But it is precisely then that the choice of a new identity is expressed through the choice for its myths of origin.

Therefore, what are the myths of origin, what are the traditions from

495. Cf. André Chouraqui writing the history of the Jewish communities of North Africa.

496. Research in historical sociology interprets the apparition of descriptive modern historiography as the response of intellectual circles facing the crises provoked by the French or the Industrial Revolutions. Cf. A. Steil, *Krisensemantik: Wissenssoziologische Untersuchungen zu einem Topos moderner Zeiterfahrung* (Opladen: Leske & Budrich, 1993). According to Steil, these intellectuals are reacting to the disappearance of the ancient order, precisely by 'doing history'. The fact of objectivizing the events allows them to distance themselves from them. Cf. too T. Römer, 'L'Ancien Testament—une littérature de crise', *RTP* 127 (1995), pp. 321-38.

which DH draws its inspiration? The Dtr partiality for the exodus has often been observed. According to Van Seters and Römer, the exilic edition of the DH contains no reference to the patriarchal traditon.[497] It seems that the Deuteronomist would have deliberately chosen to ignore the patriarchs since the 'good' ancestors are not there, and Israel has nothing to expect from them. The 'fathers' or the ancestors so often mentioned in DH, and especially in Deuteronomy, would designate originally the generations in contact with Egypt. These generations constitute an Israel that responded to an appeal and lived up to (or, by its sins, did not live up to) its vocation. If this thesis—which has been very much contested[498]—were confirmed, it would mean that the Dtr ideology is constructed in opposition to a clannish ideology that, for its part, relies first of all on the tradition of the Patriarchs, Abraham to Jacob.[499] To the 'genealogical' Israel, DH opposes a 'vocational' Israel.

This choice is not simply 'inscribed in the facts'. We can actually note that the books of Chronicles only very rarely allude to the exodus and present, according to Sara Japhet, a clannish and autochthonous Israel.[500] On this point, a comparison of DH with the Chronicler's historiography would probably open up interesting perspectives, especially since Japhet has shown the fundamentally 'optimistic' character of the ideology of the Chronicles.[501] However that may be, the file on the relation between Samuel / Kings and Chronicles deserves to be taken up

497. J. Van Seters, 'Confessional Reformulation in the Exilic Period', *VT* 22 (1972), pp. 448-59; *idem*, *Prologue to History*, pp. 227-45; Römer, *Israels Väter*, passim.

498. Cf. in particular N. Lohfink, *Die Väter Israels im Deuteronomium: Mit einer Stellungnahme von Thomas Römer* (OBO, 111; Freiburg: Universitätsverlag; Göttingen: Vandenhoeck & Ruprecht, 1991); L. Schmidt, 'Väterverheissungen und Pentateuchfrage', *ZAW* 104 (1991), pp. 1-27.

499. Cf. on this subject A. de Pury, 'Le cycle de Jacob comme légende autonome des origines d'Israël', in J.A. Emerton (ed.), *Congress Volume Leuven* (VTSup, 43; Leiden: E.J. Brill, 1991), pp. 78-96; *idem*, 'Las dos leyendas sobre el origen de Israel (Jacob y Moisés) y la elaboración del Pentateuco', *EstBib* 52 (1994), pp. 95-131.

500. Cf. W. Rudolph, *Chronikbücher* (HAT, 21; Tübingen: J.C.B. Mohr, 1955), p. ix; S. Japhet, *The Ideology of the Book* of *Chronicles and its Place in Biblical Thought* (BEAT, 9; Frankfurt: Peter Lang, 1989), pp. 379-86; P. Abadie, 'La figure de David dans les livres des Chroniques: De la figure historique à la figure symbolique. Contribution à l'étude de l'historiographie juive à l'époque postexilique' (Dissertation, Institut Catholique & Sorbonne, 1990), pp. 45-59.

501. Cf. her contribution in this volume.

again, in particular after the suggestion of Auld who considers that the two collections are almost contemporaneous and depend on a common source.[502]

8.2. *DH and Historiography*

On all sides we hear about the desire to see the very term 'historiography' defined more closely. It is especially Van Seters[503] who has compared the Deuteronomists with historians of the Greek world. On the other hand, Thompson[504] has sharply criticized the comparison of Hellenistic historiography and biblical 'historiography', since, according to him, the latter entails nothing like an inquiry on historical facts. It is obvious that Van Seters proposes an entirely different definiton of the concept of historiography: this concept will have to be refined and broadened in comparison with the systems of historicity of Mesopotamia, of Egypt and of Greece.[505]

Any historiographical enterprise implies at the same time a search for the past, therefore a certain observation of historical reality, and an intepretation of this past in function of the present, therefore a certain ideology. The 'reading' of the past goes together with the 'construction' (or the reconstruction) of the past. Noth has admirably perceived this, not only in his study of biblical historiography, but in his scientific approach, an approach as reader and builder at the same time. This is why, to our way of thinking, it is wrong to become obsessed with the antagonism between ideology and history. As DH has shown us, all through our journey, historiography is always ideological, but ideology always remains in turn rooted in history.

8.3. *What is the Future of DH?*

At the present time, the majority of scholars continue to work with the DH model. Of course, as we have seen several times, the term DH can be understood in very diverse ways. Nevertheless, all those that are

---

502. Auld, *Kings without Privilege*.
503. Van Seters, *In Search of History*. Noth, *ÜSt*, p. 12, too makes a remark going in this direction.
504. T.L. Thompson, 'Israelite Historiography', *ABD* III, pp. 206-12.
505. Cf. in this volume the contributions of M. Detienne and of J.-J. Glassner.

based on the Nothian hypothesis agree on the fact that there is a literary plan that unites the books from Deuteronomy to 2 Kings. It is all the same not astonishing that in the context of the destructuring that today affects the social sciences, the existence of a DH is questioned. This questioning amounts to a denial of the compositional unity on which Noth had especially insisted. If we imagine, for example, the process of the formation of the historical books and of Deuteronomy as a single process of gathering together, starting from the book of Kings, how in that case can we explain the presence of a system of Deuteronomistic cross-references that subdivides the history of Israel differently than the present books?[506] These interrelations really exist and if we want to leave aside the DH hypothesis, it is in that case necessary to find another explanatory model.

With that established, perhaps the Nothian thesis should be radically modified. The question of the beginning of DH is far from being settled. The recent discussion on the Pentateuch has brought out the importance of one or of several Deuteronomistic-type redactions in Genesis–Numbers. The break between Numbers and Deuteronomy is therefore much less clear-cut than it appears in the current presentations of DH. Must we therefore envisage instead a great Deuteronomistic history going from Genesis or Exodus as far as the books of Kings? But then what would be the status of Deuteronomy within this collection? If DH had combined the Pentateuch and the historical books, how can we explain the fact that many of the narrative traditions of Exodus and of Numbers are repeated in Deuteronomy? Deuteronomistic research should perhaps take up the analysis of Deuteronomy from this angle. It is not enough to postulate ten or so Deuteronomistic layers in Deuteronomy without asking about the presence or absence of these same layers in the books that surround Deuteronomy.

506. For the Deuteronomists, the period of the Judges only ended in 1 Sam. 12; next comes the period of the beginnings of the monarchy that is concluded with Solomon's discourse in 1 Kgs 8. The following period is that of the two parallel kingdoms that come to an end with the Deuteronomistic commentary of 2 Kgs 17. The demarcation of the historical books is apparently done by the insertion of non- , even post-Deuteronomistic texts: Josh. 24 and Judg. 1.1–2.5 separate Joshua and Judges; Judges 17–21, Judges and Samuel; 2 Samuel 21–24, Samuel and Kings.

Another open question is that of the chronological duration of DH. Only recently, Dietrich asserted that 'the language and thought of the Persian period as a whole represents a *terminus ad quem* for the Deuteronomistic historical writing'.[507] Knight, on the other hand, wonders about it in these terms: 'Is the usual Josianic or exilic dating of Dtr much too early, perhaps by several centuries'?[508] The history of the text shows clearly that the Dtr style is present up to the Hellenistic period. How and where must we then trace the frontier between the 'real' editors of DH and the epigones who merely 'imitate' the Deuteronomistic style? This area of research that is still almost virgin territory deserves attention.

We may conclude with a few remarks on exegetical methods. By hitting on the idea of DH, Noth, as we have seen, awakened the interest of researchers in the history of the redaction. And it is not a coincidence if, at the outset, the harshest critics came especially from those who longed for the return of the old *Literarkritik*. For scholars who use synchronic methods (close reading, narratology, etc.) DH has become a simple abbreviation to designate the unit Deuteronomy–Kings. From then on the often conflicting relation between redaction(s) and received tradition(s) disappears from the horizon of the exegete. Despite the often fairly bitter conflicts engaged in by synchronists and diachronists, these two exegetical currents come together in so far as they both favour working from the text alone. Now, during the last few years, a new exegetical trend is emerging: socio-historical criticism, an approach that seeks to introduce sociological and anthropological methods into exegesis. Socio-historical criticism tries to describe the institutions and social structures that make it possible to locate such and such biblical literature. The application of this method to DH will doubtlessly open new avenues[509] for understanding better in what historical or cultural context the emergence or the transmission of a historiographical work of this nature can be imagined. Deuteronomism remains, as we wrote

507. Dietrich, 'Martin Noth and the Future of the Deuteronomistic History', p. 159.

508. Knight, 'Deuteronomy and the Deuteronomists', p. 74.

509. Cf. the first attempts of L. Stulman, 'Encroachment in Deuteronomy: An Analysis of the Social World of the D Code', *JBL* 109 (1990), pp. 613-32; P. Dutcher-Walls, 'The Social Location of the Deuteronomists: A Sociological Study of Fictional Politics in Late Pre-Exilic Judah', *JSOT* 52 (1991), pp. 77-94.

seven years ago, a 'touchstone' for research on the formation of the Old Testament literature.[510] If Israel was able to construct its history and through that to think of and choose its identity, it owes it to a great extent to the Deuteronomists.

510. De Pury and Römer, 'La Pentateuque en question', p. 67.

Part II
ANCIENT HISTORIOGRAPHY

POSTEXILIC HISTORIOGRAPHY: HOW AND WHY?

Sara Japhet

Introduction

Postexilic historiography constitutes one segment of a much larger corpus: the historiography of Israel during the First and Second Temples. The first representatives of this literature are the great historical works in the Bible, followed by the historiography found in the Apocrypha and later works. 'Writing history' is, thus, a consistent and continuous cultural phenomenon in Israel, an immanent expression of its spiritual constitution, disposition and presuppositions. The exact literary scope of this phenomenon, as well as its precise chronological boundaries, are still a matter of scholarly debate. While it is generally accepted that the original extent of this literature was broader than what we now have in our possession, and that not all the historical works that were written over this long period have come down to us,[1] the chronological boundaries of this literary activity are the subject of a long and rather heated debate. The end of historical writing in Israel may be placed quite accurately with the two great historical works of Flavius Josephus, written after the destruction of the Second Temple by the Romans: the *Jewish War* and the *Antiquities of the Jews*.[2] The beginnings of this

1. This view is based on both the general argument that there is no reason to believe that everything written during this period was preserved and canonized and on the explicit mention of historical works in the extant biblical ones, e.g., in the books of Kings and Chronicles. See O. Eissfeldt, *The Old Testament: An Introduction* (Oxford: Basil Blackwell, 1965), pp. 132-36.

2. The time of publication can be decided fairly accurately, as between 75–82 CE for *War*, 93–94 CE for *Antiquities*. See G. Hölscher, 'Josephus', *PW*, IX (1916), pp. 1942, 1950; more recently, L.L. Grabbe, *Judaism from Cyrus to Hadrian* (2 vols.; Minneapolis: Fortress Press, 1992), I, pp. 6-9.

phenomenon, however, are far less clear.[3] Rather loud voices in current scholarship tend to deny the early beginnings of biblical historiography (as well as its authenticity) and postpone it to as late a date as possible.[4] The debate continues and no general or even partial agreement on this point has been reached. Although this debate may have an impact on the question of definition—what precisely is 'post-exilic' within biblical historiography—my attention in this paper will be given to a well-defined corpus, of less-debated provenance.[5] This corpus will include the biblical books of Ezra–Nehemiah and Chronicles and the apocryphal book of 1 Esdras.[6] I shall preface my discussion with four preliminary remarks.

(1) In this article the term 'postexilic' should be understood in a technical or chronological sense rather than an essential one. Biblical scholarship tends to ascribe a certain finality to the 'exile', that is, the destruction of Judah in 586 BCE, and view everything that followed in relation to it. The period of Return and Restoration or, from another perspective, the Persian period in the history of Israel, is commonly described as 'postexilic', and so are its social, literary and spiritual phenomena. 'Postexilic' prophecy, liturgy, poetry, and so on, are therefore common terms in scholarly literature. This terminology, however, may have been influenced by the historical picture of Ezra–Nehemiah, which has determined the historical understanding of the period for a

3. For a brief summary of the matter and the pertinent considerations, including bibliography, see N. Na'aman, 'The "Conquest of Canaan" in the Book of Joshua and in History', in I. Finkelstein and N. Na'aman, *From Nomadism to Monarchy* (Jerusalem: Yad Izhak Ben Zvi and Israel Exploration Society, 1994), pp. 218-22.

4. See, for example, J. Van Seters, *In Search of History* (New Haven: Yale University Press, 1983); *idem*, *Prologue to History* (Louisville, KY: Westminster/John Knox Press, 1992).

5. Even here, however, the range of dates proposed for the respective works spans from the second half of the sixth to the first half of the second centuries BCE. See, S. Japhet, *I and II Chronicles—A Commentary* (OTL; London: SCM Press, 1993), pp. 23-28; H.G.M. Williamson, *Ezra, Nehemiah* (WBC; Waco, TX: Word Books, 1985), pp. xxxv-xxxvi; J.M. Myers, *I and II Esdras* (AB; New York: Doubleday, 1972), pp. 8-15. My position on the matter will be expressed as we go along.

6. For recent research reviews of these works see T.C. Eskenazi, 'Current Perspectives on Ezra–Nehemiah and the Persian Period', *CRBS* 1 (1993), pp. 59-86; J.W. Kleineg, 'Recent Research in Chronicles', *CRBS* 2 (1994), pp. 43-76.

long time.[7] In fact, however, the works that are commonly identified as 'postexilic historiography' were not written under the immediate impact of destruction and exile, nor as a direct response to them. These works were composed between the fifth (or fourth) and the third centuries BCE and the destruction and exile are not their principal concern. They view these events from a distance and from varying historical perspectives, to which I will return later.

(2) My choice of corpus is based on two principles, literary and historical. From the literary point of view I restricted myself to 'historiography' proper. Works that belong to other genres were excluded, even though they may deal with historical subjects, express 'historical memory' or may be used as historical sources. The popular genre of 'historical novel', for example, Esther, Ruth, parts of Daniel, Judith and Tobit, poetry that invokes and preserves 'historical memory', and prophecy, which addresses the issues of the time and serves as an authentic and powerful historical source, should all be treated on their own. My second principle of selection is historical rather than canonical. I included 1 Esdras although it does not form part of the Hebrew Bible, but did not include other historical works from the Apocrypha, primarily the books of *Maccabees*, which come from a later period and should be viewed against a different historical and cultural background. By its genre, purpose, subject-matter and perspective 1 Esdras belongs to the same group of writings as Ezra–Nehemiah and Chronicles.

(3) The literary questions of composition, authorship and date stand outside the formal scope of the present article. I would have liked to ignore these difficult problems altogether, at least at the outset, and begin my presentation from as neutral a vantage point as possible. However, since one can speak only about one thing at a time, some order of presentation is indicated. A seemingly 'neutral', or 'formal' solution was to follow the order in which these books appear in the Hebrew Bible, that is, Ezra–Nehemiah first, and Chronicles second, but this order is problematic in itself, since the tradition of the Hebrew Bible is divided on this point. In addition to this commonly known order, which appears in many manuscripts and in the printed editions, another order is displayed in the most important mediaeval manuscripts (Len. B 19a and the Aleppo Codex), where Chronicles appears as the

---

7.   See, S. Japhet, 'People and Land in the Restoration Period', in G. Strecker (ed.), *Das Land Israel in biblischer Zeit* (Göttingen: Vandenhoeck & Ruprecht, 1983), pp. 103-25.

first book of the Hagiographa, and Ezra–Nehemiah as the last.[8] More-over, since 1 Esdras is not included in the Hebrew Scripture, its position must be determined on different grounds. If we place it after the canonical works, should the order be: Ezra–Nehemiah—Chronicles—1 Esdras, according to one tradition, or Chronicles—Ezra–Nehemiah—1 Esdras, according to the other? One may suggest, alternatively, fol-lowing the order of the Septuagint, which deviates from all the above and has Chronicles first, 1 Esdras second, and Ezra–Nehemiah last. It is clear, therefore, that this decision cannot be made on the basis of 'neutral', or 'external' factors and needs to have recourse to literary and historical considerations, which are outside the scope of this article. I will therefore present the works in what I consider to be the historical order of composition, that is, Ezra–Nehemiah, Chronicles, 1 Esdras, without actually trying to justify it.[9] I hope that some contribution to this topic will be made by the discussion as it unfolds.

(4) The topic of this article has been phrased as: 'Postexilic Historio-graphy: How and Why?' One may wonder whether the order of the questions should not be reversed. Should not we look first for the causes and motives of this phenomenon and only then turn to the man-ner and methods of its actual realization and formulation? The answer lies in the scope and nature of the sources from which we draw our data. Even when dealing with the question of 'Why?' our most impor-tant evidence remains the literary work itself, and even questions of historical and cultural background, against which these works have been written, may sometimes be decided only from the works them-selves. Facts and considerations drawn from the fields of archeology, epigraphy, sociology, economy, world history, contemporary cultures, and the history of religions, are certainly to be taken into account in understanding this background. But the relevance of such evidence must be fully justified. The 'Why?' question cannot be addressed before the 'How?' question also because the authors of the works under con-sideration did not identify themselves, their motives or their purposes in writing their books. Even if they did, it is doubtful whether we would have been satisfied with their views on the matter. The only sound methodology is thus to first analyze the nature and method of pre-sentation in each literary work and follow with its background, motives, and purpose.

8. Japhet, *I and II Chronicles*, p. 2.
9. For some notes on the separateness of the works, see below pp. 168-69.

Ezra–Nehemiah

The book of Ezra–Nehemiah is a historical description of the restoration of Israel in the land of Judah between the second half of the sixth century and the first half of the fourth century BCE, that is, a period of about 150 years.[10] The historical description is focused on three topics and periods:

1. The building of the Temple in the time of Cyrus and Darius (Ezra 1–6).
2. The return and activities of Ezra in the time of Artaxerxes (Ezra 7–10).
3. The office of Nehemiah and his enterprises in the time of Artaxerxes (Nehemiah 1–13).

The book of Ezra–Nehemiah displays a very peculiar literary method, which is not attested elsewhere in the Bible. It is composed by means of a constant and faithful citation of existing documents, either official or literary. The official documents are supplied with a narrative framework and the literary ones are left to transmit their own story.[11] The author preserves the peculiarities of language (Hebrew or Aramaic), style, contents and views of the original documents incorporated into his book, while his own additions to these documents are limited. The author's

---

10. The book opens with the decree of Cyrus in the first year of his reign, that is 538 BCE (Ezra 1.1) and ends formally with the second office of Nehemiah, which began in 433 BCE (Neh. 13.6). However, there are references within the book to later dates, and its actual chronological span is dependent on three factors: the identity of 'Darius the Persian' in Neh. 12.22—whether Darius II (423–404 BCE) or Darius III (335–331 BCE) is intended; the identity of 'Artaxerxes', whether the first or the second, in whose seventh year Ezra's activity is dated (Ezra 7.7-8), that is, either 458 or 398 BCE, and the identity of the priests mentioned in Neh. 12.11, 22, and their office. For a more general treatment of these matters, and the book's peculiar chronological method, cf. S. Japhet, 'Composition and Chronology in the Book of Ezra-Nehemiah', in T.C. Eskenazi and K.H. Richards (eds.), *Second Temple Studies 2* (JSOTSup, 175; Sheffield: Sheffield Academic Press, 1994), pp. 189-216.

11. On this method, see S. Japhet, 'Biblical Historiography in the Persian Period', in H. Tadmor and I. Eph'al (eds.), *World History of the Jewish People*, VI (Ramat Gan: Massada Press, 1983), pp. 181-82 (in Hebrew); H.G.M. Williamson, 'The Composition of Ezra I–VI', *JTS* 34 (1983), pp. 1-26; and from a different point of view, T.C. Eskenazi, *In an Age of Prose* (Atlanta: Scholars Press, 1988), pp. 87-96, 189-91.

composing hand is manifest in the book's general structure, its specific periodization, some harmonistic remarks and the material he added to his sources. The result of this peculiar method is that the book speaks to us in several simultaneous voices. The voices of the various sources and the voice of the final author may differ in many ways, and sometimes present the reader with difficult historical problems. It is only through the understanding of this method that the various aspects of Ezra–Nehemiah become clear, and that the distinctive historical view taken by the author of Ezra–Nehemiah can be grasped.

According to the historical picture drawn by Ezra–Nehemiah, the restoration of Israel's life had three central aspects, which form the focus of the book's interest.

(1) The most important aspect is the full renewal of religious life in Jerusalem and Judah. This renewal is described as occurring in several stages: the renovation of the altar and the re-establishment of regular sacrificial worship (Ezra 3.2-6); the building of the Temple and the establishment of its clerical institutions (Ezra 3.7-6.18); provision for the maintenance and prosperity of the Temple and the support of the priests and Levites (Ezra 6.9-10; 7.17-24; 8.25-27; Neh. 10.33-40; 12.44-45; 13.10-13, 30-31); the reading of the Law and the establishing of its authoritative position in the life of Israel (Neh. 8.1–9.4; 10.30; 13.1-3); the celebration of the festivals (Ezra 3.4-5; 6.19-22; Neh. 8.13-18); the strict observance of the Sabbath (Neh. 10.32; 13.15-22), and more. Renewal of religious life is the central axis of Ezra–Nehemiah. It is almost the exclusive topic of the first section of the book (Ezra 1–6) and large parts in the other sections are dedicated to it. The book thus describes the continuous and consistent effort to restore religious institutions, in the greatest possible conformity with the institutions and standards of the first Temple, though with a different economic, social, and spiritual basis.

(2) The second aspect of Israel's restoration in Ezra–Nehemiah is the concrete, physical restoration of habitation and settlement, in Jerusalem and in Judah. This aspect of the restoration is depicted in two ways:

(i)   Reference to and description of repeated acts of rehabilitation, settlement and reform throughout the whole period, such as the return of exiles and their settlement (Ezra 1.5-6, 11; 2.1-70; 7.7-9; 7.28-8.36; Neh. 2.5-9, etc.); the building and dedication of the walls of Jerusalem and the organization of its guard

(Neh. 1–4; 6.1–7.3; 12.27-43); and the populating of Jerusalem and the social care for the community (Neh. 5.1-13; 7.4-71; 11.1-2).

ii. Introduction of lists of various kinds which reflect and illustrate actual static situations and confer the feeling of an established, well-rooted community. One may mention such lists as returnees (Ezra 2//Neh. 7; Ezra 8.2-24; Neh. 12.1-8); people settled in the land (Neh. 11.3-21); participants in events and ceremonies (Neh. 3.1-32; 10.2-28); clergy (Neh. 12.1-26); lists of settlements (Neh. 11.25-35), and more.

(3) The third aspect of Israel's restoration in Ezra–Nehemiah is the establishment and consolidation of the Judaean community as a 'holy people'. Israel of the book of Ezra–Nehemiah is a community of 'returnees', people who went through the experience of the Babylonian exile and returned to Judah. Although they are traced by genealogy to 'the clans of Judah and Benjamin' (Ezra 1.5) or to the various clans to which they belong (Ezra 2, etc.), they are defined as 'returned exiles' (*benei hagolah*, Ezra 4.1 etc.) or even 'Exile' (*hagolah*, Ezra 9.4 etc.).[12] This community is fully aware of its historical role as the bearer of the history and destiny of Israel, and its members dedicate themselves to the keeping of God's will and commandments. They are also actively occupied in preserving the purity of the community through repeated acts of segregation from and expulsion of foreign elements: 'peoples of the land', 'foreign wives' or 'mixed'. This topic is a major component in the story of Ezra, but is found also in Nehemiah's memoirs and in the words of the author himself (Ezra 4.1-4; 9-10; Neh. 9.1-2; 10.31; 13.1-3, 23-27).[13]

---

12. On this aspect of Ezra–Nehemiah see in more detail, Japhet, 'People and Land', pp. 112-18.

13. It is also a major concern of biblical scholarship. In addition to the commentaries, see, among others, Y. Kaufmann, *The Religion of Israel*, IV (Jerusalem: Mosad Bialik, 1956), pp. 197-206 (in Hebrew); S. Japhet, 'Law and "the Law" in Ezra–Nehemiah', in M. Goshen-Gottstein (ed.), *Proceedings of the Ninth World Congress of Jewish Studies, Panel Sessions* (Jerusalem, 1988), pp. 104-15; D.L. Smith, *The Religion of the Landless: The Social Context of the Babylonian Exile* (Bloomington: Meyer Stone Books, 1989), passim; see the conclusion on pp. 196-97; S. Talmon, 'Esra–Nehemia: Historiographie oder Theologie?', in D.R. Daniels, U. Glessman and M. Rösel (eds.), *Ernten, was man sät: Festschrift für Klaus Koch* (Neukirchen–Vluyn: Neukirchener Verlag, 1991), pp. 343-51;

Several salient features characterize this historical picture, first and foremost its basic positive perspective. Although the book of Ezra–Nehemiah is written in a very low key and is far from idealistic exaggeration, it leaves no doubt that the people of Israel have succeeded in their enterprise of restoration. There certainly have been difficulties and occasional drawbacks, but no failures. The building of the Temple was a longer and harder process than initially anticipated, but it was completed at the right time (Ezra 6.15-16). The building of the walls of Jerusalem was met by intense opposition and intrigue, but was brought to a successful completion in the shortest possible time (Neh. 6.15). Even regarding the problem of mixed marriages, which penetrated all layers of Judaean society, the author creates an impression of success (Ezra 10.17, 19; Neh. 9.2; 10.31; 13.3). The problem was certainly difficult, but the people of Judah coped with and overcame it.

Furthermore, all the difficulties that confronted the people of Judah were caused by outsiders, by external, powerful forces. The building of the Temple was halted not because of any laxity or negligence on the part of the people of Judah, or because of their desperate economic situation,[14] but because of the hostile intervention of 'the adversaries of Judah and Benjamin' and the explicit command of the Persian king (Ezra 4.1-24). The delays in the building of the walls in the time of Nehemiah were all caused by 'foes', by adversaries who exploited every possible means to prevent the restoration of Jerusalem (Neh. 2.10, 19; 3.33-35; 4.1-5; 6.1-14). The people themselves were eager to build and cooperative in every way.

It is significant that these drawbacks are not conceived in the theological framework of 'sin and punishment'. The difficulties were temporary, practical obstacles, to be overcome by the people's adherence to their goals. They are nowhere represented as divine punishment, or even as being of divine origin, nor are the people regarded as sinful.

D. Smith-Christopher, 'The Mixed Marriage Crisis in Ezra 9–10 and Nehemiah 13: A Study of the Sociology of the Post-Exilic Judaean Community', in T.C. Eskenazi and K.H. Richards (eds.), *Second Temple Studies 2* (JSOTSup, 175; Sheffield: Sheffield Academic Press, 1994), pp. 243-65; T.C. Eskenazi and E.P. Judd, 'Marriage to a Stranger in Ezra 9–10', in Eskenazi and Richards (eds.), *Second Temple Studies 2*, pp. 266-85.

14. As depicted by Haggai and Zechariah (Hag. 1.6-11; 2.15-19; Zech. 8.10). See S. Japhet, 'The Temple of the Restoration Period: Reality and Ideology', *USQR* 43 (1991), pp. 206-207.

Only in the matter of the mixed marriages are the people presented as having committed actual sin (*ma'al*, Ezra 9.2, 4, 6, 15). However, when confronted with the nature and meaning of their acts, the people immediately repent and do everything in their power to repair their ways (Ezra 10.2-5). 'Sin' and 'punishment' are certainly valid and powerful theological concepts in Ezra–Nehemiah. They are strongly emphasized in the several confessions and prayers included in the book, and serve to explain God's ways in conducting the fortunes of his people.[15] From the perspective of this book, however, they belong either to the past or are considered as a latent threat for the future. They are not applied to the actual present of return and restoration and do not explain the realities of the time.[16]

Also characteristic of Ezra–Nehemiah are the chronological system and method of periodization, which determine the literary structure of the work.[17] Ezra–Nehemiah conceives of the Restoration as comprised of two consequent periods, each of which spans one generation. The focus of the first generation is the building of the Temple (Ezra 1–6) and the center of the second is the activities of Ezra and Nehemiah (Ezra 7–Neh. 13). An outstanding characteristic of these periods is their political system. In each of the periods the people are ruled by a 'pair' of leaders of equal status: a secular leader (Zerubbabel, Nehemiah), and a clerical one (Jehoshua, Ezra).[18] Both the method of periodization and the assumed political system express Ezra–Nehemiah's political ideology, and I will return to it later.

Another feature of the historical picture is the absence of any expressed foresight toward the future. Not only eschatology—expectations for the 'end of days'—is missing from the book, but any perspective toward the future.[19] The explicit focus of interest is exclusively the present, the

15. These confessions witness a strong sense of guilt, which is phrased mostly in conventional terminology. See Ezra 9; Neh. 1; Neh. 9, and the commentaries.

16. Except for one place in the whole book, that is, Neh. 9.36-37. On the question of origin of this prayer, see H.G.M. Williamson, 'Structure and Historiography in Nehemiah 9', in Goshen-Gottstein (ed.), *Proceedings of the Ninth World Congress of Jewish Studies*, pp. 117-31.

17. See in great detail, Japhet (above, note 10). A further developed form of this article is 'Chronology and Ideology—the Case of Ezra-Nehemiah' (forthcoming).

18. See Japhet, 'Composition and Chronology'; Talmon, 'Esra–Nehemia', pp. 351-56.

19. See also W. Rudolph, *Esra und Nehemia* (HAT; Tübingen: J.C.B. Mohr Siebeck, 1949), p. xxx.

actual moment. Thus, for example, when the building of the Temple is concluded, all we hear is that the people celebrated its dedication 'with joy' and re-established the clerical institutions (Ezra 6.16-18). Nothing is said, for example, about the role of the Temple in Israel's life, how it will serve future generations, and what its fortunes would be—so much in contradistinction to the dedication of the First Temple, expressed in Solomon's prayer and in God's response to it (1 Kgs 8.21-53; 9.1-9). This is true of all the other events recorded in the book except for the immanent danger of mixed marriages (Ezra 9.14). The attention of the book is directed solely to the present.

Moreover, any concept or fact that might be identified as, or even related to 'eschatology' is missing from the book. This is seen most emphatically in the attitude to the Davidic ideology and to the concept of political independence. There are, indeed, a few reminiscences of David,[20] and even of the kingdom,[21] but these institutions belong exclusively to the past. They are irrelevant for the present day of the community's life. The absence of any mention of the house of David, and in fact what seems to be an intentional avoidance of it, is most obvious in regard to the figure of Zerubbabel; his extended genealogy and even a reference to his Davidic ancestry, are totally missing.[22] The only occasional reference to a Davidide, probably by oversight, is to a person named Hattush, in the list of returnees at the time of Ezra (Ezra 8.2). Kingship, political power and independence, and the house of David are all ignored, I would even say, silenced, in Ezra–Nehemiah.

Another peculiar feature of the description is the role allotted to the kings of Persia in the history of Israel. These kings are presented as the

20. Ezra 3.10; Neh. 12.24, 36, 45 (mentioning also Solomon), 46, relating to various aspects of the temple's song, and Ezra 8.20 relating to the temple servants (Nethinim) 'whom David and the officers had appointed'. All these references relate to David's constitutive acts in the framework of the cult. Neh. 3.16; 12.37 mention geographical points in the city of Jerusalem connected with David: 'the graves of David' and 'the steps of the City of David'. Ezra 8.2 defines the genealogy of one, Hattush, as 'of the sons of David'.

21. See in particular Ezra 4.20; 5.11; Neh. 9.32, 34, 35; 13.26.

22. These are attested in the prophecies of Haggai (in particular, 2.21-23), the genealogy of Chronicles (1 Chron. 3.17-19), and probably also in Zechariah (6.12-13). See in detail S. Japhet, 'Sheshbazzar and Zerubbabel against the Historical and Religious Tendencies of Ezra–Nehemiah', *ZAW* 94 (1982), pp. 66-98; in particular pp. 68-80.

source of authority and initiative in all the important enterprises of the
period. The book begins with Cyrus, who in the first year of his reign
issued a decree permitting the Jews to rebuild the house of the Lord in
Jerusalem (Ezra 1.1-4). It is followed by the command of Artaxerxes to
stop the building of the Temple (Ezra 4.17-23) and the renewed effort
to build it in the second year of Darius (Ezra 5.1-2). This is followed by
the investigation of Darius (Ezra 5.3–6.5), his own decree (Ezra 6.6-12)
and the completion of the building in the sixth year of his reign (6.15).
Then the story continues with the role of Artaxerxes, in whose days
both Ezra and Nehemiah were active. His letter of authorization to Ezra
(Ezra 7.12-26) and his authorization of Nehemiah (Neh. 2.7-9; 5.14;
13.6), formed the basis for all their future enterprises.

The role of the Persian kings is expressed not merely through the
abundant narrative detail, but also in explicit, reflective statements.
They are presented as inspired by the Lord's spirit, and their acts are
seen as the way in which the Lord of Israel chose to extend his love to
his people. The best way to illustrate this astonishing trait is to cite a
few examples:

1. 'In the first year of King Cyrus of Persia...the Lord roused the
   spirit of King Cyrus of Persia to issue a proclamation...' (Ezra
   1.1).
2. 'So the elders of the Jews progressed in the building...and
   they brought the building to completion under the aegis of the
   God of Israel and by the order of Cyrus and Darius and King
   Artaxerxes of Persia' (Ezra 6.14).
3. 'They joyfully celebrated the Feast of Unleavened Bread for
   seven days, for the Lord had given them cause for joy by
   inclining the heart of the Assyrian king to them, so as to give
   them support in the work of the House of God, the God of
   Israel' (Ezra 6.22).
4. 'Blessed is the Lord God of our fathers, who put it into the
   mind of the king, to glorify the House of the Lord in
   Jerusalem, and who inclined the king and his counselors and
   the king's military officers to be favorably disposed toward
   me' (Ezra 7.27-28).
5. 'For bondsmen we are, though even in our bondage God...has
   disposed the king of Persia favorably toward us, to furnish us
   with sustenance and to raise again the House of our God,

repairing its ruins and giving us a hold in Judah and Jerusalem' (Ezra 9.9).

This view of the role of the Persian kings may be traced to well-attested biblical theological tenets, but it bears its own peculiar marks. The attitude of biblical narrative towards foreign rulers in the history of Israel is generally to regard them as oppressors and enemies.[23] From a theological perspective they were seen as the agents of the Lord in executing judgment against his people, his 'rods'.[24] Probably following the excited pronouncements of Isaiah regarding Cyrus (Isa. 44.28; 45.1-7), the book of Ezra–Nehemiah reverses the common picture as well as extends his view to all the Persian kings related to the history of Israel. These rulers were the benefactors, the agents of the Lord in bringing about the people's salvation.

These characteristics of the historical narrative are all interrelated and add up to a consistent ideology, which is the spiritual response to an actual historical reality. We should therefore turn to this historical background which may be learned, albeit in an incomplete way, from the eye-witnesses of the events, the prophets Haggai and Zechariah.

The picture drawn from the words of Haggai and Zechariah conforms in many respects to that of Ezra–Nehemiah and thus adds weight and authority to the general historical portrayal. The process of restoration that the community in Judah was undergoing; the centrality of the issue of 'building'—of the Temple and the city; the difficulties that this community was facing; the role played by the prophets Haggai and Zechariah; the figures and roles of the leaders, Zerubbabel and Joshua, form the common ground of these books. In certain other matters, however, the views proclaimed by these books are no less than diametrically

---

23. One may recall, for example, the figure of Pharaoh in all the biblical sources, or the kings who subordinated Israel during the period of the Judges. A more specific and politically oriented view is displayed in the book of Kings. See N. Na'aman, 'Criticism of Voluntary Servitude to Foreign Powers: A Historiographical Study in the Book of Kings', in D. Assaf (ed.), *Proceedings of the Eleventh World Congress of Jewish Studies, Division A* (Jerusalem: Magnes Press, 1994), pp. 63-70 (in Hebrew).

24. This is the term used by Isaiah regarding Assyria: 'Ha! Assyria, rod of my anger, in whose hand, as a staff, is my fury' (Isa. 10.5), but the idea is very common. See, H. Wildberger, *Isaiah 1–12: A Commentary* (Hermeneia; Minneapolis: Fortress Press, 1991), pp. 218-45; 424-26; G. von Rad, *Old Testament Theology*, II (2 vols.; New York: Oliver and Boyd, 1965), pp. 183-84.

opposed.[25] Two of these matters are relevant to our immediate context: the role of the Persian rulers and the question of eschatology.

In the books of Haggai and Zechariah, the Persian rulers play no role in the history of Israel, neither positive nor negative. The decrees of Cyrus and Darius on the one hand, and the command to stop the building of the Temple, on the other hand, are not even mentioned. The only references to Darius are the chronological statements in the narrative framework (Hag. 1.1, 15; 2.10; Zech. 1.1, 7; 7.1). The responsibility for the fortunes of the community lies entirely in the hands of the people themselves: their egocentric neglect at one point and their enthusiastic devotion at another, were the origins of failure and success. Israel's destiny is determined by God and the only mediators between the Lord of Israel and his people are the prophets.[26]

The counterpart of this attitude is the eschatological ideology that permeates the words of these prophets and motivates their activity.[27] This ideology may be best illustrated by the small book of Haggai, which contains two eschatological prophecies that predict the shaking of the natural world and the upheaval of the political one. The topic of the first prophecy is the Temple, and it opens with: 'In just a little while longer I will shake the heavens and the earth, the sea and the dry land. I will shake all the nations. And the precious things of all the nations shall come [here] and I will fill this House with glory, said the Lord of Hosts' (Hag. 2.6-7). The second prophecy is addressed to Zerubbabel, and opens similarly: 'I am going to shake the heavens and the earth, and I will overturn the thrones of kingdoms and destroy the might of the kingdoms of the nations. I will overturn chariots and their drivers. Horses and their riders shall fall each by the sword of his fellow' (Hag. 2.21-22). The shaking of heaven and earth and the overturning of the political powers is to be followed by the establishment of a new world order founded on two pillars: the House of the Lord in Jerusalem,

---

25. Regarding both the similarities and the differences, see Japhet, 'The Temple', pp. 199-208, 216-22. For a skeptical view of these materials, see R. Carroll, 'So what do we *know* about the Temple? The Temple in the Prophets', in Eskenazi and Richards, *Second Temple Studies 2*, pp. 34-51. D.J.A. Clines, 'Haggai's Temple, Constructed, Deconstructed and Reconstructed', in Eskenazi and Richards (eds.), *Second Temple Studies 2*, pp. 60-87.

26. See Hag. 1.13; Zech. 1.4-6; 2.12-13, 15-16; 4.9, etc.

27. On this matter, see Kaufmann, *The Religion of Israel*, pp. 219-20; 224-25; 247-51; 269-72; von Rad, *Old Testament Theology*, pp. 282-84, 288.

which is in the process of being built, and the kingship of the 'house of David', represented by the Davidic heir, Zerubbabel.[28] For Haggai, these cosmic changes are to happen 'in a little while', and they are connected with concrete, contemporary institutions. In fact, this 'end of Days' would be an aggrandized repetition of the First Commonwealth, in a reversed order of attainment. The order for the first period was 'conquest—settlement—kingship—rest', that is, the securing of political independence and power followed by the consolidation of the cultic institutions and the building of the Temple. In the new era soon to come, the building of the Temple will be achieved first, to be followed by the establishment of Davidic kingship. It is probably by the force of this comprehensive eschatological ideology that Haggai and Zechariah succeeded in changing the attitude of the people and made them build the Temple. 'That day' was at their gates!

Against the background of this ideology, the political statement of Ezra–Nehemiah is easily understandable. It is a sober reaction to the frustration from the unrealized eschatological hopes, and a declaration of confidence in the new reality. The eschatological hopes were founded on the expectation, actually the confidence, that God 'will overturn the thrones of kingdoms and destroy the might of the kingdoms of the nations' (Hag. 2.22). But the rule of the Persian Empire continued and strengthened, and seemed so solid as to last forever. In the meantime, a new reality had developed in Judah. There was now a rooted and active community, with a temple whose arrangements were being consolidated and a lifestyle that had as its center the worship of the Lord. This present situation, under the auspices and benevolence of the Persian kings, is conceived in Ezra–Nehemiah as governed by God's providence. It is 'God's steadfast love for Israel' and 'the good hand' of the Lord for Israel. The adherence to this kind of life, separation from 'the peoples of the land', and observance of the commandments of the Lord, is a guarantee for the future—survival and prosperity.

The position of Ezra–Nehemiah on the most fundamental issues of identity and continuity, is characterized by a view of partial and restricted connection with the past. In terms of identity, the book professes a distinct definition of the 'we', the community in which Israel's existence and survival is represented. This is the community of the

---

28. As phrased vigorously by Clines, 'designating him as nothing less than the universal and eschatological ruler' ('Haggai's Temple', p. 77). For a critique of the 'domesticated' interpretations of earlier commentators, see nn. 52-53.

'exile', the people from Judah, Benjamin and Levi, who came from Babylon to settle in Judah. Ezra–Nehemiah displays no interest in the fortunes of the Diaspora as such,[29] and does not recognize any other 'Israel' in the land. The 'ten tribes' of northern Israel, or 'non returned' Judaeans in the land of Judah, simply do not exist in the view of this book.

This partial and restricted connection with the past is true also in the book's view of historical continuity between the new life, which began with the Return, and the past. The destruction of Jerusalem brought about the end of the Davidic kingdom and the destruction of the Temple, but only the latter is to be renewed. The Davidic house, the monarchy, political independence, all are seen as having come to their final end. The decree of Cyrus and the period of Restoration are a new beginning, which is connected to the past through the medium of prophecy: 'to fulfill the word of the Lord spoken through Jeremiah' (Ezra 1.1). This limited fulfillment, under the Persian rule, represents the people's 'hopeful future' (Jer. 29.10-14); no other is necessary or should be hoped for. In the structure of Ezra–Nehemiah and in much of its symbolism, the restoration of the Judaean community is compared to the conquest of the land: a new revival of Israel. This revival, however, gets only as far as building the Temple, the city and the walls, and the organization of the community. No farther.

Chronicles

Moving from Ezra–Nehemiah to the book of Chronicles is like moving from one spiritual world to another; in its topic, contents, method and ideology, Chronicles presents a different world.

The book of Chronicles[30] is a comprehensive historiography, which

---

29. The Jews of the Diaspora are referred to primarily as a 'source': of returnees (Ezra 1.3, 5, 11; 2.1-67; 7.6-9; 8.1-20, 35-36; Neh. 1–2) and financial means (Ezra 1.4; 2.68-69; 8.25-34). Their history, whether of individuals or collectives, is not recorded. (How much the perspective of Ezra–Nehemiah has influenced the modern histories of the period is illustrated by the recent book of Grabbe, *Judaism*). Although the book's topic is defined as 'Judaism', diaspora Judaism is never treated on its own (*Judaism*, p. xxv). Why this fact did not affect the choice of title is another problem that the book presents.

30. I have written extensively about Chronicles and will restrict myself here to the more general features of the work and to questions of background, provenance and motivation. For a more detailed presentation of my views, see: S. Japhet, *The*

describes the history of Israel from its beginning to the end of the first Temple. It begins with Adam (1 Chron. 1.1), thus being parallel to Genesis 1, and ends with the destruction of Jerusalem and the declaration of Cyrus. Except for the last four verses (2 Chron. 36.20-23), its end parallels the last chapter of 2 Kings, and so it constitutes a 'parallel' to the entire history of Israel, from Genesis to Kings. This history is told in three parts, distinguished in their topic, contents and method.

(1) 1 Chronicles 1–9 is the introduction, which provides the basis for the historical description that follows. The 'introductory' function of this section is demonstrated by both contents and literary form. It provides answers to basic preliminary questions, such as: who is the people whose history is to be told, where does this people live, and what is the historical framework.

(2) 1 Chronicles 10–2 Chronicles 9 tells the history of David and Solomon, presented as one period. In the longest and most detailed section of the book, this period is described as the climax of Israel's history, in which it reached its peak in both worldly and spiritual achievements.

(3) 2 Chronicles 10–36 presents the history of the people of Israel during the reign of the kings of Judah. It begins with the story of the rebellion, the defection of the northern tribes from their legitimate kings, and ends with the destruction of Jerusalem and the termination of the monarchy. The book concludes with the beginning of the declaration of Cyrus, cited from Ezra–Nehemiah (2 Chron. 36.22-23).

The 'parallelic' essence of Chronicles is expressed not merely in the topic of the book but also in the details of contents and form: it follows the order of the preceding works and has the same chronological skeleton. Large parts of Chronicles are a repetition, literal or with changes, of earlier works. It is a 'parallel history' in genre, historical framework, main contents and method.[31] At the same time, however, there are also

---

Ideology of the Book of Chronicles and its Place in Biblical Thought (trans. Anne Barber; Bern: Peter Lang, 1989); *idem, I and II Chronicles.*

31. This 'parallelic' nature of the book exerted great influence on the study of the book, in ancient as well as modern time. On this matter, cf. S. Japhet, 'The Historical Reliability of Chronicles: The History of the Problem and its Place in Biblical Research', *JSOT* 33 (1985), pp. 83-88; *idem, I and II Chronicles,* pp. 28-29. For a list and classification of the parallels, see J. Kegler and M. Augustin, *Synopse zum chronistischen Geschichtswerk* (BEATAJ, 1, Bern: Peter Lang, 2nd edn, 1991).

great differences between Chronicles and the preceding historiography. From among the books of the Pentateuch, the only one that is fully represented, albeit only through its lists, is the book of Genesis. Small sections are taken from Exodus, Numbers and Joshua, but the historical portrayal of Chronicles skips over the sojourn of Israel in Egypt, the Exodus, the wanderings in the wilderness, the conquest of Canaan, the settlement, and the periods of Joshua, the Judges and Saul. History moves directly from the genealogies of the sons of Jacob to the reign of David. In the description of the monarchic period, there are numerous omissions, additions and changes in detail in the histories of David, Solomon and all the kings of Judah, as well as a systematic omission of the independent history of the northern kingdom of Israel. This intensive reworking adds up to a thoroughly new picture of the history of Israel.

This historiographical method, that is, the repetition of a story that has already been told, the founding of the historical description on earlier works to the degree of extensive literal citations, and yet the portraying of an idiosyncratic historical picture, raises the question of purpose: What was the goal of the Chronicler in his writing? Why did he make this enormous effort? Was his work intended to supplement earlier historiography or replace it?

The concept of 'supplement', which was prevalent in the earlier interpretations of the book and still survives in certain circles,[32] is not supported by the literary nature of the work. If this was the author's purpose, he could have limited himself to supplementing the books of Samuel–Kings with the few additional details that he had to offer. He certainly did not have to reiterate the historical course, or reproduce whole chapters word for word. The enormous effort put into the work clarifies the fact that the interest of the writer was not in the antiquarian knowledge of details, nor in the publishing of the 'hard facts' of history. 'Replacement' seems to be a better way of explaining the Chronicler's project, but it is refuted by the correct argument that the Chronicler alludes to facts and topics that are not brought up in his book, and thus assumes the reader's acquaintance with details that he has not provided or even suppressed.[33]

---

32. The earliest testimony for this view is the name of the book in the Septuagint: *paraleipomena*, that is, '[the book of] the things omitted' or 'left over'.

33. This is pointed out particularly by H.G.M. Williamson, *1 and 2 Chronicles* (NCB; Grand Rapids: Eerdmans, 1982).

The best way to define the author's purpose is through the concept of 'corrective history': a thorough reformulating of ancient history from a new, 'modern' perspective, responsive to its time. The new story should supplement the necessary facts where they were unknown or omitted, replace mistaken facts and explanations by historically probable and theologically valid ones, use all available sources and materials, and provide wholeness of form and meaning to the account of the past. Such a history would provide a new interpretation of the past, which would be valid for the present and lay the foundations for the future. How, then, does Chronicles respond to the central issues of his time?

Although the book of Chronicles deals with a host of subjects in the worldly and spiritual spheres—it seems, in fact, that it has touched upon every important topic that pertains to Israel's history and religion—and these subjects are scattered throughout the book as demanded by the historical course and the narrative plan, the book's composition in three sections constitutes also a representation of the super-arching components of the historical portrayal. 1 Chronicles 1–9 concentrates on the question of identity and answers the question of 'who is Israel', the protagonist of the story and the bearer of God's providence. 1 Chronicles 10–2 Chronicles 9 portrays the 'ideal', that period in the history of Israel which is the model for all times to come. And 2 Chronicles 10–36 expounds the author's philosophy of history and unveils the mysteries of the historical course. These chapters uncover the ways of God in ruling the world and display how the divine attributes were realized and demonstrated in the history of Israel. Following the depth-structure of the book but availing myself of the testimony of the work as a whole, I will present its views on these three topics.

(1) The Chronicler has a very clear view of the people of Israel: they are the descendants of the sons of Jacob, 'the children of Israel'. Although the concept of 'the twelve tribes' is an active symbol in the book, the actual constitution of Israel is not determined by this concept. Israel is the name for everyone who descends from the seed of Jacob, in the broadest possible meaning of these terms. In the first nine chapters of the book, the prevalent genre is genealogy, which is a major form for the Chronicler's conceptualization of identity. 'Who you are' is determined by 'where you come from', that is, by ancestral origin and the way in which descent from this origin is actually traced. In providing this genealogical basis for Israelite identity, the Chronicler is as inclu-

sive as possible;[34] every element in the land of Israel is made to be connected to the basic structure of the sons of Jacob. Those among the inhabitants of the land who are expressly foreigners, are regarded as 'sojourners' (*gerim*), who also form part of the people of Israel (2 Chron. 30.25, etc.). Thus, contrary to the more common function of genealogy as the means of exclusion and restriction, of setting boundaries between the legitimate and non-legitimate, the Chronicler employs the genealogical format as the way of inclusion, of stretching to the broadest limits the concept of 'Israel'.

The Chronicler traces the genealogy of Israel back to Adam, who is thus presented as the ancient father of Israel, and with it expresses his peculiar concept of Israel's election. The special relationship between the people and their God is not viewed as a result of a particular historical act at a given historical moment. It is an absolute relationship, embedded in the very creation of the world, and whose validity is similar to that between God and the universe.

Parallel to this 'inclusive' concept of ethnic identity is the Chronicler's view of geographical identity. In concrete, geographical terms he describes the borders of the land of Israel in their greatest extent, and as early as the beginning of their history at the onset of David's kingship (1 Chron. 13.5). From a theological point of view, he regards the bond between the people and the land as a constant. Settlement in the land of Israel goes back to the sons of Jacob themselves, that is, to the earliest beginnings of the people's existence. All the intermediate periods of 'exile', such as the sojourn in Egypt on the one hand, and the Babylonian exile on the other, are played down and almost ignored. The tie between the people and their land is viewed as an undisturbed continuity; it is not a result of an historical act at a historical moment, but an essential aspect of their being.

(2) The history of David and Solomon is presented in Chronicles as one successive period, and along the same lines of form and contents. Although it is not depicted as 'ideal' (some mistakes and drawbacks are to be found even here) this is the glorious period in the history of Israel, which has never been repeated. Only very few of the subsequent Davidic monarchs, particularly Hezekiah, approached it to some degree, but no one has succeeded in emulating it. The Chronicler omitted from the

---

34. See Japhet, *Ideology*, pp. 267-351; T. Willi, 'Late Persian Judaism and its Conception of an Integral Israel According to Chronicles', in Eskenazi and Richards, *Second Temple Studies 2*, pp. 146-62.

story of his sources almost all the chapters that cast a shadow, or might be understood to do so, on the figures of David and Solomon. David's sins, the struggle for his succession, Solomon's sins of idolatry, the political drawbacks in Solomon's times, and more, are all omitted in the Chronicler's story.[35] To the rest of the story which he takes from 2 Samuel–1 Kings, the Chronicler adds his own material. Most extensive additions are provided for the time of David, pertaining primarily to ceremonial celebrations and to administrative matters of the Temple and the kingdom. This huge corpus has a double function: it serves to highlight and glorify the achievements of the kings, particularly David, and to equalize their respective reigns. The long period under David and Solomon, the apex of Israel's history, was a glorious time of prosperity and success.

The model presented by David and Solomon comprises elements of all aspects of life. The state's political order is the monarchy, which for the Chronicler is the 'natural', self-evident regime, adopted by all nations. Geographical expanse, constitution of the people, economic prosperity, military prowess, political administration, international reputation and contacts, are all at their utmost level of achievement. As for the religious sphere, this period sees the building of the first Temple in its extraordinary splendor, the establishment of cultic ritual and clerical institutions, the introduction of temple music and song, and the consistent care for the most minute details of temple administration. This is also a period of almost no sin. The people are described as enthusiastic about the building of the Temple and devoted to the worship and the commandments of the Lord, while their kings are depicted as wise and devoted leaders. Only in a few issues relating to David do we trace some setbacks, but he repents and makes reparation. The history of David and Solomon is in every respect the historical model, to which every period in the history of Israel should aspire.

(3) The reign of the kings of Judah is a direct continuation of David and Solomon in the historical and political aspects, but the integrity that characterized this 'model period' has been disrupted. Based on the material taken from the book of Kings with greater or lesser omissions and additions, the history of the kings of Judah is portrayed as a continuous struggle with constant vacillations from one extreme to the other. The task of the historian, underlined in his handling of this

35. See the synoptic lists in Kegler and Augustin, *Synopse zum chronistischen Geschichtswerk.*

period, is not merely to describe the events but to explain them. This is when the principles that govern the Lord's guidance are the most manifest, and when the Lord's attributes, particularly his justice, are illustrated in the most minute details of the historical description.

The Chronicler's view of God's justice is influenced greatly by that of Ezekiel, but is transferred from the realm of the individual to the public, national arena. There is a constant correlation between 'deed' and 'reward'. Human act, good or evil, is always and immediately recompensed, and any human state of welfare or misfortune is a consequence of God's retribution, measured to fit the human conduct. Important components of this philosophy are the concepts of warning, repentance and compassion, which involve an increased emphasis on the role of the prophets in Israel's history.

Although the theological basis of this view may have other biblical expressions, the Chronicler develops it into a comprehensive, encompassing theory. More importantly, he portrays the history of Israel as a constant realization of these principles: this is how the history of Israel actually unfolded. One of the most significant consequences of this philosophy is its basic positive view of the fortunes and future of Israel. Since each and every sin is immediately punished, there is no burden of blame carried on from one generation to the next. There is no 'accumulated sin', and each generation is a *tabula rasa*, whose fortunes are decided by its own choice. It raises to the highest degree the concept of self-responsibility, but it also provides a starting point of great hope for every new generation, for the very possibility of continuity and restoration.

One of the major themes of Chronicles, which runs throughout the book, is the place of religion, in the limited sense of the term, in the history of Israel. The Temple—its site, plans, preparations for, building, furnishing, dedication and restorations; the Temple personnel and administration—priests, Levites, singers, doorkeepers, treasurers, and more; the ritual, sacrifices, music, and more; the Temple's economy and history; celebration of the Festivals, primarily Passover; the teaching of the Law; faithfulness to the Lord versus idolatry—all these are the subject of great interest and the author refers to them repeatedly and throughout his work.[36]

The major role in this field is assumed by David and Solomon, who

36. See Japhet, *Ideology*, pp. 199-265; 438-44.

bring the ark to Jerusalem, prepare for the Temple, build and dedicate it and establish the constitutive forms of ritual and administration. However, the following kings both continued in the steps of their predecessors and also initiated and executed reforms and innovations of their own. The first Commonwealth was a period of laying the foundations, of struggle and renewal in the religious life of Israel.

A comparison with the preceding Deuteronomistic historiography highlights two different aspects to this picture. The first is the great interest and the enormous literary effort put into the description of these matters and in their integration into the story; the second is the specific points of interest within the general subject. These two features reveal the Chronicler's vantage point and his reaction to issues of his time.

The Chronicler's greatest attention is given to the innovative aspects of Israel's worship and to the very questions of innovation and authority. While the sacrificial cult as established in the Pentateuch is basically taken for granted, the Chronicler deals extensively with aspects of cult administration and ritual that are not recorded in the Pentateuch. These include, among others, the introduction of the system of rotating 'divisions' for all the classes of Temple personnel; the division of the Levites to four sub-groups, Levites, singers, gatekeepers, judges and scribes (1 Chron. 23.4-5) and clear definition of their tasks; the introduction of Temple music and descriptions of ritual ceremonies in which 'song' is greatly emphasized; the presentation of various innovations in the celebration of the festivals, and more. All these reflect either the Chronicler's own reality or his concepts and aspirations. His major motive is legitimization, based on the concept of 'genealogy'. Present day institutions are legitimized by the uncovering of their origins. The 'writing of David' or the 'order of the king', which were inspired and sanctified by God or 'the command of the prophets', are the source of authority from which contemporary institutions and concepts receive their validity.

When the Chronicler's overall ideology is compared with that of Ezra–Nehemiah, his agenda becomes clear. Although the two works have several common interests and respond to similar major aspects of historical existence, they are acting against different historical backgrounds. As demonstrated above, the Chronicler's answer to the question of identity is totally different from that of Ezra–Nehemiah, and similar difference may be seen in his concept of continuity. The reader of Chronicles cannot fail to note the dominant 'future perspective' from which the book is written. This correct observation, however, has led many scholars to define the book as 'eschatology' and ascribe to it eschatological ideology. But this interpretation is entirely mistaken, if we take the term 'eschatology' to mean what it does. The Chronicler does not share the prophetic expectations for 'the end of days', and cannot be regarded as the follower of Haggai and Zechariah. He does not foresee any changes in the cosmic or even the political constitution of the world. Rather, his concept of the Lord's guidance of the world by absolute, constant principles mitigates against any concept of dramatic change.

Yet, the Chronicler is not satisfied with the reality of 'the restoration' either. In Ezra–Nehemiah the new beginning initiated by Cyrus's decree forms the basis for the restoration of Israel. In Chronicles, by contrast, the first sentences of the same decree constitute the end of the story. The decree of Cyrus is presented in Chronicles indeed as a beginning of a change, but it is not followed by fulfillment, because what has been described in the book of Ezra–Nehemiah cannot count. Fulfillment is still ahead, a matter of the future. The Chronicler's whole view of history is a clear pointer to a future, when Israel will achieve its true destiny. This is a belief in the concrete revival of Israel, in earthly, political terms within the framework of historical time. The model of that revival is the period of David and Solomon: the broadest definition of Israel both as people and land, political independence and Davidic kingdom. The guarantee for the realization of this future is what the Chronicler tried so hard to describe: the positive picture of God's providence. His guidance in justice and compassion must lead to the near revival of Israel, in all its glory.

1 Esdras

Compared with Ezra–Nehemiah on the one hand and Chronicles on the other, 1 Esdras is the least impressive work of postexilic historiography. Contrary to Ezra–Nehemiah it has no new story to tell, and unlike Chronicles, it is not a comprehensive new interpretation of the history of Israel. However, 1 Esdras is a historiography and belongs with the two earlier works also by its actual text: most of its story parallels literally either Ezra–Nehemiah or Chronicles. 1 Esdras reacts to a close historical background and its study sheds light not merely on the book's own message but on the views and positions of its predecessors as well.

1 Esdras describes the history of Israel from the celebration of the Passover by Josiah king of Judah to the reading of the law in the time of Ezra, covering a period of about 165 or 225 years.[37] As the book stands, the historical description is composed of three parts:

1. The history of the kings of Judah, from Josiah's Passover to the destruction of Judah and Jerusalem (1 Esdras 1).
2. The building of the second Temple during the times of Cyrus and Darius (1 Esdras 2–7).
3. The return and activities of Ezra the scribe (1 Esdras 8–9).

From the perspective of sources, 1 Esdras has three components:

1. 1 Esdras 1 is parallel, with minor changes, to 2 Chron. 35–36
2. 1 Esdras 2 and 5.7–9.55 parallel Ezra 1–10 and Neh. 7.72–8.13a, with some changes in order and detail.
3. 1 Esdras 3.1–5.6 are peculiar to this book and are not attested in any other source.[38]

In the period it covers, its topic, contents, and source, 1 Esdras is more similar to Ezra–Nehemiah, whereas by some of its contents, and particularly by its major characteristic of being a 'parallel history', it follows the example of Chronicles. The question of its origin and relationship to these two works is thus of the greatest significance, and probably the most discussed subject in the study of the work.[39] A stand

---

37. Josiah's Passover is dated in all biblical sources to the eighteenth year of his reign (2 Kgs 23.23; 2 Chron. 35.19; 1 Esdras 1.22), that is, 622 BCE. According to 1 Esdras, Ezra's reading of the Law followed immediately the settlement of the mixed marriages affair (1 Esdras 9.17, 37), and should be placed at the eighth year of Artaxerxes, i.e., either 457 or 397 BCE. (For these alternatives, see above, n. 10).

38. For the details see S.A. Cook, 'I Esdras', *APOT*, I, p. 1; Myers, *I and II Esdras*, pp. 1-4.

39. See E. Bayer, *Das dritte Buch Esdras und sein Verhältnis zu den Büchern Esra–Nehemia* (Freiburg: Herder Verlag, 1911); K.-F. Pohlmann, *Studien zum dritten Esra: Ein Beitrag zur Frage nach dem ursprünglichen Schluss des chronistischen Geschichtswerkes* (FRLANT, 104; Göttingen: Vandenhoeck & Ruprecht, 1970); H.G.M. Williamson, *Israel in the Book of Chronicles* (Cambridge: Cambridge University Press, 1976), pp. 12-36; T.C. Eskenazi, 'The Chronicler and the Composition of I Esdras', *CBQ* 48 (1986), pp. 39-61; A. Schenker, 'La relation d'Esdras A' au texte massorétique d'Esdras–Néhémie', in G.J. Norton and S. Pisano (eds.), *Tradition of the Text: Festschrift D. Barthélemy* (Göttingen: Universitäts Verlag, 1991), esp. pp. 238-46.

on this matter is also of great relevance for our discussion, as it might influence our understanding of the whole historiographical corpus. A quite common position on this matter is that 1 Esdras represents a fragment of an original work, which comprised in one sequence Chronicles and Ezra–Nehemiah. Those who profess this view usually bring up another literary aspect of the book, its actual extent, as both ends of the work seem curtailed. The book opens in the middle of Josiah's reign, presenting with no introduction or proposition the story of the Passover: 'and Josiah made...' (1 Esd. 1.1).[40] It ends even more abruptly with the first word of Neh. 8.13: 'They came together',[41] left as is. Could this be the original format of the work, or is the book that has come down to us only a fragment of a longer one, the boundaries of which are unknown?[42] As already indicated by the order of my presentation (which did not begin with 1 Esd.) I do not accept the view that 1 Esdras represents a fragment of an original work that comprised Chronicles and Ezra–Nehemiah. Elaboration on this point is outside the scope of this article,[43] but suffice it to say that, following other scholars before me, I

40. In Hebrew: *waya'as*, in Greek: καὶ ἤγαγεν.

41. In Hebrew: *waye'asfu*, in Greek: καὶ συνήχθησαν. The modern translations try to overcome this abruptness in various ways.

42. Eskenazi sees in the abruptness itself, especially at the end, an intentional literary device and regards it as one of the proofs that the author of this work (but not of Ezra–Nehemiah) was the Chronicler ('The Chronicler', pp. 56-59). Most scholars, including Williamson who regards 1 Esdras as independent of the Chronicler's work and of Ezra–Nehemiah, regard the present form of the book as incomplete.

43. For arguments against this view see, for the time being, Williamson (*Israel in the Book of Chronicles*), Eskenazi, 'The Chronicler', pp. 42-43. As we have shown on many other occasions, and as demonstrated by other discussions of this topic, the underlying concept of continuity between Chronicles and Ezra–Nehemiah cannot be upheld any more (for my last statement on this issue, see Japhet, 'The Relationship of Chronicles and Ezra–Nehemiah', in J.A. Emerton [ed.], *Congress Volume: Leuven, 1989* [VTS, 43; Leiden: E.J. Brill, 1991], pp. 298-313), and this fact by itself undermines the 'fragment hypothesis' for the composition of 1 Esdras. As will be evidenced in what follows, my view differs also from that of Eskenazi, who sees in 1 Esdras a separate work but attributes its composition to the Chronicler ('The Chronicler', pp. 44-61). Eskenazi has eloquently elucidated the similarities between 1 Esdras and Chronicles, but failed to consider the differences between them, some of them of the greatest significance for each of the author's world view. These differences put the possibility of a common author in serious doubt.

regard 1 Esdras as a work on its own. While it should certainly be compared with Ezra–Nehemiah and Chronicles, it has its own purpose, method and ideology.

The nature of 1 Esdras as a 'corrective history' is demonstrated in two different areas, the historical and ideological. The book exhibits an impressive effort to remove the chronological and historical difficulties presented in the story of Ezra 4, and accord the historical course a more coherent flow.[44] In the realm of ideology, 1 Esdras reacts to the same issues that were dealt by both Ezra–Nehemiah and Chronicles and this reaction determines its position vis-à-vis the previous historical books and against the background of its period.

(a) In terms of historical continuity, the picture of 1 Esdras is different from both Ezra–Nehemiah and Chronicles. While Ezra–Nehemiah opened with the declaration of Cyrus and passed in complete silence over what preceded it, and Chronicles presented Cyrus's declaration as a turning point, the continuation of which still lies in the future, 1 Esdras bridges the gap between the periods of the first Temple and the second by the very flow of the story. Destruction, exile and restoration are fully integrated into the flow of history. The fall of Jerusalem loses the severe meaning that it had in the book of Kings, and Cyrus's decree becomes one in a series of events. It no longer marks, as in Ezra–Nehemiah, the beginning of the new period nor, as in Chronicles, is it the vantage point toward a new future. The realization of the concept of continuity can be seen as the motive and purpose of the book's structure. The author does not show any interest in the actual history of the interim period, as he does not 'fill in' the bridged gap by any additional data. Nor are theological explanations given for the transition from one historical stage to the other. A direct and uneventful way leads from destruction to restoration, through the decree of Cyrus and beyond it.

(b) One of the major changes in 1 Esdras pertains to the figure and role of Zerubbabel, who becomes the central figure and the major

44. For the difficulties, see Japhet, 'Composition and Chronology', pp. 201-205; L. Dequeker, 'Darius the Persian and the Reconstruction of the Jewish Temple in Jerusalem (Ezra 4.24)', *OLA* 55 (1993), pp. 69-70. In spite of the great effort, the harmonization does not seem to have worked out. Even among those scholars who see 1 Esdras as the original form of the work, some would nevertheless view the reversal of order as a secondary element in 1 Esdras. See Rudolph, *Esra und Nehemia samt 3. Esra*, pp. xii-xiii.

protagonist of the whole period. The tendency to 'stretch' the span of Zerubbabel's office and project him from the time of Darius back to that of Cyrus is found already in Ezra–Nehemiah. Yet, he is not explicitly mentioned there at the completion of the Temple, and he is not included in the transfer of the Temple's vessels, which is presented exclusively as the role of Sheshbazzar (Ezra 1.7-11; 5.14-15). In 1 Esdras this matter is corrected at both ends of the story: Zerubbabel is mentioned by name in connection with the completion of the Temple (1 Esd. 6.27) and is referred to explicitly with regard to the transfer of the holy vessels (1 Esd. 6.18). The term of his office thus covers the entire period from Cyrus to Darius.

Moreover, the refraining in Ezra–Nehemiah from any form of glorification with regard to Zerubbabel is 'corrected' in 1 Esdras in several ways. With the introduction of the story of the three guards, of which he is the hero, he is presented as full of wisdom and piety, devoted to the welfare of his people. The Davidic descent of Zerubbabel, which is totally silenced in Ezra–Nehemiah, is reaffirmed in 1 Esdras by an explicit genealogy: 'Zorobbabel, the son of Salathiel, of the house of David, of the lineage of Phares, of the tribe of Judah' (1 Esd. 5.5).[45] He is also explicitly referred to as the governor of Judah (1 Esd. 6.27), a fact that is suppressed in Ezra–Nehemiah. Zerubbabel's wise words are cited extensively: in his answer to Darius's challenge, his negotiations with the king and his prayer (1 Esd. 4.13-63), and his personality and wisdom are greatly lauded. In 1 Esdras Zerubbabel is the central figure of the Restoration.

On the other hand, while 1 Esdras follows Haggai in calling Zerubbabel 'my servant' (Hag. 2.23; 1 Esd. 6.27), it does not adopt the eschatological perspectives of the Restoration prophets. In 1 Esdras Zerubbabel is not the bearer of any eschatological expectations, not even the hope of political renewal and independence. Due to the additions in 1 Esdras the story of Zerubbabel comes close to a 'court story', which by its very definition presupposes the authority and benevolence of the foreign rulers. In this respect, 1 Esdras follows in the wake of Ezra–Nehemiah, seeing in the Persian rule the 'good hand' of the Lord toward his people.

(c) The literary structure of Ezra–Nehemiah, which expresses its socio-political view of the period, is completely disrupted in 1 Esdras.

45. On the textual difficulty of this verse see the commentaries; also Japhet, 'Sheshbazzar and Zerubbabel', *ZAW* 95 (1983), p. 219 n. 6.

As we have seen, according to Ezra–Nehemiah the political order in Judah during the restoration period was a rule of 'pairs', a secular and a clerical ruler working together. 1 Esdras breaks up this structure in three different ways. For the first period of the restoration 1 Esdras augments the role of Zerubbabel without doing the same for the priest Jehoshua. The result of this change is that Jehoshua is no more Zerubbabel's equal but acts very much in his shadow. For the second period 1 Esdras omits altogether the story of Nehemiah and leaves Ezra as the sole protagonist of this period. And finally, by beginning his story with Josiah, the entire periodization has been changed.

This restructuring seems to express, among other things, a certain rivalry between the figures of Nehemiah and Zerubbabel. 1 Esdras recognizes in the history of the restoration period only one 'governor of Judah': Zerubbabel, 'the servant of the Lord', the descendant of the house of David.[46] Although his office is subordinate to the foreign rulers of the country, he is nevertheless the legitimate heir of the earlier monarchy. There is no political independence indeed, but in Zerubbabel the rule of the Davidic kings is somehow continued.

Conclusion

The study of the three works that constitute postexilic historiography illustrates in an unmistakable way their political dimensions. In the book of Ezra–Nehemiah Israel was asked to adjust to a political situation at the peak of the Persian period, when the Persian military and political supremacy seemed so solid as to last for ever. In reaction to earlier messianic movements it now adopted a quietist approach, which saw in the limited restoration under the Persians the grace of God. All the religious fervor and energy were to be directed to the formation of a 'pure Israel', a 'holy seed', which would secure the physical and spiritual survival of Israel, and would realize the perfect relationship between Israel and its God.

The book of Chronicles was written later than Ezra–Nehemiah, at the

---

46. In the same vein, the reference to Sheshbazzar as governor is also omitted or rephrased. The words 'whom he had appointed governor' of Ezra 5.14 are omitted, and the reference to him as the receiver of the Temple's vessels is augmented to include Zerubbabel, thus: 'they were delivered to Zerobbabel and Sanabassarus the governor'. Sheshbazzar's Hebrew title of Ezra 1.8 'the prince (*hanasi'*) of Judah' is rendered in Esd. 2.11 with the rare word: 'the appointed' (προστάτῃ).

end of the Persian or at the beginning of the Hellenistic period. For the Chronicler, the great change in the history of Israel still lies in the future but is sure to come. Chronicles is a profound 'stock taking' of all of Israel's history and faith in preparation for this change. It lays the foundations for the unbroken continuity—from the very creation of the world—between past, present and future.

1 Esdras is obviously later than Chronicles and should be dated to the Hellenistic period in the third century. Following Chronicles, it preserves the hope of a Davidide as Israel's ruler, but the general political framework for Israel's existence is very much different from the model set by Chronicles. The hope for a change in the fortunes of Israel is limited, and as in Ezra–Nehemiah the survival and welfare of Israel is dependent on the world powers.

Could it be said, then, that postexilic historiography is a 'political history'? The answer, which would apply to any part of biblical historiography, would be both in the positive and in the negative. It is positive because, as historiography, it is a response to a political situation and makes a political statement. It is also in the negative, because the term 'political' does not exhaust it. 'Pure' politics do not exist according to the most basic presuppositions of biblical faith. The world is ruled by God, and he alone conducts all that happens in it. Any statement about politics is by definition a statement about God, about his guidance and providence for the world or, more restrictedly, for the people of Israel. The two protagonists of biblical historiography, including its postexilic segment, are God and Israel. Moreover, 'history' is not merely one aspect of religion, but is the arena in which the manifestation of God's sovereignty is expressed. The role of the biblical historian, like that of any historian, is to uncover the chain of cause and effect in the actual unfolding of history. Since the primary cause of the world history is God, the principle that guides this history is the will of God and history is 'religious' in the broadest sense of the term. Yet, this 'religious' framework of the concept of history does not preclude history from being rational at the same time. God's acts in ruling the world are neither willful nor arbitrary. The world is governed by rational principles which are the divine attributes. These principles are known and understandable and were revealed to man by God's self-revelation.

The conclusions of this discussion may be summarized in a broad characterization of postexilic historiography. Very much in contrast to its Deuteronomistic antecedent, postexilic historiography has a positive message at its core and is basically optimistic. It was not written as a theodicy, aimed to justify God in the face of the destruction, or as a memorial to an extinguished past. It conceives of the political reality as the expression of the will of God, but is consigned to this reality and is operating within its framework. For postexilic historiography, the trauma of the exile is a matter of the past.

A DEBATE ON COMPARATIVE HISTORICITIES

Marcel Detienne

Let us agree on this immediately: anyone intending to engage in a comparative analysis of systems of historicity implicitly rejects all those who would accept, to whatever extent, on no matter how small a scale, the evidence of an initial division between societies endowed with a 'historical consciousness' and societies devoid of it. As much as it seems impossible to distance ourselves from our own historiographical system, to that extent it seems to us urgent to analyse its components, to be suspicious of its apparent uniformity and to question its presuppositions, so as to observe as clearly as we can the details in the consciousness of itself adopted by any society, through its construction of time or perception of the past. According to the project for a comparative survey by anthropologists and historians proposed by François Hartog and Gérard Lenclud,[1] it would be

> to put in perspective, without any immediate typological preoccupation, models for writing history by following closely their structures, their structuring logic, their practices, their internal crises, the significant discrepancies that they therefore show between themselves, as well as their circulation, their encounters, their ups and downs.

In 1983, Claude Lévi-Strauss,[2] in a Conference that gave him the opportunity to take up again the old History-Ethnology debate, presented a paradox that will help us introduce a comparative reflection: 'All societies are historical in the same way, but some frankly admit it, while others find it objectionable and prefer to ignore it.' This is a sentence that Lévi-Strauss has repeated as a firm belief: primitive

---

1. François Hartog and Gérard Lenclud, 'Régimes d'historicité, modèles de temporalité' (Document préparatoire au Colloque MRT, Anthropologie contemporaine et anthropologie historique, 1992, unpublished).
2. Claude Lévi-Strauss, 'Histoire et ethnologie', *Annales E.S.C.* (1983), pp. 1217-31.

societies are distrustful of history, they do not like it, they put up with it. Such a conviction does not commit anthropology at all, any more than the denial of physical time—the time of astronomy or of geology—by Heidegger, disposing of 'vulgar time', leads philosophers to admit that time belongs to a 'metaphysical conceptualization'. The Lévi-Straussian paradox is directed to an audience of historians, and more broadly to all those who understand the double meaning of 'historical': on the one hand, belonging to natural time just like all living things; or on the other hand, being aware that the human race, in its present state, possesses a history and that it makes it or at least works as hard at it as it can. I have concentrated my attention on this system of an anthropologist—so lucid, moreover, on so many pertinent questions, in this very area—because it puts on a show of believing that the choice is simple and free: either to admit frankly one's historicity or instead to pretend not to notice it. This is a supreme generosity towards societies called, just yesterday, archaic and endowed with mythical thinking, liking to think of itself, delighting in travelling its conceptual mazes to the point that, when the day has come, of preferring 'to withdraw' in favour of a philosophy, that emerges as the prior condition for scientific research.

It is not necessary to be a historian of history, as one knowing little about our culture, to know that thinking of the past as something else, if not as something radically cut off from the present appears, in the West at least, to be a long and difficult undertaking. Just as the objective calculation of time in the mathematical and scientific measurement of physical time as the foundation of dating and of the calendar are recent knowledge acquisitions of astronomers and mathematicians, at least in our culture. In order to have a society admit that it is historical, it is perhaps not necessary that it construct a model of linear time or that it give greater importance to a representation of the event as unforeseeable and never exactly repeating itself in the same way, nor any longer, doubtless, that it discovers the dynamism specific to the history of human actions.

In the perspective of comparative and experimental linguistics that we adopt with Hartog and Lenclud, our investigation will focus on the 'systems of historicity' and on their components, convinced that to speak of a 'system of historicity', at first, makes it possible, as Hartog and Lenclud write, to take up, in a comparative way in the field of anthropology...the various forms of historical awareness, of a semantic experience of history, of a conceptual construction of human time, without for all that postulating besides its necessary coherence, nor, as a result, making the assumption of a close correlation between a culture and a historical system.

To engage in a comparative reflection, we need general formulations and specific arguments, in other words, problematic main lines and one or several areas in order to enquire into the local configurations, to put them to the test of undergoing questioning, and in this way to move forward the formulation of the one or the other 'comparison'. Certainly, we ourselves will be led to give greater importance to the field of ancient Greece, but by referring to the comparative analyses already laid out in the collective volume *Transcrire les mythologies*.[3] Three approaches have held our attention: general reflections on memory and its relation to historical thought. Next, the analysis of what is change: the representations, the different models more specifically deployed in archaic Greece. Finally, the past, the ways of speaking of it, of thinking of it, of constructing it, and the difficulties in doing so. Here again, there will be more on Greece, so often credited with the invention of 'historical knowledge'.

Memory and Historical Thought

In the history of the human race, the memory and its development have played an important role. This acknowledgment in no way leads us to believe nor to repeat that memory spontaneously creates representations of the past; no longer should certain historians in search of a new mission be allowed to write that 'true' memory is lost or is on the way to being lost, as if there was an authentic memory reserved to societies that are fortunate and without histories or a historical consciousness. The philosophers and the historians of mnemonic activity are more attentive than the laboratory cognitive scientists to what can be called the management of the memory, not as a spatial control of a supply of information, but as an apprehension in the old days of a distance of self to self.

3.   M. Detienne (ed.), *Transcrire les mythologies: Tradition, écriture, historicité* (Paris: Albin Michel, 1994).

It has often been noted that one of the most important moments in this construction of the mnemonic took place in the fourth century CE when, in Book XI of the *Confessions*, Augustine set out to reflect on the anxieties in the experience of time. As others have done, but with a new scope, Paul Ricoeur has recently shown the complexity of the thought processes carried out by Augustine.[4] I will retain just two points: on the one hand, the development of three forms of the present; on the other hand, the spatialization of the soul as a place of distension. Three modes of the present: the present torn between narrative-memory of past things that still exist; the future with that which is already, in waiting; and the present-present in its punctuality. Three modes that are situated and experienced in the soul, a soul racked by the work of that distance of self to self that opens up a temporal space and involves the construction of a human time, critical for western ideas of history. For Augustine, all this labour is done in contrast with and in opposition to eternity and to the creation of time by the Word. Tension, rifts and expectation are actually marks of the finite, of the creature facing the eternity of the Creator. From the scepticism about time between Aristotle and Augustine, and without reducing the peculiarity of this completely western approach, we should at least remember by what long developments that distance of self to self has been discovered and progressively integrated into a certain architectonic of time. In comparison, and to invoke without waiting a culture so indifferent to our historian indicators, it would be highly heuristic to analyze the memory techniques implemented by societies like Vedic and Hindu India, since we know how much they valued the mnemonic function and its immense resources. As I. Meyerson has theorized, memory as the function of the individual past of the person seems essential to the accession of a common and collective memory without which there could not be in human groups the portrayal of a common past.[5] A hypothesis that has not been accorded much attention by anthropologists, all in all not well informed about reflection carried out under the sign of a 'historical and

4.   Paul Ricoeur, *Temps et récit. I. L'intrigue et le récit historique* (Paris: Seuil, 1983).

5.   I. Meyerson, 'Le temps, la mémoire, l'histoire', *Journal de Psychologie* (1956), pp. 333-54 [republished in *Ecrits 1920–83: pour une psychologie historique* (Paris: Presses universitaires de France, 1987), pp. 264-80].

comparative psychology', fond of calling itself between 48 and the 80s,
'the only truly marxist psychology'.[6] From this we would retain today
as something experimental the idea that, though he would have thought
like a historian and one historiographically aware 'it is necessary that
the distance of the group's present in regard to the events of groups
other than those present become clearer'. In other words, no less hypothetical, when there begins the organization of that 'present absence'
that is the past of the group, when the need becomes imperative to make
present some prior events of a group lacking memory, it is then,
perhaps, that there would be an awareness and an activity of a historian.

I return to a proposition that must be subjected to rigorous testing: a
group gifted with memory does not spontaneously develop the mind of
a historian. The Vedic memory—Vedic scholars remind us—fabricates
neither India's past nor knowledge of history, although they speak
today, and already yesterday, of Indian historians with pure intentions.
The religious memory of Israel, emphasized by the 'remember', formed
by the 'remember the privileged relationship to Yahweh', can certainly
amass genealogies, lineal descendance and compare among them the
great ancestral models, Jacob and Abraham. This memory does not lead
immediately to the institution of a historiographical discourse whose
object would be the past in itself. The problem was formerly set out by
Yerusalmi; it is now taken up again by the research of Françoise Smyth
and her Swiss colleagues.

And So to the Question of Change

How does one begin to think like a historian? A double foundation:
distance of self from self, critical space within a culture. Probably such
critical space can manifest itself in other ways than by what we call the
techniques of writing, the intellectual techniques of the written. Crude
writing will not do for evidence. It would still be necessary to see if and
how cultures made it available or made or make radical arrangements
of it.

Let us extend the hypothesis in the direction indicated by Meyerson:
besides the distance of self to self, the advent of critical space, would a

---

6.   J.P. Vernant, *L'individu, la mort, l'amour: Soi-même et l'autre en Grèce
ancienne* (Paris: Gallimard, 1989).

decisive element in the collective life not be 'a great and long experience of changes'? Experience, and, perhaps, an awareness of changes?
So many societies, at first sight, seem to have undergone upheavals and
radical changes without them being recognized, thought and theorized
about.

One of the dimensions of the first Greek city with its freedom to
create itself under the form of a radical commencement, is to put into
circulation the idea, so deplorable for moralists, that virtually all political configurations are possible. The domain of the politics becomes
the privileged area for the desired reforms, deliberated with a statement
of the reasons for change. What we are dealing with here would be
practices and theories of change. In a parallel way, in philosophical
thinking, among the Presocratics, changes play an essential role in the
composition of the living, taken in a chain that goes, so far in the
Timaeus of Plato, as to link together the plant to the god, the one and
the other forming part of what the Greeks call *zôa*, the living, as are as
also the birds, or quadrupeds and human beings.

Medical thought, in its turn, enhanced the value of change, first, in
the discovery of ways of living, the development of technical skill and,
in the actual learning of doctors, the force of new theories. But, in the
hippocratic tradition, change, *metabolē*, is likewise a category that plays
a part in defining sickness and therapy: sickness is presented as a
change in the body, itself most often coming either from a change in the
seasons, or a sudden disruption in the diet. Vice versa, adequate therapy
can require change, a change 'at the same time opposed to and pro-
portioned' to that causing the illness. This is in Greek *antimetaballein*,
responding to change with change. Thucydides, who wrote the history
of the greatest turbulence ever experienced in the Greek cities shows
himself to be very attentive to models of change. Nicole Loraaux has
rightly pointed out that the most suitable time for the disclosure of that
which Thucydides calls 'human nature'—*phusis anthrōpōn*, that is to
say that which the historian of the present intends to discover—is that
of revolutions of situations (*metabolai tōn ksuntuchiōn*). Times of tur-
moil and of passions still more perverse as they change, Thucydides
writes in this same text (3.82.2-3), 'up to the usual meaning of the
words in relation to the acts in the justifications that they would give'.
For the analyst of human nature, the extreme turbulences of a war,
without common measure with all that preceded, offer conditions for
experimentation that justify in Thucydides the feeling that he towers

above all his contemporaries in the field of 'history'. If it is a matter of understanding, there is no room for doubt. As for the ways of thinking about the very object of historical knowledge, all reservations are indispensable.

Imperceptibly, in following the advances of Thucydides in regard to the faces of change, we would be led to make him the first theorist of progress. There is certainly no other model of programs ad infinitum before the works of Condorcet. Change, as it was thought about and experienced in the different sectors of knowledge, did not in the least give rise in Greece to the idea of a dynamism of history like that which the twentieth century has produced (history, before long, with its speeding up, its fuel-injection motor and double or even triple carburettor). When the contemporary historian refers to change as the indelible mark of history, he understands it in its relation to absolute chronology, to linear and irreversible time as well as to the unpredictable, singular and purely contingent event. Event, change and time are closely linked up in our thinking as historians Modern since the eighteenth century and its philosophers have made it credible that the knowledge of the past in *itself* was the object of historical knowledge.

To discover the exoticism of this project—I was going to say of this belief—it suffices to travel to China, China ancient and modern, the country of History and Historiography as far as the eye can see and in serried ranks. But what history? And what historiographers? The work of Vandermeersch has stressed the major effects of the practice of seers, in the sacrificial area in China. These are the seers who administered the assessment of signs produced by the sacrificial devices and directly recorded on the divinatory pieces—tortoise shells and shoulder blades of bovids. These seer-scribes will be the authors of the records of everything that belongs in the ritual. Called 'seers', the first annalists descend in direct line from the 'scribe of divinations'. Divided between historians of the right hand and historians of the left hand, the annalists are personages very early inseparable from each seigniorial house and from every principality. Later, as government officials of the imperial house, the compilers of annals will devote themselves to the meticulous notation, day by day, of the doings of the lord and of the prince, and of their declarations as well as all the 'events' that occurred in the course of the reign.

The analytical history of the Chinese is and will remain until the twentieth century an affair of state. While the historians, heirs of the scribes-seers, tend, like their predecessors, to formulate the events in a writing making readable their *hidden meaning*. In this system of historicity encompassing an immense production over more than two millennia, the task of the historian-government officials remains constant: 'It was a matter of establishing what each *event* could reveal about the meaning of the general evolution of the world and what sense the general evolution of the world gives to each event'. According to one of the great historians of ancient China, Sima Qian (145–86 BCE)—who was however a traveler and a great searcher for texts across the whole Chinese world of that period—the investigations of history are intended 'to clarify the meeting point of Heaven and humanity across all that which has *changed* from Antiquity to the contemporary epoch'. The writing of history aims at describing events, and, eventually, the changes according to their *true meaning*, hidden under appearances. Chinese time does not dread anything unpredictable. Emphasized by the virtues, it unfolds in the order of the cosmos that shows in a perfectly clear manner the adherence of human nature to the universal nature. In such a thought system, how could the model of a past analyzed *in itself* be extricated? The scribe-seers who underlie the model of the historians can really be astronomers and experts in calendars, the temporality that is theirs remains a stranger to the very idea of linear time, and, through it even, to the concept of the event as something unforeseeable and unique.

Rome and its annalists are just as indifferent to the analysis of the changes in the knowledge of a past radically cut off from the present. From a distance, Roman time constructed by the pontiffs and their activities seems promising, and more open to the thorough study of human action. 'Pontifical' time takes shape in religious practices: at the beginning of each month, on the Capitol, the pontiffs announced the 'nones' (the ninth day before the ides) publicly in a loud voice. Each official announcement set in motion the intervention of the *Rex sacrorum*, a second religious personage in the Roman hierarchy: his role was to make known on the 'nones' all the religious events of the month. To this mastery of the time that comes and that begins, the pontiffs added a competence over past time. These are the ones who preserve the memory of certain facts or events that occurred: military expeditions, successes, defeats, exemplary sacrifices, marvels of all kinds, signs sent by the gods. When the end of the year arrived, the Pontifex maximus seems to have got into the habit of posting the outstanding events of the year on a tablet fastened to the wall of his dwelling. It was a sort of report, a bulletin about the health of the state of affairs between the gods and humans. In this way, the pontiff can decide the vows and the most adequate expiatory ceremonies to 'inaugurate' the year well. It definitely amounts to a mastery of time allotted to a personage who was at the same time priestly and official but endowed—Dumézil has insisted on this—with 'liberty, initiative, *movement*'. In the succession of these links between two 'civil' years, the writing of the first annalists, then of historians like Livy was going to begin. A historiographical operation with a fine future: to recount the great events of a nation, for better or for worse. Events, it must be added, that make sense in the organization of the year and of its place in the life of Rome and its 'twelve hundred years'. Rome seems like a society that has not ceased to be joined to its birth place and to be intoxicated with future prospects offered it by the progressive gradation of a series of twelve—12 days, 12 months, 12 years, 12 decades, 12 centuries. A time that expands and thus suggests for the city become capital of an empire a long duration like a destiny but without the help of any linear time. History, in the Roman style, is more a memory than a survey: *memoria*, it has been observed, in the sense of an 'awareness of the past' that establishes the present and implies a certain kind of behaviour inherited from the *majores*, from the ancestors. A past heavily present, that is authoritative but also knows how to open up in the direction of the future, that of a nation sure of itself, and for long centuries.

The Colours of the Past

Not long ago, the philosopher and historian Huizinga suggested a definition of history in these terms: 'It is the intellectual form in which a civilization becomes aware by itself of its own past'. It is a seemingly simple definition but involves several complex operations, as a genealogical investigation shows.

1.   The 'rendering of an account', that refers to this work of *self to self* that is already involved in the activity of the memory ('that distance in time of self to self').

2.   To become aware: is it a simple representation or, rather, a more or less complex architectonic construction?

3.   Finally, the *past*. How to imagine it? Where does it begin? It is not at all easy to conceive that the past *is* at the same time that it *has been*. It is a long road to arrive at the notion that the past

of a group is something other than the present of this group, something different than an evident part of the group that refers to it, speaks of it, and derives examples or authority from it. Few societies, it seems, come to think that the past is of interest as such—to have been and to be—as past, in that which is the same and that which is *other*.

In order for the *other* to appear, it is necessary that the past should have begun to be separated from the present that constitutes it and seems to justify it. Death and the dead often lead historians to propose a scenario that even seems easily observable. About 30 years ago, a reputable Turkish scholar wrote an article setting out to recognize the first forms of historiography in the ancient Turkish world. He marked out these forms of beginnings in the ritual of funeral eulogies, pronounced on the occasion of the death of princes and warriors. In a condensed form, the eulogy for the dead person was engraved on a stela. First written documents, the stele of this type constitute the most ancient written documentation for the modern, that is to say contemporary, historian of Turkey. Writing of the dead, is this written eulogy a first discourse on the past? There is no indication that it is, there is no other distance than the death so near, no reflection on what there is of the other and even in the past dealt with in a ritual.

A little later, an African ethnologist studying the production of historical writing in a contemporary Mossi country indicated, for his part, the role played by the 'masters of the word', by the storytellers (*griots*), given the responsibility professionally at the time of the king's funeral to recount in detail the acts and exploits of the deceased. But it is in no way the epiphany, in this funeral scene, of a past that *is* at the same time that it *has been*. If the writing of history seems here to be turned into the eulogy of the dead by the masters of the word, it is because in Mossi country, yesterday and today, individuals practising a sort of half-memorial, half-narrative function were and are the most qualified to take the new position of historian according to the more or less prestigious model of the white conquerors who came with their writing and a duty to do history as the foundation of the identity of a group. Elsewhere, for example, in the North and South American Indian world there appeared at the beginning of the twentieth century a history turned into myth, with the mythology being progressively historicized and becoming a narrative 'in a mythical way' of contemporary events since the arrival of the whites up to those lived by the author personally, half-spoken, half-written.[7]

Between Turkish and African ethnology, there is something like a primitive scene of the beginning of historicity or of a 'making of history' that a Hellenist might be tempted to read in turn in the epic tradition of Homer. Recently, Vernant has suggested seeing a sort of complementarity between the funerals meant to transform a warrior into a hero dying a good death, and on the other hand, the epic song, inscribing the praise of the heroic exploits in the time of the *kléos*, that is to say of immortalizing glory. There were therefore, in ancient Greece, two 'institutions' making it possible to *integrate death culturally*. On the one hand, the funerals (for example of Patroclus or of Hector) come to mark the passage with a memorizing more objective than the simple regret, an institutionalized memory round the body, the weapons and the tomb, a signifying marked by the Greek word *sèma*, with everything being organized according to the social code of a heroic culture. On the other hand, the epic song, produced and displayed by the bards—who are practically the *griots* of Greece—comes to transform an individual who has lost his life into a dead person whose presence as dead is definitively inscribed in the memory of the group.

In the Greek context, a similar scene, more archaic than primitive, is only a reconstruction. In the *Iliad* and in the *Odyssey*, the epic poets already seem no longer to have direct contact with the ritual of funerals, and we do not know if they would have therefore acted as a 'social memory' for the group in the eighth or seventh century. Certainly, in reading the epic, we can get the impression that the bard by his song 'separates' the past and the present and that, thanks to the account of the mighty deeds of men of former times, the dead become men of the past. But, in the word lists, the people of bygone days alone are called *proteroi*, 'anteriors', coming before, without any word designating the past as that which has been and can be known as *other*. The Ancestors and the Ancients, indeed even the tears of Ulysses discovering, as François Hartog suggests,[8] 'the non-coincidence of self to self', are not enough, it seems to me, to establish a *first form of the past*. Very far from being the witness to a first discovery of the 'separation' between

---

7. Cf. C. Lévi-Strauss, *Paroles données* (Paris: Plon, 1984).
8. François Hartog, 'Temps et histoire "Comment écrire l'histoire de France?" ', *Annales E.S.C.* (1995), pp. 1219-36.

past and present, Homer and the epic can be considered as one of the most formidable obstacles in Greece even to thinking of the past 'as that which has been and represents something else than the present'. A continual obstacle on the scale of the fulfilment that the Homeric epic brings in archaic if not classical culture.

Fulfilment, why? Since the seventh century BCE Homer has belonged to Greek culture, he has been part of it and, very quickly, he has represented the cultural learning of the Greeks. They learned to read and write with Homer. He meant the tradition. He was the reference, and the one who gave the measure of the disparity, of the perceptible distances. In joining the heroic past to the continuous present of archaic if not classical Greece, Homer as tradition and *paideia* reinforced the feeling that the memory of the past was alive and that the vocation of the first genealogical and historiographical writers was to take over from the poets of which he was the first.

What proofs can be given of this obstacle set up by Homer in the face of the coming of an 'autonomous thought of the past'? I will retain two. The one, drawn from Thucydides; the other, provided by Herodotus, the two most outstanding exponents of fifth-century historiography. First, Thucydides, the most innovative in the area of the writing of what we call 'history'. At the time when he began to compose the accounts of the Peloponnesian War, Thucydides, as an opening, chose to use the Homeric poems to construct the model of a condition of civilization prior to the present time. It is what he calls 'Archaiologia', 'A History of Ancient Times', that is to say, that reconstruction of the 'past', of ancient times, starting from indications (*tekmèria*), from signs that make it possible to recognize and to foresee. Homer is a witness in Thucydides' eyes to a past present in the memory and before the very eyes of his contemporaries. A past that allows the historian of the present to compare and assess the greatness of today's events compared to those of yesterday.

This archaeology serves as a prologue to a 'history' entirely turned toward the present, and without any other link with 'the past' except through the comparison with the respective greatnesses. For Thucydides, the past, the *archaiologia*, is neither interesting nor significant. It is a sort of preamble, a prelude to this present that is so new and so rich. The present is actually the basis for the understanding of the 'past', if we really wish to speak of it by referring it to the poetic memory of Homer, who offers in the second half of the fifth century the recollection and the most convincing testimony, for him and for his contemporaries. Obviously, Thucydides is in no way interested in the past, in the past as such. And Homer does not lead us in any way to separate 'that which has been' from 'that which is'.

A second proof that Homer in weaving a continuity out of tradition and memory puts obstacles in the way of a new awareness of the past is provided by Herodotus of Halicarnassus. He is, in Greece, the historian who inaugurates writing about a recent past. When it comes to defining this recent past, Herodotus seems to proceed just like Homer, and to want to act as a witness so that the great deeds shall not die out, nor fade away, like the colours of a painting in time losing their radiance. Herodotus wants to recount yesterday's exploits just as Homer sang the great deeds of Achilles and Hector so that they are not deprived of 'glory', of glorious fame. Herodotus, of course, has a very intense feeling that things fade with time, that time can change everything. But, in setting out his plan for inquiries, Herodotus describes it in opposition to Homer and the memorial tradition of the epic. He excludes from his project everything that belongs to the time of the gods and heroes. His inquiry begins with the Medic wars, in the period that is called, Herodotus says (3.122), that of the human generation; the 'time of humans' (*anthrōpèiè geneè*). Herodotus seems to be the first in Greece to separate as clearly as possible the history of the gods and the history of humans. The enquiry on the recent past intends to cut itself off from the heroic past mixed with the stories of the gods, that is to say, from everything that Homer and Hesiod represent for Herodotus. This is explained in 2.53: Homer and Hesiod lived 400 years earlier, and 'These are the ones who, in their poems, have set for the Greeks their theogonies, who attributed to the deities their appropriate titles, distributed among them honours and skills, designed their appearances'. The first recent past is based on a piece cut out; it tries to be established in a distant time with Homer, with the time of the gods and of those heroes that the genealogists of the sixth century, and also the fifth, continue to join presumptuously to their presumed descendants.

Herodotus has much less than Thucydides the feeling of living in a perpetual renewal, in a time when novelty always prevails. But it is with him that the specific object of the first 'history' emerges: a recent past that is not to be confused with the fictional work of the mystical realm. His predecessor Hecataeus of Milet has helped him in this direction: he decided at the very end of the sixth century to 'put into writing' the stories of the Greeks, discovered that these stories were numerous and set out to write them 'as they seemed to him to be true'.

Before Herodotus, and more particularly with Hecateus, there is therefore, in Greece, 'a critique of the tradition'. It could be objected that there is as it were no society that does not proceed in this way. Gérard Lenclud[9] insists on this in his reflections on tradition, published in the same volume *Transcrire les mythologies*. Are there really, Lenclud wonders, societies without the 'capacity to attend to themselves'? It is to be hoped that anthropologists, outside of any great differences of viewpoint, get down to the observation of the modes of reception of 'traditions' in the societies that have so long held the attention of ethnologists and not of historians. Cultural reflectiveness can express itself in a variety of ways. To do a critique in writing of the different versions of a same story is not a Greek privilege. It is not the same procedure as the debating in the course of a ritual about the connection between two sequences or the responding to the version of an account proposed by neighbours through another version that makes a joke of the first. The context, above all, is perhaps not the same. From earliest Japan—analyzed by François Macé[10]—with the duplicate writing of the Tradition by order of the first Emperor, the so-called 'Chinese' version makes itself conspicuous by the notation and recording of all the variants of the 'accounts of primordial times'. But the compiler does not choose, he does not decide, as did the Greek from Milet, Hecateus by name, to write the account 'as it seemed to him true'. The Chinese of the Japanese eighth century work in the service of the palace administration. These are government servants. Hecateus is a citizen of leisure. Someone else will act differently, as he likes even, without any control by the city, nor even of a social body. Other configurations are there to propose variants, to set out changes, making it possible to see or imagine how the event is transformed or not in relation to the break with the past or the forms of the temporal context. These configurations are offered to us (to the extent of our curiosity) as much by societies said to be without a history as by the series of societies said to be into history as we know it.

9. Gérard Lenclud, 'Qu'est-ce que la tradition?', in Detienne (ed.), *Transcrire les mythologies*, pp. 25-44.

10. François Macé, 'La double écriture des traditions dans le Japon du VIIIe siècle: Fondation et refondation, histoire et commencement', in Detienne (ed.), *Transcrire les mythologies*, pp. 77-102.

To compare among themselves several pictures of change, of the event, the many ways of separating, of putting at a distance from the present and from the future, is perhaps a fruitful way to reflect on what would be called historical awareness or a conceptual construction of time between anthropologists and historians.[11]

11. Additional bibliography in J. Scheid, 'Le temps de la cité et l'histoire des prêtres', in Detienne (ed.), *Transcrire les mythologies*, pp. 149-58. J. Bazin, 'Production d'un récit historique,' *Cahiers d'études africaines* 73-76 (1979), XIX, 1-4, pp. 453-83. The latest version of this paper is in Marcel Detienne, *Comparer l'incomparable* (Paris: Seuil, 2000).

HISTORICAL TIMES IN MESOPOTAMIA*

Jean-Jacques Glassner

Every human society produces a dominant period that imposes its
order, its logic, its organizational system on the social body as a whole
and results in a synthesis of the diverse remarkable times illustrating the
variety of activities to which they help to give a certain rhythm, a co-
ordination and a measurement. In Mesopotamia, it is a matter of a religious time, given a certain rhythm by the succession of feasts and
rituals that are generally considered to be cyclic, in harmony with cosmic time and glorifying the past. The collective and ritual celebrations
provide the reference points; the commemorative or funerary rituals,
more particularly, emphasize their reversibility, with the commemorative rites transposing the past into the present, the funerary rituals the
present into the past.[1]

It is a generally accepted idea that in traditional societies, this time
would be nothing more than the identical reproduction of one and the
same cycle narrated in the account of the originating myth, history itself
becoming identical with this untiringly reproduced myth. Western
societies especially show originality here, with Christianity, then the
Industrial Revolution, having given to their times their linear character,
in perpetual evolution, with history never again repeating itself. The
model of cyclic time seems to be derived from Vedic India which
elaborated the doctrine of cosmic cycles called 'yugas', within which

*   The following abbreviations are used in addition to those in IATG[2]:
ARRIM: Annual Review of the Royal Inscriptions of Mesopotamia Project; BPO:
Babylonian Planetary Omens; *JTVI: Journal of the Transactions of the Victoria
Institute*; OECT: Oxford Editions of Cuneiform Texts; SAA: State Archives of
Assyria; *SAAB: State Archives of Assyria. Bulletin*; YOS: Yale Oriental Series,
Babylonian Texts.
1.   C. Lévi-Strauss, *La pensée sauvage* (Paris, 1962), pp. 313ff.

history, with its wars, its empires and its dynasties turns out to be fleeting, even evanescent.

Of course, in Mesopotamia, the calendar year was, ideally, equivalent to the creation and duration of the life of the world; during the ceremonies that mark its beginning, the chaos and the creative act that put an end to it are regularly actualized. But the temporal horizon of a society cannot bring its repetitive activities to a standstill in immobile time; it lies as well, and no less necessarily, in its ability to imagine a future and project itself into it. It is certain that without the perception of the time to come, no social strategy is possible; but, such is the case too in Mesopotamia where, like any society based on the practice of gift and exchange, the return-gift is necessarily deferred, with the immediate restitution meaning a refusal and amounting to an insult.[2]

The Mesopotamians gave a name too to that future, *nam.tar* in Sumerian, *šīmtu* in Akkadian, 'destiny', literally 'what is allocated, destined for someone'. The choice of the term makes it quite clear that, in its principle, it is subordinated to the divine will, even if, by definition, the human kings are as much its agents as its objects.[3] This notion excludes, however, a complete fatalism; the possibility is actually always offered to each individual to get out of an adverse fate by means of an appropriate ritual.[4]

The prevailing time turns out to be, in Mesopotamia, more complex therefore than appears at first sight. At a distance from the routines of the peasant world and the immobility of the mythical universe, the Mesopotamians integrated the temporal dimension into their thought patterns and attempted to put in contact with their present and their past a future that they considered uncertain and in regard to which they never ceased enquiring of the diviners. The interest in the past that results from this is not reduced to bringing back memories; it consists as well of writing history, that putting to work of memorized pieces of information under the form of new literary genres. And what does it

2.   J.J. Glassner, 'Aspects du don, de l'échange et formes d'appropriation du sol dans la Mésopotamie du 3ᵉ millénaire', *JA* 273 (1985), pp. 11-59; for a theory on the whole thing: P. Bourdieu, *Le sens pratique* (Paris: Plon, 1980), p. 179.

3.   M. David, *Les dieux et le destin en Babylone* (Paris: Édition de Minuit, 1949), *passim*.

4.   J. Bottéro, *Mythes et rites de Babylone* (Paris: Champion, 1985), pp. 29-64.

matter if Voltaire has not yet separated from his field, because anec-
dotes, the allusions to the life of princes and governments, there is no
fear, therefore, with the question not coming up, of seeing history
restricted to a subordinate role of explaining residual phenomena; matters without any meaning are not immortalized.

In Mesopotamia, there are several historical times.[5]

In the twenty-first century BCE, at Uruk, the intellectuals in charge of
putting in shape a history of the monarchy, deal with the memory of the

---

5.   Let us briefly recall the information on instruments for measuring, sundials
and other clepsydra, that were used to establish calendars and were all based on the
movement of the stars. Time is divided up into days, into months and years. Such
is, according to the Enuma Elish (5.3-46), Marduk's project who, after having
created the constellations, endowed them with movement, defining the year as made
up of twelve months, themselves made up of three decades, and the smallest unit of
time being the day, with the alternation of day and night.

The day begins in the evening, at the setting of the sun. The night itself is made
up of three watches or six double hours, a distribution that is likewise applied to the
day; the respective length of these units varied, needless to say, according to the
seasons. Finally, the double hour in turn is divided up into units of four minutes,
themselves divided into units of four seconds.

The month is a lunar month, even if it is generally rounded off to 30 days.

The year, made up of 12 lunar months, begins most generally in the spring, but
some noteworthy exceptions show that it can begin with the summer solstice or the
autumn equinox. We perceive principally two seasons, summer and winter; in its
midst, the space of six months that separates the two equinoxes is likewise perceived and counted in the number of its divisions.

The example of Cappadocia in the Old Assyrian period is especially worth noting; there, they added up, in the space of a year, 72 sequences of five days, an
eponymous ancestor being designated for each of them; the period taken into
consideration being the 365 days, namely, approximately, that of a solar year; it
seems therefore that, in this particular case, the lunar year was disregarded.

We pass over in silence, finally, the delicate question of the equivalence between
the lunar year and the solar year, with the sovereigns taking, in an erratic way, the
decision of doubling a month or part of a month when the need was felt. It was only
about the middle of the first millennium that the Babylonian astronomers discovered the cycles of 223 lunar months, or cycles of 'Saros', and that of 235 lunar
months, or 'metonyc' cycles, long cycles, respectively, of 18 and 19 years that
allow for the calculation of the regular intercalation of a month in the calendar.

As for the existence of an era, Ptolemy states that an 'era of Nabonassar' had
begun on 26 February, 747 at the twelfth hour; however, nothing in the present state
of the sources is found to support this assertion.

past and write down a chronicle, the 'Chronicle of the Single Monarchy',[6] whose object is to legitimate the local sovereign, Utuhengal, an ambitious and brilliant epigone who presents himself as a zealous continuator of the defunct kingdom of Akkadē.

The thesis developed throughout the work relies on a double postulate: the assertion of the character at once unique and local of the monarchy; in other words, it is not divided up but, not being the exclusive privilege of one place only, it is manifested, successively, in different cities. Four cities, principally, receive it in turn: four times it fell to the lot of Kish, five times to Uruk, one time to Akkadē, three times to Ur. This synthetic vision of the movement of history brings to light the precise representations of space and time. As regards space, the choice and the order of succession of toponyms make it seem like an interplay of alternations between the North and the South of Mesopotamia, an interplay itself complicated by local rivalries.[7] As for time, it is not considered a continuous and uniform movement but a splitting up, a succession of segments that sometimes bear the same name but never have the same duration. The passage from one segment to another corresponds to a threshold that signifies the abandonment or the destruction of a city and the transfer of kingship to a new city. In total, twenty periods of unequal length follow one another throughout the chronicle.

Some manuscripts use the Sumerian *bala* to designate the periods during which the kingship is established in a city.[8] It is generally assumed that this term alludes to a circularity in time; some readily

---

6.   Most recently: J.J. Glassner, *Chroniques mésopotamiennes* (Paris: Les Belles Lettres, 1993), pp. 137-42. It is not impossible that a first version could date from the period of Akkad; even if several arguments support this, the hypothesis remains flimsy and is based on the validity of a reconstruction proposed for the end of a royal inscription (J.J. Glassner, 'Modes d'acquisition de la terre au 3e millénaire en Mésopotamie: le témoignage des kudurrus anciens', *BiOr* 52 (1995), p. 22, *sub* n. 24); it makes it possible to understand better, however, the precedence of Kish in the work.

7.   The kingship fell to the lot of cities that were foreign or associated with the political realm under consideration: Adab, Awan, Ḥamazi, Mari, Akshak, Gutium, finally Isin, that is a late addition; the names of Mari, Akshak and Adab appear in the Ebla archives; we know, besides, that Akshak is at the head of a coalition that included Kish and Mari against Lagash, and that Kish and Akshak are adversaries of Uruk; but the work was not intended to give an account of all past history.

8.   Manuscripts D and N.

compare it to a homonymous word that refers to the 'spindle', the tool that is used to twist and wind a thread when they spin at the distaff; some think that there is just one term, *bala*, the idea of circularity being derived from the primary meaning of 'spindle'.

Of course, *bala* contains, to begin with, the idea of turn, of successive or alternative rank. It means, very commonly, the alternative exercising of duties that individuals emanating from all levels of society, from the most humble person up to the governors of provinces, kings and even the gods themselves, can fulfill. An example will suffice to illustrate this; in the Empire of Ur III, some high dignitaries were obliged to pay annually a tax specific in nature that they paid in turn, thus ensuring a good distribution of its payment throughout the year; in this context, *bala* designates the levied tax, the spell of duty and the established rotation.[9] In short, the term indicates a scanning of time.

But *bala* indicates as well a duration, the period of work conscripted employees carried out or that of the alternative discharge of certain duties or functions. That duration varies, as it can go from simply one day annually to a more or less extended number of years. The word designates therefore a temporal segment, a closed interval of time, a part cut off in the *continuum* of social time. This segment is character-ized by a beginning that corresponds to the taking of office, a duration and an end indicating the stopping of the activity; a document of the Ur III period is explicit on this subject, reporting on the salaries of employ-ees who 'have gone to the *bala*, have completed the *bala* and have returned from the *bala*,' *bala.še₃ gin.na bala.a [gub].ba u₃ bala.ta gur.ra*.[10] We bear in mind that that portion of time is not linear, since at the core of the semantic field defined by the term are the ideas of rotation and of periodicity that return to the image of a circular and repetitive time, a same period characterized by the same activities being called on to happen again.

Nevertheless, if the image of the circularity of time stands out, it does not necessarily imply symmetry. We actually find that the duration of a *bala* bearing the same name is not inevitably the same; thus, in the Chronicle of the Monarchy One: Kish I lasts 24,510 years, 3 months

9.   M. Sigrist, *Drehem* (Bethesda: CDL, 1992), pp. 339-56.

10.   H. de Genouillac, *Textes économiques d'Umma* (Textes cunéiformes. Musée du Louvre, 5; Paris, 1922), 5676 rev. xi 11-13.

and one and a half days: Kish II, 3195 years; Kish III, 100 years; Kish IV, 491 years; and so on. This implies that some idea of change is like-wise present in *bala*, with the term not exclusively referring to these worlds that live, die and are reborn since earliest times, 'identical in themselves, unchanged, just like the earth, the things, without interrup-tion, have called for them' (P. Bergounioux).

It is therefore a circular time that is displayed throughout the chron-icle and we have good reason, in regard to its purpose, to speak of 'cycles'. A closer reading of the work makes it possible to discover there several temporalities that are superimposed or are interwoven.

The author of the C version uses the name *bala* to refer to temporal units that are not identified by means of a toponym but with the help of an anthroponym, whose period of existence is specified each time: '1560 years, *bala* of En-me-nunna', '1207+... years, <*bala* of Bar-sal-nunna>', '1525 (?) years, *bala* of En-men-barage-si', '745 years, *bala* of Mes-kiag-gasher', '131 (?) years, *bala* of Ku-Bawa', '157 (?) years, *bala* of Sargon'; other similar phrases are very likely restorable in the gaps of the manuscript. With *bala* speaking each time of a related group identified by the name of its founder, these units quite obviously form family cycles whose extent includes, depending on the individual case, two to four generations. But these cycles happen to be found within local cycles; thus three family cycles are present within the cycle of Kish I; others are deployed, later, inside the cycles of Uruk I, of Kish III and IV, or of Akkadē; the example of Ur III shows that a local cycle can coincide with a family cycle.

We see also that the time of a chronicle can extend simultaneously in two ways, on the diachronic level and the synchronic level. The first is obvious, it shows through behind the form of writing and the spatial system retained by the authors. The second appears with less clarity, although at least two biographical notes unambiguously indicate it; one concerns Dumuzi, the fourth king of Uruk I, who, according to Manu-script C, is the conqueror of En-men-barage-si, the second-last king of Kish I; the other concerns the founder of the Akkadē cycle, Sargon, of whom it is indicated that he served as cupbearer for Ur-Zababa, the second king of Kish IV; but, to begin with, always if we trust the chron-icle, there are at least 2560 years separating the reigns of En-men-barage-si and Dumuzi, and 91 those of Ur-Zababa and Sargon. Conse-quently, it appears that the kingship passed from Kish I to Uruk I not right after the dying out of the local cycle of Kish, but at the time of the defeat of the second last of his representatives and that it made its appearance at Uruk under the reign of the fourth representative of this cycle; besides, from the period of Ur III, the hymnic literature takes over from the chronicle, even if, in its eyes, it is no longer Dumuzi, but Gilgamesh who conquered En-men-barage-si and brought, at the same time, the kingship from Kish to Uruk.[11] A similar conclusion emerges with regard to Ur-Zababa and Sargon. In short, royal cycles and local cycles do not correspond nor necessarily coincide: if the royal cycles can only follow one another, the local cycles can partially overlap.

The concept of time expressed by means of *bala* is therefore that of a complex time, enriched with layers and formed by the superimposition of several different streams. It raises, about itself, the question of its portrayal. The Sumerian verb *bal*, which has, notwithstanding its homophony, but little relation to the noun *bala*, means, among other things, the gesticulations of a goat when it is being pursued by wolves, and ends up in a tangle of feet and stumbles,[12] or, metaphorically, of the contortion of a human body moving like a reptile.[13] We take from this metaphor a sinusoidal representation of this time that is suggested in a more convincing manner, by another route, by G. Bachelard, with his outline of the theory of 'temporal waves',[14] and, especially, by P. Bourdieu.[15] This representation has the merit of underscoring, all at once, the times of transition that correspond to the birth, the ageing and the dying out of each cycle, with the ageing coinciding with the birth of a second cycle and the death with a third, of bringing up the outstanding episodes the author of the chronicle has judged it worthwhile to note by means of brief biographical notices, of representing, finally, the synchronisms, the interweaving and the overlappings that they just emphasized. As regards the first cycle of Kish, we get the following diagram, which we can extend to the whole field of chronicles:[16]

11. J. Klein, 'Šulgi and Gilgameš: Two Brother-Peers (Šulgi O)' (*AOAT*, 25; Neukirchen–Vluyn: Neukirchener Verlag, 1976), pp. 271-92 (278, ll. 58-60).

12. A Sumerian proverb, Coll. 8 17, cited by A.W. Sjöberg (ed.), *The Sumerian Dictionary*, II (Philadelphia: University of Pennsylvania Press, 1984), p. 49b.

13. E. Chiera, *Sumerian Religious Texts* (Upland, 1924), n. 6 i 33; J. Klein, 'Šulgi D: A Neo-Sumerian Royal Hymn' (PhD dissertation, Philadelphia, 1968), p. 70, l. 173.

14. G. Bachelard, *La dialectique de la durée* (Paris: PUF, 1963), pp. 92ff.

15. P. Bourdieu, *Le sens pratique*, pp. 333-55.

16. J.J. Glassner, *Chroniques mésopotamiennes*, pp. 83-87.

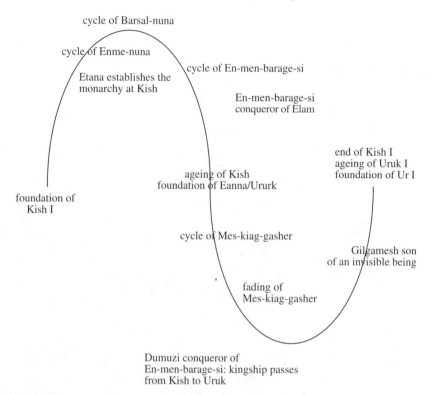

cycle of Barsal-nuna

cycle of Enme-nuna

Etana establishes the
monarchy at Kish

cycle of En-men-barage-si

En-men-barage-si
conqueror of Elam

end of Kish I
ageing of Uruk I
foundation of Ur I

foundation of
Kish I

ageing of Kish
foundation of Eanna/Ururk

cycle of Mes-kiag-gasher

Gilgamesh son
of an invisible being

fading of
Mes-kiag-gasher

Dumuzi conqueror of
En-men-barage-si: kingship passes
from Kish to Uruk

For this kind of time is actually made thinkable by reference to genealogy, the real organizational axis of the chronicle. In the image of the historians of King Entemena of Lagash who, about 2350, on the pretext of writing about the more than century-long war that had brought Lagash and Umma into conflict, narrate the history of a royal family, the chronicler brings together the events, the people and the different places on the basis of a temporal relation inspired by the genealogical links and makes use of the two dimensions of diachrony and synchrony.[17] In fact, the royal cycles follow one another in the image of human generations and, just as a family does not die with the death of the ancestor, kingship does not die with the end of a cycle but lives on with the institution of a new cycle, in the image of a son who perpetuates the family cycle; an opposition becomes clear between two successive cycles, a royal city 'conquered' or 'destroyed' being

17. At the end of the second millennium, in order to recount the creation of the world, the author of the glorification of Marduk again makes use of the same genealogical outline; it is a matter then of a divine genealogy.

replaced by a new one, just like an equivalence between two alternate cycles, a third cycle replacing the first at the moment when this one has just disappeared; in several cases, the recurrent presence of the same toponyms, each second generation, emphasizes this equivalence, as in the sequence *Kish*—Aksak—*Kish—Uruk*—Akkadē—*Uruk*—Gutium—*Uruk*—Ur. It is in a word the succession of generations that justifies the relative dating of the events, and the presence of totals, at the end of the manuscripts of the chronicle from Nippur, shows that time is measured by the number and duration of cycles, the system of dating reflecting the relations that they maintain between them.

In Akkadian, the terms *dāru* or *dūru* and their derivatives—the Sumerian da.ri$_2$ is a loan word from Akkadian—express continuity, duration or permanence; they indicate a time that is elapsing, according to a continuous state of flux, from a past gone by, sometimes distant, up to a future more or less distant.

They understand the past like the future. Puzur-Sîn of Assyria (eighteenth century) asserts that he constructed a wall at Assur, a deed, according to him, that no king had yet accomplished 'since the most remote times', *ištu dūrîm*.[18] Hammurabi of Babylon (1792–1750) supposes himself 'the descendent of an ancient royal line', *zērum dārīum ša šarrūtim*, and expresses the wish to see 'in the future', *ana dār*, his name pronounced with veneration, specifying that he had ensured 'for the future', *ana dār*,[19] the happiness of his people; his successor, Samsu-iluna (1749–1712) claims in his turn 'an ancient divine lineage', *zēr ilī dārīum*[20]; later, in the fifteenth century, a mayor of Byblos writes to Pharaoh to remind him of the fidelity of his city with regard to Egypt 'since the most remote times', *ištu dārīti*[21]; finally, and among many others, an unknown monarch proclaims himself 'king, son of a king, of [anc]ient [royal li]neage', *šarru mār šarri zē[r šarrūti dār]*.[22]

18. A.K. Grayson, 'Rivalry over Rulership at Assur: The Puzur-Sîn Inscription', *ARRIM* 3 (1985), p. 13 iii 5.

19. G.R. Driver and J.C. Miles, *The Babylonian Laws* (Oxford: Clarendon Press, 1955), p. 12, v. 1; p. 96, xxv, 1; p. 98, xxv 36.

20. F.J. Stephens, *Votive and Historical Texts from Babylonia and Assyria* (YOS, 9; New Haven: Yale University Press, 1937), p. 71 n. 35.

21. W.L. Moran, *Les lettres d'El-Amarna* (LAPO, 13; Paris: Cerf, 1987), p. 45 n. 88.

22. T.G. Pinches, 'Certain Inscriptions and Records Referring to Babylonia and Elam and their Rulers', *JTVI* 29 (1997), p. 85: 17-18.

Two more texts make it possible to define better the concept of time that they express. An inscription of Naram-Sin of Akkadē (about 2200–2150)[23] associates *ištum dār* with *šikitti nišē*, 'the creation of man', the time thus designated going back to the origins of humanity; elsewhere, the epic of Gilgamesh[24] compares *ana dūr dār* with *šīmat la iqattû*, 'a destiny that will not have an end'; the verb *qatû* means 'to put a stop, an end',[25] but when understood negatively, it means, on the contrary, the absence of a limit.

Dūru and *dāru* mean therefore a time that proceeds from a starting point, here the creation of man, elsewhere a festive activity, every date of any kind being able, besides, to be agreed upon,[26] but a time that, on the contrary, does not know any limit in the future.

Consequently, it is not surprising to see them translate the idea of eternity: thus, in the royal inscriptions of every epoch, there are numerous allusions to 'eternal' reigns, *dār*, of the kings; similarly, a seer can predict, in the case of a simple *person*, that 'the eternal protection of the god will be over the person concerned', *ṣilli ili dārû eli amēli ibašši*.[27] This 'eternity' lasts as long as their gods and their work last; Samsu-iluna[28] proclaims that the gods decreed for him 'a destiny of eternal life like (that) of the gods Sîn and Utu', *balāṭam ša kīma Sîn u Šamaš dārîum*; in the correspondence from every epoch, we can formulate for its speaker the wish for an eternal life: 'long life to a father as long as the heaven and earth last', *kīma šamû u erṣetum dārû adda lū dārî*, is

23. I.J. Gelb and B. Kienast, *Die altakkadischen Königsinschriften des dritten Jahrtausends* (FAOS, 7; Stuttgart: Steiner, 1990), p. 255: 1-4.

24. Gilgamesh VII iii 7: R.J. Tournay and A. Shaffer, *L'épopée de Gilgamesh* (LAPO, 15; Paris: Cerf, 1994), p. 166.

25. See the very beautiful verse: *ūmū iqtat ītetiq adannu*, 'the times have passed, the hour has come' (L. Cagni, *L'epopea di Erra* [Rome: Istituto di Studi del Vicino Oriente; University of Rome, 1969], p. 86, IIc 13).

26. An early Babylonian letter recounts a legal declaration according to which it is announced that a person has 'always', *dār*, slept with a certain woman, with the duration being understood as starting from a precise moment, '*ištu la-ba-aš x x*', 'since...'; the term is damaged by an unfortunate break (F. Thureau-Dangin, *Lettres et contrats de l'époque de la première dynastie babylonienne* [TCL, 1; Paris: Librairie Orientaliste P. Geuthner, 1910], p. 17 n. 10).

27. E. Ebeling, *Keilschrifttexte aus Assur religiösen Inhalts*, I (Leipzig, 1915–1919), p. 22 n. 148.

28. F. Stephens, *Votive and Historical Texts from Babylon and Assyria*, YOS 9 (1937), p. 150 n. 35.

expressed in an early Babylonian letter,[29] 'that they govern as long as heaven and earth last', *adi šamê irṣitim dārûni šunu lū muma"irute ša kal mātāti*, such is the vow formulated for the posterity of the king by a palace exorcist in a letter of the neo-Assyrian period.[30] It is contrasted with what is perishable, with futility, as is evident from remarks made by Gilgamesh, in a passage of an early Babylonian version of the epic:[31] *mannu ibrī elû ša[mâ] iluma itti Šamaš dārîš uš[bu] awīlūtumma manû ūmūša mimma ša īteneppušu šāruma*, 'My friend, who therefore can go up to heaven? These are the gods who live there forever, with the sun. As for humanity, its days are numbered: all that it does and redoes is nothing more than wind'!

They indicate, finally, a continuous time, made thinkable and manageable thanks to the calendar, marked by equal and measureable cyclical units of time, the years, the months, the days, as is emphasized by the author of a neo-Babylonian letter[32] that takes care to explain the phrase *ana dāriš*, 'forever', in these terms: *ūmu ana ūmu arḫu ana arḫu šattu ana šattu*, 'day after day, month after month, year after year'.[33]

In brief, it amounts to a time that we can represent by means of a vector, of a segment oriented in a straight line, and we come close, on the face of it, to the traditionally accepted definition, nowadays, of linear time: a time endowed with a beginning and oriented in a perspective of progress. This last category, however, is very much lacking in Mesopotamia, if we make exception for the claims of the kings of having performed exploits that none of their predecessors had accomplished before them. But let us not be fooled, when Naram-Sin of Akkad asserts that he discovered what 'no king, among the kings, had ever seen', *šar in šarrī manāma la īmuru*,[34] or strode along routes that

29. M. Stol, *Letters from Collections in Philadelphia, Chicago and Berkeley* (ABBU, 11; Leiden: E.J. Brill, 1986), p. 7 n. 59.

30. S. Parpola, *Letters from Assyrian and Babylonian Scholars* (SAA, 10; Helsinki: University of Helsinki, 1993), n. 227: rev. 20-22.

31. Gilgameš, Yale tablet iv 5-8: R.J. Tournay and A. Shaffer, *L'épopée de Gilgamesh*, p. 86.

32. R.F. Harper, *Assyrian and Babylonian Letters* (London, 1892–1914), n. 1410 r. 6.

33. For more details, cf. J.J. Glassner, *Le devin historien, Actes de la 45e Rencontre Assyriologique Internationale* (Cambridge, MA: Harvard University Press).

34. I.J. Gelb and B. Kienast, *Die altakkadischen Königsinschriften des dritten Jahrtausends* (FAOS, 7; Stuttgart, 1990), p. 235, Naramsin C 1 403-405.

'no king among the kings had travelled', *šar in šarrī la illik*,[35] when, after him, among many others, Tukulti-Ninurta I (1243–1207) recalls that he strode on mountains 'whose paths no king had yet reconnoitred', *ša šarru ia'umma arḫatešunu la idu*,[36] Tiglath-Pileser I (1114–1076) recalls the high mountains 'that no king had yet reached', *[ša a]šaršunu šarru ia'umma la iba'u*,[37] or Sennacherib (704–681) boasts of having brought back the tribute from the Medes 'whose name no king, among his ancestors, had heard the name', *ša ina šarrani abbīya mamman la išmu*[38]; in all these cases they call to mind more the feats that they accomplished and that were until then unequalled rather than the idea of progress.

In actual fact, insistence is placed more on the duration itself than on any kind of well-defined direction of time. It is really in this way that we should understand, for example, the chronological indications contained in the Assyrian and Babylonian royal inscriptions: Tiglath-Pileser I notes that Ashur-Dan I (1178–1133) and Shamshi-Adad I (1808–1776) reigned, respectively, 60 and 641 years before him[39]; Sennacherib reckons that Tiglath-Pileser I had preceded him by 418 years[40]; Nabonidus (55–539) estimates the time that separates him from Naram-Sin at 3200 years.[41] With these chronicles, it is important, first of all, to put the past in perspective and, by the great antiquity of the examples set forth, to ensure a legitimacy to the acts of the reigning sovereign.

Some Akkadian-speaking lawyers from Susa, in the early Babylonian period, used the two terms *dūru* and *pal* in one and the same formula. A loan-word from Sumerian, Akkadian *pal* always indicates the alternative cycle, one or several year(s) of a reign, indeed a reign or a

35. I. Gelb and B. Kienast, *Die altakkadischen Königsinschriften*, p. 249, NaramSin C 3 23-25.

36. E. Weidner, *Die Inschriften Tukulti-Ninurtas I und seiner Nachfolger* (*AfO* Beiheft, 12; Graz, 1959), p. 27 ii 41.

37. E.A. Wallis Budge and L.W. King, *Annals of the Kings of Assyria* (London, 1902), p. 52 iii 38-39.

38. D.D. Luckenbill, *The Annals of Sennacherib* (OIP, 2; Chicago, 1924), p. 29 ii 34.

39. A.K. Grayson, *Assyrian Royal Inscriptions*, II (Wiesbaden: Otto Harrasso-witz, 1976), pp. 17-18.

40. Luckenbill, *The Annals of Sennacherib*, p. 85: 50.

41. S. Langdon, *Die neubabylonischen Königsinschriften* (Leipzig, 1912), Nabonidus I ii 58 and passim.

dynasty;[42] it expresses as well, in the image of *bala*, some idea of change.[43]

The phrase from Susa, as is evident from the complete formula, *ana dūr u pala ana šer šerri*, where *šer šerri*, '(for) posterity', indicates the succession of generations; by associating the two ideas of time, it has as its aim to evoke all of time to come; we will translate it, in the light of what has just been said: 'for continuity and change, for posterity'.[44]

Shamshi-Adad I, in one of his inscriptions,[45] uses the term *dāru*, with the meaning 'generation'; this king recalls the 7 *dārū ītiqu*, 'the seven generations gone by', that separate one of his own achievements, the capture of the city of Nurrugum, from *šulum Akkadē*, 'the apogee (of the Empire) of Akkadē';[46] we see here an attempt to develop a chronology in terms of genealogy, the latter initiating the former, like the Chronicle of Monarchy One, a historiographic work that the same Shamshi-Adad knew well, since he had at least one copy made by his scribes, in his city of Shubat-Enlil.[47]

According to the *Enuma Elish*, when Marduk created the world from the dead body of Tiamat, he put the moon and the sun in the liver of the deceased, assigning them the task of defining the days and the months, foundations for calendar calculations, and for 'giving divinatory sentences', *dīna dīn[a]*;[48] the myth emphasizes in this way the connection that divination, including hepatoscopy, in its essence maintains with cosmic time and, consequently, with that of history. Since, if it is true that divination is interested in the prediction of the future, of which it gives, certainly, a partial vision, and, often, in short term (the date for the realization of an oracle varies ordinarily from a few days to a

42. To speak of a spindle, Akkadian uses another term, this one Semitic, *pilakku*.

43. E. Cassin, 'Cycles du temps et cadres de l'espace en Mésopotamie ancienne', *Revue de Synthèse* 90 (1929), pp. 243-44.

44. J.V. Scheil (ed.), *Actes juridiques susiens* (MDP, 22; Paris: E. Leroux, 1930), p. 8 n. 42; (MDP, 23; Paris, 1932), nn. 200:10; 203: 9; 213: 5; (MDP, 24; Paris, 1933), p. 12 n. 357; *Mélanges épigraphiques* (MDP, 28; Paris, 1939), p. 11 n. 418.

45. R.C. Thompson, 'The British Museum Excavations on the Temple of Ishtar at Nineveh', *AAA* 19 (1930–31), pl. 81 I 18.

46. For this translation, cf. Glassner, *Chroniques mésopotamiennes*, p. 22.

47. Glassner, *Chroniques mésopotamiennes*, pp. 87-92.

48. J. Bottéro and S.N. Kramer, *Lorsque les dieux faisaient l'homme* (Paris: Gallimard, 1989), p. 632, V 24.

month[49]), it appears likewise preoccupied with the memory of the past[50]: at Mari, round about 1800, a diviner inquires about the meaning to be attributed to an eclipse of the moon[51]; in Assyria, in the seventh century, other seers were put to work to elucidate the reasons for the death of King Sargon II, surprised in his camp, in a foreign land, and, due to this, deprived of burial.[52]

At least two reasons explain this attraction for times gone by; first of all, all the acts of public life, whether past, present or future, have formed or form the subject of divinatory consultations; secondly, an event of the past, because it suggests resemblances, can be the occasion to call up a historical precedent raised to the rank of example.

In fact, the approach of the diviner is far removed from that of the historian as we understand it at the present time. Certainly, he picks out the events of the past, but the simple notation of facts seems to be enough for him. Because if history, with its time fragmented into various units susceptible of repetition, is not exempt from the general laws

49. See J.M. Durand, *Archives épistolaires de Mari 1/1* (ARM, 24; Paris: Recherche sur le civilisations, 1988), pp. 57-59; in Assyria, a hepatoscopic text (E. Ebeling, *Keilschrifttexte aus Assur religiösen Inhalts*, II [Leipzig: Hinrichs, 1920–23], p. 7 n. 452) expresses itself as follows: *šumma rēš ṣēri šumēl ubāni I paṭir UD.6.KAM adanš[u...] ana UD.6.KAM ïl nakri taṣabbat*, 'if the upper part of the "back" of the right side of the "finger" displays a "crack"—the term is six days; during these six days you will take possession of an enemy city'. The same text continues with mention of 9, 12, 15, 18, 21, 24, 27 and 30 days. The exceptions to this rule are relatively rare, since the term for the realization of an oracle announced by an eclipse that takes place during the evening watch perhaps is a hundred days (H. Hunger, *Astrological Reports to Assyrian Kings* [SAA, 8; Helsinki: University of Helsinki Press, 1992], n. 336); elsewhere, a certain configuration of the liver is a sign that *šarrum [š]er šerrišu adi ŭamšim ina kussîm [uš]šab*, 'the posterity of the king will sit on the throne up to the fifth generation' (A. Goetze, *Old Babylonian Omen Texts* [YOS, 10; New Haven: Yale University Press, 1947] n. 31 v 49; *ḫamši*, 'five' means in fact numerous); or again (E. Reimer and D. Pingree, *Enuma Anu Enlil, Tablets 50-51* [BPO, 2; Malibu, 1981], p. 59, Text IX 26): *Elamtum Akkad MU.5.KAM išallal*, 'Elam will pillage Akkad for five years'.

50. Such is the case as well in ancient China: see L. Vandermeersch, 'L'imaginaire divinatoire dans l'histoire en Chine', in Detienne (ed.), *Transcrire les mythologies* (Paris: Albin Michel, 1994), pp. 103-13.

51. J.M. Durand, *Archives Epistolaires de Mari 1/1* (ARM, 26; Paris: Recherche sur les civilisations 1988), p. 221 n. 81.

52. H. Tadmor, B. Landsberger and S. Parpola, 'The Sin of Sargon and Sennacherib's Last Will', *SAAB* 3.1 (1989), pp. 3-51.

that divinatory science brings to the fore with more and more sharpness, the seer seeks more and more to define, by means of a meticulous description of occurrences, the modalities according to which are established the reciprocal relations that unite the two worlds of society and nature, longing for a plan in which the very subject matter of history is diluted.

It is noteworthy, as is shown by the use of formula c) on the liver models of Mari (see below), that the diviners would be in a position to deduce a presage of the oracle that is associated with it, so convinced are they of the reality of the reciprocal relation that unites the cosmos, nature and culture. The configuration of a sheep's liver being able to be inferred from a political or military event, Mesopotamian divination claims to assert itself as a system scientifically developed and for which, as a final authority, the gods are the guarantors.

Because the diviner has his legitimacy and his authority, precisely, from his aptitude for dialogue with the divine and from his capacity to interpret the language of the gods; the dialogue is introduced at the time prayer is addressed to them, when he poses his own question and he awaits from them a 'firm and positive' response, *annā kīna*; it is at that moment, and at that moment only, that the gods write on the envisaged medium the shape of the omen.[53] He becomes in that case the interpreter of the divine message that he reads as if it were a text, since it is thought of as a written document; besides, is it not said of Shamash, the god par excellence of divination, *[kīma t]ikip sattakki taḫāṭa ina nūrka kallatsina mātāte*, 'you scrutinize in your light all the countries like cuneiform signs',[54] *ina libbi immeri tašaṭṭar šīrī tašakkan dīnu*, 'you produce your sentence by inscribing the omen within the sheep'?[55] The diviner, like every literate person of the time, sees the whole world through the metaphor of writing, every phenomenon becoming, first of all, a graphic sign. This knowledge, however, is not enough by itself to establish his competence and his authority; he must still monopolize the word that he has granted himself and introduce a scientific and institutional discourse, making of his speciality, besides a descriptive

53. I. Starr, *Queries to the Sungod* (SAA, 4; Helsinki: Helsinki University Press, 1990), *passim*.

54. E. Ebeling, *Keilschrifttexte aus Assur religiösen Inhalts*, III (Leipzig: Hinrichs, 1920–23), p. 3 n. 361.

55. S.H. Langdon, *Babylonian Penitential Psalms* (OECT, 6; Paris: P. Geuthner, 1927), pl. 30, K 2824: 12 and duplicates.

science of the connections that nature and society maintain, a model for teaching and the place for the statement of political precepts, institutional regulations, even economic decisions.

This science did not remain fixed all through the three millennia. For the convenience of exposition, we propose recognizing in them two periods. The first can only be characterized negatively as being marked by the absence of learned tracts; it came to an end around the eighteenth century; the second is distinguished by the presence of tracts that became, progressively, genuine manuals with encyclopedic aspects.

As regards the first period, it is illustrated by the models of livers dating from the very beginning of the second millennium, where three different forms are distinguished:

a) (the figure illustrated by the model) *amūt* + a royal name, a toponym or substantive in the genetive + *ša* + event, with the verb, when there is one, being noted as preterite.[56] Thus: *amūt Išbi-Erra ša Elamtam dagilšu u Elamtam ilqā*, 'omen of Ishbi-Irra who, (although) a subject of Elam, seized Elam'; *amūt šaḫurrurim ša ummānum isḫur*, 'omen of amazement according to which the army withdrew'.[57]

b) *inūmi* + event, the verb being in the preterite, + (the liver, allusion to the model) appears in this way, the verb being likewise in the preterite.[58] For example: *inūmi Šubariū ana Išbi-Erra ištapparuma ašar šanîm Šubariū issaḫruna annium kīam iššakin,* 'when the Subarians, having exchanged messages with Ishbi-Irra, turned away in another direction, that appeared in this way'; *inūmi šarrum mâtam nakartam ana ṣērišu utirruma annium kīam iššakin,* 'when the king won over to his cause a country up until then an enemy, that appeared in this way'.[59]

c) *šumma* + event, the verb being in the present, + (the liver, allusion to the model) will appear in this way, the verb being likewise in the present; the last proposition is however optional.[60] For example, *šumma Amurrum iṣaḫḫer [kī]am iššakkan,* 'if Amurru weakens, that will appear in this way'; *šumma nakrum ana ālim ayumma tēbīam itauma*

56. M. Rutten, 'Trente-deux modèles de foies en argile provenant de Tell-Hariri (Mari)', *RA* 35 (1938), nn. 1 to 6; 8 and 9; 11; 13; 16 to 18.

57. Rutten, 'Trente-deux modèles', nn. 9 and 16.

58. Rutten, 'Trente-deux modèles', nn. 7, 10, 22.

59. Rutten, 'Trente-deux modèles', nn. 10 and 22.

60. Rutten, 'Trente-deux modèles', nn. 11, 12, 14, 15, 17 to 19, 21, 23, 24, 27, 29 to 32.

awassu uṣṣiam annium kīam iššakkan, 'if an enemy plans an attack against any city and if his plan is disclosed, that will appear in this way'.[61]

These accounts can be divided into two series, according to whether they deal with past or future time. Among the thirty-two sentences inscribed on the Mari liver models, no less than nine make reference to historical events. As so many signs unobserved until then and henceforth remarkable, such historical omens are therefore noted in writing and memorized, being a sign of the bond that unites human history to nature and to the cosmos. Divination likes to think of itself as a knowledge of reality that constantly mixes theory and practice; it is based on experience, by turning towards the past from which it draws its inspiration and by considering, at the same time, the coincidences established between social facts and natural, a priori fortuitous, configurations, as obligatory correlations that must re-occur, it rethinks the events of which it has knowledge, according to the principles that govern its own cognitive operations, extrapolating in the direction of the future the configurations and linkages from the past and looking to the establishment of homogeneous series constituted of as many specific facts, potentially repeatable, that take on the value of prototypes. Let us not deceive ourselves about this, however, with repetition not necessarily meaning symmetry, since any repetition generates a new content; the Mesopotamians do not reread indefinitely the pages of a same book and the relationship between the past, the present and the future is essentially based on similarity.

Let us choose, to illustrate this intention, a final document from Mari where it is written: *šumma dūram nakrum ṣa'ilšu*, 'if the enemy attacks a fortified town, (that will appear in this way)'; an isolated noun clarifies the ominous meaning of the sentence: *pušqum*, 'distress'. But, this term recalls a precise historical situation, the siege of Akkadē, at the beginning of the reign of Naram-Sin, with the king being besieged in his capital by the entirety of his people revolting against him. If the historical reference is therefore undeniable, the absence of the place name and the giving up of the past historic helps, on the contrary, to separate the observation from its original temporal context and makes it possible to assign it to another time, present or future, as well as to a new individual and to a different place. Conversely, it is the reciprocal

---

61. Rutten, 'Trente-deux modèles', nn. 12 and 19.

relation between the omen and the oracle, and it alone, that remains unchanged.[62]

Later, with the development of canonical tracts, the forms change. The b) formulas disappears. The c) formula comes into general use, with this distinctive characteristic, however, in that its components are reversed: *šumma* + status of the omen, with the verb most usually in the stative, rarely in the preterite, + wording of the oracle, with the verb being in the present; thus: BE BA_3 *ul-lu-ṣa-at* DIRI GABA NI_3. GA LU_2 *ana* IGI-$šu_2$ GIN-*ak*, 'if the omen dilates—success; the possessions of the person concerned will prosper'.[63] The a) formula continues in use, but it is reserved for historical omens only and is adapted to the dominant outline: *šumma* + status of the omen, with the verb in the stative, + *amūt* + royal name, place name or noun + *ša* + wording of the oracle, with the verb being in the preterite; thus: BE *ina* 15 BA_3 BUR_3. MEŠ 2 ŠUB.MEŠ BA_3-*ut man-nu* LUGAL *man-ni* NU LUGAL u_4-*um* UR_5.$UŠ_2$ DU_3-$šu_2$ *ina* $SISKUR_2$ NUN GU_4 UZU GU_4 KU_2, 'if at the right of the omen two cavities are found—omen "who is king, who is not king"; on the day of the hepatocopic consultation, during the prince's sacrifice, an ox ate the flesh of an ox'.[64]

The tracts appear as endless successions of sentences, each composed of a protasis and an apodosis, with the protasis setting out an aspect of the object studied under the form of a conditional proposition and the apodosis speaking of the consequence that is deduced from it under the form of a principal proposition. This form of expression, with the formula 'if…(in that case)…' that characterizes it and puts the emphasis on the necessary relation between the two elements of the sentence, makes the learning of the seers a hypothetical-deductive system of great logical precision. The sentences are lined up in a definite order where we find, among the logically possible arrangements that are retained, a preference for the dual or compound organization of the field of thought by mean of pairs of opposed or complementary sentences and of triads of sentences made up of a medium term between two extremes.[65] The

62. Rutten, 'Trente-deux modèles', n. 15; in an exceptional occurrence, the oracle is in the stative. In regard to *pušqum*, cf. Glassner, *Chroniques méso-potamiennes*, p. 22.

63. F. Thureau-Dangin, *Tablettes d'Uruk à l'usage des prêtres du temple d'Anu au temps des Séleucides* (TCL, 6; Paris: P. Geuthner, 1922), n. 1:3.

64. Thureau-Dangin, *Tablettes d'Uruk*, p. 88 n. 1.

65. J.J. Glassner, 'Pour un lexique des termes et figures analogiques en usage

omens concerning past events whose historicity is never doubted, are relatively numerous; we know of some two hundred and fifty of them, dispersed in the body of tracts or gathered together in collections.[66]

In a word, the seers set to work in the service of their ambition, to establish a divinatory science that claims to be objective and rational, a discourse endowed with scientific logic, through which the certitude of possessing the monopoly on truth asserts itself.

A final characteristic trait of the divinatory tracts lies in the use of the times of the verbs. The oracles about the past are written in the preterite, all the others in the present; on the contrary, with a few odd exceptions, the omens are always expressed in the stative. The boundary between the uses of these different times is rigid.

The stative is the one favoured in Akkadian to describe scientifically observed and recognized pieces of information, in the field of divination (we are mainly thinking of hepatoscopy and astrology) just as in that of medicine, astronomy or mathematics, unlike, for example, codes of law where, out of consideration for the diachrony specific to social times, the protases are in the preterite and the apodases in the present. As for meaning, this verbal time marks a state, without establishing present, past or future time, and it expresses the active or passive voice. In the pseudo-autobiography of Sennacherib, all of it written in the passive, the historical events about which the king decides to consult the seers, the death of his father and his being deprived of burial, are written in the stative[67]: the author of the account intends in that very way to assert the power of the events in question, seeking to abolish appropriately every temporal marking in order to make absolute the meaning and impact of the event.[68]

---

dans la divination mésopotamienne', *JA* 272 (1984), pp. 15-46. In regard to Mesopotamian divination in general, cf. J. Bottéro, 'Symptômes, signes, écritures', in J.P. Vernant (ed.), *Divination et rationalité* (Paris: Seuil, 1974), pp. 70-197.

66. The corpus will be collected together in a work now in preparation; for now, see Glassner, *Chroniques mésopotamiennes*, p. 37 and nn. 78 to 82.

67. Tadmor, Landsberger and Parpola, 'The Sin of Sargon', ll. 8'-9': [*ša₂ ina* KUR *na-ki-ri de-ku-ma*] *ina* E₂-*šu₂ la qeb-ru*, '[who was killed in an enemy country and] was not buried in his dwelling place' (the translation cannot render the nuances of the Akkadian language).

68. Compare the related use of the simple past tense and the nominal phrase in the historiography of the French language: J. Rancière, *Les noms de l'histoire* (Paris: Seuil, 1992), p. 100.

The use of the stative means the institution of a certain constant and lasting form of the statement; we can consider it , with E. Benvéniste,[69] as asserting outside of time a truth uttered as such; it indicates the birth of a real descriptive science assuring the advancement of singular occurrences to the rank of remarkable historical facts susceptible of being the object of a scientific analysis. Because it is a question of a discursive procedure, the omen-filled relation not being present from time immemorial, but being put in place, as we saw, at the moment when the seer appeals to the divinity. That permanence that the discourse institutes is the reflection of a scientific logic through which is expressed the certitude of holding the monopoly of the truth.

We can conjecture what possibilities the seers derived from the use of these grammatical times. As regards the movement of history, they try to discover its regularities and continuities, aiming at establishing homogeneous series constituted of so many specific and virtually repeatable facts that acquire value as prototypes. To do this, they put the past of the event face to face with a continuous present that is supposed to be that of insight. The process makes it possible to bring into conformity facts of a different nature and opens the way to the handling of the facts; with it, we pass from a history in the rough to a thoughtful history, a history that makes light of time, that settles into a perspective of a time always present, since scientific truth is so permanent.

All this does not rule out the possibility that, in a simultaneous way, the commemoration of historical events could help in strengthening the legitimacy of the divinatory discourse and, consequently, in asserting the power of the seer. An astrologer of Assurbanipal writing to his king, entangled in Elamite affairs, mentions an ancient omen, supposed to be 'from the mouth of a scholar when Nebuchadnezzar I crushed Elam', *ša pî umm[āni] kî Nabû-kudurrī-uṣur Elamtam iḫpūni*.[70] The astrologer who, obviously, refers to observations that he has made or is preparing to make himself, or whose content has been communicated to him, turns toward his sources which he cites (an exceptional fact in Mesopotamia) and situates in their proper time. In this case, the observation made in the present time and concerning the future has recourse, in order to be justified, to the prerequisite of the past; the credibility of the discourse implies that history, to be accepted, should be borne out in

69. E. Benve niste, *Problèmes de linguistique générale* (Paris: Gallimard, 1966), p. 165.

70. Hunger, *Astrological Reports to Assyrian Kings*, n. 158: Rev. 3-5.

and by this past which is at the same time its source and proof. The invocation of the past legitimizes the present.

Far from Weberian disenchantment, the Mesopotamian world is a universe populated with human beings and divinities. *Bala* in Sumerian or *dāru* in Akkadian refer to times that are, without distinction, those of one and the other. It is enough to say that the concept of time does not elude the category of the religious and that the tradition imposes its model considered as the only viable one because the only one possible. There exists, besides, a historiographic outline in which history is supposed to unfold in this instant without duration that characterizes mythical time. The myth of Erra, one of the most famous and most perfect works that Mesopotamia produced, is its most brilliant illustration. It narrates the account of the political events that took place in Babylon between 1100 and 850, but the facts are lifted out of the time of human history, and articulated and interpreted in accordance with the timeless model of a mythical account and the gods have become the actors in it.[71]

However, even if we do not see the dawning of an obvious will to transform the world, that would suppose the passing from the present toward a rationally calculated future, it appears that all these ways of conceptualizing time are characterized by their different methods of thinking of the dialectic of permanence and change, of continuity and break. Whereas the historians at the end of the third millennium thought that the last royal cycle, that of the present moment, has authority to last without end, those of the period of Isin advocate, on the contrary, the thesis of the mortality of all the cycles, even the most renowned. Later in the Sargonid period, the Assyrian historians think that history obeys a cyclic law, each cycle forming a system, and that, from one cycle to another, beyond the variations, there subsists between the time limits and the contents the same invariant connections, that did not prevent them from considering, at the same time, the reigning sovereigns as the successors, in a direct line, to the ancient monarchs reigning in ever more distant times. As for the author of the Erra myth, he shows, in his own way, that if a god abandons his city, bringing about its ruin, his return is inescapable but that the sorting out, for its part, does not necessarily happen of itself. Probably there existed, in every period, schools

---

71. Cagni, *L'epopea di Erra*, p. 86, IIc 13). Glassner, *Chroniques mésopotamiennes*, pp. 45-47.

that confronted each other in endless polemics, but we have, for now, lost all trace of them.

These various visions have in common the fact that they acknowledge, without however rejecting the notion of a trajectory inscribed in the cosmic order, that the march of historical time is neither constant nor absolutely determined, but that it is driven by an oscillatory movement and that there are thresholds where from an ascending movement it becomes a descending one, from progression it becomes retrogression.

They have in common, as well, the pursuit of meaning: to understand the relations that weave themselves among the regularities marked off and the individual pieces of information that are committed to memory. The events of which they retain the memory are not the same depending on the periods; the historians of the third and second millennia, for whom an archetypal vision of history predominates, prefer to note exceptional, astonishing or extraordinary facts; in the first millennium, on the contrary, with the neo-Babylonian chronicles, probably under the influence of Assyrian annalistic and chronographic inscriptions where it is a question of facts and dates only, a more precise knowledge and a richer casuistry about the events are revealed in the extension of the list of occurrences. But it would be committing a serious error to think that that extension does not permit anything else but a parataxic commentary, indeed that it authorizes the birth of a factual history where the various episodes, dated by reigns, by years, by months or by days, even, by hours, only exist in the reports of a vicinity, of precedence or of posteriority. Of course, 'chronicler' history (J. Rancière) remains stuck in the hesitant beginnings of life; however, beyond the surface agitation, it has for vocation to explore the underground realities and it is in the study of the continuity of institutions that it as a priority devotes itself. The question does not focus on the multiplicity of facts but on the kind of unity that makes sense of it. Perhaps it is necessary to distinguish, therefore, between two categories of events, the ones that are reproduced periodically in the range of analogy and similitude, the others that are produced just once. We cannot be positive about this.

But the central question remains that of a future not well defined beforehand that we try to know. It presupposes a tension in historical time. To make in regard to the future a statement whose claim to truth could appear to be justified or at least plausible, the Mesopotamians put to work a technique supposed to make the future accessible to them, to make it an object of knowledge. This prospective method is divination. But, we note that the authors and copyists of historiographical documents practised, in the case of a great majority of them, the professions of exorcist, of wailer or, to be more precise, of seer.[72] Their works offer the lists of the threats of change or of subversion that hang over the order of the world; they add up the countless unusual occurrences that are a sign of these threats in order to give them a significance and to guard against them; it is a matter therefore, with them, of a conservative reading of history whose final ends seem well inscribed in the preservation of the present time. To put off the payment dates endlessly!

72. Glassner, *Chroniques mésopotamiennes*, pp. 28-32.

Part III
TEXTUAL CRITICISM AND LITERARY CRITICISM

Jeroboam and the Division of the Kingdom in the Ancient Septuagint: LXX 3 Kingdoms 12.24 a-z, MT 1 Kings 11–12; 14 and the Deuteronomistic History

Adrian Schenker

1. *The Problem*

1.1. *Two Editions of the Tradition on Rehoboam and Jeroboam*

The account of the definitive division between Judah and Israel (1 Kgs 11–12; 14) appears in the ancient LXX under another form than in the MT, 3 Kgdms 12.24 a-z. Zipora Talshir, who has very recently carried out the best existing study of the account of the ancient LXX,[1] calls it Alternative History. This name implies however that this form of the narrative is derived from the first and original form. That is far from being certain. That is why I propose to call it here: *The History of Two Ambitions* (abbreviated: HA). This story actually recounts the ambition of a usurper, Jeroboam, who wishes to arrogate to himself a power that is not his, and the ambition of a new king, Rehoboam, who wishes to prove through arrogance that he is superior to his father. The meeting of these two ambitions at the time of the succession to Solomon is disastrous for the unity of the Davidic monarchy. But this account contains practically the same narrative material as MT 1 Kgs 11–12; 14. It represents therefore another 'edition' of the division of the two kingdoms.[2]

---

1.   Z. Talshir, *The Alternative Story: 3 Kingdoms 12:24 A-Z* (JBS, 6; Jerusalem: Simor, 1993). It is the English translation, in a revised form, of a study that was published in Hebrew in Jerusalem in 1989. I thank the participants in the Swiss doctoral level seminar in 1994–95 for their many valuable suggestions. This text owes much to them.

2.   J.C. Trebolle Barrera, *Salomón y Jeroboán. Historia de la recensión y redacción de 1 Reyes, 2–12; 14* (Bibliotheca Salmaticensis, Diss. 3; Salamanca and Jerusalem: Inst. Español Biblica Arqueologico / Universidad Pontificia, 1980), p. 174. Subsequently, the MT of 1 Kgs 11–12; 14 is taken just as it is. The com-

1.2. *Connection Between the Two Editions*

These two forms of the tradition concerning the schism between Judah and Israel are not independent of each other. Either they go back to a common source, or one is a modification of the other. This double written tradition is fortunate for the historian of the tradition and the exegete, since it enables them to keep their eyes on a moment in the literary development of a historical tradition and to distinguish in it an earlier point from a subsequent one within the trajectory of the tradition.

1.3. *Significance for the Deuteronomistic History Question*

1 Kings 11–12; 14 is strongly marked with the Dtr imprint in the form preserved by the MT. On the other hand, the HA is hardly marked by it at all. If the latter is later than the MT, the question comes up of knowing precisely why the Deuteronomistic marks have been eliminated from it. If, on the contrary, the HA precedes the account of the MT or is parallel to it, with the two being derived from a common source, another question comes up: how is it that this earlier or parallel form alone would be lacking the Dtr elements? Would it be a matter, in this case, of a pre-Deuteronomistic redaction of the account?

We see immediately that it is indispensable to reach certainty on the subject of the HA in its relation to the MT of 1 Kings 11–12; 14 when we study the Dtr redaction of the books of Kings.

2. *History of Research and the Method Followed Below*

The HA has certainly drawn the attention of exegetes for a long time. The history of the research was carefully retraced by Jörg Debus and by

parison of this text with the translation in the LXX, as found in all its manuscripts (besides the HA coming from the ancient LXX), should be done as well. The LXX actually preserves, besides the HA, another form of the account that corresponds in the essential points to 'the edition' of the MT, but presents in the manuscripts variants in 11.43; 12.2-3, 20. These different forms of the recent LXX are studied by J.C. Trebolle Barrera, 'Jeroboán y la Asamblea de Siquén (1 Rey. TM 12:2-3a; LXX 11:43; 12:24 d.f.p.)', *EstBíb* 38 (1979–80), pp. 189-220; T.M. Willis, 'The Text of 1 Kings 11:43–12:3', *CBQ* 53 (1991), pp. 37-44; A. Schenker, 'Un cas de critique narrative au service de la critique textuelle (1 Rois 11,43–12,2-3.20)', *Bib* 77 (1996), pp. 219-26. D.W. Gooding had already studied this more recent form of the LXX in 'The Septuagint's Rival Versions of Jeroboam's Rise to Power', *VT* 17 (1967), pp. 173-89.

Julio C. Trebolle Barrera[3]; Talshir refers to it throughout her study cited above.[4] It is enough for now to note here that reputable authors defend one or the other position, either the originality of the MT in relation to the HA that is derived from it or, inversely, the precedence of the HA and the corresponding secondary character of the MT. The latest study, that of Z. Talshir, breaks new ground with its method. Talshir dismisses immediately two approaches that have dominated the comparison of the two accounts for a long time. The first was dominated by the interest in history. It consequently measured the two narratives by way of the greatest historical probability. This meant jumping over an indispensable step in the analysis: the study of the texts as literary works outside of their place within the context of general history. They are certainly historical sources as well, but just as much narrative pieces, literary compositions. And only after their literary nature has been recognized can the evaluation of their contribution to the knowledge of what has taken place proceed. The second inadequate approach was the comparison of the corresponding elements in the two accounts without taking the trouble to understand each of the two narratives in itself. However, the components of these two accounts first of all play a role in giving a structure to the autonomous literary unity of which they form a part. It is therefore necessary to understand them in the first place in the overall literary structure, in the framework of the literary composition of which they are the components. Only then can the comparison with the parallel elements of the neighbouring story proceed.[5]

---

3. J. Debus, *Die Sünde Jerobeams* (FRLANT, 93; Göttingen: Vandenhoeck & Ruprecht, 1967), pp. 68-80; Trebolle Barrera, *Salomón y Jeroboán*, pp. 444-46.

4. *The Alternative Story*. The history of the research is succinctly summarized and discussed as well by R.P. Gordon, 'The Second Septuagint Account of Jeroboam: History or Midrash?', *VT* 25 (1975), pp. 368-93 (368-74).

5. The latest study illustrates these two inadequate approaches: D.A. Glatt, *Chronological Displacement in Biblical and Related Literatures* (SBLDS, 139; Atlanta, GA: Scholars Press, 1993), pp. 100-109. Glatt states that 300 chariots belonging to Jeroboam are *historically* improbable (p. 103), or that the Pharaoh would never have given his sister-in-law in marriage to a commoner like Jeroboam. What is possible in narrative reasoning need not be possible in historical reality. Glatt compares the term 'prostitute', applied to the mother of Jeroboam in HA, with 'widow' in the MT to conclude that the MT would not have discarded 'prostitute' if it had been found in the *Vorlage* (p. 103). He does not ask himself however what narrative function these two terms fulfil in each of the two accounts.

Talshir has achieved for the first time an analysis of the HA that avoids these two pitfalls. In this respect, her book is exemplary. She establishes first of all the proof that the HA, preserved today only in the LXX, is the Greek translation of an original Hebrew text. She tests this hypothesis by translating the text back into Hebrew, substantiating its retroversion by the appropriate biblical parallels. Then she analyses the HA specifically as an autonomous literary work, independent of the parallel account of the MT in 1 Kings 11–12; 14.[6] Only after this inter-pretation does she make the comparison with 1 Kings 11–12; 14.[7]

With this methodical premise accepted, the following question comes up: how should the two accounts be compared? Are there *solid criteria* for determining the meaning of their relationship? Does the MT depend on the HA or vice versa? When we read studies on this subject, we cannot avoid the impression that subjective assessments and reasons for greater or lesser probability are most in evidence. That is very natural since texts so close (to repeat, practically all the narrative material of the HA is found in the MT) offer little on which to base a relative dat-ing, in the absence, of course, of all external criteria.

I want to propose here a criterion that, I hope, will provide the 'Archimedean point' in establishing the relationship of the two accounts to one another. It is a matter of a narrative cycle composed of particular accounts. A useful criterion seems to be the study of the relationship between the cycle or the whole and its components. Is there an account that would be in tension with its more global literary context, either in the HA or in the MT of 1 Kings 11–12; 14? If the broader context of one of these two accounts actually does violence to one of its narrative components, whereas in the neighbouring form, the same component would be integrated perfectly, in harmony with its context, it is prob-able that the suitable context would be original, while the context presenting inadequacies shows the *re-use* of pre-existing material, ori-ginally intended for another organization of the whole.

On the level of a narrative *cycle*, in fact, the principle in textual criticism according to which the difficult reading has a better chance than the easy reading of being original does not apply. This is because homogeneity in *textual criticism* shows the spontaneous tendency of copyists to eliminate everything that is harsh in a phrase, whereas it indicates in *narrative criticism* the mutual rapport and common origin

6. Talshir, *The Alternative Story*, pp. 163-80.
7. Talshir, *The Alternative Story*, pp. 181-242.

of the accounts and of the global cycle of which the accounts are the components. The spontaneous tendency of the storyteller here will be towards the development of particular features in the individual accounts without taking into account the architecture of the whole.

We come across four narratives common to the MT and the HA that we can subject to this test of homogeneity or heterogeneity with their global context: the story of a refugee in Egypt (Hadad, prince of Edom in the MT, 1 Kgs 11.14-22, 25; Jeroboam in HA; §§d-f); the story of the loss of Jeroboam's son (1 Kgs 14.1-18; HA §§g-n); the prophetic sign of the torn garment (1 Kgs 11.29-39; HA §o); and the assembly of Shechem (1 Kgs 12.1-16 or 1-19; HA §§n-u).

3. *First Account: Hadad and Jeroboam in Egypt*

In the MT, 1 Kgs 11.14-22, 25, the account of Hadad is well anchored in the broader context. Verses 15-16 refer to 2 Sam. 8.13-14. The text contains some tension however, since it in no way affirms clearly that Edom had defected from the Solomonic Empire,[8] whereas the tendency of the account is precisely to show how the kingdom will be snatched from Solomon and his successor (cf. 11.11), and that those conquered by David, Aram (2 Sam. 8.3-12; 10.15-19) and Edom (2 Sam. 8.13-14), will regain their power, a danger for Solomon. That is explained perhaps by a concern for harmony: it is only under Rehoboam that the kingdom will be effectively dismembered, according to 1 Kgs 11.12.

But the account contains some narrative deficiency. Hadad starts a family in Egypt, thanks to Pharaoh (1 Kgs 11.18-20). He has a son, raised as an Egyptian prince (v. 20). This narrative detail has no narrative follow-up. The account has no more need of it, since it is not this son who is going to fight against Solomon and Rehoboam. Hadad acts alone (vv. 21-22, 25). The mention of the son therefore functions solely to indicate that Hadad had reestablished the Edomite royal dynasty despite the massacre of all the male children of Edom (11.15), without for all that being able to give a specific role to the crown prince.

In the HA, the account of the sojourn of Jeroboam in Egypt recalls

8.   Unless there is a correction in 11.25 of Aram to Edom; cf. D. Barthelemy, *Critique textuelle de l'Ancien Testament. I. Josué, Juges, Ruth, Samuel, Rois, Chroniques, Esdras, Néhémie, Esther* (OBO, 50.1; Freiburg: Universitätsverlag Göttingen: Vandenhoeck & Ruprecht, 1982), p. 362.

the birth of a son according to an obvious narrative necessity: it prepares for the episode of the sick child (§§g-n).

In the MT, the marriage of Hadad to the sister-in-law of the king is explained: Hadad belongs to the royal house of Edom (1 Kgs 11.14). It is an aristocratic marriage between two royal houses, and political too: Edom and Egypt are allies. On the other hand, in the HA, Jeroboam is a *nobody*, son of a prostitute, by an unknown father (§a). Actually, the HA does not give a patronymic to Jeroboam! The marriage of Jeroboam with the sister-in-law of the Pharaoh thus represents the social rise of an upstart. This rise is emphasized in §e by accentuating the rank of his wife. She is the (elder) sister[9] of the queen. This relation between the two wives who are sisters makes Jeroboam the brother-in-law of the Pharaoh, therefore his close relative. The child born of this marriage is going to be a prince!

In §d of the HA, Jeroboam wishes to return home after the death of Solomon. Shishak, the king of Egypt, tries to keep him, by offering him large compensations: 'Ask me anything you want: I will give it to you'. What is the narrative function of this royal offer? It indicates that Jeroboam knew how to make himself indispensable to the king! The latter from now on depends on him. Otherwise he would not go so far as to offer him a maximal compensation.

This consisted of the marriage that the king arranged for Jeroboam by giving him as wife that sister of the queen who had the highest rank (§e). Jeroboam was thus able to profit from a situation where the king absolutely had need of him. In this way he enters the royal family, he, a refugee who does not know who his father is!

Zipora Talshir considers this marriage a flashback.[10] She translates it

9.   For the interpretation of this passage we can refer to the critical commentary of Talshir, *The Alternative Story*, pp. 68-69. Trebolle Barrera (*Salomón y Jeroboán*, p. 121), considers §§d-e as a secondary addition, but ancient because he sees it as a *Wiederaufnahme* (resumption). Since these two paragraphs have an obvious narrative function (the social and political rise of Jeroboam to a higher rank), and since the *Wiederaufnahme* (the repeated phrase 'send me and I will go') is explained better as a repetition required for the progression of the narrative (see below), there is no longer any reason to eliminate §§d-e from the primitive narrative.

10.   Talshir, *The Alternative Story*, p. 67, 168-69. She refers to other authors who likewise postulate the flashback interpretation of the marriage of Jeroboam with the Egyptian princess or who consider the two requests of Jeroboam to be able to return home as a secondary literary doublet. These interpretations are only necessary if Jeroboam comes back for the election of a king of Israel at Shechem.

as a past anterior: 'and Shishak had given...' But the HA does not require that the assembly at Shechem follow just after the death of Solomon. It is not convoked to give the tribes of Israel the occasion to elect Rehoboam as king over them: according to the HA Rehoboam is already king of the Israelite tribes since he has succeeded his father (§a). The reason for the convocation of the assembly of Israel at Shechem is something else. It is the weight of the corvée that Rehoboam imposed just as his father did on Ephraim. It is an assembly on account of the grievances that demand a lightening of the corvée, the tax paid in hours and hard labour, and a diminution of the taxes that Israel owes the king for the supplying of his house (§p). Since the king refuses (§s), the Israelites rise up against their legitimate king, Rehoboam (§t). In revolt they reject him.

There is no reason therefore to situate the assembly of Shechem in the period that immediately follows the death of Solomon. There is room for a marriage of Jeroboam and the Egyptian princess and the birth of a baby before the assembly of Shechem. From the marriage to the birth of the baby, who is going to die at an early age (§§g-n), there is no need for more than two years, at most three.

The account of the HA in §§b-n can be read in a linear way, that is, without a flashback. Jeroboam carries out Solomon's work, becomes powerful in the kingdom, on the military level as well, to the point of worrying Solomon, who wishes to avert the possibility of a usurpation of power by seeking to eliminate physically the potential usurper. The latter flees to Egypt where he makes himself indispensable to the Pharaoh. When the news of the death of Solomon reaches Egypt, Jeroboam asks permission to return to his home in the mountain of Ephraim. The Pharaoh, absolutely dependent on him, tries to keep him through a marriage. From this marriage a son is born to Jeroboam. He again asks authorization to leave. This time he gets the permission and returns. His child, who is still a baby, falls ill and dies. The supreme ambition of Jeroboam to start a dynasty of royal blood thanks to his wife suddenly collapses. After that Jeroboam organizes the assembly at

---

But this is the perspective of the account in the MT. In the HA, there is no assembly for an election at Shechem! The latter had another purpose. It does not have to take place immediately after the death of Solomon. These interpetations of Talshir and the others show that they are reading the HA without emancipating it from the perspective of the account in the MT, instead of reading it in its own narrative perspective.

Shechem where Israel, infuriated with the weight of the corvée and the taxes, seeks from King Rehoboam some relief. All that forms a continuous and perfectly coherent narrative framework.

In conclusion, the story about Hadad in the MT prepares for nothing. It is sufficient unto itself as preparation for the future confrontation between Hadad (called 'adversary', שׂטן) and Solomon, a confrontation that will not be recounted, but just announced in 1 Kgs 11.11, as part of the future chastisement of Solomon, consisting of the snatching of a portion from his empire, Edom. In this context, the birth of an Edomite prince in Egypt is not exploited in the narrative. This prince actually plays no role and disappears from the account right after the mention of his education in the palace of the Pharaoh. That is surprising, especially since this prince would belong precisely to the generation of Rehoboam which is going to sustain, according to v. 12, the dismemberment of his kingdom. The story in the MT does not clearly say that the adversary Hadad would wrest Edom from Solomon and ignores the whole war that the Edomite prince waged against Rehoboam.

On the other hand, the account in the HA is the first part of a narrative diptych. It recounts the social and political rise of Jeroboam who succeeds in allying himself by marriage with the royal house of Egypt, even though he was himself by origin a plebeian. To consecrate the permanence of this success, there is born to him a son, a guarantee of a dynasty to come. This part is complete in itself, and each element is necessary to the organization of the narrative whole. From the point of view of the narrative adequacy of this account to its context, a presumption in favour of the originality of the HA seems well founded.

4. *Second Account: The Loss of Jeroboam's Child*

Placing this account in second place in the analysis presented here does not imply a preference for the sequence of events in the HA. It is a neutral arrangement.

The story of the death of Jeroboam's child is the last account about Jeroboam in the MT (1 Kgs 14.1-18). Its function is to give a negative assessment of the career and work of the rebel Jeroboam (1 Kgs 11.26-27): the condemnation by YHWH ending up in the extermination of the house of Jeroboam. And that extermination is inaugurated, like a pledge and sign, by the death of the son of Jeroboam, with the name Abiyya, never previously mentioned by the narrator. This brings out the divine origin of this condemnation by placing it on the lips of a blind prophet whom Jeroboam tried to fool (1 Kgs 14.2, 14.4). This double scene between the prophet and Jeroboam does not succeed in diverting the divine wrath. Verses 7-16 are the oracle of condemnation, explaining the immediate death of the child.

It must be noted that this story is not found in the LXX, except for the hexaplaric LXX.[11] In the HA, the account, which is briefer (§§g-n), stands before the separation of Judah and Israel, immediately after the return of Jeroboam from his exile in Egypt. The prophet is blind (§i), but here Jeroboam does not attempt to deceive him by the disguising of his wife. The child is known from the preceding story of the flight of Jeroboam to Egypt (§§d-f).

The prophet announces the death of the child (§§k-m) and the extermination of all the male descendants of Jeroboam, who will not even have a burial, *without giving the reasons* why the Lord had to act with such severity. Since the episode is found before the rejection of Rehoboam by Israel, this condemnation of the house of Jeroboam actually cannot be the chastisement of a fault linked to the schism between Israel and Judah.

Is the HA incomplete and unintelligible in itself here but understandable within the horizon of the MT? Talshir and others maintain this[12] and deduce from it that the HA clearly presupposes the story of the MT. Trebolle Barrerra concludes from it that the condemnation of the *dynasty* of Jeroboam (§m), incomprehensible in the framework of the HA, must have been inserted afterwards by a glossarist.[13] Talshir

11. A.E. Brooke and N. McLean, *The Old Testament in Greek*. II. *The Later Historical Books Part II. I and II Kings* (Cambridge: Cambridge University Press, 1930), pp. 263-64. Trebolle Barrera (*Salomón y Jeroboán*, p. 464 n. 334), explains this absence by supposing that with the HA being found already in its present place (after 12.24), the translator of this LXX did not want to repeat the story of the death of the child that he had just mentioned in the form of the HA that he had integrated himself in his translation. This is certainly a plausible explanation. Trebolle Barrera sees in 1 Kgs 15.29-30 LXX the proof that the translator of 1 Kgs 11–12 in the LXX knew MT 1 Kgs 14.1-18.

12. Talshir, *The Alternative Story*, pp. 219-21, 248-53. She refers to D.W. Gooding, 'Problems of Text and Midrash in the Third Book of Kings', *Textus* 7 (1969), pp. 1-29 (12); S.L. McKenzie, *The Trouble with Kings: The Composition of the Book of Kings in the Deuteronomistic History* (VTSup, 42: Leiden: E.J. Brill, 1991), p. 29.

13. Trebolle Barrera, *Salomón y Jeroboán* , pp. 152-53.

rightly rejects this makeshift solution, which introduces into the HA itself a history of the redaction. This complicates and as a result weakens the hypothesis!

Nevertheless the HA has an inner coherence. It is actually the story of the cursed ambition of Jeroboam. Unlike the MT in 1 Kgs 11.26-27, §b does not report the rebellion of Jeroboam.[14] This paragraph recounts the social and political success of the son of a prostitute and an unknown father in the service of Solomon. He is a self-made man. Having become powerful to the point of offending King Solomon himself (§b end), he flees to Egypt where, far from coming to nothing, on the contrary he pulls himself up to the highest level, to that of the Pharaoh, king of Egypt, who needs him. He actually becomes one of Pharaoh's brothers-in-law who occupies the highest rank. After the death of Solomon, this person of enormous ambition returns to Israel. If he has been a rival for Solomon, how much more is he going to become that for his successor, and thus for *the house of David*. At this point, the Lord, who has himself built the house of David, strikes him with a curse. By making the son of Jeroboam and of the sister of the queen of Egypt die, the Lord undermines the house that Jeroboam thinks he can build himself. The contrast between the house built by the Lord and that which humans wish to build without the Lord's help actually forms the theme of the HA in this narrative. This is precisely the theme of Ps. 127.1-3. It explains why the HA associates in its §l-m the death of the sick child with the extermination of all the other male descendants of Jeroboam, who do not rest in a sepulchre: there will not be a family of Jeroboam whose sons will lie down with their ancestors (cf. 1 Kgs 14.31; 15.8.24; 16.6, etc.)!

In conclusion, the accounts of the death of the son of Jeroboam are coherent narratives in their respective contexts, both in the MT and in the HA. The latter does not need the account in the MT to be complete on the narrative level. It hangs together perfectly by itself.

---

14. Talshir, *The Alternative Story*, p. 148 and plate 'The Alternative Story LXX 12:24a-z Reconstruction and Translation') chooses as a title 'The revolt of Jeroboam against Solomon'. That does not correspond to the content! The HA actually shows the concentration of political and military power in the hands of Jeroboam. He becomes a person so powerful in the kingdom and in Ephraim in particular that Solomon begins to have fears of a seizure of power. But Jeroboam has not taken the step of opening the rebellion, as in the MT. He is a very powerful and dangerous major-domo, he is not yet a rebel.

5. *Third Account: The Prophetic Sign of the Torn Garment*

In the MT (1 Kgs 11.29-39), this sign is carried out by the prophet
Ahijah of Shiloh in favour of Jeroboam before the flight of the latter
into Egypt. The prophet promises him by words and deeds from this
moment, when the two men meet alone in the country near Jerusalem
(vv. 29, 31, 37), the royal dignity over the ten tribes of Israel. Besides,
the Lord promises Jeroboam to build him a house as had been done for
David (2 Sam. 7), on condition that Jeroboam obey the divine will
(v. 38).

This passage corresponds to the religious apostasy of Jeroboam in
1 Kgs 12.26-33, which thus contravenes the condition put by YHWH to
the election of the house of Jeroboam. The same prophet Ahijah of
Shiloh will in the end take note of this contradiction between the Lord's
promise made to Jeroboam and the response of the latter, in his
message of condemnation in 1 Kgs 14.7-11. The narrative architecture
is clear in its main lines: a promise of the Lord, accompanied by a
condition at the start of the narrative; the miserable failure of Jeroboam
with regard to this condition in its culmination in the middle of the narrative; the response of the Lord condemning Jeroboam with his whole
house and his people Israel at the end of the account.

The MT, however, is in tension with the story of the torn garment on
one point. The announcement of the chastisement of Solomon in 11.13,
32, 36 actually insists that the one tribe of Judah would remain in the
house of David. The revolt at Shechem in 12.20 ends in fact with just
one tribe on the side of the Davidic dynasty, Judah. It is only in 12.21,
23 that a second tribe, required by the symbolic sign of Ahijah, makes
its single appearance. We understand why! This passage assures the
suitability between the prophetic sign of ten and two pieces and the
tearing apart of the kingdom.

In the MT, Judah alone remains attached to David because Jerusalem,
a city chosen by the Lord, is situated there (11.13, 36).

The HA has the prophetic sign accomplished not by Ahijah of Shiloh,
but by the man of God Shemaiah the Nehlamite (§o), without specifying the circumstances or the place or the date. Because in the HA this
short account is recounted in a 'flash back', a narrative procedure
especially favoured by the author of HA. Talshir has rightly drawn

attention to this point.[15] Actually, we meet the procedure of a 'flash back' to a certain extent in §§h-i. It is found in the MT 1 Kgs 11.14-25.

The man of God Shemaiah reappears in the conclusion of the HA in §y, where his message, received from God, stopped King Rehoboam dead as he took steps to bring by force of arms the ten tribes of Israel into submission. The Lord will actually assert that 'this revolt happened on my initiative' (§y *at the end*). The Lord had already said to the spokesperson Shemaiah at the starting point: 'Thus speaks the Lord about the ten tribes of Israel' (§o).

Shemaiah's two oracles thus form an inclusion with the assembly at Shechem, reported in §§n, p-y. Still better, they form the inclusion of the second part of the narrative. The HA is actually composed of two narrative arcs: the rise of Jeroboam, abruptly stopped by the Lord (§§b-n), and the definitive rejection, willed by the Lord, of Rehoboam by the ten tribes of Israel, at the instigation of Jeroboam (§§n-z).[16]

Let us draw attention to a second inclusion, doubling and reinforcing that of Shemaiah in §§o and y! It is the double mention of Jeroboam before and after the episode of the assembly of Shechem, in §§n and x. Before that assembly and before the prophetic sign of Shemaiah, the narrator tells us that Jeroboam had assembled the tribes of Israel. After the assembly, before the second intervention of Shemaiah, he tells us that Jeroboam is the military leader of these revolting tribes. During the assembly however, the overshadowing of Jeroboam is absolute. He is therefore not a cause of the revolt. He prepares it solely by channeling Israelite discontent into an explosive political protest, and he defends it, after it takes place, by organizing it on the military level. This inclusion functions therefore to characterize the personage! He organizes the discontent in Israel as an intriguer and political agitator, and after the revolt, he is going to organize as a military leader the resistance of the tribes in revolt against the king. He is a tribune and a *condottiere*.

The prophetic sign of the new garment, torn into twelve pieces of which ten are given to Jeroboam with which to clothe himself (§o), a feature missing in the parallel account of MT 1 Kgs 11.31, possesses in this way a clear narrative impact in the HA: an ambitious man cursed by God is going to clothe himself in a torn garment, that is, he will

15. Talshir, *The Alternative Story*, pp. 169, 175-76, 189.

16. J.C. Trebolle Barrera, *Salomón y Jeroboán*, pp. 148-49, 167 considers, on the basis of literary-critical analyses, the two oracles of Shemaiah in the HA (§§o, y-z) as added later.

govern over an incomplete, drastically reduced, maimed people. This is a scathing definition of this part of the people who had defected from the house of David![17] But it is God who wanted it this way. Why? The HA does not make this explicit in its own narrative. Implicitly it seems to condemn the ambition of an upstart to create for himself, by his own means, a dynasty. What is certain, on the other hand, is the condemnation without any appeal of the kingdom of Israel. For the HA, the master, a plebeian and cursed upstart, does not even merit the title of king, and in cornering power over this fraction of the people, he pitifully clothes himself in a torn garment. He is a brother of the usurper Abimelech of the book of Judges, like him a cursed ambitious man usurping a power that is not destined for him and that he does not obtain from the Lord, because the latter's favour had been withdrawn from the people, abandoned to such a master for its shame and its misfortune.

Here the prophetic sign of the torn garment is not, as in the MT, a royal investiture and a promise that God seriously makes to Jeroboam. Very much the contrary, it is a sign of derision and of chastisement for Israel. Israel is awarded by God to a man who has just been cursed! That is what Israel deserves for a leader: a usurper rejected by the Lord, and the garment of ten pieces that he wears is the sign of this.

Let us not forget that the prophet does not tear the garment into two pieces, one of ten twelfths, the other of two! No, he tears it into twelve pieces, and clothes Jeroboam with ten of these pieces.

Here the specifically *tragic* dimension of our account appears. It is understandable and legitimate that Israel revolts against an arrogant king like Rehoboam. But that inevitable and just revolt throws Israel into the arms of a plebeian and cursed usurper! It is a real tragedy! In 'the story of the two tragic ambitions for Israel', the split of the Davidic kingdom is one of the most grandiose tragic scenes of the whole Bible.

The HA reports on three occasions that two tribes remain attached to the house of David, Judah and Benjamin (§§u, x, y), while the ten others separate from it. That is in perfect harmony with the prophetic sign of Shemaiah (§o). Unlike the MT, the HA in no way maintains that the tribe of Judah alone remains faithful to the descendants of David.

In conclusion, the prophetic sign of the garment torn into ten and two

---

17. Gooding ('Rival Versions', p. 188), noted the 'sarcasm' of the picture of a future king clothed in a torn investiture garment.

pieces creates a tension in the MT, whereas it is perfectly in place in the HA.

6. *Fourth Account: The Assembly at Shechem*

The MT presents the assembly at Shechem as an assembly to elect the king (1 Kgs 12.1): 'for all Israel had come there *to make him king*'. It is an 'elective diet' of the tribes of Israel. The Israelite tribes are there in league with Jeroboam who is actively present there (vv. 2-3, 12, 15). This is doubtless why the chastisement of Jeroboam will strike Israel as well, in solidarity with him in his sin (1 Kgs 14.9-14, 15-16). However, Jeroboam is not a protagonist in the account. Only Rehoboam, the people, the elders and the young counsellors take their turn at speaking. It is true that in v. 3, the people and Jeroboam speak in unison. But subsequently, reference is only made to the people: in vv. 5, 15 and 16 by the narrator, in vv. 6, 9 and 13 by Rehoboam, in v. 7 by the older counsellors, in v. 11 by the young ones. In v. 16 the people are referred to as 'all Israel', thus forming an *inclusion* with v. 1, but Jeroboam is not mentioned. It should especially be noted that the decision to reject David (and his house, of course) is expressed uniquely by Israel. The drama is played out between Israel and Rehoboam, and between the young and old counsellors. It is not played out between Rehoboam and Jeroboam.

For that matter the election of Jeroboam as king of Israel is not the object of the account of the assembly of Shechem. It is reported as a corollary in v. 20, after the hasty departure of Rehoboam from Shechem to hide himself in safety in Jerusalem (v. 18). Verse 20 seems therefore at first sight to suggest a second elective assembly at Shechem where Jeroboam would have been effectively proclaimed king. But the announcement of v. 20, 'and when all Israel learned that Jeroboam had returned, they sent for him and called him to the assembly', partially repeats the beginning of v. 3, opening the story of the Shechem assembly. Would not the narrative (or redactional) function of this repetition, which has always raised difficulties for exegesis,[18] precisely be to

18. For it is in tension with 12.2-3. R. de Vaux, JB, *ad loc.*, sees a contradiction between these two passages; likewise M. Noth, *Könige* (BKAT, 9.1; Neukirchen–Vluyn: Neukirchener Verlag, 1968), p. 273; J.A. Montgomery, *A Critical and Exegetical Commentary on the Books of Kings* (ed. H.S. Gehman; ICC; Edinburgh: T. & T. Clark, 1951), p. 248; R.W. Klein, 'Jeroboam's Rise to Power', *JBL* 89

identify the first assembly (vv. 1-16) with the second (v. 19)? We should actually understand that the same assembly of Israel, at which Jeroboam was actively present, as the text suggests in vv. 2-3, 12 and 15, rejected Rehoboam and chose Jeroboam.

Read in the overall context, 1 Kings 11–14, the MT account shows a tension between the recounted episode in itself and its global contextual framework. The rejection of the Davidic dynasty by the tribes of Israel is actually explained by the intransigence of the king and the arrogance of his young counsellors. This is precisely the object of the narrative. The arrogance of power causes its own ruin. That is what this story wants to show. But, in the MT, its cause is different. Verse 15 states it in explicit terms. It is the effective prophetic word of Ahijah of Shiloh, 1 Kgs 11.29-39, and behind it the Lord, who has decided to punish Solomon, 1 Kgs 11.11-13. Thus the hard-line rigidity of Rehoboam and the arrogance of his young ministers are not the cause of the rejection of David and his house by Israel. They are only its occasion.[19]

In the HA, the Shechem assembly, §§n-u, is not an elective diet. Rehoboam is already king, since he has succeeded Solomon, as §a attests. Israel gathers together there in order to demand from the legitimate king a mitigation of his terms. Jeroboam clearly assembles these Israelite tribes with a view to this demand, according to §n, but the narrator does not show him taking part in the assembly.[20]

The failure of the demand, thwarted by the intransigence of the king and the arrogance of the young counsellors, leads to the uprising against the existing royal authority, that is to say, a revolt. This is an account parallel to the revolt of Sheba, son of Bichri, in 2 Samuel 20. As Sheba was not proclaimed king, since he was not the leader of the revolt, likewise Jeroboam is not made king either. By saying at the beginning of the account that Jeroboam had called together the tribes of Israel (§n), the HA hardly suggests that he played a role as leader of the revolt.

The account of the Shechem assembly conforms perfectly to the context of the whole HA. The only cause of the revolt of the Israelite tribes

---

(1970), 217-18; D.W. Gooding, 'Jeroboam's Rise to Power: A Rejoinder', *JBL* 91 (1972), pp. 529-33; R.W. Klein, 'Once More: "Jeroboam's Rise to Power" ', *JBL* 92 (1973), pp. 582-84.

19. Trebolle Barrera, *Salomón y Jeroboán*, p. 183.

20. Talshir (*The Alternative Story*, plate with translation; §n) is wrong in translating: 'and Rehoboam...went to confront him' for 'and Rehoboam...went up there'. The reference 'there', 'up there' refers to Shechem, and not to Jeroboam.

against King Rehoboam lies in what the account itself indicates: the intransigent rigidity of the king and the pride of his young wolves.

The episode of the torn garment as a prophetic sign in §o plays no part in the explanation of the revolt, since this account does not refer to it. This episode has another function, as we have seen. It explains the prohibition that the Lord will impose on King Rehoboam quelling the revolt of the tribes by war, according to the plan of §y. These two passages actually correspond, since they both have the same protagonist, Shemaiah, who does not appear elsewhere in the HA, and since they surround the story of the Shechemite assembly like an inclusion. The narrator feels obliged to explain the capitulation of King Rehoboam, formerly so uncompromising and so proud, in the face of Israel's revolt. It is explained by the will of the Lord, indicated twice.

At the same time, the bringing up of this plan for war, prohibited for Rehoboam by the Lord, provides the occasion for reintroducing Jeroboam, absent during the whole episode at Shechem. This is the other inclusion, already pointed out above, of the Shechemite assembly. It has the function of characterizing this protagonist by the role that he plays before and after the revolt of the Israelite tribes. He is the political leader of the malcontents and the military head of the rebels. He is what Sheba, son of Bichri, was in 2 Samuel 20: a skilled profiteer from discontent and a capable organizer of military resistance, of which the Lord makes use.

The war that Rehoboam planned to wage against Israel thus has a different nature in the HA than in the MT. In the latter, Rehoboam wants to force the Israelites to return to the crown of David, in the former the king wishes to bring back the rebels to submission to their legitimate sovereign.

In conclusion, whereas the account of the Shechem assembly in the MT is somewhat in tension with its broader context, the same episode recounted by the HA is homogeneous with the overall context.

7. *Conclusion of the Literary History*

It is apparent that one of the four parallel stories in MT 1 Kings 11–14 and the HA 12.24 a-z, 3 Kgdms, is homogeneous with the context as a whole in both cases. It is the story of the death of the child inflicted on Jeroboam. But in the MT, the three other stories, that of the flight to Egypt, that of the torn garment and that of the assembly of the tribes of Israel at Shechem, reveal a certain tension between the accounts considered in themselves and in their broader context. In the HA, on the contrary, the relation of these three stories with their global context presents no tension. If this observation is well founded and sound, it leads to such a consequence as this: the inadequacy of an account fitted into a broader contextual structure betrays the re-use of this pre-existing narrative piece in a new contextual arrangement. On the other hand, when an account is integrated perfectly into its global context, *the probability is strong that the context and the account were made for one another*. Applied to our case, this principle means that the HA is a unity in which the global context exactly fits and integrates its constituent narratives without grating or tension. There is therefore neither re-use of elements nor new organization of the context in the HA. In other words, it is found in an unrevised form. On the contrary, the tensions noted in the MT between three stories and their global context show new adjustments in the contextual structure and the re-use of these three elements in a modified perspective.

With regard to the relation between the two texts, then, we can posit the HA as the prior account and the MT as a rewriting of it.

Before studying the consequences of this fact for the Deuteronomistic features which are so pronounced in the MT and much more discreet in the HA, we can further corroborate the fact of the rewriting of the HA through the wording recorded in the MT. It should actually be possible to give an account of most of the divergent elements of the MT in the light of its aims, precisely discernible in the touching up that it introduces. At this point, it also becomes clear that we can ignore the hypothesis of a common lineage of the HA and the MT, since it does not seem called for by the data in order to give an explanation.

8. *Differences between the Overall Structure of the Account in the MT of 1 Kings 11–14 and in the HA*

The Account in the MT

The narrative driving force is God's project to chastise Solomon for his sin of idolatry (11.9-13). The chastisement will affect the house of David, which will lose the kingship. However, after the announcement of this chastisement, God twice decides to mitigate it. The chastisement will not strike Solomon himself, but only his son (v. 12), and it will not strike to the very end, but will spare him by leaving to the house of David the tribe of Judah, out of consideration for David and for Jerusalem (v. 13).

This announcement of the chastisement is a programme and a prologue. The narrative that follows (11.14–14.20) is its realization. In 11.11 'the slave of Solomon' who is going to receive the kingship in place of the descendant of the Davidic family is foretold. Thus the protagonists of the account are put in place and the unequal division of the Davidic kingdom is announced.

In 11.14-28 the dismemberment of the Solomonic empire initiates the execution of the project of chastisement. It takes place in three stages. First it will take away from Solomon the satellite kingdoms of Edom (vv. 14-22), and then of Damascus (vv. 23-25).[21] This happens while Solomon is still living (vv. 21 and 24). The third act is announced in vv. 26-27, 40. It no longer touches only the periphery of the empire. It reaches the kingdom itself through internal warfare. It is the revolt of Jeroboam, first while Solomon is still living, then under Rehoboam, when it will prove successful, as the account of 11.29–14.20 has precisely the task of relating. Eventually, the house of David will have effectively lost the satellite kingdoms to the south and to the north and the ten Israelite tribes. The chastisement will have displayed its announced effects.

11.28 and 12.18 seem to want to illustrate the complete reversal by a feature that has value as a sign: in 11.28 Jeroboam has charge over all the forced labour of the house of Joseph under King Solomon, while in 12.18 all Israel carried out the lynching of Adoram, the taskmaster over the forced labour that Rehoboam wanted to impose. The forced labour carried out forms an *inclusio* with the forced labour rejected.

A first time, the divine chastisement had been announced to Solomon in 11.9-13. In 11.29-39, a second time, the prophet Ahijah of Shiloh will announce it to Jeroboam by investing him, by divine mandate, with the role of enforcer of the chastisement. The announcement to Jeroboam repeats the two mitigations that God had already promised to Solomon (11.12-13 and 11.32, 34-36). Moreover, it promises Jeroboam the kingship over the ten tribes, a long-lasting royal dynasty and pre-eminence over the house of David, on condition of a perfect loyalty with regard to the Lord (vv. 37-39).

---

21. Moab and Ammon are not mentioned among the kingdoms liberated from Israelite vassalage. In the case of Moab, 2 Kgs 3.5 explains this silence, since it is only after the death of Ahab that Moab was liberated. According to 2 Sam. 12.31, the Ammonites ceased to exist as a people in the period of David.

Jeroboam resembles Hazael, king of Aram, and Jehu in 1 Kgs 19.15-16, in that a prophet appoints them as kings, by divine mandate, to carry out the chastisement intended by God. In these two cases, this royal investiture in the service of a punitive mission is manifested by a prophetic sign: here the sign of the torn garment, there, the anointing. This analogy anchors the account of the MT still more firmly in the Deuteronomistic History. This is why Martin Noth emphasizes the importance of the accounts of prophets for the Deuteonomistic History and mentions side by side the accounts of the prophets Elijah and Elisha and in particular the account of Jehu (2 Kgs 9.1–10.27) and that of Ahijah of Shiloh.[22] For Noth, 1 Kings 11–12 and 14 in the MT must be characterized as a prophetic account of Jeroboam and Ahijah of Shiloh.[23]

The investiture of Jeroboam is framed by his revolt against Solomon (11.26-27) and his escape to Egypt (11.40). It is possible that we should read the account of the prophetic sign as a 'flashback'.

After the death of Solomon, Israel, instead of recognizing the kingship of Rehoboam, rejects it (11.43–12.19) and gives it to Jeroboam (12.20). Israel separates from the house of David (12.19, negative formulation), Judah alone remaining attached to it (v. 20, positive formulation). The divine (11.12-13) and prophetic (11.32, 34-36) word has become reality. The prophetic story of Ahijah of Shiloh and of Jeroboam wants to show precisely this accomplishment of the divine word.

Rehoboam strove to nullify the division of the kingdom by force of arms, but the Lord cuts him short and sends the prophet Shemaiah to say that the chastisement decided by the Lord should not be revoked (12.21-24). Rehoboam obeys while Jeroboam fails in his duty with regard to the Lord.

Unlike Rehoboam, he actually does not disarm. And above all he introduces idolatry on a large scale in his kingdom (12.26-33) to eliminate any role for the sanctuary of Jerusalem, still chosen by God (vv. 27-28). Jeroboam prefers idolatry out of political self-interest! Religion is reduced to the rank of a means of service to the government, an absolute end.

For this sin, the Lord announces through the prophet Ahijah of Shiloh

22. M. Noth, *Überlieferungsgeschichtliche Studien: Die sammelnden und bearbeitenden Geschichtswerke im Alten Testament* (Darmstadt: Wissenschaftliche Buchgesellschaft, 3rd edn, 1967), pp. 78-80.
23. Noth, *Überlieferungsgeschichtliche Studien*, p. 72.

the chastisement of Jeroboam (14.1-18). The same prophet had transmitted the divine promise with its conditions to Jeroboam (11.37-39). Now, after the breach of these conditions, he is put in charge of promulgating the sanction.

In conclusion, the account of the MT is divided into two analogous sections: (A) sin of idolatry of Solomon—an irrevocable sanction for this sin under Rehoboam (11.9–12.24); (B) sin of idolatry of Jeroboam—irrevocable sanction for this sin (12.25-33; 14.1-18).

In the first sanction, that of Rehoboam, the Lord uses Jeroboam as an instrument of chastisement. Jeroboam receives the mission for this, thanks to a prophetic investiture, analogous to that of Jehu (1 Kgs 19.15-16). But this instrument ends up by rejecting God his ruler as well as his role as instrument in order to free himself from it. This is what is going to cause his ruin, a destiny analogous to the arrogance and the fall of the Assyrians in Isa. 10.5-11 or the Babylonians in Habakkuk 1–2.

8.2. *The Account of the HA*

We have seen that the HA equally traces two narrative arcs: the first (§§b-n) recounts the rise of Jeroboam from the nothingness of his social origin all the way up to the summit of power, but the Lord puts the axe to the root of this dynasty (§§g-n). It will not last, because it is cursed by YHWH since power does not return to Jeroboam, as it did not return to Abimelech (Judg. 9). This is a power that Jeroboam arrogates to himself. The Lord has not destined it for him. The second arc shows two things: the revolt of Israel against the Davidic king, and the irreversible character of this revolt (§§n-z).

The revolt is tragic. Yet it was easy to avoid. A little moderation by the king would have been enough. But arrogance had pushed Rehoboam headlong into the abyss. His power is legitimate, but badly managed. He wanted to appear as stronger, more powerful than his father. His personal ambition drove him to want to surpass his father, *to the detriment of the kingdom that definitively lost its unity.*

This split is actually definitive. Why? It punishes at the same time the rebellion of the tribes of Israel and the sons of Solomon, incapable of wisdom and moderation. God willed this double sanction: the revolt, as the prophet Shemaiah attests at the beginning (§o) and at the end (§y) of this second section, deprives Rehoboam of the tribes of Israel and leaves these in the hands of a cursed leader, Jeroboam. The two, Israel and Rehoboam, have each committed a fault; the two bear its consequences.

The first section is given over to Jeroboam, who is much like Abimelech of Judges 9. The second section has as its object the *hubris* of the king, Rehoboam, tragically provoking the misdeed of the revolt by the ten tribes.

The two sections of the HA are introduced by §a, which reports on the kingship that Rehoboam received in place of Solomon, exercising like him government over the whole of Israel and Judah. The HA thus recounts a revolt of part of the kingdom against the legitimate king, led by Jeroboam and made definitive by the Lord as a sanction.

9. *The Differences in Detail between the MT and the HA Explained in the Light of the Precedence of the HA*

The comparison of the narrative details has been carried out astutely by Talshir in the hypothesis of the precedence of the MT. Her analysis will allow for a confrontation on each point in regard to the plausibility of her arguments as compared with mine. Thus the solidity of the two opposing positions, that defended by Talshir and that adopted here, will be tested in the study of the details.

§a
1. *'And Rehoboam, his son, reigned in his stead in Jerusalem'*
In the MT (11.43) this clause of §a is found at the end of the story of Solomon (1 Kgs 1–11), where it forms the link with the account of the assembly at Shechem (12.1-20). This account relativizes the clause, since in 12.1 we learn immediately that 'all Israel' will meet Rehoboam at Shechem 'to proclaim him king'. (We should note that this final clause does not appear in the HA.) Rehoboam therefore succeeds Solomon without yet being king of Israel.[24] 1 Kings 12.1 is a point limiting 11.43: we conclude from it that Rehoboam is king only of Judah. This situation is analogous to 2 Sam. 5.1-5 where the tribes of Israel give

---

24. Since A. Alt, *Die Staatenbildung der Israeliten in Palästina, Kleine Schriften zur Geschichte des Volkes Israel*, II (Munich: Beck, 1953), pp. 1-65 (33-65), and *idem, Das Grossreich Davids, Kleine Schriften*, II, pp. 66-75, this distinction is considered important for understanding the monarchical institution created by David.

themselves a king in the person of David who has already been king over Judah for seven years.

On the other hand, the HA does not limit the clause 'and Rehoboam reigned in his stead at Jerusalem'. We understand here that Rehoboam inherited the whole kingdom of his father, which extended over Judah and Israel. In the view of the HA, Rehoboam is king over the tribes as a whole before the loss of the ten Israelite tribes during their revolt.[25]

In MT 11.43, the phrase 'at Jerusalem' is missing. It is found in the HA. According to 2 Sam. 5.5, David reigned at Hebron over Judah, but *at Jerusalem* over all of Israel and Judah. Jerusalem is the capital of the two parts of the kingdom. The absence of 'Jerusalem' in the MT and its presence in the HA is explained well in the light of 2 Sam. 5.5: for the HA, Rehoboam is king over Judah and Israel *at Jerusalem* as David was at Jerusalem after his anointing as king of Israel, while for the MT, Rehoboam is precisely not king over Judah and Israel and therefore does not reside as king at Jerusalem where David and Solomon had reigned over the whole kingdom. The presence of this element in the HA and the absence of 'at Jerusalem' in the MT are thus coherent in the perspectives of each of the two accounts.

The slight tension between 11.43 and 12.1 is clearly the sign of some redactional work in the MT, since, without 12.1, the readers interpret 'in his stead' quite naturally: Rehoboam takes the place of Solomon, his father, who was king over Judah and over Israel. But with 12.1, the readers are going to be informed straight away that Rehoboam is not yet king over 'all Israel'. They must therefore turn back and reinterpret 11.43 in this sense: 'and Rehoboam...reigned in his stead *over Judah*', which the text precisely does not say. The verse that follows corrects the verse that precedes.

---

25. Talshir (*The Alternative Story*, p. 185) thinks this clause is certainly secondary because 'the account of the kingship of Rehoboam over Judah could not have been recounted before the story of the division of the kingdom'. But the HA precisely does not speak of the reign of Rehoboam *over Judah*. In its view, Rehoboam began by being king like his father: over Israel and over Judah. Trebolle Barrera (*Salomón y Jeroboán*, pp. 189-90) also interprets the assembly at Shechem in the HA as a diet to elect the king, even though §a had clearly stated, from the start, that Rehoboam effectively succeeded his father on the throne.

2. *The Age of Rehoboam on Accession to the Throne*

The MT (14.21) gives Rehoboam the age of 41 on his accession to the throne and has him ruling 17 years, while the HA attributes to him the age of 16 years when he became king and a reign of 12 years.

According to the MT, Rehoboam is thus born a year before Solomon's accession to the throne, since the latter reigned 40 years (11.42). Although he was born of an Ammonite mother (14.21), she was not among the foreign royal wives responsible for the sin of Solomon by pushing him to venerate their gods (11.3-5), since they only succeeded in this when he was old (11.4). Rehoboam is born already in the time of David when his father was searching for wisdom and was loved by God.

According to the HA, on the other hand, Rehoboam was young when he acceded to the throne, in conformity with the story of the assembly of Shechem where we see him surrounded by young counsellors. 2 Chron. 13.7 calls him *na'ar*, young man. We can argue in two opposite directions. Either the HA adapts the difficult pieces of information from the MT (a king 41 years old who relies on a college of young counsellors) or else the MT wants to remove from Rehoboam any suspicion of being the son of an idolatrous mother who formed part of the circle of foreign wives fatal for the faithfulness of the old king Solomon.

3. *The Mother of Rehoboam*

In MT 14.21, 31 the mother of Rehoboam is referred to as 'Na'ama, the Ammonite'. The HA on the contrary calls her 'Na'anän, daughter of Hannün, the son of Nahash, king of the sons of Ammon'. She is thus identified as a royal princess, daughter of an Ammonite king, famous for having insulted David in the person of his ambassadors (2 Sam. 10.1-4). He had committed this insult on the advice of his counsellors. From the side of his mother, Rehoboam is therefore the grandson of a king who has brought calamity on himself and his kingdom because of his pride and because of his docility with regard to bad counsellors.

Again, it is possible to argue in two opposite directions. Either the HA explains the pride of Rehoboam and his stupid docility with regard to bad counsellors by placing him in the lineage of Hannün, king of the sons of Ammon, or else the MT clears the king of Judah of the stain of such a lineage.

4. *The Lifespan of Rehoboam*

According to the MT of 14.21 Rehoboam reached the age of 58, while in the HA he dies at 28,[26] 30 years younger. As a premature death is considered a curse, and death after a long life is on the contrary seen as a sign of blessing, it is the HA that suggests a curse on the life of Rehoboam, whereas in the MT he seems to have a normal lifespan and is therefore blessed.

5. *In Conclusion*

In the subject matter common to the HA §a and the MT 1 Kgs 11.43; 14.21, we do not find sufficient elements to prove the dependence of one of the two accounts with regard to the other. One indication, however, would lead to the diagnosis of the probable dependence of the MT in relation to the HA. This is the modification already mentioned of the significance of the last clause of 1 Kgs 11.43 by a clause of the following verse (12.1), which has no equivalent in the HA: 'and Jeroboam reigned in his stead' (11.43) is actually followed in the MT by 'for it is at Shechem that *all Israel came to make him king*' (12.1). This second clause limits the first. It seems to be the sign of a wording precisely aimed at giving a new meaning to 11.43. Moreover, the detailed comparisons are in no way opposed to the viewpoint of the HA preceding the MT. On the contrary, on this basis the comparisons give it an excellent meaning.

§b

1. *The Mother, the Father and the Home Town of Jeroboam*

In the MT, the mother of Jeroboam is called Zeruah and is a widow (1 Kgs 11.26), whereas in the HA she is called Sareira and is a prostitute. But it must be noted besides that the MT specifies several times the family name of Jeroboam. He is the son of Nebat of Ephrat (11.26; 12.2, 15; 15.1; 16.3, 26, 31, etc.). He is a native of Zereda. The HA makes no reference to any family name. Jeroboam is from the mountain of Ephraim.

To be the son of a prostitute with no known father definitely indicates a socially ignominious position in Israel. Jephthah was indeed a son of a prostitute, but his father was known and held in high regard (Judg.

---

26. Trebolle Barrera (*Salomón y Jeroboán*, p. 190) sees here a mistake of a copyist in the case of the HA.

11.1).[27] On the other hand, to be the son of a widow and of a deceased father known to everyone has nothing dishonourable about it.

One piece of evidence makes it possible perhaps to explain the more honourable ancestry of Jeroboam in the MT. The prophet Ahijah of Shiloh transmits to Jeroboam the divine promise to build a dynasty for him, if however he remains faithful to the Lord and the divine demands (1 Kgs 11.38). That promise is not found in the HA. According to the MT, Jeroboam would have therefore been able to be another David, father of a dynasty blessed by God. But would it be conceivable that the Lord would want to build a house for a son of a prostitute and an unknown father? For the MT, Jeroboam is not a man lost from the very start, he becomes lost by his sin. He was chosen by God before being rejected by God. He is like Saul.

In the HA, Jeroboam, without a father and son of a prostitute, has just one title: he is in the service of Solomon. The latter has given him the social status that he did not have at birth. He is therefore a favourite of the Davidic house! To it he owes his position.

In that way, it is possible to explain the MT as an adjustment to the infamous social origin of Jeroboam that is so inconsistent with the honour of a promise that the Lord makes to him. In the opposite direction, we can interpret the HA as secondary: it would be the result of the effort to tarnish the positive origin that Jeroboam has in the MT.[28]

---

27. In discussing the status of a son of a prostitute it is important to take into account the father: is he a man known and honoured, or is he unknown? That definitely changes the status of the child.

28. M. Aberbach and L. Smolar ('Jeroboam's Rise to Power', *JBL* 88 [1969], pp. 69-72) argue that the HA does not defame Jeroboam more than the MT and that it is not possible to distinguish the two versions on the basis of the criterion of antipathy or sympathy for Jeroboam, as Gooding had tried to do ('Rival Versions'). But I cannot agree with Aberbach and Smolar when they interpret the term 'prostitute' given to Jeroboam's mother as a neutral title. This title goes hand in hand with the absence of the name of the father: these two details together are disparaging. To explain the term 'prostitute' in the dependent version, in the face of 'widow' in the supposedly original version, Gordon ('The Second Septuagint Account of Jeroboam', p. 379) has to introduce the hypothesis of a Judaean edition of the HA. The need of secondary hypotheses to make possible the principal thesis (that is, that the HA is a secondary edition of the MT) is not a good sign in this case. Trebolle Barrera (*Salomón y Jeroboán*, pp. 192-93) gives the history of the interpretation of the label 'prostitute' that the HA attaches to the mother of Jeroboam. The link between this term and the absence of a family name has not received the attention that it deserves.

2. *The Activity of Jeroboam*

MT 1 Kgs 11.26-27 twice states that Jeroboam rebelled or raised the hand against the king. 'To raise the hand' (*herîm yad*) is related to the turn of phrase '(with) the hand held high' (*b^eyadramâ*) in Exod. 14.8 and Num. 33.3, which means 'demonstrably, not secretly'. In Num. 15.30 to sin 'highhandedly' means a sin committed publicly, that is to say, without shame, defiantly and in a provocative way.[29] Jeroboam has therefore defied the king. But the account is silent about the nature of that provocation. According to 2 Sam. 20.21 where a similar, but not identical, phrase occurs (*naśâ' yad b^emelek*, to lift up the hand against the king), it is a matter of a rebellion. The account continues here with mention of the building that Solomon had undertaken (v. 27), and relates that Solomon, on observing the young Jeroboam, who was a rich person of influence (*gibbôr hayyil*), carrying out his work, chose him to be in charge of the forced labour of the house of Joseph (v. 28). Jeroboam is not here a mere hireling, a 'slave' of Solomon as he is in the HA.

In the HA, the Greek equivalent of *gibbôr hayyil* is absent. Jeroboam does not provoke the king. He is no longer called 'a youth' (*na'ar*). On the contrary, the HA attributes to him the construction of the *Millô* at Jerusalem and the 'closing', that is, the complete fortification of the city of David (constructions attributed to Solomon by the MT, 11.27).[30]

And now here are the pluses of the HA in comparison with the MT: (1) Jeroboam constructs the *Millô* in Jerusalem making use of the forced labour of Ephraimites; (2) he builds the city of Sareira in the hill

---

29. J. Milgrom, *Cult and Conscience: The ASHAM and the Priestly Doctrine of Repentance* (SJLA, 18; Leiden: E.J. Brill, 1976), pp. 109-10; A. Schenker, 'Die Anlässe zum Schuldopfer Ascham', in *idem* (ed.), *Studien zu Opfer und Kult im Alten Testament* (FAT, 3; Tübingen: J.C.B. Mohr, 1992), p. 52 n. 15.

30. Gooding ('Rival Versions', p. 187) interprets this 'closing' as a siege of Jerusalem; likewise, Gordon, 'The Second Septuagint Account of Jeroboam', pp. 382-83. But the context is about the constructions as indicated by the reference to the forced labour of Ephraim. If the 300 war chariots were mentioned in connection with the siege of Jerusalem, it would have been necessary to place them at the point where it is recounted that Jeroboam 'closed', that is, besieged the city of David. Besides, it is difficult to imagine the use of war chariots in a siege, and still more difficult in the case of a siege of the city of David, considering the topography of Jerusalem! This term συνέκλεισεν in its context of the constructions carried out by Jeroboam and the forced labour from Ephraim corresponds perfectly with a repair of walls of the city of David.

country of Ephraim for Solomon; (3) he commands 300 war chariots; (4) he achieves a high position in the kingdom analogous to that of the pretender to the throne, Adonijah, in 1 Kgs 1.5.

The only common element between the HA and the MT is that both speak of Jeroboam in charge of the forced labour of the house of Joseph by Solomon.

MT 1 Kgs 11.26-28 is difficult, certainly, but has some consistency. Verse 26 introduces Jeroboam and mentions the challenge he is to the king. Verse 27 opens with a heading that gives notice about the whole account that follows in vv. 27-40: 'And here is the story of how Jeroboam challenged the king'. The second clause of v. 27, 'Solomon built/had built the *Millô*, closed the opening of the city of David his father' surprises because of the absence of any *waw*: there is none, although it would be a matter of a total of three clauses![31] But the general sense, suggested by v. 28, seems to be very much that of a portrayal of the circumstances: as for Solomon, it was when he was occupied in building the *Millô* and so on. At that time, he got to know the young Jeroboam, an important individual, and he promoted him to be in charge of the

31. Gordon ('The Second Septuagint Account of Jeroboam', p. 384) and Talshir (*The Alternative Story*, pp. 203-204) assume that the HA divided the MT, its basis, differently in 11.27, instead of the correct division of the MT: 'and here is the story of how Jeroboam raised the hand against the king: Solomon built the *Millô*...' (§b). The HA would have carried out this syntactical boost to explain what brought about the rebellion, namely, that it was precisely the construction of the *Millô*. This hypothesis is gratuitous. First, the HA does not speak of the rebellion of Jeroboam. This is only mentioned by the MT (11.26-27). The HA had no need therefore to explain a revolt that it had not mentioned. Secondly, the HA gives an obvious narrative function to the construction of the *Millô* and the closing of the breaches of the city of David (§b, MT 11.27) that Jeroboam undertakes as head of the forced labour of Ephraim. They actually prepare for the assembly at Shechem where the ten tribes of Israel demand the lightening of the forced labour. The latter is precisely the only *stake* in the debate between Rehoboam and Israel at Shechem! In the MT there is, in narrative terms, nothing to motivate this debate. Thirdly, the closing of the breaches of the city of David cannot be interpreted as an act of rebellion by Jeroboam. Trebolle Barrera (*Salomón y Jeroboán*, p. 194) has clearly shown this, by giving the parallels LXX 1 Kgs 2.35e; 9.23; 9.15, against the thesis of Gooding and of Gordon; cf. n. 28 above. If the repairing of the breaches is in no way a rebellion, we cannot see any more reason why the construction of the *Millô* would be a rebellion against Solomon. The context of §b (Jeroboam constructs Sareira 'for Solomon') suggests on the contrary that Jeroboam worked on all these projects in the service of his master Solomon.

forced labour of the tribe of Joseph (v. 28). The MT explains in this way the meeting of Solomon and Jeroboam and the responsibility that the king entrusted to him, and it suggests at the same time, but only in an implicit way, that the defiance of Jeroboam must have begun with the prophecy of Ahijah of Shilo (vv. 29-39). After this the account implies that the relationship between Solomon and Jeroboam will deteriorate to the point that Jeroboam has to flee to escape death (v. 40). All this is not said *expressis verbis*, but seems to be implied in several laconic verses (vv. 26-27; 40).

The HA explains neither how Jeroboam was hired by Solomon nor the origin of his talents as project manager and commander of chariot-eers. But by saying at the beginning, as a heading for the account, that he was an Ephraimite in the service of Solomon, it suggests that he is totally a creature of the latter, especially since it is only after having presented him as 'servant of Solomon' that the account finally mentions his personal name with the only genealogical indication that can be pro-vided: his mother is a prostitute; we do not know who the fathers of her children are. Jeroboam is therefore nothing socially speaking if he is not 'a servant of Solomon', a servant not of Judaean origin, but Ephraimite! Like Jephthah (Judg. 11.1-2), son of a prostitute, he had to seek for an existence elsewhere, abroad.

He begins by being head of the forced labour of the house of Joseph, next he builds for Solomon the city of Sareira in Ephraim, becomes commander of 300 chariots, then constructs the *Millô* in Jerusalem but with the forced labour of Ephraim, and finally closes the gap in the fortifications of the city of David. Thus he attains a high-ranking posi-tion in the kingdom. Solomon uses him first to control Ephraim, it seems, before using his Ephraimite forced labour for Jerusalem. That utilization of Ephraimites at Jerusalem, ironically *under the command of the Ephraimite Jeroboam*, prepares for and explains the assembly at Shechem where Israel rejects, with the help of the same Jeroboam, the king Rehoboam, harsher even than his father as regards forced labour and taxes. The role of Jeroboam at Jerusalem becomes a nuisance for Solomon, who as a result will try to get rid of him.

The work of Jeroboam reported in §b of the HA clearly answers a narrative necessity. It actually prepares for the demand of the Israelite tribes for a lightening of the forced labour, weighty precisely because of the enterprises of Solomon not only in Ephraim (construction of the town of Sareira), but at Jerusalem (the *Millô* and the repairing of the gaps in the walls of the city of David). The Israelites are requisitioned more for the profit of the house of David than for the needs of the country. In contrast, the MT says nothing about forced labour of the Ephraimites for the *Millô* and the city (11.27-28). Here Solomon is exempt from suspicion of having exploited the Ephraimites. Because of that, the MT explains less well the stake in the conflict between Rehoboam and the ten tribes of Israel—which is precisely the too heavy weight of the forced labour imposed on the house of Ephraim by Solomon.

The point of §b is thus the irony that a creature of Solomon, in his service to control militarily the hill country of Ephraim and to direct the forced labour of Ephraimites by conscripting them even for constructions in Jerusalem, is going to become the leader of Israel's rebellion against the house of David! The account, no matter how embryonic, explains perfectly the conflict between Solomon and Jeroboam while making understandable the tension between Israel, subject to the forced labour, and the house of David, which exploits them for itself.

In conclusion, the account of the HA is more plausible and more coherent than that of the MT, which is much more implicit and stylistically strange. Furthermore, the HA brings §b as a stone necessary for the narrative edifice since it explains why Rehoboam and the Israelites fall out concerning the forced labour imposed on Ephraim, while the MT does not explain this fact since, according to it, Solomon has not made use of forced labour outside of Ephraimite territory! But this observation on the characteristics of the two accounts would not be enough by itself to prove the precedence of the HA. Nevertheless it corroborates it.

§c

This text of the HA is substantially identical with the MT 1 Kgs 11.40, apart from two exceptions: according to the MT, Jeroboam was afraid, a narrative detail missing from the HA, and he sojourned *in Egypt*, while in the HA he sojourned with the king of Egypt, Shishak. The MT passes over in silence the personal relationship with the king. The HA accentuates in that way the political weight of Jeroboam and his ambition. He is dangerous for the house of David. But the two narrative presentations give a satisfactory meaning and do not make it possible to determine the direction of the dependence of one account with regard to the other.

§§d-f

The substance of this section of the HA is identical with MT 1 Kgs 11.15-22, but with two big differences: the protagonist is Jeroboam according to the HA, Hadad the Edomite according to the MT; the episode takes place before the death of Solomon in the HA, but 40 years earlier, before the death of David, in the MT.

Each of the two accounts mentions elements absent from the other. In the MT, it is the war of David and Joab in Edom and the journey of Hadad, crossing in his flight Midian and Paran on the way to Egypt (1 Kgs 11.15-18). The war of David and Joab in Edom is mentioned briefly in 2 Sam. 8.13-14; Ps. 60.1-2. Midian and Paran (Gen. 21.21; 1 Sam. 25.1) are territories bordering on Egypt and are beyond the borders of the Judaean and Israelite kingdom; by mentioning them the narrator shows that the flight and the political alliance are beyond the range of David. The HA has exclusive to it the return of Jeroboam to Sareira in the hill country of Ephraim, the rallying of the tribe of the Ephraimites up there and the building of a fortress in the same place (§f). This narrative detail forms an *inclusio* with the constructions of §b. In the beginning, Jeroboam actually 'constructs Sareira for Solomon' (§b), as a city that served as a military support for Solomon to control Ephraim. With the forced labour from Ephraim, Jeroboam also builds the *Millô* at Jerusalem, a residence for Solomon, far from the land of Ephraim (§b). On the other hand, Jeroboam, back in Sareira, a rallying place of the Ephraimites, builds a fort there, but this time *against the son of Solomon*.

We have seen above (section 3) that the marriage of Jeroboam with the sister-in-law of the Pharaoh, and the birth of a son from that union, fits well in the narrative framework of the HA, while the marriage of Hadad with the sister-in-law of the Pharaoh and the birth of a son of Hadad has no narrative function in the MT. We should conclude from that observation the precedence of the HA.

The element proper to the HA, the constructions of Jeroboam at Sareira in the hill country of Ephraim before and after his fleeing to Egypt, is itself well placed too in the narrative arrangement, while, in the MT, the details of the war in Edom—the presence of David and Joab, the extermination of the male Edomite children, the flight of Hadad by way of Midian and Paran, the child of Hadad saved from extermination and educated at the court of the Pharaoh (1 Kgs 11.15-20)—play no necessary role in the narrative whole. Furthermore, these details have nothing original about them, since they depend on biblical analogies and pieces of information like 2 Sam. 8.13-14; Ps. 60.1-2; Exodus 1–2. The same cannot be said of the element proper to the HA, since it forms a narrative *inclusio* that is not just ornamental, but makes the account progress and has no direct analogy with other biblical accounts.

§§g-n

The substance of this account is identical in the MT and the HA. The differences concern first of all its place: after the assembly of Shechem, in the conclusion of the story of Jeroboam in the MT (1 Kgs 14.1-20), but before this assembly, in the conclusion of the irresistible rise of Jeroboam in the HA. Then the deception of the prophet Ahijah by Jeroboam, found in the MT (vv. 1 and 5-6), is absent from the HA. Thirdly, the discourses of Ahijah are longer in the MT than in the HA.

We have seen above (section 4) that the two forms of the account both fit coherently in the overall context of the MT and the HA. Such is the case in regard to the place of the episode: in the MT, Ahijah condemns Jeroboam after his apostasy, when he has failed in the obedience due to the Lord and thus forfeited the promise attached to the obedience. In the HA, Jeroboam had tried to make a career for himself and found a dynasty in Israel against the house of David, like Abimelech at Shechem (Judg. 9), but the Lord cut it short by condemning the child to death (§§l-m), that death being the guarantee of the annihilation to come for all his descendants (§m). The dissimulation in the MT is easily explained since Jeroboam wants to obtain by trickery a neutral divine oracle. If he had actually revealed his identity, sinner that he is, he would definitely have received a curse. But his stratagem was of no use to him before the prophet who, although blind, is a true prophet and therefore clear-sighted. In the HA, on the other hand, such a dissimulation would not have any function. Jeroboam actually has not committed a public sin. He acts here as any other Israelite would have acted facing a grave illness in his family; he consults, not anonymously but openly, a prophet! The blindness of the prophet has a different function than in the MT, where it constitutes, with the disguise of Jeroboam's wife, a double obstacle to keep the prophet from knowing with whom he is dealing. The prophet thwarts these two obstacles, of course. In the HA, Jeroboam does not want to hide his identity. The miracle of the blind prophet who knows in advance who is coming to consult him does not have to thwart any trick. His narrative function is to indicate that the condemnation of the family of Jeroboam comes certainly from the Lord.

Finally, Ahijah refers in the MT to the words of his promise of a short while ago (11.29-39), replaced now by curses. The text establishes in this way a framework of prophetic words that surround the assembly of Shechem and the apostasy of Jeroboam (1 Kgs 12.26-33). On the other hand the HA frames the episode in another way. In §f, it shows the tribe of Ephraim assembled at Sareira *in the hill country of Ephraim* and Jeroboam building there a fortress, whereas in §n he goes to Shechem *in the hill country of Ephraim* where he assembles the tribes of Israel.

In conclusion, here the evidence is lacking to detect with certainty the precedence of one textual form in comparison with the other.[32]

§o

The account shows the same tradition on both sides. The differences were interpreted above (section 5). It was possible to conclude from them that the MT probably represents a revised form in its overall composition and that the HA is its basis.

We can still make the following observations:

(1) The account in the HA could be interpreted as a 'flashback'. This is the opinion of Zipora Talshir.[33] This interpretation is possible, but not necessary since Jeroboam has no part in the assembly of Shechem. He can therefore meet the prophet, with the account leaving him room for such a meeting at the very time when it is recounted! It is even more likely that it happened at this point in the trajectory of events. Jeroboam, in the setting of the prophetic sign, actually takes the ten pieces of the torn garment during or just before the Shechem assembly where the unity of the kingdom is torn apart and the ten pieces of Israel are there to take. This chronological sequel of the prophetic sign, accompanying or preceding the event signified that realizes it, is a perfect narrative sequence.[34]

---

32. On the other hand, we see that the conclusion of McKenzie (*The Trouble with Kings*, pp. 29-31), according to which the HA is only intelligible if we presuppose MT 1 Kgs 14, is unnecessary.

33. Talshir, *The Alternative Story*, pp. 175-76.

34. Talshir (*The Alternative Story*, pp. 168 and 175) interprets the particular syntax of §§e and o as a formal indication of a 'flashback'. But this can be very well explained as an indication of a change of scene, but within the same temporal

(2) In the MT, the *prophetic* sign consists of one act *alone*: Ahijah tears his new garment. In the HA, the sign is a sequence of *two* acts: the prophet tears his new garment which has not yet been washed, and Jeroboam takes the ten pieces to wear. The sign as such is more developed in the latter.

(3) As for the words that accompany the sign, in the MT, the prophet speaks in just one scene that takes place between him and Jeroboam and in just one long discourse (11.31-39). This consists of two parts. The first, very brief (v. 31), is the order that the prophet gives to Jeroboam: 'take for yourself ten pieces' (four words in Hebrew). The other, a long speech (vv. 31b-39), is a word of the Lord, introduced by the messenger formula. The Lord speaks to him in the first person. But at the narrative level, there are only two speakers: Jeroboam, who listens in silence, and Ahijah, who reports what the Lord has ordered him to say to Jeroboam.

In the HA, we find two utterances, delivered in two different scenes, in two dialogues with different partners. At first the Lord speaks to the prophet. That word is introduced by the word-event formula: 'and the word of the Lord was (addressed) to Shemaiah...saying'. It is made up of two parts. The first explains the prophetic sign that the prophet must carry out with his garment. It is worth noting here that it is the prophet who gives the ten pieces whereas, in the MT, God gives them. The second is a messenger formula explaining what words the prophet must use to accompany, in the name of the Lord, the sign that he is in the process of carrying out.

After this the scene changes. Now we see the prophet giving the pieces and Jeroboam taking them. In this detail it is important to see that the prophet uses a different messenger formula than that which the Lord had assigned him in the preceding scene: 'It is thus that the Lord speaks concerning the ten tribes of Israel'. The 'thus' refers to the sign of the ten torn pieces that Jeroboam eagerly takes in order to clothe himself. This second utterance is joined with the sign to such an extent that, without the sign, it remains without any content.

In comparison with the divine word of the MT, there is no question here of the house of David, nor of Solomon, nor of Rehoboam, nor of Judah, nor of Jerusalem, being symbolized by the single piece that remains opposite the ten others. It is no longer a question of God who takes away from Solomon, looks after David and gives to Jeroboam! In

sequence, without any reversion to the past.

the HA, the prophet alone gives and Jeroboam alone takes.

In the HA, sign and word are more united and in a mutual equilibrium. In the MT, the word takes priority over the sign. That does not of course prove the precedence of the HA, but perhaps increases the probability.

(4) In the MT, the prophetic sign is negative and positive at the same time. It is negative because it announces the split of the Davidic monarchy, positive because the Lord remains faithful to David and promises a dynasty to Jeroboam (v. 38). The kingdom of Israel can be born under good auspices. The Lord takes away and gives. The Lord redistributes the entire twelve parts!

In the HA, the sign is exclusively negative. Israel will fall into the hands of an ambitious man condemned by the Lord. The sign of this situation: a leader clothed in a torn and incomplete garment. It is this incomplete character that is emphasized, and not the distribution of all the parts! Here God redistributes nothing, but hands over the ten tribes to this disastrous individual, Jeroboam, who has just been cursed.

(5) This uniquely negative and pessimistic aim of the prophetic sign is initially a condemnation of Israel, not of Jeroboam. We understand here why the HA has no need of the religious apostasy of Jeroboam. Israel, the people, is to be *taken* just as the ten pieces of the torn garment are to be taken, since it is on the verge or in the process of rejecting its legitimate king. Following its uprising against the house of David, Israel has become an incomplete accumulation of pieces that belong to nobody. The first comer can snatch them up.

The situation described here presents an analogy with the fable of Jotham (Judg. 9.7-15). Into the vacuum left by the good king the tyrant rushes. In the fable, there are those who would have governed well who refuse to take on the rule, while here these are the subjects who refuse the rule of the house of David, but in the two cases, the political vacuum created by the refusal is immediately beset by a deadly power.

Tragedy looms. The house of David is represented by Rehoboam, a king with tyrannical inclinations, but in rejecting him, Israel falls into the hands of a still worse tyrant. To liberate itself, Israel sells itself, and God does not stop it.

If this interpretation is correct, it has a chance of being more original than the much more usual biblical theme of divine chastisement that we find in the MT.

All these differences between the MT and the HA, in 1 Kgs 11.29-39

248   *Israel Constructs its History*

and §o, do not make it possible to establish a certain dependence of one
on the other, but nothing stands in the way of the HA being prior to the
MT account. The indicators seem on the whole to go in this direction.

§§*p-u*

Besides the differences already discussed above (section 6), the MT
presents three pluses, not found in the HA: 1 Kgs 12.17 mentions the
Israelites living in the towns of Judah and recognizing Rehoboam; v. 18
reports the stoning of the taskmaster for the forced labour, Adoram;
v. 19 summarizes: 'and Israel has been in rebellion against the house of
David to this day'.

As for the first enigmatic plus, it limits the rejection of the house of
David by all Israel. A remnant in Israel remains faithful to him. We
should note that the stratum of the LXX that translates the MT (1 Kgs
12) is unaware of this verse. It could thus be a matter of a redactional
addition, eventually interdependent with the long redaction of the book
of Jeremiah in 31 (38), 21, and surely with the parallel of Chronicles
(2 Chron. 10.17; 1 Chron. 9.3). It is perhaps intended to account for 'the
remnant of the people' whom Shemaiah tells not to wage war alongside
Judah and Benjamin in 12.24. This remnant in Israel perhaps also
suggests an analogy with the remnant that remained faithful to the Lord
in the time of Elijah, 1 Kgs 19.18.

The lynching of the taskmaster for the forced labour at Shechem indicates the break become real between Israel and the Davidic king.
Solomon's official is assassinated, whereas, only a short time before,
Solomon himself had been able peacefully to induct Jeroboam in this
same function (11.28)! Verse 19 concludes the whole narrative.

As a consequence, the absence of v. 17 in the HA is probably original, its presence in the MT resulting from a work of compilation. The
other two pluses, however, do not present criteria to situate chrono-
logically the MT as compared to the HA.

On the other hand, in §p, the HA presents one plus that the MT does
not know: καὶ ἐβάρυνεν τὰ βρώματα τῆς τραπέζης αὐτοῦ: 'He made
heavy the maintenance of his table'. Trebolle Barrera has shown the
significance of this expression.[35] It is about the taxes of the regions to
provide the table of the king with food. It was another contribution that
was added to the forced labour and to which the king submitted the

---

35. Trebolle Barrerra, *Salomón y Jeroboán*, pp. 206-10.

Israelites (1 Kgs 5.2-3, 7). The phrase in the HA is well supported, in a nearby context, by 1 Kgs 10.5. But we cannot prove that the HA preserves here an original form that the MT would have suppressed nor the contrary, namely, that the HA introduced it secondarily.[36]

§§x-z

MT 1 Kgs 12.21-25 presents several pluses as compared to the HA: v. 21: (1) Rehoboam had therefore returned to Jerusalem; (2) he assembled the *house* of Judah and the *tribe* of Benjamin; (3) the number and quality of the soldiers are specified; (4) the war is directed against the house of Israel; (5) the objective of the war, the recovery of the kingdom for Rehoboam, is asserted.

Opposite this, the HA (§x) states: 'and it happened, at the approach of the (following) year, that Rehoboam assembled every man in Judah and Benjamin and went up to make war on Jeroboam at Shechem'. From its side, the HA has thus two pluses: the indication of the time and place of the projected war.

Verse 25 of the MT is absent from the HA, if however the notice of the building of a fortress at Sareira in the hill country of Ephraim, at the end of §f, does not represent the same tradition as the notice of the fortifications of Jeroboam in 1 Kgs 12.25.

However that may be, the differences are well explained in the perspective appropriate to each account. For the MT, Israel has rejected the kingdom of David. This is why Rehoboam fights rebellious Israel, not Jeroboam. His force is such that he would have achieved the victory. But the Lord has arranged it otherwise. Jeroboam builds himself a city at Shechem and at Penuel, as David had built himself a city. According to the HA, the fact of the war is central, and this would have had to take place at Shechem, the place of the rejection of the Davidic king.

36. Trebolle Barrera (*Salomón y Jeroboán*, pp. 210-25) studies also the difference between the phrases 'elder counsellors of Solomon' (MT 12.6) and 'elders of the people' of HA §q. On the *narrative* level, we cannot determine the difference, but, according to him, there exists a difference at the *institutional* level and as a result on the *historical* level. This opposition that the HA places between the courtiers of the new king (the 'young' counsellors) and the 'elders of the people' (the representatives of Israel) would thus be close to the historical reality. On the narrative level, the opposition reveals, both in the MT and in the HA, the typical contrast between the elderly, experienced and moderate counsellors and the young, inexperienced, but all the more intransigent and arrogant counsellors.

Conclusion of this Comparison

In conclusion, the comparison of the differences in detail of the two accounts does not make it possible to prove with certainty that the one is the redaction of the other. Nevertheless, several indications tilt towards considering the MT as an editorial textual form and the HA as an underlying basis for this redaction. These indications thus corroborate the result of the preceding narrative analysis that has compared the four accounts with their global contextual setting. That comparison had brought out a connection of appropriateness between the overall context and its four narrative components on the part of the HA, and certain distortions between the narrative parts and the global literary composition on the part of the MT.[37]

The comparison of the differences in detail has not produced examples that could only be accounted for in the hypothesis of the dependence of the HA in relation to the MT. It has definitely revealed situations that could be explained in one direction or in the other. But it in no way requires presupposing the MT as a base and the HA as a redaction of this base.

10. *Is it Possible to Situate the Two Editions of the Account of Rehoboam and Jeroboam in an Absolute Chronology?*

Jörg Debus[38] had explained the HA as a textual form of the account of Rehoboam and Jeroboam still untouched by the Deuteronomistic redaction because it is earlier than this. The reason for this opinion is the absence of grounds that would account for the omission of precisely the Deuteronomistic passages 1 Kgs 11.32-39, 43; 14.7-9, 15-16. It is actually easier to understand the relation between the two forms of the account by supposing a literary base preceding the Deuteronomistic redaction represented by the HA, and a redaction due to the Deuteronomist, recorded in the MT.

On the other hand, Talshir and McKenzie try to account for these omissions by considering the account of the MT as original and the HA as secondary in editorial and literary terms. Talshir recalls that the HA

---

37. It is necessary to note here that McKenzie (*The Trouble with Kings*, pp. 29-40) argues at times on the basis of narrative considerations as I have tried systematically to do here. But he reaches a result contrary to that reached here.

38. Debus, *Die Sünde Jerobeams*, pp. 84-87; likewise, Trebolle Barrera, *Salomón y Jeroboán*, p. 174.

never presents Jeroboam as king. As a consequence, this text could not conceive of a dynastic perspective, opening onto the future, nor recount a religious schism, since this implies a king, the only one capable of leading a whole nation into another religion. It is therefore logical that the HA would have to omit, out of concern for internal coherence, all the references to a royal dynasty and a religious policy of Jeroboam, and it is precisely that, the content of the Deuteronomistic passages of the MT, that we look for in vain in the HA.

What is more, Talshir draws attention to very visible traces in the HA of a Deuteronomistic influence, for example, in §§a and m.[39]

The ultimate argument, the most decisive, of Talshir is the impossibility of the thesis of the pre-Deuteronomistic origin of the HA. Sections x-z actually report the intervention of the prophet Shemaiah, sent by the Lord to prohibit Rehoboam from waging war against Jeroboam. The parallel passage of the MT, 1 Kgs 12.21-24, is quite closely parallel. But this section seems to be secondary in the MT, since here Rehoboam is king over Judah and Benjamin whereas, everywhere else in the MT (1 Kgs 11.13, 32, 36; 12.20), there remains for Rehoboam just one tribe alone, Judah. The kingdom combining Judah and Benjamin corresponds to the idea of the Chronicles and of the book of Jeremiah (2 Chron. 11.1; Jer. 17.26).

But §§x-z of the HA equally assume a kingdom composed of Judah and Benjamin under Rehoboam. The HA therefore cannot go back to a pre-Deuteronomistic period since clearly the notion of a kingdom of Judah and Benjamin seems to be recent, characteristic of the period that follows the Deuteronomistic redaction.[40] With good reason, Talshir refutes the expedient of declaring §§x-z an editorial addition to the HA, as Debus proposes.[41] We have actually seen that the final intervention

39. Talshir, *The Alternative Story*, pp. 243-60.

40. Talshir, *The Alternative Story*, pp. 257-59. The majority of exegetes agree that the story of Shemaiah, 1 Kgs 12.21-24 (= HA §§y-z) is the expression of a recent post-exilic tradition; cf. Trebolle Barrera, *Salomón y Jeroboán*, p. 125. But that does not mean in a secondary literary sense, as Trebolle Barrera claims (*Salomón y Jeroboán*, p. 149. This author calls this passage a *Wiederaufnahme* [resumption], giving to this technical term an inappropriate sense, since *Wiederaufnahme* presupposes the identity of a wording before and after a secondary literary insertion).

41. Debus, *Die Sünde Jerobeams*, p. 90, n. 27: the editor who had inserted the HA in the account as the MT preserved it, after 12.24, has reproduced 1 Kgs 12.21-24 to restore the context, interrupted by the insertion (*Wiederaufnahme* principle).

of the prophet Shemaiah in §§x-z forms an *inclusio* with his promise in §o. The two scenes with Shemaiah, interdependent on the narrative level, mutually influence each other, so much so that one cannot exist without the other, and the one and the other had to be present in the account from the very beginning.

This observation of Talshir is relevant, but it does not require the conclusion she draws from it, namely, that the Deuteronomistic parts in 1 Kings 11–12; 14 must be considered original parts of the account that the HA later removed.

There are actually two reasons for opposing this conclusion. The first is the comparison of the two textual forms on the narrative level. As we have seen (sections 2–6 above), such an analysis suggests the precedence of the HA and the redactional character of the MT. The second reason is the extremely painstaking explanation that must be imagined to make the contrary thesis plausible. It actually seems simpler to explain the literary development starting from the HA, without the three long Deuteronomistic discourses on the lips of the Lord (1 Kgs 11.11-13) and of the prophet Ahijah (11.29-39; 14.7-16) as well as the Deuteronomistic remarks of the narrator himself (11.4-10), and to consider the form of the MT as a compilation with a Deuteronomistic flavour working from this base.

There is actually nothing to stand in the way of assuming that the notion of the alliance between Judah and Benjamin and the mention of the prophet Shemaiah in Chronicles would have been found in the Chronicler's source and that this source would in fact be the HA.[42] It is

---

Likewise Trebolle Barrera (*Salomón y Jeroboán*, p. 149, identical argument). This argument is weak because §§x-z (=1 Kgs 12.21-24) is not necessary to restore the context supposedly interrupted by the editorial insertion of the HA. The HA actually ends at §u with the return of Rehoboam to Jerusalem (1 Kgs 12.18, 21) and the position of Judah and of Benjamin, supporters of Rehoboam (cf. 1 Kgs 12.21). The mention of Jeroboam and of his activities of fortifying Shechem and Penuel (1 Kgs 12.25) would naturally follow all that and without raising any transitional difficulty. In other words, there is no need of a suture (*Wiederaufnahme*) to bring the readers back to the point from which the supposed insertion of the HA would have banished them! In the absence of a literary necessity to restore an interrupted context, the *narrative function* of §§x-z (= 1 Kgs 12.21-24) otherwise proves more weighty. On the narrative level, this passage actually confirms and ratifies the truth of the word of God that had been announced by the prophet in §o and that surrounds, like a frame, the account of the assembly of Shechem.

42. Such a view is proposed by A.G. Auld, *Kings without Privilege: David and*

the compiler of the MT 1 Kings 11–12; 14 who limits the divine election exclusively to the tribe of Judah (11.13, 32, 36; 12.20). But this particular notion about the redaction of the MT immediately creates a tension with the prophetic sign of the garment torn into *twelve* pieces of which Jeroboam must take just ten. There remains one piece, one tribe too many. But it is precisely 12.21-24, whose material is derived from the HA, that comes to correct that incoherence, at the end of the account. It is the narrative function of the mention of Benjamin alongside Judah in the MT.

It must be noted that on the other hand no narrative tension results from the mention of Benjamin in the HA, for here the exclusive election of the tribe of Judah does not exist. Opposite the ten tribes of Israel, it is usual that there would be two others, of which one is Judah, the home of Rehoboam. The mention of the second, Benjamin, in §§x-z comes up quite naturally.

The simplest explanation seems therefore to be the following: the HA preserves the original form of the account. This was the source of the Chronicler, but also of the editor of the MT of Kings. This latter introduces into it the election of the tribe of Judah alone, which he asserts initially, at the cost of an inconsistency in the text, to be remedied there later at the end of 12.21-24 by the mention of Benjamin next to Judah.

The wording of the MT 1 Kings 11–12; 14 moreover gives greater importance to Judah than the Deuteronomistic historian does for his part. This is evident from the two following observations. First, according to 1 Kings 11–12; 14.1-18, *Judah* is not accused of the sin of infidelity with respect to the Lord, whereas Solomon, Jeroboam and Israel on the contrary are gravely guilty of it: Solomon in 11.4-13, Jeroboam in 12.26-33 and Israel according to 11.33 and 14.15-16. As for 11.33, the plural of the verbs implying sins of apostasy can actually only refer to the plural that immediately precedes them at the end of v. 32: 'out of all the tribes of Israel'. Verse 33 therefore has the function

Moses in the Story of the Bible's Kings (Edinburgh: T. & T. Clark, 1994), pp. 163-67: the Chronicler and the 'Deuteronomistic' author (that is, the authors-editors of the books of Kings) would have elaborated, each in his own way, starting from a common narrative text, a presentation appropriate to the history of the kings, and the HA would be in part this common base. According to Auld, it would be a question of two *Kompositionsschichten* (composition layers) (Deuteronomistic, Chronicles).

of providing a supplementary explanation of the fact that the Lord has handed over the ten tribes into the hands of Jeroboam. It is that they deserved it because of their ancient apostasy, prior to that of Jeroboam. In conformity with this preceding infidelity of Israel, of the people, the divine word of 14.9 recalls the infidelity of the predecessors of Jeroboam, of the king. Strictly speaking, as king of Israel, Jeroboam has not had predecessors. Since he is the first king of the ten tribes. But from reading 14.9 we must understand that in Israel, there had already been leaders, who were not kings (we can think of the book of Judges), but who had abandoned the Lord even before Jeroboam. On the other hand, Judah is innocent.

But, in the Deuteronomistic History, according to 14.22-24, the tribe of Judah has really committed the sin of idolatry under Rehoboam, still more gravely than his ancestors.[43] And it does not cease repeating it later (15.12-14; 22.44; 2 Kgs 12.4; 14.4; 15.4, 35; 21.16; 22.17; 23.25-27). However, the history of the MT 1 Kings 11–12; 14.1-18 does not breathe a word about the apostasy of Judah in the period of Solomon. This silence cannot be an accident, since, in the same context, the narrator takes care to show explicitly that Israel from its side is jointly responsible in the sin of its king Jeroboam: king and people have sinned together according to 14.16. No such thing for Judah! Solomon alone abandoned the Lord, without having drawn Judah into his sin.

Logically, Jeroboam and Israel are together condemned to extinction (14.14-15), while the sanction that will strike Solomon will be the loss of the kingdom for his son Rehoboam, except for a remnant that will be preserved for him, out of consideration for David's merit. But *Judah* is not condemned here, in contrast to 2 Kgs 22.17-20; 23.26-27 where it definitely will be.

This observation reveals a contrast between Judah and Israel in the MT 1 Kings 11–12; 14: Israel, culpable of apostasy for a long time, is

---

43. Trebolle Barrera (*Salomón y Jeroboán*, pp. 191-92), considers the name 'Judah' in the MT of 14.22 as a corruption, due to a literary initiative, replacing the original name 'Rehoboam', preserved by the LXX. This hypothesis is improbable. The plurals of v. 22 actually assume a collective subject; the summaries on the reigns of kings usually contain an appraisal of the kings, whereas this is missing here, so that the summary of the MT with Judah is unusual, while that of the LXX with Rehoboam corresponds to the ordinary outline; the description of Judah as a sinner and idolater is unique in the Deuteronomistic History. 'Judah' is clearly *lectio difficilior*.

handed over by the Lord to Jeroboam, a reprehensible king (11.33), while Judah, exempt from apostasy, is preserved for the descendant of David, a king exempt from infidelity with regard to the Lord (11.13, 32). Apostate Israel (11.33) merits an apostate king, Jeroboam, while faithful Judah is worthy of a faithful David.

In conclusion, the author of MT 1 Kings 11–12; 14.1-18 does not foresee the condemnation of Judah, unlike Israel, which is going to be erased from the map and dispersed beyond the Euphrates (14.15-16). The difference is made clear: Israel has followed its sinful king, while Solomon has not been able to lead Judah into his sin.

The remainder of the books of Kings not only does not suggest in any way the innocence of Judah from the sin of apostasy, but on the contrary indicts Judah for this sin, from the reign of Rehoboam onwards (14.22-24). Judah will merit under Manasseh, by the excess of its sins, the same condemnation as Israel (2 Kgs 23.27): it will be doomed to extinction.

This acknowledgement leads to a second difference in ideas between 1 Kings 11–12 on the one hand and the Deuteronomistic History on the other. It concerns the perpetuity of Judah, interdependent with the perpetuity of the house of David, maintained with the force of a principle in 1 Kgs 11.36: David must always have a lamp before the Lord in Jerusalem. For that lamp in the city of Jerusalem, the tribe of Judah is indispensable, since it is in view of that lamp that God gives the tribe of Judah to Rehoboam. 1 Kgs 11.39 will then reaffirm the perpetuity of the descendants of David.

In the Deuteronomistic History, the lamp is given to Rehoboam in 1 Kgs 15.4 and to the descendants of David according to 2 Kgs 8.19. This latter passage possesses a complex syntax since it attaches to the verb 'to give' two indirect objects: 'to give *to him* (to David) a lamp *for his descendants*'. In the light of 1 Kgs 15.4, where Rehoboam receives a lamp because of David, we should interpret 2 Kgs 8.19 in the sense that the Lord does not give the lamp to David, deceased, but to his living descendants, because of David.

But these descendants may lose this lamp because of their unworthiness and thus lose Judah. 2 Kgs 8.19 opens up this prospect under the reign of Jehoram, in the form of a threat not yet realized.

In conclusion, according to 1 Kgs 11.36 and according to 2 Kgs 8.19, the lamp that the Lord will make shine in Jerusalem is inseparably

Israel Constructs its History

accompanied by the gift of the tribe of Judah. For the city of Jerusalem cannot exist without Judah.

But in 1 Kgs 11.36 this lamp that shines in Jerusalem of Judah belongs to David, while, in the Deuteronomistic History, in 1 Kgs 15.4 and 2 Kgs 8.19, it is given to his descendants. The difference is that David, the just king, may never lose this lamp, whereas his descendants, often sinners, risk losing it, with the result that by losing it, they lose at the same time Judah. According to 1 Kings 11, Judah will never be lost since it is the prerogative of David, the just servant of the Lord, whereas in 2 Kgs 8.19 Judah can be lost because of its sinful kings. From one side, therefore, the perpetuity of Judah is guaranteed by the justice of David, from the other side it is threatened by the sin of the kings of Judah.

The justice of David is thus recompensed by two guarantees given by God in 1 Kings 11: the permanence and the glory of his house (v. 39) and the perpetuity of Jerusalem and Judah (v. 36). In the Deuteronomistic History, while the justice of David lays the foundation for the permanence of his house, it does not assure that of Jerusalem nor of Judah.

11. Conclusion

1. The HA seems to be an original account, reworked for an edition preserved in the MT. This conclusion is the outcome of a *narrative analysis* consisting of a comparison of the four accounts of the HA and of the MT with the narrative cycle in which they are integrated as elements. Under this aspect, the four accounts of the HA correspond well to the narrative as a whole, while in the MT, tensions emerge between these accounts and the global narrative context. These tensions reveal work done on the accounts and the context as a whole that splits their mutual homogeneity.

2. The HA shows some Deuteronomistic signs, especially in §§a and m. At the same time, these concise and dramatic accounts resemble the stories of the books of Judges and of Samuel, as the analysis has shown.

The HA can therefore be Deuteronomistic in the sense that Judges and 1 and 2 Samuel are. Like those books, it presents a narrative substance that the Deuteronomistic editor alters solely by supplying it with some Deuteronomistic touches here and there.

3. MT 1 Kgs 12.21-25 and the HA §§x-z coincide with the Chronicler's notions of history (the Judah–Benjamin pact, the prophet

Shemaiah). The simplest explanation would be to consider the HA §§x-z as the source for the Chronicler and the basis for the redaction of the MT 1 Kgs 11–12; 14.1-18. The latter introduced a specific ideology concerning Judah that makes it stand out from the rest of the Deuteronomistic history.

4. The HA does not mention the religious schism that the MT 1 Kgs 12.26-33 recounts in a detailed way. That difference would explain well why the Deuteronomistic History does not seem to have a negative attitude with regard to the cultic activities of the Northern Kingdom, since this account of the religious schism does not appear in its original statement.[44]

---

44. This observation was made by my colleague Albert de Pury in the doctoral seminar.

2 SAMUEL 5–8 AND THE DEUTERONOMIST: TEXTUAL CRITICISM OR LITERARY CRITICISM?

Stephen Pisano

Most exegetes agree in thinking that the Deuteronomistic redaction has not added very much of its own material to the text of the books of Samuel, but that it made use of ancient material and gathered it together in accordance with its own particular intentions. The various theories concerning the amount of material attributable to the Deuteronomist, as well as the nature of the material that he had available to him, constitute as many different views of the form of the text at different moments in its historical development. For this study of the Deuteronomist, it is especially instructive to study those texts where the material considered to be specifically Deuteronomistic in the MT Sam[1] is omitted, or is found in a modified form in G Sam, 4QSam[a] or in the corresponding text of Chronicles (MT Chr). These variants in the texts considered as belonging to the Deuteronomistic redaction are especially interesting, since it seems probable that we can examine better there than anywhere else how textual criticism and literary criticism should be taken into account together in order to determine the genesis of the forms of the text. From this point of view, the fundamental question is to know whether textual criticism can be utilized to discover the Deuteronomistic readings that would have been hidden in the MT Sam, or whether the corrections of MT Sam based on other forms (G Sam, 4QSam[a], MT Chr) eliminate Deuteronomistic readings from the Hebrew text of Samuel. Veijola has noted that, in the discussion of the Deuteronomistic

---

1. In this study I shall use the following abbreviations to refer to the text: MT Sam = the Masoretic Text of Samuel; G Sam = the ancient Greek translation of Samuel (based on the text of Rahlfs, unless otherwise indicated); g[L] Sam = the Lucianic text of Samuel (based on N. Fernández Marcos and J. Busto Saiz, *El texto antioqueno de la Biblia griega*. I. *1–2 Samuel* [Madrid: Instituto de Filología del CSIC, 1989]); g[O] = the Origen recension of the LXX; MT Chr = the Masoretic Text of Chronicles; G Chr = ancient Greek translation of Chronicles.

redactional activity, terminology and style are the only criteria making it possible to determine what is dependent or not on Deuteronomistic work, and about what redactional level there could be question.[2] To this we should add that it is essential to establish criteria to decide whether the text in its present form should be accepted or emended.

Parallel Texts in Samuel and in Chronicles

While examining the re-elaboration of the material of Samuel in Chronicles, it is possible to see what was the form of the Deuteronomistic text. Moreover, if we emend the Masoretic text of Samuel to make it agree with the corresponding text in Chronicles against the reading attributable to the Deuteronomistic work, the question that comes up is whether we reach in this way a pre-Deuteronomistic state of the Hebrew text of Samuel. Such an assertion would imply that the Chroniclers had available a text of Samuel that had not yet undergone a Deuteronomistic redaction—an assertion that would have little probability. Another possibility would be that the variants in Samuel that do not appear in Chronicles and have a Deuteronomistic 'flavour' would be late additions or reworkings of the text of Samuel by someone who intentionally imitated Deuteronomistic style. This option, though possible, should nevertheless be used cautiously, since it would assume a very elaborate study of the text in the period of the Second Temple. Furthermore, if we accept the hypothesis that the Deuteronomistic terms and phrases could be later, pseudo-Deuteronomistic interpolations, the criteria for detecting an authentic redaction (or redactions) will have lost their force.

The principal source of Chronicles has been shown to be different from MT Sam. The question that comes up is the following: does the text of Samuel that has served as a source for the Chronicles reflect a form of text that has not undergone Deuteronomistic redaction? When a proposal for restoring the text of Samuel on the basis of the Chronicles (or even 4QSam[a]?) excludes a typically Deuteronomistic reading, the possibility suggests itself that: (1) a stage earlier than the Deuteronomistic redaction has been reached; (2) the text of the book of Samuel that served as *Vorlage* to Chronicles reflects that older form of the text.

---

2.   T. Veijola, *Das Königtum in der Beurteilung der deuteronomistischen Historiographie* (AASF.B, 198; Helsinki: Suomalainen Tiedeakatemia, 1977), p. 13 and nn. 64 and 65.

The Variants in 2 Samuel 5–8

For the purposes of this study, a small number of cases drawn from 2 Samuel 5–8 will be examined. This will only be a sample of readings. I have chosen these chapters because it seems that it is precisely there that the activity of the Deuteronomist would have been the most intense, if not in the addition of material, at least in reshaping it according to the intention of the Deuteronomist.

In 2 Samuel, the place of chs. 5–8 in the history of the redaction has been the object of much discussion. Some authors (for example Grøn-baek[3]) consider that 'the story of David's rise' ends in 2 Samuel 5 and that 'the account of the succession' begins in 2 Samuel 9, which excludes these chapters from an older state of the text. Others, such as Nübel, Amsler and Weiser,[4] extend the story of the rise of David to 2 Samuel 9 by supposing different interpolations and literary activities. Whatever may be the broader unity integrating these chapters before the Deuteronomistic redaction, their present position within 2 Samuel as a whole as well as certain phrases used in these chapters are clearly due to the Deuteronomistic editor. Chapters 5, 6 and 8 contain disparate material collected together to show the rise of David, the role of Jerusalem, capital (2 Sam. 5) and centre of worship (2 Sam. 6), and the victories over neighbouring peoples (2 Sam. 8). In this setting, 2 Samuel 7, although extremely complex, as is shown by the great number of theories about its redaction, seems more unified, at least in the sense in which its basic material came from one or two original oracles, and that the text was modified, not by the addition of traditions originally independent, but rather by successive literary alterations or re-elaborations. Because of the importance of the Deuteronomistic editorial work that we assume in these chapters, it is useful to see how this Deuteronomistic composition and its additions are interpreted in the recent studies. Admittedly, some variants are of less importance and of limited

---

3.   J.H. Grønbaek, *Die Geschichte vom Aufstieg Davids (1 Sam. 15–2 Sam. 5). Tradition und Komposition* (AThD, 10; Copenhagen: Munksgaard, 1971).

4.   H.-U. Nübel, 'Davids Aufstieg in der frühen israelitischer Geschichts-schreibung' (ThD dissertation, Bonn, 1959); S. Amsler, *David, Roi et Messie. La tradition davidique dans l'Ancien Testament* (CTh, 49; Neuchâtel: Delachaux et Niestlé, 1963); A. Weiser, 'Die Legitimation des Königs David. Zur Eigenart und Entstehung der sogenannten Geschichte von Davids Aufstieg', *VT* 16 (1966), pp. 325-54.

interest for the specific question of the Deuteronomistic charateristics of these texts. It is more important for our purposes to keep in mind the underlying question of the form of the text before the Deuteronomistic literary activity, and of the parts that go back to this level (or to these levels) of redaction. It is precisely here that the questions of textual criticism most clearly meet the questions of literary criticism. Once there is agreement on the nature of these chapters, in a general way at least, discussion on the specific corrections of the text, based on the parallels in the Chronicles or in the material found in 4QSam^a or in the Septuagint, can help to define the new form of the texts created by the Deuteronomist and to quantify his activity in the Masoretic Text where there is a divergence among several textual traditions.

2 Samuel 5

Noth forcefully maintained that after having inserted the references to 'Ishbaal' and David in 2 Sam. 2.10a-11, the Deuteronomistic editor only intervened rarely in the section devoted to the account of the succession of David. Except for the introduction to the reign of David in vv. 4-5, the Deuteronomist would have modified the order of the verses in the chapter. According to Noth, vv. 17-25 originally would have followed vv. 1-3 directly and formed the ending of the story of the rise of David; vv. 6-10 and 12 were added, but in a period prior to the Deuteronomistic redactional work. Verse 11 would therefore have been inserted at the time of the addition of the history of the succession of David or at the time of the insertion of 8.1-14 in its present location, in ch. 8.[5]

In 2 Samuel 5, Veijola attributes to the Deuteronomist vv. 1-2, 4-5, 11, 12a, 17a (DtrG) and v. 12b (DtrN). McCarter accepts vv. 1-2, 4-5(?), 12 as belonging to Dtr[1].

2 Samuel 5.1

MT Sam: וַיָּבֹאוּ כָּל־שִׁבְטֵי יִשְׂרָאֵל

G Sam: καὶ παραγίνονται πᾶσαι αἱ φυλαὶ Ἰσραήλ

4QSam^a: [כ(ו)לשב[ט]י יש[ראל][6]

---

5. M. Noth, *Überlieferungsgeschichtliche Studien* (Darmstadt: Wissenschaftliche Buchgesellschaft, 3rd edn, 1967), pp. 55-56.

6. Cited according to S.L. McKenzie, *The Chronicler's Use of the Deuteronomistic History* (HSM, 33; Atlanta: Scholars Press, 1985); all the references to

1 Chron. 11.1
MT Chr: וַיִּקָּבְצוּ כָל־יִשְׂרָאֵל
G Chr: καὶ ἦλθεν [συνηθροίσθησαν g^L] πᾶς [+ ἀνήρ g^L] Ἰσραήλ

McKenzie notes that 'this example probably represents an intentional change on the part of the Chronicler, introducing his pan-Israel interest',[7] while McCarter accepts the consonantal text of MT Sam but vocalizes שֹׁבְטֵי 'staff-bearers'.[8] The agreement between MT Sam and 4QSam^a against MT Chr is of special interest here. G Chr agrees with Sam, whereas g^L Chr reads in the same way as MT Chr.

MT Sam: וַיֹּאמְרוּ לֵאמֹר
G Sam: καὶ εἶπαν [λέγουσιν g^L; λέγοντες g^MN] αὐτῷ
4QSam^a: לאמר
MT Chr: לֵאמֹר
G Chr: λέγοντες

For the second variant, MT Sam, וַיֹּאמְרוּ לֵאמֹר, the witnesses are more varied. G Sam has καὶ εἶπαν αὐτῷ (considered original by Thenius); 4QSam^a is in agreement with MT Chr, G Chr and g^L Sam on the briefer reading of לֵאמֹר (followed by McCarter and Anderson). While the difference between MT Sam and MT Chr could be due to the change in the principal verb (וַיִּקָּבְצוּ in place of וַיָּבֹאוּ, although G Chr follows MT Sam here in the choice of the verb: καὶ ἦλθεν), the difference could also be due to the desire to lighten the phrase by shortening it. At any rate, it must be noted that, from the point of view of the Deuteronomistic text, MT Sam should be seen either as the 'original' Deuteronomistic reading or as a later development. If the second option is right, the simple לֵאמֹר must have been the Deuteronomistic reading; but if the longer reading is that of the Deuteronomistic editor, the shorter text met in MT Chr/ 4QSam^a and preferred here by some commentators must be either an older form than the Deuteronomistic or a secondary abridgement.

F. Langlamet points out, in regard to וַיֹּאמְרוּ לֵאמֹר, that similar phrases can be found in 2 Sam. 3.18 (אמר...לֵאמֹר); 17.6 (וַיֹּאמֶר...לֵאמֹר) and

readings of Qumran texts have been verified on the microfiches of E. Tov, *The Dead Sea Scrolls on Microfiche* (Leiden: E.J. Brill, 1993), and on the photographs of R.H. Eisenman and J.M. Robinson, *A Facsimile Edition of the Dead Sea Scrolls* (2 vols.; Washington, DC: Biblical Archaeology Society, 1991).

7.   McKenzie, *The Chronicler's Use*, p. 41.

8.   P.K. McCarter Jr, *II Samuel* (AB, 9; Garden City, NY: Doubleday, 1984), following the suggestion of P.V. Reid, 'šbty in 2 Samuel 7:7', *CBQ* 37 (1975), pp. 17-20.

20.18 (וַתֹּאמֶר לֵאמֹר).[9] Langlamet attributes these phrases to a 'historian of David' before DtrG, or to the compiler of the 'rise of David'.[10] In both cases, if Langlamet's analysis is correct, the use of the finite verb with an infinitive must precede the Deuteronomistic redaction, while a correction based on the simpler form of the phrase as it is found in MT Chr/4QSam[a] would not present an older form of the text.

2 Samuel 5.2
MT Sam: בִּהְיוֹת
G Sam: ὄντος
4QSam[a]: [ת]בהיו[ת]

1 Chronicles 11.2
MT Chr: גַּם בִּהְיוֹת
G Chr: ὄντος (ἔτι ὄντος Mss d e m p t)

In this small variant between Samuel and Chronicles, גַּם could be a dittography caused by the double occurrence of the same word in the preceding phrase in Chronicles. If it was intentionally added by Chronicles, it helps emphasize the contrast between David and Saul, although the difference is slight and does not seem to be significant from the point of view of the history of the redaction. Mettinger questions the Deuteronomistic origin of vv. 1-2, saying that 5.2 is clearly dependent on 2 Sam. 7.7-8,[11] but since these verses in 2 Samuel could themselves be of Deuteronomistic origin, or at least reworked by the Deuteronomist, the question of dependence becomes a problem precisely when it is a question of determining if individual verses are Deuteronomistic or not.

2 Samuel 5.4-5
Verses 4 and 5, found in G Sam (g[L] Sam has adjusted the text in v. 5 to read 'thirty-two years and six months'), are missing from 4QSam[a].[12]

---

9. F. Langlamet, review of E. Würthwein, *Die Erzählung von der Thronfolge Davids—theologische oder politische Geschichtsschreibung?* (ThSt, 115; Zürich: Theologischer Verlag, 1974), and of T. Veijola, *Die ewige Dynastie. David und die Entstehung seiner Dynastie nach der deuteronomistischen Darstellung* (AASF,B, 193; Helsinki: Suomalainen Tiedeaketemia, 1975) in *RB* 83 (1976), pp. 114-37.

10. Langlamet, review of Würthwein and Veijola, p. 128.

11. T.N.D. Mettinger, *King and Messiah: The Civil and Sacral Legitimation of the Israelite Kings* (ConBOT, 8; Lund: Gleerup, 1976), pp. 44-45.

12. E.C. Ulrich, *The Qumran Text of Samuel and Josephus* (HSM, 19;

1 Chron. 3.4 has a briefer text in which David reigns seven years and six months in Hebron and 33 years in Jerusalem. Here, Chronicles has placed this information in a different context than Samuel by including the notice on the duration of the reign of David between the two lists of the sons of David, whereas Samuel has these lists in different locations: the list of the 'sons of Hebron' is given in 2 Sam. 3.2-5 and that of the 'sons of Jerusalem' in 2 Sam. 5.13-16, in appropriate places in the context of David's coming to power. Other notes on the duration of the reign of David are found in 2 Sam. 2.11 (seven years and six months in Hebron), and in 1 Kgs 2.11 (40 years, seven years in Hebron and 33 in Jerusalem) with the parallel in 1 Chron. 29.27. As Ulrich has brought to the fore, all the notes with the exception of 2 Sam. 2.11 mention the duration of the reign of David in Jerusalem.[13] This is why the note in 1 Chron. 3.4 seems to reproduce 2 Sam. 5.5 but not v. 4, which must indicate either that the Chronicler has omitted it or did not find it in the *Vorlage*. As Sara Japhet shows, the Chronicler took over 2 Sam. 5.5, but has modified it in part: עַל־יְהוּדָה and וִיהוּדָה וְיִשְׂרָאֵל כָּל־עַל are missing from Chronicles 'in full accord with the Chronicler's characteristic view that David was, from the very beginning, king over "all Israel" '.[14] On the other hand, Chronicles has preserved the 'seven years and a half' of the reign in Hebron even if they do not correspond to the representation that is found in 1 Chronicles 11–12, and this implies knowledge of the text of Samuel.

The presence of these verses in G Sam, their partial presence in Chronicles and their absence in 4QSam[a] suggest a more complex image

---

Missoula, MT: Scholars Press, 1978), pp. 60-62. This opinion is based on considerations of space in the fragment of 4QSam[a], which requires that בחבר[ון] belong to v. 3 and not to v. 5. ואנשי (v. 6) is situated immediately under it. In this setting it should be noted that in *The Dead Sea Scrolls on Microfiche: Inventory List of Photographs*, compiled by S.A. Reed and edited by M.J. Lundberg (Leiden: E.J. Brill, 1993), p. 21, photo PAM 40.988 is wrongly catalogued as 4Q52 Sam[b] containing 2 Sam. 3.31–4.1//5.5-14. The photo is a fragment of 4Q51 Sam[a] containing these verses (or more precisely 2 Sam. 3.31–4.1//5.3, 6-14); cf. the *Companion Volume*, p. 30 that likewise catalogues the photo as 4QSam[b]. The same wrong attribution is found in the *Dead Sea Scrolls Catalogue*, compiled by S.A. Reed, revised and edited by M.J. Lundberg, with the collaboration of M.B. Phelps (SBLRBS, 32; Atlanta: Scholars Press, 1994).

   13. Ulrich, *Qumran Text of Samuel and Josephus*, p. 62.

   14. S. Japhet, *I & II Chronicles: A Commentary* (OTL; London: SCM Press; Louisville, KY: Westminster / John Knox Press, 1993), pp. 95-96.

of the history of the text. McKenzie[15] sets out two possibilities. The first is that

> the original reading was lost in the developing Palestinian tradition, hence it is lacking in C and 4QSam[a]. The proto-Lucianic recension would have deleted the material from its OG *Vorlage* to bring it into conformity with a Hebrew text of the developing Palestinian tradition, hence it is lacking in the OL and Josephus. Finally, the material would have been restored in L to make it conform with the Rabbinic or proto-Rabbinic texts. The second alternative is that the two verses represent a secondary insertion into the Rabbinic text of S, hence it was originally lacking in the witnesses to other text types. However, the material was inserted by an early reviser into the OG, and all subsequent G manuscripts included it.

McKenzie concludes that neither alternative is completely satisfying. The first, besides its complexity, 'furnishes no good mechanism for the supposed initial haplography'. The second 'presupposes a revision of the OG toward the proto-Rabbinic text prior to the proto-Lucianic revision', a solution adopted by Ulrich.[16] McKenzie himself does not decide between the two options and simply notes that Chronicles has followed its *Vorlage* in omitting these verses.

Smith retains the hypothesis of the two verses as a redactional insertion, even if he does not agree with Budde in assuming that they may have initially had a different context.[17] Veijola considers vv. 4-5 as belonging to the redaction of DtrG,[18] whereas McCarter, although he maintains that these verses 'exhibit the stereotyped pattern of the Deuteronomistic notices on the accessions of the kings of Israel and Judah', suggests that it could be a case of a very late addition 'in the spirit of the authentically Deuteronomistic notices that pertain to the reigns of the kings of the divided monarchy'.[19] Here again, the issue is to know how the inclusion or the exclusion of these verses influences our understanding of the Deuteronomist. If they are late, we could then presume that their omission must restore the Deuteronomistic form of the text. If on the contrary they have an authentically Deuteronomistic

---

15. McKenzie, *The Chronicler's Use*, pp. 42-43.

16. Ulrich, *Qumran Text of Samuel and Josephus*, p. 62.

17. H.P. Smith, *A Critical and Exegetical Commentary on the Books of Samuel* (ICC; Edinburgh: T. & T. Clark, 1899, repr. 1969), p. 287.

18. Veijola, *Die ewige Dynastie*, p. 97 n. 112; *idem, Das Königtum*, p. 91; cf. as well Grønbaek, *Die Geschichte vom Aufstieg Davids*, p. 248.

19. McCarter, *II Samuel*, p. 133.

origin, their exclusion would not bring us closer to an older form of the text. The difficulty in the suggestion of McCarter, that they were secondarily added to the text in the Deuteronomistic spirit, is to render uncertain every other attribution of an element to the Deuteronomist.

2 Samuel 5.11-12[20]

> *2 Samuel 5.11*
> MT Sam: וְחָרָשֵׁי עֵץ וְחָרָשֵׁי אֶבֶן קִיר וַיִּבְנוּ־בַיִת לְדָוִד
> G Sam: καὶ τέκτονας ξύλων καὶ τέκτονας λίθων [τοίχου g^L La; λίθων τοίχου g^O] καὶ ᾠκοδόμησαν οἶκον τῷ Δαυιδ
> 4QSam^a: [וחרשי עץ] וחרשי קיר [וי]בנו
>
> *1 Chronicles 14.1*
> MT Chr: וְחָרָשֵׁי קִיר וְחָרָשֵׁי עֵצִים לִבְנוֹת לוֹ בָּיִת
> G Chr: καὶ οἰκοδόμους καὶ τέκτονας ξύλων τοῦ οἰκοδομῆσαι αὐτῷ οἶκον

Veijola, following Noth here, shows that v. 11 must come from the same hand as 2 Sam. 7.1a, 2, 7 since it deals with the house of David in Jerusalem.[21] It would therefore be attributable to DtrG. In the second half of the verse, however, there is textual confusion about the title given to some of the workers sent by Hiram. As McKenzie notes,[22] 4QSam^a, the Lucianic text and the Vetus Latina agree with the MT Chr in reading 'masons' (literally 'artisans of wall[s]'), וְחָרָשֵׁי קִיר, whereas G Sam, as it appears in Ms B, has τέκτονας λίθων, contrasting with the longer text (*conflatio*) of the M T Sam, which has 'artisans of stone wall(s)' וְחָרָשֵׁי אֶבֶן קִיר. This longer text is found, as should be expected, in g^O.

In the light of these variants, the important question is again the picture that we get of the history of these texts. If the Deuteronomist intervened here, and if it is the oldest form of the text attested by the witnesses that we have, where can we find this form of the text: in MT Sam, in 4QSam^a or in G Sam? In this particular case, it appears that MT Sam presents a conflated reading. We must therefore ask when the conflation took place. When Talmon suggests as a 'basic Hebrew reading'

---

20. Veijola attributes 5.11, 12a to DtrG and 5.12b to DtrN, whereas McCarter attributes 5.12 to Dtr^1, while saying that the Deuteronomist is probably responsible for the position of vv. 11-12 in this chapter.

21. Veijola, *Die ewige Dynastie*, p. 99.

22. McKenzie, *The Chronicler's Use*, p. 45.

חֲרָשֵׁי עֵץ (עֵצִים) וְחָרָשֵׁי אֶבֶן (אֲבָנִים),[23] does that take us back to the Deuteronomistic reading or to a pre-Deuteronomistic stage of the text? According to Ulrich it is '*a basic Hebrew reading*', which followed the Egyptian tradition like that found in the Greek Mss BMN, while another fundamental reading is to be found in the Palestinian texts. There is good reason to distinguish two recensions of the text. The question nevertheless remains as to whether one of them reflects the Deuteronomistic reading.

It is possible that MT Sam, 4QSam[a] and g[L] Sam would have been influenced here in varying degrees by Chronicles. In 1 Chron. 22.15, the phrase וְחָרָשֵׁי אֶבֶן וָעֵץ compared to 2 Sam. 5.11 and 1 Chron. 14.1, suggests that, when עֵץ is found in the singular, it is combined with אֶבֶן, whereas in the plural, it is combined with קִיר, which is quite logical since a wall is built with several stones. If such was the case, the original reading in 2 Sam. 5.11 would therefore be וְחָרָשֵׁי אֶבֶן, which is confirmed by λίθων of G Sam. 4QSam[a], g[L] Sam and the Vetus Latina would therefore attest the influence of the parallel text of Chronicles, whereas in MT Sam the parallel reading would have been added without supplanting the original reading.[24]

2 Sam. 5.12b
MT Sam: וְכִי נִשָּׂא מַמְלַכְתּוֹ בַּעֲבוּר עַמּוֹ יִשְׂרָאֵל
G Sam: καὶ ὅτι ἐπήρθη [ἐπήρται g[L]] ἡ βασιλεία αὐτοῦ διὰ τὸν λαὸν αὐτοῦ Ἰσραήλ
4QSam[a]: נשׂא ממלכתו

1 Chron. 14.2b
MT Chr: כִּי־נִשֵּׂאת לְמַעְלָה מַלְכוּתוֹ בַּעֲבוּר עַמּוֹ יִשְׂרָאֵל
G Chr: ὅτι ὕψος ἡ βασιλεία αὐτοῦ διὰ τὸν λαὸν αὐτοῦ Ἰσραήλ

23. S. Talmon, 'Double Readings in the Masoretic Text', *Textus* 1 (1960), p. 147; cf. Ulrich, *Qumran Text of Samuel and Josephus*, p. 99.

24. וְחָרָשֵׁי אֶבֶן is adopted by several commentators, for example, Smith, *Books of Samuel*, p. 290; A.A. Anderson, 2 Samuel (WBC, 11: Dallas: Word Books, 1989), p. 80. D. Barthélemy (*Critique textuelle de l'Ancien Testament*, I [OBO, 50.1; Freiburg / Göttingen: Universitätsverlag / Vandenhoeck & Ruprecht, 1982], p. 240) opts for the longer reading of the MT Sam: 'It is possible that this complex phrase would have been simplified in two different directions by the other witnesses to obtain a better parallel with חרשׁי עץ that accompanies it'. This would have been more probable, as would be the suggested reading 'wall stones', if the reading of the MT Sam was 'stones'. The singular אֶבֶן seems to make the shorter reading preferable here.

If we compare MT Sam and MT Chr, the significant variants appear here in the first three words. MT Chr with כִּי in place of וְכִי of MT Sam, נְשֵׂאת in place of נִשָּׂא, and the addition of לְמַעְלָה,[25] changed the thought of the passage so much that it becomes a causal assertion. Whereas in MT Sam the knowledge attributed to David is 'that the Lord has established him king over Israel and has exalted his kingdom for the sake of his people Israel', in Chronicles, this becomes 'that the Lord had established him as king over Israel *because* his kingdom was highly exalted for the sake of his people Israel'. 4QSam[a] shows that the Qumran text followed MT Sam in reading נִשָּׂא, whereas G Sam, with ἐπήρθη in Ms B and ἐπήρται in the Lucianic text, seems to support the reading נְשֵׂאת of Chronicles, as did the Syriac and the Targum of Samuel. As McCarter indicates, the language is dynastic in this verse and more appropriate in a Deuteronomistic text than in an older account of the rise of David.[26] Insofar as this anticipates the promises of ch. 7, it seems more likely that the text would be consistent in attributing to God both the establishment of David and the elevation of his kingdom, so much so that the active form נִשָּׂא here seems to be the more appropriate.

2 Samuel 5.17a

MT Sam: וַיִּשְׁמְעוּ פְלִשְׁתִּים כִּי־מָשְׁחוּ אֶת־דָּוִד לְמֶלֶךְ עַל־יִשְׂרָאֵל

G Sam: καὶ ἤκουσαν ἀλλόφυλοι ὅτι κέχρισται Δαυιδ βασιλεὺς ἐπὶ Ἰσραήλ

1 Chron. 14.8a

MT Chr: וַיִּשְׁמְעוּ פְלִשְׁתִּים כִּי־נִמְשַׁח דָּוִיד לְמֶלֶךְ עַל־כָּל־יִשְׂרָאֵל

G Chr: καὶ ἤκουσαν ἀλλόφυλοι ὅτι ἐχρίσθη Δαυιδ βασιλεὺς ἐπὶ πάντα Ἰσραήλ

In this verse of Chronicles the pan-Israelite perspective is brought to the fore by the addition of כָּל before Israel. McCarter has suggested reading the niphal נִמְשַׁח, in agreement with Chronicles, instead of the qal of Samuel in 5.17, while drawing attention to its agreement with G Sam as well. It could be however that the divergent forms are indications of a change of place of this verse and of the section in vv. 17-25 that it introduces. Noth had already suggested that vv. 6-10 had been

---

25. With the intention of accentuating the verb, as was pointed out by E.L. Curtis and A.A. Madsen, *A Critical and Exegetical Commentary on the Books of Chronicles* (ICC; Edinburgh: T. & T. Clark, 1910, repr. 1965), p. 208.

26. McCarter, *II Samuel*, p. 145.

added to the text,[27] and that originally v. 17 directly followed v. 3. The niphal form in Chronicles could be explained as a modification intended to make less difficult the occurrence of the verb (מָשְׁחוּ) distant from its antecedent to the point of no longer having a clearly identified subject. If this is the case, the *lectio difficilior* in MT Sam should be considered the earlier reading. Gronbaek thinks that v. 17 shows traces of Deuteronomistic reworking, and refers to the use of בָּקֵשׁ[28] as an indication of that. The important thing to note is that MT Sam again shows traces of a new Deuteronomistic organization of the chapter, which was smoothed away in G Sam and in M Chr. If the correction with נִמְשַׁח restored an earlier form of the text, it is difficult to explain how מָשְׁחוּ of MT Sam would have arisen.

2 Samuel 6

One of the main questions with regard to the composition of 2 Samuel 6 is its relation to the accounts of the ark in 1 Sam. 4.1–7.1. Campbell, commenting on the Deuteronomistic contribution in this chapter, maintains the position that 'the Deuteronomist found the Ark Narrative among his sources in its entirety, and that he was responsible for dislocating it to accord with his historical presentation'.[29] In its present position, ch. 6 reflects the concern of the Deuteronomist to show the

27. M. Noth, *Überlieferungsgeschichtliche Studien*, p. 55, in a note. Anderson (*2 Samuel*, p. 90) quotes N.L. Tidwell, 'The Philistine Incursions into the Valley of Rephaim', in J.A. Emerton (ed.), *Studies in the Historical Books of the Old Testament* (VTSup, 30; Leiden: E.J. Brill, 1979), p. 192, according to which there is 'little justification for assuming that the present literary context of any of these fragmentary traditions is a true reflection of or a reliable guide to its original historical sequence'.

28. Grønbaek, *Die Geschichte vom Aufstieg Davids*, p. 250 n. 101.

29. A.F. Campbell, *The Ark Narrative (1 Sam 4–6; 2 Sam 6). A Form-Critical and Traditio-Historical Study* (SBLDS, 16; Missoula, MT: Scholars Press, 1975), p. 170. Cf. also *idem, Of Prophets and Kings: A Late Ninth-Century Document (1 Samuel 1–2 Kings 10)* (CBQMS, 17; Washington, DC: Catholic Biblical Association, 1986), pp. 56-57, and especially p. 60 where he concludes that נָגִיד can be seen to have gone through three stages in its meaning. Its 'profane' use in 2 Sam. 6.21 (with 1 Sam. 25.30 and perhaps 1 Kgs 1.35), referring to David as uncrowned king of Israel, would be the oldest meaning of the term (against for example L. Schmidt, *Menschlicher Erfolg und Jahwes Initiative* [WMANT, 38; Neukirchen–Vluyn: Neukirchener Verlag, 1970], pp. 131-32, 170-71, who concludes that the use in 6.21 depended on 1 Sam. 9.16 or 2 Sam. 7.8).

election of David and of Jerusalem,[30] even if vv. 16, 20-23 did not have an original link with the rest of the chapter.[31]

2 Samuel 6.21

Veijola attributed to DtrG the recognition by David of the intervention of YHWH in his life, in v. 21aβ.[32] The textual situation of this verse is rather complicated. It is not present in the parallel of 1 Chronicles, since the Chronicler has omitted all the material of 2 Sam. 6.20b-23, apparently to avoid presenting the picture of David dancing nude before the ark.

MT Sam: וַיֹּאמֶר דָּוִד אֶל־מִיכַל לִפְנֵי יְהוָה

G Sam: καὶ εἶπεν Δαυιδ πρὸς Μελχολ Ἐνώπιον κυρίου ὀρχήσομαι· εὐλογητὸς κύριος

Several exegetes correct the Hebrew text here, on the basis of G Sam, to restore אֲרַקֵּד בָּרוּךְ יְהוָה.[33] Veijola, while he admits the possibility of an error caused by a homoeoteleuton, suggests that G represents here a stripped down form of the Masoretic Text, which is more difficult.[34] According to Veijola, if the clause אֲשֶׁר...עַל־יִשְׂרָאֵל is due to a Deuteronomistic redactor, the one place in v. 21 where he could have inserted it without disrupting the meaning was before לִפְנֵי יְהוָה, even if that meant a syntactical interruption. The secondary nature of that sentence can be detected in what follows, in v. 22, since David returns to the

30. McCarter, *II Samuel*, pp. 4-6, 174.
31. L. Rost, *Die Überlieferung von der Thronnachfolge Davids* (BWANT, 42; Stuttgart: W. Kohlhammer, 1926), pp. 107-108; he maintained the position according to which 1 Sam. 4.1b–7.1 and 2 Sam. 6 formerly formed one and the same compositional unit. Cf. also Campbell, *The Ark Narrative*, pp. 28-54. P.D. Miller and J.J.M. Roberts (*The Hand of the Lord: A Reassessment of the 'Ark Narrative' of 1 Samuel* [Baltimore: The Johns Hopkins University Press, 1977], p. 19) consider that the account began in 1 Sam. 2 but ended with 1 Sam. 7.1.
32. Veijola, *Die ewige Dynastie*, pp. 66-68; his position is based in part on the understanding of נָגִיד as a typically Deuteronomistic term.
33. J. Wellhausen (*Der Text der Bücher Samuelis* [Göttingen: Vandenhoeck & Ruprecht, 1871], p. 169) follows Thenius in suggesting this re-establishment and attributing the omission to a homoeoteleuton of יְהוָה, while he remains dubious on the subject of the second καὶ ὀρχήσομαι at the end of the verse in G.
34. Veijola, *Die ewige Dynastie*, p. 66. According to Veijola, it is possible that בְּעֵינֶיךָ should be read in place of בְּעֵינַי of the MT, and that the form of the MT would be due to the influence of the addition of v. 21aβ (Veijola, *Die ewige Dynastie*, p. 67 n. 129).

reproach that Michal had made to him in v. 20. McCarter says that the sentence in G 'Blessed be YHWH...Israel' is probably secondary from the literary point of view even if 'textually primitive', and would be a contribution of the Deuteronomistic hand responsible for the final arrangement of 5.11–8.18. If such is the case, אֲרֻקֵּךְ יְהוָה בָּרוּךְ אַרְקֵּךְ must go back to the Deuteronomist, or, more precisely, אַרְקֵּךְ could have belonged to the source of the Deuteronomist and the phrase beginning with בָּרוּךְ יְהוָה would be due to the Deuteronomist.

Mettinger[35] shows that 6.21 'is a further expression of the intentions of the author of the HDR and must originate from that work', and that the terms נָגִיד and בָּחַר, since they occur in pre-Deuteronomistic texts (נָגִיד in 1 Sam. 9.16; 10.1; 1 Kgs 1.35; 2 Sam. 5.2; בָּחַר in 1 Sam. 10.24 and 2 Sam. 16.18),[36] are indications that the text extends the allusions to the divine election of David, characteristic of this literary collection.

Whatever the origin of the term here in 6.21, since נָגִיד was used, according to Campbell and Mettinger, by different traditions and at different times, the possibility must at least be admitted that the Deuteronomistic author would have in turn used it in his own formulation. If v. 21aβ is not a late insertion, its rough syntax needs an explanation. In any case, it seems that the text of MT Sam must be seen here, because of this difficulty, as prior to the form of G Sam.

2 Samuel 7

The history of the redaction of 2 Samuel 7 has been studied so often that it would be impossible to take everything up again here, even from the particular point of view of the Dtr redaction.[37] Noth did not consider 2 Samuel 7 to be Deuteronomistic, while McCarthy has shown in a quite convincing way its Deuteronomistic nature.[38] Veijola concluded

---

35. Mettinger, *King and Messiah*, p. 45.

36. Mettinger, *King and Messiah*, p. 45 n. 56.

37. For a recent study of 2 Sam. 7, cf. G. Hentschel, *Gott, König und Tempel: Beobachtungen zu 2 Sam 7,1-7* (EThS, 22; Leipzig: Benno, 1992), with a bibliography of works that have apppeared since 1976, pp. ix-xiii.

38. D.J. McCarthy, 'II Samuel and the Structure of the Deuteronomic History', *JBL* 84 (1965), pp. 131-38; F.M. Cross (*Canaanite Myth and Hebrew Epic* [Cambridge, MA: Harvard University Press, 1973]) shows the Deuteronomistic character of this chapter, which must therefore be called a 'Deuteronomistic composition' (p. 254). J. Van Seters (*In Search of History: Historiography in the Ancient World and the Origins of Biblical Historiography* [New Haven: Yale University Press,

Israel Constructs its History

by allocating vv. 8b, 11b, 13, 16, 18-21, 25-29 to DtrG, and vv. 1b, 6, 11a, 22-24 to DtrN.[39] So for him the two original oracles must be sought in vv. 1a, 2-5, 7 and vv. 8a, 9, 10, 12, 14, 15, 17. McCarter attributes vv. 4-9a, 15b, 20-21 to the prophetic redaction, vv. 1b, 9b-11a, 13a, 16, 22b-24 (?), 25-26, 29bα to Dtr[1] and perhaps vv. 22b-24 to Dtr[2].[40] On the other hand, Mettinger sees in ch. 7 the finale of the story of the accession of David to power, made up of two pre-Deuteronomistic layers, with the original prophecy of Nathan dating from the time of Solomon (vv. 1a, 2-7, 12-14a, 16*, 17), and a dynastic redaction shortly after the death of Solomon (vv. 8-9, 11b, 14b-15, 16*, 18-22a, 27-29). In this case only vv. 1b, 10-11a, 22b-26 belong to the Deuteronomistic redaction.[41]

More recently, Mark O'Brien, in his new examination of the Deuteronomistic hypothesis, has fundamentally followed Campbell with regard to the history of the redaction of ch. 7.[42] According to O'Brien, the 'prophetic record' is responsible for the largest part of the prophecy contained in 2 Sam. 7.1-17, with the contributions of the Deuteronomist limited to vv. 1b, 11a and 13. He later suggests that the prayer of David in vv. 18-29 is pre-Deuteronomistic too, with vv. 22-24 coming not from DtrH but a later Deuteronomistic redactor.[43]

A complete analysis of 2 Samuel 7 is not possible here, but it suffices for our purpose to examine some of the verses attributed by some to the Deuteronomistic redaction.

2 Samuel 7.1b

MT Sam: וַיהוָה הֵנִיחַ־לוֹ מִסָּבִיב מִכָּל־אֹיְבָיו

G Sam: καὶ κατεκληρονόμησεν αὐτὸν κύκλῳ ἀπὸ πάντων τῶν ἐχθρῶν αὐτοῦ τῶν κύκλῳ

MT G Chr: omission

1983], p. 272) considers 2 Sam. 7 a unified Deuteronomistic prose narrative. Each of these analyses, like others not mentioned here, and the theories on the development of the text, assume that each of the successive modifications left traces of what preceded it, except perhaps Cross's theory which implies a total re-elaboration by the Deuteronomist.

39. Veijola, *Die ewige Dynastie*, pp. 68-70.

40. McCarter, *II Samuel*, p. 8.

41. Mettinger, *King and Messiah*, pp. 48-63.

42. M.A. O'Brien, *The Deuteronomistic History Hypothesis: A Reassessment* (OBO, 92; Freiburg/Göttingen: Universitätsverlag/Vandenhoeck & Ruprecht, 1989), pp. 132-39; cf. Campbell, *Of Prophets and Kings*.

43. O'Brien, *The Deuteronomistic History Hypothesis*, p. 138.

McKenzie suggests that the absence of v. 1b in Chronicles can be explained by characterizing MT Sam as 'expansionistic with this common Dtr idiom'.[44] We could wonder however whether v. 1b is a Deuteronomistic insertion, while maintaining that

> the catalogue of David's wars, which follows immediately in chap. 8, shows that David had anything but 'rest' at this point, and, indeed, it was the understanding of the last (Deuteronomistic) editor of this material that David did *not* have 'rest', as explicitly stated in I Kings 5:17-18 [5:3-4]![45]

While Caquot and de Robert attribute vv. 1-3 to the 'Zadokite' editor, they attribute v. 1b to the Deuteronomistic editor.[46]

To eliminate this half verse from the Deuteronomistic work seems not only to run counter to the frequent occurrences of this term about 'rest' with regard to enemies in the rest of the Deuteronomist's work (cf. Deut. 3.20; 12.10; 25.19; Josh. 1.13, 15; 21.42; 22.4; 23.1; 1 Kgs 5.18), but equally to go against the Deuteronomistic predilection for chronological introductions. McCarter's argument against the Deuteronomistic character of the clause, namely that the wars of David follow in ch. 8, applies equally to a later insertion; the real objection is not about its Deuteronomistic character, but its inappropriate place. It is precisely because of this difficulty that it seems more likely that Chronicles would have suppressed the sentence rather than that a late hand would have added it. In any case the other occurrences of the term show that the rest from enemies was at best temporary; its presence in 2 Sam. 7.1b looks back rather than ahead (cf. 2 Sam. 5) or, better, looks back while keeping present the concrete situation in which David found himself and above all while taking into account his intention of building the temple. From this point of view, it is linked up with the use of the

44. McKenzie, *The Chronicler's Use*, p. 63; cf. M. Weinfeld, *Deuteronomy and the Deuteronomic School* (Oxford: Clarendon Press, 1972), p. 343, who classifies 2 Sam. 7.1 with a question mark as regards its authentic Deuteronomistic character.

45. McCarter, *II Samuel*, p. 191. He suggests here that David's rest with regard to enemies in v. 1b is explained as a marginal correction of v. 11aß that later found its way into the text, but at the wrong point, some time before the translation of G but after the composition of the Chronicler's history.

46. A. Caquot and P. de Robert, *Les livres de Samuel* (CAT, 6; Geneva: Labor et Fides, 1994), p. 425: 'The compiler presumes that David could only dream of building a temple thanks to a peace gained by his victories'.

expression in 1 Kgs 5.17-19. As Hentschel indicates, the attribution of v. 1b to the Deuteronomistic stratum only applies as long as the account itself is not described as Deuteronomistic,[47] and it should be considered together with the situation of Solomon in 1 Kings 5.

2 Samuel 7.11

In Veijola's opinion, v. 11 comes 'too late after v. 10, where it is no longer a question of David, but rather of Israel',[48] while v. 12 provides a good sequel to v. 10. That is why he suggests a later origin for v. 11, which actually consists of two successive additions, first of v. 11b and then of v. 11a. In his review of *Die ewige Dynastie*, F. Langlamet has opened up a debate on this point and maintains that MT Sam and MT Chr are here corrupt. Basing himself on G Chr καὶ αὐζήσω σε and on the repetition of יהוה in v. 11, he suggests as the original text ואגדלך ובית אעשה לך.[49] According to him, the corruption began with והיה, preserved in MT Chr (also as in G Chr καὶ ἔσται, which is also found in G Sam). Subsequently, later editors hesitated between והיה and יהוה, with MT Sam opting for יהוה while omitting והיה. Once יהוה had been introduced, it could not be the subject of the preceding verb, that was then changed from the first to the third person (והגיד).

In order to evaluate these variants, it is necessary to consider the four forms in which 2 Sam. 7.11aβb-12aα (= 1 Chron. 17.10aβb-11aα) is found:

MT Sam: והניחתי לך מכל־איביך והגיד לך יהוה כי־בית יעשה־לך יהוה: כי
ימלאו ימיך

G Sam: καὶ ἀναπαύσω σε ἀπὸ πάντων τῶν ἐχθρῶν σου καὶ ἀπαγγελεῖ
σοι κύριος ὅτι οἶκον οἰκοδομήσεις αὐτῷ καὶ ἔσται ἐὰν
πληρωθῶσιν αἱ ἡμέραι σου

---

47. Hentschel, *Gott, König und Tempel*, p. 56.

48. Veijola, *Die ewige Dynastie*, p. 73.

49. Langlamet, review of Würthwein and Veijola, p. 129 n. 10. The suggested Hebrew reading behind G Chr ואגדלך is already found in E. Kautzsch, *Die Heilige Schrift des Alten Testaments, vierte umgearbeitete Auflage* (2 vols.; Tübingen: J.C.B. Mohr [Paul Siebeck], 1922–23) for 2 Sam. 7.11a (cf. as well the critical apparatus of *BHK*). The original lesson proposed is that of I.L. Seeligmann, 'Indications of Editorial Alteration and Adaptation in the Massoretic Text and the Septuagint', *VT* 11 (1961), p. 209.

MT Chr: וְהִכְנַעְתִּי אֶת־כָּל־אוֹיְבֶיךָ וָאַגִּד לָךְ וּבַיִת יִבְנֶה־לְּךָ יְהוָה: וְהָיָה כִּי־מָלְאוּ יָמֶיךָ,

G Chr: καὶ ἐταπείνωσα ἅπαντας τοὺς ἐχθρούς σου καὶ αὐξήσω σε καὶ οἰκοδομήσει σε κύριος καὶ ἔσται ὅταν πληρωθῶσιν ἡμέραι σου (Ms B)

We are immediately struck by the fact that there are no two identical text forms; every analysis of the brief prophecy in 2 Sam. 7.11b must take into account all these differences, as well as the difficulties that each presents. In MT Sam the main difficulties are the abrupt passage to the third person (וְהִגִּיד), the apparently overloaded phrase with יְהוָה that comes up twice and the simple כִּי at the beginning of v. 12. In G Sam the main difficulty, besides that of the verb in the third person, is the verb in the second person with the pronoun in the third person in οἶκον οἰκοδομήσεις αὐτῷ, apparently out of context. The manuscripts b o c₂ e₂ have οἰκοδομήσει ἑαυτῷ, Symmachus ποιήσεις, thus showing a greater literal fidelity to יַעֲשֶׂה of MT Sam while retaining the second person.

In MT Chr the difficulty consists of the waw before בַיִת, which is difficult to explain grammatically after וָאַגִּד לָךְ. G Chr is the only form in which there is apparently no problem of grammar or context, although it lacks the accusative of the internal object οἶκον. However that may be, if it attests to the original form of the text by preserving καὶ αὐξήσω σε, it must be admitted that the rest of the phrase has undergone a revision based on the text (modified or 'corrected') of MT Chr, since we would have expected καὶ οἶκον οἰκοδομήσω σοι (in place of καὶ οἰκοδομήσει σε κύριος). There is here actually some confusion in the manuscript tradition:[50]

οικοδομησει σε BSc₂] οικοδομησει (-σαι eᵃ ?) σοι ANcen: οικοδωμιση σαι g: οικοδομησαι σε h: οικον οικοδομησει σοι f: οικον οικοδομησω σοι d: οικον οικοδομησαι σοι jpqtz: οικοδομησω σοι οικον abimoye₂: *aedificabo te ego* Arm ‖ κυριος] pr ειπε biye₂: om d

Only Ms d attests a form of the text that would be that proposed by Seeligmann and Langlamet, since, besides the form of the verb in the first person and the presence of οἶκον, it omits κύριος. If this is not the

50. According to the critical apparatus of A.E. Brooke *et al.* (eds.), *The Old Testament in Greek*. I. *The Later Historical Books. Part III. I and II Chronicles* (Cambridge: Cambridge University Press, 1932), ad. loc. The lesson αὐξήσω, on the other hand, seems certain, since the only variant is represented by αὐξῆσαι in Ms h.

ancient Greek version of the original Chr here, it must be a modification by the scribes based on αὐξήσω. In regard to the form οἰκοδομήσει σε found in the ancient Greek version (Mss BSc₂), Allen suggested that 'after the omission [of οἶκον] the pronoun was adapted for the sense'.[51] Rahlfs gives καὶ οἶκον οἰκοδομήσει σοι κύριος, which is found only in Ms f, as an original Greek version which if it is correct, followed MT Chr. The fact that the form of the verb in the third person is solidly attested in the Greek tradition of Chr (Mss BANScefnc₂) suggests that it really is the original reading.

Since such is the situation of the text of Chronicles, the correction proposed as original in the Hebrew text of 2 Sam. 7.11b. ואגדלך ובית אבנה[52] (אעשה) לך loses its plausibility. It is possible, but not very likely, that G Chr preserves just one verbal form without the rest of the phrase. The verb in the third person in the second part of the clause suggests that καὶ αὐξήσω σε in G Chr is due to a reading error of ואגד לך on the part of the Greek translator.

Hentschel argues quite differently on the subject of the origin of these verses. He is perhaps the most reserved of those who attribute some redactional activity to the Deuteronomist in this oracle, since, in the Lord's discourse in vv. 5-16, he maintains that only vv. 5b and 8b show signs of Deuteronomistic re-elaboration.[53] According to him, the original discourse would be found in vv. 4, 5, 8d-9c, 12-15b, 15a. For him, vv. 9d-11b form a unity based on the use of the past historic wᵉqatal, from וְעָשִׂתִי in v. 9 to וַהֲנִיחֹתִי in v. 11. The change of person in v. 11b would therefore be the sign of a later insertion. Likewise, since Nathan's announcement in v. 11b interrupts the connection of vv. 8-9 with v. 12, it could be considered secondary. Verse 16, with its sudden change to the second person, could have been added at the same time. With these additions, the promises are no longer for Solomon and his descendants but for David and his house.[54] But Hentschel accepts the form of the prophecy in v. 11b of MT Sam as the original form, basing

51. L.C. Allen, *The Greek Chronicles. Part II: Textual Criticism* (VTSup, 25; Leiden: E.J. Brill, 1974), p. 47.

52. Cf. Seeligmann, 'Indications of Editorial Alteration', p. 209; Langlamet, review of Würthwein and Veijola, p. 129 n. 10. Allen (*The Greek Chronicles. Part II: Textual Criticism*, p. 106) indicates that neither Curtis nor Rudolph accept ואגדלך as the original reading in Chr.

53. Hentschel, *Gott, König und Tempel*, p. 68.

54. Hentschel, *Gott, König und Tempel*, p. 53.

himself on its presence in the Greek, Syriac, Old Latin and Vulgate versions.[55]

While it seems that no form prior to that of MT Sam can be arrived at for 2 Sam. 7.11b, the main question is whether this form of the text was the *Vorlage* of the Deuteronomistic redaction. If the latter had not formulated it, as Veijola would suggest, it would have at least taken it over and incorporated it into the final form of the oracle. On the other hand, if any of the numerous corrections suggested is accepted, that will change both the idea of the Deuteronomistic form and the history of the redaction of this section of the oracle. First, the suppression of the evidence that it is out of place or the elimination of anything that interrupts the flow of the oracle immediately calls into question the very criteria that led Rost to consider it a remnant of the ancient oracle.[56] Then, under the various and more acceptable forms that Seeligmann, Cross or Langlamet have proposed, to name just a few commentators, the notion that we get of the Deuteronomistic redaction finds itself modified. If the verse fits in perfectly with the development of the oracle, as would have to be the case in its corrected form, it can no longer be said that it shows specific indications of Deuteronomistic activity. Evidently what could or could not be the type of work carried out by a Deuteronomistic editor should not be a decisive factor in choosing for or against the correction of the text, but the idea that we have of this work follows from the way that we see the 'original' form of the verse. This verse 11b is particularly significant since the intervention attributed to an editor here is representative of the type of work that the editor or editors would have accomplished throughout the whole Deuteronomistic History undertaking.

2 Samuel 7.13a
MT Sam: הוּא יִבְנֶה־בַּיִת לִשְׁמִי
G Sam: αὐτὸς οἰκοδομήσει μοι οἶκον τῷ ὀνόματί μου
MT Chr: הוּא יִבְנֶה־לִּי בָּיִת
G Chr: αὐτὸς οἰκοδομήσει μοι οἶκον

The Deuteronomistic nature of this half-verse is questioned by only a few (for example, Mettinger, Hentschel). McCarter suggests that the refusal of a temple (vv. 5b-7) and the promise of a dynasty (vv. 11b-16)

55. Hentschel, *Gott, König und Tempel*, p. 17.
56. Rost, *Die Überlieferung von der Thronnachfolge Davids*, p. 59. Rost notes as well that since the period of the Chronicler there were several attempts to modify the text (p. 57).

'are joined together in a precarious unity by v. 13a', so much so that the half-verse is more probably editorial.[57] The variant in 2 Sam. 7.13a, MT Sam לִשְׁמִי/ MT Chr לִי, is significant in the context of the Deuteronomistic redaction. Gese,[58] Mettinger[59] and Cross,[60] and others, are in favour of a correction to לִי in the Hebrew text of Samuel, on the basis of Chr and partially of G Sam.

To make a judgment in this case it is necessary to consider other references to the construction of the temple in the books of Kings and in Chronicles. In 1 Kgs 5.19 Solomon sends a mission to Hiram and quotes the words of the Lord addressed to David, הוּא־יִבְנֶה הַבַּיִת לִשְׁמִי (G Kgs οὗτος οἰκοδομήσει τὸν οἶκον τῷ ὀνόματί μου). The parallel text in 1 Chron. 22.10 has the same reading. This is quoted again in 1 Kgs 8.18 in the prayer of Solomon at the dedication of the temple: לִבְנוֹת בַּיִת לִשְׁמִי (G Kgs τοῦ οἰκοδομῆσαι οἶκον τῷ ὀνόματί μου); in 2 Chron. 6.8, 9 the text also contains לִשְׁמִי. It is therefore only in G 2 Sam. 7.13 (where the reading is *conflata*) and in the parallel text in 1 Chron. 17.12 that we find לִי. Elsewhere Chronicles has no difficulty with keeping the expression לִשְׁמִי. The greatest probability consists then in attributing v. 13a and לִשְׁמִי to the Deuteronomist. If such be the case, the variant in 1 Chron. 17.12 needs an explanation, especially in the light of the fact that לִשְׁמִי is found in 1 Chron. 22.10 and in 2 Chron. 6.8, 9.

The Chronicler seems to have modified slightly several phrases in this chapter, some of which could have had an influence on the expression לִשְׁמִי. In 1 Chron. 17.4 the Lord prohibiting David's building a house is made explicit, whereas in 2 Sam. 7.5 there was a question ('Are you going to build me a house?'). In 1 Chron. 17.13 the reference to infidelity made in 2 Sam. 7.14b ('If he does evil, I will correct him with a rod such as mortals use and with blows inflicted by human beings') is omitted, and the text continues with the promise that the Lord will not take away his steadfast love from him, even if the explicit mention of Saul is omitted too. The possessive pronouns too are dif-

---

57. McCarter, *II Samuel*, p. 222.

58. H. Gese, 'Der Davidsbund und die Zionserwählung', *ZTK* 61 (1964), pp. 10-26.

59. Mettinger, *King and Messiah*, p. 56.

60. Cross, *Canaanite Myth and Hebrew Epic*, p. 247 n. 117. Cross maintains that 'in either case the reading is Deuteronomistic', even if לִי would seem to be less clearly so.

ferent between Samuel and Chronicles, so much so that in 2 Sam. 7.16 it is the house of David, the kingdom and the throne that will be made firm whereas in 1 Chron. 17.14 the son and his throne are the ones going to be strengthened in the house and the kingdom of the Lord. The reference to 'my house [of the Lord]' in 1 Chron. 17.14 (בְּבֵיתִי) in opposition to 'your house [of David]' (בֵּיתְךָ) in 2 Samuel seems to indicate that Chronicles, in this chapter at least, has simply seen the house in question as the dwelling of the Lord, and was preoccupied with the parallelism between the prohibition of building a house and the construction of this house by the son, whereas the concept, important for Deuteronomistic theology, according to which the temple was the place where the Lord's name dwelt is less significant. This desire to maintain the parallelism could explain the change made by Chronicles from לִשְׁמִי to לִי. If such be the case, the form of G in 2 Sam. 7.13 could be explained as the combination of these two readings, with the possibility that the ancient Greek version of Samuel had originally followed Chronicles.[61]

The alternative explanation consists of seeing the corrections of the text to לִי as a return to the 'original' Deuteronomistic expression, and of considering לִשְׁמִי as a late (post-exilic? rabbinic?) modification of the text. As Weinfeld has noted, however, there are no examples in the Deuteronomistic literature of the temple considered as a house of the Lord; the temple is always built there for his name.[62] If לִי is the reading to be retained in v. 13a, the text must be pre- or post-Deuteronomistic.

That the original reading of 7.13 would have contained at the same time לִשְׁמִי and לִי, as Hentschel suggests,[63] basing himself on G Sam, seems much less probable. We find this formula in none of the other occurrences of the expression in the different allusions to the prophecy; besides, to speak of an 'overloaded text', as Langlamet does, seems to postulate what is in question, since it is necessary to render an account in one way or another of this fuller form.

Once again in this example we find ourselves confronted with the question of a reading frequently identified as Deuteronomistic, for which however a correction is proposed in order to reach a state of the

---

61. Cf. McCarter, *II Samuel*, p. 194.

62. Weinfeld, *Deuteronomy and the Deuteronomic School*, pp. 193-94.

63. Hentschel, *Gott, König und Tempel*, pp. 18-19, following the suggestion of Langlamet in his review of Würthwein and Veijola, p. 131 n. 14; Mettinger (*King and Messiah*, p. 53) suggests this too.

text prior to that of MT Sam. It is difficult to see here, as in the other cases, to what state of the text such a correction would lead us, especially for a reading such as 7.13a that seems so clearly Deuteronomistic. Recourse to an insertion in accord with the style of the Deuteronomist, but due to a later hand, runs up against the difficulty already met of attributing Deuteronomistic characteristics to supposed later insertions.

Conclusions on the Subject of 2 Samuel 7

In the light of the numerous divergent opinions on these redactional levels, perhaps two things alone produce unanimity among the commentators: (1) the text is made up of different layers, or of different oracles; (2) a Deuteronomistic editor is responsible in some way for its final form. It seems to me that one of the main questions that must be asked is to what extent the preceding redactional levels left their traces on the following form, or, in other words, to what extent such traces can be distinguished in the text. The central affirmation of the first part of the oracle, vv. 5-11a, at least in its present form, fits in well with the aim of the Deuteronomist. Verses 5-7 explain why the Lord does not wish a temple to be built by David; verses vv. 8-11a tell the story of David linked with that of the people. The repeated reference to David as 'my servant' in vv. 5 and 8 recalls the title specific to Moses (cf. Deut. 34.5; Josh. 1.1, 2, 7, 13 etc.).

That 2 Samuel 7 is a Deuteronomistic composition, at least in its final form, seems beyond doubt. One of the first characteristics of Deuteronomistic compositions is actually the role of the discourses that the principal actors in the primitive history of Israel, Moses, Joshua and Samuel, have all pronounced, discourses that present the Deuteronomistic point of view on the meaning of that history. In Deuteronomy 31, Joshua 23 and 1 Samuel 12, the discourses summarize the activities of these key figures. 2 Sam. 7.18-29 seems to fulfil that function with regard to the figure of David in the Deuteronomistic history. It is the longest discourse in the entire collection in which he is present; it is actually the only discourse strictly speaking that he pronounces. As far as the content goes, it seems quite probable that the same hand is responsible for 2 Sam. 7.18-29 and 1 Kings 8, which is also the longest discourse pronounced by Solomon. This seems to run counter to the position of Mettinger who considers that the editor of the history of the rise of David is responsible for David's response to the oracle.[64]

---

64. Mettinger, *King and Messiah*, pp. 52-61.

2 Samuel 8

For Veijola, ch. 8 is a Deuteronomistic composition in the sense that it organizes the materials coming from official archives. In its present form, it is the work of DtrG, who introduces in ch. 8 specific re-elaborations or additions in vv. 14b-15.[65] 1 Chronicles 18 has the same material in the same order, with a few minor variants. If the effective author of the composition of this chapter in its present state was the Deuteronomist, it will be necessary to assume that the Chronicler had this form of the chapter available, and any modification would be attributable to the Chronicler's own reformulation. Budde suggested that vv. 7-13 were an addition to the text, based on the occurrence of the same formula in vv. 6 and 14.[66] Hertzberg rejected Noth's position according to which ch. 8 had been compiled by the Deuteronomist; he is favourable to the suggestion of Kittel who saw in the chapter an annalistic arrangement of the heroic deeds of David, as well as that of Alt according to which it originally had been joined to 2 Sam. 5.17-25.[67]

2 Samuel 8.14

The state of MT Sam 8.14 is not clear and the first part of the text could be somewhat disrupted.

MT Sam: וַיָּשֶׂם בֶּאֱדוֹם נְצִבִים בְּכָל־אֱדוֹם שָׂם נְצִבִים וַיְהִי כָל־אֱדוֹם עֲבָדִים לְדָוִד

G. Sam: καὶ ἔθετο ἐν τῇ Ἰδουμαίᾳ φρουρὰν ἐν πάσῃ τῆς Ἰδουμαίᾳ (+ ἔθηκεν ἐστηλωμένους g^OL) καὶ ἐγένοντο πάντες οἱ Ἰδου-μαῖοι δοῦλοι τῷ βασιλεῖ (Δαυειδ g^L)

1 Chron. 18.13

MT Chr: וַיָּשֶׂם בֶּאֱדוֹם נְצִיבִים וַיִּהְיוּ כָל־אֱדוֹם עֲבָדִים לְדָוִיד

G Chr: καὶ ἔθετο ἐν τῇ κοιλάδι φρουράς καὶ ἦσαν πάντες οἱ Ἰδουμαιοι παῖδες Δαυειδ

65. Veijola, *Die ewige Dynastie*, pp. 95-97; cf. also McCarter, *II Samuel*, p. 251.

66. K. Budde, *Die Bücher Samuel* (KHAT, 8; Tübingen/Leipzig: Mohr, 1902), pp. 237-38; cf. too, more recently, Caquot and de Robert, *Les livres de Samuel*, p. 447: 'The ancient passage seems to have been expanded in vv. 7-12 by a Deuteronomistic redactor preoccupied with the history of the temple treasure'.

67. H.W. Hertzberg, *I & II Samuel: A Commentary* (OTL; Philadelphia: Westminster Press, 1964), p. 290 (translation by J. Bowden of *Die Samuelbücher* [ATD, 10; Göttingen: Vandenhoeck & Ruprecht, 1956]).

In MT Sam the 'plus' בְּכָל־אֱדוֹם שָׂם נְצִבִים is generally considered to be a conflation,[68] or a 'synonymous reading'.[69] McCarter suggests that 1 Chron. 18.13 could have sustained a haplography producing the disappearance of the 'plus' of the text, whereas MT Sam is a *lectio conflata*.[70] If such is the case, the question comes up of when the conflation would have taken place. If the text of 1 Chron. 18.13 contained it originally, it would be an ancient reading. The text of G Sam contains a part of the longer text of MT Sam, omitting only שָׂם נְצִבִים (which is present in g^{OL}, in an adjustment to the text of MT Sam). The Vulgate presents no equivalent for בְּכָל־אֱדוֹם, and the Vetus Latina and the Syriac have no equivalent for בֶּאֱדוֹם and שָׂם נְצִבִים. There is therefore no agreement among the ancient versions, which would be evidence of attempts to amend the verse, since the missing parts in the versions are precisely those that are repetitive. Hertzberg suggested that the 'plus' in MT Sam constitutes 'presumably some indication of the content of the passage originally in the margin'.[71] There is no evidence making it possible to attribute the repetitive text to the Deuteronomistic editor. The shorter text such as is found in 1 Chron. 18.13 may be the earliest form of the text.

2 Samuel 8.15a
MT Sam: וַיִּמְלֹךְ דָּוִד עַל־כָּל־יִשְׂרָאֵל
G Sam: καὶ ἐβασίλευσεν Δαυειδ ἐπὶ (+ πάντα Mss MNgin) Ἰσραήλ

1 Chron. 18.14a
MT Chr: וַיִּמְלֹךְ דָּוִיד עַל־כָּל־יִשְׂרָאֵל
G. Chr: καὶ ἐβασίλευσεν Δαυειδ ἐπὶ πάντα Ἰσραήλ

Some commentators (for example, McCarter) follow G Sam in eliminating כָּל from the text of Samuel. The absence of 'all' in G could have been the original reading of Samuel, since the addition certainly agreed with the pan-Israelite perspective of Chronicles. If such is the case, the Deuteronomistic text would have been preserved in G Sam.

Conclusion

From the few cases that we have examined it is not possible to reach a firm conclusion. On the other hand, it is possible to distinguish at least

---

68. Cf. Anderson, *2 Samuel*, p. 130.
69. Talmon, 'Double Readings', p. 177.
70. McCarter, *II Samuel*, p. 246.
71. Hertzberg, *I & II Samuel*, p. 289, note e.

some tendencies in the recurrent interpretation of the Deuteronomistic material of 2 Samuel 5–8. In the perspective of the development of the text, the choices from textual criticism can sometimes play a part in making it possible to attribute verses or sections to the Deuteronomistic redaction. The cases where G Sam agrees with MT Chr (for example, 2 Sam. 5.17a משחו vs נמשׁה) naturally indicate a collusion between the text of G Sam and that of MT Chr, perhaps already on the level of material from Samuel that the Chronicler had available, but in the passages considered to be Deuteronomistic there is no indication that G Sam / MT Chr transmit a more ancient text form. A text such as 2 Sam. 5.17a would actually seem to indicate just the contrary, since the qal plural מָשְׁחוּ is a sign of the (Deuteronomistic) rearrangement of the text, while G Sam and MT Chr have smoothed out the difficulty arising from the excessive distance of the subject in relation to the verb.

One of the greatest problems is to know to what extent the successive redactional layers have left traces in the text, and to what extent the successive redactions have obliterated or modified the signs of earlier forms of the text. A case such as 2 Sam. 7.11b indicates how a text can be considered Deuteronomistic or not, depending on whether we acknowledge that the text can be corrected in order to obtain a form prior to that which we now have in MT Sam. From a methodological point of view, it is possible that better defined criteria would be necessary to reach an agreement of the history of the redaction.

Another question, related to the preceding ones, concerns the way in which the editors (Deuteronomistic or others) worked. It is sometimes suggested that a phrase that seems to be Deuteronomistic can in fact be attributed to a later (anonymous) hand who would have inserted into the text a reading having Deuteronomistic characteristics. Here again, the notion that we develop of the history of the text will influence the judgments on the readings attributed to particular redactional layers.

At the end of our examination of the traces of specifically Deuteronomistic redactional activity, the conclusion seems to emerge from the test cases studied that MT Sam, aside from a few exceptions, tends to confirm the existence of such traces, and that the variants do not necessarily bring us closer to textual forms that would be more authentically Deuteronomistic or that would certify with the necessary evidence a more ancient reading.

Part IV

DIACHRONIC AND SYNCHRONIC METHODS

THE TROUBLE WITH KINGSHIP*

Steven L. McKenzie

1 Samuel 8–12, which recounts the beginning of monarchy in Israel, is
a notorious crux. My decision to treat it as the topic of this paper was
sparked by my observation of certain literary features in these chapters
to which scholars as a whole have not given sufficient attention and by
McCarter's contribution to the 1993 symposium celebrating the 50th
anniversary of Noth's recognition of the Deuteronomistic History.[1] My
thesis is that 1 Samuel 8–12* is a unified composition by a single
author/editor, the Deuteronomist (Dtr). The sources behind these chapters had not previously been redacted together, and while additions
have been made to Dtr's version of these chapters, there is no evidence
of later, systematic editing. In other words, I think Noth was basically
correct that 1 Samuel 8–12* was Dtr's composition.[2] However, in addition to differences in details of literary-critical analysis, I disagree with
Noth on two important points. First, his understanding of these chapters
as a whole as anti-monarchical does not take stock of the complexity of
the statements about this issue in the Dtr passages. Secondly, contrary
to Noth's conclusion that Dtr's intervention in these chapters was
atypical,[3] I believe 1 Samuel 8–12* furnishes a very good example of
his compositional techniques for the entire History.[4]

*   My thanks to Dr M. Patrick Graham and Professors Ralph Klein, Gary
Knoppers and John Van Seters for their reading and helpful comments on this
paper. I remain, of course, responsible for its content.
    1.   P.K. McCarter, Jr, 'The Books of Samuel', in S.L. McKenzie and M.P.
Graham (eds), *The History of Israel's Traditions: The Heritage of Martin Noth*
(JSOTSup, 182; Sheffield: Sheffield Academic Press, 1994), pp. 260-80.
    2.   M. Noth, *Überlieferungsgeschichtliche Studien: Die sammelnden und
bearbeitenden Geschichtswerke im Alten Testament* (Tübingen: Max Niemeyer, 3rd
edn, 1967), pp. 54-60.
    3.   Noth, *Studien*, p. 54.
    4.   My conclusions for this passage are thus similar to those of my earlier study

The individual units within 1 Samuel 8–12 have been well defined since Wellhausen as 8.1-22; 9.1–10.16; 10.17-27a; 10.27b–11.15; 12.1-25.[5] In the first part of this paper, I will examine these units concentrically because the overall unity and message of the section emerges most clearly this way. I will begin with 10.17-27a, arguing that it is Dtr's composition. Next, I will treat the three units in chs. 9–11, looking especially for signs of Dtr's editing. Then, I will look at all of chs. 8–12 to show how Dtr forged a unit on the beginning of monarchy. However, chs. 8–12 are also closely connected to their context:[6] the reference to Samuel's work as a judge in 7.15-17 binds ch. 7 to ch. 8 (esp. vv. 1-3), and the link between 10.8 and 13.7b-15 ties the account of Saul's reign in chs. 13–15 to that of his designation as king in chs. 8–12. Hence, the second part of the paper will deal with important issues for both chs. 8–12 and the entire Deuteronomistic History raised by this context. In chs. 13–15, there is the question of a pre-Dtr source continuing from chs. 8–12 as well as the continuation of Deuteronomistic themes. In ch. 7, the references to Mizpah raise the matter of the date of this section and of the entire Deuteronomistic History.

1. *1 Samuel 8–12*

a. *10.17-27a*

This passage, along with chs. 8 and 12, formed Wellhausen's 'late source'[7] in 1 Samuel, which, since Noth, has been widely associated with Dtr.[8] Recent attempts to find other redactors in this text, either before or after Dtr, have focused on vv. 17-19 and have been led, respectively, by Birch[9] and Veijola.[10] Birch's denial of Deuteronomistic

of Kings, *The Trouble with Kings: The Composition of the Book of Kings in the Deuteronomistic History* (VTSup, 42; Leiden: E.J. Brill, 1991).

5.   J. Wellhausen, *Prolegomena to the History of Ancient Israel* (Gloucester, MA: Peter Smith, 1973), pp. 245-56. The true beginning of the unit in 10.27b–11.15 has become clear since Wellhausen from the reading of 4QSam[a]. See R.W. Klein, *1 Samuel* (WBC, 10; Waco: Word Books, 1983), pp. 102-103 and P.K. McCarter, Jr, *1 Samuel* (AB, 8; Garden City, NY: Doubleday, 1980), pp. 199-200.

6.   See M.A. O'Brien's plea for considering the broader context in *The Deuteronomistic History Hypothesis: A Reassessment* (OBO, 92; Freiburg/Göttingen: Universitätsverlag/Vandenhoeck & Ruprecht, 1989), p. 98.

7.   Wellhausen, *Prolegomena*, pp. 247-56.

8.   Noth, *Studien*, pp. 54-55.

9.   B.C. Birch (*The Rise of the Israelite Monarchy: The Growth and Develop-*

writing in 10.17-19 is unconvincing. The closest parallels to these verses (esp. Judg. 6.7-10;[11] cf. Judg. 2.1-5; 10.11-16; 1 Sam. 7.3-4; 12.6-25) are widely recognized as Deuteronomistic, especially in their language about bringing Israel up from Egypt (v. 18).[12] The subsequent statements about saving Israel from the 'hand' of Egypt and from its oppressors also find similarities in Deuteronomistic contexts.[13] Even the wider context of 10.17-27a evinces traces of Deuteronomistic language and ideology, including the notion of YHWH choosing (בחר) and the designation 'all the tribes of Israel' (v. 20).[14]

Indeed, Veijola has put forth a compelling case for seeing all of the

ment of 1 Samuel 7–15 [SBLDS, 27; Missoula, MT: Scholars Press, 1976], pp. 42-54) is followed by McCarter (*1 Samuel*, pp. 189-96). See the critique by J. Van Seters, *In Search of History: Historiography in the Ancient World and the Origins of Biblical History* (New Haven: Yale University Press, 1983), p. 253. M. Weinfeld (*Deuteronomy and the Deuteronomic School* [Oxford: Oxford University Press, 1972], p. 82 n. 3 and p. 168) also apparently denies 1 Sam. 8–12 to Dtr. But his contention that these chapters preserve a tradition of opposition to monarchy from the time of Saul is not supported by close literary scrutiny.

10. T. Veijola, *Das Königtum in der Beurteilung der deuteronomistischen Historiographie: Eine redaktionsgeschichtliche Untersuchung* (AASF.B, 198; Helsinki: Suomalainen Tiedeakatemia, 1977), pp. 39-52. See also W. Dietrich, *David, Saul und die Propheten: Das Verhältnis von Religion und Politik nach den prophetischen Überlieferungen vom frühesten Königtum in Israel* (BWANT, 122; Stuttgart: W. Kohlhammer, 2nd edn, 1992), pp. 94-95.

11. Judg. 6.7-10 may be a late insertion, since it is missing from 4QJudg[a] (cf. R.G. Boling, *Judges* [AB, 6A; Garden City, NY: Doubleday, 1975], p. 125 and McCarter, *1 Samuel*, p. 192). This points out a crucial flaw in Birch's use of form to determine the date (eighth century) and provenance (prophets) of the texts in Samuel (see esp. *Rise*, pp. 83-84). Later writers, such as Dtr, obviously borrowed and adapted older forms to their own purposes. C. Westermann's *Basic Forms of Prophetic Speech* (Philadelphia: Westminster Press, 1967), upon which Birch relies heavily for his discussion of judgment oracles, does not give adequate consideration to this phenomenon.

12. See F.M. Cross, *Canaanite Myth and Hebrew Epic: Essays in the History and the Religion of Israel* (Cambridge, MA: Harvard University Press, 1973), p. 253. Van Seters (*In Search of History*, p. 253 n. 15) notes that 'the practice of citing the *Heilsgeschichte* prior to the pronouncement of an accusation [is a clear indication] of Dtr authorship'.

13. See G.F. Moore, *A Critical and Exegetical Commentary on Judges* (ICC; New York: Scribner's, 1895), p. 182. Veijola (*Das Königtum*, pp. 42-43) lists further Deuteronomistic parallels.

14. Veijola, *Das Königtum*, pp. 50-51.

story in 10.17, 19b-27a as Dtr's (Veijola: DtrG's) composition. His argument counters Eissfeldt's commonly held proposal that vv. 20-24 contain two originally separate versions of Saul's designation as king: one (vv. 20-21bα) in which he is selected by lot, and a second (vv. 22-25) where he is chosen because of his height.[15] The principal support for Eissfeldt's proposal has to do with Saul's absence from the ceremony at which he is chosen by lot (v. 21). But Van Seters has argued on the basis of Lindblom's work that this is in keeping with the practice of lot casting in antiquity.[16] Also, Veijola notes that Saul's hiding shows his awareness that the lot will fall on him so that it presumes the story in 9.1–10.16![17] Thus, 10.19b-27a is best explained as Dtr's composition, not as fragments of older tradition.

Dtr composed this material on the basis of motifs and information available elsewhere in the Saul story and the Deuteronomistic History. Lot casting was familiar from the stories about Achan (Josh. 7.16-18) and Jonathan (1 Sam. 14.38-42). Dtr borrowed the motif but adapted it so that Saul could not be found after the lot had selected him. The tradition of Saul's extraordinary height came to Dtr in 9.2. The 'law of the kingship' in v. 25 is a literary device by which Dtr marks this event as an important transition in Israel's history and prepares for his presentation of Samuel in ch. 12 'as the one responsible for providing the legal and sacral framework for the newly instituted monarchy'.[18] As for

15. O. Eissfeldt, *Die Komposition der Samuelisbücher* (Leipzig: J.C. Hinrichs'sche, 1931), p. 7. In this view, the second version is fragmentary because its beginning has been replaced by v. 21bβ in order to connect the two. The unusual reading of the MT in v. 22, which is often cited as another support, is probably simply erroneous. Based on the LXX, McCarter (*1 Samuel*, p. 190) reads הבא האיש עד הלם, suggesting that the MT reflects the misinterpretation of עד as עוד and the subsequent loss of the article before איש. The best explanation for the first עוד in v. 22 is not that a previous oracle has been omitted (so F. Crüsemann, *Der Widerstand gegen das Königtum: Die antiköniglichen Texte des Alten Testaments und der Kampf um den frühen israelitischen Staat* [WMANT, 49; Neukirchen–Vluyn: Neukirchener Verlag, 1978], p. 56 and O'Brien, *Reassessment*, p. 117) but that YHWH is envisioned as speaking through the lot-casting process (so J. Lindblom, 'Lot-Casting in the Old Testament', *VT* 12 [1962], p. 166 n. 1).

16. Van Seters, *In Search of History*, p. 252; Lindblom, 'Lot-Casting', pp. 164-78.

17. Veijola, *Das Königtum*, p. 39.

18. A.D.H. Mayes, 'The Rise of the Israelite Monarchy', *ZAW* 90 (1978), p. 10 n. 37. On Dtr's use of the deposit of a document to mark an important transition as in Josh. 24 and 2 Kgs 22, see H.J. Boecker, *Die Beurteilung der Anfänge des*

the last two verses of this passage (10.26-27a), which will be treated in more detail below, the expression בני בליעל is common elsewhere in the History, and the idea of bringing a gift to the king could be derived from 10.3-4.[19] The reference to the Matrites may be based on some older tradition about Saul; since the patronymic is unattested elsewhere, it is impossible to say where Dtr got it. Otherwise, there is no need to posit any source behind this story; Dtr has simply borrowed motifs and adapted them to his purposes.

While I agree with Veijola that Dtr wrote 10.17, 19b-27a, I believe he is wrong to assign vv. 18-19a to a second Deuteronomist (DtrN).[20] In the first place, there is a good literary reason for including vv. 18-19a in the unit. Without them, it is not clear why Samuel assembles the people or for what role Saul is chosen, since the reference to a king is found precisely in v. 19a. Veijola's reasoning has to do primarily with the notorious question of the view of monarchy in the Deuteronomistic History. He contends that vv. 18-19a regard kingship negatively while the rest of this text regards it positively. But there are ambiguities and subtleties in the text as a whole that Veijola overlooks. First of all, vv. 18-19a do not condemn monarchy *per se* but accuse the people of trusting in a king instead of in YHWH, who saved them in the past. It is a matter of faith, not of the assessment of the institution of kingship. Secondly, there are hints in 10.17-27a as a whole that Dtr views the change to monarchy under Saul with a wary eye. The use of lot casting elsewhere in the Deuteronomistic History to seek out an offender may cast a shadow on the process here.[21] The 'law of the kingship' (v. 25)

Königtums in den deuteronomistischen Abschnitten des I. Samuelbuches: Ein Beitrag zum Problem des 'Deuteronomistischen Geschichtswerks' (WMANT, 31; Neukirchen–Vluyn: Neukirchener Verlag, 1969), pp. 51-56. The expression 'law of the kingship' obviously plays on 1 Sam. 8.9 and probably Deut. 17.14-20, but since it is a literary device, the question of its exact contents is moot.

19. See Veijola, *Das Königtum*, p. 51 n. 89.

20. See also A. Moenikes, *Die grundsätzliche Ablehnung des Königtums in der Hebräischen Bibel: Ein Beitrag zur Religionsgeschichte des Alten Israel* (BBB, 99; Weinheim: Beltz-Athenäum), pp. 30-33, whose literary arguments are similar to Veijola's.

21. McCarter, *1 Samuel*, pp. 195-96. It seems unlikely that the use of the lot to assign guilt in Josh. 7 and 1 Sam. 14.38-44 is coincidence (*contra* D.V. Edelman, *King Saul in the Historiography of Judah* [JSOTSup, 121; Sheffield: Sheffield Academic Press, 1991], p. 56 n. 1; cf. Acts 1.26), although the Achan episode may be a late addition (so Van Seters, *In Search of History*, pp. 327-28).

makes the point that the king must subordinate himself to the law and thus implies that kings have a tendency to regard themselves as above it. Also, the depiction of Saul here is ambiguous. Does he hide out of humility (cf. 9.21) or ineptness? Some find him less than inspiring (v. 27a). His height, which here so impresses Samuel (v. 24), is shown to be meaningless and even deceptive in the David story.[22] Saul's success, after all, is due not to his ability but to YHWH's spirit (10.10; 11.6). Samuel's speech in 10.17-19, thus, fits perfectly with Dtr's message in 10.17-27a as a whole. In demanding a king the people evince a lack of faith. YHWH accedes to their demand and chooses a king for them. But the king must submit to the law of YHWH and will be effective only because of and so long as YHWH's spirit is upon him.

The fact that vv. 17-19 are in the form of a prophetic judgment oracle does not, *contra* Birch (see above), preclude Dtr's authorship. Dtr shaped the form to his own purposes by having Samuel give the instructions for choosing a king in v. 19 where one expects to find the announcement of judgment. This is yet another hint of Dtr's wary attitude toward the people's demand for a change in leadership. In composing this oracle, Dtr has drawn on surrounding material in chs. 8–12. The language of v. 18, especially הלחצים, anticipates the story in ch. 11[23] and recalls that of ch. 8, especially the accusation of rejecting God (8.7),[24] and the people's statement of their determination to have a king (8.19).

b. *1 Samuel 9–11*
1. *10.14-16; 10.26-27a; 11.12-14.* While the tensions between the three units in 9.1–10.16; 10.17-27a; and 10.27b–11.15 have been noticed by scholars as evidence of their original independence, the indications of editorial unity have not received full consideration. The best such indication is the notices near the end of each unit that serve to bind them to

22. A point made overtly in 16.1-13, which is a later addition, but more subtly in ch. 17.

23. הממלכות is probably a gloss even if it is an old form of the word 'kings'. Cf. McCarter, *1 Samuel*, p. 192.

24. Birch (*Rise*, pp. 23-24, 50) contends that Dtr's characteristic verb for abandoning YHWH is עזב and that מאס is non-Deuteronomistic. But as he points out, the sense of the two verbs is different, the former referring to religious apostasy, not the choosing of a human ruler. Dtr's use of מאס in 10.19 indicates his familiarity with 8.7 and suggests his authorship of both texts.

each other. 10.14-16 relates an odd interview between Saul and his uncle—odd because it is he rather than Saul's father who questions him and because the uncle appears unexpectedly, is nameless (not identified as Ner, 14.50), plays no other role in the stories about Saul, and is never mentioned again. These factors combine to indicate that the interview is entirely fictional and editorial. Its function is to make clear what is implicit in 9.27—that Saul's anointing was a private matter, thereby creating a need for the story of Saul's public designation as king in 10.17-27a.

The devices at the ends of the other two units have a similar function. After Saul's election by lot to kingship, he returns home to Gibeah with a circle of loyal warriors (10.26).[25] Others, however, called בני בליעל, question the choice of Saul and bring him no gift, thus refusing fealty (10.27a). Then, following Saul's victory over Nahash, his loyal troops (העם) call for the execution of these בני בליעל but are refused (11.12-13).[26] Efforts to find old, historical traditions in these verses are misdirected,[27] as their function again is purely editorial. Samuel's dismissal of the people in 10.25 and Saul's return home in 10.26 prepare for the account in 10.27b–11.15, in which Saul summons all Israel to war from his family estate in Gibeah. Similarly, the mention in 10.26 of the army (החיל) that accompanies Saul to Gibeah sets the stage for his military exploit in ch. 11, even though in the latter he is obviously alone. The references to Saul's detractors in 10.27a and 11.12-13 are closely related and serve to unite the accounts in 10.17-27a and 10.27b–11.15. The man who was publicly designated king at Mizpah now proves that he can save his people from their enemies. Finally, Samuel's summons to 'renew' the kingship in 11.14 is widely recognized as editorial. The story in ch. 11 was originally independent and did not presuppose that Saul was king (see below). Its original ending (11.15) offered the alternative explanation that Saul came to be king because of his military

---

25. Reading בני החיל with 4QSam[a] and the LXX against the MT, which has lost בני. The superior reading obviates Crüsemann's argument for different hands in vv. 26-27 (*Widerstand*, pp. 55-56).

26. The LXX has Samuel refuse the request, but the MT reading ('Saul') is the *lectio difficilior*, since the people address Samuel in v. 12.

27. Birch (*Rise*, pp. 52, 60-62) recognizes that 10.26-27a has 'been intentionally composed as a transition section' (p. 52) but fails to see that 11.12-13 was also 'intentionally composed' for the same reason, so that he labors to find genuine history in both texts.

prowess. Only secondarily and editorially was Saul's accession here turned into a 'renewal' in order to make room for the previous two versions of his ascent in which he was chosen by a prophet and by lot.

While scholars have recognized the editorial nature of these three devices, they have not generally perceived how they work together as part of a single, redactional process, whose focal point is the Dtr account in 10.17-25. The interview with Saul's uncle in 10.14-16 stresses the private nature of Saul's anointing and makes way for his public designation in 10.17-25, while the references to Saul's return home and his detractors (10.26-27a; 11.12-13) bind the stories of his anointing and designation to that of his proving. The term 'kingdom' (מלוכה) in 10.16 and 11.14 signals their composition by the same hand.[28] The three versions of Saul's becoming king have been editorially linked into a unit, and since 10.17-27a, at the heart of that unit, is a Dtr composition, the editorial work must be ascribed to Dtr.[29]

2. *9.1–10.16.* Schmidt's 1970 monograph succeeded in isolating the original tale beneath this passage.[30] Since subsequent treatments have not

28. Veijola, *Das Königtum*, p. 82. It is also used in 14.47, which is part of Dtr's framework for Saul's reign. See below. The concern for a deliverer in 10.27a, expressed with the verb ישׁע, also betrays Dtr's hand. Cf. Boecker, *Beurteilung*, pp. 21-23, 58-59; Veijola, *Das Königtum*, pp. 76-79.

29. B. Halpern (*The Constitution of the Monarchy in Israel* [HSM, 25; Chico, CA: Scholars Press, 1981], pp. 111-48) has argued that Dtr followed an established pattern in structuring these accounts. He has been followed in this by Edelman (*King Saul*, pp. 27-36) and V.P. Long (*The Reign and Rejection of King Saul: A Case for Literary and Theological Coherence* [SBLDS, 118; Atlanta: Scholars Press, 1989], esp. pp. 173-94; also 'How Did Saul Become King? Literary Reading and Historical Reconstruction', in A.R. Millard, J.K. Hoffmeier, and D.W. Baker [eds.], *Faith, Tradition, and History: Old Testament Historiography in its Near Eastern Context* [Winona Lake, IN: Eisenbrauns, 1994], pp. 271-84). But there are really only two stages to this pattern—designation (9.1–10.16) and confirmation (ch. 11)—so that 10.17-27a is left unexplained. The attempt to force this pattern on 1 Sam. 7–12 leads Halpern, on the one hand, to an untenable source reconstruction (pp. 149-74) and Edelman and especially Long, on the other, to a harmonization of the more blatant tensions in the narrative. Long's effort ('How Did Saul Become King?') to reconstruct history on the basis of his literary treatment is particularly unacceptable. The 'pattern' involved in Saul's accession is best understood as Dtr's invention, since his editorial creativity is the cohesive element in these chapters.

30. L. Schmidt, *Menschlicher Erfolg und Jahwes Initiative: Studien zu Tradition, Interpretation und Historie in den Überlieferungen von Gideon, Saul und*

improved on Schmidt's and in general have failed to appreciate his arguments,[31] it is worthwhile to review them here. Schmidt's analysis depends on three important observations. First, like most scholars, Schmidt perceives 9.1-13* to be the beginning of the old story.[32] But he also notes the correspondence between the two needs of Saul and his servant at the beginning of the story and the two 'signs' in 10.2-4. They need to find out about the lost asses, and they lack bread. The two men near Rachel's tomb tell Saul that the asses have been found and that, as Saul feared, his father has begun to worry about him. The three men at the oak of Tabor give two loaves of bread, one each for Saul and his servant. This correspondence indicates that the third sign—Saul's encounter with the prophets—is a later addition, and this is confirmed by the fact that only this third sign is described in detail. Thus, 10.5-6, 10-13 are secondary.

Schmidt's second observation relates to Samuel's promise in 9.19 to tell Saul 'all that is on your mind' the next morning. It is widely recognized that this promise, along with the first sign in 10.2, is contradicted

---

David (WMANT, 38; Neukirchen–Vluyn: Neukirchener Verlag, 1970), pp. 63-80.

31. For bibliography on this passage, see G. Bettenzoli, 'Samuel und das Problem des Königtums', *BZ* 30 (1986), pp. 222-36; A.F. Campbell, *Of Prophets and Kings: A Late Ninth Century Document (1 Samuel 1–2 Kings 10)* (CBQMS, 17; Washington, DC: Catholic Biblical Association of America, 1986), p. 18 n. 2; J.M. Miller, 'Saul's Rise to Power: Some Observations Concerning 1 Sam. 9.1–10.16; 10.26–11.15 and 13.2–14.46', *CBQ* 36 (1974), pp. 157-74; and N. Na'aman, 'The Pre-Deuteronomistic Story of King Saul and Its Historical Significance', *CBQ* 54 (1992), pp. 638-58.

32. Schmidt finds three glosses in this material: 9.9, which is clearly editorial; 9.13aγ (אחרי־כן יאכלו הקראים), which will be treated below; and the reference to Saul's height in 9.2b, which is the one detail in his isolation of the old story with which I disagree. Schmidt (*Menschlicher Erfolg*, p. 98) sees v. 2b as a gloss that entered the text with the addition of 10.17-27a, and he is followed in this by Campbell (*Of Prophets*, p. 19) and Miller ('Saul's Rise', pp. 158-59). But this assumes that 10.17-27a is based on old tradition rather than being Dtr's composition, as I have argued. In fact, there is no good literary indication that 9.2b is secondary. It explains further why Saul was regarded as handsome (טוב). It also serves as an indication of Saul's distinction and ability as a military leader, which he is called to exercise in 10.7. Indeed, A. Weiser (*Samuel: Seine geschichtliche Aufgabe und religiöse Bedeutung* [FRLANT, 81; Göttingen: Vandenhoeck & Ruprecht, 1962], p. 55) has shown that Saul's height is part of the portrait of Saul here as an exemplary candidate for king. Hence, v. 2b is not superfluous to the old story but fits well within it and contributes to it.

by Samuel's revelation in the next verse (9.20) that the asses have been found, so that 9.20-21 must be an addition. But Schmidt observes that the reason for Samuel's delay in the original story must have been that he was unfamiliar with Saul's circumstances and needed to consult God overnight before he could reply. Hence, those parts of the present story that indicate Samuel's foreknowledge—9.15-17 and the banquet scene in 9.22b-24a, where Saul is given the place of honor 'at the head of the invited guests'—must also be additions. 10.1, which corresponds with 9.15-17 in its language about anointing Saul *nāgîd* in order for him to save Israel, is later[33] and so is 9.13aγ, with its mention of the 'invited guests'.

Schmidt's third observation has to do with the identification of the 'seer' with Samuel. As most scholars have recognized, the seer was originally nameless. This is a form-critical issue as well as a literary-critical one. 'The anonymous seer is a suitable folklore character, but the famous prophet is not.'[34] The mention of Samuel in 9.14b without introduction is abrupt and suggests secondary identification. Schmidt also notices that the setting of v. 14b ('in the middle of the city') contradicts v. 18's location of the encounter 'in the middle of the gate'. Thus, v. 14b is an addition, and the nameless seer has been systematically identified throughout the story as Samuel. This means further that 10.8 is secondary, since it depends on the identification of the seer with Samuel and prepares for the latter's rejection of Saul in 13.7b-15. The story originally ended with 10.7, 9. These verses refer to 'signs'— plural rather than singular as in the secondary verse, 10.1. The reference in v. 9 to God giving Saul another heart also stands in tension with the addition in 10.6, where he becomes 'another man' only after his encounter with the prophets.

---

33. With the majority of scholars, but against Schmidt, I read with the LXX in 10.1, the MT having suffered a long haplography. See Klein, *1 Samuel*, p. 83 and McCarter, *1 Samuel*, p. 171. On the apparent tension of this reading with 9.16, see below.

34. McCarter, *1 Samuel*, p. 186. Birch (*Rise*, pp. 34-35) sees the identification of the seer with Samuel as part of the original story's 'dramatic flair'. It is true that Saul's ignorance that the seer is Samuel in the present version of the story furthers the presentation of Saul's origins as rustic and humble. But this is an editorial concern (9.21) rather than an interest of the original tale. Van Seters agrees with Birch in this matter, even though in prophetic *legenda*, which Van Seters correctly identifies as the genre of this old tale, it is common for prophets to be unnamed (e.g. 1 Kgs 13; 20; 2 Kgs 9).

The original tale behind 9.1–10.16, therefore, consisted of 9.1-8, 10-13aαβb, 14a, 18-19, 22a, 24b-27; 10.2-4, 7, 9 without the identification of the seer as Samuel. As with other prophetic *legenda*, the needs of characters in crisis, in this case Saul and his servant, are met through the clairvoyance of a 'man of God'.[35] This particular tale is an example of elaborated *legenda,* since its ending is tailored to Saul's identity as the main character. As Schmidt showed, the expression, 'do what your hands find to do' (10.7) was a commission to exercise one's 'God-given' capability—in Saul's case, military prowess (v. 9). It did not refer to any specific battle or action by Saul, and efforts to connect it with subsequent stories have not proved convincing.[36]

In the material that remains after the isolation of the original tale, Schmidt finds two layers of redaction, one in 9.13aγ, 20-21, 22b-24a; 10.1, 13b-16, whose principal concern was the anointing of Saul as *nāgîd*, and the other in 10.5-6, 10-13a, which incorporated the aetiology for the *māshāl*, 'Is Saul also among the prophets?'[37] Schmidt makes a number of important observations regarding the first redactional layer, and it is worthwhile to review these before examining his case for distinguishing the aetiology as the work of a separate redactor.

First of all, the connecting rubric in 10.14-16 is also part of the redactional overlay. Its focus, the 'matter of the kingdom' (דבר המלוכה), is that of the overlay—the issue 'on which Israel's desire is fixed' (9.20).

35. On the genre of the prophetic *legenda*, see A. Rofé, 'The Classification of the Prophetical Stories', *JBL* 89 (1970), pp. 427-40; 'Classes in the Prophetical Stories: Didactic Legenda and Parable', in *idem, Studies in Prophecy* (VTSup, 26; Leiden: E.J. Brill, 1974); and especially *The Prophetical Stories* (Jerusalem: Magnes Press, 1988). On other attempts to define the genre of the tale in 1 Sam. 9.1–10.16 see Boecker, *Beurteilung*, pp. 12-16.

36. Especially Miller ('Saul's Rise'), whose argument that this story originally continued in ch. 13 has not gained a following. Indeed, ch. 13 presupposes a much different and later time, since there Saul has a grown son, Jonathan. Also, the locations do not match. The Philistine garrison in 10.5 is at Gibeath-elohim (= Gibeah, 10.10). In ch. 13 Saul is at Michmash (v. 2) and Gilgal (v. 7) but not Gibeah. No location is given for the garrison he defeated (v. 4). These differences make it unlikely that ch. 13 ever served as the direct continuation of 9.1–10.16, even at an editorial level (*contra* Dietrich, *Saul, David*, pp. 63-73). The only clear connection between the two texts is 10.8, which prepares for 13.7b-15. But literary analysis of 9.1–10.16 as well as the differences between 9.1–10.16 and ch. 13 indicate that 10.8 was a late addition.

37. Schmidt, *Menschlicher Erfolg*, pp. 81-102. Schmidt does not include 9.2b, 9; 10.8 in either layer. He sees these as later, independent additions and glosses.

Both the rubric in 10.14-16 and the overlay recognize that Saul's designation by anointing in this story is only one stage in his rise to kingship as it is now described in chs. 9–11. The overlay and the editorial rubric work together, therefore, to bind those chapters into a unit. The overlay and hence chs. 9–11 as they now stand also presuppose the larger, surrounding context. The sudden identification of the seer with Samuel presumes the reader's acquaintance with at least some of chs. 1–8. Similarly, the reference in 9.16 to saving the people from the Philistines suggests familiarity with the 'Ark Narrative' in chs. 4–6 and anticipates Saul's battles with the Philistines in chs. 13–14 and continuing throughout 1 Samuel.[38]

These considerations indicate that the overlay, or at least what Schmidt identified as the first layer of it, is Deuteronomistic, and this is supported by the language of these verses. The term נחלה reflected in 10.1 (LXX) most clearly betrays this provenance, as other scholars have observed, and the theme of saving YHWH's people from their enemies in 9.16 and 10.1 is the same as that found in Dtr's presentation of Judges.[39] Other expressions in these verses that have been cited as Deuteronomistic include 'uncover the ear' (9.15) and 'God is with you' (10.7bβ).[40]

---

38. On the tension between 9.16 and 7.7-11 see the discussion of ch. 7 below. There is also a tension between 9.16 and 10.1 (LXX), the latter referring to Saul saving Israel 'from the hand of their enemies all around', while the former mentions only the Philistines. The difference leads Schmidt (*Menschlicher Erfolg*, p. 85 n. 3) to follow the MT in 10.1. It is also one of the reasons that Veijola (*Das Königtum*, pp. 75-76) assigns 9.16a to the old tale but 10.1b to DtrG. But Schmidt's solution results in a tension between 9.16 and ch. 11 where Saul defeats Ammonites, not Philistines, and Veijola's is countered by the great similarity between the two verses and by the Deuteronomistic language in 9.16. In my view, this tension is overblown. The two verses work together to unite the story of Saul's ascent to kingship with the surrounding context. The Philistines are Israel's greatest enemy, as shown in the rest of 1 Samuel, and the people's prime concern in calling for a king. But Dtr also wanted to include the account of Saul's victory over the Ammonites (ch. 11), and besides, he knew that Israel had other enemies in addition to the Philistines (14.47).

39. Cf. Klein, *1 Samuel*, p. 90; Van Seters, *In Search of History*, pp. 255-56; and Weinfeld, *Deuteronomic School*, p. 328, whose list of Deuteronomistic expressions includes עם (ו)נחלה.

40. See Cross, *Canaanite Myth*, pp. 252-53. If Cross is right about 'God is with you' the old legend may actually have ended with v. 7bα. But this expression is not exclusively Deuteronomistic. Cross also cites 'all that is on your mind' in 9.19 as

The term *nāgîd*, found only in the overlay in this passage (9.16 and 10.1), also assumes the larger context, not only of the beginning of the monarchy in Israel but also of the entire Deuteronomistic History, and illustrates Dtr's skill as an author. Since *nāgîd* means 'one who is designated', it obviously presupposes that Saul will become the king whom the people have requested (8.4, 19), as he does in 10.17-27 (cf. 11.14-15).[41] But the term also carries military connotations and may have arisen as a title for a military commander.[42] Dtr shaped 9.1–10.16 to describe Saul's commission as a military leader before the institution of monarchy (cf. Judg. 6; Exod. 3).[43] But he also had Saul designated by anointing, a rite associated specifically with kingship. In this way, Saul's designation as *nāgîd* provided a transition from the period of the judges to that of the monarchy.[44] It was both a call to military action and an anointing as king. It also begins an important subtheme that culminates in the promise—crucial for Dtr—of an eternal Davidic dynasty:[45] Saul was initially anointed *nāgîd* (1 Sam. 9.16; 10.1, LXX),

Deuteronomistic language, but Schmidt's literary-critical analysis showed otherwise.

41. See McCarter, *1 Samuel*, pp. 178-79; Halpern, *Constitution*, pp. 1-11. T.N.D. Mettinger's argument (*King and Messiah: The Civil and Sacral Legitimation of the Israelite Kings* [Lund: Gleerup, 1976], pp. 151-84) that *nāgîd* was the title for an official 'king designate', however, relies almost exclusively on 1 Kgs 1.35.

42. W. Richter, 'Die *nagid*-Formel', *BZ* 9 (1965), pp. 71-84. Cf. Cross, *Canaanite Myth*, p. 220 n. 5. But contrast Halpern, *Constitution*, pp. 1-11.

43. Birch (*Rise*, pp. 35-40) contended, on the basis of the work of N. Habel ('The Form and Significance of the Call Narratives', *ZAW* 77 [1965], pp. 297-323), that a pre-Dtr, prophetic editor imposed the form of a prophetic call narrative on the original tale underlying this passage, and he has been followed by Klein (*1 Samuel*, p. 84) and Mayes ('Rise', p. 14). But Birch also showed that the story in 9.1–10.16 varies substantially from the 'form' elsewhere. For example, Saul's call is not direct, but mediated through Samuel. Van Seters (*The Life of Moses: The Yahwist as Historian in Exodus–Numbers* [Louisville, KY: Westminster/John Knox, 1994], p. 44) argues persuasively that the model here and in Judg. 6 was 'the holy war ideology of the late monarchy period...the creation of Dtr and unrelated to the origins of the prophetic call narratives'.

44. Schmidt, *Menschlicher Erfolg*, pp. 88-93. On the wordplays with *nāgîd* as further evidence of Dtr's creativity in this passage, see Edelman, *King Saul*, pp. 44-45.

45. Cf. Mettinger, *King and Messiah*, pp. 151-84; Van Seters, *In Search of History*, pp. 266-68.

but his kingdom was rejected (13.14) in favor of David (21.30; 2 Sam. 5.2; 6.21), who was promised an eternal kingdom (2 Sam. 7.8) as a reward for his faithfulness.

Schmidt's arguments for separating the aetiology in 10.5-6, 10aβ-13a as a distinct redactional layer are based on two observations.[46] First, he notes that the plural ויבא in v. 10aα is disruptive since Saul alone is the subject in the immediate context. The plural fits well, however, as an introduction to the conversation with Saul's uncle in vv. 14-16, since the uncle addresses both Saul and his servant. Secondly, like most scholars, Schmidt observes that the MT's reading in v. 13, 'he came to the high place' (ויבא הבמה), makes no sense. But unlike most scholars, Schmidt prefers the LXX here (εις τον βουνον = הגבעה) to the conjectural reading, הביתה. The LXX reading contradicts the mention of Gibeah in v. 10a. Schmidt sees this as a confirmation of the LXX in v. 13 as the *lectio difficilior*, and he contends that vv. 10aβ-13a were inserted into the text using the technique of *Wiederaufnahme* in the repetition of 'he/they came to Gibeah'. Thus, the aetiology in these verses as well as the prediction of it in vv. 5-6 are secondary insertions.[47]

Schmidt's argument is again well reasoned and may be correct, but there are a few considerations that weaken his case. First, Schmidt depends heavily on the LXX reading in 10.13. He is correct that 'to Gibeah' here is the *lectio difficilior*, but it so blatantly contradicts v. 10 that one must question whether an editor would have been so clumsy. Moreover, the reading הביתה in v. 13 is not without textual support, since Josephus (*Ant.* 6.58) seems to have found such a reading in his text of Samuel. Finally, the singular 'sign' in 10.1 (LXX) seems to refer in the present story to Saul's prophesying, since this is the only one of Samuel's predictions in vv. 2-6 whose fulfillment is subsequently detailed. If vv. 5-6, 10aβ-13a are taken as later additions, it becomes less clear exactly what the one confirmatory sign was.[48] In light of these considerations, it may be better to see the incorporation of this aetiology also as the work of the editor who added the overlay to the original story behind 9.1–10.16, namely Dtr.[49]

---

46. Schmidt, *Menschlicher Erfolg*, pp. 115-17.

47. Schmidt also takes שם in v. 10aα as an addition from the same hand.

48. Schmidt (p. 85 n. 3) avoids this problem because he reads with the MT in 10.1.

49. The doublet to this aetiology in 1 Sam. 19 is a post-Dtr addition. As

Whatever the situation with the aetiology in 10.5-6, 10aβ-13a, the most important conclusion for our immediate purposes is the recognition that the primary editor in 9.1–10.16 was Dtr. It was he who transformed the old story of Saul's search for his father's asses into an account of his anointing as king by Samuel. This was part of Dtr's overall presentation of the transition to monarchy in chs. 9–11, since it was also Dtr who wrote the endings in 10.14-16; 10.26-27a; 11.14-15 that serve to bind their respective stories into a unit which presents Saul's rise to the throne in stages.

3. *10.27b–11.15*. From a literary-critical perspective, the account of Saul's rescue of Jabesh-Gilead is more straightforward than that of 9.1–10.16. Besides the framework in 11.12-14, later additions are present only in the mention of Samuel in 11.7 ('and after Samuel') and possibly in the reference to Judah in v. 8. Otherwise, the story is independent and self-contained. Its original beginning, which can now be reconstructed from the Qumran evidence (see n. 5), shows that the story is not a fragment of a longer account, and there are no connections within the original story to 9.1–10.16 or 10.17-27a or to any of the surrounding material. The story did not originally presuppose that Saul was king. Thus, in vv. 3-5 the messengers do not go straight to Saul for help, but he learns only indirectly of Jabesh's plight when the messengers 'happen' to come to Gibeah in their trek through 'all the territory of Israel'. Also, in the original ending of the story in v. 15 the people make Saul king for the first time in response to his successful leadership against Nahash.

The original story, however, has been transformed by editorial additions into the final stage of Saul's movement to kingship. The insertion of Samuel in a leadership role in 11.7 presupposes the background of chs. 1–10 and helps to incorporate 10.27b–11.15 into the context, where the theme is the transition of leadership. 11.12-13 is part of the frame, with 10.26-27a and 10.14-16, which allows the three accounts to be read sequentially: in 9.1–10.16 Saul was anointed privately; in 10.17-

Schmidt (*Menschlicher Erfolg*, p. 103) points out, it presupposes David's acquaintance with Samuel in 16.1-13, itself a post-Dtr addition (cf. Van Seters, *In Search of History*, pp. 261-64). While it is possible that both versions of the aetiology were added later, it seems more likely that they come from different levels of writing, since their perspective on Saul is so different. This is another reason for attributing the incorporation of the aetiology in ch. 10 to Dtr.

27a he was designated publicly; in 10.27a he is king *de jure*; and by the end of ch. 11 he has proven himself and becomes king *de facto*. 11.14 furthers the editorial unity by having Samuel refer to 'renewing' the kingship in the assumption that Saul has already been made king. Allusions to this story in the surrounding material (e.g. 10.1 and 12.12) are also from Dtr and contribute to the overall unity of chs. 8–12.

The obvious original independence of the story in ch. 11 is important for what it indicates about the composition of chs. 9–11. While less obvious, the tale behind 9.1–10.16 was also originally independent. Neither story was connected with any other material in the surrounding chapters prior to Dtr's editorial work. He tied them together with the framework texts in 10.14-16; 10.26-27a; 11.14-15 and with his composition of 10.17-27a. I might add that despite the presence of post-Dtr additions and glosses, there is no evidence of any systematic redaction of chs. 9–11 beyond Dtr's. This will be of greater concern in what follows.

c. *1 Samuel 8–12*

1. *1 Samuel 8*. The perception of an anti-monarchical *Tendenz* in this chapter was put forward by Wellhausen and assumed by Noth.[50] The same perception has led more recent scholars to assign the bulk of the chapter either to a pre-Dtr (especially prophetic) writer[51] or to a later Deuteronomist (DtrN).[52] But assumed ideology is a poor criterion for source division, and these redactional distinctions lack strong literary support. A better approach is to focus first on the literary shape of the chapter and then to try to understand its ideology on its own terms.

That this chapter as it stands is a Deuteronomistic composition is apparent from the sprinkles of Deuteronomistic language, especially in v. 8 ('from the day I brought you up from Egypt', 'abandon' [עזב], and 'serve other gods') and v. 18 ('cry out'), but also throughout the chapter: 'like all the nations' (vv. 5, 20),[53] 'reject' (מאס, v. 7), 'warn' (העיד + ב, v. 9), and 'refuse to hear' (v. 19).[54]

50. Wellhausen, *Prolegomena*, pp. 254-56; Noth, *Studien*, pp. 54-57.

51. So McCarter, *1 Samuel*, pp. 16-20, 159-62; cf. Birch, *Rise*, pp. 21-29. On previous attempts, particularly by Weiser (*Samuel*, pp. 25-45), to find an even earlier narrative behind this chapter, see Boecker, *Beurteilung*, pp. 11-16.

52. So Veijola, *Das Königtum*, pp. 53-72 and Dietrich, *David*, pp. 90-93, 168.

53. Birch, *Rise*, p. 22.

54. On these last three expressions see Veijola, *Das Königtum*, pp. 54-60.

Some scholars have postulated a pre-Dtr source behind all or part of vv. 1-7, where they perceive older information and a tension regarding the reason for the people's demand for a king, i.e., whether it was prompted by Samuel's old age and the misbehavior of his sons or the people's rejection of YHWH in order to be like the nations.[55] But while the sons' names may preserve older tradition, the details about their judgeship in vv. 1-3 are artificial and reflect Deuteronomic concerns.[56] Nor does the tension concerning the people's demand indicate different hands. Verse 5 mentions Samuel's age and his wayward sons as well as the desire to be like the nations, and it is Deuteronomistic.[57] This is similar to 1 Kings 11–12, where Dtr gives a theological reason (Solomon's sin) in addition to political and economic ones for the division of the kingdom.

It has also been proposed that the 'right/custom of the king' in vv. 11-17 was an independent document—either a recounting of

55. Birch, *Rise*, pp. 26-27; Dietrich, *David*, pp. 90-91; Moenikes, *Ablehnung*, pp. 23-29.

56. O'Brien (*Reassessment*, pp. 109-10) points out the similarity of vv. 1-3 to the judgment formulas in Kings and to concerns for social justice in Deuteronomy. Van Seters (*In Search of History*, p. 251) notes that the reference to Beersheba is anachronistic and that Dtr likely borrowed the motif of the rebellious sons from the story of Eli. Moenikes's contention (*Ablehnung*, pp. 23-24) that v. 2b alone is redactional overlooks these indications of Dtr's hand in vv. 1-3 as a whole, and his explanation of the motivation for adding v. 2b is weak.

57. Efforts to explain the Deuteronomistic nature of this verse redactionally disagree widely and are not convincing. Birch (*Rise*, pp. 26-27) sees only the last phrase of v. 5 as Dtr's insertion into the prophetic account in vv. 1-7. But there is no real literary evidence for this view, and it does not explain the tension described above. McCarter's recognition of the similarity of v. 5 to Deut. 17.14 forces him to speak of his Prophetic History as 'proto-Deuteronomic' (*1 Samuel*, p. 156). Dietrich (*David*, pp. 90-91) takes vv. 6-20a as an insertion by DtrN into the old Samuel-Saul story in vv. 1-5 + 20b. But this makes for an odd case of *Wiederaufnahme*, since it leaves v. 20b hanging. Veijola (*Das Königtum*, pp. 54-55), similarly, gives vv. 6-22a to DtrN but then assigns vv. 1-5 to DtrG because of the Deuteronomistic language in v. 5. O'Brien (*Reassessment*, pp. 109-12) attributes vv. 1-6a to Dtr because of v. 5 but vv. 6b-7aα + 9-10 and 7aβb-8 to separate additions within a later DtrN stage of redaction. Moenikes (*Ablehnung*, pp. 23-30) also sees vv. 7aβb, 9, 18-22a on the one hand and vv. 8, 10 on the other as successive reworkings of a basic account in vv. 1-7aα, 9, 11-17, 22a. Since 10.18-19 have been shown to be of a piece with the Dtr unit in 10.17-27a, there is no reason to see 8.7aβ-8 as an insertion by *Wiederaufnahme* into Dtr's unit in ch. 8.

Israel's experience with a king or a treaty document—because of its lack of Deuteronomistic language and concerns.[58] But the content of these verses—essentially a list of items that the king will require—does not leave room for Deuteronomistic language. Also, since the passage's concern is the social, not theological, consequences of the specific demand for kingship, it is not surprising that this is not an issue for Dtr elsewhere. Finally, v. 18, which is Deuteronomistic, is the capstone to vv. 11-17, so that there is no good reason to posit an older document behind these verses or to deny their authorship to Dtr.[59]

If this chapter is a literary unit, how is the tension regarding the reason for the people's request and God's response to it to be explained? Recent scholars have pointed out that it is the people's request for a king (v. 6), not the institution of monarchy *per se*, that is condemned as rejection (v. 7) and abandonment (v. 8) of YHWH.[60] Although there is no explanation as to why the request is evil, there are hints. Verse 20 reveals the real reason for the people's request—they want a king to fight their battles.[61] Their request evinces a lack of faith in YHWH. By placing their trust in a human leader, they abandon YHWH, just as they have abandoned him previously by trusting other gods (v. 8). This allusion to apostasy also shows that their urge to be like the nations is an implicit rejection of the uniqueness of YHWH and his desire for the distinctiveness of his people.[62] YHWH accedes to their request for a king, because there is nothing inherently wrong with kingship. But the people are naïve to think that it will be advantageous to them, since monarchy tends toward oppression—the point of vv. 11-

---

58. Cf. Crüsemann, *Widerstand*, pp. 61-62; Veijola, *Das Königtum*, pp. 60-66; Klein, *1 Samuel*, pp. 73-74.

59. Similarly, Birch, *Rise*, pp. 24-25.

60. G.E. Gerbrandt, *Kingship According to the Deuteronomistic History* (SBLDS, 87; Atlanta: Scholars Press, 1986), esp. pp. 143-54; Klein, *1 Samuel*, p. 79.

61. The three expressions in v. 20: 'judge us' (וּשְׁפָטָנוּ), 'go out before us' (וְיָצָא לְפָנֵינוּ), and 'fight our battles' (נִלְחַם מִלְחֲמֹתֵנוּ) are synonymous in this context. They refer not to three different functions but to the same function, a military one. On this entire issue, see Boecker's useful discussion (*Beurteilung*, pp. 19-35, esp. 32-34).

62. Compare Weiser, *Samuel*, p. 38: 'Wenn Israel werden will wie die anderen Völker, dann gibt es seine besondere Eigenart, das Volk Jahwes zu sein, auf und verfällt dem Einfluß einer heidnischen Königsideologie, in der es sein Vorbild sieht und seine vermeintliche Rettung sucht.'

18. Still, the form of government is not the real problem. It is, rather, the people's relationship to YHWH.

2. *1 Samuel 12*. According to Noth, Dtr wrote this speech as one of the structural pillars for his History; with it he brought the period of the judges to a close.[63] Scholars, by and large, have continued to affirm the Deuteronomistic nature of the chapter.[64] There can be little doubt that vv. 6-25 with their recitation of salvation history and their call to the people to choose obedience to YHWH are Deuteronomistic. The theophany in vv. 16-19 is part of the Deuteronomistic composition and not an older tradition, as Boecker has shown: YHWH's show of power both warns of the consequence of disobedience and answers the people's lack of trust in their request for a king in ch. 8.[65] Birch contends, on the basis of the formula 'Samuel said to the people' in the MT, that v. 6 begins a new unit in which Dtr radically expands the older address by Samuel.[66] However, McCarter, who accepts Birch's basic conclusion, shows that this formula is one of two variants that have been conflated in the MT and that the other, shorter variant is preferable.[67] This means that v. 6 does not begin a new unit, so there is no reason for distinguishing vv. 1-5 from vv. 6-25. The chapter is unified.[68]

63. Noth, *Studien*, p. 10. On these speeches as such, see now R.W. McLean, ' "These are the Words": Speeches in the Deuteronomistic History' (PhD dissertation, Vanderbilt University, Nashville, TN, 1994).

64. For a detailed treatment of the Deuteronomistic language in this chapter, see Veijola (*Das Königtum*, pp. 84-91), who ascribes it to his DtrN.

65. Boecker, *Beurteilung*, pp. 82-85. *Contra* Weiser, *Samuel*, p. 87.

66. Birch, *Rise*, pp. 64-65.

67. McCarter, *1 Samuel*, p. 210. The variants are ויאמר עד at the end of v. 5 and ויאמר שמואל אל העם עד at the beginning of v. 6 (reconstructed from the MT and LXX).

68. 12.12 implies that the demand for a king was motivated by the Ammonite threat in 10.27b–11.15, which is not mentioned in ch. 8. It seems best to regard this verse, with Noth (*Studien*, p. 60; cf. Boecker, *Beurteilung*, pp. 75-76; McCarter, *1 Samuel*, p. 215) as a free interpretation of the stories in chs. 8–11. For all of its awkwardness, the statement binds ch. 8 with chs. 11–12 and thus serves to reinforce the unity of the material on the advent of monarchy in chs. 8–12. The references to YHWH's anointed in 12.3, 5 also presuppose 9.1–10.16 and must have been written by the editor of chs. 8–12 as a whole, i.e., Dtr, despite Crüsemann's objections (*Widerstand*, p. 63). As with ch. 8 and 10.17-27a, Moenikes (*Ablehnung*, pp. 33-39) again divides this chapter between a *Grundschicht* and two *Bearbeitungen*. His literary arguments rely heavily on his conclusions for those two texts, which I have

Ideologically, Samuel's speech is much the same as the Dtr texts in ch. 8 and 10.17-27a. The message is linked with an extensive review of the *Heilsgeschichte* (vv. 8-11). The demand for a king is sinful because it shows a lack of faith in YHWH as their king (vv. 12, 19-20). Samuel's leadership is contrasted with the king's: he has not *taken* from the people (12.1-5) what the king will *take* (חקל; 8.11-17).[69] But there is no indication that monarchy *per se* is evil or else YHWH would surely not allow it. Boecker rightly stresses 12.14-15 (cf. vv. 20-21) as a key passage in the Deuteronomistic History that succinctly expresses Dtr's view of kingship: Israel's success or failure depends not on their form of government but on their obedience to YHWH.[70]

Attempts to assign ch. 12 to a later hand on the basis of differences in ideology or outlook are unconvincing. O'Brien finds the following features of the chapter to be different from DtrH:[71] (1) the use of the verb *mlk* in v. 2 for the establishment of the king; (2) different elements in the cycle of sin and deliverance in vv. 10-11; (3) the focus on the people rather than the king in vv. 14-15; and (4) the portrait of Samuel as both prophet and judge, conflated in vv. 1-5 rather than sequential, and as a preacher of the law in vv. 14-15 rather than an interpreter of history within the scheme of prophecy and fulfillment. But these differences are not significant and in some cases not real. (1) The reference to appointing a *nāgîd* was transitional in Dtr's usage, as shown above; he now uses *mlk* because the transition has occurred and Saul is king. (2) The cycle in vv. 10-11 is not so different from the one in the book of Judges and is essentially the same as in Judg. 10.6-10, so that O'Brien is forced to see this latter text also as secondary. (3) As is common in these speeches, Dtr sets the alternative of obedience or disobedience before the people in vv. 14-15, although the king is mentioned. The people are the focus because they have demanded a king. In Dtr's

---

countered. I shall argue below that his ideological arguments are equally unacceptable.

69. Boecker, *Beurteilung*, p. 70.

70. Boecker, *Beurteilung*, pp. 79-82.

71. O'Brien, *Reassessment*, pp. 109-28. Veijola's conclusion for ch. 12 (*Das Königtum*, pp. 84-91), while similar to O'Brien's, is argued differently. For one thing, Veijola is more consistent, since he recognizes the similarity of ch. 12 to ch. 8, assigning the bulk of both to DtrN, while O'Brien gives most of ch. 8 to DtrH (= DtrG). As with his treatment of ch. 8, Veijola's assignment of ch. 12 to DtrN on the basis of vocabulary is overly subtle and grounded in the perception of ideological differences.

account of the monarchy, the fates of king and people are intimately connected, precisely because the people respond to the king's lead by either going astray or obeying. (4) In 1 Samuel 1–6 Samuel's roles as priest and prophet are conflated, so that he is actually a prophet before he is a judge! His preaching of the law in vv. 14-15 is a function of his role not so much as prophet but as a leader in the tradition of Moses and Joshua. One must recall Noth's initial observation, reinforced by Boecker, that this is one of a series of texts that Dtr composed to structure his History by marking the boundary between two great periods in Israel's history.

Veijola contends that the whole of ch. 12 was inserted into the work of DtrG because it separates the first element of DtrG's standard accession formula, the statement of how the king came to power (11.15), from the other two elements, his age at accession and the length of his reign.[72] The weakness of this argument is exposed by close inspection of the other accession formulas in Samuel and Kings, where the situation is more complicated than Veijola acknowledges. The first element is stereotyped in the synchronisms between the kings of Israel and Judah in the book of Kings: 'X began to reign over Judah/Israel in the Y year of Z, king of Israel/Judah.' It is also stereotyped for the kings of Judah after the fall of Israel, but in these cases it is part of the death and burial formula of the predecessor: for example, 'Hezekiah slept with his ancestors, and his son Manasseh succeeded him' (2 Kgs 20.21; cf. 21.18, 26; 23.30; 24.6, 17). However, for Ishbaal (2 Sam. 2.8-9) and David (2 Sam. 5.1-3), who had no synchronism and whose succession of the previous king was more complicated, the information about how they came to the throne is not formulaic but in narrative form. The notice that Rehoboam reigned in Judah, which precedes his accession formula (1 Kgs 14.21), is a literary device that gives notice of the narrative's return to Rehoboam following the long section on Jeroboam in 1 Kgs 12.25–14.20. Thus, the statement of how a king came to power was not a part of the accession formula. This is also indicated by 2 Kgs 23.31-36; 24.6-8 where the writer included a good deal of additional information between the descriptions of how Jehoiakim and Jehoiachin came to the throne and their actual accession formulas.

Dtr typically explained how a king came to power before giving the accession formula, but the nature of his explanation varied. In the case

---

72. Veijola, *Das Königtum*, pp. 91-92.

of Saul, he spent chs. 8–11 explaining how Saul became king. He had Samuel 'supervise' this transition in 10.17-27a, where Samuel directed the ceremony in which Saul was chosen by lot, and then by inserting this account between the stories in 9.1–10.16 and 10.27b–11.15, which he had revised to include Samuel. But this meant that the structural and transitional speech that Dtr wrote for Samuel could only go where ch. 12 now stands—after the account of the passing of power and before that of Saul's reign proper in chs. 13–15*.

Results and Ramifications

Scholarly work on 1 Samuel 8–12 has been dominated by the assumption that Dtr took a negative view of monarchy. Noth's identification of Wellhausen's 'late source' as Dtr forced him to conclude that Dtr had been uncharacteristically heavy-handed in 1 Samuel 8–12 in order to counter his pro-monarchical sources, which he left essentially intact. Noth downplayed the importance of the promise to David for the Deuteronomistic History and thus overlooked the tension that his view of 1 Samuel 8–12 caused with the rest of the History. Von Rad and Cross highlighted the Davidic promise in 2 Samuel and 1 and 2 Kings,[73] but neither of them explained how it influenced Dtr's portrait of the beginning of the monarchy. Forced to account for Dtr's positive view of King David, recent scholars have reverted to the dichotomy between pro- and anti-monarchic writers, positing a pre-Dtr, prophetic editor or a later, nomistic Dtr. But the presupposition about Dtr's ideology remains the basis for much of this work, making it methodologically suspect.[74]

In my view, 1 Samuel 8–12* is a purposeful unit composed by Dtr, and there is no sound reason for positing any other redactor. Noth was correct about Dtr's sources being independent narratives and notices

73. G. von Rad, 'Die deuteronomistische Geschichtstheologie in den Königs-büchern', in *Gesammelte Studien zum Alten Testament*, I (TBü, 8; Munich: Chr. Kaiser Verlag, 1958), pp. 189-204; Cross, *Canaanite Myth*, pp. 274-89.

74. See the discussion of Boecker, *Beurteilung*, pp. 1-6. Note the following statements, which apply as well to more recent scholarship: '...in gleicher Weise wurde es allgemein üblich...die Beurteilung des Königtums als den entscheidenden Maßstab für die literarkritische Zuordnung der einzelnen Abschnitte zu benutzen' (p. 1) and 'Aber auch neuere Untersuchungen sind zu nennen, die...eben diese Einstellung zum Königtum zum Kriterium ihrer literarkritischen oder traditions-geschichtlichen Überlegungen machen' (p. 2). Cf. Halpern's remarks on method in *Constitution*, pp. 149-51.

that had not previously been compiled. Dtr revised the stories in 9.1–
10.16 and 10.27b–11.15 and put them together around his own composition in 10.17-27a, using the rubrics in 10.14-16; 10.26-27a; 11.12-
14 as adhesive. He then added the people's demand for a king, with the
responses from Samuel and YHWH, in ch. 8 and Samuel's farewell
speech in ch. 12. Some post-Dtr additions have crept into chs. 8–12, but
they also appear to be isolated rather than part of a systematic redaction.

Dtr's attitude toward kingship in these chapters can be described as
ambiguous or ambivalent at worst. It is certainly not the decidedly anti-
monarchical stance that so many scholars have tried to make it. The
people's request for a king was a sin, because it showed their lack of
faith in YHWH. But 1 Samuel 8–12 never says that kingship itself is
sinful. Indeed, by 10.27a, those who oppose the new king are called
bᵉnê bᵉlîyaʻal and in ch. 12, the establishment of the monarchy appears
as the latest of YHWH's *heilsgeschichtliche* deeds.[75] This same ambi-
valence surfaces in Dtr's retrospect on the monarchy as a whole: kings
caused Israel and Judah a great deal of trouble, but they also brought
some rewards. Israel went through a series of wicked royal houses, but
Judah was ruled by a single dynasty because of David's faithfulness.
Tracing that dynasty from David through Zedekiah, the evil monarchs
outnumber the good ones by only two, and until the last four kings there
are actually more good than evil![76] Thus, Dtr may be suspicious of
monarchy, but he does not see it as evil. After all, 1 Samuel 8–12 ends
with YHWH endorsing monarchy provided that the king and his subjects
remain faithful. This faithfulness to YHWH is Dtr's primary concern.

2. *1 Samuel 7, 13–15*

a. *Saul's Reign: 1 Samuel 13–15*
Dtr's dating formula in 13.1 begins his account of Saul's reign, and his
notices in 14.47-52 mark its end.[77] Saul's recruitment of soldiers in

75. Points stressed, respectively, by Boecker (*Beurteilung*, pp. 59-61) and
Weiser (*Samuel*, p. 90).

76. Those judged basically good by Dtr are: David, Solomon, Asa, Jehoshaphat,
Joash, Amaziah, Azariah, Jotham, Hezekiah, and Josiah. Those judged evil are:
Rehoboam, Abijam, Jehoram, Ahaziah, Athaliah, Ahaz, Manasseh, Amon, and then
following Josiah, Jehoahaz, Jehoiakim, Jehoiachin, and Zedekiah.

77. 13.1 has been omitted from the LXX apparently because of its corruptions
regarding both Saul's age at accession and the length of his reign. See McCarter,

14.52 sets the stage for David's appearance in 16.14-23. The inter-
vening material in 15.1–16.13, therefore, is a later addition because it
lies outside of Dtr's notices in 14.47-52 and interrupts the transition to
David as the focal character. This also accounts for the doublet between
13.7b-15 and ch. 15 regarding Saul's sin and the statement in 15.35,
contradicted by the subsequent narrative, that Samuel did not see Saul
again before he died.[78]

As hinted earlier (n. 36), the battle story for Saul in chs. 13–14 was
originally independent of the material in chs. 8–12 and presupposes a
much later time. Saul is no longer a young man but has a son, Jonathan,
who is a warrior in his own right. There is a good deal of confusion in
the present account about the respective roles of Saul and Jonathan in
the conflict with the Philistines as well as its geographical setting. Birch
observed that much of the confusion is attributable to the insertion of
the references to Gilgal in vv. 4b, 7b-15a.[79] Although he tried to
attribute these verses to a pre-Dtr, prophetic writer, there are good
reasons for seeing them as Dtr's handiwork.[80] In vv. 13-14, the expressions 'you did not keep the commandment which YHWH your God
commanded you', 'YHWH would have established your kingdom over
Israel forever', and 'a man after his heart', as well as *nāgîd* are all

---

1 Samuel, pp. 222-23. On the Deuteronomistic origin of 14.47-51, cf. Veijola (*Das Königtum*, pp. 79-82), who notes the similarity to 10.1. See also Edelman, *King Saul*, p. 96. I think it more likely than Veijola that Dtr had source material for the summary of military successes in 14.47-48 and less likely than he that a separate source underlies the list of Saul's children in 14.49-51, which was readily available from narrative sources.

78. See Wellhausen, *Prolegomena*, pp. 260-64 and most recently Van Seters, *In Search of History*, pp. 258-64.

79. Birch, *Rise*, pp. 75-86. It may be that all of v. 4 is later. This would account for the tension introduced by the reference to Saul's defeat of a Philistine garrison in v. 4a. There is nothing outside of this verse to indicate the existence of a separate tradition or doublet for this event.

80. Birch, *Rise*, pp. 80-85. Birch's case is again based on form. Specifically, he argues from Westermann's *Basic Forms* that the prophetic judgment speech reflected in Samuel's oracle originated before the period of the writing prophets and disappeared shortly after that period began. But since Westermann assumes that the narratives containing oracles from pre-writing prophets in the Deuteronomistic History are historical, Birch's argument is essentially circular. Moreover, in this case Birch is forced to admit that the 'older oracle' has been adapted and 'represents something of a variant...since it is completely embedded in a narrative context' (p. 80), and it attests 'a late development in the form' (p. 83).

Deuteronomistic.[81] More importantly, these verses are concerned with and contribute to some of Dtr's key themes. They prepare the way for David and begin the contrast between him and Saul which will dominate the rest of 1 Samuel. An especially important part of that contrast is the way these verses set the stage for the promise of an enduring Davidic dynasty in 2 Samuel 7. Saul, like Jeroboam later on (1 Kgs 11.38; 14.8), contrasts with David. Each of them had the same opportunity for a dynasty, but only David was faithful enough to receive it.[82]

While Dtr did not deny Saul's military effectiveness (14.47-48), the story he chose to represent this in chs. 13–14 did not present Saul positively. It cast Jonathan as the hero and Saul as the maker of a foolish vow that nearly negated the victory.[83] Dtr enhanced the negative tone of the story by inserting the Gilgal episode in 13.7b-15a. This incident was a crucial element in Dtr's all-important theme of the Davidic promise. It not only explained why Saul's dynasty did not last but also prepared the way for the 'man after God's own heart' who would take Saul's place.[84]

b. *1 Samuel 7 and the Date of the Deuteronomistic History*
It is widely recognized that ch. 7 is inseparable from Dtr's narrative in chs. 8–12. Samuel's role as a judge, mentioned first in 7.6, 15-17, is presupposed by 8.1-5, and both attest Deuteronomistic revision.[85] In 7.15–8.5, Dtr plays on the juridical and militaristic senses of *šāpat* as

---

81. Veijola, *Die ewige Dynastie: David und die Entstehung seiner Dynastie nach der deuteronomistischen Darstellung* (AASF.B, 193; Helsinki: Suomalainen Tiedeakatemia, 1975), p. 56.

82. The theme also reaches back to Eli (1 Sam. 2.35), whose household was replaced by that of a 'faithful priest', not coincidentally, during David's reign.

83. The fact that Jonathan's violation is never properly atoned for casts an ominous shadow over his future and may be a hint, together with Samuel's denial of a dynasty for Saul, that Jonathan will not succeed his father.

84. The fact that only Saul's dynasty, not his reign, is condemned in 13.7b-15 is not a point in favor of retaining ch. 15 at the same level of writing. Indeed, one of the indications that ch. 15 is secondary is the fact that Saul's reign continues so long, at least in literary terms (the rest of 1 Samuel!) after he is rejected as king. For Dtr, Saul himself is not rejected as king. His reign continues so that the contrast between Saul and David may be presented. What is important for Dtr is that Saul's 'house' will not endure. Compare Dtr's pattern in the book of Kings for the Israelite dynasties described in McKenzie, *Trouble*, pp. 61-80.

85. On the Deuteronomistic revision of the traditional material behind 7.15-17, see Veijola, *Das Königtum*, pp. 34-35.

part of his description of the transition to monarchy.[86] Deuteronomistic
language occurs throughout ch. 7, especially in vv. 2-4, 13-14.[87] Verse
2 is typical of Dtr's editorial technique. It links the 'Ark Narrative',
which ends in v. 1, with the rest of ch. 7* by mentioning both the
residence of the ark at Kiriath-jearim and the repentance of the people
as a prelude to Samuel's instructions in vv. 3-14.[88] Whatever traditional
material may lie behind vv. 5-12, Dtr has bracketed and revised it for
his purposes.[89]

Chapter 7 also fits well with chs. 8–12 in Dtr's overall theological
perspective on the beginning of kingship. YHWH's deliverance of his
repentant people in ch. 7 balances their defeat at the hands of the
Philistines in ch. 4 and accords with Dtr's cyclic portrayal of history in
Judges, all the while demonstrating that a king is unnecessary if Israel
will but trust in YHWH.[90] The artificiality of Samuel's portrait corresponds to his transitional role in Dtr's program. As the last judge, his
career is paradigmatic in its incorporation of both deliverance and legal
functions.[91] The depiction of Samuel in this chapter also includes a role

86. So Dietrich (*David*, pp. 90-91), although he mistakenly assigns this linking
device to a pre-Dtr narrative rather than to Dtr.

87. See McCarter, *1 Samuel*, pp. 142-44 and Veijola, *Das Königtum*, pp. 30-31
for lists of Deuteronomistic terminology in these verses. Verses 3-4 have been
taken as an interpolation because of the repetition in vv. 3 and 5 of the announcement that Samuel addressed the people (cf. Dietrich, *David*, p. 87). This may be
correct, although vv. 3-4 make clear the otherwise unknown sin which the people
confess in v. 6.

88. This is Van Seters's observation (*In Search of History*, pp. 352-53), and it
holds true whether one reads ויפנו with the LXX (McCarter, *1 Samuel*, p. 141) or
ויניהו with the MT (Klein, *1 Samuel*, p. 64).

89. Birch, *Rise*, pp. 17-21, Dietrich, *David*, pp. 86-88, Klein, *1 Samuel*, pp. 64-
71, McCarter, *1 Samuel*, pp. 142-51, and O'Brien, *Reassessment*, pp. 105-106, all
find Deuteronomistic expansions of an older story in vv. 5-17. The statement in
v. 13 that the Philistines did not again enter the border of Israel stands in tension
with the following chapters. Some (e.g. McCarter) explain this tension by positing
an earlier source that Dtr has preserved. But it is probably better to understand this
statement, as its context in v. 13b suggests, as limited to Samuel's lifetime (so also
Veijola, *Das Königtum*, p. 78).

90. Cf. Boecker, *Beurteilung*, pp. 93-98.

91. Both Veijola (*Das Königtum*, pp. 30-38) and McCarter (*1 Samuel*, pp. 143-
45) observe the similarity of ch. 7 to Judg. 20, which is usually considered a late
addition. McCarter further points out that the description of Samuel as a deliverer
here is drawn largely from the framework of Judges and from Judg. 10.6-16. I see

as intercessor (vv. 5, 8); it is the means by which he delivers Israel. While this differs from the activity of other judges, it corresponds with that of prophetic figures such as Moses (Num. 21.7; Deut. 9.20), Jeremiah (Jer. 7.16; 11.14; 15.1, 19; 18.20; 29.7, 18; 37.3; 42.2, 20), and Samuel himself (1 Sam. 12.19, 23).[92] It is yet another way in which Dtr's Samuel combines otherwise distinct offices as a transitional figure.

The solidarity of ch. 7 with chs. 8–12 as Dtr's handiwork looms large in the consideration of the date of the Deuteronomistic History because of McCarter's recent revisitation of one of Wellhausen's arguments for the exilic date of his 'late source'.[93] The argument has to do with the references in these chapters to Mizpah as a place of assembly for Israel. 'Discussions of the provenance and literary history of this "Mizpah material" should be controlled by what we can establish about the history of Mizpah itself.'[94] Since it was only after the destruction of Jerusalem in 586 BCE that Mizpah gained prominence, these references, all but one of which occur in ch. 7, point to an exilic setting.[95]

McCarter treats the 'Mizpah material' (7.2–8.22; 10.17-27a; 12.1-25) as a separate strand or revision placed into Dtr's account, a position that is untenable in light of the foregoing literary analysis. Except for a few later additions, chs. 7–12 is a single composition by Dtr. The individual references to Mizpah cannot be removed as glosses,[96] nor can the 'Mizpah material' be isolated as a separate thread, nor could the entire six chapters be attributed to a later editor. But if the Mizpah argument is valid, and if chs. 7–12 form an integral part of Dtr's History, then the

---

no basis for Weiser's assertion (*Samuel*, pp. 16-21) that the combination of offices in the person of Samuel preserves genuine historical memory.

92. See Van Seters's discussion of intercession in these texts in *The Life of Moses*, pp. 171-75.

93. Wellhausen, *Prolegomena*, p. 256; McCarter, 'Books of Samuel', pp. 278-80.

94. McCarter, 'Books of Samuel', p. 278.

95. On the history of Mizpah and the case for its identification with Tell en-Nasbeh see the chapters by J. Muilenburg in *idem* and C.C. McCown (ed.), *Tell en Nasbeh*, I (New Haven: Yale University Press, 1947), pp. 13-49. Our knowledge of Mizpah's history is unaffected by the correctness of this identification, since it is based on literary sources.

96. As Muilenburg did with the references to Mizpah in Judg. 20–21 (*Tell en Nasbeh*, pp. 24-27) and as Birch (*Rise*, p. 13) erroneously accused him of doing in 1 Sam. 7–12.

notion of a pre-exilic date for the History is in jeopardy, and the arguments used to support it must be reconsidered.[97]

Obviously, this is not the place for a full reassessment of the date of the Deuteronomistic History, but a preliminary proposal is in order. Mizpah served as the capital for Gedaliah (2 Kgs 25.23), whose rule apparently lasted only seven months (2 Kgs 25.25), and there is no mention of the site again in extant sources until long after Gedaliah's assassination. Thus, the Mizpah references suggest a setting early in the exile, although the historical data for Mizpah by itself does not allow more specificity. However, the ending of the Deuteronomistic History in 2 Kings 25 provides important additional clues. I have long agreed with Friedman's contention that the notice of Jehoichin's release in 25.27-30, which presently concludes the History, is secondary.[98] There is a gap of nearly 25 years between the assassination of Gedaliah reported in 25.26 (586 BCE) and the release of Jehoiachin (c. 562). Included in that 25-year period was a third Babylonian incursion in c. 582 (Jer. 52.30), about which the text of 2 Kings is silent. It seems likely, therefore, that the History initially ended with the report of Gedaliah's assassination and the flight of part of the population to Egypt. This suggests that the History was written shortly after Gedaliah's assassination in 586 and no later than the exile of 582.[99] Noth's procedure of dating the History shortly after the last event it recorded was right in principle, but he was misled by the failure to recognize 25.27-30 as secondary.

This date may help to explain Dtr's ambivalent view of monarchy. So soon after the destruction of Jerusalem, he may have been able to maintain hope in the Davidic promise. It may even be that the Davidic promise in Dtr's History is a reflection of his support of the continuation of

---

97. My own tentative dating of the History to Josiah was based largely on the importance of the Davidic covenant in it. See McKenzie, *Trouble*, pp. 117-34, esp. pp. 133-34.

98. R.E. Friedman, *The Exile and Biblical Narrative* (HSM, 22; Chico, CA: Scholars Press, 1981), pp. 35-36; 'From Egypt to Egypt: Dtr[1] and Dtr[2]', in B. Halpern and J. Levenson (eds.), *Traditions in Transformation* (Festschrift F.M. Cross; Winona Lake, IN: Eisenbrauns, 1981), pp. 189-91.

99. This is similar to Dietrich's date of 580 for DtrG, although my proposal and the argument for it are more precise. Cf. W. Dietrich, *Prophetie und Geschichte: Eine redaktionsgeschichtliche Untersuchung zum deuteronomistischen Geschichtswerk* (FRLANT, 108; Göttingen: Vandenhoeck & Ruprecht, 1972), pp. 139-44.

the Davidic line against the non-Davidid, Gedaliah.[100] Perhaps this is also why Dtr does not mention Jeremiah, who favored Gedaliah. These are little more than speculations, of course, and they call for much more thought and research. I only hope that this proposal and its ramifications will be deemed worthy of further consideration by others.

100. See J.M. Miller and J.H. Hayes, *A History of Ancient Israel and Judah* (Philadelphia: Westminster Press, 1986), pp. 421-26, who contend that Gedaliah, whose title is never given in the Bible, was actually appointed king.

HISTORY AND LAW: DEUTERONOMISTIC HISTORIOGRAPHY AND DEUTERONOMIC LAW EXEMPLIFIED IN THE PASSAGE FROM THE PERIOD OF THE JUDGES TO THE MONARCHICAL PERIOD

Walter Dietrich

1. *Government of the Judges and Monarchy*

All through two, even three biblical books, Deuteronomistic historiography describes, with a surprising fullness, the pre-monarchical period of Israel. According to the internal chronology of the work, there were no less than two centuries during which Israel, become a people and settled in the country, lived without a king and state institutions. And when finally, we come to the foundation of the state, this in no way appeared, in the eyes of Deuteronomistic historiography, to be real progress: it would rather be a risky, even perilous, step.

Unlike Deuteronomistic historiography itself, historical-critical exegesis for a long time regarded the pre-monarchical period as a kind of awful emptiness.[1] Living outside the structures of the state could only mean living in chaos. Martin Noth was the first to succeed in finding some good aspects to the pre-monarchical period.[2] His thesis, according to which the Israelite tribal confederation would have been formed into an amphictyony, became widely dominant, at least in germanophone research, for more than a generation. It even gave rise to a whole series of secondary hypotheses. Since then, this thesis has lost practically all its appeal. Nevertheless, it has been replaced by other models that assume as well the possibility of a harmonious existence amongst the tribes before the emergence of the state.[3]

---

1. This is not surprising, inasmuch as critical exegesis has been carried on under the enlightened auspices of the state and most often in state institutions.

2. See his *Das System der zwölf Stämme Israels* (BWANT, 4/1; Stuttgart: Kohlhammer, 1930). It is not by chance that this work appeared in a period when in Germany state-controlled gigantomania began to assert itself.

3. Cf. F. Crüsemann, *Der Widerstand gegen das Königtum: Die antikönig-*

However, under no circumstances does Deuteronomistic historiography describe this way of existence as ideal or exemplary. According
to the programmatic introduction in Judges 2, there rapidly developed,
after the brilliant beginnings under Moses and Joshua, an alienation
between Israel and Yahweh. By way of chastisement, God causes
enemies from outside to penetrate into the country. These, it is true, are
always expelled again by deliverers sent by God, if Israel repents at all,
but not without that implying for Israel long periods of suffering. What
is more, the succession of charismatic leaders obviously tends towards
decadence.[4] Moreover, interspersed in the narrative, the so-called Minor
Judges[5] are not in a position to prevent the proliferation of the
deviations and violence among the tribes. The longer the period of the
judges continues, the more we are present at the eruption of troubles
and civil wars.[6] Towards the end of the period, we even see strange and
brutal scenes increase,[7] and it is quite logical that the book of Judges

*lichen Texte des Alten Testaments und der Kampf um den frühen israelitischen
Staat* (WMANT, 49; Neukirchen–Vluyn: Neukirchener Verlag, 1978), pp. 194-97;
N.K. Gottwald, *The Tribes of Yahweh: A Sociology of the Religion of Liberated
Israel 1250–1050 B.C.E.* (Maryknoll, NY: Orbis Books, 1979), pp. 489-589; N.P.
Lemche, *Early Israel. Anthropological and Historical Studies on Israelite Society
Before the Monarchy* (VTSup, 37: Leiden: E.J. Brill, 1985), pp. 202-205; R. Neu,
*Von der Anarchie zum Staat: Entwicklungsgeschichte Israels vom Nomadentum zur
Monarchie im Spiegel der Ethnosoziologie* (Neukirchen–Vluyn: Neukirchener Ver-
lag, 1992), pp. 179-81; R. Albertz, *Religionsgeschichte Israels in alttestamentlicher
Zeit*, I (Grundrisse zun Alten Testament, 8.1; Göttingen: Vandenhoeck & Ruprecht,
1992), pp. 104-106. In works like these, the contemporary intellectual climate could
have had its influence, particularly by inspiring in them a certain mistrust in regard
to state authority.

4.   Othniel, odourless and colourless—and nevertheless the only irreproachable
one among all the judges, and what is more, Judaean—will have been invented and
placed at the head of the list by the Deuteronomistic historiographer with the
express purpose of laying down the principle and setting off the sequence of
decline: Ehud was audacious, but not really noble; Gideon led to idolatry, and his
son violently usurped power; Jephthah let himself be led into tragic violence; Samson was a brawler and womanizer; Eli was responsible for the loss not only of the
ark but also of Israel's sovereignty.

5.   Cf. the lists in Judg. 10.1-5; 12.7-15 and, in regard to them, the bold hypothesis of M. Noth, 'Das Amt des "Richters Israels" ' (1950), repr. in *Gesammelte
Studien zum Alten Testament*, II (TBü, 39; Munich: Chr. Kaiser Verlag, 1969),
pp. 71-85.

6.   Judg. 9; 12.1-7.

7.   It is therefore not surprising that Noth, who is thought to have in common

comes to an end with the following report:[8] 'In those days, there was no king in Israel; each [man] did what seemed right in his own eyes' (Judg. 21.25). This formula is obviously Deuteronomistic[9] and it expresses a clearly negative judgment on the pre-monarchical period. We now await the monarchy, and this is not long in announcing itself in 1 Samuel 1 with the appearance of 'solicited' (שָׁאוּל),[10] which then materializes, beginning in 1 Samuel 9, in the person of Saul.

In Deuteronomistic historiography, this feature favourable to the monarchy (and critical in regard to the judges) is in annoying contradiction with the thesis defended by Martin Noth, the 'father of Deuteronomistic Historiography',[11] a thesis according to which 'the Deuteronomist' would have judged in an entirely negative way the foundation and institution of the monarchy.[12] The main witness in support of this interpretation is found by Noth in the supposed anti-monarchical sequence within 1 Samuel 7–12, a sequence considered by earlier research to be late, idealistic and remote from historical events. Noth gave this sequence a central place in Deuteronomistic historiography, since in it are reflected, according to him, the terrible experiences linked up with monarchy as well as the traumatism of the lost sovereignty.[13]

with Deuteronomistic historiography a certain sympathy for this form of organization in pre-monarchical Israel, considered the so-called 'appendices' of Judg. 17–21, including the stories of Samson (Judges 13–16), as 'additions' foreign to the work of the Deuteronomist: *Überlieferungsgeschichtliche Studien: Die sammelnden und bearbeitenden Geschichtswerke im Alten Testament* (Tübingen: Max Niemeyer, 3rd edn, 1967), p. 54 n. 2, and p. 61. For the genealogy of this idea, cf. T. Veijola, *Das Königtum in der Beurteilung der deuteronomistischen Historiographie: Eine redaktionsgeschichtliche Untersuchung* (AASF.B, 198; Helsinki: Suomalainen Tiedeakatemia, 1977), p. 16 n. 4.

8. Like a refrain, this phrase is found in Judg. 17.6; 18.1; 19.1; 21.25.

9. Veijola, *Das Königtum*, pp. 15-16.

10. The verb שׁאל is a key word in 1 Sam. 1.

11. This title had been applied to Noth, perhaps without malicious intent, by O. Eissfeldt (*Einleitung in das Alte Testament unter Einschluss der Apokryphen und Pseudepigraphen* [Tübingen: J.C.B. Mohr, 3rd edn, 1964], p. 323).

12. Since Julius Wellhausen (*Die Composition des Hexateuchs und der historischen Bücher des Alten Testaments* [Berlin: Georg Reimer, 3rd edn, 1899], pp. 240-45), the anti-monarchical texture within 1 Sam. 7–12 is held to be late. Noth was the first to assign it a decisive place in Deuteronomistic historiography's 'theology of history' (*Überlieferungsgeschichtliche Studien*, pp. 55-60).

13. Again, it is perhaps not by chance that the *Überlieferungsgeschichtliche*

Criticism of the monarchy was certainly formulated long before the beginning of the first book of Samuel. Israel had already had occasion—and also the inclination!—to institute the monarchy: did it not offer power to Gideon following his victory over the Midianites, and was not this power defined as hereditary, that is to say, making dynastic monarchy acceptable? But Gideon declined this offer by replying:

> I will not rule over you.
> And my son will not rule over you.
> But YHWH will rule over you (Judg. 8.23).

This wording too seems to be Deuteronomistic. It asserts—nothing less!—that the installation of a human sovereign amounts to a deposition of YHWH. Israel subsequently experienced this with the 'son' of Gideon, Abimelech, who on his own initiative had appropriated power over large parts of central Palestine and provided a first disastrous incarnation of monarchy. Only the least worthy and most brutal subjects are inclined to become kings. This is how Jotham's fable perceives the king, with pity on his poor subjects![14]

What is the correct interpretation then? That the Deuteronomistic tradition regarded the system of judges as insufficient and the monarchy necessary and good—or that it considered the monarchy as useless and evil, while the system of judges represented in its eyes a form of political organization in conformity with Israel's vocation? Are the two viewpoints opposed to one another or are they compatible? Do they convey a form of dialectical thought? Or do they reveal divergent positions, stemming from different chronological, political and theological contexts?

Studien appeared in 1943, in a period when the (German) state had transformed itself into a hybrid monster and was already doomed to disaster. To put this in perspective and to follow the history of the research, cf. S.L. McKenzie and P.M. Graham (eds.), *The History of Israel's Traditions: The Heritage of Martin Noth* (JSOTSup, 182; Sheffield: Sheffield Academic Press, 1994).

14. Jotham's fable is according to Martin Buber (*Königtum Gottes* [Heidelberg: Schneider, 3rd edn, 1956], p. 24) the strongest anti-monarchical poem in world literature. Veijola (*Das Königtum*, pp. 103-14) has tried to endorse the thesis according to which this poem was only introduced at a late stage of the redaction and set out a new emphasis, at the opposite extreme from the plaintive refrain on the absence of a king in Judg. 17.6, etc.

2. *Law of the Judges and Period of the Judges*

Anyone who has read the Deuteronomistic historiography from its beginning does come to it without having been prepared for the debate that permeates it, in the book of Judges as well as in 1 Samuel, on the matter of the alternative judges/kings and the respective merits and dangers of each of these two forms of government. Already on the other side of the Jordan, even before the conquest, Moses reflected on the question and established ordinances concerning the future organization of the people of Israel. In Deuteronomy 16–18, the fundamental political offices of the future Israel are given their juridical foundation. Apart from the office of priest and that of prophet (Deut. 18), it is precisely a question of the office of judge (Deut. 16.18–17.13) and that of king (Deut. 17.14-20). We must keep this in mind when, in reading the historiographical work, we come across, almost everywhere, these same institutions. Besides, this is an especially illuminative example of the fullness and scope of the thematic and historical frameworks that give structure to the work as a whole.[15]

We know that the Deuteronomic Law was intended to be a substitute for the Code of the Covenant (Exod. 21–23), which is older. But it is precisely in the articles on the offices, on which the older code was silent, that the Deuteronomic Law could legislate with the most originality and freedom. It is not absurd to assume that that happened with regard to the real history of Israel: the authors of Deuteronomy 16–18 knew that there had been judges and kings in Israel (just like priests and prophets), and they wanted the details of the exercise of these functions to be regulated in the Torah.

Consequently, the following question comes up: did the laws regulating public functions reflect the real practice at a given moment in history, or were they intended to be a more active influence on the behaviour of the judges and kings? Or again, did they belong to a period in which there were no longer either judges or kings and in which the laws concerning them could only be of service as a

---

15. This is to answer C. Westermann, *Die Geschichtsbücher des Alten Testaments: Gab es ein deuteronomistisches Geschichtswerk?* (TBü, 87; Gütersloh: Chr. Kaiser Verlag, 1994), who has published the most recent—and not very convincing—attack on the existence of a Deuteronomistic historiography in the form of a continuous work. See my review in *TLZ* 120 (1995), pp. 332-34.

retrospective reflection. Their goal would then be to verify whether the conduct of the judges and kings had been in conformity or not with the divine will. In other words, are these laws Deuteronomic or Deuteronomistic?

It is not possible to give a unequivocal response to this question. In regard to the *law for the judges*, it is less the heroes of the book of Judges—whether it be question of the 'Minor' or the 'Major' Judges—who seem to be envisaged than holders of a function in the monarchical period. Several indications point in this direction: in the book of Judges, the שֹׁפְטִים are always the unique holders of this function, and nowhere do we see them associated with the שֹׁטְרִים as in Deut. 16.18. Furthermore, their function is to be in charge of the whole of Israel, whereas according to Deut. 16.18 the judges should exercise their office in all the 'gates', that is to say in all the fortified towns. And it goes without saying that in the period of the judges there was no appeal court in Jerusalem to which the difficult cases could be referred (Deut. 17.8-13). Finally, according to Deut. 16.18, it is up to Israel to 'appoint' judges for themselves (נתן ל), whereas the heroes of the period of the judges were 'seized' (צלח) by the spirit of YHWH—or found themselves in some other way called by YHWH—and even the 'Minor Judges' 'went up' (קום) or simply 'judged/governed' (שׁפט) without having been invested by Israel.

We can conclude from these considerations that Deut. 16.18–17.13 is not intended to be a theoretical prospectus on the Deuteronomistic book of Judges, but is to be explained rather as an attempt in the Josianic period to regulate the judicial institution in Judah.[16] It is in this perspective that the specific tasks attributed to these judges are justified: they had, basically, to apply the positive law (מִשׁפָּט 16.19) in an incorruptible spirit and ensure in this way that there was justice (צדק 16.20). Then, more specifically, they had to proceed against every violation of

---

16. Cf. H. Niehr, *Rechtsprechung in Israel: Untersuchungen zur Geschichte der Gerichtsorganisation im Alten Testament* (SBS, 130; Stuttgart: Katholisches Bibelwerk, 1987), pp. 96-99; U. Rüterswörden, *Von der politischen Gemeinschaft zur Gemeinde: Studien zu Dt 16,18–18,22* (BBB, 65; Frankfurt: Athenäum, 1987), pp. 89-90. On the other hand, C. Schäfer-Lichtenberger (*Josua und Salomo: Eine Studie zu Autorität und Legitimität des Nachfolgers im Alten Testament* [VTSup, 58; Leiden: E.J. Brill, 1995], p. 367) understands the laws relative to various public functions as the expression of a theological reflection on the social constitution of Israel, in view of its post-exilic reorganization. In my opinion, the attribution of the whole passage to the Deuteronomistic redaction is not justified.

the commandment on exclusive veneration of YHWH (16.21-22; 17.1-7). This latter preoccupation is perfectly explainable in the context of the religious policy of Josiah and the disputes that arose from this.

If the law on judges is Deuteronomic, this does not mean that the Deuteronomistic historiographers could not have considered it under its historiographic aspect as well, or, to express it in a more general way, that they would not have been concerned about placing their historiography under the illumination of the Law. The mere fact that the office of judge is the first to be dealt with in the law on public offices shows the will of the Deuteronomists to conform to the development of their historiography. Anyone coming from Deuteronomy 16, who discovers in Judg. 2.16-19 the programme of the period of the 'judges' and, next,[17] reads what the accounts say about the exercising of 'judgment' by these 'judges',[18] could not do anything else but establish a link with the institution of judge foreseen by the Torah and, as a result, consider that institution to be legitimate and beneficial. On the other hand, such a one will be shocked when—in the continuation of the narrative and, strangely, to an ever increasing extent—the judges will be seen to be failing at their task. Gideon, Jephthah, and even more, Samson, are certainly valiant heroes, endowed with the spirit of God, and yet they do not show themselves leaders of Israel totally worthy of confidence, especially when it comes to religious matters. Eli no longer possesses divine power. As for his sons and the sons of Samuel, they no longer even meet the minimal requirements of impartiality expected of a judge and formulated in Deut. 16.18-20.

This means that it is in the Deuteronomic law on judges that Deuteronomistic historiography, without having to say so, draws its criteria for an assessment of the individual 'judges' and of the period of the judges as a whole. In the perspective of this historiography, it is precisely to the extent that the judges are less and less able to respond to the demands of the Torah that they prepare the transition towards the monarchy.

17. It is true that the judges already appear earlier in the texts, but always as functionaries among others, therefore without any specifically great importance: Josh. 8.33; 23.2; 24.1. All these passages are Deuteronomistic or even later.

18. Judg. 3.10 (Othniel); 4.4 (Deborah); 15.20; 16.31 (Samson); 1 Sam. 4.18 (Eli); 7.15 (Samuel)—all Deuteronomistic passages. The references that could be pre-Deuteronomistic are found in the list of Minor Judges in Judg. 10.1-5; 12.7-15 and in the notice in 1 Sam. 7.16.

Israel Constructs its History

3. *Foundation of the State and Monarchy*

Moses as legislator foresaw that one day,[19] Israel would find itself obsessed with the following idea:

> I want to appoint over me a king like all the nations round me! (Deut. 17.14b)

And, in the days of Samuel, the Israelite Elders actually came to find the prophet and said to him:

> Appoint a king for us[20] to judge/rule over us like all the other nations [have]! (1 Sam. 8.5)

It is hardly thinkable that these two passages would have been formulated independently from one another. We can envisage three possibilities: either Deuteronomy 17 is older, and 1 Samuel was formulated to echo it; or the two passages are due to one and the same author; or again, it is 1 Samuel 8 that has priority, and Deuteronomy 17 is formulated in the intention to prepare this scene.

Although the verbal near-correspondences (שׂים, מלך, כל הגוים) could suggest the second possibility, that of a synchronic origin, some nuances and divergences that are apparently not arbitrary separate the two texts and call for an explanation. These differences all indicate an influence going from 1 Sam. 8.5 to Deut. 17.14.[21] If in Deuteronomy 17, it is the people[22] who are the sovereign power and express the desire

---

19. The formula for historicizing 'when you reach the land that YHWH your God is giving you, and have taken possession of it and settled there' (Deut. 17.14) is met in a quite similar form several times and provides at the same time the redactional basis for the following text. A pre-Deuteronomistic textual form can hardly be reconstructed. See the attribution of Deut. 17.14-20 to the phase of Deuteronomistic reelaboration by authors such as H.D. Preuss (*Deuteronomium* [EdF, 164; Darmstadt: Wissenschaftliche Buchgesellschaft, 1982], p. 54) and E. Otto (*Theologische Ethik des Alten Testaments* [Theologische Wissenschaft, 3.2; Stuttgart: W. Kohlhammer, 1994], p. 195).

20. The change of preposition between Deut. 17.14 and 1 Sam. 8.5 is striking. If the ל of the latter text has the same meaning as the על of the former, then the formulation of Deut. 17.14 could be still more critical in regard to the monarchy than that of 1 Sam. 8.5.

21. Rüterswörden, *Studien*, p. 58, votes in the opposite direction. He considers 1 Sam. 8.5—without any discussion—to be Deuteronomistic.

22. F. Crüsemann (*Die Tora: Theologie und Sozialgeschichte des alttestament-*

to have a king, it is the Elders who appeal to Samuel, and this latter step is evidently easier to imagine, since it is more concrete. In 1 Sam. 8.5 the king is pictured being entrusted with the mission of שפט. If Deut. 17.14 passes over this definition in silence, that is probably due to the fact that in the Deuteronomic code a law on שפטים has just been announced and the offices of 'judge' and 'king' must be clearly distinguished. The preposition על, used in Deut. 17.14, often has a negative connotation: 'from above', 'against', but that is never the case with the preposition ל used in 1 Sam. 8.5. In 1 Sam. 8.5, the desire to have a king is motivated by referring to what is done among 'all the nations', whereas Deut. 17.14 speaks of 'all the surrounding nations'. The difference would seem minimal, but the term (ות)סבב refers to the Dtr concept of the conquest according to which Canaan would have been entirely emptied of its inhabitants by the Israelite conquest and other nations no longer existed after that except in the 'surroundings': it is therefore from these regions exterior to the country that the nations would have continued to be a threat hanging over the Israelites, whether that would be through warlike incursions, through incitements to idolatry,[23] or even by the propagation of the monarchy. If all the indications are not misleading, Deut. 17.14 is an intended and consciously varying anticipation of 1 Sam. 8.5. So it is from the formulation of the Law that the description of the historical development sustains a sudden deep shadow.

If we read the account in 1 Sam. 8.1-22 for its own sake, we get the impression that the Elders have good reasons to desire the establishment of a king:[24] they formulate this desire relatively innocently and in

lichen Gesetzes [Munich: Chr. Kaiser Verlag, 1992], p. 257) contends that the Deuteronomic 'you' is in principle addressed to the *'ām-hā'āreṣ*, but that is impossible, if only because of the *Šema' Yiśrā'ēl* of Deut. 6.5.

23. Deut. 6.14; 12.10; 13.8; Judg. 2.12, 14; 8.34. Joshua (Josh. 21.44) and David (2 Sam. 7.1; 1 Kgs 5.18) succeeded—for a limited time—in giving 'rest' from these enemies. For the distinction between these two notions of the conquest—that in which foreign peoples only survived in the *surroundings* of the country and that in which there were also some of the people who remained *in* the country—cf. R. Smend, 'Das Gesetz und die Völker: Ein Beitrag zur deuteronomistischen Redaktionsgeschichte', in H.W. Wolff (ed.), *Probleme biblischer Theologie* (Festschrift G. von Rad; Munich: Chr. Kaiser Verlag, 1971), pp. 494-509, reprinted in R. Smend, *Die Mitte des Alten Testaments: Gesammelte Studien*, 1 (BEvT, 99; Munich: Chr. Kaiser Verlag, 1986), pp. 124-37.

24. They could refer not only to the institutions of all the other peoples, but also

all good conscience.[25] It is only if we read the account in the light of Deuteronomy 17 that we surmise that the people of Israel are about to procure a king not 'for' themselves, but 'over' or even 'against' themselves, and that evolution is going to lead the people to submit themselves to the 'surrounding nations', not materially at first, but on the spiritual plane. In that perspective, Samuel's negative reaction to the desire for the institution of the monarchy is not surprising: 'It displeased Samuel that they should say: "Give us a king to judge us". And Samuel prayed to YHWH' (1 Sam. 8.6). It has been wondered whether 'the narrator' had not tried here to put Samuel in an ambiguous light: Samuel, as a holder of the office of judge, would have been personally affected by the demand for a 'king to judge us', and his reaction would reveal his sensitiveness. So it would only be after a painstaking process of soul therapy that God would have brought Samuel to better sentiments.[26] As a matter of fact, on one point, all—Samuel, God and Moses—are in agreement: the monarchy is dangerous!

Nevertheless, it is true that God answers Samuel in a tone that seems to support the interpretation I have just outlined: Samuel is asked to give in to the desire of the people, since it is not he who happens to be 'rejected', but God personally, 'so that I would no longer be king over them'! Here placed in opposition, with an intransigence that takes one's breath away, are two concepts that in the imagination of the whole ancient Near East, not merely in that of the Israelite and Judaean monarchical periods, were in no way felt to be incompatible; just the contrary, earthly kingship and divine kingship support one another.[27] In

---

to the obvious failure of Samuel's sons. Clearly, the office of judge carried out by these latter does not present an organizational form that would be satisfactory in the long term.

25. Veijola (*Das Königtum*, pp. 54, 68) has observed that the justifying reference to other peoples in 1 Sam. 8.5 has no pejorative intention. But he attributes this passage to a (first) Deuteronomist who, for his part, would have thought in terms still entirely pro-monarchical.

26. Cf. L.M. Eslinger, 'Viewpoints and Point of View in 1 Samuel 8–12', *JSOT* 26 (1983), pp. 61-76; R. Polzin, *Samuel and the Deuteronomist: A Literary Study of the Deuteronomic History* (Bloomington and Indianapolis: Indiana University Press, 1993), pp. 83-88.

27. Cf. M. Dietrich and W. Dietrich, 'Zwischen Gott und Volk: Einführung des Königtums und Auswahl des Königs nach mesopotamischer und israelitischer Anschauung', in *Und Mose schrieb dieses Lied auf* (Festschrift O. Loretz; AOAT, 250; Münster: Ugarit Verlag, 1998), pp. 215-64.

the presence of such stakes, the questionings and the sensitivities of Samuel are not of great weight.

However, this is only one of two responses of God, both being introduced by the same words: 'Listen to the voice of the people (respect their voice)' (8.7, 9). We are here obviously in the presence of a resumption (*Wiederaufnahme*) by means of which the passage in 8.7-9 has been secondarily introduced. Previously, the text pursued another aim: Samuel should give in to the desire of the people, but not without having beforehand 'warned' them, and it is in this context that he proclaims to the people the 'right of the king' (מִשְׁפַּט הַמֶּלֶךְ). In doing this, Samuel presents to them the famous catalogue that lists, in a sarcastic tone, all that a king 'takes' (לְקַח—the key word in 8.11b-17a) without giving in exchange the least thing. The king has only rights, the people only duties. It is all summed up in the last sentence: 'You, you will be slaves to him' (8.17b).

Research in recent years has made it likely that this 'right of the king', far from being a Deuteronomistic creation,[28] results from a pre-Deuteronomistic satirical tract belonging to a movement opposed to the monarchy, a traditional movement that steadfastly continued in Israel.[29] In 1 Samuel 8, this tract served as a scathing commentary in the face of the somewhat naïve aspiration of the people (8.5); it is actually the whole social structure of Israel, the tract claims, that will find itself weakened by the monarchy. It is as if it was a matter here of making understood what it will mean for Israel to have a king 'over' or 'against' itself (Deut. 17.14). And it is certainly not by chance that this precise formulation comes up twice in the redactional framework of 8.11-17. God instructs Samuel to communicate to the people the 'rights of this king' who will be 'king over them (עֲלֵיהֶם)' (8.9). Subsequently, 'the people refuse to listen to the voice of Samuel[30] and say: "No, there must in any case[31] be a king over us (עָלֵינוּ)" ' (8.19).

---

28. Cf. already M. Noth, *Überlieferungsgeschichtliche Studien*, p. 57.

29. Crüsemann, *Der Widerstand gegen das Königtum'*, pp. 66-73; Veijola, *Das Königtum*, pp. 60-66.

30. This wording presents a subtle response to the request repeatedly directed to Samuel to listen at last to the voice of the people. Samuel listens, even if it is reluctantly, but as for them, they do not listen to him. This is probably the way that we must understand the scene.

31. This is the best way to render לֹא כִּי אִם. Or else, it is perhaps necessary to follow the textual variant that suggests a לֹּה for לֹא; cf. *BHS*.

The following sentence is particularly striking: 'and we, we wish to be, we too, like all the nations' (8.20a). In 8.5, the Elders, to support their demand for a king, had evoked in a quite pragmatic way the customs of 'all the nations'. Here, the desire is that of Israel, and it is aimed at its adaptation, even its assimilation to 'all the nations'. And it is in this way that the second fear mentioned in Deut. 17.14 is taken up again and fully developed: with the monarchy, Israel opens itself up with no holding back to the influences of 'all the surrounding nations'.

This prediction is in complete opposition to the hope that the people express: 'Our king will judge us, he will march out at our head and will fight our battles' (8.20b). Justice within, security without, that is what they expect from the monarchy. According to the prediction, the monarchy will bring the exact opposite: injustice within, submission and assimilation to outsiders![32] From a diachronic point of view, the phrases describing the kings' activity of 'judging' and the relation with 'all the nations' constitute, in 8.20 as in 8.5, a resumption (*Wiederaufnahme*), that is to say, they indicate that now the account of the request for the monarchy is going to continue.[33] The substantial insertion of 8.6-20

32. Still again, it has been presumed that the Deuteronomist had only an extremely limited ability to judge in regard to the monarchy. His one and only criterion, the interpreters say, was that of the Deuteronomic cultic law; cf., for example, R. Albertz, 'Die Intentionen und die Träger des deuteronomistischen Geschichtswerks', in R. Albertz, F.W. Golka and J. Kegler (eds.), *Schöpfung und Befreiung: Für Claus Westermann zum 80. Geburtstag* (Stuttgart: Calwer Verlag, 1989), pp. 37-53. K. Zobel even turns to the old opinion of Wellhausen, who had described the Deuteronomistic redactional layer in the historical books as 'Judaic digestive mucus'. He acknowledges that the Wellhausian metaphor 'is certainly not very delicate but fundamentally it corresponds well to the reality of things' (*Prophetie und Deuteronomium: Die Rezeption prophetischer Theologie durch das Deuteronomium* [BZAW, 199; Berlin and New York: W. de Gruyter, 1992], p. 131 n. 86), without taking into account the anti-Judaic tendency of such an expression. The Deuteronomism must not be underestimated. The introduction to the history of the monarchy, as it has fashioned it in 1 Sam. 8, blames the monarchy for the failures of an entirely different kind: the social failure and the selling off of the identity of Israel to the foreigner (by which we can understand either the institution of the monarchy as such, or the participation of the Israelite and Judaean kings in alliances or in struggles for influence in the international context of the Near East).

33. When I proposed (*David, Saul und die Propheten: Das Verhältnis von Religion und Politik nach den prophetischen Überlieferungen vom frühesten Königtum in Israel* [BWANT, 122; Stuttgart: Kohlhammer, 2nd edn, 1992], p. 92) separating this passage from v. 20b, I already actually felt that the 'rapid succession' of

certainly had the effect of reorientating strongly the tendency of the account to disapprove of the monarchy. Nevertheless, already in the earlier version, more favourable to the monarchy, Samuel submitted the demand[34] of the people to God[35] and already in this version we find the response: 'Listen to their voice'.[36] Plainly, at this level of the account, the invitation is continued—away from any contesting or criticism of the monarchy—by order of God: 'and establish for them a king'[37] (8.21, 22a). It is only in 8.22a and in 8.5 that the king is granted 'to' the people (preposition לְ), and not placed 'over' or 'against' them (preposition עַל).[38] There we have confirmation that we are definitely back on the same textual level.[39]

We still have to deal with 1 Sam. 8.18, which forms the present closing of the proclamation of the Law by Samuel: 'That day, you will cry out because of this king that you will have chosen for yourselves, but that day, YHWH will not answer you.' The slightly cumbersome repetition of בַּיּוֹם הַהוּא, and especially, the abrupt shift from the relation between the king and the people to the opposition of the relation between the people and YHWH,[40] shows us that we are no longer in the presence of the old account but that again the redactor makes the rules. Israel's call for help (זָעַק) is very much reminiscent of the analogous

different layers could be laborious. Here, a simplification is conceivable.

34. In place of the Elders, here it is a question of the people (עַם). However, that is not sufficient indication to propose a process of diachronic literary criticism.

35. In 8.21 Samuel addresses himself to the 'ears of God'. This is an attractive anthropomorphism and an unusual one, which is replaced in 8.6 by the 'orthodox' form of a plea.

36. It is here that the model is found for the analogous phrases in 8.9 and 8.7.

37. The etymological figure of the Hebrew expression is difficult to imitate in English: 'Make a king for them a king'!

38. *BHS* indicates two Hebrew manuscripts that have, in 8.22, עֲלֵיכֶם. However, precisely because of the rarity of לְ, the MT must be preferred.

39. The allocation of 8.22b can remain in suspense. This half-verse is in any case redactional, since it represents a transition by means of which the long account of 9.1–10.16 was inserted into the context of 1 Sam. 8 and 10.17-27a. Samuel had to be provided an occasion on which to make the acquaintance of the one who had been chosen by God to take on the monarchy, before being able, in 10.17-27a, to proceed to the election and public acclamation of this king.

40. This relation here is obviously of a completely different kind from that in 8.7-9. YHWH does not feel 'rejected' as king of Israel, but does not come to the aid of Israel in distress.

situation so frequently described in the book of Judges,[41] except for the difference that now the enemies are no longer from outside Israel, but it is their own kings who move Israel to tears. And contrary to what formerly happened, YHWH this time will no longer respond to the cries of distress. We must pay attention in particular to the use of the concept of 'election' (בחר). It is Israel who elects, and the object of its election is not a particular king, but the king as such, the monarchy as an institution.

The approach is different in the Deuteronomic 'Law of the King': 'The one that you establish at your head must absolutely be a king *elected* by YHWH your God' (Deut. 17.15a). Taken together, the two passages, Deut. 17.15 and 1 Sam. 8.18, state approximately the following: YHWH does not 'elect' the monarchy. The monarchy is a matter for Israel to decide. The latter certainly has not been left in ignorance in regard to the consequences of this decision. The only reservation is that from the moment when Israel decided to establish the monarchy, YHWH reserves the right to 'elect' the king of the moment. In other words: the monarchy as an institutional form is not a good choice, but precisely for that reason it is important that God should be able at least to elect good kings. What that means in particular is what the Deuteronomistic historiography sets out to demonstrate in regard to the first kings of Israel. (And once again, it must be concluded that the passage concerning the Law of the King could hardly have received its present formulation without having undergone the influence of the Deuteronomistic reflection).

The long account about Saul, 'who set out to look for the she-donkeys of his father and found the royal crown' (1 Sam. 9.1–10.16), centres thematically on the following question: will it be possible, and if so how, to bring about the meeting of the first king of Israel elected by YHWH and Samuel, who is the one who must confer on him the anointing? The term for 'election' (בחר) is not used yet in this episode, but it will be in 10.17-24, in the account of the accession of Saul to kingship. Here, Samuel presents to the people the one who has been designated by lot and who was finally found hidden among the baggage, saying to them: 'Do you see the one whom YHWH has elected?', at which the people break out in a great royal ovation (10.24). The terms correspond exactly to those of Deut. 17.15a, and here again, we

---

41. Judg. 3.9, 15; 6.6, 7; 10.10; cf. too 1 Sam. 7.7, 8 and elsewhere.

have every reason to think that the historical account is prior and that the legal prescription was formulated in a way to anticipate it.[42] If we have kept in mind the Torah, then, in reaching the account of Saul's election, we react with confidence and relief, saying to ourselves: since there must be a king, it may as well be that one!

We know that, according to the biblical description, the harmony between Saul and Samuel as well as with God did not last long. Some minor escapades with regard to the orders of Samuel are enough to have Saul 'rejected' (מאס).[43] This is not the place to follow up the grave historical and theological questions that this raises.[44] What matters for our purpose is to note that the rejection of Saul is accompanied by a new election. In the account of the anointing of David (1 Sam. 16.1-13), the verbs מאס and בחר function as key words: God has rejected Saul, but not only him, but also the elder brothers of David, so close in many ways to Saul; God has 'rejected' them (16.1, 7) or, at least, has 'not elected' them (16.8, 9, 10). In enjoining Samuel to anoint the youngest, David (16.12), it is this latter who is designated as 'the elected'. And in 2 Sam. 6.21, David reveals to Michal, the daughter of Saul: 'YHWH elected me, rather than your father'.

In the Deuteronomistic prayer of dedication of Solomon's temple, the divine election of David is confirmed (1 Kgs 8.16) and extended through the insistence on the Solomonic succession of David to the entire Davidic dynasty.[45]

---

42. For the arguments in favour of a pre-Deuteronomistic nucleus in 10.17-24, cf. Dietrich, *David, Saul und die Propheten,* pp. 94-99; and P. Mommer, *Samuel, Geschichte und Überlieferung* (WMANT, 65; Neukirchen–Vluyn: Neukirchener Verlag, 1991), pp. 69-91. Another point of view is found in Veijola, *Das Königtum,* pp. 39-52, who holds, with many precursors, that almost the entire section of 10.17-27 is Deuteronomistic.

43. 1 Sam. 15.23, 26.

44. On this subject, cf. the history of research present in W. Dietrich and T. Naumann, *Die Samuelbücher* (EdF, 287; Darmstadt: Wissenschaftliche Buchgesellschaft, 1995), pp. 47-55, and the theological considerations in W. Dietrich, *Die frühe Königszeit in Israel: 10. Jahrhundert v. Chr.* (Biblische Enzyklopädie, 3: Stuttgart: Kohlhammer, 1997), pp. 282-89.

45. It need not be recalled that the kings of the house of David were not infallible. However, the basic sympathy of the Deuteronomist for the Davidic dynasty is not called into question; cf. T. Veijola, *Die ewige Dynastie: David und die Entstehung seiner Dynastie nach der deuterononomistischen Darstellung* (AASF.B, 193; Helsinki: Suomalainen Tiedeakatemia, 1975). In regard to the kings

By way of assessment, we can conclude that the prescription of Deut. 17.15a can be considered as respected at the time of the election of Saul and, after his rejection, at the time of the designation of David (and his successors). We can say as much in regard to the strange clause in 17.15b (about which we shall have to speak again), a clause that provides that only an Israelite ('from among your brethren')—and in no case a foreigner—should be installed on the throne. By and large, this means that it is true that Israel made a bad choice in opting for the monarchy, but God limited the damage in seeing to the good election of kings.[46] What is expressed here is certainly a critical attitude, but above all a practical one in regard to the monarchy.

Even greater is our surprise when we read in 1 Samuel 12, in the long farewell discourse of Samuel, the following phrase: 'And here then is the king *you have chosen*, whom you asked for' (12.13a). It is Saul who is intended, personally, and not the institution of the monarchy. We perceive a contradiction here, a slight but significant one: Saul in no way ascended the throne in accordance with the Torah and as 'elected' by YHWH; it is the Israelites who elected him. Saul is here included in the negative verdict that, in 8.18, fell on the whole institution: as first king, he cannot be different from the institution that he inaugurated. They both emanate from a bad human choice. We get the impression that, in place of a pragmatically critical attitude in regard to the monarchy, a much more fundamental rejection appears here that tolerates no exception.[47] The whole passage is actually steeped in a radically anti-monarchical perspective: if the pre-monarchical period as a result benefits from an extremely favourable light,[48] the desire for the monarchy is presented, for its part, as a shameless and useless affront against 'YHWH, your God, your King' (1 Sam. 12.6-12). By thunder and rain

---

of Northern Israel, on the other hand, it is never a question of divine election (בחר), but rather of rejection: not only of the kings but of the people (מאס), 2 Kgs 17.20.

46. Or in that case, when the very first election was revealed to be disastrous, in the quick rejection of the one elected.

47. In 1 Kgs 11.34 we certainly read—and perhaps in the context of the same literary level—of the divine 'election' of David, but this election is confirmed immediately, and therefore conditioned in some way, by the statement according to which David obeyed all the 'commandments and laws' of God.

48. The only negative thing each time is the infidelity of Israel towards YHWH. But YHWH, in turn, always reacts promptly as soon as the people repent and call for divine help.

YHWH confirms for the terrified people to what extent they are charged with sin by establishing the monarchy (12.16-19), and it is only after the intercession of Samuel and through the rigorous observance of the commandments that Israel recovers, even if this is only a small chance for survival (12.14-15, 20-25). That does not leave room for the slightest doubt: here again we hear the voice of that Judaism focused on the Torah and hostile to any form of state-controlled existence, such as was established in the post-exilic period.

That same voice we sense again in 1 Sam. 10.*18, 19a[49]: has not YHWH delivered Israel from Egypt and from all the other pillaging kingdoms?[50] Such is the question that Samuel asks and he adds this particular reflection: 'But as for you, you have today rejected (מאס) your God...by saying: "No! Set up a king over us" '! The 'rejection' of God as the real king over Israel was already the question in 8.7, then again in 12.13. Turning to the monarchy is turning away from God. Such is definitely the conviction of this layer, probably the latest in our textual complex. You can almost put your fingers on its post-exilic origin. We are in the situation of post-exilic Judaism confronted with the basic problem of its way of life: should Israel be organized again under the monarchical system 'like all the nations', or must they try to find a different kind of existence, more in keeping with their status as the people of God?[51] It is in this context that the passages of Judg. 8.22-32 and 1 Sam. 8.7-8; 10.18-19a; 12.6b-13a, 14-24 must be situated.[52]

Conversely, the texts of 1 Sam. 8.1-5, 20b-22a; 10.17, 19b-27 are openly favourable to the monarchy. The question of whether these texts

---

49. 10.18 without the introduction ויאמר שמואל אל־בני ישראל required for v. 19b.

50. Here and in v. 19 we find this extremely positive view of the period of the judges.

51. Cf. W. Dietrich, 'Gott als König: Zur Frage nach der theologischen und politischen Legitimät religiöser Begriffsbildung', *ZTK* 77 (1980), pp. 251-68.

52. It is not so certain that 12.1-6a and 12.13b would also belong to the same context. In these verses, the newly elected Saul is bathed in a more favourable light: at the side of God he serves as a witness when Samuel makes his 'management report', then, in v. 13b, he is designated as the one that YHWH has given to the people. Not only is v. 13b slightly redundant, but after the sternness and the contempt for Saul that show up in v. 13a, we cannot help perceiving a certain tension. Perhaps these verses belong to the literary layer that was merely *critical* with regard to the monarchy and that determined the line of 1 Sam. 8, but that here would have been considerably covered by the later layer, resolutely *hostile* to the monarchy.

should be considered as Deuteronomistic and/or pre-exilic here remains in abeyance.[53]

The redactional layer that I refer to in 1 Sam. 8.6, 9-10, 18-20a, (22b); 12.1-6a, 13b is not hostile to the monarchy, but it is not less critical of it. Its intervention begins much earlier in the Deuteronomistic historiography, in Deut. 17.14-15. Consequently, the passage introducing the Law of the King should be considered not as Deuteronomic but as Deuteronomistic.[54] Obviously, this redactor turned his attention to a long history of the monarchy, mainly an unfortunate history, of whose final failure he was probably already aware. This is why we have reasons for situating this redaction (at the earliest) in the exilic period.

On which of these levels must Judg. 21.25 be situated and, similarly, the derogatory presentation of the regime of the judges, as it appears above all in the second part of the book of Judges and at the beginning of the first book of Samuel? We are certainly no longer on the level of the redaction radically hostile to the monarchy, since it permits itself in 1 Samuel 12 a very positive view of the period of the judges. Perhaps it is necessary to opt for a parallel with the pro-monarchic description that we have found in 1 Sam. 8.1-5. But we could think of a third position, that of the moderate criticism of the monarchy. For just as the latter is able to combine, in its appreciation of the monarchy, criticism and pragmatics, it could have had the same ambivalent attitude with regard to

53. According to my analysis (*David, Saul und die Propheten*, pp. 76-102), we are in the presence here of a pre-Deuteronomistic 'History of Samuel and Saul', fed by traditions from the northern part of Israel; this history had the task of presenting and interpreting the passage from the period of the judges to that of the kings. Besides the passages indicated in 1 Sam. 8 and 10.17-27, we must attribute to this history mainly 1 Sam. 1–3, an initial form of 1 Sam. 7 as well as 1 Sam. 11 and 14.47-52. For a similar argumentation on many points, but with a greater interest in the historical figure of Samuel, cf. Mommer, *Samuel*, pp. 51-91.

54. Crüsemann (*Die Tora*, p. 275) does not share this opinion. He considers that what is demanded in Deut. 17.14-15 corresponds 'so closely to historical developments following the assassination of Amon or accompanying the enthronement of Josiah or that of his successor that we can scarcely speak of a coincidence'. In other words, Deut. 17.14-15 is Deuteronomic and pre-Josianic, in such a way that at the time of the accession of Josiah to kingship, already that law had to be observed. But the historicizing introduction in 17.14a allows only for understanding that the matter in question relates to the establishment of the *monarchy* and not the installation of certain *kings*. That is why we find in Deut. 17.14-15 and in 1 Sam. 8.5 the verb שׂים, whereas in 2 Kgs 21.24; 23.30, it is the verb מלך in the hiphil that is used.

the regime of the judges. We would in that case be led to consider that the two institutions had had, in their respective periods, their merits and their flaws and that one and the other (and each of their representatives) must be allowed to measure itself by the good will of God with regard to Israel. If that is the way it was, we would have put our finger on the basic version of the Deuteronomistic historiography: its author would be at the same time a historian concerned about a well-balanced description and a theologian impelled by a genuine critical sense.

4. *Monarchical Government and Limitation of Power*

The Deuteronomic 'Law of the King' (Deut. 17.14-20) not only offers guidelines for the institution of the monarchy in Israel, but also specifies what the people had the right to expect or not expect from the kings.

> One from your own community you may set as king over you;
> you are not to put a foreigner over you who is not of your own community.
> But he must not acquire many horses for himself
>   or make the people return to Egypt,
>   since YHWH has said to you: 'No, you will not return that way again!'
> He must not procure a great number of wives either,
> and his heart must not go astray.
> As for silver and gold, he must not procure a great quantity...
>   so that his heart will not look down on other members of his community.

It has been observed several times already that the triple prohibition of accumulation—horses, wives and riches—indicates an astonishing closeness to the accounts of the reign of King Solomon:[55] Solomon took a great interest in horses (1 Kgs 5.6, 8; 10.25, 28, 29;), in women (1 Kgs 11.1, 7), in silver (1 Kgs 7.51; 10.21, 22, 25, 27, 29) and in gold (1 Kgs 6.20-35; 7.48, 49, 50, 51; 9.11, 14, 28; 10.2, 10, 11, 14, 16, 17, 18, 21, 22, 25).

Again, we are induced to ask ourselves the question: which came first, the Law or the history? That main question can be subdivided into some subordinate questions: Would it only be the late period—and then probably on the basis of Deut. 17.16-20—that would have attributed to

---

55. The idea that there could be a connection between the history of Solomon and the Law of the King is an old one. To retrace its genealogy, cf. Zobel, *Prophetie und Deuteronomium*, p. 131 n. 84 (he himself rejects the idea).

King Solomon all his horses, his women and his riches?[56] Or did there exist a 'Book of the Acts of Solomon', which the initial author of the Deuteronomistic historiography quotes as one of his sources in 1 Kgs 11.41, and did it contain at least a part of the allegations that we have just mentioned? And if we admit that the second possibility is the valid one, did the Deuteronomic legislators try to draw lessons from history and elaborate the consequences for the future of the Judaean monarchy?[57] Or would the authors of the Deuteronomistic historiography, after the end of the Judaean monarchy, have given to the Law of the King a form that drew its pejorative connotation from the description of the luxury and grandeur of the reign of Solomon? And if it was this way, does Deuteronomism speak about this question in just one voice, or can we perceive there divergent tendencies concerning what is illuminating about the Solomonic era?

The 'Law of the King' in Deuteronomy 17, in the aspects we have considered up to now, presents a coherent and constant structure. Each specific injunction is followed by a supplementary piece of information:[58] 'Set up a king that YHWH has elected—*but only someone who comes from your community*; he must not have many horses—*and he*

---

56. The commentary of E. Würthwein (*Die Bücher der Könige, 1 Könige 1–16* [ATD, 11.1; Göttingen: Vandenhoeck & Ruprecht, 2nd edn, 1985]) goes in this direction, in an especially pronounced way for example on pp. 115-16.

57. This is basically the thesis of Crüsemann (*Die Tora*, pp. 274-77), even if he has no intention of denying the existence of Deuteronomistic additions. Several researchers have tried to define these additions more closely, by separating them from an earlier state of the text, whether this would be Deuteronomic or even pre-Deuteronomic: F. García López, 'Le roi d'Israël: Dt 17, 14-20', in N. Lohfink (ed.), *Das Deuteronomium: Entstehung, Gestalt und Botschaft* (BETL, 68; Leuven: Peeters–Leuven University Press, 1985), pp. 277-97 (p. 287); Rüterswörden, *Studien* (1987), pp. 52-66; Zobel, *Prophetie und Deuteronomium*, pp. 112-19. The results from these inquiries concur along broad lines. M. Rose (*5.Mose*, I [ZBK.AT, 5; Zürich: Theologischer Verlag, 1994], pp. 72-84), relies on these and pursues them even further: the three bans on accumulation (horses, women, riches) would come from a tradition of Northern Israel, critical in regard to monarchy (according to him, these reproaches fit not only Solomon, but just as much the Omride dynasty of the 9th century). The Deuteronomic legislators would have taken up these norms and expanded them with vv. 15b, *18-20. As for v. 15a, the further information on the bans on accumulation, and a good part of vv. 18-20, they would be due to two Deuteronomistic redactions.

58. Perhaps we must interpret in this way the sequence in 17.14bα and 17.14bβ: Israel decide to give themselves a king—*like all the nations round about*.

must not make Israel return to Egypt; he must not have many wives—
and his heart must not go astray[59]; he must not accumulate great
riches—*and his heart must not look down on other members of his
community*.[60]

We could wonder whether an earlier version of this text was limited
to the specific injunctions, and whether the precise details were added
subsequently.[61] If such was the case, we would be tempted to opt for the
model 'Deuteronomic law/Deuteronomistic commentary'. However, it
is fruitless to attempt to separate a text of a law that would be
formulated in general terms from a commentary that would perform the
application of the law to the Deuteronomistic presentation of the beginnings of the royal period. It actually appears that the basic injunctions
already refer in a way that could not be clearer to the first kings of
Israel, as they are described in the Deuteronomistic historiography.
Why would the observation that we have made in regard to the subject
of election (Deut. 17.15) not apply also to the three injunctions for
moderation? Here, the Deuteronomistic historiography already integrates into the Torah the scale according to which it thinks the accounts
of the birth of the Israelite state and the reign of Solomon should be
read.

That observation excuses us from any attempt at distinguishing
several literary levels *within* Deut. 17.14-17:[62] the attempts in this

59. This statement gives the impression of being a little abrupt. We can certainly complete it using 1 Kgs 11.3, 6-8.

60. It is absolutely necessary to attach 17.20aα here, because the introductive
לבלתי duplicates in an awkward way ולבלתי that opens 17.20aβ. And while v. 20aβ
with its nomistic tendency excellently corresponds to vv. 18-19, v. 20aα relates
very well—as much on the syntactical level as on the semantic (the concepts of
'heart' and 'community') and thematic levels (against the insolence of the sovereign)—to vv. 16-17. Conversely, v. 17b without v. 20aα would remain the only
prohibition without a motivation.

61. In this sense, cf. among others Rüterswörden, *Studien*, pp. 60-61; Rose,
5.Mose, pp. 73-79.

62. An attempt of this kind is undertaken by P. Särkiö, *Die Weisheit und Macht
Salomos in der israelitischen Historiographie: Eine traditions- und redaktionskritische Untersuchung über 1. Kön 3–5 und 9–11* (Schriften der Finnischen
Exegetischen Gesellschaft, 60; Helsinki and Göttingen: Finnische Exegetische Ges,
1994), pp. 224-28; illustrative chart, p. 228. But for him, the oldest layer
(vv. 14abα, 15a as well as the ban on accumulations and, curiously, v. 20aα without
מאחיו!) is already Deuteronomistic (DtrH). This layer, subsequently, was twice
expanded: by DtrN[1] (especially in the pieces of information concerning the ban on

direction are always complicated and do not really end up being successful. What are the literary facts that should force us to separate the particular injunctions from the pieces of information that accompany them? The three injunctions about moderation do not form in any way a polished block of text that would let itself be isolated from its context. Already the beginning with רק (17.16) indicates that the sentence depends on something that preceded it. And why was it necessary, at the time of the third injunction, that the object of the covetousness all of a sudden precedes the verb, and why this מאד stuck on at the end (17.17b)? This state of affairs is not very favourable to the thesis according to which a basic text hidden under our present text, but it is explained very well by the fact that in 1 Kings 3–11 it is still much more a question of silver and gold than of horses and wives.

Let us examine more closely the detailed stipulations in Deut. 17.15-17, 20aα. In v. 15, we find the prohibition of letting a foreigner (איש נכרי) who is not a part of the 'community' of Israel accede to the throne.[63] If we confine ourselves to the history of the Israelite monarchy, even to that of the Judaean monarchy, at what moment would such a possibility have arisen?[64] The only king who would expressly be

accumulation and in v. *20), then by DtrN[2] (especially in vv. 18-19). Such fine dissections are difficult to make convincing and still more difficult to prove.

63. It is only in this case that a solid argument in favour of a diachronic terracing of layers can be advanced: from the moment when YHWH has the prerogative in the election of the king, is not the case envisaged by v. 15b excluded straight away (cf. Särkiö, *Die Weisheit und Macht Salomos*, p. 225)? Such a conclusion however would be fallacious. YHWH elected Saul, then David, directly, and neither one nor the other is a foreigner. But the Davidic dynasty, whose representatives are no longer elected directly, could very well have (half-)foreigners accede to the throne. We will have to speak shortly of the case of Solomon's descendants. In this context, it is interesting to recall the ancestry of the prophet Zephaniah. According to Zeph. 1.1, this prophet is the son of the 'Cushite' and great-grandson of an Ezekiah who could be the king of the same name. In this hypothesis, an Ethiopian element would have entered by marriage into the Davidic line.

64. Sometimes, one has referred to the case of Ben Tab'el of Isa. 7.6 and to the obscure events reported in 2 Kgs 21.23-24. But in the first case, it is a matter of a deliberate interference directed from a foreign country, and in the second, we are not informed about the intentions of the putschists. Queen Athalia (2 Kgs 1) was an Israelite from the North, but that did not make her a נכריה. Jezabel (1 Kgs 17–21) was Phoenician, but she was not queen. The origin of usurpers in the Northern Kingdom is not always known, but in no case do we find the term (נכרי) in this

put in contact with foreign customs is Solomon. Certainly, Solomon was not a foreigner himself, but according to 1 Kgs 11.1 'he loved many (!) foreign women (נשים נכריות[65])'—and among them, they insist, a daughter of Pharaoh! For 'all the foreign wives' he built, according to 1 Kgs 11.8, places of worship dedicated to non-Israelite deities. Very obviously, the possibility is never mentioned that one of these wives could have been considered for the exercising of royalty, but it is no less natural to suppose that nevertheless some of them gave Solomon sons who could have been in line for the succession. Thus it is in view of this apparent risk, illustrated by the example of Solomon, namely the risk for Israel, or for Judah, of letting themselves be subverted by a foreigner within the royal house, that the requirement of Deut. 17.15b could have been formulated.

The account about the many wives of Solomon does not seem, originally, to have been reported with the intention of discrediting the reign of this king. The goal was, on the contrary, to emphasize the glory:[66] 'Solomon loved[67] many foreign wives... He had seven hundred main wives and three hundred concubines', 1 Kgs 11.*1a, 3a[68] informs us, and this in the same tone that is used elsewhere to inform us that Solomon composed three thousand proverbs and one thousand and five

---

context. It is true that from the eighth century onwards there were increases in influence on the part of foreign powers over the politics of Israel and Judah, but it was never claimed that the great kings of Assyria, for example, would have bestowed the Israelite crown or the Judaean crown on their own leader. Manasseh himself, the one whom the Deuteronomists liked to treat as a lackey of the Assyrians, has an irreproachable ancestry: there is no reason to attribute to his mother Hephzibah a foreign origin.

65. איש (Deut. 17.15) and אשה/נשים (1 Kgs 11.1-8) are more closely connected than is the case in the German language (or French); but in English, there is just as close a connection between *woman* and *man*.

66. Cf. E. Würthwein, *Die Erzählung von der Thronfolge Davids—theologische oder politische Geschichtsschreibung?* (ThSt[B], 115; Zürich: Theologischer Verlag, 1977), p. 131. These indications 'orininally did not intend to report anything pejorative; on the contrary, it is with admiration that they spoke of the great number of wives'.

67. The verb 'love' should be understood, not in a necessarily erotic sense, but (also) as a term from political and diplomatic language, having a sense close to 'form bonds with', 'show reverence for'; cf. K. Doob-Sakenfeld, 'Loyalty and Love: The Language of Human Interconnections in the Hebrew Bible', *Michigan Quarterly Review* 22 (1983), pp. 190-204.

68. Verses 1b-2 are probably secondary. See below.

songs and that in his architectural enterprises he employed seventy thousand labourers and eighty thousand stonecutters.[69] It definitely seems that the 'Book of the Acts of Solomon' had a fondness for fantastic numbers. That Solomon's harem was made up of many foreign women must have seemed in the eyes of this author therefore as a very special claim to fame. It is in a tone filled with respect that this book, in another passage, reports that Solomon was able to count among his wives even a daughter of Pharaoh.[70]

Later commentators on the history of Israel would have different values.[71] When they came across the adjective 'foreign' in their source, they wanted to make clear what type of women it concretely involved: beside the Egyptian princess, they list 'Moabite, Ammonite, Edomite, Sidonian, Hittite' women.[72] These women originate from those nations (גוים) of which YHWH had said to the Israelites: 'You are not to go to them, and they are not to enter your place, or they will sway your hearts towards their gods'; it is precisely to these nations that Solomon became attached because of his love affairs[73] (1 Kgs 11.1b, 2). And immediately there happened what was bound to happen: 'his wives swayed his heart' (11.3b) so that he erected near Jerusalem 'high places' for the principal deities of the countries from which his wives originated (11.7-8).[74]

The list in 11.1b is nothing else but an invented development of 'peoples round about' (הגוים סביבות) mentioned in Deut. 17.17. The observation that the 'heart' of Solomon was 'swayed' by the wives helps to recall the warning of Deut. 17.17, that the 'heart' of the king

69. 1 Kgs 5.12, 29.

70. 1 Kgs 3.1—probably repeated editorially in 11.1.

71. Zobel (*Prophetie und Deuteronomium*, p. 132) tries to demonstrate that these values belong to the prophetic movement, and he thinks that he must question the possibility that the prohibition in Deut. 17.17a could equally have been provoked by 'the effects of the bad example of Solomon'. There, it is the— 'Deuteronomistic'!—serpent that bites the tail!

72. This list can hardly be pre-exilic. Cf. the exilic addition of strophes concerning (not Sidon, certainly, but) Tyre and Edom in Amos 1.3–2.16, and in connection with this, H.W. Wolff, *Joel und Amos* (BKAT, 14.2; Neukirchen–Vluyn: Neukirchener Verlag, 2nd edn, 1975), *ad loc.*; W. Dietrich, 'JHWH, Israel und die Völker beim Propheten Amos', *TZ* 48 (1992), pp. 315-28.

73. Here, the root אהב has a clearly erotic meaning.

74. The passage 11.4-6, including perhaps besides the connective או in 11.7, is probably of tertiary origin.

could be 'swayed' by many wives. It is in regard to Solomon that we understand that the stake is not polygamy but polytheism. And the peculiar structure of 11.2 ('the nations about whom YHWH had said: "You are not to go to them" ') recalls the identical formulation of Deut. 17.16b where it is the return to Egypt that is designated as a route 'about which YHWH has said: "You are not to return by this route" '.[75]

We thus arrive at a point at which the network of connections between the Law of the King and the history of Solomon is especially dense. Deut. 17.16a decrees that the king 'must not acquire many horses for himself and must not return the people to Egypt in order to increase the number of his horses'. There have long been questions about what this could mean: the delivery of Israelite or Judaean slaves in return for expensive war chariots, the voluntary subjection of Judah to Egypt with a view to thus escaping from the imperialist claims of Assyria or of Babylon?[76] To the extent that the Law of the King is Deuteronomistic, nothing of all that is excluded. But the most obvious interpretation remains the reference to the history of Solomon. We have already noted the Egyptian princess. Further, in 1 Kgs 10.28-29, there is mention of the lucrative market in Egyptian horses and Egyptian chariots,[77] mounted by the commercial agents of Solomon.

The reference to Egypt in the formula for the consecration of the golden bulls (the 'calves') that the first king of Northern Israel, Jeroboam I, installed in the newly established state sanctuaries at Bethel and Dan, is especially significant: 'Here are your Elohim, Israel; these

75. It is not clear what ban could be alluded to here. Rose (*5.Mose*, pp. 81-82) refers to passages such as Exod. 13.17; 14.13; Deut. 1.40-42; 28.68 and Hos. 8.13; 9.3. N. Lohfink would see there an echo of Hos. 11.5 ('Hos. XI 5 als Bezugstext von Dtn. XVII 16', *VT* 31 [1981], pp. 226-28). For the Deuteronomist who holds the pen here, it probably sufficed to watch the direction set by God; that direction going from the Exodus to the Conquest would always appear to be totally clear. In this sense, it amounts to a citation from memory that is not only very free but already interpretative, analogous to what must probably be postulated for 1 Kgs 1.17, 30.

76. Cf. Isa. 30.1-3, 15-17; 31.1-3. Whoever is not afraid of later datings can consider 2 Kgs 23.33-35, Jer. 37 or Ezek. 17.

77. It is possible that the *judgment* passed on that situation by the—in my opinion Deuteronomistic—author of Deut. 17.16 would have been provoked essentially by what Zobel (*Prophetie und Deuteronomium*, p. 121, in reference to Isa. 30.15-16; 31.1) has called 'the critical distance in regard to horses...in the prophetic movement'.

brought you up out of the land of Egypt' (1 Kgs 12.28). The Judaean redactors of this text cannot refrain from accusing Jeroboam of polytheism, even of worship of beasts. Actually and in its first sense, the formula celebrates nothing else but the God of the Exodus. It is probably not by chance that this God is not called YHWH here: 'YHWH' had been monopolized by the Davidic dynasty and established on Zion. But as true as was the deliverance of Israel from Egypt under the leadership of Moses, just as true was the deliverance under Jeroboam: then as now, God had helped the people free themselves from Egyptian shackles.

It is not the Judaean narrators of 1 Kings 12, any more than the authors of the book of the history of Solomon, but the Deuteronomistic historiographers who insinuate that they have perfectly understood the secret analogy between the regime of Solomon and that of the Pharaohs. The fearsome symbol of the slavery in Egypt was forced labour (Exod. 5). It is not by chance that the personal union between the Judaean South and the Israelite North is broken precisely over this question: the Northern tribes demand a reduction in the forced labour (1 Kgs 12.4). In 1 Kgs 5.27-32, the organization of the forced labour under Solomon is described, and in conformity with the spirit of the book of the acts of Solomon, from which it is taken, this description has a completely positive connotation; the royal enterprises are there glorified. A first Deuteronomistic redactor gives from the outset, however, an opposite signal that is totally negative: in the Law of the King of Deuteronomy 17, he warns that no king must send Israel back to Egypt. But that is just what Solomon has done: he has put Israel back in the grip of Egypt—by the women, by the horses, by the forced labour!

Later, a new Deuteronomistic editor could not allow such an insinuation to continue.[78] In 1 Kgs 9.15-24, he returns to the theme of forced labour: 'This is the account of the forced labour that King Solomon levied', in order to carry out his many architectural projects. There follows a list, apparently ancient, of the Solomonic warehouse and garrison cities, then, contradicting the older version of 1 Kgs 5.27-32, it is specified that the workers compelled to labour for these projects had not been taken from among the Israelites but only from the indigenous Canaanite population, insofar as these had survived the conquest (9.20-22). The fact that the redactor of these verses refers here to the more recent—and less radical—history of the conquest in the book of Joshua

---

78. Cf. W. Dietrich, 'Das harte Joch (1. Kön 12, 4): Fronarbeit in der Salomo-Überlieferung', *BN* 34 (1986), pp. 7-16.

makes it possible to determine to what historical and spiritual group he belonged: this redactor was from post-exilic 'nomistic' circles within the Deuteronomistic movement.[79] Their main concern was to base the existence of Israel—or of Judaism—on a meticulous observance of the Torah and on a strict separation with respect to all that was non-Jewish.

This is not the first time that we come across traces of this nomistic thinking. A particularly impressive witness to this stream is presented to us in the final paragraph of the Law of the King, in Deut. 17.18-20. This paragraph has obviously been added secondarily to what precedes it.[80] The introduction already betrays a rather ponderous resumption: 'And when he is seated on his royal throne...' (v. 18). The theologian who begins to speak here intends to make clear what, in his opinion, will determine the success or failure of the monarchy: obedience or disobedience to the Torah. In this passage, 'the Torah' no longer refers to the teaching given orally by Moses, but designates a written document of which copies can be made. The control of this treasure—on which the continuance not only of individual kings but of the entire dynasty depends—is given into the hands of the 'priest Levites' (which already brings us close to the book of Chronicles). It is by their good offices that the king will have to have prepared a copy of the Torah, in order to be able, rather than reigning, to spend his life in studying. We do not know of a single real king who would have carried out such a programme.[81] Even the pious Josiah remained far short of the proposed ideal, since he did not content himself with studying the Torah, but forcefully directed the affairs of state. But the author of our passage

79. See R. Smend, 'Das Gesetz und die Völker: Ein Beitrag zur deuteronomistischen Redaktionsgeschichte', in H.W. Wolff (ed.), *Probleme biblischer Theologie* (Festschrift G. von Rad; Munich: Kaiser, 1971), pp. 494-509, and W. Dietrich, 'Niedergang und Neuanfang: Die Haltung der Schlussredaktion des deuteronomistischen Geschichtswerkes zu den wichtigsten Fragen ihrer Zeit', in B. Becking and M.C.A. Korpell (eds.), *The Crisis of Israelite Religion: Transformation of Religious Tradition in Exilic and Postexilic Times* (Leiden: E.J. Brill, 1999), pp. 45-70.

80. Contrary to Schäfer-Lichtenberger (*Josua und Salomo*, pp. 80-81) who considers the whole passage 17.14-20 to be from one Deuteronomistic level.

81. In what probably corresponds to the same redactional level, the accomplishment of this programme is explicitly questioned in so far as Solomon is concerned: 1 Kgs 6.12; 9.4-7; 11.9-13. David, for his part, is seen to be much closer to the ideal, see 1 Kgs 2.3-4; 9.4; 11.4, 34, 38; and in this regard, cf. Veijola, *Die ewige Dynastie*, p. 141 n. 104.

does not care about the realities of the control of a state. The only thing on which he sets his heart is the utopia of a theocratic society. He who wants kings only in the context envisaged here in fact does not want kings.[82]

In this passage given over to the Torah of the King, just one small notation, v. 20aα, seems to be from the older version of the Law of the King. It expresses an ideal that is not as unrealistic as the one just considered: the king must make sure not to let 'his heart look down on other members of the community'. To answer that expectation, he must—not study the Torah, but—give up accumulating excessive riches (Deut. 17.17b). Earlier, I listed the passages that mention the enormous quantities of precious metals that passed through the hands of Solomon or were piling up in his coffers. The book of the acts of Solomon, from which most of these passages must have been drawn, tried to inundate the Solomonic era with gold and silver. How would the reader, coming from Deuteronomy 17, not be frightened by it? The Deuteronomists, in doing this, preoccupy themselves less with the origin of this wealth than with its effects: the wealth leads the king to insolence and to contempt for his 'community'.[83] This is scarcely a problem merely in Antiquity and with monarchs.

82. T. Römer ('The Book of Deuteronomy', in McKenzie and Graham [eds.], *The History of Israel's Traditions*, pp. 178-212, especially p. 202) rightly feels that Deuteronomy as a whole is negative in regard to monarchy: Deuteronomic Israel 'is a people who does not really need a king'; only Deut. 17.14-20 deals with this set of themes. Crüsemann interprets the Law of the King itself as 'an astonishingly complete dispossession of the monarchy' (*Die Tora*, p. 277), but by continuing to connect it with Josiah, he situates it in a much too positive way. In reality, it visualizes—beyond the foundation of the Israelite state and the deployment of state power under Solomon—an Israel that is defined neither by the state nor by the monarchy.

83. It is in my opinion arbitrary, from the literary point of view, and theologically doubtful to consider as secondary the component מאחיו in the warning of v. 20aα (as for example García López, 'Le roi d'Israël', p. 286; Zobel, *Prophetie und Deuteronomium*, pp. 148-49). Then, the heart of the king would no longer be raised above the citizens of his country, but above God! But is not the former the usual temptation of sovereigns? And what one does 'to the least of my community', does this not touch the Lord personally (Mt. 25.40, 45; cf. Prov. 19.17; Isa. 58.7)?

WHEN JOSIAH HAS DONE HIS WORK OR THE KING
IS PROPERLY BURIED: A SYNCHRONIC READING
OF 2 KINGS 22.1–23.28

Françoise Smyth

The account in 2 Kgs 22.1–23.28 takes the form of a double expansion
of the reports of the reigns that comprise the characteristic material of
this book of Kings. Two long sequences deal with the finding of the
book during the work on the restoration of the temple and implement-
ation of the Josianic reform, inserted between two sub-sequences on the
celebrations of the Covenant and of the Passover. The sequential distribution of the narrative sheds light on an outlook, the articulations of
which serve to validate the historiographical project whose conclusion
is here introduced as well as it is correlated to its pre-monarchical
prolegomena.

22.3-20 comprises the 'finding of the book' sequence with a royal
address to the high priest (vv. 4-7), a discourse being done under the
sign of the *'emunâ* and outlined by the designation of its actors as
'doing' something (*'śh*), thus taking over from the previous account of
the king's 'doing' right (v. 2).

'Those who do the work' are therefore at the heart of a plan of action
moving in a circle: a royal word sends Shaphan the scribe to Hilkiah the
high priest (vv. 3-4) who transmits to Shaphan an object destined for
the king (vv. 8-10). The account is again marked by the exchange of
gifts: vv. 4-7 handle the gift of money that, coming from the people,
passes from hand to hand in view of the restoration of the house of
YHWH, or the exact duplication of the programme of reform of Joash
(2 Kgs 12.1-17), in exchange for which the book of the Law is given to
the scribe who reads its words to the king. The origin of the book
'found' by the priest is the place where the money is 'found', in the
house.

Just as the sub-sequence 'project of restoration' bequeaths to the reader a surplus of meaning through the concept of *'ᵉmunâ*, that of the exchange carried out (vv. 8-10) shapes a concept of *qara*, reading, with Shaphan as an indispensable actor or mediator.

Between these two sub-sequences, as a contractual scene of all that is going to follow, or as the basic enigmatic premiss, there is the formula of Hilkiah, 'I have found in the house of YHWH the book of the Law': as such, it supplies a system of referential elements that the text will move around in order to bring the structurings into play and show how the originality of the combinations come to light in a particular context. (It is not a matter of simple 'narrative logic' whose abusive exploitation would in the long run neutralize the surface of the text nor of an inter-textuality that is passive or meant solely for the diversion of a cumula-tive reading.) Using the whole of this text as a model will allow us to explore the meaning of this declaration that sets up the narrative with-out explanation, in an act that exhumes the book instead of depositing it or that exhumes a book instead of exhuming a foundation stone.

Ensconced in the middle of the first two sub-sequences ('I have found...the book of the Law'), the third, as long as the first two to-gether, opens with a decisive formula: 'As soon as the king heard the words of the book of the Law'. The important spatial code has so far organized the narrative in such a way that the acts of gift and counter-gift are structured. It is now the temporal code (*wayyᵉhi*) that quickens the action and stamps on it a characteristic urgency or even imminence, whereas the book 'that has been found' no longer moves about and forces attention on 'this place', the new-ancient name of Jerusalem, the chosen.

The first sub-sequence mobilized money and men, the last one mobi-lizes several actors defined as much by their genealogy as by their roles. Only the priest and the scribe preserve their mediator roles: in place of the three classes of artisans of the temple, three royal officials (the inclusion of *mlk* in v. 12 emphasizes this royal aspect) are associated with them. No longer on assignment to the temple, but on a hermeneut-ical quest (without many other legitimate examples—cf. the 'witch of Endor') with a woman, admittedly a prophetess (of course), but situated as if in a move backwards, in comparison with an officer (a subordi-nate?) of the temple: a conjugal genealogy (whereas the mother of the king was known by the name of her own father) and a residence outside the old city. Whatever is said of her, there is not much of a relationship with Deborah from the perspective of a Deuteronomistic whole, but more so with the anti-model of the medium of Endor (1 Sam. 28) and maybe, earlier on, with a Miriam with traditional traits lost (that of a known tomb and the elusive mention in Mic. 6.4).

The instantaneous speech of the king (vv. 11-13) provides starting blocks with the order to consult YHWH, based on a judgment oracle against Judah, against 'us' (the king and the people), itself justified by a nodal historical summary, 'our ancestors have not obeyed the words of this book' and its criterion, that rejoins negatively with what the author says in v. 2: 'Our ancestors did not obey the words of this book *to do (la'aśot) according to all that is written*': the king historian, mixing up moreover his own ancestors and those of the people, or royally authorizing the verdict of the historian responsible for the text that we read, a verdict essentially falling on each of the kings of the dynasty, particularly the immediate ancestors of Josiah. From the point of view of the account, the king, here, is the figure of History and, as such, he is not, despite the appearances, a prophet, but on the contrary the one who sends someone to consult YHWH.

Three actors are in place: the king (and his servants, then his people); the book stemming from the temple; YHWH (and the divine fury) from whom to seek advice. Three times, in these few lines, 'the words of the book' give a certain rhythm to the thought that makes the reader go from the oral—the king heard the words—to the written: 'all that is written (*hakkatûb*) in it' or 'about us'. The considerable movement steers this same reader to the concept of an foundation object that structures the opening of the text, gives it to the reader as a site for judgment but determines, for lack of the house of YHWH, the consultation of someone elsewhere, which will mean the prophetess. The royal intuition comes to a stop at the reading of a past informing the immediate present, the history, and the royal sequence moves then to Huldah. We might see some significance in these names of small mammals that replace the theophoric names predominating otherwise in the historical accounts.[1]

No matter what its genesis, the double discourse of the completed text (vv. 16-17 and 18-20) does not erase the enigmatic effect of the juxtaposition of two addressees who are only one for the reader: 'the

---

1. Along with Akbor ('mouse') and Shaphan ('badger'), Huldah's name suggests a very small field animal. The imagination readily contrasts it with the royal uranian name of Deborah, even if the effect is not intended and it corresponds to the contemporary onomastic usage.

man who sent you to me' having to be 'the king of Judah who sent you to consult YHWH'.

The first judgment oracle announces the imminence of the fulfilment of 'what is said in the book that the king of Judah has read'. The messengers of an anonymous personage understand from the prophecy only the confirmation of the obvious sense of the Law as an interpretation of the historical calamity occurring in 'this place' (inclusion). The role of the king is therefore limited to that of a reader (no more need of a scribe): it dates the text; the event will not be confused with a general rule but it also has a function as a colophon; the book that interprets these events for every reader will always be the one that the king read. And every reader who thus examines how the prophecy in its turn is linked to the Law happens to occupy a formidable crucial space but has the aid of a discernment that is in the first place royal. The second oracle concerns the royal person in his connection to what YHWH 'has said' or 'is going to bring' 'on this place' (inclusion: see v. 16). But whereas the first displaced the reader in its reference to the text that was read, the latter focuses the reader's attention on a new exchange correlated to that which set up the account in vv. 4-10. This king of Judah was able to do what was necessary on hearing the words of the book interpreted as words of YHWH, 'before me', as Shaphan read them before the king (v. 10b). The text thus lays out, in vv. 19b and 20a, in counterpoint to the destruction announced for 'this place', a new space for reading: to this mourning 'before me' corresponds the 'well as to me (*gam 'anoki*), I have heard you, and here I am'; three times there is the divine pronoun in the first person in a very close encounter introduced by the king, within the great inclusion that ties together the two discourses 'I am the one who is going to bring disaster upon this place' (vv. 16a, 20aγ).

Just as the preceding sub-sequences gave the reader responsibility for a lexicon to explore ('read', 'the writing', 'the words of the book' at the core of the account and the concept of *emounah* to conclude the discourse of Josiah, the virtual restorer of the temple), this one leaves the reader with the enigma of a rather obscure *bᵉšālôm* (in peace). The king counted, as Jehoash did in the past, on the 'honesty' of the temple artisans and YHWH promises him the peace of the ancestral tombs. The correlation of these details (indicated by *bᵉr...*) could be emphasized by the recurrence of the verb *'sp*: it was about the people's money collected in the temple by those on guard at the entrance in v. 4; and now, twice, in v. 20, it is a question of the king personally, gathered to his ancestors in their tombs (without his eyes seeing the disaster, in contrast to what the situation of Zedekiah will be—do the readers know this? Are the readers invited to read on in order to know it?).

If this salvation oracle has nothing exciting for the average readers, they could certainly believe that the royal logic adapts to it and accepts the lesson regarding the reading of the book that opens such a space for reciprocity between the king and YHWH even in the circumstances of a radical judgment.

No matter what inventive acrobatics might be necessary so that this *bešālôm* would have a plausible meaning in the perspective of the historical destiny of Josiah duly reported later on, in this text the concept is quite pregnant: the circumstances of the death of the king produce for him the great blessing of not knowing yet the horror that rains on Jerusalem and enables him to rejoin, practically to close, the dynasty of the elect established by his ancestor David, with whom he forms an inclusion. 'Your ancestors', YHWH says, a sort of reconciliation in the thoughts of the readers instead of the rupture indicated by 'his ancestor' (v. 20) and 'our ancestors' (v. 13); gathered together in death, this royal line constitutes a unity, a privileged subject matter for history, a useful object for remembrance (v. 13b) but not a promise of a future: there is the extreme proximity of Josiah and YHWH, but their exchange of dialogue takes place in a peacefulness of tombs; the displacement of the promise to David is a radical one; is it not moreover what must be explained? The lineage of Josiah is still-born just like the project to restore the temple of Solomon, notwithstanding the integrity of the royal project, of the popular participation and of the mobilization of the artisans. In fact, the readers left in want of a temple have found a book that deprives them of an honourable ascendancy and throws them on the mercy of the prophetic interpretation of Israel's history to the extent of making the early death of its best king (but all the same he reigned 31 years) a blessing of YHWH. The narrator, here, far from making Huldah prophesy the wrong way, ventures a paradoxical interpretation of the end of the monarchy, and, if the restoration of a temple accomplishes the promises of every enthronement, the king and project-manager is here anointed when well buried. It is as such that he seals the destiny of the dynasty, a dead counter-sign of the end of the city (and of its inhabitants). The temple is not restored in the account; in its place, there is the narrow space of the penitential liturgy where the divine response makes a detour through the obligatory mourning for a monarchy well arrayed in the peace of its tombs.

The word of YHWH reported by Huldah and his own messengers to the king (v. 20b) seems, however, in the completed text, to be the initiator of the text that follows, in 23.1-24 or 25 (v. 24 forms an inclusion with 22.8-10 and v. 25 with 22.2). But it is the sequence as a whole on the finding of the book and the immediate effects of this that informs the account of royal reform.

There are some new actors for the sub-sequence on the Covenant (vv. 1-3): the elders assembled (always *'sp*) a harvest of humans instead of money and the involvement of 'all the people' (23.2 and v. 30; we find 'all the people' again in the correlative sub-sequence of vv. 21-23 on the Passover, after the long journey through the enclosed reform).[2]

The report on the Covenant is itself divided in accordance with four royal acts.

In v. 1, the king, just as in 22.3, 'sends' (*wayyišlaḥ*) a summons to all the elders of Judah and Jerusalem. It is no longer a summoning of the court with power delegated to the scribe, but a move towards the outside, the setting in motion of Judah and Jerusalem as a people or inhabitants (the same ones that the oracle of Huldah affected).

In v. 2, just as Shaphan received the royal order about it in 22.4, the king 'went up', without the intervention of the priest, as was obligatory for the scribe, to the 'house of YHWH', with all the people, among them the priests and the prophets without any specific function. It is that

---

2. Are the two episodes of entrance into the Covenant and the celebration of the Covenant like two pillars of a portico around the central purification ritual, or must we see the second one as a transformation of the first as a result of the passage through this same itinerary enclosed between them? From the point of view of the readers' experiences, there is some progression: the first cultic act, substituted for those of the sacrifices according to the calendar, establishes a precedence of the king and its imitation by 'all the people', signified by the use of the same verb *'md*: the subject-people fall into step (on the spot?) with the royal initiator of the contract. The second cultic act, the real Passover, is again a Josianic initiative but the assembly celebrates the collective feast without a royal model; the real subject is the Passover that 'is done' or not done in the right way. The people, after the great sacrificial destruction, no longer abide by a Covenant behind their king, but, upon an injunction at two levels ('do... as it is written'), 'concelebrate' a new ritual: a real success, and one familiar to the readers, of what will be called 'the Josianic reform'.

totality that forms a liturgical person (cf. Jon. 3.7) and the addressee of the third royal deed: the reading of the book. The exemplary Deuter-onomistic nature of the scene is of less interest to us than the displace-ment in the chain of references to the first sequence, expressed in particular in the definition of the object read to all the people: 'the words of a book' as those that caused the close exchange between the king and YHWH in 22.11-19 in reference to the connection that the king established between them and the sin of 'our ancestors' (22.13).

The book had been identified by the priest (22.8) and acknowledged by the narrator (v. 11) as 'a book of the Law'. Josiah has spoken of it as 'found' (v. 13) in reference to the lucky find of Hilkiah (v. 8) 'in the house of YHWH', object of the first royal initiative. This information is summed up in 23.2, with an important extra meaning 'the words of the Book of the Covenant, the one found in the house of Yhwh': the reader leaves the plain logic of the discovered and incriminating Law to find restored the contractual perspective that generates action, whether just or not. Thus the temple destined for destruction, source of words for dying, is also a source of words for living: the activity of Josiah is described as hurried and extremely energetic, with scarcely any con-nection to the double oracle of Huldah, but perhaps in continuity with the interrupted account about a vague impulse towards restoration. The quest for the oracle had for the time being brought about the royal read-ing; the reading in the hearing of all the people substitutes the con-tractual logic for that of the threats of the Law, but it is a matter of the same book stemming from somewhere else, 'found' in the temple, without any real place of origin and without any real date, recognizable by its effects alone. The effect of the contract is ritualized in v. 3, out-lined as it is by the inclusion formed by 'And the king stood (*wayya'amod*) on or near the *'ammûd'*, with the last words of this short text 'and all the people stood fast (*wayya'amod*) in the covenant (*babb^erith*)'. Whatever the place designated by *'ammû* might be, a podium or a pillar, it is royal (2 Kgs 11.14), but confused with neither the palace nor the temple, of which it probably marked the entrance, unless it was rather the functional space between the two areas. It also suggests a connection of the account with that of the exodus of the people led by the ambiguous column of light and of darkness, signify-ing YHWH's simultaneous absence from and closeness to the people. This narrative inclusion is itself surrounded by another, larger one, that encloses it: 'the words of the Book of the Covenant' (v. 20) and 'the words of this covenant, written in this book' (v. 3). On a still larger scale, the mention of 'all the people' in v. 2 is correlated with that of 'all the people' at the end of v. 3. The heart of this first ritual is made up of three infinitives that indicate its purpose: to walk (behind YHWH), to keep or put into practice the whole Law, to uphold the terms of the agreement; the central proposition explicitly concerning the law sets out three objects that are as many aspects of it. The literary structure of this small unit culminates therefore in this agreement in regard to the Law that can only be understood in a future perspective, initiated here by the king, but mobilizing all the people.

We meet up with the king and all the people again in 23.21-23, in regard to the Passover, it too celebrated as a collective ritual of obedience to the agreements of the covenant. The repetitive style of this sub-sequence is close to that of v. 3. There are three mentions of the Passover (corresponding to the three mentions of the Covenant), linked up with a reference to 'what is written in the Book of the Covenant' (v. 21), but, this time, the role of the king is greater: it is he, indirectly, who is the principal agent; it is he who has the Passover 'carried out' and the narrator emphasizes for the benefit of the readers, in v. 22, that this is unique in the history of the leaders of Israel, judges and kings taken together, before making a large inclusion with 22.3 and the first act of that eighteenth year of Josiah. There remains a surplus of meaning with the note 'at Jerusalem', a rather sceptical one, concerning the judges but appropriate in connection with the unfinished project of the restoration of the temple or the content of the oracle of Huldah the Jerusalemite about 'this book'. In any case it brings the attention of the readers back to the 'book found by Hilkiah in the temple of YHWH' (v. 24). If the repetition of the root *'md* recalls the exodus, the Passover is referred to just as much, and the following notice, which closes the account in v. 25 and allies Josiah with Moses, is introduced perfectly as well. The book that was found, the book of the Law, the book of the Covenant, this book is indeed that of the 'law of Moses' that is recognized as the one that incited repentance (*šwb 'el Yhwh*) and in the first place royal repentance, without any precedent and without any future. This is to say that v. 25 could be a sort of colophon: the possibility of a just monarchy and even the Davidic model (cf. 22.2) are buried with Josiah. At the core of the sequence, the mention of the days of the judges, of the kings of Israel and Judah, invites a collective remembrance for a negative reading which is, strangely, the project for a history (where diachronists will have no trouble in seeing that of the Deuteronomistic historian).

Putting the account of these two great ritual acts, even the Josianic ritual reform, in a rhetorical correlation lays out in a way the long journey of a sacrificial type that the reader experiences to go from one, which operates as a foundation, to the other which is in the nature of the calendar celebration that evidently the readers personally practice, after having buried any possible nostalgia for the royal or proto-royal periods.

This journey is really the undertaking of the king.

Even a synchronic reading appeals here to classical literary criticism in order to receive authorization not to treat 23.4-20 as a narrative unit but rather, for example, to consider vv. 16-20 as an expansion on the theme of the fulfilment of the prophecy applied to Bethel-Samaria and of the motif of tombs running all through these two chapters. The reading of the finished account makes a sort of instructive detour, rhetorically indicated by the action of Josiah at Bethel in v. 16 (*wayyipen*) and his return to the scene at Jerusalem in v. 20 (*wayyašab*), which the final redaction moreover arranges well in order to make a royal 'round trip' from Jerusalem (vv. 4-5) to Jerusalem. A series of concentric correlations organizes the royal activity rather loosely:

Burning of the Asherah (of Jerusalem—of Bethel)	vv. 4 and 15b
Against the works of the kings of Judah and of Israel	vv. 5 and 15a
Defilement of the Wadi Kidron, dump	vv. 6 and 12
Desecration on the theme of fire	vv. 10 and 11

That is to say:

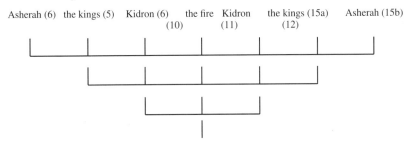

Asherah (6) the kings (5) Kidron (6)   the fire Kidron   the kings (15a)   Asherah (15b)
                                    (10)   (11)   (12)

On the other hand, a geographical organization starts from the heart of the temple; its high priest (access to the cella), and even the guardians (of the threshold; cf. those of 22.4!), cast off the objects dedicated to the three figures of vitalist worship reputed to be Canaanite and to the 'celestial army' of an Assyrian type that gave it its uranic character, to the 'outside of Jerusalem', then to Bethel to the north. The high places of the towns of Judah and in the neighbourhood of Jerusalem in v. 5 are then purified of 'pagan' servants of the same cult.

Three mentions of Asherah give a certain rhythm to this sub-section from the first 'out of the temple' up to the 'graves of the people' (?) (v. 6b) while passing by the Kidron (v. 6a). The mention, so unexpected, of Bethel in this first context suggests that its troubles have something of the programmatic. A diachronic study of the emergence of a radical monotheism must probably therefore be concerned about Asherah more than Baal as an anti-Deuteronomistic *pièce de résistance*.

More widely, v. 8 deals with the towns of Judah and their high places from Geba to Beersheba. Structurally, the mention of the high places of the Gates of Jerusalem brings back the thread to Jerusalem, just as that of the houses of those consecrated did in v. 7, and especially calls to mind Joshua in a negative context (not that the text imputes any responsibility in the affair to him, but his name, here, sounds bad). A synchronic reading of the text does not make it necessary to read v. 9 as a follow-up to v. 8, but establishes instead a literary break. However, if the first sub-sequence repeatedly attacked Asherah, the latter names the high places three times, and those of the city would be perfectly framed by the priests (vv. 8a and 9a): this is a possible redactional or editorial concern.

With the sub-sequence of vv. 10-12, the centripetal movement is confirmed with the profanation of the Topheth in the valley of Ben-Hinnom and the horses of the sun at the entrance to the house of YHWH. Josiah is here sweeping up very close to the temple. In regard to the fire of *Mlk*, despite the weakness of the definition of it, each (*'iš*) is affected—in the masculine, complementary to the feminine (*našîm*) of v. 7—whereas the existence of horses and blazing chariots of the sun are attributed to the kings of Judah.

Just like the cult objects of v. 4, the altars of v. 12 are destined for the Kidron: coming from the palace or the temple, they are royal, associated with the names of Ahaz and Manasseh. It is moreover king against king that shapes this matter of the altars: as in v. 3, where the great purification begins, then in v. 13, in the following sub-sequence, the royal title is mentioned in the operations that directly oppose Josiah to one or some of the predecessors named.

With vv. 13-14, it is the area 'facing Jerusalem' that is cleansed of the high places of foreign gods due to Solomon himself; through these, it is the Sidonians, Moabites and Ammonites who are aimed at, with their abominations destined for the worst profanation.

To the three indigenous forms of pagan divinity within the city of v. 4 correspond at the end of the programme the three forms of divinity imported from the neighbouring peoples who have circumvented Jerusalem.

We have seen that the sacrificial and violent ritual that takes up the centre of this second sequence is, rhetorically and in the experience of the readers, framed by the two serene liturgies that limit it, the entrance into the Covenant and the celebration of the Passover at Jerusalem, that is to say at the living heart of the system of purification that has swept broadly from the temple as far as Bethel (and perhaps Samaria, in the text) and Beer-sheba. The almost orgiastic character of this anti-poly-theistic outburst is in no way repeatable; the only meaning that it has is cathartic, once and for all, foundation or earlier boundary of the memory like the account of a deluge at the frontier of an ancient, non-renewable order. We could just as easily say that the Josianic deed recounts in an abyss a possible historiography with as a sole referent a God more solitary than unique and making the destruction of Jerusalem (and of its inhabitants) the place of a heuristic theophany.

Earlier than Josiah, the royal history, modelled on that of Joshua, has therefore been traversed, that of a mythic, Solomonic Israel, then of Judah, in which we find Ahaz and Manasseh. As an appendix, but also in rhetorical correlation with v. 4b, we finally encounter Jeroboam, the one responsible for the 'sin of Israel'. In his ritual purification spring cleaning, Josiah not only founded the account of an unholy history but also marked off the geography of a defiled land (high places, altars), burning, reducing to dust, and defiling with human bones; in the very logic of the text, that was a royal conquest in the name of YHWH, round a city called holy. It defines at the same time a necessary and horrifying reading of the dynastic record. Historiography discovers here a programme founded on a ritual: a record of royal culpability and of the participation of the people in the same fate, in a history of death without burial. At the heart of this ritualization of the effects of Huldah's oracle, the king who makes history by putting history in perspective uses the cleansing arm, fire, against two opposite aspects of the fire of dis-obedience, the one, chthonic, of the horrible *topeth* and the other, the splendid radiance of the horses and the chariot of the sun.

Instead of crossing the sea where there was born an Israel destined for the fury of YHWH on account of the conduct of its kings, it is in the landscape of fire and ash, of desecrated tombs and scattered bones that the reader goes round in trepidation, on the order of the king to the high priest (v. 4). Bethel, a possible theological recourse against the curse of Jerusalem, shares its verdict and its fate, as a frontier where the ashes come to settle.

It is there that the probable expansion of vv. 16-20 takes place. In the completed structure, it has at least three functions. The anecdote of vv. 16-18 articulates the prophecy and its fulfilment (v. 17) for historiography, within a programme dominated by the Law, basically, canonical. A new Elijah, Josiah, mentioned in v. 19 as well as in v. 16, faces the kings of Israel in the towns of Samaria corresponding to those of Judah (v. 5), constituting, in the deconstruction, the conditions for a possibility of a 'Great Israel'. Finally, this literary subset deals abundantly with tombs and bones, emphasizing the privilege of the two prophets, of the South and the North, whose bones are spared.

The great royal liturgy reaches in v. 21 the celebration of the Passover, on the other bank of this 'passage' to monotheism, a journey of fire and sword, of death and ashes, consuming the work of the past by initiating at the same time a hermeneutical origin of all that history that is already cannonical (Judges-Kings) and 'the eighteenth year of King Josiah' as a beginning of the cultic history of the readers (from which comes their reading of the collective memory).

The account has therefore produced a considerable and irreversible displacement of the obvious indicators and references in the text, upsetting all the endogenous or foreign forms of the sacred, as if the book dug up in the temple implemented, through the royal mediation, the work of the scroll of Zechariah 5. But in reality, in the experience of the readers, it is clear that this same account is on the contrary a foundation of an order already known to the reader and one with its rules already assumed. The immense Josianic spring cleaning takes place in the quasi-jubilation of a reference to the practical experience of the readers, mixing up in the same dustbin Baal, Asherah, the Army of the Heavens, Molech, the Sun, Astarte, Chemosh, Milcom and the specific local characteristics of Yahwism, the high places, renouncing the works of Judah like those of Israel, making a clean space, apart from some prophetic tombs, to found in the geographical and historical precariousness a liturgy of the word addressed to the whole crowd of potential readers

(23.2). It assassinates the past of the ancestors for the prize of a future radically dependent on YHWH alone, in the only reliable reference to the Law of Moses that is no longer a prisoner of the temple, and of the example of Josiah, as v. 25 defines them together. It forms a people who are not without a history; but its strict allegiance to the God of the Covenant requires a penitential historiography like that carried out by Josiah (22.13) in response to which the historical experience becomes the place of a theophany and of its hermeneutic perceived as much by the historical king as by the prophetism that forms a pair with him.

What is left of the temple of which it is said that it becomes with the Josianic reform the cult centre of all Israel? Like the Law, the purifying fire that goes out from it ravages the religious country but the programme for its restoration does not succeed any more than that of its construction by David, while he was alive. However, it is here the place of a decisive exchange and of a spatial metaphor no less decisive, that of the gathering together (*'sp*) at the beginning of the first sequence (22.4) and of the second (23.1), the object besides of the only promise made to Josiah, gathered together with his ancestors and in the peace of their tombs.

The exchange is fundamental, and allows the passage, by the mediation of the book found/given, from the relationship of debt (gift of money against gift of the book, all in 'good faith') to that of belief that the king ritualizes through the mediation of the prophetess (faithful response of Josiah to the reliability of the Law). It is a matter, even if the figures are reversed, of a model, opposed to the sacrificial logic, known besides from the Indo-European world. We may mention here the characteristic elements of the description of this model in a recent article of M. Linder and J. Scheid[3] commenting on the formula of Cicero: 'Religion is the consciousness of cultic duties toward the gods'. Thus Numa, founder and before that mythical reformer of Roman cult enacts rules for ritual; clarified by Egerius as to their meaning, he recorded his revelations in a book that he had buried with him. For the people, there is the proper observance of ritual, including that for the goddess of good faith, Fides.[4] It is a matter therefore of an orthopraxy

3. M. Linder and J. Scheid, 'Quand croire c'est faire: Le problème de la croyance dans la Rome ancienne', *Archives des Sciences Sociales des Religions* 81 (1993), pp. 47-62.

4. Cf. the correspondence between contract-*credo* and *sraddha* = belief. See E. Benveniste, 'Créance et croyance', in *Le vocabulaire des institutions*

that can be contrasted with what is habitually understood by a religion of the book with its supposed weight of doctrine.

The text of 2 Kings 22 and 23, despite the ethical implications of 23.3 and its book disinterred rather than buried, establishes a necessary connection between the *'ᵉmunâ* (*fides*) practised in the undertaking of restoration and the uprightness of the king reforming cultic practices. This religion, here more than ever explicitly 'of the book', is not expressed in terms of doctrinal orthodoxy but in terms of ritual orthopraxy (we must note the importance of the verb *'āśâ*, 'to do'). Monotheism outlines its doctrinal exclusivism here in a great display of royal and collective activity with a ritual connotation or expression. The account methodically throws out the excess religious figures of the temple, of Jerusalem, of Judah and Israel and constructs a complete societal structure: Shaphan, in service to the right of the king, Huldah and her mantic function, the assembly of the people already represented in the collection (22.4) and carried through in the complementarity of the rituals of the Covenant and of the Passover. A surreptitious inclusion substitutes the Passover for the restoration of the temple and sends away the high priest famous solely for finding the Law without any further explanation about the confusion over which he presided in the house of YHWH before the great and violent cleansing where the king voiced his justice and at the same time ritualized his interpretation of the history and of the divine word. In his personal history, Josiah testifies to the fulfilment of the words of the book that he put into practice and of the prophecy in which he actually dies and is then gathered together with the bones of his ancestors. What is constructed from the work and the person of him who allows the readers to say 'our ancestors' and 'us' (22.13) is as a matter of fact a royal tomb. The oracle that he solicits buries him. The monarchy established according to the rigour of the written Law of YHWH has no other proper future except that of the blind peace of the tombs. The people itself will experience the fury, the destruction, but also the purification and finally the sequence of Passovers modelled on what Josiah instituted, which the Israel of the readers has celebrated ever since. The readers are summoned to a royal obedience, that which Deuteronomy (23.3) preaches to them and which makes them stand (*'md*) as the subjects that they are

européennes, I (Paris: Ed. de Minuit, 1969), pp. 171-79, cited by Linder and Scheid, 'Quand croire c'est faire' and brought to my attention by J. Lambert.

of the Covenant and of the account, therefore, of the history to which the kings give the chronology.

There remains the scribe or secretary, the true servant of the book that was read. In one sense, he disappears with the first sequence, the founding sequence, of the account. In reality, he dominates the whole text. First of all explicitly assisting in acquiring the text, in having it read and in its intepretation (in the intervention with Huldah), he is later, for the reader, the narrator of a series of remarks that help in their turn to produce intelligent readers. Having recounted a history of the great purification (can we speak of a reform?) by Josiah, and through it, that of the monarchy and even of the time of the judges, it is he who suggests the reference to David and to Moses (22.2 and 23.5), giving the reader the necessry criteria for a sound judgment. He is not satisfied, however, with this putting in a perspective where each recognizes the elements said to be of the Deuteronomistic historiographic framework. The burial of the monarchy, which takes place in a great racket of bones being scattered, profaned or profaning as the unfinished project of restoring the temple destined for destruction, creates the vacuum for the elaboration of Jewish eschatology. Based on the recognition of the power of YHWH to take over and make the present calamity come across to the readers, to make them even bypass the mausoleum of the kings bad or good in order to take away the history—there remains some of it, since there are readers—by the history that ends with Jerusalem and the royal chronicle, this eschatology is just like the figure of Josiah who dies in the history where he assumes a function as last king but is excluded from that same history ('Your eyes shall not see all the disaster...', v. 20) and, contrary to all narrative logic, transcends it in the useless institution of a celebration of Covenant and Passover (only the mourning—cf. 22.19—was useful). This double institution, like a new sanctuary where the Law beomes effective, contains the possibility of new life: a past, 'what was written' and the reference to critical historiography, the cultic present and the future promised by the accomplishment of the prophecy, become the subject for belief for the readers (Josiah is quite dead before the fall of Jerusalem). Thus there is a passage from the credence-good faith of 22.3-7 to the belief-faith of the readers attentive to canonical historiography, guided by the reliable testimony of the good scribe. But this 'passage' is towards the expectation of the signs of a greater reliability, that of YHWH whose words recorded in a book prompted people to consult YHWH in the

person of the prophets. If what was announced by the book has happened, those who acquiesce in the great Josianic conflagration can
await on the ashes of Jerusalem the fruits, promised to them too, of
their new allegiance to the exclusive God who assembles them for a
collective ritual after the close of royal history and that of the first
temple, on the threshold of a purified space. It is for prophecy, sub-
sumed in the person of Huldah, to formulate the responses of the satisfied God after those of the jealous God. Or else, even, for the scribe-
reader to construct the positive exegesis of the catastrophe announced
once and for all. The king is dead, long live the new people, whose eyes
have seen and will see!

Part V

THE SOURCES OF DEUTERONOMISTIC HISTORIOGRAPHY

THE SOURCES OF THE DEUTERONOMISTIC HISTORY:
RESEARCH ON JOSHUA 1–12

Jacques Briend

For M. Noth, the Deuteronomistic work (Dtr) consisted of the books of Joshua, Judges, Samuel and Kings, which are marked, to a greater or lesser extent, by the literary activity of a 'Deuteronomistic'[1] author who by his vocabulary, his style and his ideas refers to Deuteronomy, to its Law and to its discourses. Noth's thesis is at the same time appealing and debatable.

It is appealing because of its simplicity, which explains to some extent the success that it has met. It remains debatable because it does not succeed in taking into account the data that an attentive reading of this vast literary corpus discovers. For fifty years, Noth's hypothesis has been examined, discussed, nuanced, but it remains an obligatory starting point.

All the same, the idea of a single author for such a diverse work remains a difficulty. What is more, while important studies have been undertaken of the books of Kings, the others that open the DH, strangely enough the books of Joshua and Judges, have been somewhat forgotten. As S.L. McKenzie recognized,[2] what one observes in the books of Kings is not necessarily true for the rest of the DH. That is so true that in a contribution to the debate on the composition of that History, I.W. Provan[3] suggested in 1988 that the book of Judges had only been joined to the books of Samuel and Kings at a late period. The

---

1. M. Noth, *Überlieferungsgeschichtliche Studien* (Tübingen: Niemeyer, 1943, 2nd edn, 1957), pp. 3-4.

2. S.L. McKenzie, *The Trouble with Kings: The Composition of the Books of Kings in the Deuteronomistic History* (VTSup, 42; Leiden: E.J. Brill, 1991), p. 19.

3. I.W. Provan, *Hezekiah and the Books of Kings* (BZAW, 172; Berlin and New York: W. de Gruyter, 1988), pp. 164-68.

book of Joshua also prompted him to raise some questions in regard to its final composition and date.[4]

Not being able to take up all the books that make up the DH, I intend to examine the book of Joshua, at least the first part of it (Josh. 1–12), in regard to which we must recall that Noth had earlier prepared a commentary;[5] such an examination is needed in order to be more specific about the extent of the written text that served as the base for the Dtr redaction. Our goal in reading these chapters is therefore to distinguish what belongs to a pre-Dtr text and its sources in relation to a redaction whose coherence we take for granted, at least along its main lines. The task is difficult. To carry out this discernment we will utilize all the resources of literary criticism so as to obtain multiple criteria. However, I shall leave aside questions of textual criticism, which in the case of the book of Joshua are numerous. As a general rule I shall follow the MT.

In this search for a written document earlier than the Dtr redaction, we will be led to discern written or oral sources utilized in the document or documents that are the beginnings of the future book of Joshua. This distinction between document and sources is necessary in this study on Joshua 1–12. The study is divided into five sections; I do not pretend to be able to examine the whole biblical text.

1. A Starting Point: Joshua 9

If we leave aside for the time being the text of Josh. 9.1-2 and its special role, Josh. 9.3-27, which relates the story of the ruse of the Gibeonites and the status imposed on this group by Joshua, can serve as a starting point for research on the sources and the document at the disposal of the first Dtr redaction. Without redoing an analysis of this text which has already been carried out,[6] we can draw from it some

4. Provan, *Hezekiah*, p. 170 and n. 36.
5. M. Noth, *Das Buch Josua* (HAT, 7; Tübingen: Mohr, 1938, 2nd edn, 1953).
6. On this text, see J. Briend, 'Israel et les Gabaonites', in E.M. Laperrousaz (ed.), *La protohistoire d'Israel: De l'exode à la monarchie* (Paris: Cerf, 1990), pp. 121-67; J. Briend, 'Gabaon à l'époque perse', *Transeuphratène* 5 (1992), pp. 9-20 extends the first study and focuses on the Deuteronomistic and priestly redactions. K. Lawson Younger (*Ancient Conquest Accounts: A Study in Ancient Near Eastern and Biblical History Writing* [JSOTSup, 98; Sheffield: JSOT Press, 1990], pp. 200-204) concerns himself with Josh. 9 strictly from the point of view of a specialist in comparative linguistics.

conclusions on the question that preoccupies us.

The text begins by recounting the ruse of the Gibeonites. Very quickly the reader can pose the following question: Who is the interlocutor of the Gibeonites? The man of Israel or Joshua? All indications suggest that it is 'the man of Israel', the original interlocutor of the Gibeonites. It is moreover the only account in the book where we come across this designation, which has a collective value. Furthermore, since the presence of Joshua is predominant in the accounts of Joshua 2–8, it is difficult to think that the phrase 'the man of Israel' had been introduced belatedly in the text. After all, in v. 6, the insertion of Joshua and the detail 'in the camp, at Gilgal' compelled the redactor, who wanted to accentuate the role of Joshua, to make a displacement of the mention of 'the man of Israel' to the middle of the verse and the man of Israel becomes in some way dependent upon Joshua. On the other hand, in v. 7 'the man of Israel' becomes the subject of the sentence and it is he who directly speaks to the Gibeonites/Hivites.

Behind the present text we can recover an account prior to the 'Joshua' redaction that presents only 'the man of Israel' (cf. below, Document 1). This account establishes itself as a written source for the one who introduced the personage of Joshua. This entry of Joshua into the text is a necessity for this redactor, not simply to make a connection with what preceded, for if that is the case (cf. Josh. 9.3), it is not the main reason, but rather to attribute to Joshua an authoritative function that will allow him in the continuation of the text to determine the status of the Gibeonites.

If this hypothesis about the reading is accepted, several conclusions follow from it.

First of all, on the basis of Josh. 9.3, it must be admitted that the 'Joshua' redactor knew the accounts that we have in Joshua 6–8, which suggests developing research in the direction of these chapters.

On the other hand, we have a written source that calls for a negative judgment on the attitude of the Israelites (9.14); the compiler extends this and completes it by having Joshua grant a juridical status to the Gibeonites: 'Joshua made them wood-carriers and water-carriers...for YHWH's altar down to this day' (Josh. 9.27).

The document composed by the 'Joshua' compiler underwent some additions (cf. below, Document 2). If we examine them, it becomes possible to verify that there were more recent interventions by redactors on this first document. The first such intervention could be described as

Dtr. This is noticeable in Josh. 9.9bβ-10 in the account of the ruse and in Josh. 9.16*, 17, 24a, 26, 27* for the second part of the text. The intention of these interventions is clear, even if we cannot know whether they were made at the same stage. Josh. 9.9bβ-10 is a confession of faith by the Gibeonites that recalls that of Josh. 2.10 and takes up again some well-documented expressions in Deuteronomy 1–3. To some extent, this confession of faith justifies in the eyes of the redactor the fact that they had not exterminated the Gibeonites. This order for extermination given by God to Moses in Deut. 7.23 is recalled in Josh. 9.24a. This logic is already present in Josh. 9.17: 'The Israelites set out and reached their cities on the third day. The cities were Gibeon, Chepirah, Beeroth, and Kiriath-jearim'. The binomial 'set out—reach'[7] indicates a military action on the part of the Israelites and the Gibeonites really risk death as the continuation of the text shows (v. 26). For the redactor, the cities named must be 'cities where you must not leave any living being alive' according to the prescription of Deut. 20.16. As we have seen, Josh. 9.17 and Josh. 9.26 are verses that match each other. The temporal indications, 'after three days' (v. 16; cf. Josh. 3.2), 'the third day' (v. 17), 'on that day' (v. 27) come under this Dtr redaction, which could be characterized as a 'rhetoric of conquest' according to the phrase of R.H. O'Connell.[8] By itself, the phrase 'at the place that YHWH has chosen' (v. 27b), occurring after the formula 'to this day', could belong to another Dtr hand, concerned about the law of centralization of the altar (Deut. 12).

Finally, the text bears witness to a priestly insertion as well (cf. below, Document 2) which is mainly found in vv. 18-21.[9] This is prepared for by a part of v. 15 and it explains the mention of the 'community' in v. 27. The vocabulary and the intention that presides over this insertion leave no doubt about the attribution.

Before leaving Joshua 9, it is advisable to pay some attention to the introduction to the account that we have just examined. The vocabulary, the style and the content of Josh. 9.1-2, at least if we remove the list of regions and that of peoples that must be attributed to the Dtr redaction,

7.   R.G. Boling and G.E. Wright (*Joshua*; AB, 6; Garden City, NY: Doubleday, 1982], p. 266), noted the warlike connotation of the verbal binomial.

8.   R.H. O'Connell, 'Deuteronomy VII 1-26: Asymmetrical Concentricity and the Rhetoric of Conquest', *VT* 42 (1992), pp. 248-65.

9.   J. Halbe, 'Gibeon und Israel', *VT* 25 (1975), pp. 613-16; Briend, 'Gabaon à l'époque perse', pp. 18-20.

actually set these verses apart. We are dealing here with a relay-text that, like Josh. 5.1, is intended to prepare for Joshua 10–12. All the kings who are beyond the Jordan form a coalition and assemble their troops to wage war against Joshua and against Israel.[10] This project is only carried into effect beginning with Joshua 10. We shall therefore have to devote the last part of our research to the literary unit formed by chs. 10–12. They represent an addition to the work of the 'Joshua' compiler.

2. *The Conquest of Ai (Joshua 7–8)*

Chapters 7 and 8 of the book of Joshua are closely connected to each other from the point of view of the sequence of events, since the largest section of Joshua 7 recounts the discovery of the culprit responsible for the first setback at the time of the conquest of the city of Ai by Joshua, with chapter 8 recounting the conquest of that city. The search for sources is more difficult here than in Joshua 9, but I shall show that it is possible with a fair degree of certainty to distinguish a written source and its reworking by the 'Joshua' compiler.

Joshua 7.1-5
Should one set out to find a beginning for this ancient account, one cannot find it in Josh. 7.1. This verse is a sort of general superscription that is only interested in the presence of a guilty person among the people. This superscription has been composed in two stages.

In a first stage it was composed by a Deuteronomistic redactor: 'Achan, son of Carmi, son of Zabdi, son of Zerah,...took something that fell under the ban, and the wrath of YHWH was kindled against the Israelites' (v. 1b). This divine reaction has its counterpart at the end of the text in 7.26aβ. The main preoccupation of the redactor revolves around the ban as put into practice in holy war and its violation by an Israelite whose genealogy is given to us.

This first superscription is supplemented by a generalization traceable to a priestly hand: 'The Israelites broke faith in regard to the ban' (v. 1a). The verb מעל followed by the noun of the same root and by an object introduced by a preposition belongs to the vocabulary of the book of Ezekiel, of P and of the Chronicler.[11] To this priestly hand also

---

10. Cf. Briend, 'Israël et les Gabaonites', pp. 124-30.
11. The verb is found 35 times in the Old Testament: outside of Josh. 7.1 and

belongs the precise detail 'of the tribe of Judah'. The term מַטֵּה, very rare in the book of Joshua (Josh. 7.1, 18; 13.29; 14.2-3), comes under priestly vocabulary.

It is only in Josh. 7.2 therefore that an account begins with Joshua sending explorers with the idea of conquering Ai. This account, which continues up to v. 5, recounts how the first attempt at conquest meets with a military setback. God does not intervene in this account. On the other hand, beginning with Josh. 7.6 a lamentation scene occurs; in this setting Joshua addresses God (vv. 7-9), then God intervenes in order for Joshua to discover the guilty one (vv. 10-15). The reader discovers at that time that the military defeat is connected with the guilt of an Israelite. From v. 6 up to v. 26, the text is no longer interested in the conquest of Ai, but in the theological reason for the military setback. To what extent does this account of the search for the guilty person influence the account of Joshua 8 that recounts the taking of Ai? Such is the question that should be asked.

Joshua 8.1-29

In Joshua 8 we are in the presence of a very simple narrative structure, even if the text is not without some internal tensions. We have the following sequence:

> discourse of Yhwh with Joshua (vv. 1-2),
> orders given for the ambush (vv. 3-9),
> execution of Joshua's orders (vv. 10-25),
> conclusions (vv. 26-29).

At this stage, we can already make some observations. In the first place, God's discourse (vv. 1-2) is very overloaded.[12] But is this discourse needed for the development of the narrative? We do not find

Prov. 16.10, it is found 7 times in the book of Ezekiel (14.13; 15.8; 17.20; 18.24; 20.27; 39.23, 26), in the priestly texts (Lev. 5.15, 21; 26.40; Num. 5.6, 12, 27; Josh. 22.16, 20, 31) and in the Chronicler (1 Chron. 2.7; 5.25; 10.13; 2 Chron. 12.2; 26.16, 18; 28.19, 22; 29.6; 30.7; 36.14). To these references should be added Ezra 10.2, 10; Neh. 1.8; 13.27; Dan. 9.7).

12. Noth (*Das Buch Josua*, p. 50) considered with good reason that several phrases in Josh. 8.1-2 were Deuteronomistic (vv. 1a ['Do not be afraid or dismayed'], 1b, 2a). The order 'Take with you the whole fighting force' (v. 1a) could belong to the ancient redactor of Josh. 10–12, since the phrase 'the whole fighting force', very rare in the Old Testament, occurs, outside of Josh. 8.1, 3, in Josh. 10.7 and 11.7.

there, oddly, any reference to the setback suffered at the time of the first attack on Ai (cf. Josh. 7.2-5). The order given by God: 'Take with you..., go up against Ai...' (v. 1a) is carried out in v. 3a. We have there the beginning of the execution, but at the same time an anticipation since the execution is reaffirmed in 8.10.

Still more interesting is the fact that the setting up of the ambush precedes the departure of the army in v. 9, and is then repeated in v. 12, once the army is deployed.

Finally, no reference is made to God's discourse from v. 10 onwards. Joshua is in charge of the action and, if we put aside v. 18 to which we must return, God does not intervene any more in this section of the text, which runs from v. 10 to v. 29. To some extent the account that begins in v. 10 is sufficient unto itself; what is indispensable in it, in order to understand the stratagem used, is the account of the first attempt (Josh. 7.2-5) and not the unity formed by Josh. 8.1-9.

According to the observation that we have just made, we can propose a hypothesis for reading that can make it possible both to understand the double sending out of an ambush, a doublet that has disturbed the textual transmission[13] as well as the understanding of the account, and to discover how the 'Joshua' composer worked from a written source. This composer has in the first place taken up again the beginning of an account of the conquest of Ai (Josh. 7.2-5), then interrupted it to make room for an account of the search for the one culpable in the military setback (Josh. 7.6-26). He only takes up with the written source again in 8.10. In Josh. 8.1-9 the composer has imprinted in the text a religious dimension with a discourse of God and has made Joshua the intermediary who faithfully carries out God's orders. It is in this way that he opens ch. 8 with a brief divine discourse where God appears as the commander in chief: 'YHWH said to Joshua: "...Get up, go up against Ai... Place then an ambush against the city"' (vv. 1-2*). In 7.2 it is Joshua who gave the orders; from now on it is God who commands.

---

13. On this subject we should recall the remark of J. Wellhausen quoted by D. Barthelemy (*Critique textuelle de l'Ancien Testament* [OBO, 50.1; Freiburg: Universitätsverlag; Göttingen: Vandenhoeck & Ruprecht, 1982], p. 11): 'It is worth noting that *G has eliminated almost all the inconsistencies created by the duality of the versions [of the capture of Ai]. Thus vv. 12 and 13 are missing as well as in v. 14 the two opposing temporal references and finally all of v. 26... The best witness, on the contrary, that could be brought to *M amounts to being able to continue the literary analysis to such an extent and with such preciseness.'

The change is clear. Joshua is the one who obeys God and transmits in the field the orders necessary for an ambush planned by God. This conveying of orders for the ambush (8.3b-9) is due almost totally to the compiler[14] and results from a narrative process that we find elsewhere in Joshua 3–6.

Consequently, it is only in Josh. 8.10-25 that we can again find the ancient account that follows after Josh. 7.2-5 (Document 3), but these verses do not escape all intervention by the 'Joshua' compiler, as well as a Deuteronomistic redaction.

We can attribute to the compiler some points introduced into the ancient account, but any such contribution in comparison with the written source at times remains difficult to specify. He will be credited with the piece of information in v. 10, 'he and the elders of Israel' (cf. Josh. 7.6), with all of v. 11 and v. 16a as well as v. 17a. Verse 18 has its own characteristic. It is an order from God to Joshua, but its location is at first sight strange. Why here and not at the beginning in Josh. 8.1-2? The order from God and its immediate execution by Joshua is a reminder that the victory comes from God. Such is the meaning of the sicklesword brandished by Joshua.[15] It is an efficacious sign of the divine power: it is neither a signal given for the ambush, as v. 19 says, since in that case the orders given for this in Josh. 8.3-9 should have spoken of it; nor is it a signal maintained until the complete execution of the anathema as 8.26, a Dtr verse, wants.

The Dtr redaction is not limited to this v. 26. It plays a part in 8.14 with the mention of the 'king of Ai', disrupting a text that, originally, knew as participants only 'the men of Ai'. This insertion was prepared for in 8.1-2 by several phrases in God's discourse: 'Do not be afraid or dismayed... See, I give into your power the king of Ai, his people, his city and his land. You shall do to Ai and its king as you did to Jericho and its king...' That promise of conquest had been renewed in 8.7b: 'YHWH your God, has delivered it into your hand', to which is added the recommendation of 8.8: 'According to YHWH's order you shall act'. Prepared for in this way, the mention of the king of Ai must have been introduced into an account that made no mention of him, since the Dtr redaction is interested in the kings of cities and especially in their death.

---

14. In Josh. 8.3-9 we will not attribute to the compiler v. 3a (cf. v. 1: 'fighting force'), v. 7b and in v. 8 the formula 'according to YHWH's word you will act'.

15. O. Keel, *Wirkmächtige Siegeszeichen im Alten Testament* (OBO, 5; Freiburg/Göttingen: Universitätsverlag/Vandenhoeck & Ruprecht, 1974), pp. 11-82.

In the continuation of the warlike account, the interventions of this redaction are minimal.[16] On the other hand, when it comes to describing the consequences that follow from the capture of the city, the intervention becomes more extensive. We can with certainty ascribe to this redaction v. 22b ('and they struck them down until there was left neither survivor nor fugitive'), v. 23 ('they captured the king of Ai and brought him to Joshua') and vv. 26, 28-29, which report the anathematization of all the inhabitants, the total destruction of the city and finally the death of the king of Ai.

In conclusion, the examination of Joshua 7–8 has made it possible to discover a written source taken up by the 'Joshua' compiler. Faced with a warlike account in which Joshua held the central role, the compiler made God intervene as the one who gives orders to this same Joshua. God in that case becomes the author of the victory. We are witnessing the Yahwization of the ancient account.

The Dtr redaction intervenes in an already constituted text and makes use, still more than in Joshua 9, of this rhetoric of conquest of which there has already been question. The repeated mention of 'all Israel' in Josh. 8.15, 21, 24 insists on the inseparable binomial formed by the human leader and the people.

Beyond these first results, research would have to be continued by taking an interest in the Achan episode (Josh. 7.6-26). It would be a question of verifying whether this account is built on a written or oral source. The second hypothesis is the more probable, but it would require a precise examination. What can be said is that the 'Joshua' compiler associated this account with that of the conquest of Ai, that the culprit was a Judaean and that the genealogy of Achan is partly Judaean and partly from the tribe of Reuben. These pieces of information make it possible to situate the compiler who uses these various sources, but does not hesitate to implicate a Judaean. In the text of Josh. 7.6-26, the religious, indeed liturgical, motivations of the compiler are very clear. It is a matter of providing a reason explaining why God has not given victory to the Israelites. The lamentation of Joshua (7.6-8*), the orders of God to Joshua (7.9-15), and their faithful execution by the leader of the people (7.16-18) are mainly the work of the compiler.

Research would also have to interest itself in the contacts that exist between Joshua 8 and Judges 20 where the same stratagem is used, that

16. We must nevertheless attribute to the Deuteronomic redaction the mention of 'and all Israel' in v. 15, v. 21 in its entirety and perhaps v. 17b.

of an ambush and a simulated flight. But such an examination would take us too far from the more immediate question of the sources used by the compiler and the state of the document on which a Deuteronomistic redactor or redactors intervened.

3. *Jericho (Joshua 5.13–6.24)*

Before taking up the account of the fall of the rampart of Jericho (Josh. 6.1-24), it is necessary to begin the research from the text that precedes it, the theophany of the commander of the army of YHWH (Josh. 5.13-15), which we can consider an introduction for the account that we find in Joshua 6.[17]

The Manifestation of the Commander of YHWH's Army (5.13-15)
This enigmatic account never fails to raise numerous questions. The location of the scene is placed 'at Jericho' (v. 13a). This difficult reading of the MT in the face of some versions[18] deserves consideration, since it can preserve an indication that the account has an origin and a meaning independent of its present context, but that at the same time the reader is prepared for the acccount that is going to follow in Joshua 6.

Joshua is granted a vision: 'Joshua raised his eyes and saw: right there...' Such a sequence is not very frequent in the Old Testament but it is met in Gen. 18.2; 24.63; 33.1; 37.25 (cf. Gen. 22.13; 31.10). We are in the presence of an account of a vision. Is it a theophany? The continuation of the text tends in that direction: 'right there a man was standing before him, a drawn sword in his hand' (v. 13). The drawn sword can be a sign of threat or a sign of victory. The vision is ambiguous and Joshua's reaction shows it: 'he said to him: "Are you one of us or one of our adversaries?"' The response that Joshua receives is only clear if we make the negation focus on the second part of the question: 'No, for I am the commander of the army of YHWH' (v. 14).

17. E. Jacob, 'Une théophanie mystérieuse, Josué 5,13-15', in R. Kuntzmann (ed.), *Ce Dieu qui vient: Mélanges offerts à B. Renaud* (LD, 159; Paris: Cerf, 1995), pp. 131-35.
18. In actual fact the MT is supported by the Greek and the Targum; on the other hand the Vulgate (*in agro urbis*), the Syriac ('in the plain of Jericho') and the Arabic version ('in the vicinity of Jericho') give the preposition *b^e* a broad meaning, as is done by most translators.

What clarifies the response is that the man declines to identify himself. The warlike role of the personage and his celestial status are thus made clear. But how is the title put forward to be understood? Normally, 'commander of the army' is a title given to a royal official who heads the army. Here the army is celestial, but when the biblical texts mention such an army, they do not say that it has a commander. This commander is actually God personally. Through anthropomorphic language Josh. 5.13-14 presents God as the real commander of the army, including that of Israel. Is it not This One who goes out at the head of the army (Judg. 4.14; 5.4; 2 Sam. 5.25)? Is this not The One who gives the victory?

This is the interpretation that seems to be required. After having declined to reveal his identity, the interlocutor of Joshua declares: 'I have now come'. This coming is that of God. The reader would expect some preciseness on the purpose of that coming,[19] but there is no indication of this. We get the impression of a truncated text whose meaning can only be discovered in its link with Joshua 6. However that may be, Joshua reacts and his reaction indicates the presence of God: 'Joshua fell on his face to the ground and worshipped'. This is a normal reaction in the setting of a theophany.

At the end of v. 14 a prostrate Joshua is ready to listen: 'He says to him: "What does my Lord have to say to his servant?" ' The reply is found in v. 15, but the narrator offers a citation of Exod. 3.15. The linking is strange. But if we keep in mind the literary phenomenon of citation and of the will that it expresses of comparing the figure of Joshua and that of Moses, which is a characteristic of the Dtr redaction (cf. Josh. 1.5; 3.7; 4.14), we can in that case assume that the listening that Joshua displayed in 5.14 has its normal outcome in Josh. 6.2: 'YHWH said to Joshua'.

In conclusion, Josh. 5.13-14 is an account of a vision that very probably comes from a source, but one that is truncated. For the 'Joshua' compiler, this short account serves as an introduction to the following account, which opens with the orders given by God to Joshua (6.2-5); in addition, it has the function of indicating to the reader that the taking of Jericho is the work of YHWH. The drawn sword is a sign of victory as the sicklesword pointed by Joshua will be in Josh. 8.18. The reader is

19. The motif of the coming of God is not clearly indicated by the text, as is recognized by Jacob. 'Une théophanie mystérieuse', p. 134. On Josh. 5.13-15, see Keel, *Wirkmächtige Siegeszeichen*, pp. 82-88.

informed that the whole of Joshua 6 is perhaps not to be read as a war-like account. But discussion on this point is far from being closed.[20]

The Rampart of Jericho (Joshua 6.1-25)

Reading Joshua 6 raises a difficult question: what was the content of the text before the intervention of a Dtr redaction? The response is found in part in the link established between Josh. 5.13-14 and Josh. 6.2. The original account opens with God's orders to Joshua (6.3-5). Only the verses which are directly linked to the execution of this order should be retained to reconstruct the original account before the intervention of Dtr redactors. Thus the coherence between God's order and its execution by Joshua should serve as a guide.

What God orders is that during six days the people (designated by the second person plural in the order) are to circle the city once each day. The seventh day (v. 4*), the people must circle the city seven times; at a fixed signal, provided by the trumpets, the people must give a tremendous shout, the rampart will crumble and the people must go up, each one charging straight ahead. This scenario must therefore be carried out in two stages.

The execution of the march, opened in v. 12 with the formula 'Joshua rose early in the morning', is described in v. 14: 'They marched round the city...once and they returned to the camp; they did this for six days'. We recognize here therefore the first stage of the divine order.

The second stage of the execution concerns the seventh day. We find it first in v. 15a (except for: 'in the usual manner') where it is a question of seven tours of the city, then in v. 16, which mentions the sound of the trumpets, finally in v. 20b, which repeats almost word for word v. 5. From this v. 20b we will not retain the last words: 'and they took the city', not found in v. 5 and intended to introduce the anathema, a decisive preoccupation of the Dtr redaction.

This rapid sketch of the literary form based on a link between order and execution does not take into account the complexity of the text. On the one hand, from v. 6, Joshua transmits orders either to the priests, or to the people, of which we must render an account. On the other hand, the text definitely seems to make the ark have a part in the march round

20. L. Schwienhorst (*Die Eroberung Jerichos* [SBS, 122; Stuttgart: Katholisches Bibelwerk, 1986], p. 47) considers that the basic account in Josh. 6 contains elements coming from accounts of the war of YHWH and of the conquest of a city. The basic account proposed in Document 4 is notably different.

the city and the priests are the carriers of the ark just as they are the ones who sound the trumpets.

The sequence order–execution is no longer that of the text. As we have been able to see in Joshua 8, the compiler made Joshua the one who transmits God's orders; from a binary structure we pass to a compound structure where Joshua becomes a transmitter of orders whether to the priests or to the people. The narrative elaboration of the binary source-text does not stop there and we must attribute to the 'Joshua' compiler an adaptation of the text to the Jerusalem liturgy, from which we get the presence of the ark, of priests who are carriers of the ark and finally of priests who sound the trumpets before the ark. In this adaptation, Joshua becomes the one who gives the signal for the shout (v. 10), which was not essential since this role was fulfilled by the sound of the trumpet (vv. 5, 20b).

All these modifications of a simpler source-text occur between v. 6 and v. 14 where we see a liturgical production adapted by the compiler.

It is this text (cf. below, Document 4) that is going to complete and modify the Dtr redaction. With v. 1, this redaction separates Joshua 6 from its normal introduction and Jericho becomes a besieged city. In v. 2 it uses a formula to have God announce the conquest of the city: 'See, I have handed Jericho and its king over to you'. In v. 16 the formula is repeated by Joshua: 'for YHWH has given the city to you'. It is Joshua too who announces in the same discourse that the city is anathema with all that is found in it (v. 17a). This anathema is accomplished in v. 21 and the city is destroyed by fire (v. 24a). The application of the anathema to the city of Jericho will be able from then on to serve as a paradigm in the following chapters of the book. The intention that governs the Dtr redaction is here evident.

In conclusion, the compiler had available to him a binary text in which there appeared orders in the second person plural and an account of an execution. On this basis he develops a text in which Joshua is introduced as leader of the people and in which he transmits God's orders with great faithfulness. It is this text that the Dtr redaction transforms into an account of holy war.

4. *The Beginning of the Document (Joshua 1–3)*

I have proposed that the end of the document due to the 'Joshua' compiler stops at Josh. 9.27, which leaves open the incorporation of Joshua 10–12 into this first document. A question comes up before that:

where can we discover the beginning of the document that ends in Joshua 9?

We cannot make the beginning of the text coincide with the formula of Josh. 3.1: 'Joshua rose early in the morning', a formula that we have met in Josh. 6.12; 7.16; 8.10. F. Langlamet[21] acknowledges, at least in an implicit way, that this signal-formula cannot serve as a narrative opening, since it always presupposes an earlier element. The solution adopted by Langlamet, which consists of transferring this formula to the beginning of Josh. 3.6, does not seem to be a good solution. If we examine the other examples of the formula in Joshua 6–8, we discover that this signal-formula has as a function to announce the execution by Joshua of God's orders. But in Josh. 3.1 we have nothing of the sort and the account in Joshua 2 contains no order from God.

If we look for an order from God that explains the use of the signal-formula in Josh. 3.1, we must go back as far as Josh. 1.1-2, which, today, opens the book of Joshua. Certainly, Josh. 1.1 consists of an opening that forms a transition from Deuteronomy 34 and the death of Moses, but there we also find the expression 'YHWH said to Joshua' which we have in Josh. 6.2; 7.10; 8.1, where the divine order is only separated from the signal-formula by the transmission of Joshua's orders to the people or to a part of the people. God's order in Josh. 1.2, reduced to its essentials, focuses on the crossing of the Jordan: '...rise, it is time, and cross the Jordan here, you and your people...' In its simplicity we have there the beginning of the document that continues in Josh. 3.3 (except for 'you and the sons of Israel'), then in 3.5 (cf. below, Document 5).

Such a beginning reflects well the purposes of the compiler: it is a matter of immediately establishing the sequence of events as ordained by God. For the redactor, the crossing of the Jordan is a marvellous act of God in favour of the Israelites that is only equalled by the exodus from Egypt. This interest in the crossing of the Jordan is borne out by the space accorded the event in Joshua 3–4, chapters for which the compiler had sources at his disposal. This same interest in the crossing and its significance for Israel are very clear in the lamentation prayer pronounced by Joshua: 'Ah! Lord God, why have you made this people cross the Jordan?... What shall I say now that Israel has turned its back towards its enemies?... All the inhabitants of the land will hear of it...'

---

21. F. Langlamet, 'La traversée du Jourdain et les documents de l'Hexateuque', *RB* 79 (1972), p. 9 and n. 13.

(Josh. 7.7*-9*). The crossing of the Jordan had been willed by God personally, as is stated in Josh. 1.1-2.

Despite the arguments just advanced, locating the beginning of the document in Josh. 1.1-2 can seem a rash option. The most important objection stems from the presence in Joshua 2 of the account about Rahab and the hospitality she shows to Joshua's messengers. There can be no question of carrying out here a study of this text,[22] but we can at least briefly touch on the time when this account found a place in the document. The sending out of explorers by Joshua could be considered part of the necessary preparations for the crossing of the Jordan and was therefore inserted between Josh. 1.1*-2* and 3.1, but it certainly seems that this happened at quite a late period. There is actually no reason to think that this Rahab account had been inserted by the compiler. The passage was integrated into the document when the account about Jericho (Josh. 6) was already elaborated, so that it has had no influence on it. However, it is hard to think that the Rahab text would have been introduced by the Dtr redaction. The study of Josh. 6.22-23, 25 makes it possible to conclude that v. 25 is an older conclusion on the lot of Rahab than that of vv. 22-23. These latter verses call to mind the oath of which there is question in Josh. 2.12, 17, 20, and thus explain why Rahab and her house escaped the anathema. It is therefore very probable that the account of Joshua 2 only made its way into the document at a late date, but prior to the Dtr redaction.

If there was any need of it, Josh. 6.25 recalls that the episode about Rahab and her house, despite the differences in vocabulary and style, maintains quite close connections with Joshua 9, since Rahab, like the Gibeonites, 'dwells in the midst of Israel to this day' (6.25).[23]

With these pieces of information on the time when Joshua 2 could find a place within the 'Joshua' document, it seems to me that we have discovered the beginning of the document. There still remains Joshua 10–12 about which to make a decision in order to complete this survey on the state of the text before the intervention of the Dtr redaction.

22. On Josh. 2, see J.P. Floss, *Kunden oder Kundschafter?* (St Ottilien: EOS Verlag I, 1982; vol. II, 1986), and the long review by F. Langlamet, *RB* 96 (1989), pp. 563-81 (p. 580 n. 13). At what stage of the composition of Josh. 2 did it become part of the future book of Joshua? May we consider that Josh. 2 was not a part of Dtr G as J. Van Seters thinks (*In Search of History* [New Haven and London: Yale University Press, 1983], p. 274)? An answer to these questions remains difficult.

23. Briend, 'Israël et les Gabaonites', p. 132.

5. A Supplementary Text (Joshua 10–12)

As I have stated in discussing Josh. 9.1, the written document due to the 'Joshua' compiler stops at Joshua 9, but it received an addition in Joshua 10–12 that cannot be attributed to the Dtr redaction, even if the latter is strongly present in these chapters.

The Battle near Gibeon (Joshua 10.1-15)

Like Josh. 9.1, Josh. 10.1-15 begins with a formula rare at the beginning of an account, וַיְהִי כִשְׁמֹעַ, but the subject of the activity is not originally the king of Jerusalem. The subject here, as is indicated by the plural verbs and v. 5, must be 'all the kings of the Amorites' (cf. Josh. 5.1). That being said, the beginning of the account strives to form a link with Joshua 9, but the vocabulary and the style show that it is not the work of the same redactor (cf. below, Document 6).

The analysis of the text has already been done elsewhere[24] and we will only take up some elements of the text. The first thing to observe is that it is only in v. 8 that God speaks to Joshua and assures him of the victory. The war narrative is therefore transformed into an account of holy war, which is confirmed by vv. 10-11.

From v. 12* onwards we leave the actual account and have a citation from the book of the Just (cf. 2 Sam. 1.15; 1 Kgs 8.53 LXX), as is stated very clearly in v. 13b. This verse is an interpretation by the redactor that follows upon that of the Deuteronomistic redactor (v. 13a).

The account has its own coherence without vv. 12-14. It is an account of holy war in which the victory is the work of God.

The Dtr redaction has transformed the account in order to describe a coalition of five kings against Israel (Josh. 10.3-4, 5*), perhaps modelled on Josh. 11.1. That redaction has drawn from the list of kings in Josh. 12.7 and is based on the mention of five kings in the cave of Makkedah. It is to this redaction that we must also attribute the anathema pursued against Ai and Jericho and recalled in 10.1.

The Cave for the Five Kings (Joshua 10.16-27)

About this text we will simply say that from an account in which Joshua is informed of the presence of five kings in the cave of

---

24. J. Briend, 'Israël et les Gabaonites', pp. 167-82. See also B. Margalit, 'The Day the Sun Did Not Stand Still: A New Look at Joshua X 8-19', *VT* 42 (1992), pp. 466-91 and the bibliography given on p. 488.

Makkedah (v. 17) the Dtr redaction has formed an account about the death of the kings united against Israel in the preceding text. We find in Josh. 10.23 the same list of kings as in Josh. 10.5.

The Conquest of the Five Cities (Joshua 10.28-39)

This part of the text should be read while keeping in mind the modifications introduced by the Dtr redactor. Originally, we had a rapid and therefore schematic conquest of the five cities by Joshua (cf. below, Document 6). With a series of formulas and an unremitting interest in the kings of the five cities mentioned, the Dtr redaction has transformed the primitive text in an important way.

The conquest of Makkedah (v. 28) must be attributed to the Dtr redaction for reasons of context and vocabulary. The taking of that city by Joshua is strange, since the preceding episode (vv. 16-27) situated at Makkedah presupposed the conquest of that city. Verse 21 even supposed that Joshua's camp is established at Makkedah, which the redaction of v. 43 forgets.

What confirms this solution is the fact that the three following accounts open with the same verb 'marched on' (עבר), which ensures the literary unity of the sequence and indicates that the beginning is in v. 29.

Verse 33 is also an addition to the primitive text with its mention of the king of Gezer. The use of the adverb אז at the beginning of the verse indicates this, since it often draws attention to an addition. It is more important to note the verbal sequence 'come up, help, attack' already used in Josh. 10.4, a verse that comes under the Dtr redaction. The word 'people' refers here to the population of a city (cf. Josh. 8.1), whereas the same word designates for example in Josh. 10.21 the army of the tribes. Finally, the formula 'until there was no longer any survivor' is familiar in the Dtr redaction (Josh. 8.22; 11.8; cf. Deut. 3.3).

If we leave out of consideration the formulas due to the Dtr redaction, we can find a list of five cities that must coincide in an artificial way with the death of the five kings recounted in vv. 17-27. The text is therefore very schematic and raises the question of the sources used for such a description.

The conclusion of ch. 10 in its initial state is found in v. 42. The Dtr redaction emphasizes more the result of these conquests: the whole country to the south is cleared of its inhabitants and the boundaries can be pointed out (vv. 40, 41).

The Battle near the Waters of Merom (Joshua 11.1-9)

The account that opens ch. 11 of the book of Joshua bears many resemblances to that which began ch. 10. Both of them mention a coalition against Israel; both present themselves as an account of holy war in which God gives victory to the Israelites. Here Joshua appears as the one who faithfully executes God's orders (11.9) (cf. below, Document 7).

The mention of Jabin, king of Hazor, probably comes from Judg. 4.2; that of Jobab, king of Madon, could be attributed to the Dtr redaction, but it seems that the latter was content to introduce two names of cities drawn from Josh. 12.20.

If we set apart v. 3, the account has not been retouched by the Dtr redaction.

The Conquest of Hazor (Joshua 11.10, 11*)

This conquest of the city of Hazor is the object of just a brief notice. The mention of the death of the king could definitely be the concern of the Dtr redaction like the greatest part of v. 11 as well.

The conclusion of the ancient document is found in Josh. 11.16*-17.

The List of the Cities (Joshua 12)

Without insisting on the reasons for this attribution, we may suppose that the ancient document closed with the list of cities that we find in Josh. 12.7-24.

According to a proposal of M. Wust[25] we can find the introduction to this list in Josh. 12.1 if we at least keep the first words: 'Here are the kings of the land...' This list began, as is normal, with the mention of Jerusalem and it proceeds by indicating the cities distributed to the south and to the north. The mention of Tirzah (v. 24) at the end of the list could have been made belatedly. It could be due to a redactor who knew that Tirzah had been a royal city of great importance in the past and that for this reason it deserved to be represented in the list.

The Dtr redaction modified Joshua 12 by introducing into it a description of the land beyond the Jordan (12.1-6) and by offering a new introduction to the list of cities with the description of the land to

---

25. M. Wust, *Untersuchungen zu den siedlungsgeographischen Texten des Alten Testaments*. I. *Ostjordanland* (Tübingen Atlas des Vorderen Orients, B, 9; Wiesbaden: Dr Ludwig Reichert, 1975), p. 53.

the west of the Jordan (12.7-8) and with the mention of the cities of Jericho and Ai (12.9).

To the question raised at the beginning, namely, that of the sources of the Deuteronomistic History, I have tried to respond with a study of the literary whole constituted by Joshua 1–12. Despite its brevity, this study has made it possible to bring to light the existence of a written document whose main points are found in Joshua 3–9. The beginning of this document is to be sought in Josh. 1.1*-2*. This document, which I conjecture to be based upon oral or written sources, was extended in two stages, first by chs. 10–12, then by Joshua 2.

The document extended in this way was taken up again by a Dtr redaction that we discern in most, if not all, of the chapters. This redaction is quite uniform, but it is above all a rereading of past history and presents two contrasting aspects.

On the one hand this document offers a unitary vision of the people, whence the phrase 'all Israel' that comes up unceasingly (16 times), whereas in the second part of the book of Joshua we only meet it once (Josh. 23.2). It is a people of one mind that, under the leadership of Joshua, crosses the Jordan.

This perspective opens the way to understanding that the Transjordanian tribes (Reuben, Gad and the half-tribe of Manasseh) had participated in the crossing and in the conquest (Josh. 1.12-18) and only returned to their territory after having accompanied the other Israelites (Josh. 22.1-8).

The land possessed is at the same time in Transjordan and Cisjordan. The picture of the territory given in Joshua 12 is twofold (Josh. 12.1-6 and 12.7-24) and thus offers a description of the land that is not limited by the Jordan.

In this rereading, the referent is Moses whose orders and activity Joshua recalls (Josh. 1.13-15, 17). The Gibeonites themselves recall the orders from Moses (Josh. 9.24b). Finally, Joshua himself receives from God a promise of assistance as successor to Moses (Josh. 3.7; 4.14). In Josh. 3.15 he receives from God an order almost identical to that heard by Moses (Exod. 3.15).

On the other hand, this Dtr redaction offers a vision of violence, while manifesting a marked hostility to the cities and their kings. The war accounts (Josh. 8; 10–11) or accounts interpreted as such (Josh. 6) are only of interest to this redaction as a way to make mention of the anathema, that is to say of the total devotion to God of persons and goods. The death of the kings is expressly emphasized each time that it is possible and the radicalism of the presentation is evident in the repetition of formulas such as 'he did not leave a survivor' or 'he dedicated to anathema every person who was found there' (Josh. 10.28). What was originally a schematic account relating the conquest of five cities becomes under the pen of the Dtr redactor a picture in which no one is spared (Josh. 10.28-39). The redaction is here under the influence of Deut. 7.1-6, 17-26, which gives rise to this rhetoric of conquest that strikes the reader of the book of Joshua. To understand such violence, we cannot forget that it is a matter of a rereading of past history and of a desire to explain what had to be done so that Israel would not fall into infidelity. Such a vision presupposes the exile and the need to understand this event by rereading the past. This drive to understand it in its beginnings from the post-exilic period.

If the distinction beween a written document and the Dtr redaction is correct, at least in its main lines, it entails two consequences. The first concerns the pre-exilic document which is based on varied sources quite short in length; the historian who is interested in the period of the installation of the tribes should take note of this situation of the text. The second, which is more the concern of research on the DH, is the issue of whether the Dtr redaction present in Joshua 1–12 is found again, and to what extent, in the other books that have a part in that History as Noth understood it. On this point the research and the discussion remain open.

APPENDIX

Document 1

Joshua 9

Introduction

1.　　Now, when all the kings who are beyond the Jordan—in the high country, in the foothills and all along the coast of the Great Sea, in the vicinity of Lebanon—the Hittites, the Amorites, the Canaanites, the Perizzites, the Hivites, and the Jebusites, heard of this,

2.　　they formed an alliance to wage war against Joshua and against Israel.

The account of the ruse (9.3-15)

3.   *The inhabitants of Gibeon*
      learned what Joshua had done to Jericho and to Ai, but they made use of
      trickery
4.   *setting out to change their appearance, they took used sacks for their
      donkeys, old wineskins, torn and patched up,*
5.   *worn-out and patched sandals on their feet, wearing worn-out clothes; all
      the bread in their provisions was dry, and crumbling.*
6.   *They went to find (the man of Israel)* Joshua in the camp, at Gilgal *and they
      said to him* (and to the man of Israel): *'We come from a distant country.
      Now then, make a treaty with us.'*
7.   *The man of Israel said to the Hivite: 'Perhaps you dwell in the midst of
      me? How will I be able then to make a treaty with you?'*
8.   They said to Joshua: 'We are your servants.' Joshua said to them: 'Who are
      you? Where do you come from?'
9.   *They said to him*: 'Your servants come from a very distant country in the
      name of YHWH your God, for we have learned of his renown...
10.   ...
11.   *Our elders and all the inhabitants of our country have told us: "Take
      provisions with you for the road; go to meet them and you shall say to
      them: 'We are your servants; now then, make a treaty with us' ".*
12.   *Here is our bread: it was hot when we stocked up in our houses the day
      when we left to go to you; and now here it is dry, in crumbs.*
13.   *And these wineskins, new when we filled them, here they are torn; our
      clothes and our sandals are worn out as a result of a very long journey.'*
14.   *The men partook of their provisions, but they did not consult the mouth of
      YHWH.*

The statute (9.16-27)

16.   But...after they had concluded a treaty with them, they learned that they
      were their neighbours and that they dwelt in the midst of them.
17-21. ...
22.   Joshua called them and spoke to them saying: 'Why have you deceived us
      by saying: We live very far away from you, while in fact you live in the
      midst of us?
23.   Now then you are cursed and you shall not cease being servants...for the
      house of my God.'
24.   They replied and said: '...We very much feared for our lives faced with
      you and we have done this thing.
25.   And now we are in your hand; do with us according to what will be good
      and just in your eyes.'
26.   ...
27.   Joshua made them...wood-cutters and water-carriers...for Yhwh's altar to
      this day...

Document 2

Joshua 9 and its redactions

1. Dtr redaction(s)

vv. 9bβ-10.
v. 16*: 'after three days'
v. 17: 'the Israelites set out and entered their cities on the third day, and their cities were Gibeon, Chepirah, Beeroth and Kiriath-jearim'.
v. 24a*: 'It is because they had told your servants that the Lord your God had ordered Moses, his servant, to give you all the land and to exterminate all the inhabitants before you'.
v. 26: 'This is what he did for them and he delivered them from the hand of the Israelites who did not kill them'.
v. 27b*: 'in that day'; 'in the place that YHWH has chosen'.

2. Priestly intervention

v. 15a*: 'in order that they may live'.
v. 15b: the leaders of the community swore an oath to them.
vv. 18-21 (in full)
v. 27a*: 'for the community and'

Document 3

The conquest of Ai

Joshua 7.2-5
2. Joshua sent the men...to Ai which is near Beth-Aven... The men went up and spied out Ai.
3. They returned to Joshua and said to him: 'Do not let all the people go up! Let about two or three thousand men go up and attack Ai. Do not weary all the people up there, since they are few in number.'
4. About three thousand men taken from the people went up there, but they fled before the men of Ai.
5. The men of Ai killed about thirty-six of them and they pursued them beyond the gate of the city as far as Shebarim and killed them on the slope. The heart of the people melted away and became like water.

Joshua 8.10-25
10. Joshua *rose early in the morning and* inspected the people; he went up, *he and the elders of Israel,* at the head of the people to Ai.

11.   *All the people* (of war) *who were with him went up, approached and came facing the city, and they camped on the north side of Ai, the valley being between him and Ai.*

12.   He took about five thousand men and he placed them in ambush between Bethel and Ai, to the west of the city.

13.   The people set up the whole camp, that was to the north of the city and its rear to the west of the city; and Joshua passed that night in the middle of the valley.

14.   But as soon as (they saw), the men (of the city) hurried to get up and went out...for combat...at the Crossroad facing the Arabah...

15.   Joshua...(was defeated) before them...

16.   *All the people who were in the city were called for help to pursue them.* They pursued Joshua and they were drawn away from the city.

17.   *There was not a man left in Ai* (and Bethel) *who did not go out behind Israel.* They left the city open and pursued Israel.

18.   *YHWH said to Joshua: 'Point the sicklesword that is in your hand towards Ai because I am going to deliver it into your hand.' Joshua pointed the sicklesword that he had in his hand towards Ai.*

19.   The ambush rose quickly from their position and they ran, entered into the city, captured it and hurried to set fire to the city.

20.   The men of Ai returned; they looked and saw the smoke from the city rising to the sky. None of them had the power to flee this way or that. The people who fled towards the wilderness turned back against the pursuers.

21.   ...

22.   Those came out from the city to engage them and they fled...in the middle, some on one side and some on the other...

23.   ...

24.   ...

25.   The number of those that fell that day...was twelve thousand, all the people of Ai.

Document 4

Joshua 5.13-15

Theophany by way of an introduction

13.   But, while Joshua was at Jericho, he lifted his eyes and saw: and there was a man standing in front of him, his drawn sword in hand. Joshua advanced towards him and said to him: 'Are you for us or for our adversaries?'

14.   He said: 'No, but I am the commander of the army of YHWH. Now, I am coming.' Joshua fell face down on the ground and did homage and said to him: 'What does my lord have to say to his servant?'

15.   ...

Joshua 6.1-25

Collapse of the walls of Jericho

1. ...
2. YHWH said to Joshua:
3. 'You shall go round the town...once; thus you shall do for six days.
4. But...the priests shall carry...trumpets...in front of the ark. The seventh day, you shall go round the town seven times and the priests shall sound the trumpet.
5. Now,...when you hear the sound of the trumpet, all the people shall shout with a great shout, and the wall will collapse on the spot, and the people shall go up, each one straight ahead.'
6. Joshua, (son of Nun) called the priests and said to them: 'Carry the ark of the covenant and let...the priests carry...trumpets...before the ark of YHWH.'
7. And he said to the people: 'Go forward and march round the town...'
8. Now, as soon as Joshua had spoken to the people,...the priests carrying...the trumpets...passed before YHWH...
9. ...
10. To the people Joshua gave orders saying: 'You shall not shout, you shall not make your voice be heard and let no word come from your mouth until the day when I shall say to you: Shout, then you shall shout.'
12. Joshua rose early in the morning and the priests carried the ark of YHWH.
13. ...
14. They marched round the town...once and they returned to camp; this they did for six days.
15. The seventh day, having risen at dawn, they marched round the city...seven times...
16. The seventh time, the priests sounded the trumpets and Joshua said to the people: Shout...
17-19 ...
20. ...Now, when the people heard the sound of the trumpet, the people shouted a great shout, and the wall collapsed on the spot, and the people went up into the city, each one straight ahead.

Document 5

The beginning of the document

Joshua 1

1. ...YHWH said to Joshua: '
2. ...Rise, cross the Jordan here, you and all the people...'

Joshua 2.1-24 + 6.22-23, 25

Joshua 3

1.   Joshua *rose early in the morning*. They set out from Shittim and came to the Jordan…They passed the night there before they crossed.

2-4.   …

5.   Joshua said to the people: 'Sanctify yourselves, for, tomorrow, YHWH will work wonders among you.'

Document 6

The battle near Gibeon (Joshua 10.1-15)

1.   Now, when * all the kings of the Amorites * learned…that the inhabitants of Gibeon had made peace with Israel and that they were in their midst,

2.   then they were afraid, since Gibeon was an important city, like one of the royal cities…and all its men were warriors.

3.   …

4.   …

5.   the…kings of the Amorites…assembled, went up,…besieged Gibeon and attacked it.

6.   The men of Gibeon sent messengers to Joshua in the camp at Gilgal, saying: 'Do not let your hand be estranged from your servants; come up to us quickly; save us, help us, because all the Amorite kings who live in the mountains have formed a coalition against us.'

7.   Joshua went up from Gilgal, he and all the fighting force with him…

8.   YHWH said to Joshua: 'Do not fear; none of them shall stand before you.'

9.   Joshua came upon them suddenly; he had come up all night from Gilgal.

10.   YHWH threw them into a panic before Israel and inflicted a great defeat on them at Gibeon; he pursued them toward the ascent of Beth-horon and struck them down as far as Azekah.

11.   Now, while they fled before Israel and were in the Beth-horon descent, YHWH threw down huge stones from heaven on them…

12.   Then Joshua spoke to YHWH…and he said in the presence of Israel: 'Sun, stand still over Gibeon, Moon, over the valley of Aijalon!'

13.   …Is that not written in the book of the Just? The sun stood still in the middle of the heavens and it did not hurry to set for almost a whole day.

14.   Neither before nor since has there been a day like this when YHWH obeyed a man, for YHWH fought for Israel.

The cave of the five kings (Joshua 10.16-27)

Pre-exilic text: vv. 17-21, 22, 24, 26-27.

Dtr redaction: vv. 16, 23, 25.

The conquest of five towns (Joshua 10.28-39)

28.   ...
29.   Joshua...went on from Makkedah to *Libnah* and he fought against Libnah;
30.   ...and he struck it with the edge of the sword.
31.   Joshua...went on from Libnah to *Lachish*; he besieged it and attacked it.
32.   ...and he took it (on the second day) and he struck it with the edge of the sword...just as he had done to Libnah.
33.   ...
34.   Joshua...went on from Lachish to *Eglon*; (he besieged it) and (attacked it).
35.   (He captured it) that day and he (struck) it with the edge of the sword.
36.   Joshua...went up from Eglon to *Hebron* and (he attacked it).
37.   (He captured it) and (he struck) it with the edge of the sword.
38.   Joshua...turned towards *Debir* and attacked it.
39.   He captured it...as well as all the towns and (he struck) them with the edge of the sword.

Conclusion

40-41   ...
42.   Joshua captured all these kings and their land in a single sweep, because YHWH, (God of Israel), fought for Israel.
43.   ...

N.B.   The text is revisable from the point of view of distribution between the document and the Dtr redaction. The verbs in parentheses are in the plural in the MT.

Document 7

The battle near the waters of Meron (Joshua 11.1-9)

Pre-exilic text

1.   Now, when Jabin, king of Hazor, heard of it, he informed Jobab, king of Madon,...
2.   and all the kings in the North...
3.   ...
4.   They came out, they and all their troops with them, a great number of people, as numerous as the sand along the seashore, with very many horses and chariots.
5.   All these kings gathered and came to camp together near the waters of Meron to fight Israel.

6. YHWH said to Joshua: 'Do not be afraid of them, for tomorrow, at this very hour, I will hand over all of them cut to pieces before Israel; you shall maim their horses and you will burn their chariots.'
7. Joshua, and all the warriors with him, came upon them without warning at the waters of Meron and they fell upon them from the mountain.
8. YHWH delivered them into the hand of Israel; they attacked them and pursued them as far as Sidon the Great, as far as Misrephoth-maim and as far as the plain of Mizpah to the east...
9. Joshua did to them as YHWH had told him: he maimed the horses and burned their chariots.

The taking of Hazor (Joshua 11.10-11)

Pre-exilic text

10. At that time Joshua turned back and captured Hazor,...for Hazor was in the past the capital of all these kingdoms.
11. ...and he handed over Hazor to be burned.
12-15 ...

Conclusion (Joshua 11.16-23)

Pre-exilic text

16. Joshua took all that land...
17. from Mount Halak that towers over Seir as far as Baal-gad in the Lebanon Valley at the foot of Mount Hermon; he took all their kings, struck them and put them to death.
18-20. ...
21. (post-exilic text)
22-23. (post-exilic text)

Joshua 12: the list of towns

Pre-exilic text

1. These are the kings of the land...
2-9 ...
10. the king of Jerusalem, one; the king of Hebron, one; (as far as v. 23)

Part VI
THE MILIEUS OF THE DEUTERONOMISTS

DOES 'DEUTERONOMISTIC HISTORIOGRAPHY' (DTRH) EXIST?

Ernst Axel Knauf

> Ist das deuteronomistische Geschichtswerk (dtrG) noch zu retten? Nach
> so vielen schrafsinnigen und widersprüchlichen exegetischen Analysen...
> denkt mancher Experte oder manche Expertin: 'Requiescat in Pace—
> 1943 bis 1993—ein erfülltes Leben für eine Hypothese!'... Hat O'Brien
> das DtrG gerettet? Ich habe Zweifel daran.[1]

I stopped believing in the existence of a 'Deuteronomistic historiographical work' (DtrH) some time ago. But my position receives, I
think, the backing of the articles of this collection as a whole, but in an
indirect way and so to speak contrary to the liking of their authors. My
contribution will be limited to a short list of arguments against the
hypothesis of the existence of 'DtrH'.[2]

1. 'Can the Deuteronomistic History (DtrH) still be saved? After so many
exegetical analyses at the same time discerning and contradictory...several experts
think: ' "Requiescat in pace—1943–1993—a long and beautiful life for a hypothesis!"... Has O'Brien saved the DtrH? I doubt it', E. Gerstenberger, *BZ* 39
(1995), pp. 114-15. I must thank A. Bühlmann for having clarified my article as
regards style and argumentation.

2. I will try not to repeat the arguments of C. Westermann, *Die Geschichtsbücher des Alten Testaments: Gab es ein deuteronomistisches Geschichtswerk?*
(TBü, 87; Gütersloh: Chr. Kaiser Verlag, 1994), a book filled with good observations, although it contains opinions on the sociology of the literature of ancient
Israel and of the ancient Near East that are a little out of date. It is essential to preserve the term 'DtrH' in this article, because the phrase 'Deuteronomistic Historiography' (or DH) does not take into account enough, nor exactly enough, the nature
of the phenomenon. There has never been any question that the prophetical books,
including the former prophets, had been composed in a 'Dtr' way. Those who maintain that Joshua–2 Kings constitute a sort of historiography will be able to continue
to speak of a DH; but these books do not form a *Geschichtswerk*, i.e. an historical
literary construct conceived by one author or a homogeneous group.

A Preliminary Note: Dtr Theology and Dtr Texts

'Dtr' designates a literary style (probably influenced by the rhetoric of Assyrian annals, especially those of Esarhaddon) as well as a group of theological notions such as those of the 'conquest of the promised land' and of the 'covenant' (that is to say the $b^e r \hat{\imath} t$, which means 'vassal treaty'). This style and this theology are both derived from Assyrian imperialism.

As a general rule, we expect to see Dtr theologians expressing themselves in the Dtr style. But there are some exceptions: the theology of texts in the Dtr style of Jeremiah is quite at variance with that of Kings.[3] In the Pentateuch, we find Dtr theology in priestly style (for example, Num. 25.6-18; 31.1-54),[4] and conversely priestly theology in Dtr style (for example, Gen. 15; Deut. 9.4-6), which indicates the way in which the Torah was composed (see below). Since the Dtr texts have been produced over a long period—from the court of Josiah up to the final additions to the book of Jeremiah in the second century BCE—Dtr style conceals a vast multiplicity of theological positions.[5] Thus, the content must always be taken into consideration.

The DtrH of Martin Noth and the DtrH Today

For Martin Noth, the Dtr was a distinctive theologian, and the artisan of the whole literary complex from Deuteronomy 1 to 2 Kings 25 (except for some later additions), a work that would therefore reflect his purpose. Today, two different possibilities are envisaged: either that there

---

3. Thus Albertz in several places, most recently in this collection.

4. Cf. N. Lohfink, 'Die Schichten des Pentateuch und der Krieg', in *idem* (ed.), *Gewalt und Gewaltlosigkeit im Alten Testament* (QD, 96; Freiburg: Herder, 1983), pp. 51-110 (97); *idem*, *Studien zum Pentateuch* (SBAB, 4; Stuttgart: Katholisches Bibelwerk, 1988), pp. 255-315 (301).

5. Cf. also the warning of N. Lohfink, 'Gab es eine deuteronomistische Bewegung?', in W. Gross (ed.), *Jeremia und die 'deuteronomistische Bewegung'* (BBB, 98; Weinheim: Beltz Athenäum, 1995), pp. 313-82; *idem*, *Studien zum Deuteronomium und zur deuteronomistische Literatur*, III (SBAB, 20; Stuttgart: Katholisches Bibelwerk, 1995), pp. 65-142, with which I agree in principle except for the history of Israel as it is recounted by the Dtr authors, which Lohfink does not recognize as a theological construction (it constitutes therefore, *pace* Lohfink, a sort of school).

were two editions of DtrH, one Josianic and the other exilic (the view of the Cross school), or that there were several editions or redactions,[6] designated as DtrH ('historian'), DtrP ('prophetic'), DtrN ('nomistic'), each being susceptible to subdivisions into several layers, DtrN[1], DtrN[2], etc. (the view of the Smend school). But while the Cross theory seems too simple (especially when we consider the history of the text; see below), the Smend redactions do not necessarily cover the whole DtrH, but perhaps only some sequences or some books: however, this is already a step in the right direction. A third theory, a very attractive one, but unfortunately not yet worked out in detail, has been proposed by N. Lohfink, according to whom the literary history of DtrH began with a DtrL, made up of Deuteronomy* and Joshua*.

This history of the redaction could really turn out to be more complicated than any of the three schools has envisaged it.[7] In any case, Noth's Dtr has been abandoned by everyone. We will see later that H, that is to say the historiographical work, must be abandoned as well.

In Search of the Lost Author, or a Mistake about Category

Noth's Dtr hypothesis, with its kerygma[8] that relates to his own historical situation, resembles the attempts already seen in the nineteenth and early twentieth centuries (as was the case for J,[9] E, P in the Pentateuch) to circumvent the *scandalon* of the Old Testament literature, which arose from the polyphony of the text and the anonymity of the authors. This is why theoretical authors are introduced (if not invented). Now the Torah and the Prophets are not a literature of authors

---

6. 'A Deuteronomist seldom comes alone', as H. Weippert remarked very pertinently some years ago.

7. The five redactions of Kings as they have been established by H. Weippert ('Die "deuteronomistischen" Beurteilungen der Könige von Israel und Juda und das Problem der Redaktion der Königsbücher', *Bib* 53 [1972], pp. 301-39; the fourth added 1 Kgs 3–11, the fifth 1 Kgs 1–2) are irreconcilable with the two main theories.

8. In regard to this problematic idea, cf. A. de Pury and E.A. Knauf, 'La théologie de l'Ancien Testament: kérygmatic ou descriptive?', *ETR* 70 (1995), pp. 323-34.

9. Let us note that the body of J texts is often called a *Geschichtswerk* (historical work) as well, while P is really such a work according to the historiographical criteria that were current in the ancient Near East.

(*Autorenliteratur*), but a literature of tradition (*Traditionsliteratur*),[10] after the fashion of the Talmud. Written after and under the influence of Hellenism, the latter cites its authorities: 'Rabbi Gamaliel said..., but Rabbi Nicodemus said...' (a procedure unknown to the Old Testament). Now that the search for a Dtr author (or redactor) turns out to be a mistake in regard to category (quite comparable to the situation of the Pentateuch), and that it is besides rather unlikely that there would have been just one Dtr school, how many good reasons are there for still maintaining the DtrH hypothesis?

In Search of Biblical History, or a Second Mistake about Category

The interest of some theologians in 'historiography' seems to be inversely proportional to the understanding that they have of history. We may note that the history of 'scientific historiography' begins with L. von Ranke and G. Droysen. Prior to them, nobody, not even Herodotus and Voltaire, knew what history was: they merely recounted stories, they constructed legends—religious, moral, political legends. The category of 'what really happened', just like the rational methods needed to construct a critical history, dates from the nineteenth century;[11] and since then, it has become impossible to call a work 'historiography' which has nothing to do with history as it happened. There certainly was an interest in history in the centuries preceding that revolution—but it was rather a way of appropriating tradition. Today, intellectual honesty requires that we emphasize the fundamental difference that exists between 'traditional historiography' and our way of perceiving history.

Even if we conclude that speaking of a 'historiographic' literary genre in the ancient Near East is a reasonable thing, it remains very doubtful that the heroic legends of Judges or the great novelistic work(s) of 1 and 2 Samuel would be included in it. The Akkadian chronicles and the 'Annals of the Kings of Israel and Judah', often cited

10. Cf. O. Kaiser, *Grundriss der Einleitung in die kanonischen und deuterokanonischen Schriften des Alten Testaments*, I (Gütersloh: Gerd Mohn, 1992), pp. 24-32; E.A. Knauf, *Die Umwelt des Alten Testaments* (NSK-AT, 29; Stuttgart: Katholisches Bibelwerk, 1994), pp. 221-37.

11. Cf. E.A. Knauf, 'From History to Interpretation', in D. Edelman (ed.), *The Fabric of History: Text, Artefact and Israel's Past* (JSOTSup, 127; Sheffield: JSOT Press, 1991), pp. 26-64.

Israel Constructs its History

in 1 and 2 Kings, but unfortunately lost to us, probably belong to this literary genre. On questions of historical interest, the reader is referred to these annals by the redactor(s) of 1 and 2 Kings, which offer, not a historiographic work, but rather a philosophy of history: factual history is presupposed in these books, but is not recounted. The novelistic accounts about Saul, David and Absalom in 1 and 2 Samuel have their parallels in the ancient Near East; however, they are found not in Akkadian historiography, but in the Aramaic tales of the *Amherst Papyrus*.

It is the Greek (and Christian) canon that groups together the Torah and the Former Prophets as 'historical books'.[12] Although the relation between God and history is foundational for the Christian faith, particularly in regard to the incarnation (which is as much a liturgical as a historical fact), the exegete of the Old Testament must read and make us read what is written there, not what was read by earlier generations. For their part, they assumed that importance was added to the biblical account by emphasizing its 'historicity'; in my opinion, they have lessened that importance. Historical truth—hypothetical like all human truth—has no useful purpose where there is question of a spiritual truth, since the truth of faith and hope is expressed *by* stories rather than *in* history.[13]

If there are already inadequate reasons for thinking that the 'Dtr' is found in 'DtrH', there is less satisfactory reason for assuming the existence of a 'Dtr historiographical work'.

The History of the Text

Unlike the Pentateuch, where variant readings are minimal, the edition of 1 and 2 Samuel and 1 and 2 Kings[14] translated by the LXX is not the

12. Cf. my article 'Die Mitte des Alten Testaments', in M. Weippert and S. Timm (eds.), *Meilensteine* (Festschrift Herbert Donner; ÄAT, 30; Wiesbaden: Otto Harrassowitz, 1995), pp. 79-86.

13. Cf. D. Ritschl and H. Jones, *'Story' als Rohmaterial der Theologie* (ThExh, 192; Munich: Chr. Kaiser Verlag, 1976); D. Ritschl, *Zur Logik der Theologie: Kurze Darstellung der Zusammenhänge theologischer Grundgedanken* (Munich: Chr. Kaiser Verlag, 2nd edn, 1988), pp. 45-47; 81-83; 98-102; and from the other side, for 'the historical Israel', P.R. Davies, *In Search of 'Ancient Israel'* (JSOTSup, 148; Sheffield: Sheffield Academic Press, 1992).

14. And also, but to a lesser extent, of Joshua and Judges, while the differences between MT Jeremiah and LXX Jeremiah are glaring.

same as the one preserved in the MT.[15] That indicates that there were several 'Dtr schools' with their own texts up to the third and second centuries BCE.[16] Furthermore, this fact characterizes the 'Former Prophets' as deuterocanonical texts up to the second century, texts that left more redactional freedom to the *tradentes* than was the case with the Torah (including Deuteronomy). The redactional history of Joshua–2 Kings did not stop either in 562 BCE, or in 520 or 515 BCE.

DtrH and Pentateuch

The Pentateuch, which was not composed from various sources, nor in several layers,[17] is today very far away from the questions that were formerly the subject of such agitated debate.[18] The Pentateuch results from a long theological (and political) discussion between the main schools of the 'priestly milieus loyal towards the Persians' (P) and the 'Dtr nationalists' (D). Although the content of many of the prophetic books is presupposed by the compilers of the Pentateuch (cf. Gen. 6.13 P and Amos 8.2; Gen. 9.13 P and Ezek. 5.16-17), that does not mean that any prophetic book (including the former prophets) was completed before the Torah. If the evolution of the Pentateuch contains neither the classical pre-Dtr Yahwist, edited and continued by the Deuteronomistic authors, nor the post-Dtr Yahwist of Van Seters and others (pre-supposing DtrH), it is DtrH that remains in suspense. As was noted 20

15. Cf. the contribution of A. Schenker in this volume.

16. This date also applies to the late Dtr redactions in Jeremiah; cf. C. Levin, *Die Verheissung des neuen Bundes in ihrem theologiegeschichtlichen Zusammenhang ausgelegt* (FRLANT, 137; Göttingen: Vandenhoeck & Ruprecht, 1985), p. 196; A. Schenker, 'La rédaction longue du livre de Jérémie doit être datée du temps des premiers Hasmonéens?', *ETL* 70 (1994), pp. 281-93.

17. Cf. E. Blum, *Zur Komposition des Pentateuch* (BZAW, 189; Berlin: W. de Gruyter, 1990), pp. 229-85; 333-60. While Blum himself is not totally free from the idea of layers, it is R. Albertz (*Religionsgeschichte Israels in alttestamentlicher Zeit*, II [ATD, 8.2; Göttingen: Vandenhoeck & Ruprecht, 1992], pp. 497-504) who has reconstructed a historically conceivable evolution of the Pentateuch, with two principal groups in dialogue; cf. also Knauf, *Umwelt*, pp. 171-75. I am not reluctant to call this model of the evolution of the Pentateuch a 'model for discourse', despite E. Henscheid, *Dummdeutsch: Ein Wörterbuch* (Stuttgart: Reclam, 1993), p. 61.

18. For the questions that were raised, A. de Pury and T. Römer (eds.), *Le Pentateuque en question* (Geneva: Labor et Fides, 2nd edn, 1991), is still worthwhile. Unfortunately, the most attractive answer is not presented there in sufficient detail.

years ago, DtrH presupposes at least a 'book of Exodus'.[19] Joshua–
2 Kings does not contain therefore a coherent view of Israel's history,
but is inserted from the outset in a more wide-ranging library bringing
together various books of the same kind. The present way of understanding the Pentateuch implies the two following points concerning
the interpretation of 'DtrH': on the one hand that the notion of an
author in regard to it (with perhaps the exception of 1 and 2 Kgs) and
the idea of precisely defined compilations be abandoned, and on the
other hand that there should be an attempt to describe more precisely
the theological discourses that these books contain, as well as their political options.

Deuteronomy Did Not Belong to DtrH

For H. Donner, DtrH never consisted of more than the books of Joshua
to 2 Kings. It is Deuteronomy that is cited there as normative law.[20]
What other historiographic work would use its first volume as an absolute authority? To maintain the difference between the canonical
'fundamental law' and the application of that law, that is, in brief, the
difference between the sacred text and its exegesis—a decisive difference for the voices recorded in the Prophets and the Ketubim
(= Writings)—Deuteronomy and the following books must be clearly
separated.

Besides, S. Mittmann has already shown that Deuteronomy 1–3, far
from serving as an introduction to DtrH, was used to insert Deuteronomy in the Pentateuch.[21] Furthermore, it is only because the central
place, the Sinai pericope, is taken up by P texts, that Deuteronomy is
relegated to the 'plains of Moab'; it is because of Gen. 14.18-20, with
an allusion to the only legitimate Judaean sanctuary, that Deuteronomy
27, alluding to the only legitimate Samaritan sanctuary, has been
inserted.[22]

---

19. Cf. S. Mittmann, *Deuteronomium 1,1–6,3 literarkritisch und traditions-
geschichtlich untersucht* (BZAW, 139; Berlin: W. de Gruyter, 1975), p. 178.

20. Cf. H. Donner, ' "Wie geschrieben steht". Herkunft und Sinn einer Formel',
SbWGF, 29.4 (1992), pp. 147-61 (repr. in *idem, Aufsätze zum Alten Testament aus
vier Jahrzehnten* [BZAW, 224; Berlin: W. de Gruyter, 1994], pp. 224-38).

21. Cf. Mittmann, *Deuteronomium*, pp. 164-69; cf. also M. Weippert, 'Fragen
des israelitischen Geschichtsbewusstseins', *VT* 23 (1973), pp. 415-42.

22. Cf. Knauf, *Umwelt*, p. 173; cf. B.J. Diebner, ' "Auf einem der Berge des

Joshua Did Not Belong to DtrH

Noth invented DtrH while writing a commentary on the book of Joshua. It is this book that today calls this hypothesis most into question. Against Noth, it must be maintained that the 'few additions in the style of P' are really additions due to the P school[23] (at least P^S, if not P^g).[24] Like the Torah, Joshua was produced by the dispute between two parties, D and P. That does not make Joshua the sixth book of the Hexateuch, but rather a supplement to the Pentateuch, and as a result the first deuterocanonical book. Josh. 22.10-24 ('PD'—Priestly with Dtr influence) may actually reflect the problem of the Jews of Elephantine.

It would probably be possible to construct by means of literary criticism an original book of Joshua* that might go back to the time of Josiah and would be contemporaneous with Dt* (here, in my opinion, lies the *particula veri* of the theory of a 'DtrL'); but the mimimalist 'DtrH*' thus reconstituted would not compel greater recognition than the 'J' of Weimar or that of Levin—two options in an ocean of probabilities. It seems to me however that the Josianic Joshua* eludes any possibility of reconstruction. The story of the spies of Joshua 2 introduces an account of a military conquest of Jericho that would fit in well with Josianic tendencies. But with Jericho conquered, the original military exploit is suppressed in favour of a liturgical procession, a procession that could have been carried out without the activity of the spies.[25] We observe

Landes Morija" (Gn 22,2) oder: "In Jerusalem auf dem Berge Morija" (2 Chr 3,1)', *DBAT* 23/24 (1987), pp. 174-79; *idem*, 'Gottes Welt, Moses Zelt und das salomonische Heiligtum', in T. Römer (ed.), *Lectio difficilior probabilior? L'exégèse comme expérience de décloisonnement* (*Mélanges offerts à Françoise Smyth-Floentin*) (BDBAT, 12; Heidelberg: Wissenschaftlich-theologisches Seminar, 1991), pp. 127-54 (131).

23. Cf. the contribution of J. Briend in this collection.

24. Thus N. Lohfink, 'Die Priesterschrit und die Geschichte' (VTSup, 29; Leiden: E.J. Brill, 1978), pp. 189-225 (194-95; 222 n. 30) (repr. in *idem*, *Studien zum Pentateuch*, pp. 213-53 [219; 223 n. 30]); *idem*, 'Die Schichten des Pentateuch und der Krieg', pp. 80-82 (repr. in *Studien*, pp. 284-86).

25. Cf. V. Fritz, *Das Buch Josua* (HAT, 1.7; Tübingen: J.C.B. Mohr [Paul Siebeck], 1994), p. 68; K. Bieberstein (*Josua-Jordan-Jericho, Archäologie, Geschichte und Theologie der Landnahmeerzählungen Josua 1–6* [OBO, 143; Freiburg: Universitätsverlag; Göttingen: Vandenhoeck & Ruprecht, 1995], p. 298) proposes the opposite solution. Furthermore, Bieberstein provides the best arguments so far advanced in favour of 'DtrL' (*Josua-Jordan-Jericho*, pp. 299; 386-87).

here a real 'demilitarization of war'—Joshua 6 is therefore to be attributed to DP (Dtr school under Priestly influence).

Judges Did Not Belong to DtrH

The geographical data of the core of Judges provide enough arguments for the hypothesis of Richter relating to a 'book of saviours' originally composed in Israel (of the North): Ehud/Benjamin, Deborah-Barak/Naphtali, Gideon/Manasseh, Jephthah-Gilead. This book, which evidently seeks paradigms of deliverance from foreign oppression (without any king of Israel being involved), could definitely have been composed at Bethel after 720 BCE (that is to say at the same time as the book of Hosea). The additions are attributable to several Dtr schools: the royalist group added Judges 17–21, while the anti-royalist group inserted Judges 9.[26] A third group, the history teachers of the Second Temple school, added a chronology that was adapted in part to the Priestly chronology, in part to the chronology of Kings (that is to say, the annals of Israel and Judah), so that the general framework in which the book was inserted by this school is not the 'DtrH', but the whole 'historical library' of Genesis to 2 Kings.

Samuel Did Not Belong to DtrH

The books of Kings appear firmly linked to those of Samuel by the end of the 'history of the succession' (1 Kings 1–2), which would make 2 Samuel 21–24 a post-Dtr addition (because these additions presuppose the present state of separation of the books). But beginning the history of Solomon with 1 Kings 1 is rather a sign of the mentality of the 'history professors' mentioned above than of that of the Dtr. We have already seen that the content of Samuel does not belong to the historiographic genre of the ancient Near East; as a consequence, neither the history of David nor the history of Solomon is found in the 'annals' that served as a source of 1 and 2 Kings.[27] As Westermann has already remarked, the differences in literary genre that exist between Judges, Samuel and Kings do not allow for attributing these three books to a common 'work'. Just as the Dtrs of Kings act as censors, the Dtrs

26. Cf. the contribution of W. Dietrich in this collection.
27. Cf. Knauf, *Umwelt*, pp. 22, 122, 128.

of Samuel behave as narrators: 2 Samuel 7 (royalist)–1 Samuel 1–3; 7–8; 12 (anti-royalist).

What Is Left of the DtrH: The Books of Kings

We can appreciate now the good sense of Albertz, who limited his comparison between the Dtrs of DtrH and Dtrs of Dtr-Jeremiah to a comparison between Kings and Jeremiah that remains entirely valid.[28] The end of the books of Kings, 2 Kgs 25.27-30, is a lamentably unsatisfactory end for the great drama which unfolded since Genesis 1 (or Exod. 1). That end is only acceptable as an opening of a history that will continue, and its continuation is indicated by texts such as, e.g., Ezra 7; 9.1-6, 11; Mic. 5.1-5; Hag. 2.21-23. This is to say that 1 and 2 Kings fits better into the prophetic books for which they serve as an introduction, than into the 'historical' books of which it hardly forms the conclusion.

The History of the Canon is Not Acquainted With DtrH

The canon as a historical *fait accompli* provides pertinent information on the intention of the final redaction of the books that constitute it, as we have just seen. When we consider the Psalms, which present as a whole the systematic theology of the Old Testament we find no attestation of the 'DtrH'. The following are attested in the Psalms: the Torah (Pss. 74; 95; 135), the Torah with Joshua as a supplement (105; 114; 136[?]), the 'former prophets' Joshua–2 Kings (44; 66; 68; 129[?]) and the 'historical books' Genesis–2 Kings (78; 80; 81[?], 89; 102; 103[?]; 106; 136[?]). These divisions should be sufficient both for theology and for exegesis.

The Duty of the Exegete

Exegesis as an attentive reading of the text must note the differences, the singular characteristics of each text and, finally, reconstruct the

28. Cf. R. Albertz, 'Die Intentionem und die Träger des deuteronomistischen Geschichtswerks', in *idem*, F.W. Golka and J. Kegler (eds.), *Schöpfung und Befreiung* (Festschrift C. Westermann; Stuttgart: Calwer Verlag, 1989), pp. 37-53; *idem*, *Religionsgeschichte Israels*, II, pp. 383-84; 387-413.

theological debate of which the Old Testament is the proceedings.[29]
Exegesis should not harmonize differences, nor transform its difficulties
into pious platitudes. The hypothesis of a 'DtrH' encourages the second
set of intentions but hardly the first. It must be abandoned.

29. As the Göttingen school mainly does, with regard to 'DtrH'.

IS THERE A DEUTERONOMISTIC REDACTION
IN THE BOOK OF JEREMIAH?

Thomas Römer

1. *Jeremiah and the Deuteronomists:*
The Contribution from the History of Research[1]

1.1. *The Discovery of the Dtr Phenomenon in Jeremiah*

Since the works of de Wette and of Ewald, the presence of redactions of a 'Deuteronomistic' (Dtr in what follows) type in the historical books as well as in the Pentateuch has been the subject of scientific debate. The Dtr phenomenon appeared ever larger, in relation to the book of Jeremiah, exegetes soon took note of the presence of texts strongly resembling, in their style as well as in their themes, Deuteronomy or Dtr texts. For Kuenen, that observation simply meant that the redactors of the historical books were 'men of the same mind as Jeremiah, knowing and imitating his writings'.[2] But towards the end of the nineteenth century, such an explanation was no longer sufficient to satisfy historico-critical exegesis. It was Bernhard Duhm (1847–1928) who set forth, in his commentary on Jeremiah,[3] the thesis of a Dtr redaction of this book, leaving to the 'historical Jeremiah' only some 60 short poems. From then on, it became necessary to explain the presence of the 'Dtr' texts in the book of Jeremiah.

1.2. *The Elaboration of a 'Documentary' Theory for the Book of Jeremiah*

S. Mowinckel[4] proposed a theory that had an enormous influence on subsequent research. This was strongly inspired by the documentary

1. Cf. also the history of the research in the present volume.

2. A. Kuenen, *Histoire critique des livres de l'Ancien Testament. I. Les livres historiques* (Paris: Michel Lévy Frères, 1866), p. 428.

3. B. Duhm, *Das Buch Jeremia* (KHAT, 11; Tübingen: J.C.B. Mohr [Paul Siebeck], 1901).

4. S. Mowinckel, *Zur Komposition des Buches Jeremia* (Oslo: Jacob Dybwad, 1914).

theory triumphant at that time in research on the Pentateuch. The Scandinavian scholar actually distinguished four sources from which the book of Jeremiah had taken form:

> The 'A' source: a collection of Jeremiah's oracles, contained in Jeremiah 1–25, and compiled by a redactor R^A in Egypt.
> The 'B' source: the biography of Jeremiah, contained in Jeremiah 19–20* and 26–44*, compiled by a redactor R^B between 580–480.
> The 'C' source: the prose discourses, written in a Dtr style: Jeremiah 7; 11; 18; 21; 24; 25; 32; 34; 35; 44, compiled by a redactor R^C about 400 in Babylon (or eventually in Palestine).
> The 'D' source: the collection of salvation oracles in Jeremiah 30–31, whose origin and date Mowinckel did not specify. (The final additions to the book would be found in the oracles against the nations in Jeremiah 46–52.)

Mowinckel explains the relation between the three main sources by making use of the redactional theory concerning the formation of the Gospels. The relation between B and A would be comparable to that existing between Mark and 'Q', the relation between C and A-B would correspond to that of John in relation to the Synoptic Gospels.

We should note that for Mowinckel the C source is situated in the middle of the Persian period.[5] This document in Dtr style contained only the public discourses of the prophet, and their insertion into the whole book was due to some redactor whose motives remain obscure.

1.3. *The Transformation of a Source into a Compilation*

Subsequently Mowinckel's model was modified. It was realized that the Dtr style was not limited to just the prose discourses, but also appeared within the oracles (for example, 23.1-8) and in the narrative sections (for example, ch. 36). Bright noted: 'When B opens his mouth, he talks like C'.[6]

Starting from these observations, 'D' will be transformed into a compilation, especially due to the works of J.P. Hyatt and W. Rudolph.

5.　According to Mowinckel, C presupposes the definitive ideology of Judaism, and is therefore later than Ezra; cf. *Zur Komposition des Buches Jeremia*, pp. 39, 48-51.

6.　J. Bright, 'The Prophetic Reminiscence: Its Place and Function in the Book of Jeremiah', in *Biblical Essays 1966. Proceedings of the 9th Meeting 'Die Ou-Testamentiese Werkgemeenskap in Suid-Afrika' in Pretoria* (Stellenbosch: Ou-Testamentiese Werkgemeenskap, 1966), pp. 11-30 (17).

As early as 1942,[7] Hyatt considered that the 'Deuteronomic Editors' would have wanted, at a later date, to make Jeremiah a supporter of Josiah's reform. In a 1951 article,[8] he specified that 'the "school" of writers we call the Deuteronomists' was at the same time responsible for the edition of the Dtr historiography and for that of Jeremiah 1–45. Rudolph, in his 1947 commentary, took up Mowinckel's model and terminology but gave them a more 'conservative' aspect.[9] As for 'C', he envisages the possibility that its author could be the principal compiler of the book.[10]

The idea of one or several Dtr redactions of Jeremiah henceforth dominated research. In the English-speaking world, it was made popular by E.W. Nicholson,[11] who insisted on the omnipresence of the Dtr ideology and style in the 'prose sermons', as well as in the so-called biographical texts. According to him, these texts find their *Sitz im Leben* in the preaching and teaching addressed to the exiles in Babylon.

1.4. *Questioning and Confirmations*

This consensus was however contested by a minority of exegetes who considered that the so-called Dtr character of certain texts corresponded to a *Kunstprosa*, a language very widespread in Judah during the seventh and sixth centuries BCE.[12] On this view, there is nothing to

7.   J.P. Hyatt, 'Jeremiah and Deuteronomy' (1942), in L.G. Perdue and B.W. Kovacs (eds.), *A Prophet to the Nations: Essays in Jeremiah Studies* (Winona Lake, IN: Eisenbrauns, 1984), pp. 113-27.

8.   J.P. Hyatt, 'The Deuteronomic Edition of Jeremiah' (1951), in Perdue and Kovacs (eds.), *A Prophet to the Nations*, pp. 247-67. Cf. also his commentary, *The Book of Jeremiah* (IB, 5; New York: Abingdon Press, 1956), pp. 775-1142.

9.   W. Rudolph, *Jeremia* (HAT, I/12; Tübingen: Mohr Siebeck, 1947, 3rd edn, 1968). According to Rudolph, B was written by Baruch, and C is often based on the authentic words of Jermiah. Jer. 30–31 belongs to an independent source, but forms part of A, as do a certain number of the oracles against the nations.

10.   'Es ist nicht ausgeschlossen, daß der Verfasser der C-Stücke zugleich der Hauptredaktor des Jeremiabuches war' (*Jeremia*, p. xx).

11.   E.W. Nicholson, *Preaching to the Exiles: A Study of the Prose Tradition in the Book of Jeremiah* (Oxford: Basil Blackwell, 1970).

12.   Cf. J. Bright, 'The Date of the Prose Sermons in Jeremiah' (1951), in Perdue and Kovacs (eds.), *A Prophet to the Nations*, pp. 193-212. J. Holladay, especially in his monumental commentary: *Jeremiah 1. A Commentary on the Book of the Prophet Jeremiah Chapters 1–25* and *Jeremiah 2. A Commentary on the Book of the Prophet Jeremiah Chapters 26–52* (Hermeneia; Philadelphia: Fortress Press, 1986–1989); H. Weippert, *Die Prosareden des Jeremiabuches* (BZAW, 132; Berlin

prevent attributing the 'C' texts to the prophet himself who would simply have had recourse to the same language as the editors of the Dtr historiography. It is in this way that H. Weippert rejects any Dtr influence, considering the prose discourses as the words of YHWH directly transmitted by the prophet. Independently of the theological prejudices which such a view implies, the thesis of a *Kuntsprosa* available for whoever wished to utilize it presents a problem. It hardly takes into account the diversity of styles and concepts within the book of Jeremiah itself and the parallels between certain texts of Jeremiah and those of the Dtr historiography are too close to be explained solely by recourse to a common language.

It is to W. Thiel that the credit is due for having tried to demonstrate in detail the presence of a Dtr redaction in Jeremiah.[13] That redaction (present in Jer. 1–45) presupposes, according to him, the Dtr historiography (DH). It actually seems that the Dtr redaction of Jeremiah cites DH on several occasions, and this right from ch. 1, where Jeremiah is, in the account of his vocation, presented as the worthy successor of Moses (cf. Jer. 1.7, 9 with Deut. 18.18). Like DH, 'Dtr Jeremiah' is preoccupied with the explanation of the fall of Judah and by the question if there is a future for the people of the covenant. Such a future is only possible if the people return to the foundation of their relation with YHWH (namely, the Deuteronomic Torah). The sermons giving alternatives (*Alternativpredigen*) in Dtr Jeremiah are to be understood in this sense (Jer. 7.1-15; 22.1-5; 17.19-27). As for style, Thiel notes that Dtr Jeremiah uses the same stereotypical turns of phrase as the redactors of DH; 'Dtr' phraseology limited to the book of Jeremiah appears to be created from Jeremianic phrases. Thiel dates the Dtr redaction of Jeremiah after the death of Jehoiachin (cf. Jer. 22.25-27) and before the end of the exile (about 550) and locates it in Judaea.[14] Thiel also remarked

and New York: W. de Gruyter, 1972).

13. W. Thiel, *Die deuteronomistische Redaktion von Jeremia 1–25* (WMANT, 41; Neukirchen–Vluyn: Neukirchener Verlag, 1973); *Die deuteronomistische Redaktion von Jeremia 26–45* (WMANT, 52; Neukirchen–Vluyn: Neukirchener Verlag, 1981).

14. The localization of the Dtrs in Palestine is still quite popular in present research; its basis seems to be a footnote in M. Noth's *Überlieferungsgeschichtliche Studien: Die sammelnden und bearbeitenden Geschichtswerke im Alten Testament* (Darmstadt: Wissenschaftliche Buchgesellschaft, 3rd edn, 1967 [1943]); English translation: *The Deuteronomistic History* (JSOTSup, 15; Sheffield: Sheffield Academic Press, 1981), p. 110 n. 1; such a localization seems to me to be not too

that the Dtr redaction of Jeremiah was not the last intervention in the book. Thus, the announcement of judgment in 16.10-13, typically Dtr, is 'corrected', even 'neutralized' in the present text of Jeremiah by vv. 14-15, which assume the presence of a post-Dtr redaction (or Dtr^2). Thiel's survey, with results often agreeing with Hyatt's intuitions,[15] seemed to have definitively demonstrated the existence of a Dtr redaction in Jeremiah, in immediate local and temporal proximity with DH. That vision of the formation of Jeremiah is introduced in a number of commentaries.[16] However, the consensus was only apparent.

2. Two Recent Challenges

2.1. The 'Dtr Redaction' of Jeremiah—a Research Pipe Dream?

To demonstrate the presence of a Dtr redaction in Jeremiah, scholars especially emphasized the identical vocabulary and turns of phrase between the DH and Jeremiah. But, as Pohlmann and others[17] point out, Dtr style is very easy to imitate and is met with up to the New Testament period. All we have to do is think of the books of Ezra–Nehemiah and Chronicles, of texts like Zechariah 1; Jonah 3; Daniel 9; Baruch 1–3, and even Acts 7.[18] Furthermore, the 'pluses' of the MT in comparison with the *Vorlage* of the LXX[19] are often composed of Dtr phrases, thus

logical in relation to the 'Golah-centrism' of many Dtr texts. Furthermore, the Dtr milieu was probably that of the intelligentsia who were deported by the Babylonians to Babylon.

15. Cf. the very handy synopsis established by S. Herrmann, *Jeremia: Der Prophet und das Buch* (EdF, 271; Darmstadt: Wissenschaftliche Buchgesellschaft, 1990), pp. 80-81.

16. Cf., for example, the commentary of D.R. Jones, *Jeremiah* (NCB; Grand Rapids: Eerdmans, 1992).

17. K.F. Pohlmann, *Studien zum Jeremiabuch: Ein Beitrag zur Frage nach der Entstehung des Jeremiabuches* (FRLANT, 118; Göttingen: Vandenhoeck & Ruprecht, 1978), pp. 16-18; H.-J. Stipp, *Jeremia im Parteienstreit: Studien zur Textentwicklung von Jer 26,36-43 und 45 als Beitrag zur Geschichte Jeremias, seines Buches und judäischer Parteien im 6. Jahrhundert* (Athenäum Monographien Theologie; BBB, 82; Frankfurt: Hain, 1992), pp. 39-41.

18. Cf. T. Römer and J.D. Macchi, 'Luke, Disciple of the Deuteronomistic School', in C.M. Tuckett (ed.), *Luke's Literary Achievement* (JSNTSup, 116; Sheffield: Sheffield Academic Press, 1995), pp. 178-87.

19. These 'pluses' are dated to the Persian period (Y. Goldman, *Prophétie et royauté au retour de l'exil: Les origines littéraires de la formation massorétique du livre de Jérémie* [OBO, 118; Freiburg: Universitätsverlag; Göttingen: Vandenhoeck

showing that the presence of Dtr texts in Jeremiah in no way implies that these should be considered contemporaneous with DH. Pohlmann, in his analysis of Jeremiah 24 and 37–44, identified in the book of Jeremiah a redaction with an ideology favourable to the Babylonian Golah (cf. in particular the vision of the good and bad figs in Jer. 24). The segregationist tendency expressed in these texts makes them appear to be contemporaneous with the work of the Chronicler. Pohlmann envisages therefore a date about 400 BCE. We should immediately note that this analysis remains a partial one to the extent that Pohlmann does not discuss Dtr texts like Jeremiah 7; 11, and others.[20]

However, the questions raised by Pohlmann remain valid. Can we furthermore gather together all the texts with a Dtr appearance under just one redaction? R.P. Carroll, for his part, while attributing an important role to these Dtr circles for the production of the book,[21] notes: 'So few of the elements constituting the book are datable, and the social background of many of them equally obscure, that the book may represent many and various political movements from the fall of Jerusalem to the Greco-Roman period'.[22] He compares the situation reflected by the book of Jeremiah to that of primitive Christianity, which is characterized by a cohabitation of several interpretations of the 'Jesus event'.[23]

& Ruprecht, 1992]), the Hellenistic period (H.-J. Stipp, *Das masoretische und alexandrinische Sondergut des Jeremiabuches: Textgeschichtlicher Rang, Eigenarten, Triebkräfte* [OBO, 136; Freiburg: Universitätsverlag; Göttingen: Vandenhoeck & Ruprecht, 1994], pp. 142-43), even the Hasmonaean period (P. Piovanelli, 'La condamnation de la diaspora égyptienne dans le livre de Jérémie [*JrA* 50,8–51,30 / *JrB* 43,8–44,30]', *Trans* 9 [1995], pp. 35-49; A. Schenker, 'La rédaction longue du livre de Jérémie doit-elle être datée au temps des premiers Hasmonéens?', *ETL* 70 [1994], pp. 281-93).

20. In his book *Die Ferne Gottes—Studien zum Jeremiabuch* (BZAW, 179; Berlin and New York: W. de Gruyter, 1989), Pohlmann criticizes in passing the analyses of these chapters by Thiel, without however proposing an in-depth argument.

21. 'Whose interests are promoted by this construction of the book? Deuteronomistic circles are the most likely candidates for locating an ideology of the word which would serve their purposes in the second temple period' (*Jeremiah* [OTL; London: SCM Press, 1986], p. 78). He also envisages 'post-Deuteronomistic circles'.

22. R.P. Carroll, *Jeremiah* (OTG; Sheffield: JSOT Press, 1989), p. 107.

23. Cf. R.P. Carroll, *From Chaos to Covenant: Uses of Prophecy in the Book of Jeremiah* (London: SCM Press, 1981), pp. 25-26.

The questioning of the idea of a coherent Dtr redaction is presented differently in W. McKane's commentary. After a detailed analysis of Jeremiah 1–25, he concludes that the book of Jeremiah came into existence owing to successive and continual additions of which the last stage is composed of the MT.[24] McKane sums up the formation of Jeremiah with the image of a 'rolling corpus'. A poetic nucleus (which is not necessarily Jeremianic) can give rise to ('trigger') the composition of other texts in verse, or can lead the redactors to create ('generate') some prose texts, without these processes necessarily having in view the comprehensive edition of the book or important parts of it.

McKane returns in a certain way (using a better argumentation) to the position of Duhm at the beginning of this century. Is everything in that case to be redone? Are the Dtr texts in Jeremiah beyond all systematization? To these questions another problem is to be added: that of the 'ideology' of the Dtr texts of Jeremiah compared with those of the DH.

2.2. A Family Quarrel? Are the Deuteronomists of Jeremiah opposed to the Deuteronomists of Deuteronomy–2 Kings?

It has long been wondered that DH, unlike 2 Chronicles, does not mention Jeremiah. H.-J. Stipp and others interpreted this omission as a sign of the hostility of the redactors of DH towards the prophet.[25] In that case, must the thesis still be supported according to which the book of this same prophet would have undergone one or several Dtr redactions? For some authors, the Dtr family was divided into two main factions: that which edited DH and that which dealt with the book of Jeremiah. According to Hardmeier, the account of 2 Kings 18–19 (Jerusalem miraculouly spared from the Assyrian assault) shows that the Dtrs supported an ideology of a 'Zionist' or royal type, convinced of the inviolability of the temple, even after the catastrophe. Since their heroes

---

24. 'MT is to be understood as a commentary or commentaries built on pre-existing elements of the Jeremianic corpus' (W. McKane, *A Critical and Exegetical Commentary on Jeremiah* [ICC; Edinburgh: T. & T. Clark, 1986], I, p. lxxxiii).

25. H.-J. Stipp, 'Probleme des redaktionsgeschichtlichen Modells der Entstehung des Jeremiabuches', in W. Gross (ed.), *Jeremia und die 'deuteronomistische Bewegung'* (BBB, 98; Weinheim: Beltz Athenäum, 1995), pp. 225-62 (232); C. Hardmeier, 'Die Propheten Micha und Jesaja im Spiegel von Jeremia xxvi und 2 Regum xvii–xx. Zur Prophetie-Rezeption in der nach-josianischen Zeit', in J.A. Emerton (ed.), *Congress Volume. Leuven 1989* (VTSup, 43; Leiden: E.J. Brill, 1991), pp. 172-89 (188-89).

are Hezekiah and Josiah, they are hoping for the restoration of the Davidic dynasty.[26] These 'hardliners'[27] would have been in bitter opposition to the pro-Babylonian policy of the Shaphanites,[28] who would be the Dtr editors of Jeremiah and the minor prophets. In such a context, Albertz understands the (Dtr) discourse on the temple (Jer. 7), denouncing the confidence of the people in this place and explaining its destruction owing to the disobedience of Judah to the Torah, as a polemic against the vision of the temple in DH.[29] Stipp goes further and notes 'a deep trench between the redactors of DH and the authors of the Dtr passages in Jeremiah'.[30] If such inconsistency really exists between DH and Jeremiah, is it still possible to speak of a common milieu?

The challenges that I have just presented risk disrupting considerably what exegesis considered as established on the subject of the formation of the book of Jeremiah. They necessitate two inquiries. First, the questioning of a coherent Dtr redaction obliges us to raise the question of the compositional intentions of an eventual Dtr redaction. The second issue is that of the ideological and theological differences between the book of Jeremiah and DH. Do these differences exist, and in the event of an affirmative response, how must they be explained?

3. *Two Inquiries*

3.1. *Does a Dtr-Constructed Redactional Objective Exist in Jeremiah?*
The book of Jeremiah in its present form[31] can easily be subdivided

26. Hardmeier ('Die Propheten Micha und Jesaja') suggests seeing partisans of Ishmael, murderer of Gedaliah, in these Dtrs, but in doing so we are dealing with an out-and-out novel.

27. This is Hardmeier's term ('Die Propheten Micha und Jesaja', p. 187).

28. Hardmeier ('Die Propheten Micha und Jesaja') and Stipp ('Probleme des redaktionsgeschichtlichen Modells') consider 2 Kgs 19.2-7 as a polemic against the exhortation to submit to Babylon, very prevalent in the Jeremianic tradition (cf. Jer. 21.2-10; 37.9-10).

29. R. Albertz, 'Die Intentionen und Träger des deuteronomistischen Geschichtswerks', in *idem* (ed.), *Schöpfung und Befreiung* (Festschrift C. Westermann; Stuttgart: Calwer Verlag, 1989), pp. 37-53 (46). Cf. earlier F.K. Kumaki, *The Temple Sermon: Jeremiah's Polemic Against the Deuteronomists (Dtr 1)* (Ann Arbor and London: University Microfilms International, 1980), who considers Jer. 7 as a polemic of the prophet Jeremiah against the Dtrs of the time of Josiah.

30. Stipp, 'Probleme des redaktionsgeschichtlichen Modells', p. 232.

31. For convenience and out of habit I base myself on the Masoretic Text. The different arrangement in LXX Jeremiah especially concerns the place of the oracles

according to the following units: after the introduction (Jer. 1: date, vocation and visions), a first unit, Jeremiah 2–6, contains a collection of oracles, mainly in verse, announcing the enemy from the North and calling on the recipients to change their conduct; ch. 7 (the first discourse on the temple) introduces a unit going as far as Jeremiah 24, gathering together discourses and lamentations, symbolic acts and the 'confessions'. These various genres are all concerned with the difficult announcement of the judgment. The vision of good and bad figs concludes this section with the announcement of salvation for a small group (the deportees of 597). Jeremiah 25 can be described as a 'turning point', resuming the themes of chs. 7–24 and preparing for what follows. The following unit goes from ch. 26 to ch. 35 and is introduced by the second version of the discourse on the temple (Jer. 26). In these chapters, announcements of salvation predominate. The conclusion in Jeremiah 35 can be compared to Jeremiah 24: it is a matter again of a promise made to a small group (the Rechabites). Jeremiah 36 (the burnt scroll, the counter-reform of Jehoiakim) introduces the narrative part of the book (often called 'the passion of Jeremiah': the conflicts of the prophet with Zedekiah, his imprisonment, the fall of Jerusalem, his forced descent into Egypt, followed by the sermon against the Egyptian diaspora). This unit ends with the announcement of salvation addressed to an individual: Baruch (Jer. 45). There follow the oracles against the nations (Jer. 46–51) and the historical appendix (Jer. 52; cf. 2 Kgs 24.18–25.30).

The reminder about the organization of the book makes apparent a certain desire for structuring, especially in the case of the two central parts, with both beginning with a discourse on the temple (Jer. 7 and 26) and ending with a promise of salvation to a restricted group (Jer. 24 and 35). This plan, established on the synchronic level, will nevertheless be of use in detecting the eventual intentions of a Dtr redaction. We are actually going to see that these structurally important chapters are strongly marked by the Dtr style that, as we have seen, is characterized by a certain number of stereotyped turns of phrase.[32]

---

against the nations. If LXX has preserved the 'original' plan of Jeremiah, which is quite possible, it would change nothing in the Dtr compositional intentions (ignoring the oracles against the nations), as I will try to demonstrate.

32. Cf. the lists in M. Weinfeld, *Deuteronomy and Deuteronomic School* (Oxford: Clarendon Press, 1972) and Bright, 'The Date of the Prose Sermons in Jeremiah', appendix A.

The main themes in these phrases are: obedience or disobedience in response to the voice of YHWH, the warning against the veneration of 'other gods', the uninterrupted sending of the prophets, 'servants of YHWH', the recalling of the coming out of Egypt, the covenant concluded (with the ancestors), the gift of the land (to the ancestors), the sins of the ancestors, and so on. Of course, the mere inventory of this phraseology does not demonstrate the existence of a structured Dtr redaction. However, the distribution of some of these formulas in the book of Jeremiah can suggest the existence of such a redaction.

Let us take the example of the gift of the land to the ancestors. This phrase, which plays a large role in DH,[33] appears for the first time in Jeremiah in ch. 7 (vv. 7 and 14),[34] which is probably Dtr,[35] and its final attestation is found in 35.15. In these two chapters, the gift of the land to the ancestors is envisaged conditionally (obedience to YHWH), and it is met again a third and final time in Jer. 25.5-6:[36] 'If every one of you turn back from your evil behaviour…then you will remain[37] on the land that I[38] have given to your ancestors…' In the same way, Jeremiah 25

33. Cf. for this point and for the following T. Römer, *Israels Väter: Untersuchungen zur Väterthematik im Deuteronomium und in der deuteronomistischen Tradition* (OBO, 99; Freiburg: Universitätsverlag; Göttingen: Vandenhoeck & Ruprecht, 1990), pp. 368-70 and 441-43.

34. Jer. 3.18 speaks of the land 'given for a heritage' (נחל in place of נתן) and belongs to a passage that is generally considered to be a post-exilic addition forming part of the final retouches to the book; cf. Thiel, *Die deuteronomistische Redaktion von Jeremia I–25*, p. 92; McKane, *Jeremiah*, pp. 76-77.

35. An attempt to reconstruct an 'authentic' oracle reworked by the Dtrs has often been made, but this is hardly possible, as T. Seidl has very well demonstrated: 'Jeremias Tempelrede: Polemik gegen die joschijanische Reform? Die Parallel-traditionen Jer 7 und 26 auf ihre Effizienz für das Deuteronomismusproblem in Jeremia befragt', in Gross (ed.), *Jeremia und die 'deuteronomistische Bewegung'*, pp. 141-79; and J.P. Floss, 'Methodische Aspekte exegetischer Hypothesen am Beispiel von Theo Seidls Beitrag zur "Tempelrede" ', in Gross (ed.), *Jeremia und die 'deuteronomistische Bewegung'*, pp. 181-85.

36.   אם היטיב תיטיבו את דרכיכם ואת מעלליכם   7.5
         שובו נא איש מדרכו הרעה ומרע מעלליכם   25.5
       שבו נא איש מדרכו הרעה והיטיבו מעלליכם   35.15

37. We find in Jer. 25 a paronomasia with the roots שוב and ישב, quite comparable to that produced by שוב and שבה in 1 Kgs 8.46-48.

38. According to the LXX; the MT has 'YHWH'. For the priority of the LXX, cf. most recently G. Wanke, *Jeremia. I. Jeremia 1,1–25,14* (ZBK.AT, 20,1: Zürich: Theologischer Verlag, 1995), p. 224.

expressly refers to Jeremiah 7[39] and already prepares for the statements of Jeremiah 35.[40] We get the impression that Jeremiah 7, 25 and 35 function as 'pillars' of the Dtr composition of Jeremiah. It is hardly conceivable that the relations between these three chapters would be a simple result of chance.

Within the whole of Jeremiah 7–35, other connections become evident. Jer. 11.1-13 is a long Dtr sermon[41] taking note of the breach of the covenant by the people being addressed who are reproached for returning to the sins of 'their first ancestors'[42] (הראשנים האבות, 11.10). Despite the Dtr insistence on the theme of the ancestors, the latter are not characterized as ראשנים in the Dtr literature[43] except in this place. In the book of Jeremiah this phrase is only understandable in connection with the other key text on the covenant, Jer. 31.31-34. This text, whose Dtr character seems difficult to call into question,[44] functions, on the

39. Cf. 7.13//25.3-4; 7.25//25.4; 7.24, 26//25.4; 7.6, 9//25.6; 7.18-19//25.6-7; 7.34//25.10-11; cf. also the synopsis in Römer, *Israels Väter*, p. 459.

40. Cf. in particular 25.3-6 and 35.14-15 and the synopsis in Thiel, *Die deuteronomistische Redaktion von Jeremia 1–25*, p. 267.

41. Cf. for example McKane, *Jeremiah*, pp. 244-46; Wanke, *Jeremia*, p. 119.

42. This quite uncommon phrase probably refers in the Dtr context to the 'original sin' of the people, namely, the veneration of the golden calf; cf. for more details, T. Römer, 'Les "anciens" pères (Jér 11,10) et la "nouvelle" alliance (Jér 31,31)', *BN* 59 (1991), pp. 23-27.

43. Just one other text in the Old Testament has the same construction, Isa. 43.27: אביך הראשון חטא. Job 8.8 puts דר רישון and אבות parallel. In Deut. 19.14; Isa. 61.4; Qoh. 1.11 ראשנים is used to designate ancestors in general; Lev. 26.45 mentions a covenant concluded with the ראשנים after the Exodus; Ps. 79.8 is quite close to Jer. 11.10, since it speaks of עונות ראשנים.

44. In spite of numerous attempts to attribute Jer. 31.31-34 to the prophet Jeremiah, the Dtr character of this pericope can, in my opinion, scarcely be contested (cf. especially S. Herrmann, *Die prophetischen Heilserwartungen im Alten Testament: Ursprung und Gestaltwandel* [BWANT, 85; Stuttgart: W. Kohlhammer, 1965], pp. 179-81; 195-97; S. Böhmer, *Heimkehr und neuer Bund: Studien zu Jeremiah 30–31* [Göttinger Texte und Arbeiten, 5; Göttingen: Vandenhoeck & Ruprecht, 1976], pp. 75-77; Thiel, *Die deuteronomistische Redaktion von Jeremia 26–45*, pp. 24-26). C. Levin (*Die Verheissung des neuen Bundes in ihrem theologiegeschichtlichen Zusammenhang ausgelegt* [FRLANT, 137; Göttingen: Vandenhoeck & Ruprecht, 1985], p. 60) detects four layers (Dtr and post-Dtr) in these verses; this appears to me too complicated. He is right all the same in considering v. 33, which announces the inscription of the Torah in the heart of each one (cf. the tension between 'the days are coming', v. 31a and 'after these days' in v. 33a), as a late addition. Verse 34 could be situated on the same redactional level.

compositional level, as the response to the report of Jer. 11.10-12 and takes up again word for word the phrases of Jer. 11.4 and 10:

31.32a   לא כברית אשר כרתי את אבותם ביום...להוציאם מארץ מצרים

11.10   בריתי אשר כרתי את אבותם   11.4   ביום תוציאי אותם מארץ מצרים

In the same way the recalling of the breaking of the covenant in 31.32b clearly refers to 11.10.

31.32b   אשר המה הפרו את בריתי

11.10   הפרו...את בריתי

If Jer. 11.1-13 and 31.31-34* can be understood as the two poles[45] of the Dtr reflection on the *berît*, we understand as well that the utilization of the adjective ראשון in 11.10 refers ahead to חדש in 31.31. This pair 'old [first]–new' is found frequently in exilic texts.[46] Isa. 42.9 is especially interesting: הראשנות הנה באו וחדשות אני מגיד: 'See, the former things have passed, and now I announce new things'. In Jer. 31.31-34, it is in comparison with the ancestors that the 'newness' of the covenant is described. Just as in Deut. 5.3, the ancestors symbolize the past in order to insist on the fact that the covenant in question will be 'present'.[47] In the case of Jer. 31.31-34 that means: the covenant will be new because God does not take into account the ancient times to which the אבותם הראשים of 11.10 referred. Thus this unique phrase is at the service of a bipolar structure by means of which the Dtr editors of Jeremiah seek to link together the explanation of the catastrophe and the hope of a new beginning.

Other examples of the compositional bonds between the different Dtr texts of Jeremiah could be added to the remarks that I have just set out (for example, Jer. 7.21-24 'prepares for' 11.1-5; Jer. 30.1-3 and Jer. 31.31-34 frame the Dtr edition of the 'book of consolation').[48] It seems

In that case, Jer. 31.31-32 can scarcely be considered as going beyond the ideology of a Dtr horizon, as has recently been suggested; cf. G. Fischer, 'Aufnahme, Wende und Überwindung dtn/r Gedankengutes in Jer 30f.', in Gross (ed.), *Jeremia und die 'deuteronomistische Bewegung'*, pp. 129-39).

45. It is in relation to Jer. 11 that the surprising conclusion of 31.32 makes sense: ואנכי בעלתי בם can be understood as an allusion to לקטר לבעל in 11.13: Israel has served Baal while forgetting that its 'true Baal' is YHWH.

46. Isa. 42.9; 43.19; 48.6; 62.2; 65.17; 66.22; Jer. 31.22; Ezek. 11.19; 18.31; 36.26; Lam. 3.23.

47. For the interpretation of this text, cf. Römer, *Israels Väter*, pp. 45-53.

48. Cf. N. Lohfink, 'Die Gotteswortverschachtelung in Jer 30–31', in L. Rup-

therefore that the idea of a coherent Dtr redaction of Jeremiah must be recognized. This first redaction, however, did not necessarily include the whole book in its present form. We have seen that Jeremiah 7, 25 and 35 constituted the three pillars of Dtr Jeremiah, and they could really mark out the extent of the first Dtr redaction of the book which would comprise the two large sections 7–24 (25)—(25) 26–35. A number of observations confirm this possibility. First, as I have mentioned, the formula of the gift of the land to the ancestors is found for the first time in Jer. 7.7 and for the last time in 35.15. Several typically Dtr phrases are attested only within this portion of Jeremiah. קרא ולא ענה is found only in 7.13, 27 and 35.15; היטיב מעלליכם occurs in 7.3, 5; 18.11; 26.3 and 35.15; the introductory formula 'the word that came to Jeremiah from YHWH' is used only between 7.1 and 35.1.[49] Jeremiah 7 is the first, Jeremiah 35 the last of the prose discourses constructed according to the same plan.[50]

In this perspective, L. Stulman's study[51] provides some supplementary arguments. His charts show that the Dtr phrases that are attested both in Deuteronomy–2 Kings and in Jeremiah are found in 77 per cent of the cases within these chs. 7–35. On the other hand, the turns of phrase declared 'Dtr' in the research, but limited to Jeremiah, appear in 56 per cent of the cases outside of this collection. Stulman's analysis confirms the thesis of a Dtr redaction of Jeremiah closely linked to DH, and extending from Jeremiah 7 to 35. H. Cazelles and C. Levin have moreover envisaged Jeremiah 35 as the conclusion of a Dtr or exilic redaction of Jeremiah.[52] Furthermore, the collection Jeremiah 2–6[53]

pert *et al.* (eds.), *Künder des Wortes* (Festschrift J. Schreiner; Würzburg: Echter Verlag, 1982), pp. 105-19 (106).

49. In 44.1 'from YHWH' is missing. For the occurrences cf. Pohlmann, *Studien zum Jeremiabuch*, p. 167.

50. Cf. Nicholson, *Preaching to the Exiles*, p. 34.

51. L. Stulman, *The Prose Sermons in the Book of Jeremiah: A Redescription of the Correspondences with Deuteronomistic Literature in the Light of Recent Text-critical Research* (SBLDS, 83; Atlanta: Scholars Press, 1986), pp. 33-44.

52. Cf. H. Cazelles, 'La production du livre de Jérémie dans l'histoire ancienne d'Israël', *Masses ouvrières* 343 (1978), pp. 9-31 (24-25); Levin, *Die Verheissung des neuen Bundes*, p. 158.

53. For the redactional history of this section, cf. in particular M. Biddle, *A Redaction History of Jeremiah 2:1–4:2* (ATANT, 77; Zürich: Theologischer Verlag, 1990) and R. Liwak, *Der Prophet und die Geschichte: Eine literar-historische Untersuchung zum Jeremiabuch* (BWANT, 121; Stuttgart: W. Kohlhammer, 1987).

bears no traces indicating a Dtr redaction. In the same way, the accounts of Jeremiah 37–52 are not really typically Dtr.[54] The whole of Jeremiah 1–44 (45)[55] is consequently due to one or several late Dtr (Dtr² Jeremiah) or post-Dtr redactions. In Jeremiah 1 (dating and vocation), a mixture of Dtr style and post-exilic prophecy can be observed;[56] at the end of the book, chs. 43–44 seem to express the situation of a well installed Egyptian diaspora: these texts probably reflect, therefore, the context of the Persian period.[57] Finally, the redactional work on the book will have continued at least until the end of the Hellenistic period, as the differences between the LXX and the MT especially indicate.[58]

Let us return now to the problem of the link between the first Dtr redaction of Jeremiah and DH. As we have seen, some authors postulate an almost insurmountable opposition between Dtr Jeremiah and DH. But an examination of the key Dtr texts of Jeremiah makes that thesis difficult to support.

Thus, the sermon of Jeremiah 11 on the covenant prescribed for the ancestors (cf. Judg. 2.20) at the time of the coming out of Egypt (11.3-4) corresponds to the wording of DH. The idea that *berît* and exodus are closely linked is also found in the Dtr redaction of the historical books, as Deut. 29.24 and 1 Kgs 8.21 show. Obedience to the *berît*, to which Jeremiah 11 commits the people, without any doubt alludes to the *berît* concluded with Israel by Moses, as appealed to in the book of Deuteronomy. It is a matter therefore, on the literary level, of an explicit

54. Cf. below.

55. I shall not go into the problem here of the oracles against the nations.

56. Cf. S. Herrmann, *Jeremia* (BKAT, 12.1; Neukirchen–Vluyn: Neukirchener Verlag, 1986), pp. 52-55.

57. Cf. A. de Pury and T. Römer, 'Terres d'exil et terres d'accueil. Quelques réflexions sur le judaïsme postexilique face à la Perse et à l'Egypte', *Trans-euphratène* 9 (1995), pp. 25-34 (30-31).

58. At this level, it becomes extremely difficult to know whether it is a matter of an intervention with a comprehensive design or simply occasional corrections. Here the thesis of the 'rolling corpus' (McKane) finds its justification. A special problem is presented by the many doublets within the book, showing the complexity of the redactional process; cf. on this point the contribution of J.D. Macchi, 'Les doublets dans le livre de Jérémie', in A. Curtis and T. Römer (eds.), *The Book of Jeremiah and its Reception. Le livre de Jérémie et sa réception* (BETL, 128; Leuven: University Press and Peeters, 1997), pp. 119-50.

reference to the book of Deuteronomy;[59] this constitutes the perspective from which Jeremiah 11 depicts an anti-history of salvation for which the addressees bear the whole responsibility.

The Dtr version of the vision of the good and bad figs is characterized by the idea that the punishment by YHWH of the people implies the removal of all the inhabitants of Palestine[60] (24.8-10; cf. also Jer. 25.11, Dtr). This same ideology is found at the end of DH (cf. 2 Kgs 25.21 and 25.26)[61] and in a certain way as well in the prayer of 1 Kings 8.[62]

We must come back to the central text in the discussion of Dtr ideology in the book of Jeremiah, namely, the discourse on the temple of Jer. 7.1-14 (15).[63] This text, which has played an important role in the discussion of the 'historical Jeremiah', is clearly a production of Dtr redactors,[64] leaving no possibility of reconstructing an authentic oracle.[65] But can we say, with Stipp and others, that this text rejects the temple and is opposed to the cultic theology of DH?[66] The structure of the text is that of a sermon in the form of an alternative. After an introduction, v. 3 sums up the aim of the text: 'Amend your ways...and I will let you dwell in this place'. There follow two sections that present an alternative to the hearer. The first section (vv. 4-7) begins with an exhortation ('Do not trust in lying words'), followed by a 'citation' of

59. The allusions in Jer. 11 to the book of Deuteronomy are many. Some examples: the appeal 'to listen to the voice of YHWH' and the covenant formula in v. 4 and in v. 5 is a combination of Deut. 7.8 and 8.18. The announcement that YHWH is going to bring upon Israel the words of the covenant (v. 8 MT), even disaster (v. 11), means the realization of the potentiality of the curses in Deut. 28.15-69.

60. Cf. Pohlmann, *Studien zum Jeremiabuch*, p. 28.

61. Verse 21 notes that 'Judah was deported far from its land', and v. 26 concludes the first version of DH with the descent of the rest of the people (who according to v. 26 no longer belonged to 'Judah') to Egypt, thus realizing the last curse of Deut. 28.68.

62. Verse 46 speaks of the exile of the sons of Israel without envisaging the population left in the country.

63. Verse 15 is probably an addition (cf. Rudolph, *Jeremia*, p. 54). Without this verse, the two parts of the discourse both end with a recalling of the gift of the land made to the ancestors (v. 7 and v. 14).

64. The list in Stulman (*The Prose Sermons in the Book of Jeremiah*, pp. 33-44) brings to light 92 Dtr turns of phrase in Jer. 7.1-15.

65. For the history of research and the Dtr character of this text, cf. recently Seidl, 'Jeremias Tempelrede'.

66. Cf. below.

these words, then the following verses define a condition expressed in prescriptions which are both social (do not oppress, etc.) and cultic (do not run after other gods). At the end of the announcement of this condition, we meet again the promise of v. 3: 'then I will make you dwell[67] in this place', a place identified as the 'land I have given to your ancestors'. The second section (vv. 8-14) takes up again the vocabulary of the first section, but passes to specifics: in place of 'do not trust in lying words', we find in v. 8: 'Here you are, relying on lying words'. The social and cultic prescriptions become accusations (for example, the fact of running after other gods, v. 9). In v. 2, those addressed have been summoned to listen; v. 13 says on the contrary 'you have not listened', and introduces the announcement of judgment: just as the ancient sanctuary of Shilo has been destroyed, YHWH will do the same to 'the place[68] that I have given to you and your ancestors' (v. 14).

This structure makes it clear that the goal of the discourse is not criticism of the temple as sanctuary.[69] It is a popular magical and blind confidence in the temple that is denounced; vv. 10-11, in characterizing the temple as the place where the שׁם of YHWH has been proclaimed (cf., for example, 1 Kgs 8.29-30), show a high esteem for the temple.[70] Jeremiah 7 wishes above all to explain the reason for the destruction of the temple by linking up its cult to the obedience to the Deuteronomic Torah. It is because the ethical and cultic prescriptions of Deuteronomy have not been respected that the destruction of the temple and the deportation have been produced. For the Dtrs of Jeremiah, the temple is not important as a place of ritual sacrifices (cf. Jer. 7.22), but as a privileged place where Israel can invoke the one who brought them out of Egypt and the one who is to be honoured by respect for the *berît* (cf. Jer. 10.24 and Deut. 5.33). It follows that there is no tension between the theological conception of Dtr Jeremiah and of DH. T. Seidl states it

67. It is necessary to retain in vv. 3 and 7 the MT as the more difficult reading against Aquila and the Vulgate which read 'I will dwell with you'. For the 'authentic Jeremiah' the MT causes a problem, but not for the situation of the Dtr redactors.

68. Jer. 7 maintains a certain ambiguity as regards מקום, which can mean at the same time the country and the temple (the two gifts from YHWH to the people). Such use of מקום occurs also in Deuteronomy; cf. 1.30-31; 9.7; 11.4-5; 26.9; 29.7.

69. Cf. Carroll, *Jeremiah* (OTL), p. 209: 'The sermon is not a statement against the temple worship'.

70. Cf. E. Holt, 'Jeremiah's Temple Sermon and the Deuteronomists: An Investigation of the Redactional Relationship between Jeremiah 7 and 26', *JSOT* 36 (1986), pp. 73-87 (75).

very clearly: 'Jer. 7 does not show any difference with the deuteronomic law or with the Deuteronomistic History. On the contrary, there
is a convergence with the deuteronomi(sti)c corpora of the OT, concerning central themes and intentions.[71]

This convergence can also be emphasized on the redactional level.
Jeremiah 7 seems to me to be conceived as a guarantor of DH's key text
on the temple, namely, 1 Kings 8, the great prayer of Solomon at the
time of the inauguration of the sanctuary. These two chapters refer to
one another on different levels. Both discourses envisage and explain
the destruction of the temple and the exile; the two texts weave a close
link between the temple, the city and the land (cf. 1 Kgs 8.48). In DH
the phrase about the gift of the land to the ancestors appears for the first
time in 1 Kings 8, in Jeremiah for the first time in Jeremiah 7. 1 Kings
8.34 wonders as Jer. 7.7 does about the conditions that Israel must fulfil
in order to dwell in 'the land given to the ancestors'. In 1 Kgs 8.36 as in
Jer. 7.3, 5 it is a question of 'good ways' in which the addressees are
called to walk. And in a general way, 1 Kings 8, like Jeremiah 7, deals
with 'good utilization' of the temple. The possibility of the destruction
announced by Solomon (1 Kgs 8.46-51) is confirmed by the prophecy
in Jer. 7.8-15. Such links demonstrate a wish to put DH and Dtr Jeremiah in contact.[72] There is not therefore competition but rather con-
cordance! This acknowledgment is valid for all the great Dtr texts in
Jeremiah. Thus Rendtorff has underlined for Jer. 25.1-13 the 'clear connections with the summary Deuteronomistic interpretation of the
history of Israel in II Kings 17'.[73] It seems consequently that the Dtr
sermons in Jeremiah play the same compositional role as the 'chapters
of reflection' (according to Noth's terminology) in DH. Furthermore,

71. Cf. Seidl, 'Jeremias Tempelrede', p. 175: 'Jr 7 zeigt keinerlei Divergenz
zum deuteronomischen Gesetz oder zum DtrG, konvergiert vielmehr mit den klass-
ischen deuteronomischen und deuteronomistischen Textkorpora des AT in zentralen
Themen und Anliegen'.

72. Other parallels can be found: for example, 1 Kgs 8.29 and Jer. 7.10; the
importance of the coming out of Egypt: 1 Kgs 8.21, 51 and Jer. 7.22 (this verse is
not, strictly speaking, part of the temple discourse, but of the large unit 7.1–8.3 that
can be considered a Dtr vade mecum of good and bad worship). We may also recall
that Jer. 7 has many parallels with 2 Kgs 17, another key DH text (2 Kgs 17.3//Jer.
7.22; 2 Kgs 17.14//Jer. 7.24; 2 Kgs 17.16-17//Jer. 7.9, 31; 2 Kgs 17.18//Jer. 7.15,
and so on).

73. R. Rendtorff, *The Old Testament: An Introduction* (London: SCM Press,
1985), p. 204.

the fact that the end of DH (2 Kgs 24–25) and Jeremiah 52 deal with the same events[74] shows that at a given moment the Dtr school wanted to establish 'cross-references' (Lohfink) between the two literary units.[75] However, the question of the absence of the prophet Jeremiah in 2 Kings 24–25 remains open. What is the reason therefore for this 'prophetic silence'[76] of DH with regard to Jeremiah?

3.2. *How Is Jeremiah, Missing from DH, Transformed into a Spokesperson for Dtr Ideology?*

The absence of Jeremiah from DH is explained, according to Koch, by the fact that the historical Jeremiah had announced an irreversible judgment, which could not be accepted by the Dtr redactors. This thesis presents a double problem: the criteria allowing for the reconstruction of the 'authentic' message of the prophet are at least ambiguous. Can it be postulated that the oldest texts of Jeremiah contain only announcements of calamity, as Pohlmann, for example, claims?[77] And can we be sure that the first edition of DH would have had as a priority the intention to bring a message of hope to its addressees?[78] Koch's solution is therefore weighed down with too many hypotheses.

We have seen that there is no ideological difference between DH and Dtr Jeremiah.[79] However, such is not the case for certain texts that seem

74. This is not the place for a discussion on the complex relations that exist between these chapters; cf. on this subject C.R. Seitz, *Theology in Conflict: Reactions to the Exile in the Book of Jeremiah* (BZAW, 176; Berlin and New York: W. de Gruyter, 1989), pp. 266-69.

75. N. Lohfink, 'Gab es eine deuteronomistische Bewegung?', in Gross (ed.), *Jeremia und die 'deuteronomistische Bewegung'*, pp. 313-81 (360).

76. Cf. K. Koch, 'Das Profetenschweigen des deuteronomistischen Geschichtswerks', in J. Jeremias and L. Perlitt (eds.), *Die Botschaft und die Boten* (Festschrift H.W. Wolff; Neukirchen–Vluyn: Neukirchener Verlag, 1981), pp. 115-28.

77. Pohlmann, *Die Ferne Gottes*, pp. 115-17. Pohlmann goes still further by stating that only the texts announcing calamity without referring to YHWH form part of the ancient nucleus (p. 181). The idea of a late 'Yahwisation' of the judgment oracles seems to me to misjudge the very essence of biblical and semitic prophetism in general.

78. Let us recall that for Noth, the Dtr editor wanted to draw up a report of failure without any perspective on the future. This thesis was subsequently criticized, but this discussion is far from being closed.

79. If we accept Noth's thesis on the intention of DH, we could see the announcement of Jer. 31.31-34 contradicting the report of failure by DH. That apparent contradiction disappears if we situate Dtr Jeremiah a little later than DH

partially to reflect the 'historical Jeremiah', or to speak more prudently, another tradition on Jeremiah, especially chs. 32 and 37–43. The symbolic act of Jeremiah 32 (the buying of a field by Jeremiah) receives in v. 15b[80] the following interpretation: 'Houses and fields and vineyards will still be bought in this land'.[81] Here, the hope is very clearly nourished that life is going to continue in Judah in spite of the first (and the second?) deportation. Such a view is opposed to that of DH according to which 'Judah was deported entirely from its land' (2 Kgs 25.21; cf. also 25.26 where all the people remaining leave Palestine and make for Egypt). According to Jer. 39.14 and 40.2-6, the prophet chooses to remain with the non-exiled population in Judah, which implies the continuity of the relation between YHWH and the people in the land (cf. again 27.11). In these texts, we can observe with Seitz 'hopes for continued existence of the remnant community in the land'.[82] According to 40.6, Jeremiah becomes an adviser to Gedaliah, the governor installed by the Babylonians. 40.10-12 describes the prosperity of the community in the land: the people who took refuge with neighbours returned and benefited from an overabundant harvest, which is evidently the sign of a divine blessing. But these notices are missing in 2 Kings 25. The text of DH even seems to want to 'downplay the potential rule of Gedaliah'.[83] DH's reticence in comparison with the Jeremianic tradition can thus be explained by the fact that this tradition in its pre-Dtr form was clearly situated on the side of the non-exiles (39.14; 40.6; 42.10).[84] C.R. Seitz has shown that the nucleus of

(as is done, for example, by Thiel, *Die deuteronomistische Redaktion*).

80. According to the very critical Levin, we have here the trace of a word of the historical Jeremiah; cf. *Die Verheissung des neuen Bundes*, p. 159.

81. In the following verses, which probably belong to a Dtr redaction, this perspective is changed in favour of the Golah.

82. Seitz, *Theology in Conflict*, p. 223.

83. Seitz, *Theology in Conflict*, p. 217. According to Seitz, for the DH the only legitimate head is Jehoiachin (2 Kgs 25.27-30). This assertion depends on the (Nothian) thesis according to which these verses form the conclusion of the exilic edition of the DH. This view does not inevitably compel acceptance; cf. for example R.E. Friedman, 'From Egypt to Egypt: Dtr[1] to Dtr[2]', in B. Halpern and J. Levenson (eds.), *Traditions in Transformation: Turning Points in Biblical Faith. Essays Presented to Frank Moore Cross, Jr.* (Winona Lake, IN: Eisenbrauns, 1981), pp. 167-92.

84. Cf. K.F. Pohlmann, 'Erwägungen zum Schlusskapitel des deuteronomistischen Geschichtswerkes. Oder: Warum wird der Prophet Jeremia in 2. Kön. 22–25

418   *Israel Constructs its History*

Jeremiah 37–42 (together with some other texts) could have formed a 'scribal chronicle', written by a member of the community remaining in the land who relates the events of 597–587 from the perspective of the population remained in the land.[85] The situation of the non-exiled is legitimated by the figure of Jeremiah. The descent into Egypt in 43.7 (which forms, according to Seitz, the original end of this chronicle)[86] is described as an action contrary to the will of God for whom life must continue in Judah (42.12). It is after the final deportation of 582 that this text would have arrived in Babylon where it would have been adapted to the perspective of the exiled, indeed even the Deuteronomists.

We can thus propose the following thesis for the 'Deuteronomization' of the Jeremianic tradition: the redactors of DH and the 'historical' Jeremiah (even certain traditions circulating in regard to him) are in conflict about the significance of the exile. Because of Jeremiah's position in favour of the non-exiled population, DH omits mentioning him (unlike Chronicles).[87] The Dtrs nevertheless could not totally ignore this prophet. Consequently, they compiled a Dtr version of Jeremiah 7–35*[88] insisting on the conformity of the message of the prophet with Dtr thought, without however speaking of his 'biography'. From the time when this biography or chronicle was known among the exiles as well, a second Dtr redaction of Jeremiah (Dtr^2 Jeremiah), showing some stylistic and ideological differences from DH and Dtr Jeremiah,[89]

nicht erwähnt?', in A.H.J. Gunneweg and O. Kaiser (eds.), *Textgemäss: Aufsätze und Beiträge zur Hermeneutik des Alten Testaments. Festschrift E. Würthwein* (Göttingen: Vandenhoeck & Ruprecht, 1979), pp. 94-109.

85. Seitz, *Theology in Conflict*, especially pp. 282-96. For Seitz, it is a matter of an eyewitness of the events, perhaps a member of the Shaphanite family (p. 285: 'though it cannot be established with absolute certainty').

86. Cf. his chart, p. 283.

87. This fact is a supplementary argument in favour of my thesis. As S. Japhet showed, the Chronicles have an indigenous vision of the origins of Israel, unlike Ezra–Nehemiah (cf. 'Composition and Chronology in the Book of Ezra–Nehemiah', in T.C. Eskenazi and K.H. Richards [eds.], *Second Temple Studies. II. Temple Community in the Persian Period* [JSOTSup, 175; Sheffield: JSOT Press, 1994], pp. 189-216).

88. As I have already emphasized, it is within these chapters that the Dtr style is most pronounced, unlike chs. 2–6 and 37–43.

89. For more details, cf. Römer, *Israels Väter*, pp. 422-91.

was imperative. It integrates the chs. 2–6*[90] and 37–43* with the help of chs. 1 and 44–45 and frames the new edition of Jeremiah, revised and corrected, with the leitmotif of the disobedience of the ancestors (2.5 and 44.9).[91] This theme shows a certain scepticism in the face of the optimistic attempts at restoration. We can therefore situate this second Dtr redaction in the Persian period. Let us mention again the fact that Dtr^2 Jeremiah transforms the Dtr formula of the 'land given to the ancestors' into that of the 'Torah given to the ancestors' (44.10);[92] this formula could express the interests of a Golah transformed into a diaspora, for which the Torah becomes the means par excellence to speak of the relation between YHWH and Israel. For this redaction, the status of the prophet Jeremiah can only be defined in relation to this written Torah, as Jeremiah 36 clearly shows, and this gives to the 'scribal chronicle' of Jeremiah 37–43 a new perspective for interpretation.[93]

4. By Way of a Conclusion: The Scroll and the Prophet (Jeremiah 36)

Despite the repeated attempts to utilize Jeremiah 36 as a historical document,[94] it should first of all be read as a theological statement[95] seeking to interpret the reasons for the catastrophe and to define that status of the prophetic word in the face of a written support. This account of the burnt scroll has numerous parallels with the account of the scroll found in 2 Kings 22–23.[96] It matters little to us here to know

90. It is a matter of an independent collection that has probably been subjected to a specific redaction before being integrated into the 'great book' of Jeremiah; cf. Liwak, *Der Prophet und die Geschichte*.

91. Cf. also 3.25; 7.26; 17.23; 34.13. 16.11 and 23.27 belong to Dtr Jeremiah.

92. Cf. Römer, *Israels Väter*, pp. 467-70.

93. For the redactional framing of chs. 37–43 by ch. 36 and chs. 44–45, see in particular Seitz, *Theology in Conflict*, pp. 289-91: 'Chs. 36 and 45 are made to function together as framing units' (p. 289). Cf. also Stipp, 'Probleme des redaktionsgeschichtlichen Modells', p. 254, who speaks of a 'Dtr sound, but post-Dtr text-group'.

94. Cf. recently K. Seybold, *Der Prophet Jeremia: Leben und Werk* (Urban Taschenbücher, 416; Stuttgart: W. Kohlhammer, 1993), pp. 29-30.

95. Cf. especially Carroll, *Jeremiah* (OTL), pp. 662-68.

96. Cf. C.D. Isbell, '2 Kings 22–23 and Jer 36: A Stylistic Comparison', *JSOT* 8 (1978), pp. 33-45; Carroll, *Jeremiah* (OTL), pp. 663-64; G. Minette de Tillesse, 'Joiaqim, repoussoir du "Pieux" Josias: Parallélismes entre II Reg 22 et Jer 36', *ZAW* 105 (1993), pp. 352-76.

about the literary dependence of these two accounts;[97] what is important is the fact that the two texts should be read and understood in relation to each other.[98] The two accounts are linked together around the 'publication' of a written text, previously unknown to the people and the king (Josiah in 2 Kgs 22, Jehoiakim in Jer. 36). The scroll is transmitted to the king in 2 Kgs 22.8 by the secretary Shaphan; in Jer. 36.11-19, it is also the Shaphanite family that plays the intermediary role. The message of the book is characterized by the root רעה (2 Kgs 22.16; Jer. 36.31) and by the following announcement: 'Great is the anger (and the wrath) of YHWH' (2 Kgs 22.16; Jer. 36.7). The announcement of the divine wrath calls for a reform, a conversion to avoid the disaster (2 Kgs 23.1-25; Jer. 36.3, 7). The reaction of the two kings is described in an antithetical way: Josiah tears (קרע) his clothes, a visible sign of his repentance (2 Kgs 22.11, 19); Jehoiakim and his servants do not tear (לא קרעו) their garments (Jer. 36.24). Josiah listens (שמע) and this listening implies obedience (2 Kgs 22.11, 18, 19), while Jehoiakim listens without listening (Jer. 36.24). Josiah burns the objects for illegitimate worship (we find seven times the root שרף for five different objects: 23.4, 6, 11 [2×], 16, 20). Jehoiakim on the contrary burns the book (שרף in 36.25, 27, 28, 29, 32).[99] After these reactions, Josiah is rewarded with the announcement of a burial 'in peace' (22.20),[100] unlike Jehoiakim who is denied at the same time a successor and a burial (36.30).

It follows therefore that the two texts contrast two archetypes of behaviour in the face of the divine word and that they can be read as two accounts of reform and anti-reform. Josiah shows in an exemplary

97. According to Isbell, Jer. 36 depends on 2 Kgs 22–23; Minette de Tillesse defends the reverse relation.

98. In 2 Kgs 22–23, a second Dtr redaction in the Persian period can be detected, inserting the motif of the book that was found; cf. on this subject T. Römer, 'Transformation in Deuteronomistic and Biblical Historiography: On "Book-Finding" and other Literary Strategies', *ZAW* 109 (1997), pp. 1-11.

99. Contrary to what Isbell states ('2 Kings 22–23 and Jer. 36'), the number of attestations is not identical in the two texts.

100. It has often been observed that this announcement is in tension with the death of Josiah on a battlefield (2 Kgs 23.29). Verse 30 notes however that he was buried in his tomb, and in a (post-)exilic perspective בשלום has probably been understood in the sense that the king did not have to live through the cataclysm of 597–587; cf. E. Würthwein, *Die Bücher der Könige: 1 Kön. 17–2 Kön. 25* (ATD, 11.2; Göttingen: Vandenhoeck & Ruprecht, 1984), pp. 451-52.

way what should be done to avoid the catastrophe: Jeremiah 36 shows that this chance was not taken.[101] 2 Kings 22 and Jeremiah 36 can however also be read as reflections on the relation between the prophetic word and the book. In Jeremiah 36, Jeremiah is absent from the actual account (v. 5: there was an 'obstacle'); he appears only in the prologue and the epilogue. The central stake is the obedience in regard to the דברי הספר (36.22). The same phrase appears in 2 Kgs 22.16, where the oracle of the prophetess Huldah consists of a confirmation and an exegesis of the words of the book. The prophets are in retirement in relation to the book, which means that the two accounts insist on the priority of the book in relation to the prophetic word (Jer. 36 also ends with the production of another book). If 2 Kings 22 and Jeremiah 36 come from a Dtr milieu, they can therefore be considered as an attempt at a 'taking over' of the prophetic milieu by the Dtr scribes. This is in accordance moreover with the idea (whose origin is perhaps 'Dtr')[102] according to which the Persian period would imply the end of prophecy (cf. Dan. 9.24; *B. Bat.* 12b).[103]

For the book of Jeremiah, ch. 36 forms in some way the outcome of the Dtr transformation of the prophet. After having been transformed from a prophet for those not exiled into a Dtr preacher (Dtr Jeremiah), Jeremiah now becomes (Dtr^2 Jeremiah) the producer and the guarantor of the book that will give to post-exilic Judaism the means *par excellence* to find its identity. Jeremiah 36 is therefore also the account of a transfer of authority: the written word has replaced the prophet. 36.32 speaks of 'many other words' that were added to the new book edited by Jeremiah and Baruch,[104] which is probably an allusion to other Dtr and post-Dtr redactional interventions. But that is another story...

---

101. This is why Jer. 36 is dated to 605, the year of the battle of Carchemish whose outcome definitively made the Babylonians the dominant power in the ancient Near East. The oracles of Jer. 4–6 announcing the arrival of the enemy from the North are going to be realized; cf. Carroll, *Jeremiah* (OTL), p. 663.

102. Cf. R.F. Person, *Second Zechariah and the Deuteronomic School* (JSOTSup, 167; Sheffield: JSOT Press, 1993), pp. 193-99, who refers especially to Jer. 23.33-40 (Dtr).

103. 'From the day when the temple was destroyed, divine inspiration was taken away from the prophets and given to the wise' (*B. Bat.* 12b).

104. An edition that corresponds in our terminology to Dtr^2 Jeremiah.

Part VII
DEUTERONOMISTIC IDEOLOGY AND
THEOLOGY OF THE OLD TESTAMENT

DEUTERONOMISTIC IDEOLOGY AND
THEOLOGY OF THE OLD TESTAMENT

Martin Rose

Those responsible for the doctoral-level seminar (see Foreword) chose for the final session a title that issues a challenge that I take up only hesitantly, since the term 'ideology' is loaded with very diverse associations of ideas[1] which risk leading our considerations astray rather than setting them on the right track. In part at least my hesitation is explained by the fact that my thinking, marked by its German-speaking origin, perhaps associates with the term 'ideology' too many *negative* connotations. In the *German* language the somewhat pejorative usage is clearly dominant; the definition of 'ideology' in the 'Duden' reference dictionary is revealing:

> Designates an [artificial] theory, a [false] view of the world.[2]

A theory is artificial (*weltfremd*) if its interpretations are not the product of concrete experiences, but a sort of perverted knowledge of these experiences; ideology is an inauthentic theory that is arrived at in regard to the world (*unechte Weltanschauung*).

Another dictionary[3] specifies the origin of this negative understanding; it is under the influence of the writings of Marx that the pejorative sense is imposed on the German language:

> The common modern meaning of the term 'ideologie' is influenced by Marx, on a deprecative notion for interpretations of social reality behind which stand a certain interest.[4]

---

1.   Cf. below in this volume the presentation of A.D.H. Mayes with his detailed discussion of the understanding of the 'nature of ideology'.
2.   K.H. Ahlheim, *Fremdwörterbuch* (Der Grosse Duden, V; Mannheim: Dudenverlag, 2nd edn, 1966), p. 292: 'Bezeichnung für eine [weltfremde] Theorie, eine [unechte] Weltanschauung'.
3.   *Der Große Knaur*, IX (Munich: Lexikographisches Institut, 1982), p. 3722.
4.   'Von Marx beeinflußt ist ferner auch die heute gebräuchl. allg. Bed. des

This citation defines the usual meaning (*heute gebräuchlich*) as an interpretation of reality (for example, social reality: *gesellschaftliche Wirklichkeit*), behind which are hidden certain interests. The ideology conceals the real situation, with the goal as a general rule of exercising power or of maintaining it.

These are the meanings of the term 'ideology' that are conveyed by the German language. In French, on the other hand, the ideas of Feuerbach, of Marx and of Engels have not exerted as strong and direct an influence on the understanding of the word 'ideology'. The definition of the *Petit Robert* contains no evidence to imply that a pejorative understanding would be dominant:

> An assemblage of ideas, beliefs and doctrines specific to an epoch, to a society or a class.[5]

It is on the basis of this last definition that I will organize the 'concluding theological remarks' that those responsible for this doctoral-level seminar asked me to make. However, before the main part of my paper (sections 2-4), I shall summarize some of the indispensable exegetical presuppositions for a correct understanding of my theological evaluation.

1. *The Starting Point: A Literary Work*

It seems to me important to emphasize that we have no way to approach the question of Dtr ideology other than on the basis of a *literary* work. We do not have any other information at our disposal on this milieu that we call 'Dtr'; for example, neither on its authors, nor on their life, their formation and their eventual professional activity. Notes about this Dtr movement and its authors from *other* contemporaries would be very

Begriffs I. als abschätzige Bez. für Interpretationen der gesellschaftl. Wirklichkeit, hinter denen bestimmte Interessen stehen.'

5.   *Le Petit Robert*. I. *Dictionnaire alphabétique et analogique* (Paris: Dictionnaire Le Robert, 1984), p. 957 (repeated in the 1993 edition). Cf., for example, G. Dumézil's definition: '*Ideology*, that is to say an idea and an appreciation of the great forces that sustain the world and society, and their connections. Often this ideology is only implicit and must be drawn out by an analysis of what is plainly said about the gods and especially their activities, about the theology and especially about the mythology, that leads to a certain restoration of the primacy of this kind of document' (*Rituels indo-européens à Rome* [Paris: C. Klincksieck, 1954], p. 7).

interesting for us. But unfortunately, we have just one source of information: a literary work. Now this is far from constituting a satisfactory basis for a solid evaluation; but we have no other alternative: we must start from what remain for us as documents of the period.

If I speak of a 'literary work', I am thinking especially of Dtr Historiography (DH). But we can also, carefully, expand the scope of our observations, since it has been proved that a redaction in Dtr style is evident in other biblical writing, especially in the book of Jeremiah. However, let us confine ourselves initially to the work of the DH. It is there that we must look for the fundamental criteria for analysis; other texts in Dtr style can be used only in the second phase of the argumentation.

If the title of my first section includes the phrase 'literary work' to characterize the Dtr texts, it must be remembered that this is not an indisputable (written) *fact*, but a *theory*. Among the biblical books, we do not find a writing entitled (for example) 'Deuteronomistic History'; this phrase is no older than the innovative *theory* worked out and proposed by M. Noth.[6] In recalling the name of Noth, I want to emphasize that I am quite aware of the *presuppositions* of the considerations that follow: I presuppose a *thesis*. The work of DH remains for me a hypothesis, which has however met with a fairly wide consensus in Old Testament research. It is therefore a strongly probable theory.[7]

According to Noth's thesis of, DH comprises Deuteronomy, Joshua, Judges, 1 and 2 Samuel and 1 and 2 Kings. I am expressly repeating this listing out of concern for clarity: I do not agree with the compromise solution that consists of making DH begin with the book of Joshua out of respect for the Jewish tradition and its distinction between the 'Torah' and the 'prophetic books' (*nebi'îm*).[8] Noth's thesis actually

6.   M. Noth, *Überlieferungsgeschichtliche Studien: Die sammelnden und bearbeitenden Geschichtswerke im Alten Testament* (Darmstadt: Wissenschaftliche Buchgesellschaft, 3rd edn, 1967 [1943]); ET: *The Deuteronomistic History* (JSOTSup, 15; Sheffield: Sheffield Academic Press, 1981). For details on this thesis, cf. above, the introductory account of A. de Pury and T. Römer.

7.   Cf. for the opposite view, the recent study of Hartmut N. Rösel, *Von Josua bis Jojachin: Untersuchungen zu den deuteronomistischen Geschichtsbüchern des Alten Testaments* (VTSup, 75; Leiden: E.J. Brill, 1999).

8.   This tendency to compromise also appears (unfortunately) in the *Traduction Oecuménique de la Bible* (*TOB*) (édition intégrale; Paris: Éditions du Cerf, Société Biblique Française, 1988). On the one hand, we find in it many comments that bear

destroys the unity of the Pentateuch (and the Torah) by excising Deuteronomy, which he makes the programmatic introduction of a great historiography. Indeed Joshua does not have the characteristics of the first
part of a literary work: from a literary and exegetical point of view, the
first verses of this book do not lend themselves to functioning as an
opening of a literary work;[9] the beginning of Deuteronomy, on the other
hand, possesses all the elements necessary for such a function.[10]

out the acceptance of the idea of a Dtr Historiography; but for the overall structure
of the Old Testament, the editors are anxious to preserve the tripartite division:
'The Pentateuch', 'The Prophetic Books' and 'The Other Writings' (to this is added
a fourth, supplementary, part, 'The Deuterocanonical Books'). Among the 'Prophetic Books', the *TOB*, faithful to the Jewish tradition, distinguishes between the
'Former Prophets' and the 'Latter Prophets', and the introduction to the Prophetic
Books is found before Joshua (pp. 417-21). It is perfectly in keeping with the
Jewish tradition to consider Joshua, Judges, 1 and 2 Samuel and 1 and 2 Kings as
prophetic books, while the author of the introduction to the *TOB* wants to attribute
this collection to the Dtr historian (p. 420): 'This is also the standpoint of the
historian to whom we owe the collection of Joshua to Kings and who is often
referred to as a "Deuteronomistic Historian" '. A little later, on the same page, the
author of the introduction speaks of the 'historiographical work of synthesis as is
found in the collection of the *Former Prophets*', and on p. 421, he clearly expresses
himself on the *beginning* and the *end* that he claims for this historiographical work
as he understands it: 'Beginning with the promise of God to Joshua to give him the
land (Josh. 1.1-9) and ending with the mention of the elevation of Jehoiachin, the
work often so disparate is presented under the sign of unity'. It seems to me that
this formulation clearly indicates that its author is thinking of a work that forms a
literary unity beginning in Josh. 1.1-9 and ending with the last verses of the books
of Kings ('the mention of the elevation of Jehoiachin'). This delimitation does not
correspond to what follows from the thesis of Noth, but is dictated by a desire for
compromise that wants to honour at the same time both the Jewish tradition *and* a
fundamental result of present exegetical research. It is a compromise that probably
convinces nobody, neither the Jews, nor the exegetes from the Christian tradition.

9.   In the first three verses of Joshua, Moses' name is mentioned four times.
The beginning of this book clearly refers, therefore, to the accounts of the death of
Moses, to his relationship with Joshua, the 'auxiliary of Moses', and also to the
promise given to Moses, presupposed as known to the readers of Joshua. That
naturally obliges us to understand Joshua not as the beginning of an independent
work, but as the development of the account begun in Deuteronomy.

10.   Deuteronomy begins with: אֵלֶּה הַדְּבָרִים אֲשֶׁר דִּבֶּר מֹשֶׁה אֶל־כָּל־יִשְׂרָאֵל בְּעֵבֶר
הַיַּרְדֵּן ('These are the words that Moses spoke to all Israel, beyond the Jordan...').
This verse has the style quite usual in a title; cf. Exod. 35.1: אֵלֶּה הַדְּבָרִים אֲשֶׁר־
צִוָּה יהוה... ('These are the words that YHWH has commanded...') and also the beginning of Jeremiah: ...דִּבְרֵי יִרְמְיָהוּ בֶן־חִלְקִיָּהוּ...אֲשֶׁר הָיָה ('The words of Jeremiah,

If we want to define the intention of a literary work (or its 'ideology'), we must especially concentrate on the texts that occupy a key position in the whole work. It is probable that the author would have grasped the opportunity to use a key text to highlight his message or his theology. The introduction and the conclusion of a literary work provide just such privileged occasions. If the two, the beginning and the end, agree in coming up with a comparable set of themes, we can speak of a real 'framework'.

1.1. *The Framework: The Question of the Land*

The 'framing' criterion can be applied exactly to the literary work that makes up DH: 'the question of the land' is present in its opening just as in its final verses. We find at the *beginning* of the work the order from God to take possession of the land (Deut. 1.8: 'I have set the land before you; go in and take possession of this land!'), and at the *end*, the theme of the loss of this land dominates, in so far as DH coming to an end at the Babylonian exile.

On many occasions during this doctoral-level seminar, we have mentioned and discussed the problems of the *end* of this literary work. At first sight, 2 Kgs 25.27-30 is well suited to mark the end of this historiography. But what could the *function* of these verses be in the whole Dtr work? With what *objective* could the Dtr author have mentioned, at the very end of his work, this event of the 'return to favour of Jehoiachin'? What is the *interpretation* therefore that must be given to these verses? The research above proposes contradictory and difficult interpretations.[11]

According to Noth, the whole DH has just one function: to explain the fall of Jerusalem and the destruction of the temple. What God had already announced to Moses is finally realized: the disobedience of the people has led to the final disaster.

son of Hilkiah, one of the priests who were in Anatoth...') as well as that of Amos: ... הָיָה אֲשֶׁר ... עָמוֹס דִּבְרֵי ('The words of Amos who...'). Without wanting to present an exhaustive discussion of this question, it seems evident to me that there is no problem in seeing in Deut. 1.1 the beginning of an independent work (cf. M. Rose, *5. Mose.* I. *5. Mose 12–25—Einführung und Gesetze.* II. *5.Mose 1–11 und 26–34—Rahmenstücke zum Gesetzeskorpus* (ZBK.AT, 5.1, 5.2; Zürich: Theologischer Verlag, 1994).

11. Cf. also the presentation of the history of research in the article of H. Weippert, 'Das deuteronomistische Geschichtswerk: Sein Ziel und Ende in der neueren Forschung', *ThR* 50 (1985), pp. 213-49.

In a categorical manner, Noth[12] affirms that, for the Dtr, the notice of the amelioration of the personal fortunes of King Jehoiachin did not have as its function to indicate the dawn of a new future. According to him, that quite marginal event does not allow for an interpretation of such great significance. This notice is not introduced therefore in the perspective of a new future that is eventually approaching, but solely as the latest historical information. Noth emphasizes that the Dtr author always shows scrupulous respect (*Gewissenschaftigkeit*) and accuracy in his use of documents; this same attitude also affects the last event in connection with the history of the Judaean monarchy: it is mentioned as a 'simple fact'.

Noth's position is very clear: the theological function of DH is to present the end of the kingdoms of Israel and of Judah as a judgment of God on the disobedient people. The final catastrophe is not due to chance, but is the logical consequence of the behaviour of the people of Israel and of their kings. According to Noth, everything is centred on this theme of the *end*, without there being the least perspective on the future: the Dtr author considered the national catastrophe as something definitive and irrevocable, and he expressed no hope, not even the most modest, for the future. The note on the change in Jehoiachin's situation should not be read therefore as a positive sign.

This rejection of any positive perspective has led to protests by many exegetes. We may mention, for example, G. von Rad who, in 1947, four years after the publication of Noth's study, proposed another interpretation of this final notice of DH;[13] he also presented his divergent position in his *Theology of the Old Testament* in 1956. Von Rad does not question that the function of DH consists of explaining the end of the kingdom of Judah as a judgment of God on the people: 'His work is a great "doxology of judgment" transferred from the cultic to the literary sphere...he also set himself the task of giving a detailed theological explanation of how the saving history ended in the catastrophes of 722 and 587'.[14] Up to here, von Rad does not differ from Noth. But he adds a second point:

> But the Deuteronomist saw yet another word at work in history, namely, the promise of salvation in the Nathan prophecy, and it, as well as the threat of judgmemt, was effectual as it ran through the course of history. Had it too creatively reached its goal in a fulfilment? The Deuteronomist's history leaves this question open. Yet, closing as it does with the

---

12. *Überlieferungsgeschichtliche Studien*, p. 108.

13. G. von Rad, 'Die deuteronomistische Geschichtstheologie in den Königsbüchern', in *Deuteronomium-Studien*, B (FRLANT, 58; Göttingen: Vandenhoeck & Ruprecht, 1947), pp. 52-64 (repr. in *Gesammelte Studien zum alten Testament*, I [TBü, 8; Munich: Chr. Kaiser Verlag, 1958], pp. 189-204; ET: 'The Deuteronomic Theology of History in I and II Kings', in *The Problem of the Hexateuch and Other Essays* [Edinburgh: Oliver & Boyd; New York: McGraw–Hill, 1966], pp. 205-21).

14. G. von Rad, *Theology of the Old Testament*, I (New York: Harper & Row, 1962), p. 343.

note about the favour shown to Jehoiachin (2 Kgs 25.27-30), it points to a possibility with which YHWH can resume the work of salvation.[15]

Von Rad therefore gives the text of 2 Samuel 7 a constitutive function in the history of salvation, and he interprets the final notice on Jehoiachin by linking it with this fundamental oracle of Nathan, which is concerned with the whole Davidic dynasty. According to von Rad, the whole DH should be read from the point of view of the connection between the word of God and its fulfilment: '[the author's] concern was rather with the problem of how the word of YHWH functioned in history. This word operates in two ways: as law it acts destructively; and as gospel, it works as salvation.'[16] Thus, von Rad gives the end of the historiography a totally different interpretation: he recognizes in it a sign of *hope* that the Dtr author wanted to put at the end of his work;[17] the change in condition should be read as a modest but tangible sign that YHWH, God of Israel, does not abandon the people. To go back to the New Testament term used by von Rad, I could say: this final note should be read as a 'gospel' text.

Who is right: Noth or von Rad? This clear-cut opposition between two options gave rise, in the continuation of exegetical research, to a lively discussion among exegetes. Noth's opinion on the question of the interpretation of the end of the DH has not found many supporters. Most exegetes tend to see there a *positive* sign consciously put by the Dtr author at the end of his work. The *Traduction Oecuménique de la Bible* is also of this opinion: 'The favour granted to the king of Judah in exile is a note of hope for a better future'.[18]

Refuting Noth's interpretation does not mean, however, that it is necessary to adhere to that of von Rad. Other solutions can be thought up. There is, for example, the view of H.W. Wolff who was satisfied neither with Noth's suggestion, nor with the quasi-'evangelic' interpretation of von Rad. The title of his article, 'Das Kerygma des deuteronomistischen Geschichtswerks', indicates that Wolff set himself the task of defining the central message of this historiography, its 'kerygma'.[19] In the

15. Von Rad, *Theology of the Old Testament*, I, p. 343.

16. Von Rad, *Theology of the Old Testament*, I, pp. 343-44 (cf. also below, §§3.1 and 3.2).

17. Cf. also E. Zenger ('Die deuteronomistische Interpretation der Rehabilitierung Jojachins', *BZ* 12 [1968], pp. 16-30), who expresses himself strongly in this sense (p. 30): '…blickt hoffnungsvoll auf die sich anschickende Erfüllung der dem David gegebenen Verheissung'.

18. *TOB*, p. 747 n. x; cf. also p. 636: 'the books of Kings end on a note of hope…'

19. H.W. Wolff, 'Das Kerygma des deuteronomistischen Geschichtswerks', *ZAW* 73 (1961), pp. 171-86 (repr. in *Gesammelte Studien zum Alten Testament* [TBü, 22; Munich: Chr. Kaiser Verlag, 2nd edn, 1973 (1964), pp. 308-24]; ET: 'The Kerygma of the Deuteronomic Historical Work', in W. Brueggemann and H.W. Wolff [eds.], *The Vitality of Old Testament Traditions* [Atlanta: John Knox Press, 3rd edn 1978 [1975], pp. 83-100).

notice of the liberation of Johoiachin, Wolff does not read, contrary to von Rad, an allusive reference to the oracle of Nathan, because, normally, the Dtr author likes to emphasize the relation between a prophecy and its fulfilment, whereas the text of 2 Kgs 25.27-30 contains no reference at all to the Nathan oracle (2 Sam. 7). An invitation to hope cannot be the 'kerygma' intended by this theological work. But Wolff emphasizes that a message with a more important theological weight must be awaited, and he finds it in the call to conversion, with a return to fidelity towards God. He can indeed show that all the great central texts of the Dtr author always return to the verb שׁוּב ('to return') and to the theme of the repentance necessary if Israel is to recover its relationship with God. The observations made by Wolff seem to me very interesting, but I ask myself whether his arguments are really sufficient.

These three coryphaei of German exegesis (Noth, von Rad and Wolff) have only touched on criteria of content in determining the central message of this historiography. However, must not things be nuanced, if a *literary* analysis made with the help of *literary*, linguistic and formal criteria tends to undermine the hypothesis of the *unity* of this work and emphasizes instead its literary heterogeneity?[20] Is it not necessary to think of several 'kerygmata', if DH is composed of *several* literary levels? The *theological* assertions should be controlled by rigorous exegetical work, and the observations about the *content* by *formal* criteria such as language, style, stereotypical formulas, and so on.

R.D. Nelson, a student of F.M. Cross and therefore inclined to deny the literary unity of the DH, has undertaken stylistic analyses.[21] Like his teacher, he assumes *two* Dtr layers, that of an author from the period of Josiah and that of a redactor from the time of the Babylonian exile. With regard to the *end* of these two versions, the first would consist of the praise of King Josiah (2 Kgs 23.25), while the redaction from the exilic period would have continued the history up to the account about

---

20. W. Dietrich (cf. his contribution above in this volume), representing the 'Göttingen school', proposes distinguishing three literary levels in the DH: DtrH, DtrP and DtrN. For my part, I am content with recognizing there *two* literary layers, that of the *author* of DH and that of a *redactor* who is also responsible for the Yahwist Historiography (M. Rose, *Deuteronomist und Jahwist: Untersuchungen zu den Berührungspunkten beider Literaturwerke* [ATANT, 67; Zürich: Theologischer Verlag, 1981]; 'La croissance du corpus historiographique de la Bible—une proposition', *RTP* 118 [1986], pp. 217-36; cf. also *5. Mose.* Whatever the details, I join those who no longer agree with the idea of unity of authorship defended by Noth.

21. Cf. his doctoral thesis of 1973, published in 1981 under the title *The Double Redaction of the Deuteronomistic History* (JSOTSup, 18; Sheffield: JSOT Press, 1981).

the liberation of Jehoiachin. Nelson has worked on the Dtr phrases that sum up the reign of each Israelite and Judaean king, and he has concluded that the texts concerning the last kings are briefer than those that concern the predecessors of Josiah. Nelson observes an analogous conciseness in the use of sources taken up by this exilic redactor, with the text of 2 Kgs 25.22-26 being just a brief summary drawn from Jeremiah (Jer. 40.7–41.8).

The *two* versions of the end of the Historiography also establish the tone that Nelson recognizes in the two forms of the work. The first version, dating from the period of Josiah[22] and ending with the praise of this king, is considered a piece of propaganda from his court. The exilic redactor on the other hand would have made it a 'doxology of judgment' as Noth had proposed. The first layer is marked by a strong tendency toward idealization, while the second knows only resignation and expects neither a return to the country, nor a continuation of the Davidic dynasty. The *end* of the work decides therefore its entire interpretation.

I affirm that I have some doubts about the idea of a 'piece of propaganda' from the period of Josiah. Likewise, the *literary* arguments adduced by Nelson are not sufficient to separate as neatly as he would wish the text that goes up to the period of Josiah from the chapters that follow.[23]

I am convinced that the *end* of the work decides its whole interpretation, and it seems to me necessary to outline the view that I have reached on the final part of the DH. I am of the opinion that on this subject exegetical research has not sufficiently taken into account the fact that the last chapter of the books of Kings has parallels in Jeremiah (Jer. 39–41 and 52) with, most often, minimal differences.[24]

22. Cf. also the redaction 'RII/Dtr1' of E. Eynikel, *The Reform of King Josiah and the Composition of the Deuteronomistic History* (Oudtestamentische Studiën, 33; Leiden: E.J. Brill, 1996).

23. For example, 2 Kgs 24.2-4 should be read as the fulfilment of the prophetic announcement of 2 Kgs 21.10-15; likewise, 24.13-14 stands in line with 20.12-19. These two correlations form part of a much larger system ('prophecy and fulfilment') which does not respect the frontier between the two versions laid out by Cross and Nelson.

24. The textual situation is more complicated due to the fact that the text of LXX Jeremiah differs considerably from the Hebrew text (Y. Goldman, *Prophétie et royauté au retour de l'exil: Les origines littéraires de la forme massorétique de Jérémie* [OBO, 118; Freiburg: Universitätsverlag; Göttingen: Vandenhoeck & Ruprecht, 1992]). The book of Jeremiah is the result of a very complicated transmission process that took place differently in the Greek tradition than in the Hebrew tradition, or to formulate it in geographical terms, differently in the Jewish diaspora in Egypt than among the Palestinian Jews. In the context of my contribution, the problem of the Greek version of Jeremiah can only be mentioned without going into its details.

1. Jeremiah 52 is an adjunction that, originally, did not form part of the book of Jeremiah. The last words *before* this adjunction indicate the end of the book (51.64): עַד־הֵנָּה דִּבְרֵי יִרְמְיָהוּ ('up to here the words of Jeremiah'). This is in conformity with the literary tradition of the ancient Near East to indicate the end of a book by repeating the title, here: דִּבְרֵי יִרְמְיָהוּ ('the words of Jeremiah'). On the literary and formal level, this evidence about an adjunction is obvious.

This comment however does not authorize the neglect of this text. It can be important from two points of view. First, with regard to the *material*, it can contain more precise information than the other chapters, even if its own *textual* and *literary* form is later. That means that it is necessary to distinguish between the age of the *material* and that of its present *textual* form. Verses 28-30, for example, without a precise analogy in the other texts, can contain especially valuable information. Secondly, the text of Jeremiah 52 can also be important from the point of view of questions about the *transmission* of the text, since a comparison of the grammatical and linguistic variants of the two texts indicates that the text of Jeremiah 52 is less corrupt and tampered with than that of 2 Kings 25.[25]

In short, from the *textual* point of view, ch. 52 of Jeremiah, as a whole, turns out to be an addition, but with regard to *details*, it can be quite an important witness.

2. With regard to the connection between the other two texts (Jer. 39–41 and 2 Kgs 25), we can imagine two possibilities: that 2 Kings 25 influenced the redaction of Jeremiah 39–41, or conversely that the text of 2 Kings 25 is an *extract* from the more detailed account of Jeremiah. The two opinions may be read in the works of exegetes.[26] My research on this subject has led me to think that the text of Jeremiah 39–41 is older than that of 2 Kings 25. I have compared all the parallels, and it seems to me difficult to understand the longer texts of Jeremiah as a secondary expansion;[27] the text of 2 Kings 25 is instead a sort of *résumé*.[28]

25. With regard to the 10 textual differences between the two versions, in 9 cases the text of Jer. 52 seems preferable to that of 2 Kgs 25.

26. The commentator in the *TOB* (p. 1016 n. h), for example, is of the opinion that the definitive redaction of Jer. 39 was influenced by the other two texts; for the opposite opinion, we may mention Nelson, who defends the hypothesis that the text of 2 Kgs 25.22-26 is just a brief summary drawn from Jer. 40.7–41.8; *The Double Redaction*, p. 86: 'an abridgement'.

27. In this context, just one example should suffice, that of the description of the assault on Jerusalem (Jer. 39.2b-4 compared to 2 Kgs 25.4). While the text of Jeremiah is clear and describes a logical progression, the parallel sentence of the book of Kings does not even have a verb; the translations must add one ('they made their escape') to make the text understandable. In the text of the book of Kings, King Zedekiah is not expressly mentioned among the runaways, even if the following verses especially recount his fate and that of his sons. The names of the Babylonian military commanders in Jeremiah do not give the impression either of being fanciful or a secondary addition; the redactor of 1 and 2 Kings on the other hand replaces them with the general remark 'and the Chaldeans [had] surrounded the city'.

28. Two examples: Jer. 41.1-3 is summarized in just one verse (2 Kgs 25.25),

In short, the textual elements of chs. 39–41 of Jeremiah seem to be older than the parallel texts of the other chapters (this *general* orientation does not however exclude some exceptions that would indicate a different relationship).

3. If 2 Kings 25 is essentially written up on the textual base of Jeremiah 39–41, it is not out of the question that 2 Kings would have ended *before* this ch. 25 (whose content seems to me to be taken over from Jeremiah), which would imply that the DH comes to an end with 2 Kgs 24.20. The Dtr work would therefore have ended with a theological note: 'And this happened because of the anger of YHWH against Jerusalem and against Judah with the result that he expelled them far from his sight'. A similar remark is found at the end of the account of the fall of the northern kingdom, Israel, in 2 Kgs 17.22-23: 'The people of Israel imitated all the sins that Jeroboam committed; they did not depart from them until YHWH removed Israel far from his sight as he had foretold through all his servants the prophets'. The two texts would include therefore the formula according to which YHWH rejected Israel and Judah 'far from his sight' (מֵעַל פָּנָיו); the national catastrophe is interpreted as a manifestation of God as Judge who does not tolerate the sin of his people. It is the theological interpretation that inspires the whole Dtr work and that, as a consequence, seems to me appropriate to appear in the final note of the work.

Verse 23 of ch. 17 continues the subject of the fate of the kingdom of the north, Israel: 'So Israel was exiled far from their own land to Assyria until this day'; the *TOB* rightly adds the explanation: 'When the people of God did not *move away* from the sin of idolatry, God *moved* them *away* from his presence by the exile: the Promised Land is only given to Israel if the latter remains faithful to the Lord. This theme is constantly met in Deuteronomy.'[29] The two key terms of 'Promised Land' and 'exile' form the frame for DH that begins immediately before the conquest of the country and ends with the mention of the deportation (גלה מֵעַל אַדְמָתוֹ; 'deporting far from its land'). Parallel to this note that, in 2 Kings 17, concerned the kingdom of the north, we can expect a comparable remark for the kingdom of the south, Judah. It is however not found yet in 24.20, but with an identical wording to that of ch. 17, in 25.21: 'It is thus that Judah was deported far from its land'; גלה מֵעַל אַדְמָתוֹ. I think therefore that we possess there (in 25.21) the second element of the final note of the DH.[30] With regard to the kingdom of the *north*, Israel, the two elements ('far from the sight of YHWH' and 'far from the land') are found together in just one verse (17.23), while concerning the kingdom of the *south*, Judah, they are separated from each other. But this separation is due to a redactional and secondary interpolation whose title is found in 24.20b: 'Zedekiah revolted against the king of Babylon'. The later redactor wanted therefore to give more details on the end of

and Jer. 41.16-18 as well (2 Kgs 25.26).

29. *TOB*, p. 727 n. q.

30. Cf. also W. Dietrich, *Prophetie und Geschichte: Eine redaktionsgeschichtliche Untersuchung zum deuteronomistischen Geschichtswerk* (FRLANT, 108; Göttingen: Vandenhoeck & Ruprecht, p. 142): '...läßt sich kein besserer Schlusssatz für sein Buch denken als 2.Kön 25,21b'.

Judah and composed this supplementary part by drawing from Jeremiah. He inserted this supplementary account *before* the old mention of the deportation ('deported far from its land'), which is completely logical, since the revolt of Zedekiah precedes the deportation. However, the redactor has thus destroyed the connection between the two elements of the final notice: he has left the first ('far from the face of YHWH') *before* the account of the revolt of Zedekiah (in 24.20), and thus, this primitively *final* element now has an *introductive* function: it introduces the final phase of the history of Judah.

If I attempt an evaluation of my comparative research on the three texts, I retain two points that concern the literary and redactional aspects.

a) Originally, there were *two* different versions of the end of Judah and of Jerusalem, that which we now find in Jeremiah, and that of the primitive form of DH. In Jeremiah, the accounts are quite detailed; many recount the relations of the prophet Jeremiah with the king Zedekiah; they are equally detailed about the history *after* the fall of Jerusalem, concerning the rule of the administrator Gedaliah, his assassination and the flight of another part of the population to Egypt. These people took the prophet Jeremiah along with them, against his will, and he still carried on his prophetic activity in Egypt. Despite the importance of the years of Zedekiah in the accounts of Jeremiah, it must be supposed that the primitive end of the DH was content to mention the strict minimum; they were no longer so interested in this last king of Judah, nor in a detailed description of the destruction of Jerusalem and of the temple (in 587). The main emphasis was put on the deportation; the first and probably the most important deportation had already taken place under King Jehoiachin.[31] It is therefore necessary to take account of *two* circles which had transmitted the narratives relating to the land of Judah/Jerusalem; one of which is easy to define: it should be sought among the disciples of Jeremiah. They described how their teacher was involved in political affairs (the 'biography' of Jeremiah). At the end of his life, Jeremiah was in *Egypt* and, very probably, a number of his disciples with him. It is there, in Egypt, that we must situate this circle that recounted the end of Judah from Jeremiah's perspective: the Jerusalem catastrophe is the fulfilment of his prophecies. The other circle, which created the DH, is not interested in the prophet Jeremiah, but in the question of the possession of the country and in that of its loss. For

31. Cf. below, Section 2.1.

the people in this circle, the *deportation* is, from a theological point of view, the most significant event.

b) While the primitive version of the DH ends with the theological note about the 'anger of YHWH' and the deportation 'far from the Promised Land', its second (redactional) version is marked by a tendency towards literary harmonization, the most important political information from the accounts of Jeremiah being taken up again in order to be integrated redactionally in the Dtr work. The redactor of this second layer manifests therefore a particularly *literary* concern, that is to say, a tendency towards harmonization between the pieces of information provided in the two literary works, Jeremiah and the DH in its primitive version.

To sum up, I locate the *end* of the DH neither with the mention of Josiah (against Cross and his disciples), nor with the note on the liberation of Jehoiachin (against Noth and many other exegetes), but in the final *theological* remark of 24.20a and 25.21b:

> And this happened because of the anger of YHWH against Jerusalem and against Judah so that he rejected them far from his sight. Thus Judah was deported far from its land.

מֵעַל אַדְמָתוֹ are for me the very last words of the Dtr work. At the beginning of the work (in Deuteronomy), Israel is presented as being outside its land ('beyond Jordan in the Wilderness'), and the same thing also applies now to Israel at the end of this historiography: it is in exile in a foreign land. It seems to me absolutely justified to speak of a 'frame' that casts a strong light on a preoccupation of the author and holds together the whole work. It is evident that the theme of this frame, 'the question of the land', provides important elements in the elaboration of the Dtr ideology (we will return to this); but in this first and introductory section, we are discussing for the moment only the *literary* aspects. I am therefore convinced that the criterion of *framing* is of the utmost importance in discerning the literary cohesion of this work of DH, and for its interpretation.

1.2. *Principal Themes: History, Prophetism, Law*

A second important aspect for the understanding of DH as a literary work is the recurrence of certain main themes: the interest in *history*, the central role filled by the *prophets*, and the importance of the *law*. These three key terms also recall the three redactional layers postulated by the 'Göttingen school' (DtrH, DtrP, and DtrN).[32] The researchers of that 'school' have recognized something important by stressing these three themes; but I do not see the necessity of using them for *literary* aims in developing different redactional layers in the DH. The *three* terms are constituent *together* of the literary conception of the work.

We can go further: this criterion of the main themes is not only significant on the purely quantitative level, it is also significant in terms of the (qualitative) level of their position in the work: the importance that the author wants to give to these themes is discernible in their repeated variation in the great programmatic discourses that punctuate DH. It is therefore not only the *framing* that guarantees the literary cohesion of the work, it is the *great discourses* too. Once again, we can therefore say that the criterion of *content* and that of *form* mutually support one another, since the three main themes (from the perspective of *content*) are especially present in the great discourses (from the perspective of *form*). A characteristic of the *content* is united with a characteristic of the *literary form*.

We will return later to these three themes, when we take up their function in the context of Dtr *ideology*.

1.3. *Stylistic Features*
As a literary work, DH is also marked by certain stylistic features. Its stereotyped vocabulary must be mentioned as well as the repetition of certain turns of phrase and formulas.[33] Likewise on the level of syntax, the Dtr style shows some typical preferences, for example, rhetorical expansions very often using constructions with infinitives.[34] These two stylistic features are frequently attested throughout DH which supports the hypothesis of a literary work going from Deuteronomy to 2 Kings.

1.4. *Heterogeneities*
If we speak of the DH as a literary work, we cannot pass over in silence the aspect of heterogeneity that marks it. This historiography includes

---

32. Cf. above, n. 20.

33. Cf. the work of M. Weinfeld (*Deuteronomy and the Deuteronomic School* [Oxford: Clarendon Press, 1972]) who, in an extraordinarily useful appendix, lists all the phrases typical of the language of these Dtr authors.

34. Cf. N. Lohfink, 'Gab es eine deuteronomistische Bewegung?', in W. Gross (ed.), *Jeremia und die 'deuteronomistische Bewegung'* (BBB, 98; Weinheim: Beltz Athenäum, 1995), p. 323 (with n. 42).

sections that demonstrate an interest in very different themes, written in a very different style from which the typically Dtr expressions are absent. A critical reader will find numerous incoherences in the description, tensions between several narrative elements and repetitions of certain themes. There are two main reasons for this phenomenon of thematic, literary and stylistic heterogeneity:

a) The author has made use of numerous sources[35] which are very faithfully reproduced, even if they are not always entirely in accordance with his own conceptions of the history of Israel. This use of sources is beyond doubt, since the consultation and use of such documents is expressly mentioned in Kings. Therefore the first reason for the heterogeneity of the work is found in the tension between *tradition* and *interpretation*, more precisely between the traditon reproduced and cited on the one hand, and the interpretation added by the Dtr author on the other.

b) This tension between the tradition and Dtr's own interpretation does not, however, explain *all* the literary problems of the work. Some passages, using the *same* Dtr vocabulary, take up quite different themes. What is more, a careful and very discriminating study of the stereotyped expressions can show that it does not suffice to speak globally of a 'Dtr style', but that certain nuances are imperative. The second reason for the heterogeneity of the work is therefore connected with the redactional reshaping that this work has undergone; it is a matter of the tension betwen the concept of the Dtr author ('interpretation') and the concepts of a futher redaction. This redaction remains quite close to the primitive intention, so that exegetes speak of a 'Dtr school', but the differences are too great to postulate just one Dtr author, as Noth proposed.

If we assume several literary layers in DH, it also becomes necessary to qualify each time the definition of Dtr ideology. But the author and the redactor being quite close in time and in theological thinking, I will limit myself in the following (Sections 2-4) to just one evaluation process, while adding however occasional remarks on the modifications occurring in the redactional process.

---

35. Cf. above, J. Briend, 'The Sources of the Deuteronomistic History', pp. 360-87.

2. *'Epoch—Society—Class'*[36]

2.1. *The Epoch*

The fundamental event that marks the whole period is that of the destruction of Jerusalem in 587 BCE. DH ends with the mention of that event; it does not describe its details,[37] but limits itself to giving its theological interpretation and to recalling the consequence considered to be the most important: the loss of the national land and the deportation of the population:

> And that happened because of the anger of YHWH against Jerusalem and against Judah so that he rejected them far from his sight. It is for this reason that Judah was deported far from its land (24.20a and 25.21b).

If the end of the work is seen in this specific formulation, the notice on the favour shown to Jehoiachin (2 Kgs 25.27-30) must be considered a later *redactional* addition. There is no need to date DH according to this brief redactional note mentioning an event of the year 561, but according to the fundamental event that is at the origin of the work and its ideology, the ruin of Jerusalem and the deportation. We must start therefore from the year 587.

The Dtr work should not, however, be dated exactly to this year as if the author had immediately after the destruction of Jerusalem set out to compose his history; we can imagine therefore one of the following years. Personally, I do not, however, rule out the possibility that the author might have begun to prepare his work even *before* that key date of 587.

I consider this author of DH as belonging to the *first* deportation in 598, together with the young King Jehoiachin.[38] From a historical point

---

36. I repeat that the main part of my paper (Sections 2-4) will be structured according to the definition that the *Petit Robert* gives of 'ideology'. I shall begin with the *last* terms of that definition and then go back to the first ones.

37. Cf. above, §1.1.

38. At first sight, my research leads to a result quite close to that of C.R. Seitz (*Theology in Conflict: Reactions to the Exile in the Book of Jeremiah* [BZAW, 176; Berlin and New York: W. de Gruyter, 1989]). Therefore the claimed 'originality' of my result (cf. thesis 7, below at the end of my contribution) may be contested. I must point out however that on the literary and redactional level, Seitz develops a quite different concept according to which the first edition of the DH would have ended with 2 Kgs 24 (p. 200: 'Ch. 24 formed the original conclusion of the primary edition of Kings') and should be situated immediately after the first deportation

of view, it is probable that this first deportation would have been the most important. According to Jer. 52.28-30,[39] the number of deportees are divided up as follows:

> 3023 persons for the first deportation, in 598;
> 832 persons for the second deportation, in 587;
> 745 persons for a third deportation, in 582 or 581.

The quantitative difference between the first deportation and the other two is very marked. It was also the most important from the social point of view, since, in this first one, all the elite of Jerusalem were affected (the prophet Ezekiel was part of that first wave). The deportees did not really recognize Zedekiah as a legitimate king.[40] It is in this milieu, among the elite of the nation, that I look for the circle of DH. Certainly, as historians, they have not suppressed the mention of the last king, Zedekiah, but for them, the main part of the divine judgment took place already *before* his accession to the throne, i.e. with the events of the deportation of Jehoiachin and of the elite of the nation. The final catastrophe at Jerusalem in 587 is just the completion of what had begun with the first deportation. The circle that is the milieu of DH must therefore be sought in *Babylon* among the deportees, around King Jehoiachin.

The final remark of the work corresponds perfectly to this proposition, mentioning only the deportation; it does not give a theological commentary on the fall of the holy city, nor on the destruction of the temple of YHWH. The shock of the year 598 was evidently the massive deportation,[41] and the events of the year 587 only constituted, for this author, the final fulfilment of what he had already lived through in 598.[42]

(p. 202: 'the composition of 2 Kgs 24 took place shortly after the events of 597 themselves'), that is to say in ignorance of the final catastrophe of 587, supposition which seems to me highly improbable.

39. For the historical evaluation of these verses, cf. the general remarks made in §1.1 above).

40. We may recall, for example, that the dates of the book of Ezekiel are counted from the reign of Jehoiachin, the deported king; they are bent on ignoring the reign of Zedekiah.

41. Compare the figures given by Jer. 52.28-30 (cf. above).

42. I am quite aware of the extent of the consequences of my hypothesis, which gives up on according the *temple* a *central* place in the thinking of the Dtr author. At first sight, the whole programme of the centralization of cult (cf. Deut. 12) as

The theme of the loss of the land and that of the deportation are constitutive of the work as a whole, which must therefore be dated from the Babylonian exile, *after* 587 and probably *before* 561, the date of King Jehoiachin's return to favour.

I situate the *redactional* layers noted in DH during the first years of the Persian period, i.e. perhaps between 530 and 520, at the time of the return of the first Jews and the reconstruction of the temple. Events of such importance must have had an influence on the contemporary ideology.

2.2. *The Society*

What was the 'society' that produced the ideology that the DH expresses?

Even if the composition of the Dtr work dates from the experience of the exile, the thought that it reflects is oriented rather, in a conservative manner, towards the heritage of the past. For the authors, it would be very important to gather together the *traditions* of Israelite society, preserve all the traditional laws, as they are now found in Deuteronomy, even if most of them were no longer applicable in the situation of the exile: without a monarchy, without a national government, without a temple, and so on. But this society was still profoundly marked by all this heritage: by the accounts focusing on the theme of the land (the conquest according to the book of Joshua), the military campaigns (in Joshua and in Judges), the birth of the monarchy in Israel and in Judah, the accounts concerning the temple, its construction and the cultic reforms, and the narratives brought together in the many prophetic cycles. In the period of the exile, all that belonged to the past; but these

well as the idea of the divine election of Jerusalem seems to invalidate this proposition, but it is important to distinguish more clearly between a *Deuteronomic* heritage and its *Deuteronomistic* use (cf. *5. Mose*, I, p. 26); it is true that the Israelite traditions (of the northern kingdom) were revived by the royal court of Jerusalem (and among these the ideas formulated in Deut. 12), but that does not mean that they would have been considered by all as being therefore *central*. The Dtr author was certainly not a descendant of the ancient fugitives from the kingdom of the north (i.e. from the milieu of the 'Deuteronomic' tradition), nor a member of the priesthood of the Jerusalem temple either (like, for example, the prophet Ezekiel); his social background is to be sought rather in the circles of the ancient ruling families of Jerusalem (cf. for more details §2.3: 'class'). For them, there were more 'existential' and central questions than that of the sacrificial cult and its centralization.

traditions were gathered together in a literary work, since these authors diagnosed well that the fundamental identity of their society, their thought and their ideology were still determined by all these traditions, despite the situation of radical rupture implied in the deportation and the exile.

We could try to describe with some preciseness the society that was the bearer of this ideology especially with regard to its economic organization, its social structure, and so on. I limit myself to formulating a summary in the following terms: it was marked by national traditions, a national monarchy, a national religion, and so on, but these elements were at the same time called into question by the most recent events, i.e. by the national catastrophe and the massive deportation. The *traditional* identity of this society was still predominant, but seriously called into question. Here we find the *two* aspects that characterized this society.

2.3. *The 'Class'*

In accordance with the definition of the *Petit Robert*,[43] I retain the term 'class', which most certainly reflects the influence exerted by Marxist thought on the understanding of the notion of 'ideology', but I use it here as equivalent to 'social group'. This section will deal with the 'milieu', understood in the restricted sense of 'group', to which the author of DH belonged.

He belonged to the *first* deportation, i.e. that of the year 598, the one that especially struck the ruling strata of Jerusalem, according to 2 Kgs 24.14:

> Nebuchadnezzar deported...all the leaders, all the rich, ten thousand deportees, all the metalworkers and the ironsmiths; there remained only the poorest of the land.

'All the rich people', all the elite of the society, all the leadership of the nation were consequently deported into Babylonian exile. 2 Kgs 24.14 can even sum it up in these terms: 'He deported *all* Jerusalem'. This overall formulation does not really conform to the reality of 598: a king of the Davidic dynasty still remained in Jerusalem, King Zedekiah, installed by Nebuchadnezzar, as well as his family, his ministers and certain officials of the court. This remark, however, speaks of the deportation of '*all* Jerusalem', reflects the sentiment of the exiles of

43. Cf. above, n. 5.

598: with them, Jerusalem had already, in principle, lost *everything*. The author, who speaks of '*all* Jerusalem' in regard to the *first* deportation, would certainly therefore have belonged to part of that ancient elite of the people. This also explains his great erudition, since he is soundly informed on the history of his people and must have had access to the royal annals expressly mentioned among his sources.

To understand well the situation of this author in exile, we must not think that all the people of the first deportation had been destined for the slave market, for work camps, or for the forced labour required for the projects of the central government. That deportation was also intended to provide *hostages* who guaranteed the submission of the conquered country and its pacification. A minority of this elite was therefore not dispersed in the Babylonian region and forced into state works, but lived directly under the control of the royal palace, certainly on the whole as prisoners, but not worn out by physical labour and therefore capable of devoting themselves to historical and theological reflections.

It is in this specific milieu that I situate the author of DH: a member of the ancient elite of Jerusalem and now still living in privileged circumstances in Babylon. But he does not write a history in praise of the past: his work involves on the contrary a 'mea culpa': the deportation is the result of the sins against God. The mention of 'the anger of YHWH' actually dominates the final note of the work: 'This happened because of the anger of YHWH' (24.20a). It is, on the part of the author, the theological expression of a *critique* of his people's history. If he had not given a theological explanation in the sense of the 'anger of YHWH', he would have incriminated *God* for not having sufficiently protected his people against the enemy armies. This theological move as such is not uncommon; other peoples have given comparable explanations of military defeats. But *who* has sinned? There we have perhaps the most interesting point: it is not the priests, it is not the great landowners either, regularly criticized by the prophets, nor the judicial authorities in the towns who have manipulated the law; the author would have had there the occasion to revive numerous prophetic impulses. But he speaks explicitly only of the sins committed by the *kings*. Nevertheless, this criticism, included implicitly also the ruling classes to which the writer probably belonged. This 'mea culpa' is therefore a criticism which is not lacking some elements of *self*-criticism.

The 'mea culpa' is the first step in the return to YHWH so much demanded by the prophets; it is the first step in the act of שׁוּב: 'to return' to YHWH.[44]

To sum up concerning the question of the social 'class': the author of DH must have been a member of the elite very close to the ancient royal court, capable however of an astonishing critical distance and of a remarkable theological judgment; or, formulated in the opposite way, he must have been a genuine theologian, but also an expert in royal history and politics. In short, he was a *theologian* of great ability or a *scholar* with a remarkable theological profile.

3. 'Ideas—Beliefs—Doctrines'

3.1. *The Identity*

The most important idea that is expressed in this work is that of the quest for *identity*. The author raises the question of what kind of identity to propose to all those Jews scattered in the world of the Near East: in Babylon, in Syria-Palestine and in Egypt. The first element of the response is the concept of the *unity of the nation*. This concept is surprising, seeing that the whole history of the people had been marked by conflicts, at first conflicts among the tribes and then between the two brother kingdoms, Israel and Judah. But for the primitive history of the people, for its ideal history before the conquest of the country, the author conceives of a united people, composed of twelve tribes under the guidance of a sole leader, Moses, and after him, Joshua. The author of this literary work calls this people 'Israel', giving it thus the name of the kingdom of the north that this historiography harshly condemns. At first sight, this is an astonishing phenomenon, it seems to me. But it can be explained by the fact that at the time of our author, the name 'Israel' no longer corresponded to a concrete political reality; for 150 years the term had been synonymous with the 'past' and 'tradition'. This loss of a concrete political meaning certainly facilitated the revival of the term 'Israel' to designate from now on a primitive unity of all the Israelite

---

44. In this way, I can take up some of the observations made by Wolff, 'Kerygma'; cf. also Dietrich (*Prophetie und Geschichte*, p. 141): 'DtrG schreibt eine Ätiologie des Nullpunkts, an dem er und seine Zeitgenossen stehen. Zugleich aber scheint er sich und seine Zeitgenossen daran erinnern zu wollen, daß es für Israel während seiner ganzen Geschichte eine—und nur diese eine—Möglichkeit zum Überleben und zum Wiederaufleben gegeben hat: die Rückkehr zu Jahwe'.

and Judaean tribes. This idea is also inspired by the period of David when *all* the tribes were united under just one sceptre. The period of the migration in the desert has therefore been painted in analogous colours.

The second element of response employed by the author to develop the idea of identity is that of the possession of a national land: the identity must be guaranteed by attachment to a *country*. This theme is of primordial importance[45] (the conquest of the land is the first event recounted in this History), particularly important for the first generation of the exile that had suffered the separation. Later, for the second and third generations, things would change appreciably: after the fall of the Babylonian Empire, in 537, only a minority was even ready to return to the land of the ancestors. But our author is a member of the *first* generation for whom the theme of the land is absolutely central. The idea of the unity of the nation is linked to that of the land: right from the beginning of the history of the settlement in the land, Israel received this land as נחלה divided among all the tribes; the unity of the land guaranteed the identity of Israel, the 'land of YHWH' became the 'land of Israel'.

The third identifying point developed by the Dtr author is the *law*. One law alone is constitutive: it is that law found in the temple in the time of Josiah, and it is declared a 'law of Moses', the law that Moses received on the mountain of God, at Horeb. It is the ideal law, almost the 'constitution' of the nation. I emphasize that this definition does not correspond to the real situation of the time, but to an ideological concept. The period certainly knew of *several* juridical codes in Israel, and it suffices to read a little in our Pentateuch to have an idea of the enormous diversity in the juridical tradition. But to guarantee the idea of an identity, the Dtr author retains one law alone, and he presents it in all its details in the first part of his work. The Israelite and Jewish identity is guaranteed by obedience to the law, to *this* law.

The fourth identifying point is developed around the theme of the common *religion*: *one* nation, only one YHWH, only one legitimate sanctuary! That view did not correspond to the real facts in the history of Israel, which was marked instead by great religious diversity in the Yahwist tradition. But for this Dtr author, the quest for *identity* is much more important than a neutral description of history. If the multi-religious situation in the land of Babylon (in this 'supermarket of

45. Cf. also the remarks made in §1.1.

religions') is kept in mind, we can see how it was essential for the survival of the Yahwist religion to develop a religious identity in the sense of a *unity* of the faith in YHWH.

We are here introduced to the second term in the definition of the *Petit Robert*: 'the beliefs'. I will speak of it under just one aspect.

3.2. *The Logic in the History*

DH in its first version must be read in the light of the tension that exists between the situation *before* the conquest of the land (the theme in Deuteronomy) and that of the *loss* of the land mentioned in the final theological account (2 Kgs 24.20a and 25.21b). Consequently, in my way of understanding it, DH did not end on a note of hope, as is stated by the exegetes who consider the account of the liberation of Jehoiachin as the original end of this historiography, but it ended with the theological comment on the theme of the 'anger of YHWH', which must be read in all its radicalism. As far as this aspect is concerned, I agree with the interpretation of Noth, who defends the idea that the Dtr work is a vast 'judgment doxology' that leads to an understanding of the national catastrophe as an action of God-as-Judge who could no longer tolerate the sins of his people; the end of the work is devoid of any 'dawn of a new future'.[46] The *explicit* message of the end of the work refers the reader to the judgment of God; but the same work, as a whole, *implicitly* bears another message as well. This divine judgment manifested in the Jerusalem catastrophe is not the first; the author mentions still others, for example, those at the beginning of the history of Israel in its own land, those from the period of the Judges. We may cite, for example, the description of Judg. 2.14-15:

> The anger of YHWH was kindled against Israel: he gave them over into the hands of pillagers who plundered them, and he sold them into the power of their enemies surrounding them. They were no longer able to withstand their enemies. In all their sorties the hand of YHWH was against them to bring misfortune, as YHWH had warned and sworn to them; and they were in great distress.

The same terms used here to describe a situation in the time of the Judges could also describe the situation after the Jerusalem catastrophe. The Dtr author suggests therefore imagining a future after the Jerusalem

---

46. 'Überlieferungsgeschichtliche Studien', p. 108: 'Morgenrot einer neuen Zukunft'; ET: 'The Deuteronomistic History', p. 98: 'to herald a new age'.

catastrophe in a way analogous to his vision of the time of the Judges, even if he does not dare to speak of it *explicitly*. 'The Israelites cried out to YHWH, and YHWH raised up for them a deliverer who saved them.' By assuming that there is an *implicit* hope at the end of DH, I find myself quite close to the idea of Wolff, who considered the theme of 'conversion' (שוב) as the central 'kerygma' of this historiography.[47] But let us emphasize once more that the *end* of DH is not yet marked by the concrete and express expectation of a deliverer or of a conversion; it speaks explicitly only of the *judgment*. But in an implicit way, it calls for the sincere acceptance of the divine judgment, its theological understanding and for a profound conversion to YHWH.

The Dtr author has faith in the 'logic in history'. This means that history is not marked by a profound absurdity, but that it is—in a certain perspective—completely reasonable ('logical'). I shall develop this aspect in four points.

a) The 'logic in history' was particularly important for the people in the Babylonian exile: a *meaning* had to be given to the national disaster. For a profoundly human life, it is not enough to *survive* a catastrophe physically, but it is necessary to try to give a *meaning* to what one has experienced. The national catastrophe was a shock that gave rise to many questions, and the people who were really mature had to look for answers. In this way their responses were based on the principle of the 'logic in history'.

b) In this 'logic in history', it is the *law* that occupies a central position: the law had been given right from the beginning of the history of Israel, but Israel had not respected it. 'Logic' demands punishment for those guilty. Thus the Babylonian exile is declared a logical consequence of not respecting the law. History is explained in terms of behaviour with regard to the law.

c) Another aspect of the 'logic in history' is defined by the relationship between prophecies and their fulfilment. Nothing is left to chance: *God* is the ruler of history. In an extraordinarily precise way, a (Dtr) formulation in Amos defines this theological conception of the relationship between prophecy and history: 'The Lord God does nothing without revealing his secret to his servants the prophets' (Amos 3.7).

---

47. Cf. Wolff, 'Kerygma', in Brueggemann and Wolff, *Vitality*, pp. 90-100.

d) This observation can be generalized in speaking of the 'word of God', as the law as well as the prophecies are 'word of God', and very often in DH the prophets have no other function than reminding people about fidelity to the law. This functioning of the word of God, either in the form of the law, or in that of prophecies, reveals the 'logic in history'. We could expand von Rad's statement that: 'The word of God becomes history',[48] and yet say that it 'becomes a clear and reasonable history'. It is the word of God alone that makes the history of Israel function, and this in a demonstrable way. This is what the Dtr theologians believed; this was their conviction (their 'belief').

I find this theological concept of history, born in a situation of profound depression, very impressive. These theologians do not allow themselves to be so depressed by the catastrophe and by the situation of the exile as to be left in a resigned passivity, but, *active*, they conceive of a historical work, in a writing activity that is the opposite of resignation or depression: if resignation had taken over, why still write a history of Israel? These Dtr theologians still await something, even if they do not dare to say it in an explicit way. This 'something' is perhaps a miracle; it is perhaps like an Easter after a Good Friday: something that they could not expect, but in regard to which they could remain open. The Dtr theologians have not yet reached their 'Easter', they are still living in the situation of their 'Good Friday'. They speak of the end in an absolutely sober manner, without hiding anything or embellishing it, in an almost blunt manner, as primitive Christianity spoke of the cross of Jesus. 'All has been fulfilled'—the anger of YHWH is brutally realized in the deportation of his people. I find it impressive that a history ends with the description of a catastrophe and its theological interpretation.

But this reflection on the situation of the end is astonishingly *creative*: the *whole* history that Israel has lived in its land, and not only one or other period of its past, is reviewed in a critical manner. It is here that a profoundly *historical* thought is born: unlike popular accounts and the annals of the royal court, this new literary genre that historiography represents does not limit itself to occasional accounts, but lives with a totalizing interpretation, that is to say with an understanding that covers all that is recounted. *Historical* consciousness is born out of

48. Cf. M. Rose, 'L'Ancien Testament: livre d'une attente. Le concept d'histoire comme clef d'interprétation dans l'oeuvre de Gerhard von Rad', *RTP* 121 (1989), pp. 407-21 (cf. also von Rad, *Theology of the Old Testament*, I, pp. 343-44).

the situation of the end.[49] It is in this final situation that is discovered the dimension of irreversibility that is constitutive of historical thought. Without experience of the *end*, we cannot speak of an era nor of a whole history. This experience is, certainly, distressing, but it opens a revolutionary new dimension, that of history.

To interpret a period and its final catastrophe is *one* indispensable condition for being open to an 'Easter event'. The Dtr historians also had to take a decision on the *beginning* of their history, an opening which had to take on a *programmatic* character. Wherever there is a programme, there is also the perspective for an eventual future. It is evident that for a pascal event to be fully realized, there is still need of something else: merely interpretation of the catastrophe would not be enough. But those who try to understand what has happened, are already on the *way* to Easter if they interpret the events from the point of view of *God*. This author *speaks* of the end of Israel without adding anything to it, but he *thinks* of an open future, or, to invoke the terms of the New Testament: he *speaks* of the cross, but *thinks* of the possibility of a resurrection.

3.3. *The Bipolarity*

Belief or conviction is a resolute opinion, but from this I distinguish 'doctrine', a term also mentioned in the definition given in the *Petit Robert*. With the term 'doctrine', I associate something much more rigid. What is the 'doctrine' that defines the orientation of the Dtr theologians? In my opinion, they are completely set in a dualistic way of thinking (and it is here that certain criticisms regarding their theology must be made). Their bipolar view takes effect on several subjects:

a) First, they set up an opposition between the goodness of God and human culpability. In a radical way, responsibility for the national catastrophe is attributed to humans; *God* did everything to direct his people on a path to salvation and happiness, but Israel did not want to listen. God is *just*, his punishment is *justified*; the guilty are elsewhere: they are the kings and the ruling classes of the population.

b) The Dtr work is marked by a second bipolarity: that existing between an idealized origin and then a sequel necessarily decadent. The ideal origin is described, for example, by the fact that at the mountain of God, Israel as a whole is considered worthy to hear the word of God,

---

49. In this context, I could return to some elements of the article of M. Detienne; cf. pp. 174-88.

the ten commandments (Deut. 5.4, 23-25). The march in the desert in the direction of the promised land takes place, from one stage to the next, with the people perfectly obedient,[50] as is the case too for the conquest of the land on the other side of the Jordan. Each stage of the march is introduced by an order of God followed by the faithful accomplishment by the people. The time of Moses is the period of the ideal beginning; that is the conception of DH.

However, the later redaction has ruined this ideal period by inscribing the revolt of the people from the beginning, at the mountain of God (Deut. 9.7-24; cf. Exod. 32) and likewise already in the first chapter of Deuteronomy (Deut. 1.19-45).[51] As for the *original* concept of DH, it must be remembered that it was marked by the radical bipolarity between an ideal beginning and its sequel.

c) A third bipolarity is that which the Deuteronomist sees between the tradition proper to Israel and all the bad influences coming from other peoples. As a result, the disastrous development begins from the moment when Israel is established in the land of Canaan without completely eliminating all the local population. It is the ideology of a radical separation; and I understand clearly that a population in exile, a hopeless minority, sees security in such a doctrine of separation. Separation best guarantees the maintenance of identity; it is an identity gained by demarcation.

4. An 'Assemblage' of Ideas (A Theological System)

I will consider the theological system that I perceive in the Dtr ideology under two aspects: I see there certain strong points, but equally some weak points.

4.1. The Strong Points

a) The most important point, in the theological process of Dtr interpretation, is the attempt to give a *response* to the questions of the time. I will not discuss the validity of this response; but this strenuous endeavour to give *responses* is, as such, very impressive. There is also the fact that the desire to respond is, in itself inspired by an unquestionable

50. For the details, my exegesis of the most ancient narrative framework of Deuteronomy may be consulted: 'Jahwe: Herr und Gebieter der Geschichte', in *5. Mose*, II, pp. 371-470).

51. Cf. the 11th 'stage' in *5. Mose*, II, pp. 471-522.

consistency. This is a very different process from that of the prophets, for example, who, for their part, wished rather to *question* their contemporaries and among whom a *consistent* concept was not really imperative. As far as DH is concerned, on the other hand, I find it remarkable that, in a situation of complete disorientation, theologians took the trouble to propose consistent responses.

b) The second positive aspect is the mastery of the vast amount of material received from the tradition. The traditions composed in this literary work are of a very disparate nature, from the point of view of their literary form and their content. There are annals of the royal court, lists, prophetic accounts, and so on. All this traditional material is not only recovered, assembled and built up, but remarkably structured as well. Thanks to a redactional framework (cf. §1.1), to great programmatic discourses and to certain leading ideas (cf. §1.2), this work attests to a character of undoubted *unity*. This unity given to a history of four centuries is impressive: it is not only a collection of various texts, but it is a genuine theological historiography; I do not hesitate to call it the first historiography of Israel.[52]

c) The third strong point is that of 'simplicity' (in the positive sense of the term). The situation of the time was anything but simple; it was marked rather by a total upheaval: the dispersal of the population, the disruption of economic conditions, the disorientation of religious hopes, and so on. In such a situation of break-up, a 'simple' response can help enormously, and the response *was* simple: 'Israel has sinned'. There we have the whole response. Certainly, this response will later be proved to be *too* simple; but let us emphasize first that a response must be given in relation to the *concrete situation*, and I have the impression that a *simple* response was *at that time* the only valid response.

4.2. *The Weak Points*

As for the weak points, I will reverse the order of the three points of §4.1:

a) The ideological concept was ultimately *too* simple; it did not make it possible to resolve the problems. The description of an *ideal* time, for example, was obviously conceived in view of a model for an eventual future. This model described, in Deuteronomy, under the form of an ideal beginning, was in the end too idealistic, too simple and unreal. The model was not really practical.

---

52. Cf. Rose, *Deuteronomist und Jahwist*, pp. 325-28.

b) The same thing is true of the concept of *unity*: it proved impossible to impose on all the religious currents of Israel this concept of *unity* envisaged by the Dtr theologians. The description of the history of Israel was *too* standardized. It suffices to think, for example, of the priestly circles, which are underrepresented in DH.[53] This 'deficit' has prompted the development of concurrent descriptions of the history like those that we possess in the priestly writing (P) and in the Chronicler's history.[54] The *unity* of the description of the history of Israel and the unity of the theological *concept* could not be maintained. The diversity of the religious currents dominated more and more to the detriment of the concept of *unity*.

c) *Responses* once given need to be modified when the situation changes. New questions come up in a new situation. The successive redactional revisions of DH express this feeling that the responses given under the shock of the deportation are no longer really suitable for the new questions posed by the second and third generation following this overwhelming event. The unity of the response gives way to the multiplicity of responses.

5. *Perspectives: What I Retain for (My) Theology*

5.1. *Up-To-Date*
The 'up-to-date' nature of the theological concepts of the Deuteronomists in their time must be mentioned as an important aspect for *all* theology. By that, I am not thinking of a modernism at any price, but of

---

53. For example, we may mention what little space the sacrifices occupy in the history of the inauguration of the temple of Solomon (1 Kgs 8): the introduction (vv. 14-21) does not lead to a sacrifice, to an act of purification, to a hymn or a procession, but to long prayers; sacrifices are only mentioned at the end, in the narrative framework (vv. 62-66). The same observation is also true for the description of the event that, according to the fundamental text of Deuteronomy, took place at the mountain of God, at Horeb: there is not a word mentioning a sacrifice. Everything is speech: the communication of the law, the declaration of the people about respecting all the commandments given by God, the fixation in writing of the commandments received, and so on. The celebration is not sanctioned by any specific ritual worship, by any sacrifice. All the great gatherings of the people take place without any sacrifice being mentioned: cf., for example, Josh. 24; 1 Sam. 12 and 2 Kgs 23.1-3.

54. Cf. my description in 'La croissance du corpus historiographique de la Bible', pp. 217-36; especially the graph on p. 233.

a sensitivity that theologians must develop in order to grasp the questions of their time. The Dtr theologians are not learned historians carrying out a theoretical enquiry in a critical and neutral manner; it is visible everywhere in their work that they are engaging with questions of their time. History must be recounted so that comtemporaries understand something of their own situation. The theologian who is really moved by *current* problems will speak of the *history* of the faith in a transparent way: a history at *two* levels.

5.2. *Coherence*

What can be observed in the Dtr ideology is required of *all* theology: all theologians should do their best to give maximal coherence to their thought. It is obvious that we can no longer go back to the Dtr responses in order to give coherence to *our* thought. But the criterion of 'coherence' as such seems to me indispensable; the accumulation of theological knowledge still does not make one a theologian. How can we gain such coherence? Personally, I would give the following response: coherence is only guaranteed by a rigorous *hermeneutical* reflection. This means that a theological reflection is only complete and coherent on condition that its *presuppositions* are also integrated into the process of reflection. For example, these might be the presuppositions which are influenced by the factors of belonging 'to an epoch, to a society or to a class' (to return to the three terms of the *Petit Robert*). I would say that today the criterion of 'coherence' no longer relates solely to the *responses* that are given, the *results* or the *theses*; it is the *whole* process of theological reflection that must be coherent, from presuppositions to conclusions. Evidently, the Dtr theologians did not spell out their presuppositions; but today, hermeneutical reflection seems to me indispensable.

5.3. *The Process of Tradition and of Interpretation*

A fundamental point in all theology is the need of the journey that goes from tradition to interpretation. In my theological work, I always feel bound to a precise tradition, for example, to the biblical tradition and to the Christian tradition. However, I am not an archivist of this tradition, but an *interpreter*. The interpretations that I give of the tradition are never to be understood as a result, but rather as a journey always to be taken up again; the vitality of the theology depends on the vivacity of this process of interpretation. If the tradition becomes a straitjacket, the theologian risks becoming a fundamentalist or a sectarian; if, on the other hand, the interpretation is no longer controlled by tradition, the theologian becomes an elegant rhetor or a sort of sophist. As for me, I would like to be a theologian who lives in the *process* of tradition and interpretation, like the Deuteronomists who respected their traditions while giving new interpretations.

5.4. *A Meaning to Life*

The theologian must give 'a meaning to life'! The Deuteronomists attempted this by speaking of the necessity of a שׁוּב, of a 'return' to YHWH. The *meaning* that they gave to the life of the exiles was, in the last analysis, to describe humans before God, humans as sinners, but called to conversion (שׁוּב). In a comparable way, I cannot give another meaning to life than that defined by this orientation of humans towards transcendence. The temptation is always great to take concrete steps on the path towards transcendence and towards eternity: to construct pyramids that will be admired for millennia, to write works that will become part of world literature, to create foundations that perpetuate the patron's name or to do good works inscribed in the book of life. In all these activities, a meaning that a person wants to give to life can actually be found. But the 'meaning' according to Dtr theology is different: it is first of all to accept one's sin; today, we would say to accept one's failure and one's limits. The redactional revision that DH underwent can teach us that such a theology risks becoming too negative, since in the continuation of the history of the theologies several steps have been taken to correct it, for example, in elaborating a 'Yahwist' history and a 'Priestly' one. But the theology that seems to me the strongest and to which I adhere is that which adds to the (Dtr) dimension of the fall of humanity the *love* of God: the theology of Jesus. This theology, *prepared for* by the Dtr theology of the fall of humans, *announced* in the Yahwist theology of grace,[55] has been *fulfilled* in its complete form through the *life* and the message of Jesus.

Ten Concluding Theses

1.   The *hermeneutical presuppositions* that could have had an influence on the interpretation of the text must be determined and clarified.

---

55. Cf. Rose, 'La croissance du corpus historiographique de la Bible', p. 232.

2. I would insist on avoiding any impression of ('positivist') objectivity in my exegetical results, and it seems to me important to become aware of my own *exegetical pre-suppositions*.

3. Exegetical analysis must begin from the *specificity* of each text (pericope, book, work), as far as can be expected, to discern its intention.

***

4. The book of Deuteronomy is the only text that can form the *beginning* of a work as vast as DH.

5. The thorny problem of the *end* of DH will only find a response by being linked with the redaction-history method.

6. Certain texts of DH occupy a *key position* in the organization of the whole.

***

7. The originality of my research on the *period* and *milieu* of DH lies in the argument that we must look for the author of this work among the Judaeans of the first deportation (598).

8. The theological interest that this work reflects is that of the articulation between the two poles of the quest for *identity* and the search for a *'logic' in history*.

9. The three central themes (law, prophetism, [historical] experience) of DH have influenced the formation of the *whole* Old Testament *canon (tora, nebi'îm, ketubîm)*.

***

10. The DH induces me not to remain a historian (philologist, exegete, linguist, archaeologist, and so on), but to become a *theologian*.

DEUTERONOMISTIC IDEOLOGY AND THE THEOLOGY OF THE OLD TESTAMENT

Andrew D.H. Mayes

The title of this paper suggests not an attempt to assess the contribution of the deuteronomistic history to the theology of the Old Testament, but that a contrast is to be drawn between them. On the one hand, there is the ideology of a deuteronomistic history that belongs to a particular time and place; on the other hand, there is the theology of the Old Testament which has a normative role independent of those circumstances.[1] This kind of contrast is, I believe, present in several studies which suggest that the descriptive approach to the Old Testament provides us with the ideology of its various writers whereas the normative approach of theologians today provides us with a non-ideological theology, or, indeed, that within the Old Testament itself one may distinguish between those parts of it which may be characterized as ideological and those belonging to a higher theological plane.

---

1. For discussion of the nature of Old Testament theology, with particular reference to its descriptive and normative aspects, see especially the essays by Eissfeldt ('The History of Israelite–Jewish Religion and Old Testament Theology') and Eichrodt ('Does Old Testament Theology Still Have Independent Significance within Old Testament Scholarship?'), and the introductory essay by Ollenburger ('From Timeless Ideas to the Essence of Religion'), in B.C. Ollenburger, E.A. Martens and G.F. Hasel (eds.), *The Flowering of Old Testament Theology* (Winona Lake, IN: Eisenbrauns, 1992). For a recent discussion of the relationship of theology to historical criticism, see J.J. Collins, 'Is a Critical Biblical Theology Possible?', in W.H. Propp, B. Halpern and D.N. Freedman (eds.), *The Hebrew Bible and its Interpreters* (Winona Lake, IN: Eisenbrauns, 1990), pp. 1-17. For Collins, biblical theology cannot ignore the ideological use of God-language, and can become compatible with historical criticism only if, as a sub-discipline of historical theology, it is understood as an open-ended and critical enquiry into the meaning and function of God-language.

An important part of our task is a clarification of terms. The first section of this paper will, therefore, attempt to define the nature of ideology, with particular reference to Israelite religious thinking. The second will concern itself with the deuteronomistic history and try to provide an account of deuteronomistic ideology and the major stages of its development. The third section will then return to the question of Old Testament theology, but will confine itself to just one aspect, suggested by the preceding account of deuteronomistic ideology.

I

(1) In 1976 P.D. Miller discussed the implications for Israelite religion of the view that no human thought is immune to the ideologizing influences of its social context.[2] Miller notes that 'ideology' may mean, in a neutral way, 'a description of the way things are in a society, the values, ideas and conceptions of a society which cause it to do or act as it does'.[3] But it commonly has a pejorative sense: it is a partial view of the way things are, a view which is a function of the conditions of the person who holds it; the ideas expressed are to be interpreted in the light of those conditions and are not to be taken at face value. Two quotations emphasize this partial nature of ideology:

> An ideology is a selective interpretation of the state of affairs in society made by those who share some particular conception of what it ought to be...

> [An ideology is] that composite myth by which a society or group identifies itself, not only for itself but also for other societies and groups. An ideology posits the group's goals and the justification of these goals in terms of which the group deals with other groups and with conflicts within the group; it defines and interprets the situation; it aims to overcome indifference to the common good; it reduces excessive emphasis on individual action. It makes possible group action.[4]

2.   P.D. Miller, 'Faith and Ideology in the Old Testament', in F.M. Cross, W.E. Lemke and P.D. Miller (eds.), *Magnalia Dei—The Mighty Acts of God: Essays on the Bible and Archaeology in Memory of G. Ernest Wright* (New York: Doubleday, 1976), pp. 464-79.
3.   Miller, 'Faith and Ideology', p. 465.
4.   The first quotation is from Winston White, the second from J.L. Adams; for both see Miller, 'Faith and Ideology', p. 466.

Ideology defined in this way is clearly present in the Old Testament. Israel's early poetry, Exodus 15, Deuteronomy 33 and Judges 5, is thoroughly ideological. The material interests of Israel, particularly its acquisition of land, are projected as the interests of Yahweh also. There is no self-criticism, relationships with other groups are hostile, and there is no demand for justice and righteousness. In the work of the Yahwist ideological elements are also to be found: the description of Israel as descended from a common ancestor, as a chosen people whose ancestors received divine promises of land and posterity, is a thoroughly ideological description. But self-interest is also transcended in J: the divine blessing on Israel is fully realized only in the context of universal blessing (Gen. 12.1-3), and there is a demand for justice and righteousness in Israel (Gen. 18.17b-19). In J, therefore, faith and ideology are intertwined. The deuteronomic conquest traditions represent an ideological presentation of the past, a justification for certain actions and practices on the basis of Israel's self-understanding as the chosen people. Israel's action in dispossessing the former inhabitants is projected as fulfilling the purposes of Yahweh. A check is kept on ideology, however, by a covenant framework, with its demand for Israel's obedience.

In Miller's view, therefore, it is clear that ideology is an expression of material interests: where the religion of Israel identifies Israel's material interests with the will of Yahweh, that religion is ideological. But on the basis of certain objective criteria it is possible to distinguish ideology from that which transcends self-interest and so is non-ideological.

(2) There are, I believe, problems with this view. First is the clear implication that some forms of human thinking stand so close to material circumstances that they may be held to be caused by them. Thus, the material and physical circumstances of Israel—its possession of the land of Canaan, or the threat to its continued possession—were the cause of the ideology of the divine promise of land to the patriarchs. This is a materialist view of ideology, one that has often been traced back to Marx. In modern times it appears explicitly in the work of Marvin Harris and Norman Gottwald, but is an understanding of ideology that was in fact criticized by Marx and then subsequently by Clifford Geertz and Paul Ricoeur.[5] The essence of the critique is: how can

5. Cf. C. Geertz, *The Interpretation of Cultures* (New York: Basic Books, 1973); P. Ricoeur, *Lectures on Ideology and Utopia* (New York: Columbia Uni-

physical conditions be transformed into mental conditions? Physical causes have physical effects, not mental effects. The idea that physical conditions can cause thought cannot explain the transformation of the one into the other, and does not reckon with the subjective, conscious human activity in the creation of those material conditions which are reckoned to cause human thinking.

Geertz has argued that the foundation of ideology lies rather in what he calls 'the autonomous process of symbolic formulation'.[6] We can understand how ideas arise, an ideology is formed, only if at the most basic level of human existence there is a symbolic dimension. That is, physical reality does not just impinge itself on the human mind; if it did do so, we would exist in a state of chaos. Rather, physical reality is *recognized* by the human mind by the symbolic ordering of reality in perception. This symbolic ordering is ideology, and its basic function is to integrate: an ideology is a coherent body of shared images and ideas which provides for those who share it 'a coherent, if systematically simplified, overall orientation in space and time'.[7] It is a culture pattern which provides 'a blueprint for the organization of social and psychological processes, much as genetic systems provide such a template for the organization of organic processes'.[8]

This basic function of ideology is, according to Ricoeur, fundamental to any other role it may have. In general, ideology is representation of reality, that through which reality is experienced, expressed and mediated. It also carries a pejorative sense, however, because, as in Marx,

---

versity Press, 1986). The problem identified by Geertz and Ricoeur may well in part also lie behind the refusal by M. Weber (*From Max Weber: Essays in Sociology* [ed. H.H. Gerth and C. Wright Mills; London: Routledge & Kegan Paul, 1948], pp. 269-70) to accept the term 'ideology' as a way of defining the relationship between religious belief and economic interests. The classic study is, of course, K. Mannheim, *Ideology and Utopia* (London: Routledge & Kegan Paul, 1936).

6. Geertz, *Interpretation*, p. 207.

7. This is a statement by Erik Erikson, quoted in Ricoeur, *Lectures*, p. 258; cf. also J.H. Kavanagh, 'Ideology', in F. Lentricchia and T.M. Claughlin (eds.), *Critical Terms for Literary Study* (Chicago: University of Chicago Press, 1990), pp. 311-12: ideology is a social process, working on and through every social subject.

8. Geertz, *Interpretation*, p. 216. Cf. also I. Hodder, *Reading the Past* (Cambridge: Cambridge University Press, 1986), p. 3: 'material culture is an *indirect* reflection of human society...it is ideas, beliefs and meanings which interpose themselves between people and things'.

ideology achieves 'reversal': what are in reality human ideas come to be understood as autonomous, as having other than human origin, as simply being the way things are. One instance of this understanding of ideology as distortion of reality is religion: the divine is a human idea, objectified and alienated from its originator to become the active subject. Ideology is now the means by which the processes of real life are obscured; it conceals self-interest, often in terms of divine mandate.[9]

Ricoeur[10] argues that the distorting function of ideology presupposes a prior integrating function; ideology can distort only because it originally constituted. Moreover, there is a connecting link between these two functions of ideology, where ideology serves not to integrate nor to distort reality but rather to legitimize. As soon as a differentiation appears between a ruling group and the rest of the community, ideology comes in to legitimize the authority of the ruling group. 'Ideology occurs in the gap between a system of authority's claim to legitimacy and our response in terms of belief.'[11]

Ideology is not, therefore, to be understood as mental superstructure to material infrastructure, but as symbolic representation through which reality is experienced and brought to expression. It is active at all levels, including the most basic level of material infrastructure. Ideology at first integrates, providing the symbolic system which constitutes the community; division in the community leads to the need for the ruling group to justify its authority, and now ideology functions to legitimate; then, ideology functions to distort by obscuring the real process of life. These three functions stand in a temporal as well as logical relationship: 'logically if not temporally the constitutive function of ideology must precede its distortive function'.[12]

(3) All of this is extraordinarily suggestive for our understanding of the nature of Israelite religion, which illustrates the functioning of ideology at all three levels. On the level of integration, Israelite religion provides a symbolic system that maintains community, a role that Robertson Smith long ago assigned to religion in the ancient world, a view then adopted by Emile Durkheim, and, most recently for Israelite religion, by Norman Gottwald. Robertson Smith argued:

---

9. Cf. Ricoeur, *Lectures*, pp. 4-5.
10. Ricoeur, *Lectures*, pp. 12-14.
11. Ricoeur, *Lectures*, p. 183.
12. Ricoeur, *Lectures*, p. 182.

A man did not choose his religion or frame it for himself; it came to him
as part of the general scheme of social obligations and ordinances laid
upon him, as a matter of course, by his position in the family and in the
nation... Religion did not exist for the saving of souls but for the preservation and welfare of society...[13]

This is clearly echoed in Durkheim's argument that religious beliefs
'are not merely received individually by all the members of [the] group;
they are something belonging to the group, and they make its unity'.[14]
Religion belongs to what Durkheim calls the collective representations
of society; individuals are born into these collective representations
which are imbued in the consciousness of those individuals. The function of religion is to unify and to integrate through articulating the fundamental common beliefs of the group. In relation to the religion of
Israel, the function is described by Gottwald thus:

When I refer to ideology in ancient Israel, I mean the consensual religious ideas which were structurally embedded in and functionally correlated to other social phenomena within the larger social system.[15]

The religious cult and ideology are potent organizational and symbolic
forces in establishing and reinforcing the social, economic, political and
military arrangements normative for community.[16]

Religion as ideology is a function of social relations. It performs first
an integrating function that is both the logical and the temporal basis for
its other functions, which follow from that primary function but also
reflect social and economic changes in the community—the emergence
of a distinction between a ruling group and the remainder of the community, a ruling group whose role had to be justified and legitimated. In
Israel, the rise of charismatic leadership and then monarchy represented
threats to Israel's unity which had to be averted by a process of legitimation. Ideology as legitimation is the claim which re-unites the ruler
and the ruled. Charismatic leaders claimed to be designated by Yahweh;

13. W. Robertson Smith, *Lectures on the Religion of the Semites* (New York:
Ktav, 3rd edn, 1969 [1889]), pp. 28-29.

14. E. Durkheim, *The Elementary Forms of the Religious Life* (London: George
Allen & Unwin, 1976 [1912]), p. 43. For a study of Durkheim and his influence on
Old Testament study, cf. A.D.H. Mayes, *The Old Testament in Sociological Per-
spective* (London: Pickering & Inglis, 1989), pp. 27-35, 78-90.

15. N.K. Gottwald, *The Tribes of Yahweh: A Sociology of the Religion of Liberated Israel 1250–1050 B.C.E.* (London: SCM Press, 1980), pp. 65-66.

16. Gottwald, *Tribes of Yahweh*, p. 489.

clan elders claimed leadership on the basis of immemorial tradition. Ideology performs an increasingly distorting role, however, the more extravagant became the claims that were made. The king is not only designated by Yahweh, he is the son of Yahweh; he stands in an exclusive covenant relationship with the deity. At this stage, ideology distorts in two interconnected respects: first, in presenting Yahweh's designation as an autonomous divine act, whereas in truth it is a wholly human action; secondly, in that it obscures the real conditions of power in the exercise of royal rule. Religion as distorting ideology conceals social division, by promoting it as something willed by Yahweh.

With this appreciation of ideology, we have a framework for understanding Israelite religion which is not materialistic, for, as we have seen, the idea that there is a causal relationship between material circumstances and thinking is inadequate. Human thinking is present at all stages, even the most basic, of human existence in the world. Only if this is so is it possible to understand the possibility of human thinking being at all related to material circumstances, for these circumstances of themselves cannot give rise to human thinking.

(4) The analysis of Geertz and Ricoeur is in many respects clear and convincing; it does, however, present some problems, in particular its assertion that ideology functions primarily in an integrative way. First, there is little evidence to support the idea that there was ever to be found a fundamental range of common values and beliefs, common symbols and representations, which functioned solely as a unifying influence, 'a sort of social cement', in society.[17] Secondly, it is clear that Geertz, Ricoeur and also Gottwald have doubts about a primary integrative function of ideology. Ricoeur observes that 'while ideology serves... as the code of interpretation that secures integration, it does so by justifying the present system of authority', and, later, asks 'whether we are allowed to speak of ideologies outside the situation of distortion and so with reference only to the basic function of integration... Is there ideology where there is no conflict of ideologies?... integration without confrontation is pre-ideological.'[18]

In line with this, Gottwald believes that the Israelite religious ideology functioned *'to provide explanations or interpretations of the distinctive social relations and historical experience of Israel and also to*

17. J.B. Thompson, *Studies in the Theory of Ideology* (Cambridge: Polity Press, 1984), pp. 130-33.

18. Ricoeur, *Lectures*, pp. 13, 259; cf. Geertz, *Interpretation*, p. 219.

*define and energize the Israelite social system oppositionally or pole-
mically over against other social systems*.[19] Gottwald's argument is
that Israel emerged in the context of a *conscious* social revolution
directed against the hierarchic state system of the environment: 'Israel's
tribalism was politically conscious and deliberate social revolution'.[20]
The role of ideology cannot, then, be understood simply in terms of
integration and constitution; rather, from the beginning, it belongs in a
context of opposition to other ideologies and thus has a legitimating
function.[21]

II

(1) This discussion has a bearing on our understanding of the ideology
of the deuteronomistic history. My approach here will be similar to that
adopted by Gottwald to Second Isaiah. Gottwald argues that the text of
Isaiah 40–55 has an integrity of its own, but is also connected in a
variety of ways with the social life within which it existed. The text is
both determined and a determinant. As determined, it expressed the
interests of a politico-religious oligarchy which, exiled to Babylon, sees
itself as representing the cosmic-political order once established, and
soon to be re-established, in Jerusalem. As determinant, it functioned in
making the deliverance and restoration so palpable that the aristocratic
oligarchy in Babylon will make that deliverance take place so soon as
the opportunity should arise. Thus the text of Second Isaiah is a weapon
in the struggle to maintain the role and status of a former ruling class
faced with dissolution in Babylon, by motivating it to work for the

---

19. Gottwald, *Tribes of Yahweh*, p. 66.

20. Gottwald, *Tribes of Yahweh*, p. 325.

21. It is clear that a further problem with Miller's presentation is that although
he believes that ideology expresses material interests, he essentially views ideology
as an intrinsic characteristic of certain statements and beliefs in themselves, rather
than as characteristic of certain statements in relation to social and material conditions. Thus, the belief that Israel is the people of Yahweh is an intrinsically ideological statement. On this, however, see T. Eagleton, *Ideology: An Introduction* (London: Verso, 1991), p. 9: '[ideology] concerns the actual uses of language between
particular human subjects for the production of specific effects ... exactly the same
piece of language may be ideological in one context and not in another; ideology is
a function of the relation of an utterance to its social context'; cf. further, *Ideology*,
pp. 16-17, 22-23. This view harmonizes well with the function of ideology described above.

restoration of the homeland with itself exercising the role of leader-ship.[22]

Although Gottwald's approach assumes the unity of the text of Second Isaiah, rather than the literary complexity evident in the deuteronomistic ideology, his understanding of the text as a discourse concerned with 'who is saying what to whom for what purposes'[23] is appropriate to our understanding of the deuteronomistic history. The ideology of the deuteronomistic history in all its phases is also to be understood within the framework of social and political relationships, concerned with the promotion of a world view which translates itself into political attitudes, and not simply as the expression of the particular interests of a single social or religious group. It is thus misleading to think in terms of Levites, reforming priests, prophets or scribal schools as providing an adequate explanatory context for the deuteronomistic history, for these of themselves do not constitute the political realities which shaped the social context of the ideology. Agrarian societies such as Judah were chiefly divided into a ruling class, a retainer group and peasants, and struggles for power were confined to the ruling class with little impact on the living conditions of the common people. Those involved in such power struggles were spread across various social roles, and involved priests, prophets and royal officials active in different political factions. Factional politics at work in late monarchic Judah may not be easy to reconstruct in detail, but in broad contours they certainly involved struggles for power and influence on the king on the part of nationalistic groups and their opponents. On both sides of the divide a mixed elite of prophets, priests, scribes and officials was

22. Cf. N.K. Gottwald, 'Social Class and Ideology in Isaiah 40–55: An Eagletonian Reading', *Semeia* 59 (1992), pp. 43-57. Gottwald notes that Second Isaiah assigns the political role of the Davidic dynasty to Cyrus while the moral and religious leadership is assigned to the aristocratic oligarchy of the returning exiles, and that it is this which distinguishes Second Isaiah from Ezekiel, who provides for a Judahite prince, and from the deuteronomistic history, which sees Jehoiachin as the focus of hope for restoration; for Second Isaiah, the Davidic dynasty has no role to play. A critical response to Gottwald is provided by the essays of C.A. Newsom and J. Milbank in the same issue of *Semeia* (J. Milbank, '"I will gasp and pant': Deutero-Isaiah and the Birth of the Suffering Subject—A Response to Norman K. Gottwald's "Social Class and Ideology in Isaiah 40–55"', *Semeia* 59 [1992], pp. 59-71; C.A. Newsom, 'Response to Norman Gottwald', *Semeia* 59 [1992], pp. 73-78).

23. Eagleton, *Ideology*, p. 9.

involved.[24] The appearance of a wide variety of such influences in the deuteronomistic history is a reflection of its role in the ideological dimension of those factional politics.

(2) Noth's fundamental conclusion that the deuteronomistic history was essentially the product of a single author has for long been the subject of critical discussion. Most reaction has tended to promote one or other of two major alternatives.[25] The Smend school has elaborated a

24. Cf. P. Dutcher-Walls, 'The Social Location of the Deuteronomists: A Sociological Study of Factional Politics in Late Pre-Exilic Judah', *JSOT* 52 (1991), pp. 77-94. See further, R. Albertz, *A History of Israelite Religion in the Old Testament Period* (London: SCM Press, 1994), pp. 195-231. As far as the postexilic period is concerned, it is clear that the rather simplistic contrast between theocratic and eschatological groups, which has been promoted especially by P.D. Hanson, *The Dawn of Apocalyptic* (Philadelphia: Fortress Press, 1979), cannot provide a reliable picture of the political and social realities of that time. For a critical treatment of Hanson which, while restoring a more credible exegesis of Second and Third Isaiah, still remains, however, too confined to the religious dimension of postexilic conditions, cf. B. Schramm, *The Opponents of Third Isaiah* (JSOTSup, 193; Sheffield: Sheffield Academic Press, 1995), pp. 81-111. For further discussion cf. also Albertz, *A History of Israelite Religion*, pp. 437-50, and R.F. Person, *Second Zechariah and the Deuteronomic School* (JSOTSup, 167; Sheffield: JSOT Press, 1993), pp. 149-54.

25. Cf. N. Lohfink, 'Recent Discussion on 2 Kings 22–23: The State of the Question', in D.L. Christensen (ed.), *A Song of Power and the Power of Song: Essays on the Book of Deuteronomy* (Winona Lake, IN: Eisenbrauns, 1993), pp. 45-47. Various reviews of the history of the study of the deuteronomistic history are available. For a recent short survey, see S.L. McKenzie, 'Deuteronomistic History', *ABD*, II, pp. 160-68. More extensive accounts are provided by, for example, A.D.H. Mayes, *The Story of Israel between Settlement and Exile: A Redactional Study of the Deuteronomistic History* (London: SCM Press, 1983); H. Weippert, 'Das deuteronomistische Geschichtswerk. Sein Ziel und Ende in der neueren Forschung', *TRu* 50 (1985), pp. 213-49; M.A. O'Brien, *The Deuteronomistic History Hypothesis: A Reassessment* (OBO, 92; Freiburg: Universitätsverlag; Göttingen: Vandenhoeck & Ruprecht, 1989); S.L. McKenzie and M.P. Graham (eds.), *The History of Israel's Traditions: The Heritage of Martin Noth* (JSOTSup, 182; Sheffield: Sheffield Academic Press, 1994). I leave out of account here two approaches defending the unity of the deuteronomistic history. One, promoted by H.D. Hoffmann (*Reform und Reformen* [ATANT, 66; Zürich: Theologischer Verlag, 1980), followed by Albertz (*History of Israelite Religion*, p. 388) uses a traditio-historical approach to try to retrieve Noth's own understanding of the nature of the work of the deuteronomistic historian; the other is a significant literary argument by Robert Polzin (*Moses and the Deuteronomist: A Literary Study of the Deuteronomic His-*

theory of successive deuteronomistic redactional layers (DtrH, DtrP and DtrN), none of which is to be dated before the exile, while the Cross school has maintained a genuine deuteronomistic author, dating his work to the pre-exilic period, and proposing an exilic supplement. Cross[26] distinguished two major themes in the deuteronomistic history: that which focusses on the sin of Jeroboam and his succcessors, which brought judgment on the Northern Kingdom, and that of grace and hope, with David as the symbol of faithfulness. The interrelation of these two themes is the overall concern of the first edition of the deuteronomistic history. It reaches its climax in the account of Josiah's destruction of the cult of Jeroboam and his attempt to restore the Davidic kingdom, an account seen as propaganda for Josiah's reform.

As a work supporting the reform of Josiah, the pre-exilic deuter-onomistic history is structured on three major figures: Moses, David and Josiah. Josiah is not only a Davidic king, but the true successor to David as the ideal king who lived by the law of Moses.[27] Moses is the prototypical royal ruler and lawgiver who, like Hammurabi, established the constitution of his people; it is by that law that David lived and it is that law which Josiah sought to enforce. Founded on an act of apostasy from that law, rejecting Jerusalem as the chosen place of Yahweh, the Northern Kingdom was doomed to failure from the start, but in the Southern Kingdom hope for the future could be discerned in its history. Yahweh's election of Zion holds back his judgment on his people. In the depiction of the reigns of Asa and Jehoshaphat (1 Kgs 15.12-13; 22.47), but especially the reigns of Hezekiah and Josiah (2 Kgs 18; 22–23), the deuteronomist showed how political and military crisis was overcome in the past through cultic reform, as adopted by Josiah in particular.

tory [New York: Seabury, 1980], for a discussion of which see my *The Story of Israel*, pp. 19-21.

26. Cf. F.M. Cross, *Canaanite Myth and Hebrew Epic* (Cambridge, MA: Harvard University Press, 1973), pp. 274-89.

27. On 2 Kgs 23.25 as the conclusion to the first edition of the deuteronomistic history, cf. G. Vanoni, 'Beobachtungen zur deuteronomistischen Terminologie in 2 Kön 23, 25-25, 30', in N. Lohfink (ed.), *Das Deuteronomium. Entstehung, Gestalt und Botschaft* (BETL, 68; Leuven: Leuven University Press, 1985), pp. 357-62. As Vanoni notes, only of Josiah is it said that he turned to Yahweh 'with all his heart and with all his soul and with all his might', thus fulfilling the chief commandment of the deuteronomic law, Deut. 6.5.

Rainer Albertz has argued that the reform of Josiah, based on the deuteronomic law, was a comprehensive national, social and religious movement which exploited Assyrian weakness to reconstitute an Israelite state.[28] Rejecting any possibility of distinguishing different redactional layers in the deuteronomistic history,[29] however, he believes that this history is effectively an ideological reinterpretation of the Josianic reform document, the deuteronomic law, which adapted it to the particular needs of the exilic period. Its authors are to be sought among the survivors of the ruling stratum who had remained at home after 587 BCE. For these, it was the king, the temple and the worship of Yahweh alone which were of decisive importance, and the king and his attitude to the temple and the worship of Yahweh are the criteria of judgment on the national history. The concern of the deuteronomists is to provide a theological account of the events of 587 BCE which might show their Judaean contemporaries the way out of their crisis: not in the popular syncretism then flourishing, but rather in the exclusive worship of Yahweh focused on Jerusalem, as established in Josiah's reform.[30]

The crucial problem in this account lies in the ideological disjunction which it posits between the demands of the deuteronomic law and the deuteronomistic history; but this disjunction lies also in the incompatibility between the deuteronomic law as presently constituted and the reform of Josiah. For if the social law of the deuteronomic code is downplayed by the deuteronomistic historian, it equally clearly played little or no part in the reform of Josiah. The subordinate role of the king in the lawcode hardly legitimates the role of Josiah in the reform, for that law does not see the king as the source of authority in Israel.[31] In other words, Albertz is right in his ideological reading of the deuteronomistic history as concerned with the Davidic monarchy and the Jerusalem temple, but wrong in linking this with the exilic period rather than the pre-exilic, and wrong also in his use of the deuteronomic law in much its present form to describe the reform of Josiah as a comprehensive, national, social and religious movement of renewal.

---

28. Albertz, *History of Israelite Religion*, pp. 199-201.
29. Albertz, *History of Israelite Religion*, pp. 387-88.
30. Albertz, *History of Israelite Religion*, pp. 397-99.
31. Cf. N. Lohfink, 'Distribution of the Functions of Power: The Laws Concerning Public Offices in Deuteronomy 16.18–18.22', in Christensen (ed.), *A Song of Power*, p. 347.

The original deuteronomic lawcode was probably designed to accompany and legitimate the reform of Josiah. The reform was a royal act with political and religious motives aimed at centralizing the faith and loyalty of Israelites on Jerusalem and the Davidic king.[32] If the deuteronomic lawbook was to provide overall ideological legitimation, however, it is unlikely that it contained the range of laws which now characterizes it. Rather, the laws which conform to its purpose are those which, apart from the laws on clean and unclean animals in Deuteronomy 14,[33] are found in Deut. 12.2–16.17. It is here that the central sanctuary and the exclusiveness of the worship of Yahweh are extensively treated and it is this law which has especial relevance to Josiah's reform.

This deduction conforms with recent analysis of the redaction of the deuteronomic law. It has been noted that the laws on officials in Israel in Deut. 16.18–18.22 constitute a distinct section, disjointed from what precedes and showing clear signs of an exilic redaction.[34] Braulik has argued that Deuteronomy 19–25, least affected by deuteronomic language, without centralization laws, making frequent reference to the Book of the Covenant in Exodus 21–23, and differing from the earlier part of the deuteronomic law in their relationship to individual commandments of the decalogue (whereas chs. 12–18 'correspond to the decalogue only in some rather vague and generalized respects'), was integrated into the deuteronomic law only after chs. 12–18 were already there.[35] The exilic redaction to which these sections belong was a major

32. On the geographical extent of the reform, cf. Lohfink, 'Recent Discussion', p. 39. For the pre-exilic deuteronomistic account of Josiah's reform, see Mayes, *The Story of Israel*, pp. 128-32.

33. On the dietary regulations of Deut. 14 as a late Priestly addition to the deuteronomic law, see A.D.H. Mayes, 'Deuteronomy 14 and the Deuteronomic World View', in F. Garcia Martínez *et al.* (eds.), *Studies in Deuteronomy in Honour of C.J. Labuschagne on the Occasion of His 65th Birthday* (Leiden: E.J. Brill, 1994), pp. 165-81.

34. Cf. Lohfink, 'Distribution', pp. 345-46, who points to the role of the book of the law in the law of the king, the inconsistency between the law of Deut. 18.1-8 and 2 Kgs 23.9, and the regulations for differentiating between true and false prophets in Deut. 18.21-22, as particular indications of an exilic background to this section of the deuteronomic law.

35. G. Braulik, 'The Sequence of the Laws in Deuteronomy 12–26 and in the Decalogue', in Christensen (ed.), *A Song of Power*, pp. 313-35 (321-22, 333-34); *idem*, 'Die dekalogische Redaktion der deuteronomischen Gesetze', in G. Braulik

revision in a very different setting than that of the original deuteronomic law and of the first edition of the deuteronomistic history, and
pursued its own ideological purposes and needs.

The legitimating function of the first edition of the deuteronomistic
history, with its focus on divine promises relating to the temple and the
Davidic king, was overtaken by the events of 587 BCE. The supreme
role claimed for the king and temple had not justified itself in history,
and there emerged an urgent need for a fresh interpretation of events as
they developed in the latter part of the exilic period. The revision of the
deuteronomistic history involved an extensive reorientation of the work
which involved the deuteronomic lawbook as well.

The deuteronomic lawbook in its present form is a much expanded
edition of the original one that appeared in the first edition of the
deuteronomistic history. The emphasis on cultic unity and purity was
maintained, but was extended into a concern for the constitution and
everyday life of this people in its relationship with Yahweh. By
legislating for positions of leadership within Israel (16.18–18.22), and
by decisive intervention into the spheres of property and family law
(19.1–25.19), the lawbook is now aimed not simply at proper
establishment of the centralized cult, but rather more comprehensively
at the whole religious and social order in Israel: the intention now is to
legislate for an integrated and unified society with a constitutional
monarchy. Earlier ideologies represented specific interests in Israelite
society; the expanded deuteronomic law aimed at an ideology for the
whole of Israel, in which the king is no longer the guarantor of
prosperity and salvation, but Yahweh has his covenant directly with
Israel as a whole, and his relationship with his people is a covenant
relationship with a personal, internalized and ethical emphasis rather
than one guaranteed through the king at the state sanctuary.

The original pre-exilic deuteronomistic history was transformed by
a comprehensive redaction, traceable from Deuteronomy 4 to 2 Kgs
25.27-30. It constitutes a creative retrieval of tradition to meet the needs
of an emerging people without statehood, in which Yahweh's relationship is directly with his people and the role of the king little more than
that of an exemplary Israelite. Thus the connection between the interests of the state and the interests of Yahweh is broken,[36] not simply

(ed.), *Bundesdokument und Gesetz: Studien zum Deuteronomium* (Freiburg: Herder,
1995), pp. 1-4.
    36. Albertz's description of the theological syntheses achieved by deuteronomic

through sophisticated theological reflection, but within the framework of the end of statehood, when a new legitimation had to be developed. The state had been destroyed, political institutions formerly legitimated by the pre-exilic deuteronomist at an end; the emerging remnant, dependent on a foreign power, is compelled to establish its religious identity without recourse to political organs of statecraft.

(3) Aspects of the movement between the first and subsequent editions of the deuteronomistic history can be illuminated by the work of Mary Douglas and Jürgen Habermas. Douglas has considered the intellectual dimensions of the move from a society characterized by mechanical solidarity to one characterized by organic solidarity:[37] just as societies develop by increasing institutional diversification and proliferation, so also there is 'a comparable movement in the realm of ideas'.[38] This does not mean simply increasing complexity, because undifferentiated societies often exhibit highly complex, diversified and elaborate cosmologies. Rather, the development may be described on the basis of

> the Kantian principle that thought can only advance by freeing itself from the shackles of its own subjective conditions. The first Copernican revolution, the discovery that only man's subjective viewpoint made the sun seem to revolve round the earth, is continually renewed. In our own culture mathematics first and later logic, now history, now language and now thought processes themselves and even knowledge of the self and of society, are fields of knowledge progressively freed from the subjective limitations of the mind.[39]

---

theology (*History of Israelite Religion*, pp. 224-31) may be better related to the later stages of the work of the deuteronomistic movement rather than to the Josianic period to which Albertz relates them. On the place of origin of this later stage of the work of the deuteronomistic movement, whether Palestine or the exile, see the discussion in Schramm, *Opponents of Third Isaiah*, p. 57; T. Veijola, 'Martin Noth's *Überlieferungsgeschichtliche Studien* and Old Testament Theology', in McKenzie and Graham (eds.), *The History of Israel's Traditions*, p. 126.

37. On this development, which comes to expression especially in the sociology of Durkheim, see Mayes, *Old Testament in Sociological Perspective*, pp. 28-29.

38. Cf. M. Douglas, *Purity and Danger: An Analysis of the Concepts of Pollution and Taboo* (London: Routledge & Kegan Paul, 1966), pp. 77-78.

39. Douglas, *Purity and Danger*, p. 78

In undifferentiated cultures the

> world revolves around the observer who is trying to interpret his experi-
> ences. Gradually he separates himself from his environment and per-
> ceives his real limitations and powers.[40]

Habermas has used cognitive psychology to understand the moral development not only of the individual but of society.[41] The stages of ego development, through which the individual passes until no longer accepting traditional assertions, values and norms, provide a model for the evolution of a society's self-understanding. Both child and society move from a cognitive and moral egocentrism to being able to think reflectively with full awareness of the relative standpoint of the self. In terms of social development this means a move from a world view marked by the mythological legitimation of social structures to the eventual point of a break with mythological thought and its replacement by a cosmology founded on philosophical reflection. Such learning pro-cesses are prompted by contingent circumstances, and, in the case of Israel, these would have to include the effect on Israel's self-under-standing of contact with the world powers of that day.

In Israel the mythological legitimation of royal and religious struc-tures of society came under the radical criticism of the classical proph-ets, which effectively broke down the egocentrism of the traditional Israelite world view and left the way open to a more reflective, non-mythological universalism. The deuteronomistic theology of Israel's election shows Israel gradually freeing itself from cognitive and moral egocentrism, representing the outcome of that struggle to fit traditional Israelite belief to an emergent universalism. Yahweh's relationship with his people is now a matter of free choice. This development was a creative response to, though at the same time an inevitable outcome of, Israel's encounter with a world view which constituted an alternative attraction to traditional Yahwism. Deuteronomy is an explicit ideology, re-appropriating, systematizing and legitimizing traditional Israelite belief in the face of alternative possibilities, an example of what Haber-mas has described as the 'endogenous' learning process: an internal development of existing potential in response to contingent conditions.

---

40. Douglas, *Purity and Danger*, p. 80.
41. J. Habermas, *Communication and the Evolution of Society* (London: Heine-mann, 1979), pp. 95-129; cf. also A.D.H. Mayes, 'On Describing the Purpose of Deuteronomy', *JSOT* 58 (1993), pp. 26-27.

Lohfink has rightly argued that the deuteronomistic systematization of tradition is to be seen in terms of new ideas 'present in the tradition but not so self-evident' being realized; it represents 'long present possibilities' of Israel's own culture, 'a systematization which proceeds from a new conceptual viewpoint which was previously foreign to the systematized material or at most only dimly perceived in it'.[42]

Deuteronomistic theology is, then, an explicit ideology developed in response to the conditions of late-seventh-century and early-sixth-century Judah, as a means by which the newly emerging Israel, the people of Yahweh, might identify itself, both for itself and for others, articulating its goals and justifying them through an account of how it related to others and how it overcame its own internal conflicts.

III

(1) In my view, a clear distinction between ideology and theology can scarcely be established: one may speak of a more or less adequate ideology, or of a more or less adequate theology, but both connote a systematic expression of ideas, the articulation of a world view in opposition to others. This position differs from that of Miller and Brueggemann.[43] For Miller, as already noted, ideology is the expression of self-

42. N. Lohfink, 'Culture Shock and Theology', *BTB* 7 (1977), pp. 17, 19. Lohfink, who has clearly recognized the relationship of Deuteronomy to a situation of culture shock, has related this culture shock to the impact of the Assyrians on Judah. The increasing weakness of Assyria through the seventh century and their eventual collapse before the power of the Babylonians make it more likely, however, that it is the confrontation with Babylon and the effects of the fall of Judah and Jerusalem which lie at the heart of this culture shock. While the significance of culture shock should not be underestimated, it is also true, of course, that the deuteronomistic history is not to be interpreted solely in terms of an assertion of Israelite values over against a non-Israelite alternative. That is to say, there is implicit in the deuteronomistic edition of Deuteronomy a call for Israel to reform through rejecting those practices which were very much a feature of her own culture. In this respect, the deuteronomistic edition of Deuteronomy stands very much in line with the pre-exilic prophetic critique of Israel.

43. Brueggemann's approach to Old Testament theology has marked similarities to that of Mendenhall and Herion to the Old Testament and Israelite history (cf. G.E. Mendenhall, 'The Conflict between Value Systems and Social Control', in H. Goedicke and J.J.M. Roberts [eds.], *Unity and Diversity* [Baltimore: The Johns Hopkins University Press, 1975], pp. 169-80; G.A. Herion, 'The Role of Historical Narrative in Biblical Thought', *JSOT* 21 [1981], pp. 25-57). There is the same

interest; faith is that which transcends self-interest and is marked by self-criticism, by a positive relationship between Israel and the nations and by the demand for justice and righteousness. Brueggemann, similarly, recognizes the legitimating ideological role of most of the Old Testament, but attempts 'to identify those passages in which there is a breakthrough to a non-ideological, non-legitimating theology which is open to new possibilities of speaking of Yahweh'. The Old Testament fully participates in what Brueggemann thinks of as the common, conventional theology of its time, but it also struggles to be free of that theology and is 'open to *the embrace of pain* which is experienced from "underneath" in the processes of social interaction and conflict'. Thus the God of Israel is variously presented as a god much like the other ancient Near Eastern gods, but also as a God who, unlike the gods of common theology, 'is exposed in the fray...a God peculiarly available in Israel's historical experiences'.[44]

For Brueggemann, the common, conventional theology in which the Old Testament shares is concerned with order in creation, guaranteed by God, beyond history; it is a theology which serves the interests of the ruling class which leads back the current social structure to its origins in order in creation. It expresses the relationship between Yahweh and Israel in contractual terms: Israel sins, Yahweh reacts in anger to destroy her. Yet the crushing orthodoxy of conventional, contractual theology is also questioned: Yahweh is patient, holding to his promises, even in the face of disobedience, and so not to be confined to the closed theological categories. This dysfunction in the relationship between God and Israel comes to expression whenever the dominance of structure legitimation comes under question; it is a cry, not only of Israel, but of

operating paradigm which distinguishes urban and rural, privileged and oppressed, the same value judgments, the same attempt to find values objectively stated in the Old Testament and somehow free of any ideological distortions. Suggestive as these studies are, they cannot succeed in providing the disinterested justifications of certain values which their authors seek. Brueggemann's approach comes to expression in many of the essays in the two volumes of his collected essays (*Old Testament Theology* [ed. P.D. Miller; Minneapolis: Fortress Press, 1992]; *A Social Reading of the Old Testament* [ed. P.D. Miller; Minneapolis: Fortress Press, 1994]). The essay in which it is developed in most detail is 'A Shape for Old Testament Theology', in *Old Testament Theology*, pp. 1-44, reprinted in abbreviated form in Ollenburger, Martens and Hasel (eds.), *The Flowering of Old Testament Theology*, pp. 409-26.

44. Brueggemann, 'A Shape for Old Testament Theology', pp. 4-5.

Yahweh too, against the limitations of conventional theological categories, a restless probing which refuses to be satisfied with contract
theology.[45] It is this which must form the primary material for Old
Testament theology. In breaking with conventional theology Yahweh is
brought much closer to the pain that Israel experiences. The theological
counter-theme does not supersede or nullify conventional theology, but
stands in tension with it, 'an ongoing tension, unresolved and unresolv-
able',[46] which must be maintained in all fruitful biblical theology.

It is unlikely that such a distinction between ideology and faith/the-
ology is in the end tenable. That theology or faith can somehow be non-
ideological presupposes that ideology is simply a direct reflection of
material circumstances on the part of the privileged, while faith or theology is the protest against, and the rejection of, the oppression which
ideology thus involves. But ideology always has a polemical function:
from the beginning it belongs in the context of opposition to other ideologies. The 'embrace of pain' which Brueggemann believes to characterize the primary material of Old Testament theology is Israel's breakthrough to new ideologies which arise as the old and traditional fail to
maintain conviction in the face of developing conditions. The contribution of deuteronomistic theology or ideology to the theology or ideology of the Old Testament is, therefore, not to be understood in terms of
a contrast between ideology and a non-ideological theology, but rather
in terms of how the Old Testament has received the deuteronomistic
history. It is the history of the deuteronomistic history in its reception in
the Old Testament which brings to light the themes and concepts which
are considered by the Old Testament to be of fundamental importance
and which may consequently be held to express the deuteronomistic
contribution to Old Testament theology.

---

45. So, Hos. 11.1-7 concludes its conventional theology with the declaration:
'My people are bent on turning away from me; so they are appointed to the yoke,
and none shall remove it'; but what immediately follows breaks with this conventional theology and cannot be separated from this passage: 'How can I give you up,
O Ephraim. How can I hand you over, O Israel! How can I make you like Admah!
How can I treat you like Zeboiim! My heart recoils within me, my compassion
grows warm and tender. I will not execute my fierce anger, I will not again destroy
Ephraim; for I am God and not man, the holy one in your midst, and I will not come
to destroy.'

46. Brueggemann, 'A Shape for Old Testament Theology', p. 414.

(2) Political developments in the postexilic period, while at first per-haps favouring the ideology of the revised deuteronomistic history, in the end made it clear that the revision of that history did not go far enough. The initial period of the return, the building of the temple and the existence of a descendant of Jehoiachin, Zerubbabel, provided a social and historical context within which the deuteronomistic history could provide a meaningful foundation for the new community. For at least three reasons, however, this role could not be maintained. In the first place, the Persian administration could not tolerate the apocalyptic nationalism of the prophets, with their proclamation of a restored Davidic monarchy and the rise of Jerusalem to become a world centre ruled by a priest-king (Hag. 2.23; Zech. 2.5-9, 16), and the sudden disappearance of Haggai, Zechariah and Zerubbabel may indicate Persian intervention to subdue this subject people.[47] The deuteronomistic history, with its emphasis on temple and monarchy, became increasingly irrelevant to these changed conditions. Secondly, even though temple and monarchy played a less emphatic role in the second edition of the deuteronomistic history, there was little possibility that the work could command the adherence of the diaspora. The deuteronomistic prayer of Solomon in 1 Kings 8 makes reference to the effectiveness of the temple for the exiles when they turn towards it in prayer (1 Kgs 8.48), but that tended to increase rather than decrease the significance of the temple as central sanctuary, and thereby to undermine the integrity and validity of the communities of the diaspora in their own right. Thirdly, even though the second edition incorporated the social and ethical concerns of prophecy, still that history could not be reconciled with the radical cultic critique of the prophets, particularly in the form in which that critique was developed in the deuteronomistic edition of Jeremiah. The radical questioning of the Jerusalem temple and its effectiveness in maintaining Yahweh's relation with his people was hardly compatible with a presentation of Israel in history for which the temple had the

---

47. Cf. Albertz, *History of Israelite Religion*, pp. 450-54. Alternatively, or, indeed, in addition, one might suggest that the promotion of Zerubbabel met opposition from within the land, and that it was in the context of inner-Judaean conflict that the claims his supporters represented were suppressed. For the divided world of postexilic Judaism, see R.P. Carroll, 'So What Do We *Know* About the Temple?', in T.C. Eskenazi and K.H. Richards (eds.), *Second Temple Studies* (JSOTSup, 175; Sheffield: JSOT Press, 1994), pp. 34-51, and D.J.A. Clines, 'Haggai's Temple, Constructed, Deconstructed and Reconstructed', in the same volume, pp. 60-87.

central role which the deuteronomist considered appropriate.

Those same conditions which meant that the deuteronomistic history could not adequately function as a foundation document for the postexilic community also form the context for the emergence of the Pentateuch. The literary processes involved need not be developed here, but should be understood along the lines sketched out by Rendtorff, Rose and more recently Blum.[48] As a document which has appropriated Deuteronomy from the deuteronomistic history the Pentateuch may be seen as a response, providing ideological corrections and modifications, to the deuteronomistic history. The Pentateuchal response introduces a greater emphasis on the social and ethical demands which the deuteronomistic history had tended to downplay; it emphasizes the role of priesthood and sacrifice; it avoids the title Yahweh Zebaoth with its unmistakable royal associations, although it also develops deuteronomistic references to Yahweh as creator (Deut. 4.32) into a creation theology (Gen. 1); through its emphasis on promise and on the law as that which was to be obeyed in the land, its orientation is to the future rather than to the past; the Pentateuch, much more than the deuteronomistic history, holds out for Israel a strong and explicit hope to sustain it in its powerlessness.

This suggests that the theme which should be a major focus of a study of deuteronomistic theology, and how that theology was received in the wider Old Testament context, is how the deuteronomist perceives the nature of Israel in its relationship to Yahweh and how the Pentateuch responds to that perception. This theme is suggested also by our earlier discussion of ideology in general and deuteronomistic ideology in particular, for if ideology is essentially to do with world view as legitimation for present social and political arrangements, then the perception of the nature of Israel must be the focus also for a discussion of deuteronomistic ideology.

(3) The deuteronomistic perception of the nature of Israel and its relationship with Yahweh developed between the first and second editions of the history: the first edition perceives Israel as a royal state, with the king as successor to Moses in the role of lawgiver and

---

48. Cf. R. Rendtorff, *Das überlieferungsgeschichtliche Problem des Pentateuch* (BZAW, 147; Berlin: W. de Gruyter, 1977); M. Rose, *Deuteronomist und Jahwist* (ATANT, 67; Zürich: Theologischer Verlag, 1981); E. Blum, *Studien zur Komposition des Pentateuch* (BZAW, 189; Berlin: W. de Gruyter, 1990). See also the discussion in Mayes, *The Story of Israel*, pp. 139-49.

mediator between Israel and Yahweh; the revision, introducing theological commentary such as 2 Kgs 17.7-23 and 34b-41,[49] effected a change of interest from the king to Israel as a whole: it is on the people and not on the king that responsibility for the welfare of Israel rests. The revision of the deuteronomic law aims at a sharper definition of this new perception of Israel. This code now presents 'the divinely authorized social order that Israel must implement to secure its collective political existence as the people of God';[50] it is a comprehensive social charter that sets political objectives and in particular safeguards each individual as a person possessing a sphere of genuine autonomy.

The deuteronomic law does have a community dimension, but equally clearly aims at the reformation of individual attitudes and practices; each individual's relationship with Yahweh is to be characterized by that exclusiveness which had hitherto characterized official Yahwistic religion.[51] The fundamental concern with individual attitudes and practices accounts for a notable feature of the lawbook to which Stuhlman in particular has drawn attention:[52] Deuteronomy's concern with the nature and survival of Israel fits rather uneasily with a certain lack of clarity in the definition of Israel. The attitude towards those who do not belong to the people is clearly expressed in the demand that when Israel enters the land all centres of foreign worship are to be destroyed, there is to be no inter-marriage with the Canaanites, and Israel is to be separate, 'a people holy to the Lord your God' (Deut. 7). But the nature of the membership of this Israel is obscure. It is not based on genealogical descent; Ammonites and Moabites are excluded, but not Edomites who, in the third generation, may be accepted (Deut. 23.4-9); marriage with a foreign woman taken captive in war is permitted (Deut. 21.10-14); Israelites should constantly care for the *gērîm*, who must include true foreigners and not simply Israelites away from home, living in her

49. Cf. Mayes, *The Story of Israel*, pp. 126-27.

50. S.D. McBride, 'The Polity of the Covenant People: The Book of Deuteronomy', *Int* 41 (1987), p. 233. McBride's study is intended as a correction to the presentation of the deuteronomic law as teaching or instruction, a view promoted by Noth and von Rad in particular, rather than as constitutional law. See the discussion in Mayes, 'On Describing the Purpose', pp. 13-33.

51. Cf. Albertz, *History of Israelite Religion*, pp. 210-16.

52. L. Stulman, 'Encroachment in Deuteronomy: An Analysis of the Social World of the D Code', *JBL* 109 (1990), pp. 613-32.

midst. This lack of consistency is defined by Stuhlman as an incongruity between ideology and social reality: the ideology is one of clear distinction and separation; the social reality, of Israel in her world, is one where the boundaries are insufficiently clear to make this possible. Stuhlman has shown that the 'outsiders' and 'foreigners' against whom Israel is warned are groups *within* the community, deviants involved in religious and social practices which are not true to the community as understood by Deuteronomy and must be purged so as to sustain internal coherence of ideology and social reality. The deuteronomic lawcode aims to restore a people whose social and political (and religious) boundaries have been broken down, in which Israelites faithful to the past are confused with Israelites assimilated to the peoples of the environment. It tries to persuade faithful Israelites to separate themselves from those who threaten her with internal disintegration.

(4) A useful way of understanding the nature of Israel in Deuteronomy, and appreciating how that understanding is modified in the Pentateuch is made available by Eilberg-Schwartz's distinction between societies where the status of the individual is ascribed and those in which it is achieved.[53] Ascribed status depends upon qualities such as age, sex and kinship ties, whereas achieved status is based upon success in achieving certain goals. In the former, the freedom of individuals to have control over their lives is severely restricted; the world is experienced objectively as a given, and objects are designated as taboo or impure because of their objective inherent qualities. Where status is achieved, on the other hand, the world and one's place in it are not fixed and immutable; just as one's status depends on one's action in the world, so also impurity and pollution are not objective qualities but rather result from what one does and derive from within.

Eilberg-Schwartz has used this approach to make essential distinctions between the priestly community, on the one hand, and the early Christian community on the other. In the priestly community, membership is determined by genealogical descent (ascribed); correspondingly, the priestly law understands impurity as an intrinsic quality of certain kinds of objects. In the early Christian community, on the other hand,

---

53. H. Eilberg-Schwartz, *The Savage in Judaism: An Anthropology of Israelite Religion and Ancient Judaism* (Bloomington: Indiana University Press, 1990), pp. 195-216.

genealogical descent is replaced by commitment to belief; correspondingly, objective impurity is replaced by the view that pollution derives from the conscious acts of individuals.

The principle alerts us to an important distinction between deuteronomistic and Pentateuchal perceptions of community. For the deuteronomistic history, status in society is achieved; one becomes a member of the Yahwistic community by commitment to belief, and not through genealogical descent. Correspondingly, it is from within that evil has to be rooted out and abolished. 'In the deuteronomic view, sanctity is not a taboo that inheres in things which by nature belong to the divine realm but is rather a consequence of the religious intentions of the person who consecrates it.'[54] For the Pentateuch, membership of the Israelite community is by genealogical descent, so that society and the world are objective givens, and impurity is an objectively intrinsic quality of certain objects. It might be conceded that in the deuteronomic law there is a tendency towards the Pentateuchal understanding of community, especially in laws relating to Moabites, Ammonites and physical imperfection (Deut. 23.2-9 [EVV 1-8]), where status is ascribed rather than achieved. Similarly, in the deuteronomistic history a source of weakness and danger to Israel is recognized to be inter-marriage. Yet in general, Deuteronomy and the deuteronomistic history do not adopt a genealogical understanding of the constitution of Israel. 'For them, Israel's identity depended on its vocation and the response to its call.'[55]

Thus, a remarkable development through the different stages of the deuteronomistic history to the creation of the Pentateuch is centrally related to the nature of community, and to Israel in its relationship to Yahweh. In the first edition of the deuteronomistic history, Israel is a state with its constitutional monarchy; in the second, Israel is a theocracy with power effectively removed from the monarchy, seeking to achieve a new self-understanding as an open yet confessional commu-

---

54. M. Weinfeld, *Deuteronomy and the Deuteronomic School* (Oxford: Oxford University Press, 1972), p. 215.

55. T. Römer, 'The Book of Deuteronomy', in McKenzie and Graham (eds.), *The History of Israel's Traditions*, p. 207. For this reason, if for no other, I would tend to agree with Römer's view that the identification of the fathers in Deuteronomy as the patriarchs Abraham, Isaac and Jacob, rather than as the ancestors of the present generation and especially those who had come out of Egypt in the exodus, belongs to a post-deuteronomistic stage when Deuteronomy was being connected to the Pentateuch.

nity, with widely dispersed social and political arrangements subject to divine authority; in the Pentateuch, this community is both more sharply and objectively defined, and set in a reflective, universalistic context. This development reflects the struggle of Israel to bring to expression a self-understanding appropriate to both its historical context and its own social development.

(5) The social development which distinguishes the first edition of the deuteronomistic history from the second and from the Pentateuch is the loss of independent statehood and Israel's reduction to the status of a dependent or 'pariah' people.[56] The second edition of the deuteronomistic history reflects a transitional stage in this social development in the sense that, betraying a concern to call Israel to a fresh self-understanding, it is an ideology which stands opposed to possible alternative views of how Israel should develop, views perhaps such as those expressed through postexilic apocalyptic prophecy; with the emergence of the Pentateuch, however, it is the deuteronomistic view which is established as the only acceptable understanding.

In this context, the second edition of the deuteronomistic history may be described, using the terminology applied by Gottwald to Second Isaiah, as both determined and as a determinant.[57] It is determined in the sense that it took shape within the social and political context of exile and loss of statehood; it is a determinant in the sense that it projects an identity for the new Israel which is that appropriate to the status of a pariah people, living in economic and political dependence. This is what Israel was in the process of becoming; this is the Israelite identity confirmed and established in the Pentateuch.

---

56. The term is, of course, that used of postexilic Judaism by Weber (*From Max Weber*, p. 189). See also the discussion in Mayes, *Old Testament in Sociological Perspective*, pp. 20, 37, 45, 47-48, 80, 84, 144.

57. The limitations of the term 'determined' will be clear from our discussion of the meaning of 'ideology'; more appropriate, probably, is 'motivated'.

INDEXES

INDEX OF REFERENCES

OLD TESTAMENT

Genesis		14.8	239	14.13-19	83
1	159, 476	14.13	339	15.30	239
3	87	15	458	21.7	312
4.17-24	88	16	39	25.6-18	389
4.25-26	88	18	86	31.1-54	389
4.26	88	19–24	39	33.3	239
5.28-29	88	20.2-6	87	35	92
6.13	393	20.22–23.33	108		
9.13	393	21–23	319, 468	Deuteronomy	
12.1-3	458	32–34	39	1–Josh. 22	96
14.18-20	394	32	450	1–2 Kgs 25	389
15	389	32.7-8	87	1–4	87
18.2	369	32.9-15	87	1–3	51, 103,
18.16-33	87	32.19-20	87		363, 394
18.17-19	458	32.20-32	87	1	83
21.21	243	32.34	87	1.1	428
22.13	369	34.1	87	1.3	103
24.63	369	34.4	87	1.5-18	103
26.5	39	34.8-10	87	1.8	428
31.10	369	34.11-12	87	1.19-45	450
33.1	369	34.14-28	87	1.19-33	83
37.25	369	34.28-29	87	1.37	83
		35.1	427	1.40-42	339
Exodus				3.3	376
1–2	244	Leviticus		3.10	58
3	298	5.15	365	3.12-22	103
3.7-8	87	26.40	365	3.18-20	103
3.15	370, 378	26.45	409	3.20	273
4.1	87			4–30	51
4.5	87	Numbers		4	469
4.8-9	87	5.6	365	4.2	25
5	340	5.12	365	4.19-20	64
13	39	5.27	365	4.25-31	58
13.3-16	83, 87	11.28	25	4.30	135
13.17	339	13–14	83	4.32	476

Deuteronomy (cont.)		16–18	319	19.14	409	
4.44–5.27	87	16	321	19.16-19	110	
5–30	107	16.1-15	110	20	110	
5–11	109	16.18–18.22	110, 468,	20.16	363	
5.2-3	87		469	21.8-21	110	
5.3	410	16.18–17.13	319, 320	21.10-14	110, 477	
5.4	450	16.18-20	321	22.5	110	
5.23-25	450	16.18	320	22.13-21	110	
5.33	414	16.19	320	22.23-27	110	
6.2–9.6	87	16.20	320	23.2-9	479	
6.4–30.20	39	16.21–17.1	110	23.4-9	477	
6.4-9	111	16.21-22	321	23.10-15	110	
6.4-5	64, 109	17	105, 322,	23.18-19	110	
6.5	466		324, 334,	24.7	110	
6.10-13	109		340, 342	25.13-16	110	
6.12-26	111	17.1-7	321	25.17-19	110	
6.12-19	103	17.2-7	110	25.19	273	
6.14	323	17.8-13	110, 320	26.1-11	110	
6.28-30	111	17.14-20	290, 319,	27	394	
7	477		322, 333,	28	65, 104,	
7.1-6	379		341, 342		106	
7.8	413	17.14-17	335	28.15-69	413	
7.17-26	379	17.14-15	332	28.20-27	111	
7.23	363	17.14	302, 322,	28.68	339, 413	
8.18	413		323, 325,	29.24	412	
9.4-6	389		326, 332,	31	51, 103,	
9.7-24	450		334		280	
9.9-29	87	17.15-17	336	31.1-8	25	
9.20	312	17.15	328, 330,	31.7	103	
9.28	87		334-37	31.9-12	87	
10.1-15	87	17.16-20	333	31.14-23	25	
11.29-30	51	17.16-17	335	33	458	
11.29	103	17.16	336, 339	34	51, 373	
12–26	51	17.17	335, 336,	34.5	280	
12	110, 363,		338, 342	34.10-12	25	
	440, 441	17.18-20	334, 341	34.10	26	
12.2–26.15	109, 110	17.18-19	335, 336			
12.2–16.17	468	17.18	341	*Joshua*		
12.10	273, 323	17.20	335, 336,	1–24	116	
12.18	468		342	1–12	27, 40,	
13.1	25	18	319		113, 361,	
13.2-6	110	18.1-8	110, 468		378, 379	
13.8	323	18.10-12	110	1–11	102	
14	468	18.18	402	1–3	60, 372	
14.22-27	110	18.21-22	468	1	49, 60, 62,	
15	105	19–25	110, 468		67, 103,	
15.19-23	110	19	92		112, 383	
15.22-24	110	19.1–25.19	469	1.1-9	25, 427	

1.1-6	62	5.13	369
1.1-2	373, 374, 378, 383	5.14	369, 370
		5.15	370
1.1	280, 373	6–8	373
1.2	62, 280	6	114, 370-72, 374, 378, 396
1.4	62		
1.5	370		
1.6	62, 103	6.1-25	371, 383
1.7-9	67	6.1-24	369
1.7	62, 280	6.1	372
1.11	60, 91	6.2-5	370
1.12-18	378	6.2	370-73
1.12	103	6.3-5	371
1.13-15	378	6.4	371
1.13	103, 273, 280	6.5	371
1.15	91, 273	6.6	371, 372
1.17	378	6.12	371, 373
2–12	112, 113	6.14	371
2–9	50	6.15	371
2–8	112, 362	6.16	371, 372
2	60, 113, 114, 373, 374, 378, 395	6.17	372
		6.20	371
		6.21	372
		6.22-23	374, 384
2.1-24	384	6.24	372
2.6-10	37	6.25	374, 384
2.10	363	7–8	364, 368
2.12	374	7	290, 364
2.17	374	7.1-5	364
2.20	374	7.1	364, 365
3–9	378	7.2-5	366, 367, 381
3–6	367		
3–4	114, 373	7.2	365, 366
3.1	373, 374	7.5	365
3.2-4	60	7.6-26	366, 368
3.2	60, 363	7.6-8	368
3.3	373	7.6	365, 367
3.5	373	7.7-9	365
3.6	373	7.7	374
3.7	370, 378	7.9-15	368
3.15	378	7.9	374
4.14	370, 378	7.10-15	365
5.1	364, 375	7.10	373
5.13–6.24	369	7.16-18	289, 368
5.13-15	369, 370, 382	7.16	373
		7.18	365
5.13-14	370, 371	7.26	364, 365

8	113, 364-66, 368, 372, 378		
8.1-29	365		
8.1-9	366		
8.1-2	365-67		
8.1	365-67, 373, 376		
8.2	365		
8.3-9	365, 367		
8.3	365-67		
8.5	372		
8.6	372		
8.7	367		
8.8	367		
8.9	366		
8.10-25	365, 367, 381		
8.10	366, 367, 372, 373		
8.11-25	382		
8.11	367		
8.12	366		
8.13	366		
8.14	366, 367, 372		
8.15	368		
8.16	367		
8.17	367, 368		
8.18	367, 370		
8.19	367		
8.20	372		
8.21	368		
8.22	368, 376		
8.23	368		
8.24	368		
8.26-29	365		
8.26	366-68		
8.28-29	368		
8.29	366		
8.30-35	51, 112		
8.30	103		
8.33	321		
9	361, 363, 364, 368, 373-75, 379, 381		

Joshua (cont.)		10.40-43	385
9.1-2	361, 363, 379	10.40	376
9.1	375	10.41	376
9.3-27	361, 380	10.42	376
9.3	362	10.43	376
9.6	362	11	377
9.7	362	11.1-9	377, 385
9.9-27	381	11.1	375
9.9-10	363	11.3	377
9.14	362	11.6-9	386
9.15	363	11.7	365
9.16	363	11.8	376
9.17	363	11.9	377
9.18-21	363	11.10-11	386
9.24	363, 378	11.10	377
9.26	363	11.11	377
9.27	362, 363, 372	11.16-23	386
		11.16-17	377
10–12	364, 365, 372, 374, 375, 378	12	49, 377, 378, 386
		12.1-6	377, 378
10–11	378	12.1	377
10	113, 376, 377	12.7-24	377, 378
10.1-15	375	12.7-8	378
10.1	375	12.7	375
10.2-14	27	12.9	378
10.3-4	375	12.20	377
10.4	376	12.24	377
10.5	375, 376	13–22	112, 114
10.7	365	13–21	115
10.8	375	13	67
10.10-11	375	13.1-7	114
10.12-14	375	13.1-6	67
10.12	375	13.29	365
10.13	27, 375	14–22	114
10.16-27	375, 376, 384	14.1-5	115
10.17-27	376	14.2-3	365
10.17	376	19.49-51	115
10.21	376	20	92, 368
10.23	376	21.42	273
10.28-39	376, 379, 385	21.43-45	62, 112
10.28	376, 379	21.44	323
10.29	376	22–24	40
10.33	376	22.1-8	378
		22.1-6	112
		22.4	273
		22.5	36
		22.10-24	395

22.16	365		
22.20	365		
22.31	365		
23–24	67		
23	49, 50, 67, 87, 109, 112, 115, 116, 280		
23.1	273		
23.2	321, 378		
23.11	36		
24	86, 109, 112, 115, 116, 139, 289, 452		
24.1-28	64		
24.1	321		
24.3	116		
24.4	116		
24.28-33	37		
24.29	26		
24.33	26		
Judges			
1–2.5	67		
1	27, 36, 53, 59, 119		
1.1–2.9	67		
1.1–2.5	116, 119, 139		
2	316		
2.1-5	64, 288		
2.6–16.31	61		
2.6–13.1	117		
2.6–3.6	43		
2.6-23	37, 116		
2.6-10	87, 119		
2.11–12.6	102		
2.11-23	49		
2.11-19	87		
2.12-23	103		
2.12	323		
2.14-15	446		
2.14	323		
2.16-19	321		
2.17	67		
2.20-21	67		
2.20	412		

2.23	67	7.16-22	118	17–21	36, 43, 53,
3–16	119	7.22-25	117		96, 117,
3	62, 120	8.3-4	117		121-23,
3.7–12.15	36	8.5-21	118		139, 317,
3.7-11	117	8.5-9	117		396
3.9	328	8.10-14	117	17–18	122
3.10	321	8.14-21	117	17.6	317, 318
3.12	117	8.22-32	331	18.1	317
3.13	117	8.22-23	117	18.30	30
3.14	117	8.23	318	19–21	122
3.15-26	117	8.28	117	19	122
3.15	117, 328	8.29	117	19.1	122, 317
3.16-26	118	8.31	117	20–21	122, 312
3.27-29	117	8.34	323	20	311
3.30	117	9	233, 234,	21.25	122, 317
4.1	117		244, 316,		
4.2-3	117		396	*1 Samuel*	
4.2	377	9.1-7	117	1–10	300
4.4	117, 321	9.7-15	247	1–8	297
4.6-9	117	9.8-15	118	1–6	306
4.11	117	9.16	117	1–4	123
4.14	370	9.19-21	117	1–3	123, 332,
4.17-22	117, 120	9.23-24	117		397
4.17	117	9.25-41	118	1	317
4.23-24	117	9.41-45	117	1.1-3	123
5	118, 120,	9.50-54	118	1.3	123, 124
	458	9.56-57	117	1.4-28	123
5.4	370	10.1-16	120	2	270
5.24-27	120	10.1-5	118, 121,	2.1-10	37
5.31	117		316, 321	2.12-17	123
6	298	10.6-16	43, 311	2.12-16	124
6.1-2	117	10.6-10	305	2.19-21	123
6.2-5	117	10.10	328	2.22-25	123, 124
6.6	328	10.11-16	288	2.27-36	43, 124
6.7-10	64, 288	10.17–12.6	120	2.35	310
6.7	328	11.1-11	118	3	123
6.11-17	117	11.1-2	241	4–6	124, 297
6.11	118	11.29-40	27	4	124, 311
6.18-24	118	11.30-31	120	4.1–7.1	269, 270
6.25-32	120	11.34-40	120	4.18	321
6.25-27	117	12.1-7	316	7–12	95, 293,
6.31	117	12.7-15	120, 121,		312, 317
6.32-34	117		316, 321	7–8	125, 397
7.1	117	12.8-15	118	7	38, 123,
7.3-11	117	13–16	36, 117,		287, 297,
7.11-16	118		121		308, 310-
7.11	117	15.20	321		12, 332
7.13-21	117	16.31	321	7.1	270, 311

1 Samuel (cont.)		8.6	303, 324,	9.14	295, 296
7.2–8.22	43, 312		327, 332	9.15-17	295
7.2-4	311	8.7-9	325	9.15	297
7.2	311	8.7-8	302, 331	9.16	269, 271,
7.3-14	311	8.7	291, 302,		295, 297,
7.3-4	37, 288,		303, 325,		298
	311		327	9.18-19	296
7.3	36, 311	8.8	301-303	9.18	295
7.5-17	311	8.9-10	332	9.19	294, 297
7.5-12	311	8.9	290, 301,	9.20-21	295, 296
7.5	311, 312		302, 325,	9.20	295, 296
7.6	310		327	9.21	291, 295
7.7-11	297	8.10	302	9.22-24	295, 296
7.7	328	8.11-18	303	9.22	296
7.8	312, 328	8.11-17	302, 303,	9.24-27	296
7.12	37		305, 325	9.24	421
7.13-14	311	8.17	325	9.27	292
7.13	311	8.18-22	302	10	300
7.15–8.5	310	8.18-20	332	10.1	271, 295-
7.15-17	287, 310	8.18	301, 303,		99, 301,
7.15	321		327, 328,		309
7.16	321		330	10.2-6	299
8–12	29, 56,	8.19	291, 298,	10.2-4	294, 296
	124, 286-		301, 325	10.2	294
	88, 291,	8.20-22	331	10.3-4	290
	301, 304,	8.20	301-303,	10.5-6	294, 296,
	307, 308,		326		299, 300
	310-12	8.21	327	10.5	296
8–11	304, 307	8.22	302, 327,	10.6	295
8	38, 56, 88,		332	10.7	294-97
	287, 291,	9–11	287, 291,	10.8	287, 296
	301, 302,		297, 300,	10.9	295, 296
	304, 305,		301	10.10-13	294, 296,
	322, 325,	9	317		299, 300
	326, 331,	9.1–10.16	287, 289,	10.10	291
	332		291, 293,	10.13-16	296
8.1-22	287, 323		296, 298-	10.14-16	291-93,
8.1-7	302		301, 304,		296, 297,
8.1-6	302		307, 308,		300, 301,
8.1-5	302, 331,		327, 328		308
	332	9.1–10.6	296	10.16	293
8.1-3	287, 302	9.1-13	294	10.17-27	43, 125,
8.3	302	9.1-8	296		287, 288,
8.4	298	9.2	289, 294,		290-94,
8.5	301, 322-		296		298, 300-
	27, 332	9.9	294, 296		302, 304,
8.6-22	70	9.10-13	296		305, 307,
8.6-20	302	9.13	295, 296		308, 312,

10.17-27 (cont.)		11.12-13	292, 293,
	327, 329,		300
	332	11.12	292
10.17-25	293	11.14-15	298, 300,
10.17-24	328, 329		301
10.17-19	56, 287,	11.14	292, 293,
	288, 291		301
10.17	289, 290,	11.15	292, 300,
	331		306
10.18-19	290, 302,	12	37, 38, 49,
	331		50, 56, 70,
10.18	288, 291,		88, 125,
	331		139, 280,
10.19-27	289, 290,		289, 304-
	331		308, 330,
10.19	290, 291,		332, 397,
	331		452
10.20-24	289	12.1-25	43, 287,
10.20-21	289		312
10.20	288	12.1-6	331, 332
10.21	289	12.1-5	304, 305
10.22	289	12.2	305
10.24	271, 291,	12.3	304
	328	12.5	304
10.25	289, 290,	12.6-25	288, 304
	292	12.6-13	331
10.26-27	290-93,	12.6-12	330
	300, 301,	12.6	304
	308	12.8-11	305
10.26	292	12.10-11	305
10.27–11.15	287, 291,	12.12	301, 304,
	292, 300,		305
	304, 307,	12.13	330-32
	308	12.14-24	331
10.27	291-93,	12.14-15	305, 306,
	301, 308		331
11–14	125	12.16-19	304, 331
11–12	304	12.19-20	305
11	92, 291-	12.19	312
	93, 297,	12.20-25	331
	301, 332	12.20-21	305
11.3-5	300	12.20	36
11.6	291	12.23	312
11.7	300	12.24	36
11.8	300	13–15	287, 307,
11.12-14	43, 291,		308
	300, 308	13–14	297, 309,
			310

13	296		
13.1	308		
13.2	296		
13.4	296, 309		
13.7-15	287, 295,		
	296, 309,		
	310		
13.7	296		
13.13-14	309		
13.14	299		
14.38-44	290		
14.38-42	289		
14.47-52	308, 309,		
	332		
14.47-51	309		
14.47-48	309, 310		
14.47	293, 297		
14.49-51	309		
14.50	292		
14.52	309		
15	309, 310		
15.1–16.13	309		
15.23	329		
15.26	329		
15.35	309		
16–22	125, 126		
16–18	92		
16.1-13	291, 300,		
	329		
16.1	329		
16.7	329		
16.8	329		
16.9	329		
16.10	329		
16.12	329		
16.14-23	309		
17–19	125		
17	37		
18	37		
19	299		
21.11-26	37		
21.30	299		
23–25	125		
24	37		
25	28		
25.1	243		
25.28	70		
25.30	70, 269		

1 Samuel (cont.)		5.17	261, 268,	7.11-12	274
26	37, 125		269, 283	7.11	70, 126,
27	125	5.25	370		272-77,
28	125, 345	6–2 Kgs 2	45		283
28.3-5	37	6	124, 260,	7.12-15	276
28.3	26		269, 270	7.12-14	272
29–30	125	6.16	126, 270	7.12	272, 274,
31	125	6.20-23	126, 270		275
		6.20	271	7.13	64, 70,
2 Samuel		6.21	269-71,		272, 277-
1–5	125		299, 329		80
1.15	375	6.22	270	7.14-15	272
2–4	127	7–21	127	7.14	272, 278
2.8-9	306	7	43, 58, 63,	7.15	272, 276
2.10-11	261		64, 224,	7.16	70, 126,
2.11	264		260, 268,		272, 276,
3.2-5	264		271, 272,		279
3.9-10	70		280, 310,	7.17	272
3.18	70, 262		397, 430,	7.18-29	272, 280
3.31–4.1	264		431	7.18-22	272
5–8	70, 260,	7.1-17	272	7.18-21	272
	283	7.1-3	273	7.20-21	272
5	260, 261,	7.1	266, 272-	7.22-26	272
	273		74, 323	7.22-24	64, 272
5.1-3	261, 306	7.2-7	272	7.25-29	272
5.1-2	261, 263	7.2-5	272	7.25-26	272
5.2	70, 263,	7.2	266	7.27-29	272
	271, 299	7.4-9	272	8	128, 260,
5.3	264, 269	7.4	276		261, 273,
5.4-5	261, 263,	7.5-16	276		281
	265	7.5-11	280	8.1-14	261
5.4	263, 264	7.5-7	280	8.3-12	218
5.5-14	264	7.5	276, 278,	8.6	281
5.5	235, 263,		280	8.7-13	281
	264	7.6	272	8.7-12	281
5.6-14	264	7.7-8	263	8.13-14	218, 243,
5.6-10	261, 268	7.7	266, 272		244
5.6	264	7.8-11	280	8.14-15	281
5.11–8.18	271	7.8-10	64	8.14	281
5.11-12	266	7.8-9	272, 276	8.15	282
5.11	261, 266,	7.8	269, 272,	9–20	126, 127
	267		276, 280,	9	260
5.12	261, 266,		299	9.16	271
	267	7.9-11	272, 276	10–12	127
5.13-16	264	7.9	272, 276	10.1-4	236
5.17-25	261, 268,	7.10-11	272	10.5-6	299
	281	7.10	272, 274	10.10-13	299
		7.11-16	277	10.10	299

10.13	299	5.12	338	9.15-24	340
10.14-16	299	5.17-19	274	9.15	240
10.15-19	218	5.17-18	273	9.20-22	340
11–12	27	5.18	273, 323	9.23	240
11–1 Kgs 2	92	5.19	278	9.28	333
12	69	5.27-32	340	10.2	333
12.31	231	5.29	338	10.5	249
13–14	127	6.6	223	10.10	333
15–20	127	6.11-13	37	10.11	333
16.18	271	6.12	341	10.14	333
17.6	262	6.20-35	333	10.16	333
20	228, 229	7.48	333	10.17	333
20.18	263	7.49	333	10.18	333
20.21	239	7.50	333	10.21	333
21–24	43, 122, 139	7.51	333	10.22	333
		8	52, 77, 139, 280, 413, 415, 452, 475	10.25	333
1 Kings				10.27	333
1–16	128			10.28-29	339
1–11	234	8.14-53	49, 50	10.28	333
1–2.35	127	8.14-21	452	10.29	333
1–2	126-28, 390, 396	8.16	329	11–14	228, 229
		8.18	278	11–12	214, 217, 232, 252-55, 214, 215, 217, 222, 257, 302
1.5	240	8.21-53	153		
1.17	339	8.21	412, 415		
1.30	339	8.22-61	37, 87		
1.35-37	70	8.23	36		
1.35	269, 271, 298	8.29-30	414	11	92, 93, 256
		8.29	415		
1.46-48	70	8.31-61	55	11.1-8	337
2.1-4	128	8.33-53	106	11.1-2	337
2.3-4	341	8.34	415	11.1	238, 333, 337, 338
2.3	70	8.36	415		
2.4	36, 70	8.44-51	64	11.2	338, 339
2.10-12	128	8.46-51	415	11.3-5	236
2.11	264	8.46-50	135	11.3	335, 337, 338
2.35	240	8.46-48	408		
2.46	128	8.48	37, 415, 475	11.4-13	253
3–11	128, 129, 336, 390			11.4-10	252
		8.51	58, 415	11.4-6	338
3	37	8.53	375	11.4	236, 341
3.1	338	8.62-66	452	11.6-8	335
3.4-15	129	9.1-9	153	11.7-8	338
5	274	9.4-7	341	11.7	333, 338
5.2-3	249	9.4	341	11.8	337
5.6	333	9.6-9	64	11.9–12.24	233
5.7	249	9.11	333	11.9-13	230, 231, 341
5.8	333	9.14	333		

1 Kings (cont.)		11.32	224, 231, 232, 251, 253, 255	12.24	93, 214, 222, 229, 248, 251
11.11-13	228, 252				
11.11	218, 221, 231	11.33	253, 255	12.25–14.20	306
11.12-13	231, 232	11.34-36	231, 232	12.25-33	233
11.12	218, 221, 230	11.34	330, 341	12.25	249, 252
		11.36	224, 251, 253, 255, 256	12.26-33	224, 232, 245, 253, 257
11.13	224, 230, 251, 253, 255	11.37-39	231, 233	12.27-28	232
11.14–14.20	231	11.37	224	12.28	55, 340
11.14-28	231	11.38	224, 238, 247, 310, 341	12.31–13.34	54
11.14-25	225			13	133, 295
11.14-22	218, 231			14	93, 214, 215, 217, 232, 245, 252-54
11.14	219	11.39	255, 256		
11.15-22	243	11.40	231, 232, 241, 242		
11.15-20	243				
11.15-18	243	11.41	334	14.1-20	244
11.15-16	218	11.43–12.19	232	14.1-18	218, 221, 222, 233, 253-55, 257
11.15	218	11.43	215, 234, 235, 237, 250		
11.18-20	218				
11.20	218, 232	12	36, 93, 248, 340	14.1-16	228
11.21-22	218			14.1	227, 244
11.21	231	12.1-20	234	14.2-3	228
11.23-25	231	12.1-16	218	14.2	222
11.24	231	12.1	227, 234, 235, 237	14.3	227
11.25	218			14.4	222
11.26-28	240	12.2-3	215, 227	14.5-6	244
11.26-27	221, 223, 231, 232, 239-41	12.2	237	14.5	227
		12.4	340	14.6	227
11.26	237, 240	12.6	249	14.7-16	222, 252
11.27-40	240	12.12	227	14.7-11	224
11.27-28	242	12.15	227, 237	14.7-9	250
11.27	239, 240	12.17	248	14.7	69, 227
11.28	231, 239-41, 248	12.18	231, 248, 252	14.8	37, 69, 310
11.29–14.20	231	12.19	232, 248	14.9-14	227
11.29-39	218, 224, 228, 231, 241, 245, 247, 252	12.20	215, 224, 232, 251, 253	14.9-11	69
				14.9	227, 254
		12.21-25	249, 256	14.11	227
11.29	224	12.21-24	54, 232, 251-53	14.12	228
11.31-39	246			14.13	69, 227
11.31	224, 225, 246	12.21	224, 249, 252	14.14-15	254
				14.15-16	227, 250, 253, 255
11.32-39	250	12.23	224	14.15	227, 228
				14.16	227, 254

14.18	227	9.30	129	18.17-19	130
14.19	228	9.35	129	18.36-37	130
14.20	227	9.36	69	19.2-7	406
14.21	236, 237,	10.1	129	19.9-36	130
	306	10.2-3	129	19.36-37	131
14.22-24	254, 255	10.7-9	129	19.37	94
14.22	254	10.12	129	20.1-18	131
14.31	223, 236	10.17	69	20.12-19	432
15.1	237	10.31	37	20.12	130
15.4	255, 256	11–12	130	20.13	130
15.8-24	223	11.14	349	20.21	306
15.12-14	254	12.1-17	343	21.10-15	432
15.12-13	466	12.4	254	21.10-14	69
15.29-30	222	13	133	21.16	254
15.29	69	14.4	254	21.18	306
16.1-4	69	15.4	254	21.23-24	336
16.3	237	15.34	254	21.24	332
16.11-12	69	17	104, 139,	21.26	306
16.26	237		415	22–23	33, 104,
16.31	237	17.1	63		108, 131,
17–21	336	17.3	415		132, 419,
19.15-16	232, 233	17.7-23	37, 49, 87,		466
19.18	248		477	22	108, 289,
20	295	17.7-20	64		356, 420,
21.19	69	17.13	43		421
21.20-24	69	17.14	415	22.1–23.38	343
22.38	69	17.16-17	415	22.2	63, 343,
22.44	254	17.18-21	43		345, 348,
22.45	133	17.18	415		350, 357
22.47	466	17.19-20	43	22.3-20	343
		17.20	330	22.3-7	357
2 Kings		17.22-23	434	22.3-4	343
1	336	17.23	63, 434	22.3	348, 350
2.23.24	64	17.24-34	64	22.4-10	346
3.5	231	17.24-33	54	22.4-7	343
8.19	255, 256	17.34-41	477	22.4	346, 348,
9–10	132	17.34-40	64		351, 355,
9	295	17.37	43		356
9.1–10.27	232	17.41	54	22.8-10	343, 344,
9.1-6	129	18–20	130		348
9.7-10	69	18–19	95, 405	22.8	349, 420
9.10-12	129	18	466	22.10	346
9.13	129	18.4	130	22.11-19	349
9.16	129	18.7-8	130	22.11-13	345
9.17-21	129	18.9	130	22.11	349, 420
9.22	129	18.13-16	130	22.12	344
9.23	129	18.13	131	22.13	347, 349,
9.24	129	18.17–19.9	131		355, 356

2 Kings (cont.)

22.15-18	69
22.16-17	64, 345
22.16	346, 420, 421
22.17-20	254
22.17	254
22.18-20	345
22.18	420
22.19	346, 357, 420
22.20	64, 346-49, 420
23	356
23.1-25	420
23.1-24	348
23.1-3	348, 452
23.1	348, 355
23.2	348, 349, 355
23.3	349, 352, 356
23.4-20	351
23.4-5	64, 351
23.4	353, 354, 420
23.5	352, 354, 357
23.6	351, 352, 420
23.7	352
23.8	352
23.9	352, 468
23.10-12	352
23.10	351
23.11	351, 420
23.12	351, 352
23.13-14	352
23.13	352
23.15	63
23.16-20	351, 354
23.16-18	354
23.16	351, 354, 420
23.17	354
23.19-20	64
23.20	351, 357, 420

23.21–25.30	64
23.21-23	348, 350
23.21	350, 354
23.22	350
23.23	94, 167
23.24	348, 350
23.25-27	254
23.25	63-66, 94, 348, 350, 355, 466
23.26–25.30	64
23.26-30	64
23.26-27	254
23.27	255
23.29	420
23.30	306, 332, 348, 420
23.31-36	306
23.33-35	339
24–25	416
24	94, 439, 440
24.2-4	432
24.2	69
24.6-8	306
24.6	306
24.13-14	432
24.14	442
24.17	306
24.18–25.30	407
24.20	434-36, 439, 443, 446
25	94, 97, 104, 135, 313, 417, 433, 434
25.4	433
25.7	94
25.21-26	106
25.21	54, 69, 87, 94, 413, 417, 434, 436, 439, 446
25.22-30	87
25.22-26	432, 433
25.23	313

25.25	313, 433
25.26	50, 65, 313, 413, 417
25.27-30	37, 50, 58, 63, 65, 97, 135, 313, 397, 417, 428, 430, 431, 439, 469

1 Chronicles

1–9	159, 161
1.1	159
2.7	365
3.4	264
3.17-19	153
5.25	365
9.3	248
10–2 Chron. 9	159, 161
10.13	365
11–12	264
11.1	262
11.2	263
13.5	162
14.1	266, 267
14.2	267
17.4	278
17.10-11	274
17.12	278
17.13	278
17.14	279
18.13	282
18.14	282
22.10	278
22.15	267
23.4-5	165
29.27	264

2 Chronicles

6.8	278
6.9	278
10–36	159, 161
10.17	248
11.1	251
12.2	365
13.7	236

26.16	365	6.6-12	154	2.10	151
26.18	365	6.9-10	149	2.19	151
28.19	365	6.14	154	3.1-32	150
28.22	365	6.15-16	151	3.16	153
29.6	365	6.15	154	3.33-35	151
30.7	365	6.16-18	153	4.1-5	151
30.25	162	6.19-22	149	5.1-13	150
35–36	167	6.22	154	5.14	154
35.19	167	7–Neh. 13	152	6.1–7.3	150
36	79	7–10	148	6.1-14	151
36.14	365	7	397	6.15	151
36.20-23	159	7.6-9	158	7	150
36.22-23	159	7.7-9	149	7.4-71	150
		7.7-8	148	7.72–8.13	167
Ezra		7.12-26	154	8.1–9.4	149
1–10	167	7.17-24	149	8.13-18	149
1–6	148, 149,	7.27-28	154	8.13	168
	152	7.28–8.36	149	9	116, 152
1.1-4	154	8.1-20	158	9.1-2	150
1.1	148, 154,	8.2-24	150	9.2	151
	158	8.2	153	9.32	153
1.3	158	8.20	153	9.34	153
1.4	158	8.25-34	158	9.35	153
1.5-6	149	8.25-27	149	9.36-37	152
1.5	150, 158	8.35-36	158	10.2-28	150
1.7-11	170	9	152	10.30	149
1.8	171	9.1-6	397	10.31	150, 151
1.11	149, 158	9.2	152	10.32	149
2	150	9.4	150, 152	10.33-40	149
2.1-70	149	9.6	152	11.1-2	150
2.1-67	158	9.9	155	11.3-21	150
2.68-69	158	9.11	397	11.25-35	150
3.2-6	149	9.14	153	12.1-26	150
3.4-5	149	9.15	152	12.1-8	150
3.7–6.18	149	10.2-5	152	12.11	148
3.10	153	10.2	365	12.22	148
4	169	10.10	365	12.24	153
4.1-24	151	10.17	151	12.27-43	150
4.1-4	150	10.19	151	12.36	153
4.1	150			12.37	153
4.9-10	150	*Nehemiah*		12.44-45	149
4.17-23	154	1–13	148	12.45	153
4.20	153	1–4	150	12.46	153
5.1-2	154	1–2	158	13.1-3	149, 150
5.3–6.5	154	1	152	13.3	151
5.11	153	1.8	365	13.6	148, 154
5.14-15	170	2.5-9	149	13.10-13	149
5.14	171	2.7-9	154	13.15-22	149

Nehemiah (cont.)
13.23-27   150
13.26   153
13.27   365
13.30-31   149

Job
8.8   409

Psalms
44   397
60.1-2   243, 244
66   397
68   397
74   397
78   397
79.8   409
80   397
81   397
89   397
95   397
102   397
103   397
105   397
106   397
114   397
127.1-3   223
129   397
135   397
136   397

Proverbs
16.10   365
19.17   342

Ecclesiastes
1.11   409

Isaiah
1–39   80, 81
1.2-7   80
1.10-17   80
1.18-20   80
1.21-26   80
5   81
7.6   336
10.5-11   233
10.5   155

30.1-3   339
30.15-17   339
30.15-16   339
31.1-3   339
31.1   339
40–66   28
40–55   463
42.9   410
43.19   410
43.27   409
44.28   155
45.1-7   155
48.6   410
58.7   342
61.4   409
62.2   410
65.17   410
66.22   410

Jeremiah
1–45   401, 402
1–44   412
1–25   400, 405
1   402, 407,
            412, 419
1.7   402
1.9   402
1.30-31   414
2–6   407, 411,
            418, 419
2.5   419
3.18   408
3.25   419
4–6   421
7–35   409, 411,
            418
7–24   407, 411
7   78, 400,
            404, 406–
            409, 411,
            414, 415
7.1–8.3   415
7.1-15   402, 413
7.1-14   413
7.1   411
7.3   411, 414,
            415
7.5   411, 415

7.6   409
7.7   408, 411,
            414
7.8-15   415
7.9   409, 415
7.10   415
7.13   409, 411
7.14   408
7.15   415
7.16   312
7.18-19   409
7.21-24   410
7.22   414, 415
7.24   409, 415
7.25-26   79
7.25   409
7.26   409, 419
7.27   411
7.31   415
7.34   409
9.7   414
10.24   414
11   78, 400,
            404, 410,
            412, 413
11.1-13   409, 410
11.1-5   410
11.2   414
11.3-4   412
11.3   413, 414
11.4-7   413
11.4-5   414
11.4   410, 413
11.5   413
11.7   413
11.8-14   414
11.8   413, 414
11.9   414
11.10-12   410
11.10-11   414
11.10   409, 410
11.11   413
11.13   410, 414
11.14   312, 413,
            414
11.15   413
11.21   413
11.26   413

11.46	413	30.1-3	410	40.10-12	417
15.1	312	31	248	41.1-3	433
15.19	312	31.22	410	41.16-18	434
16.10-13	403	31.31-34	41, 78, 79,	42.2	312
16.11	419		409, 410,	42.10	417
16.14-15	79, 403		416	42.12	418
17.19-27	402	31.31	409, 410	42.20	312
17.23	419	31.32	410	43–44	412
17.26	251	31.33	409	43.7	418
18	400	31.34	409	44–45	419
18.11	411	32	400, 417	44	400
18.20	312	32.15	417	44.9-10	79
19–20	400	34	400	44.9	419
21	248, 400	34.13	419	44.10	419
21.2-10	406	35	78, 400,	45	407, 419
22.1-5	402		407, 409,	46–52	400
22.25-27	402		411	46–51	407
23.1-8	400	35.1	411	51.64	433
23.27	419	35.14-15	409	52	407, 416,
23.33-40	421	35.15	408, 411		432, 433
24	79, 400,	36	104, 131,	52.28-30	433, 440
	404, 407		400, 407,	52.30	313
24.8-10	413		419-21		
25	78, 400,	36.3	420	*Lamentations*	
	407-409,	36.5	421	3.23	410
	411	36.7	420		
25.1-13	415	36.11-19	420	*Ezekiel*	
25.3-6	409	36.22	421	2.3-7	81
25.3-4	409	36.24	420	5.16-17	393
25.4	409	36.25	420	11.19	410
25.5-6	408	36.27	420	14.13	365
25.6-7	409	36.28	420	15.8	365
25.6	409	36.29	420	17	339
25.10-11	409	36.30	420	17.20	365
25.11	413	36.31	420	18.24	365
26–44	400	36.32	420	18.31	410
26–35	411	37–52	412	20	81
26	131, 407,	37–44	79, 404	20.27	365
	408	37–43	417-19	36.26	410
26.3	411	37–42	418	39.23	365
26.9	414	37	339	39.26	365
27.11	417	37.3	312		
28	104	37.9-10	406	*Daniel*	
28.1-4	105	39–41	432-34	9	403
29.7	312, 414	39.14	417	9.7	365
29.10-14	158	40.2-6	417		
29.18	312	40.6	417	*Hosea*	
30–31	400	40.7–41.8	432, 433	1.1	76

Hosea (cont.)		9.17	76	6–7	79	
1.5	76	10.9-10	76	6.2-8	79	
1.6-7	76	10.12	76	6.4	345	
2.1-3	76	10.13-14	76	6.9-16	79	
2.8-9	76	11	76			
2.10	76	11.1-11	76	*Habakkuk*		
2.15-18	76	11.1-7	474	1–2	233	
2.19-20	76	11.5	339			
2.22-25	76	12	76	*Zephaniah*		
3.1-5	76	12.1	76	1.1	336	
4	76	12.5-7	76			
4.3	76	12.10-12	76	*Haggai*		
4.6	76	12.14	76	1.1	156	
4.7-12	76	13.14	76	1.6-11	151	
4.13	76	14.2-10	76	1.13	156	
4.14	76	14.10	76	1.15	156	
4.16	76			2.6-7	156	
4.17	76	*Amos*		2.10	156	
5.2	76	1.1	75	2.15-19	151	
5.4	76	1.2	75	2.21-23	153, 397	
5.13	76	1.3–2.16	338	2.21-22	156	
5.15–6.3	76	1.9-13	75	2.22	157	
6.5	76	2.4-5	75	2.23	170, 475	
6.11–7.1	76	2.10-12	75			
7.4	76	3.1	75	*Zechariah*		
7.10	76	3.3	75	1	403	
7.12	76	3.7	75, 447	1.1	156	
7.15	76	5.25-26	75	1.4-6	156	
7.16	76	8.2	393	1.7	156	
8.4-5	76	9.7-8	75	2.5-9	475	
8.6-7	76			2.12-13	156	
8.13-14	76	*Jonah*		2.15-16	156	
8.13	339	3	403	2.16	475	
9.2-4	76	3.7	349	4.9	156	
9.3	339			5	354	
9.6	76	*Micah*		6.12-13	153	
9.8-9	76	1–3	79	7.1	156	
9.14	76	5.1-5	397	8.10	151	

OTHER ANCIENT REFERENCES

Apocrypha		2.11	171	8–9	167
1 Esdras		3.1–5.6	167	9.17	167
1	167	4.13-63	170	9.37	167
1.1	168	5.5	170		
1.22	167	5.7–9.55	167	*Baruch*	
2–7	167	6.18	170	1–3	403
2	167	6.27	170		

New Testament

Matthew

25.40   342
25.45   342

Acts

1.26   290
7   403

Talmuds

b. B. Bat.

12b   421
14b-15a   26

Josephus

Ant.

6.58   299

Classical

Herodotus

2.53   186
3.122   186

Thucydides

3.82.2-3   179

INDEX OF AUTHORS

Abadie, P. 137
Aberbach, M. 238
Achenbach, R. 98, 109
Ackroyd, P.R. 57, 127
Adams, J.L. 457
Aejmelaeus, A. 92
Ahlheim, K.H. 424
Ahlström, G.W. 124
Albertz, R. 86, 98, 104-106, 316, 326,
    389, 393, 397, 406, 465, 467, 469,
    470, 475, 477
Alexander, L.V. 62
Allen, L.C. 276
Alt, A. 46, 47, 76, 234, 281
Amit, Y. 122
Amsler, S. 260
Anbar, M. 116
Anderson, A.A. 262, 267, 269, 282
Assaf, D. 155
Augustin, M. 159, 163
Auld, A.G. 89-91, 102, 114, 119, 120,
    138, 252, 253

Bachelard, G. 195
Baker, D.W. 293
Barré, L.M. 130
Barredo, M.A. 80
Barrick, W.B. 116, 133
Bartelmus, R. 116, 121
Barth, H. 59, 80
Barthelemy, D. 92, 218, 267, 366
Baumgartner, W. 121
Bayer, E. 167
Bazin, J. 188
Bechmann, U. 119
Becker, U. 71, 116, 118, 120
Becking, B. 97, 341
Begg, C. 107, 135
Ben-Zvi, E. 71, 80

Bentzen, A. 59, 84
Benveniste, E. 208, 355
Berges, U. 98
Bertheau, E. 43
Bettenzoli, G. 294
Beyerlin, W. 117
Bickert, R. 71
Biddle, M. 411
Bieberstein, K. 91, 395
Birch, B.C. 287, 288, 291, 292, 295, 298,
    301-304, 309, 311, 312
Blum, E. 83, 85, 86, 96, 104-106, 116,
    393, 476
Boecker, H.J. 56, 103, 289, 293, 296,
    303-308, 311
Bogaert, P.-M. 78, 90
Böhmer, S. 409
Boling, R.G. 65, 118, 288, 363
Bottéro, J. 190, 201, 207
Bourdieu, P. 190, 195
Braudel, F. 136
Braulik, G. 108, 110, 468
Brekelmans, C. 81, 83, 96, 97, 108, 132
Brettler, M.Z. 83
Briend, J. 111, 113, 123, 361, 363, 364,
    374, 375, 395, 438
Bright, J. 400, 401, 407
Brooke, A.E. 222, 275
Brooke, G.J. 91, 93
Brueggemann, W. 58, 430, 447, 472-74
Buber, M. 318
Budde, K. 35, 45, 265, 281
Budge, E.A.W. 200
Buis, P. 107
Butler, T. 115

Cagni, L. 198, 209
Calov, A. 27, 28
Caloz, M. 83

Calvin, J. 28
Camp, L. 130
Campbell, A.F. 125, 132, 134, 269-71, 294
Caquot, A. 92, 273, 281
Carlson, R.A. 70
Carr, D.M. 129
Carroll, R.P. 78, 156, 404, 414, 419, 421, 475
Cassetti, P. 123
Cassin, E. 201
Cazelles, H. 411
Chan, T.-K. 83
Chiera, E. 195
Chouraqui, A. 136
Christ, F. 57
Christensen, D.L. 465, 467, 468
Claughlin, T.M. 459
Clements, R.E. 80, 104, 108, 129
Clines, D.J.A. 156, 157, 475
Coggins, R. 134
Colenso, J.W. 40, 41
Collins, J.J. 456
Coogan, M.D. 131
Cook, S.A. 167
Cooke, G.A. 89
Cortese, E. 96, 115, 119, 134
Cox, C.E. 91
Cross, F.M. 63-66, 68, 72, 73, 92, 94, 95, 271, 272, 278, 288, 297, 298, 307, 390, 431, 432, 436, 457, 466
Crüsemann, F. 86, 105, 110, 289, 292, 303, 304, 315, 322, 325, 332, 334, 342
Cryer, F.H. 85
Curtis, A.W.H. 112, 276, 412
Curtis, E.L. 268

Daniels, D.R. 77, 150
David, M. 190
Davies, J. 112, 134
Davies, P.R. 392
Debus, J. 93, 215, 216, 250
Dequeker, L. 169
Detienne, M. 97, 138, 176, 187, 188, 202, 449
Dever, W. 131
Diebner, B.J. 108, 132, 394

Diestel, L. 27-29
Dietrich, M. 324
Dietrich, W. 67-70, 94, 123-25, 131, 135, 140, 288, 296, 301, 302, 311, 313, 324, 329, 331, 338, 340, 341, 396, 431, 434, 444
Dillmann, A. 40
Dohmen, C. 122
Donner, H. 394
Doob-Sakenfeld, K. 337
Douglas, M. 470, 471
Driver, G.R. 197
Droysen, G. 391
Duhm, B. 41, 42, 74, 399, 405
Dumézil, G. 425
Durand, J.M. 202
Durkheim, E. 460, 461, 470
Dutcher-Walls, P. 140, 465

Eagleton, T. 463, 464
Ebeling, E. 198
Edelman, D. 98, 290, 293, 298, 309, 391
Eilberg-Schwartz, H. 478
Eisenman, R.H. 262
Eissfeldt, O. 60, 61, 127, 144, 289, 317, 456
Emerton, J.A. 82, 85, 89, 137, 168, 269, 405
Engels, F. 425
Engnell, I. 55
Eph'al, I. 148
Erikson, E. 459
Eskenazi, T.C. 145, 148, 151, 156, 162, 167, 168, 418, 475
Eslinger, L. 98, 324
Ewald, H. 35-40, 399
Eynikel, E. 101, 131, 432

Fewell, D.N. 99
Fichtner, J. 56
Finkelstein, I. 145
Fischer, G. 410
Floss, J.P. 114, 374, 408
Fohrer, G. 38, 60, 61, 102, 103, 118
Foresti, F. 71, 125
Freedman, D.N. 456
Fricke, K.D. 56
Friedman, R.E. 65, 106, 313, 417

Fritz, V. 81, 91, 113-15, 395
Fuss, W. 84

García López, F. 107, 108, 334, 342
Garcia Martínez, F. 91, 468
Garrone, D. 98
Garscha, J. 81
Gautier, L. 44
Geerth, H.H. 459
Geertz, C. 458, 459, 462
Gelb, I.J. 198-200
Gelin, A. 47
Genouillac, H. de 193
Gerbrandt, G.E. 303
Gerstenberger, E. 388
Gese, H. 75, 278
Gibert, P. 31
Glassner, J.-J. 138, 190, 192, 195, 199, 201, 206, 207, 209, 211
Glatt, D.A. 216
Glessman, U. 150
Goedicke, H. 472
Goetze, A. 202
Goldman, Y. 78, 90, 403, 432
Golka, F.W. 98, 326, 397
Goncalves, F.C. 130
Gooding, D.W. 215, 222, 226, 228, 238-40
Gordon, R.P. 124, 216, 238-40
Gorg, M. 85, 121, 122, 128
Goshen-Gottstein, M. 150, 152
Gottwald, N.K. 458, 460-64, 480
Gourgues, M. 62
Grabbe, L.L. 144, 158
Graf, K.-H. 35
Graham, M.P. 106, 112, 116, 123, 128, 134, 286, 318, 342, 465, 470
Gramberg, C.P.W. 35
Gray, J. 63, 118
Grayson, A.K. 197, 200
Gressman, H. 45, 46
Gronbaek, J.H. 260, 269
Gross, W. 105, 131, 389, 405, 408, 410, 416, 437
Gunn, D.M. 99, 127
Gunneweg, A.H.J. 71, 75, 94, 418

Habermas, J. 470, 471

Halbe, J. 363
Halpern, B. 65, 293, 307, 313, 417, 456
Hanson, P.D. 465
Hardmeier, C. 130, 131, 405, 406
Harper, R.F. 199
Harris, M. 458
Hartog, F. 174, 175, 184
Hasel, G.F. 456, 473
Haudebert, P. 76, 86, 96, 101, 203, 251
Hauret, C. 83, 107
Hayes, J.H. 314
Heidegger, M. 175
Henscheid, E. 393
Hentschel, G. 271, 274, 276, 277, 279
Herion, G.A. 472
Hermann, W. 57
Herrmann, S. 77, 403, 409, 412
Hertzberg, H.W. 56, 281, 282
Hobbes, T. 30
Hodder, I. 459
Hoffmann, H.-D. 97, 99, 132, 465
Hoffmeier, J.K. 293
Holladay, J. 401
Holladay, W.L. 77
Hollenberg, J. 89
Holmes, S. 89
Holscher, G. 45, 59, 144
Holt, E. 414
Holzmann, H.J. 35
Hunger, H. 202, 208
Hyatt, J.P. 77, 400, 401, 403

Isbell, C.D. 419, 420
Israel, F. 98

Jacob, E. 369, 370
Janssen, E. 57
Japhet, S. 137, 145-48, 150-53, 156, 158, 159, 162, 164, 168-70, 264, 418
Jenni, E. 46, 55, 56
Jeppesen, K. 70
Jepsen, A. 53, 54, 73
Jeremias, J. 72, 79, 416
Jirku, A. 46
Johnstone, W. 86
Jones, D.R. 403
Jones, H. 392
Judd, E.P. 151

Jungling, H.W. 122

King, L.W. 200
Kaiser, O. 33, 59, 60, 71, 72, 75, 78-80,
    94, 109, 117, 126, 127, 391, 418
Kallai, Z. 115
Kaufmann, Y. 150, 156
Kautzsch, E. 274
Kavanagh, J.H. 459
Keel, O. 367, 370
Kegler, J. 98, 159, 163, 326, 397
Kenik, H.A. 129
Kienast, B. 198-200
Kilian, R. 80, 85
Klein, J. 195
Klein, R.W. 71, 227, 228, 286, 287, 295,
    297, 298, 303, 311
Kleineg, J.W. 145
Knauf, E.A. 59, 102, 113, 119, 120, 129,
    390, 391, 393, 394, 396
Knight, D.A. 62, 140
Knoppers, G.N. 94, 286
Koch, K. 416
Koopmans, W.T. 115
Korpell, M.C.A. 341
Kosters, H.W. 40
Kottsieper, I. 85
Kovacs, B.W. 401
Kraft, R.A. 92
Kramer, S.N. 201
Kraus, H.-J. 27-31, 34, 39
Kruger, T. 81
Kuenen, A. 38-41, 64, 73, 399
Kumaki, F.K. 406
Kuntzmann, R. 369

Laberge, L. 62
Lagarde, P. de 89
Lambert, J. 356
Landsberger, B. 202, 207
Langdon, S. 200, 203
Langlamet, F. 69, 126, 263, 274-77, 279,
    373, 374
Laperrousaz, E.M. 361
Leclerq, J. 107
Lemaire, A. 132-34
Lemche, N.P. 121, 316
Lemke, W.E. 457

Lenclud, G. 174, 175, 187
Lentricchia, F. 459
Levenson, J.D. 65, 74, 313, 417
Lévi-Strauss, C. 174, 184, 189
Levin, C. 71, 72, 78, 85, 116, 130, 132,
    393, 395, 409, 411, 417
L'Hour, J. 109, 116
Lindars, B. 93, 118
Lindblom, J. 289
Linder, M. 355, 356
Lingen, A. van der 125
Liwak, R. 81, 411, 419
Loersch, S. 33
Lohfink, N. 72, 86, 94, 96, 104, 105, 107,
    108, 110, 112, 113, 131, 137, 334,
    339, 389, 390, 395, 410, 416, 437,
    465-68, 472
Long, V.P. 293
Loraaux, N. 179
Loza, J. 83
Luckenbill, D.D. 200
Lundberg, M.J. 264
Lust, J. 81, 82, 92, 96, 97, 108, 132

Macchi, J.D. 403, 412
Mace, F. 187
Macholz, G.C. 56
Madsen, A.A. 268
Mannheim, K. 459
Marcos, N.F. 258
Margalit, B. 375
Margalith, O. 121
Martens, E.A. 456, 473
Marx, K. 425, 458
Masius, A. 28-30, 39
Mathys, A.P. 123
Mayes, A.D.H. 65, 66, 95, 109, 111, 118,
    134, 289, 298, 424, 461, 465, 468,
    470, 471, 476, 477, 480
Mays, J.L. 62
McBride, S.D. 110, 477
McCarter, P.K. Jr 123, 125, 126, 261,
    262, 265, 266, 268, 270-73, 277-79,
    281, 282, 286-91, 295, 298, 301,
    302, 304, 308, 311, 312
McCarthy, D.J. 271
McCown, C.C. 312
McKane, W. 78, 405, 409, 412

McKenzie, S.L. 34, 65, 66, 68, 93-95,
    101, 105, 106, 112, 116, 123, 125,
    128, 131, 133, 134, 222, 245, 250,
    261, 262, 265, 266, 273, 286, 310,
    313, 318, 342, 360, 465, 470, 479
McLean, N. 222
McLean, R.W. 304
Meinhold, A. 44
Mendenhall, G.E. 472
Meonikes, A. 66
Merendino, R.P. 109
Mettinger, T.N.D. 263, 271, 272, 277-80,
    298
Meyerson, I. 177, 178
Milbank, J. 464
Miles, J.C. 197
Milgrom, J. 239
Millard, A.R. 119, 293
Miller, J.M. 294, 296, 314
Miller, P.D. 124, 131, 270, 457, 458, 463,
    472, 473
Minokami, Y. 129, 130
Mittmann, S. 103, 394
Moenikes, A. 66, 290, 302, 304
Mommer, P. 123, 125, 329, 332
Montgomery, J.A. 227
Moore, G.F. 288
Moore, R.D. 132
Moran, W.L. 197
Morgan, T. 29
Movers, F.C. 89
Mowinckel, S. 77, 115, 399-401
Muilenburg, J. 312
Mullen, E.T. 100
Myers, J.M. 145, 167

Na'aman, N. 145, 155, 294
Nauerth, C. 108, 121, 132
Naumann, T. 76, 123-25, 329
Nebeling, G. 109, 202
Neef, H.-D. 120
Nelson, R.D. 64, 65, 135, 431-33
Neu, R. 316
Newsom, C.A. 464
Nicholson, E.W. 57, 77, 104, 401, 411
Niehr, H. 131, 320
Niemann, H.M. 122
Nissinen, M. 76

Noort, E. 128
Norton, G.J. 167
Noth, M. 24, 25, 34-37, 44, 46-64, 67-70,
    73, 74, 82, 100, 102, 103, 105, 107,
    112-18, 120-25, 128, 132, 138-40,
    227, 232, 261, 266, 269, 271, 281,
    286, 287, 301, 304, 306, 307, 313,
    315-17, 325, 360, 361, 365, 379,
    389, 390, 395, 402, 415, 416, 426-
    31, 436, 446, 465, 477
Nubel, H.U. 260

O'Brien, M.A. 74, 94, 95, 107, 116, 118,
    132, 272, 287, 289, 302,305, 388,
    465
O'Connell, R.H. 363
Ollenburger, B.C. 456, 473
Otto, E. 79, 322
Ottoson, M. 113
Otzen, B. 70

Parpola, S. 111, 199, 202, 207
Peckham, B. 65, 66, 94, 112
Perdue, L.G. 401
Perlitt, L. 72, 81, 97, 111, 416
Person, R.F. 82, 421, 465
Pfeiffer, R. 45
Phelps, M.B. 264
Pinches, T.G. 197
Pingree, D. 202
Piovanelli, P. 404
Pisano, S. 89, 90, 92, 167
Pohlmann, K.F. 79, 81, 94, 106, 167, 403,
    404, 411, 413, 416, 417
Polzin, R. 99, 324, 465
Preuss, H.D. 62, 74, 94, 95, 109-11, 131,
    322
Propp, W.H. 456
Provan, I.W. 94-96, 360, 361
Pury, A. de 42, 59, 72, 76, 120, 126, 137,
    257, 390, 393, 412, 426

Rad, G. von 58-61, 64, 68, 102, 155, 156,
    307, 429-31, 448, 477
Radjawane, A.N. 56, 57
Ranciere, J. 207, 210
Ranke, L. von 391
Reed, S.A. 264

Reichert, A. 83
Reid, P.V. 262
Reimer, E. 202
Renaud, B. 79
Rendtorff, R. 66, 85, 86, 415, 476
Reuss, E. 35, 40
Reuter, E. 108, 109
Reventlow, H. Graf 27, 28
Richards, K.H. 148, 151, 156, 162, 418, 475
Richter, W. 117, 118, 120, 298, 396
Ricoeur, P. 177, 458-60, 462
Ritschl, D. 392
Robert, P. de 92, 273, 281
Roberts, J.J.M. 124, 270, 472
Robertson Smith, W. 460, 461
Robinson, J.M. 262
Rofe, A. 91, 92, 98, 132, 133, 296
Rogerson, J.W. 33-35
Römer, T. 42, 56, 72, 78, 97, 101, 103, 106, 116, 120, 126, 129, 132, 134, 136, 137, 342, 393, 395, 403, 408-10, 412, 418-20, 426, 479
Rose, M. 83-85, 101, 112, 131, 134, 335, 339, 428, 431, 448, 451, 454, 476
Rosel, H.N. 121, 426
Rosel, M. 150
Rost, L. 45, 46, 125, 126, 128, 270, 277
Roth, W. 71, 104
Rowley, H.H. 45
Rudolph, W. 77, 137, 152, 169, 276, 400, 401, 413
Ruppert, L. 411
Ruprecht, E. 130, 131
Rutersworden, U. 110, 320, 334, 335
Rutten, M. 204-206

Saiz, J.B. 258
Sarkio, P. 335, 336
Schäfer-Lichtenberger, C. 320, 341
Schearing, L.S. 105, 130
Scheid, J. 355, 356
Scheil, J.V. 201
Schenker, A. 90, 91, 93, 167, 215, 239, 393, 404
Schicklberger, F. 124
Schmid, H.H. 84
Schmidt, H. 45

Schmidt, L. 103, 137, 269, 293-300
Schmidt, W.H. 75
Schmitt, G. 115, 132
Schmitt, H.C. 132
Schneid, J. 188
Schramm, B. 465, 470
Schwienhorst, L. 114, 371
Sedlmaier, F. 81
Seeligmann, I.L. 274-76
Seidl, T. 408, 413, 415
Seitz, C.R. 79, 94, 416-19, 439
Seitz, G. 109
Sellin, E. 43
Seybold, K. 80, 419
Shaffer, A. 198, 199
Shakespeare, W. 127
Sigrist, M. 193
Simon, R. 31
Sipila, S. 91
Sjoberg, A.W. 195
Skweres, D.E. 83
Smelik, K.A.D. 124
Smend, R. 32, 34, 35, 41, 59, 60, 67, 68, 70-74, 86, 94, 114, 116, 118, 121, 323, 341, 390, 465
Smith, D.L. 150
Smith, H.P. 265, 267
Smith-Christopher, D. 151
Smolar, L. 238
Smyth, F. 66, 132
Soggin, J.A. 57, 71, 106, 118
Sonderlund, S. 78
Sonnet, J.P. 132
Specht, H. 122
Spencer, J.R. 116
Spieckermann, H. 71, 130
Spinoza, B, de 29-32
Spronk, K. 94
Stade, B. 130
Stähelin, J.J. 40
Starr, I. 203
Steil, A. 136
Stephens, F.J. 197, 198
Steuernagel, C. 40
Steymans, H.U. 111
Stipp, H.-J. 66, 105, 132, 403-406, 413
Stol, M. 199
Strecker, G. 146

Stulman, L. 78, 90, 140, 411, 477, 478
Suzuki, Y. 107, 108
Sweeney, M.A. 80

Tadmor, H. 148, 202, 207
Talmon, S. 150, 152, 267, 282
Talshir, Z. 93, 214, 216, 217, 219, 223-25, 228, 234, 235, 240, 245, 251, 252
Thenius, O. 89
Thiel, W. 77, 78, 402, 404, 408, 409, 417
Thompson, J.B. 462
Thompson, R.C. 201
Thompson, T.L. 138
Thureau-Dangin, F. 198, 206
Tidwell, N.L. 269
Tigay, J.H. 92
Tillesse, M. de 107, 132, 419, 420
Timm, S. 130, 392
Togan, A.Z.V. 57
Tournay, R.J. 123, 198, 199
Tov, E. 78, 91-93, 262
Trebolle Barrera, J.C. 93, 214-16, 219, 222, 225, 228, 235, 237, 238, 240, 248-52, 254
Tuck, R. 30
Tuckett, C.M. 403

Uehlinger, C. 131
Ulrich, E.C. 263, 265, 267

Vandermeersch, L. 180, 202
Vanoni, G. 94, 466
Van Seters, J. 84, 85, 97, 100, 113-16, 118, 119, 127, 128, 137, 138, 145, 271, 286, 288-90, 295, 297, 298, 300, 302, 309, 312, 374, 393
Vater, J.S. 33
Vaux, R. de 227
Veijola, T. 67-70, 106, 122, 124, 127, 259, 261, 263, 265, 266, 270, 272, 274, 276, 277, 279, 281, 288-90, 293, 297, 301-306, 309-11, 317, 318, 324, 325, 329, 341, 470
Vermeylen, J. 75, 79-81, 86-88
Vernant, J.P. 178, 184, 207
Visaticki, K. 108
Volz, P. 46

Walchi, S.H. 129
Walkenhorst, K.-H. 107
Wanke, G. 408
Watanabe, K. 111
Weber, M. 459, 480
Weidner, E. 200
Weinfeld, M. 75, 104, 108, 111, 117, 273, 279, 288, 297, 407, 437, 479
Weippert, H. 66, 77, 133, 134, 390, 392, 394, 401, 402, 428, 465
Weiser, A. 60, 61, 77, 102, 260, 294, 301, 303, 308, 312
Wellhausen, J. 34, 35, 39, 40, 42-44, 73, 74, 82, 89, 124, 126, 270, 287, 301, 307, 309, 312, 317, 326, 366
Werner, W. 80
Westermann, C. 38, 61, 102, 288, 309, 319, 388
Wette, W.M.L. de 32-35, 39, 40, 399
Whybray, R.N. 127
Wildberger, H. 155
Willi, T. 162
Williamson, H.G.M. 145, 148, 152, 160, 167, 168
Willis, T.M. 215
Winkler, H. 66
Wolff, H.W. 57, 58, 67, 75, 323, 338, 341, 430, 431, 447
Wolter, H. 110
Woude, A.S. van der 82, 124
Wright Mills, C. 459
Wright, G.E. 363

Wurthwein, E. 38, 61, 71, 94, 97, 101-103, 117, 127, 263, 276, 279, 334, 337, 420
Wust, M. 114, 377

Yee, G.A. 76

Younger, K.L. 113, 119, 361

Zenger, E. 430
Zobel, K. 326, 333, 338, 339